THE BUILDINGS OF SCOTLAND

EDITOR-IN-CHIEF: NIKOLAUS PEVSNER
JOINT EDITORS: COLIN MCWILLIAM AND
JUDY NAIRN

LOTHIAN
EXCEPT EDINBURGH

COLIN MCWILLIAM

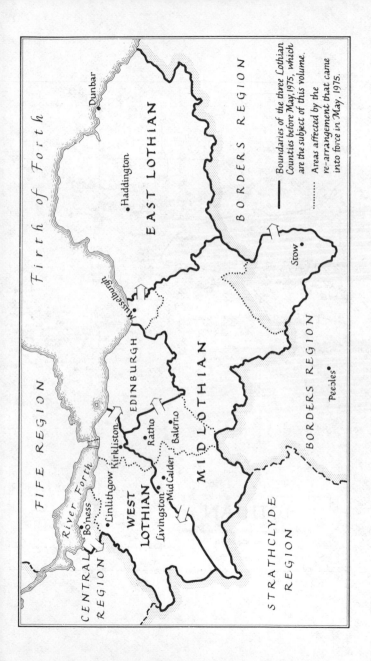

Boundaries of the three Lothian Counties before May, 1975, which are the subject of this volume.

Areas affected by the re-arrangement that came into force in May, 1975.

Firth of Forth

Dunbar

BORDERS REGION

EAST LOTHIAN

Haddington

Stow

Musselburgh

EDINBURGH

BORDERS REGION

Peebles

MIDLOTHIAN

FIFE REGION

River Forth

Bo'ness

Linlithgow

Kirkliston

Ratho

Balerno

Mid Calder

Livingston

WEST LOTHIAN

CENTRAL REGION

STRATHCLYDE REGION

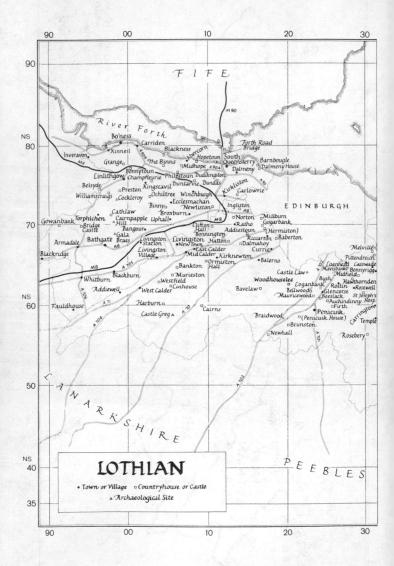

LOTHIAN

- Town or Village
- Countryhouse or Castle
- Archaeological Site

Of many donors who have made possible the publication of this volume, special acknowledgement is due to the former County Councils of EAST LOTHIAN, MIDLOTHIAN AND WEST LOTHIAN who worked, as their successors are still working, for the conservation of good buildings and places in Lothian.

THE BUILDINGS OF SCOTLAND

Lothian
except Edinburgh

BY COLIN MCWILLIAM

★

THE MEDIEVAL CHURCHES
BY CHRISTOPHER WILSON

PENGUIN BOOKS

Penguin Books Ltd, Harmondsworth, Middlesex, England
Penguin Books, 625 Madison Avenue, New York, New York 10022, USA
Penguin Books Australia Ltd, Ringwood, Victoria, Australia
Penguin Books Canada Ltd, 2801 John Street, Markham, Ontario, Canada
Penguin Books (NZ) Ltd, 182–190 Wairau Road, Auckland 10, New Zealand

—

First published 1978

—

ISBN 0 14 0710.66 3

—

Copyright © Colin McWilliam, 1978

Made and printed in Great Britain
by Butler & Tanner Ltd, Frome and London
Set in Monophoto Plantin

TO
THE MEMORY
OF MY PARENTS
EDGAR AND MARGARET
MCWILLIAM

Map References

*

The numbers printed in italic type in the margin against the place names in the gazetteer of the book indicate the position of the place in question on the index map (pages 4–5), which is divided into sections by the 10-kilometre reference lines of the National Grid. The reference given here omits the two initial letters (formerly numbers) which in a full grid reference refer to the 100-kilometre squares into which the country is divided. The first two numbers indicate the *western* boundary, and the last two the *southern* boundary, of the 10-kilometre square in which the place in question is situated. For example, Haddington (reference 5070) will be found in the 10-kilometre square bounded by grid lines 50 and 60 on the *west* and 70 and 80 on the *south*; Loanhead (reference 2060) in the square bounded by grid lines 20 and 30 on the *west* and 60 and 70 on the *south*.

The map contains all those places, whether towns, villages, or isolated buildings, which are the subject of separate entries in the text.

CONTENTS

CONTENTS

FOREWORD

BY COLIN MCWILLIAM

THE first move towards The Buildings of Scotland was made by Sir Nikolaus Pevsner. He found two authors, the other one being David Walker. None of us however could find any money towards the cost of research – the collection and collation of material before we visited the buildings and wrote our descriptions of them. The second move was made by the National Trust for Scotland, who took the sort of initiative they have taken in so many other ways in the cause of preservation north of the Border, and wrote to Sir Nikolaus offering to underwrite a Buildings of Scotland series if he would organize the writing. Thus it became possible. Ivison Wheatley was then the Trust's Secretary, and still manages on their behalf the administration of the charitable funds which he on behalf of the Trust has raised and is still raising for the series. The Trust's part in the stocktaking of Scottish buildings is no new thing. It was the grandfather of their present Chairman, the Marquess of Bute, who commissioned the 'Bute Lists' of old houses in Scottish towns some forty years ago; they were prepared by the late Ian Lindsay, who followed them up by his scholarly and catholic supervision of the official lists prepared under the 1947 Planning Act. His work is now carried on the same spirit by David Walker in the Scottish Development Department.

The Pilgrim Trust, the Russell Trust and the Scottish Arts Council are most generously making grants to the Trust towards the costs of research for the whole series, and for this volume contributions also came from the County Councils (as they then were) of East Lothian, Midlothian and West Lothian and from the Scottish Georgian Society. Their confidence in the project must be gratefully acknowledged, and so (in another way) must that of Penguin Books. The National Trust for Scotland itself is also contributing directly from its own funds.

Readers of The Buildings of England will, I hope, find themselves at home in our presentation of The Buildings of Scotland. The format is durable and unchanged, and so are the objectives: to present all the buildings that merit attention on architectural grounds, to do it for the whole country, and to do it with all possible speed. For that other B of E hallmark, the knowledge and judgement of one man and his personal view which throws the facts into relief, we have no substitute.

But I hope the reader, when confronted by at least four different authors in the course of the series, will notice a certain consistency of viewpoint which stems from the relative smallness of Scotland (B of S may fill a quarter of the shelf space of B of E) and from the sympathy that exists between historians working in Scotland. We all know that the good buildings of Scotland are diminishing week by week, many of them unnoticed, and believe that the best hope is to make them better known.

Certain general policies have been adopted for this series. In two ways we break with B of E practice. Metric measurements are used except when they would distort the sense, and church plate is not mentioned. Other points will also occur to the reader. Victorian architecture is very strongly represented; this is not merely a matter of fashion but of fact. I hope that those who use this book will be impressed by the quality of what has been described, and see the reason for the inclusion of much else that has simply been mentioned; a building of indifferent quality by an unknown architect or by no architect may still be valuable or remarkable in its context. The same applies to stained glass, which is mentioned in all cases where the artist is known, and in a few more where a window or set of windows seemed to me to have any pretension to quality. I have not dared to attempt a comparative account of Victorian and later stained glass in Lothian, but I hope this will be possible in later volumes. Church organs, which are on the borderline between one sort of aesthetic effect and another, are always included if their maker's name is known, even when their housings are of little or no merit. With post-Victorian buildings, as with the whole body of vernacular work, it has been necessary to be selective. In general anything that is remarkable in itself, or contributes positively to the character of a place, has been put in. Finally there is the matter of Scottish building terms. There is a diverse and lively vocabulary of such terms* but they are adopted in B of S only where they represent a characteristically Scottish way of doing things (crowstep, pend) or are in familiar use (astragal, rhone). These terms are included in a revised glossary.

Boundaries must be explained. This volume covers the three former counties of Midlothian (but not Edinburgh), East Lothian and West Lothian as they were just before the local government reorganization of 1975. It consequently covers all the new Lothian Region apart from the capital city. All the entries in the gazetteer are amalgamated into a single alphabetical run, and the initials ML, EL, or WL after the name of a place indicate the county to which it belonged just before reorganization. In some cases these initials are followed

* Glen L. Pride: *Glossary of Scottish Building*, 1975.

by an asterisk and note indicating that the place is not included in the new Lothian Region, or that within the region it is not included in the district bearing the name of its old county. Midlothian, East Lothian and West Lothian are now the names of three of the four districts making up the Lothian Region. The fourth is the City of Edinburgh and this, containing probably the largest concentration of noteworthy buildings in Britain, will be the subject of a separate volume written by David Walker.

In the gazetteer are two kinds of entry. Under the name of a town or village is included everything within it or immediately adjacent to it and (at the end) such buildings in the vicinity as are conveniently visible from the road like farms and bridges. Under their own names are the country houses, however small, and their lodges and other subsidiary buildings. An entry in brackets shows that the building concerned has not, for whatever reason, been personally visited. Here it must be said that mention in B of S in no way implies that a building can be visited or its grounds entered. Information on those buildings which may be visited can be obtained from The National Trust for Scotland, 5 Charlotte Square, Edinburgh.

Acknowledgements for the Lothian volume are numerous and I must begin with the researchers: Katherine Michaelson who prepared the notes for visits, Ierne Grant who added to them, and John Gifford, now Senior Investigator of Historic Buildings in the Scottish Development Department, who extracted the relevant entries from periodicals not only for Lothian but for the whole of Scotland. The typing was done by Val Mackenzie, Vera Steele, and Christine, my wife. Dr Graham Ritchie and Gordon Maxwell of the Royal Commission on the Ancient and Historical Monuments of Scotland (hereafter abbreviated to RCAHMS) wrote the introductory sections and gazetteer entries for Prehistoric and Roman Lothian respectively, and Christopher Wilson did the same for all the medieval churches in Lothian (or the medieval parts of them) and also wrote the entry for Linlithgow Palace, a monument of great importance where I became stuck. Katherine Michaelson supplied invaluable information on the topography of Lothian, Robert Scott Morton on its farm buildings. Many other contributors of unpublished information are individually acknowledged by footnotes in the gazetteer, but I must thank them now. Help and advice were also given by Stewart Cruden, Inspector of Ancient Monuments for Scotland; by Dr Kenneth Steer and John Dunbar of the RCAHMS, and by Catherine Cruft and Richard Emerson of the National Monuments Record for Scotland which is part of that Commission's establishment; and by David Walker and the other Historic Buildings Investigators of the Scottish

Development Department. Their personal interest in B *of* S *is a bonus in addition to their individual writings and the official publications for which they are collectively responsible: the* DOE *Guidebooks,* RCAHMS *Inventories and* SDD *Lists. I am especially grateful to Professor Alistair Rowan of University College, Dublin, who is the author of The Buildings of Ireland, for his help. For swift and skilful work on line drawings I am indebted to Ian Stewart, Richard Andrews, H. A. Shelley (town plans) and Reginald Piggott (Lothian maps). I would also like to thank Judy Nairn of Penguin Books for her constructive and sympathetic editing of the typescript. Last and most important, I must thank the owners of country houses and other private properties for agreeing to let me see them, for their hospitality, and for their tolerance of the necessary speed of most of my visits. Ministers, priests and church officers were generous in letting me into their churches, many of which are understandably locked. I hope that these and all others who helped in the writing of Lothian will accept what I have written, even where praise is qualified, as a token of my gratitude.*

Finally, there are doubtless errors and omissions in this volume and I shall be grateful to anyone who takes the trouble to tell me about them.

INTRODUCTION

TOPOGRAPHY AND BUILDING MATERIALS

THE name Lothian, as applied to the Region newly constituted in 1975, is not a new one. 'Laudonia' appears on approximately the same territory in Bishop Leslie's map of Scotland in 1578, 'Louthiana' in John Blaeu's in 1654. John Slezer's *Theatrum Scotiae* (1693) uses the name Midlothian for the central county of the three. So does Sir John Sinclair's *Statistical Account of Scotland* (1791–9), but it calls the other two Linlithgowshire and Haddingtonshire. The *New Statistical Account* (1830s) goes further, giving Midlothian the name of Edinburghshire, and throughout the C19 each county was usually thus named, after its principal town. Quite early in the C20, however, the three Lothian names were restored and are now applied to three of the four Districts of the Lothian Region. The fourth, the City of Edinburgh, is excluded from this volume, which would otherwise have been at least twice the size. But Edinburgh and its site are and have always been so important to the three Lothians that they cannot be entirely left out of the present description.

Lothian is defined by hills and water. Part of what is loosely called the midland valley of Scotland, it lies along the S side of the broad estuary of the river Forth. Its long coastal plain, which extends westward into the former county of Stirlingshire, has a surface of boulder clay laid down by the W–E glacial drift. Over most of West Lothian it is heavy and mainly devoted to grazing; the exception is the area round Linlithgow where the clay is lightened by river silt. In East Lothian, similarly lightened and then intensively improved from the C18 onwards, the soil is some of the richest in Scotland. Here is the greatest concentration of water-mills, notably along the Tyne, and the greatest number of substantial farm buildings, each equipped with its octagonal horse-gang in which one to six horses toiled round the central spindle to drive the threshing machine of the type patented by Andrew Meikle the East Lothian millwright in 1788. Cobbett's *Tour* (1832) describes the county in scathing terms as the supplier of huge quantities of grain to the greedy capital. In order to give fair shares of this fertile land and of the poorer upland grazing, the parishes along the SE border of the county are laid out as long parallel strips, each one ascending into the hills. The parish of Stow in Midlothian had to make do with a terrain of bald hills only. It is not typical of Lothian, and indeed it now forms part of the Borders Region.

The *Statistical Account* shows that enclosure and improvement were well under way at the end of the C18, though the old run-rig system still survived at Currie ML. The lime industry played as important a part in agricultural improvement as in the building trade, and although the most famous of the C18 kilns are at Burdie-house which is now in Edinburgh, some good examples can be seen in the rest of Lothian; one of the best is at Skateraw, In-nerwick EL.

The Lothian coastline is most dramatic along the blunt pro-montory of East Lothian. It consists of volcanic cliffs and crags of assorted colours and, notably at Tantallon, great lumps of sand-stone displaced by their movement. Here the castle is sited on a tall volcanic vent and its red stonework is mixed with green basalt. Here also begins a chain of spectacular volcanic plugs; the Bass Rock projecting from the sea, North Berwick Law which is the landmark of that town, and the long ridge of Traprain Law to the S, each of the two inland crags having its rocky tail in the lee of the W–E glacial drift. Then there are the small-scale volcanic hills of Garleton, matched by the deep green Bathgate Hills of West Lothian with their intimate bumpy landscape and the switchback roads round Cairnpapple. West Lothian also has its crag-and-tail formation, at Dechmont Law near Bangour; it is rivalled by the flat-topped red bings left behind by the oil-shale industry from the century of intensive production that ended in 1962. But the most obvious group of crags-and-tails is that in whose midst the City of Edinburgh is sited – inconveniently but strategically; the castle rock and its attendant hills stand guard in the narrow gap between the Pentlands and the Forth. Lothian's SE and E boundary is formed by two other ranges, the Moorfoots and the Lammermuirs, and corresponds roughly with the South-ern Uplands Fault. The W boundary is the river Avon.

An eventful geological history has provided a very great variety of building stones. No builder in search of rubble or ashlar for any sort of work has had to look far from his site for a quarry. Although Gosford House is said to have been built of Angus stone and Whittingehame's pale stonework certainly came from Cullalo in Fife, these are exceptional cases. The availability of excellent ashlar (and the masons to shape it) was especially helpful for the construction of farm buildings with their wide arched entries and arcaded cartsheds. Loudon (1839) remarked on the princely appointments of Greendykes Farm, Gladsmuir EL, but the form- 108 ally designed farm steading (even monumental, as at Rosebery 107 ML) was already common in East and Midlothian, and in the latter half of the C19 the majority of new farm buildings were to be designed by specialist architects, e.g. *Robert Bell* at Carlowrie WL and Thurston EL, or by firms that were best known for their bank offices or country houses. From the C18 virtually all farm stead- ings, especially in East Lothian, are developments of the court- yard plan first promoted in Lord Belhaven's *Countryman's Rudi- ments*, published in 1699.

Lothian's basic material is calciferous sandstone, and the most famous quarries are those just outside Edinburgh and now within it, like Craigleith and Hailes, which supplied stone for the city's Georgian development. In the Victorian period these were suc- ceeded by Hermand (near West Calder), Dalmeny and Binny, all to the w. These stones are pale and dense, and Binny, rather warmer coloured than the others, had already been used for the Georgian house of that name in West Lothian. Mutual to Midlothian and East Lothian is a broad carboniferous wedge on whose w flank the coal measures extend from Prestonpans south- ward to Tranent, Newbattle and the Midlothian coalfields. From here to the east, beginning with the lightly banded stones of Tranent and Dalkeith, the general pattern is variegated with a rusty iron colour that sometimes provides elaborate figuring, sometimes a choice of warm shades so that many an East Lothian steading is a patchwork of buff and yellow, orange and dark brown. In the far NE corner Dunbar produces two extremes of colour in its own freestone, the creamy white of Catcraig and the deep Dunbar Red whose source (true to its name for once) is the Old Red Sandstone. All three counties have patches of the im- mensely hard volcanic stone which in Scotland is called whin, so intractable that it is no use for dressings; but its square cleft shapes, laid in courses, give a regular pattern to rubble walls. In North Berwick the gaps in coursed whinstone are made up with neat vertical rows of little pin-stones.

Such impervious walls need no further protection. Nor, of course, do the ashlar fronts that most builders, especially towards the E, could afford from the beginning of the C19. But where a rubble wall is softer it has to be covered with harling (originally lime based, with a fine aggregate), only the dressings being

66 exposed. In the C17 even as grand a house as Newhailes ML had an entrance front treated in this way, but to the ordinary lairds' houses harling supplies much of their character – an abstract sculptural quality that dignifies the most workaday composition. In the stone-conscious days of the C20 the best of East Lothian 95 housing was sometimes harled and sometimes of well built rubble, e.g. at Macmerry. The hard, variegated stone from the Rattlebags quarry was a favourite for all classes of house, and is still in use at the new abbey buildings at Nunraw. But proper stone walling is now a rarity; the modern equivalent of harling, which can be applied to bricks or concrete blocks just as well as to rubble, holds the field and tenuously maintains a tradition.

Pantiles (rather than slates which had to come from the West of Scotland) cover the roofs of most of the C18 farms and cottages, especially to the E – orange-red over orange-brown walls; there is no evidence that they were in general use in the previous century. Their manufacture was concentrated in the central coal districts, e.g. near Inveresk and at Prestonpans. So was the making of the purple-red common bricks for the Victorian miners' rows of Newtongrange and Rosewell ML, and the brighter coloured bricks of the East Lothian farm chimneys when steam power took from horses the job of powering the threshing machines. Broxburn WL and the other shale villages produced their own bricks, slightly pinker than those of Midlothian.

The C20 has introduced some new materials and building types 115 to Lothian, and the big industrial sheds of Cockenzie Power Station EL and the best Livingston WL factories are quite at home in the functional Scottish tradition. Development control are important, however. Overcoming a wretched backlog of C19–20 industrial blight, the local planning authorities have established a tradition of constructive control, especially of building materials. East Lothian, with its most obviously vulnerable heritage, was the pioneer. But the traveller in Lothian is not often confronted with recent follies; indeed the last twenty-five years have seen a general improvement. Conservation has won its point.

THE LOTHIANS IN PREHISTORY

BY J. N. GRAHAM RITCHIE

THE earliest evidence for human settlement in Lothian is provided by the small groups of hunters and fishermen who penetrated the wood- and scrub-lands that still covered the area in
the fifth millennium B.C. Seasonal forays from north-east England
introduced these hunters to the resources of south-east Scotland
and most particularly to the richness of the Tweed Valley. In the
Lothians some of the favoured hunting spots and temporary
camps of these mesolithic people may be indicated by the chance
finds of their flint implements at Hedderwick and Gullane and
on Traprain Law E L, and at Kaimes Hill and Arthur's Seat in Edinburgh. Perhaps more permanent occupation is shown by the substantial heaps of oyster shells, with occasional examples of mussel,
cockle, periwinkle and winkle, at sites on the banks of the River
Avon near Bo'ness W L and also on the island of Inchkeith in the
Forth. There were traces of hearths and fires within the heaps
of shells but there is no information about the settlement sites
of this period, nor any indication whether the shellfish were a
seasonal or a permanent source of food. Radiocarbon dates from
material retrieved from the shell-heap at Inveravon W L show that
the occupation may be as early as the fifth millennium B.C.

The first groups of farmers practising a mixed economy of
stock-breeding and agriculture probably arrived in the Lothians
by way of north-east England before 3500 B.C. The deep clayey
loams of the East Lothian lowlands proved too heavy for the
primitive ploughs of these farmers, and they seem to have
settled on the sandy littoral, with some upland communities presumably concentrating on stock-breeding. No habitations or
ritual sites of neolithic date have yet been discovered in the Lothians, but scatters of midden material including pottery and bone
near Gullane and North Berwick E L are evidence of the existence
of nearby settlements. The earliest pottery in south-east Scotland
is similar to that from Yorkshire and suggests that the new settlers
came from this area; one example of a typical round-based pottery
vessel is from Roslin M L. The main evidence of the presence of
neolithic farmers is provided by the discovery of the stone axes
with which they created clearings for fields and cut down fodder
for their animals. The choice of stone suitable for the making
of such polished stone axes is a remarkable illustration of the

complexity of neolithic economy; at Cairnpapple Hill WL, for example, fragments of axes from as far afield as Graig Lwyd in North Wales and Great Langdale in Westmorland have been found associated with the first phase of this important sanctuary site.

The excavation of the series of ritual and burial monuments on the top of Cairnpapple Hill provides a key for an understanding of the types of site and finds dating to the first half of the second millennium B.C. The site is therefore, exceptionally, described in greater detail here than in the gazetteer. In the first period the site consisted of a number of small pits, six of which contained deposits of cremated bone, associated with a setting of standing stones; this period dates to before 2000 B.C. and may be compared to the first period of Stonehenge (Wiltshire). It has been suggested that the axe fragments mentioned above were broken during the initial clearance of the site, and certainly the first period may be associated with late neolithic traditions rather than with the intrusive burial rituals of period two. The second period would have been the most visually impressive when it was constructed. It was a henge monument, that is an oval earthwork consisting of a ditch and outer bank with entrance causeways to N and S. Within the henge was an oval setting of twenty-six standing stones and perhaps a central setting of stones represented only by a series of hollows in the ground. A burial with an early example of a type of pot known as Beaker ware, which may originally have come from the Rhineland, was found beside one of the uprights of the stone circle. Perhaps rather later in the second period a small kerb-cairn surrounded a grave pit containing an inhumation burial accompanied by two later Beaker vessels and two wooden objects with a standing stone at one end of the grave. This small cairn may be compared to that which originally contained the Cat Stane, near Turnhouse, Edinburgh. The number of cist burials (individual coffins often with crouched inhumations) in East Lothian suggests a concentration of the newcomers in that area, but discoveries of such vessels at Bathgate WL and Juniper Green, Edinburgh, are evidence of Beaker presence in the west.

In the third period at Cairnpapple, the hill-top was chosen as the site of a cairn of large stones covering two cists, the central one containing the remains of an inhumation burial associated with a Food Vessel pot; the standing stones of the second period were taken down and some at least were used as kerb-stones at the base of the cairn to help to retain the considerable weight.

About the middle of the second millennium B.C. this already substantial cairn was enlarged to a diameter of 30 m., apparently to cover two further burials in inverted Cinerary Urns. Finds of such pottery vessels are more frequently made in natural hillocks or as secondary deposits in already existing cairns, and the remodelling and enlarging of the Cairnpapple mound must surely indicate that the burials were those of people of some importance. The final period of activity on the site is represented by four graves for extended inhumation burials, the date of which is not known but is probably within the early first millennium A.D.

Increasingly, in studying the social structure of individual areas, archaeologists have been basing their ideas on the distribution of certain types of monument, chiefly those which imply an organization greater than the family unit. For the Lothians in the first half of the second millennium B.C., Cairnpapple is clearly a site of paramount importance, first as a ritual centre or meeting-place and latterly as a burial site that could be seen from a considerable distance. It may even be that the axes made of stones from as far away as North Wales are evidence of long-distance exchanges which went on at this focal point; be that as it may, the construction of the henge monument required a considerable amount of communal effort in digging out the ditch and constructing the bank and stone circle. Similar ceremonial centres exist for adjoining areas, e.g. at Huntingtower near Perth, and probably at Balfarg near Markinch in Fife. The burial cairns of periods three and four at Cairnpapple may be compared to other hill-top cairns in the Lothians such as those on the summits of Caerketton Hill in Edinburgh, and Spartleton and Harestone Hills near Hopes EL. It is possible that these were deliberately sited in such conspicuous positions, high above the tree-line, so that they could be seen from several settlements on the lower ground. The finds from the cairns on Cairnpapple Hill, for example, mirror those from cairns on less conspicuous sites or indeed from cists or burial deposits unaccompanied by any covering mound. No inferences about the structure of society can be drawn from the objects themselves.

Standing stones make an important contribution to the Lothian landscape, and it is tantalizing that so little is known about them. The Loth Stone near Traprain Law EL, traditionally said to cover the remains of Loth, the eponymous king of Lothian, is one of the few to have been scientifically excavated, but nothing was found which could shed light on its date. There were no datable finds in the stone holes of the circle at Cairnpapple Hill. Certain stones of East Lothian – Pencraig Hill, Kirklandhill and near Traprain for example – are among the most outstanding. The stone circles on Kingside Hill and Mayshiel on the other hand are low and unimpressive. No satisfactory overall purpose for standing stones and stone circles can be proposed. Some clearly acted as a focus for Bronze Age burials, others may have had an astronomical significance, yet others may have indicated territorial boundaries. Equally puzzling are the rock carvings known as cup-marks, sometimes surrounded by a circle (cup-and-ring marks); some standing stones are thus decorated, like the Caiystane in Edinburgh and the stone at Easter Broomhouse, Spott EL, but the decorated surfaces on boulders or rock outcrops at Glencorse church ML and on Tormain Hill, Edinburgh, give a better impression of such prehistoric art.

The introduction of a knowledge of metallurgy seems to be linked with the arrival of the makers of Beaker pottery in the late third millennium B.C. The range of tools and weapons and the improvements in functional shape and manufacturing techniques can best be seen in the displays of the National Museum of Antiquities of Scotland. The century between about 700 and 600 B.C. saw the start of a period of social and technological change that lasted for some seven hundred years in southern Scotland until the advent of the armies of Rome altered the character of local life.

There had been increasing trade contact between east Scotland and the continent in the C8 B.C. reflected by imported bronze wine-containers and horse harness, and this contact can be seen to have continued into the C6 B.C. Most of the imports coming into Scotland were luxury goods like bronze jewellery and the fashionable new swords, but there was a flourishing local bronze industry producing more prosaic equipment such as the axes needed for cutting timber for house-building. Moulds used in manufacturing bronze axes, swords and spearheads have been found on Traprain Law EL, indicating that the hill-top was settled by a small self-supporting community in the C7–6, before the ramparts of the later tribal capital were built.

The settlement on Traprain Law was also one of the earliest in Scotland to obtain the new metal: iron. Conservative and resistant to change, the inhabitants seem to have been lured into accepting iron; the familiar socketed axe was copied in the new material, despite the technical difficulties of hammering out in iron a form of tool designed to be cast in bronze. If we can judge from the number of objects that survive, the manufacture of iron tools and weapons seems never to have matched the flourishing industry enjoyed by the old bronzesmiths, at least not before the Roman period. Bronze itself continued to be used for fine metalwork including sword scabbards, neck ornaments, brooches and horse harness.

The centuries following 600 B.C. were marked by more than just technological advances, for there were also social changes so radical that they have left their impression even on the tangible archaeological record. There is reason to believe that the population had been expanding during the latter part of the Bronze Age, and, with the increased craft specialization seen in the bronze industry, the social framework seems to have become more stable and organized. For the first time it is justifiable to think in terms of tribes as political and economic units. For the first time, too, we know something of the language of the inhabitants of southeast Scotland; but the mechanics of how the Brittonic or P-Celtic language may have been introduced cannot be inferred from the present archaeological evidence.

One effect of social stabilization was to make the remains of houses and farmsteads easier for the archaeologist to find. Communities began to enclose their timber houses within protective fences and banks which were sufficiently substantial for traces of them to remain today. The settlement of Braidwood ML in the foothills of the Pentlands was originally surrounded by a double line of sturdy timber fencing, and shallow grooves in the turf still mark the position of the fences and the round wooden houses that they enclosed. More obvious still are the upstanding banks and ditches which were built to replace the stockades when the timbers had rotted.

Even a small undertaking like the building of Braidwood required communal effort, but the extent of social organization is most clearly seen behind the imposing remains of hill-forts. By the C7 B.C. social pressures were such that protection of life and property was required on a grand scale; the rampart of these early fortifications might be of earth with a stone or timber revetment presenting a sheer vertical face to the outside world; it might be built wholly of stone, or timber beams might be used as an internal framework to strengthen a rampart of either earth or stone. It is known from radiocarbon dating of burnt timbers found in excavation that the latter technique, described as timber-lacing, was popular among the earliest fort-builders in the C7 B.C.

Timber-lacing had been in use on the continent for several centuries before its appearance in Scotland, and it has been suggested that the idea was brought over by immigrants from north Germany. There is certainly evidence for trade contacts with that area, but nothing to prove physical immigration of people; the idea of strengthening ramparts with wooden beams may have evolved independently in the two areas simply as a sensible method of achieving a stable line of defence. Timber-lacing, however, had its drawbacks, for the beams were liable to rot eventually and could be replaced only by the drastic measure of dismantling the rampart. In the case of stone walls the wooden framework presented a fire hazard of dramatic effect: as the beams smouldered, the slots in the stonework became flues and the carbon acted as a flux, resulting in temperatures high enough to fuse or vitrify the stones into a distorted mass. Whether such a fire happened by accident or by enemy action, its effect was to cut short the useful life of the fort wall. One of these vitrified forts can be seen at Harelaw EL, and traces of unburnt timber-lacing were found during excavations at the entrance into the fort at Castle Law ML.

A century or so before the arrival in Scotland of the Roman army, some fort-builders had adopted the device of multiple ramparts as a way of strengthening the defence and at the same time increasing the visual effect of the fort. At The Chesters, Drem EL, a magnificent multivallate fort was built in a quite unstrategic position overlooked by higher ground; the primary object here must surely have been to impress rather than to defend.

A few monuments appear to be intrusive into Lothian, as their main distributions are outside this region – one broch at Bow ML and two souterrains at Castle Law ML and at Crichton ML are examples of sites which occur in the north-west of Scotland and Tayside respectively. At Bow the foundations of what was once a substantial stone-walled tower survive; it has not been scientifically excavated, but an enamelled brooch of Roman date in the shape of a cock has been found. Some indication of the date of the souterrain at Castle Law, which was constructed in the hollow between the outer ramparts of the fort, is given by the discovery of Roman pottery, glass, and an enamelled brooch. That at Crichton, which is about 15 m. in length underground, uses about seventy blocks of Roman dressed masonry in its construction.

If Cairnpapple Hill can be used as the key site in the second millennium B.C. to illustrate the continuity of sanctity of a single site and to suggest something of the web of interrelationships in economic and social organization, the comparable site in the first millennium B.C. is Traprain Law EL. The earliest evidence links it with the fourth period at Cairnpapple, as four Cinerary Urns and a small accessory vessel were discovered in 1920, one of them still containing the remains of the cremation burial; this is of considerably earlier date than the next stage of activity in the C7–5 B.C. which has already been reviewed. The sequence of ramparts shows that Traprain was by its size one of the most important sites of the region, and it may well have been one of the citadels of the Votadini, the major tribe in this area. Excavation has produced a large quantity of objects illustrative of life in the early centuries of the first millennium A.D., but, because of the unsatisfactory nature of the site plans, it is difficult to build up a picture of the houses and streets of one of the earliest attempts at urbanization in south-east Scotland.

THE ROMAN PERIOD

BY GORDON S. MAXWELL

IN considering the Roman occupation of Lothian it is necessary to make two basic assumptions: first that the historical and archaeological information now available to us, although lacking in detail, nevertheless provides a satisfactory general picture of the period; and second that by A.D. 80, the date of their earliest invasion of Scotland, the Romans had amassed enough intelligence about the northern British tribes to have had a good reason for all their troop dispositions in the subsequent campaigns. The remarkable distribution of Roman monuments in the area under discussion – at least seven forts and fortlets and twelve temporary camps in the western half, but not a single example in the eastern – clearly demands an explanation that goes beyond appeals to the random nature of archaeological discovery or to the inscrutable rigidity of the military mind.

In the Roman period Lothian formed the northernmost riding of the *civitas Votadinorum*, whose tribal territory extended from the Tyne to the Forth. The area was first brought under Roman rule when the governor of the province of Britannia, Gnaeus Julius Agricola, followed up a single-season campaign against the Brigantes of northern England with a fast-moving thrust that penetrated as far N as the estuary of the Tay. This operation, dating most probably to A.D. 80, may well have taken the form of a pincer-movement designed to isolate the Selgovae, who held middle and upper Tweeddale. It did not apparently involve any reconnaissance of Votadinian territory away from the main invasion route, which, leaving the Tweed near Melrose, drove northwards through Lauderdale to cross the Lothian river Esk near Dalkeith or Inveresk, and the Almond near Cramond or Newbridge; thence it followed one of the E–W coastal ridgeways, seeking a crossing of the Forth a little to the NW of Stirling.

When the tide of battle had swept on, road-building commenced along the line of the advance, with garrison-posts of different sizes set at intervals along the route to maintain security. In later times the sector of the road S of the Esk remained in use over long stretches, and became known as Dere Street. A second road, possibly following the course of the pincer's western claw, was constructed on the SE side of the Pentland Hills, effecting a junction with the first somewhere in the vicinity of Dalkeith

ML, at Eskbank perhaps. It is somehow not inappropriate that these roads, among the first structures of the Roman period to be built, should also be among the last to disappear. Although now much attenuated in their course by cultivation and by urban development, they represent the most extensive and abiding monuments to Roman imperial achievement that the area can furnish. The best preserved stretches are to be found between Eight Mile Burn and Carlops ML, lying to the N of the A702, and SW of the A68 at Soutra ML, where Dere Street wheels majestically over the watershed into Lauderdale.

No military posts of the later CI A.D. have yet been identified in Lothian with any degree of certainty, but it seems very probable that there were garrisons at that time in the vicinity of both Cramond (Edinburgh) and Inveresk ML, while the remoteness from any known road-system of the small fort of Castle Greg WL, on the NW side of the Pentland Hills, may indicate that it, too, belongs to an early phase of frontier policy. It was examined by Sir Daniel Wilson in 1852, but no plan was then published, and the objects recovered during the excavation were inadequately described and have since been lost. The fortlet, defended by a rampart of turf and two ditches, measures approximately 58 m. by 50 m. (0.3 hectares); its garrison probably did not exceed two *centuriae*. Temporary camps intended to accommodate Roman armies on the march and possibly dating to the Agricolan campaigns of A.D. 80 have, however, been recognized S of Pathhead MI on the A68 (NT 397634), on the r. bank of the Esk NE of Dalkeith ML (NT 345693), and in the fields to the S of Inveresk EL (NT 347710). Unfortunately, none of these survives above ground level; their existence was betrayed by crop-markings recognized in the course of aerial reconnaissance.

It is not known whether the CI forts in Lothian were peacefully evacuated in A.D. 86/7, when the Roman garrison in Scotland appears to have been drastically pruned, or were maintained as forward strongpoints in association with Newstead on the Tweed, and like it suffered violent destruction *c.* 105. Certainly from that latter date until *c.* 140 they lay empty. However with the arrival of the governor Q. Lollius Urbicus in 139 there came a change of policy: the frontier was moved northward from the Tyne-Solway isthmus, where it had lain as a continuous barrier since *c.* A.D. 122, to the narrow strip of land between Forth and Clyde. Here was constructed the Antonine Wall, a predominantly turf-built rampart 4.5 m. in average thickness and more than 3 m. high; it was guarded by nineteen forts disposed along the line of the barrier at intervals of just over two Roman miles from each other. At the same time throughout Scotland, even to the N of the Wall, many old Agricolan *castella* were renovated and enlarged for their new garrisons, and the road-system, after forty years of neglect, was brought back into use; in fact the only surviving Roman milestone in Scotland,* which was found near Ingliston ML (c. NT 1372), records road repairs dating to c. AD 140.

The ANTONINE WALL, named in modern times after the Emperor Antoninus Pius in whose reign it was first built, is Scotland's major Roman field monument. Its course may be followed for about 6.5 km. on the westernmost fringe of the old territory of Lothian, from its eastern terminus at Bridgeness WL (NT 013813), where was found the magnificent distance-slab* dedi- 1 cated by men of the Legio II Augusta, as far as the River Avon, immediately W of the site of the recently discovered Wall-fort of Inveravon WL (NS 952797). At each end of this sector aerial reconnaissance has identified the sites of four of the labour camps that accommodated the legionary *vexillatio* engaged in wall construction; the camps, grouped in pairs, lie a little way to the S of the frontier line.

No trace of the Wall itself can now be seen above ground level in these parts, but the presence of the massive, 12-m.-wide ditch that lay to the N of the barrier is indicated in places by a barely detectable dip or hollow in boundary wall and field surface. The approximate sites of two more Wall-forts are known at Kinneil WL (NS 983805) and Bridgeness, Bo'ness WL, although the role of the latter as a terminal fort may have been taken by the known station at Carriden House WL (NT 025808). This last, which was located from the air in 1945 by Professor St Joseph, although its existence had long been suspected because of the numerous finds of Roman coins and inscriptions, is the only site in Lothian whose Roman name has come down to us. An inscribed altar ploughed up in 1956 some way to the E of the fort identifies it as the Castellum Velunia(s) mentioned in the C7 Ravenna *Cosmography* list of stations on the Antonine Wall. The inscription also indicates that Carriden fort, itself about 1.6 hectares in extent and capable of accommodating a 500-man *cohors*, or infantry regiment, possessed a *vicus*, or officially recognized civilian settlement, immediately adjacent; traces of such a settlement were subsequently identified in aerial photographs.

Carriden would doubtless have supplied some of the logistical

---

* Now in the National Museum of Antiquities in Edinburgh.

needs of the Wall garrison, but the great bulk of material probably
passed through Cramond (*see Buildings of Scotland: Edinburgh*)
situated beside an excellent harbour at the very mouth of the River
Almond. Excavations at this site, which occupies an area of about
2.4 hectares, have shown that much of its interior was given over
to workshops or storehouses throughout the C2 occupation. Inveresk at the mouth of the River Esk (ML, formerly including
Musselburgh) was apparently not provided by nature with the
same harbourage facilities. Nevertheless, probably thanks to its
position near the head of Dere Street, the Inveresk fort served
as the focus for an extramural civil settlement of exceptional size
and importance, quite possibly the nearest thing to Romanized
urban development anywhere in Scotland. The first indication of
the existence here of a Roman site was the discovery as early as
1565 of an altar dedicated to Apollo Grannus by an Imperial *procurator*. In the late C18, and again in the C19, a number of hypocausted structures was uncovered during building operations or
the improvement of parkland some distance to the E of the parish
church, while popular accounts spoke of hard cobbled floors 'that
resisted the plough' in fields lying to the N E of the village. However,
it was not until 1946 that the fort itself was discovered in excavations conducted by Sir Ian Richmond on the W side of the church.
Facing W towards the crossing of the Esk, the fort measured about
185 m. by 145 m. (2.7 hectares) over the ramparts. Although the
identity of the garrison is unknown, the internal plan together
with the area of the fort led the excavator to suggest that it had
housed an *ala quingenaria* or 500-man cavalry regiment. As was
the case with Cramond, occupation appears to have commenced
c. A.D. 140 and continued with one brief interval until some date
in the later C2.

More recent excavations have shown that an extensive civil
settlement or *vicus* lay to the S and SE of the fort, consisting of
handsomely built stone structures, some equipped with hypo-
causts, probably disposed along streets leading to the E gate of
the fort. At present it seems that such ribbon-development could
extend over an area of about 10 hectares; a stone pine-cone finial
found in a field 700 m. SE of the church probably indicates the
existence of a Roman cemetery lying on the limits of the inhabited
area. To the S and SE of the village crop-markings identified on
aerial photographs have revealed the sites of temporary camps
associated with at least one of the known Roman invasions of Scotland as well as an extensive system of fields, enclosures and tracks
dating to the Roman period; the system, which resembles

examples found in large numbers in the Upper Thames Valley or the East Riding of Yorkshire, is, in its extent and complexity, unique in Scotland.

The fact that to the E of Inveresk the Votadinian territory appears to have contained no permanent Roman garrisons may not be a coincidence; for the discovery here of an altar dedicated to Apollo by an Imperial *procurator* clearly suggests that Roman civil administration had no unimportant role to play in the surrounding area. If we are to claim that in the life of the community occupying the *oppidum* on Traprain Law EL we can see the hand of Rome, surely it is at Inveresk that we may hope to detect the immediate source of that influence during the C2. The recent discovery in Inveresk churchyard of a second altar mentioning the *procurator* Q. Lusius Sabinianus confirms that such a hope is not ill founded.

To the list of the known Antonine sites we may safely add the presumed site near Crichton, S of Pathhead ML, whose existence is indicated by the blocks of Roman masonry incorporated in the fabric of a souterrain. Roman coins and a bronze *patera* or skillet have been found in nearby fields. The position, approximately halfway between the fort of Inveresk and the fortlet of Oxton in Berwickshire, both in use in Antonine times, makes it probable that the Crichton post was another fortlet of the same period, intended to provide additional security on the main trunk route between the Tweed and the Forth.

The duration of the Antonine occupation of Scotland is still a matter for academic debate. Whether the first phase lasted from A.D. 140 until 155 or 158 is uncertain, and although most authorities would agree that reoccupation took place after only a very brief interval, estimates of the closing date of the second phase range widely – some putting it as early as 163, others as late as 197. At present it seems possible that some forts in southern Scotland may have been held for only part of the second Antonine phase – some, we know, were never reoccupied after the end of the first – but there are others, especially on the Antonine Wall, which must have been garrisoned until at least the 170s. On balance, the frontier war of the early 180s still presents the most likely pretext for the final evacuation of the Antonine frontier, although by that time many of the outpost and hinterland forts may already have been long in ruins.

This, however, is not the end of the story, for at both Pathhead and Inveresk air photographs have revealed evidence in the form of crop-markings of the largest class of temporary camp known anywhere in the Roman Empire, c.65 hectares in extent. Intended to house the field army of the Emperor Septimius Severus and his son Caracalla during their campaigns against the Maeatae and the Caledonii in 209–11, they lie approximately 9.5 km. apart, plainly marking the end of two consecutive stages in the progress through Scotland of a battle group numbered in tens of thousands of men. The campaigns, which may have penetrated as far N as the Moray Firth, resulted in the construction of a legionary base at Carpow, on the S shore of the Tay near Newburgh, and a re-occupation of the Antonine post at Cramond, together with some kind of military presence at Newstead.

Once more the fort on the Almond saw service as a works depot and stores base, and once more the civil settlement round the fort enjoyed a time of prosperity, although only for a handful of years, until a revision of frontier policy under Caracalla necessitated a return to the line of Hadrian's Wall. We need not, however, imagine that with the departure of the legionary and auxiliary garrisons c. 212–15 all Roman contacts with Lothian suddenly ceased. The provision of long-range patrols (*exploratores*) operating from the outpost forts of Hadrian's Wall ensured that for the rest of the C3 military and political control of the nations lying immediately outside the military frontier and as far N as the Tay rested with the O.C. Northern Command. In such a system of frontier control we may be sure that the peaceful co-existence between Roman and native that had been fostered in the civil settlements of the Lothian forts had no small part to play. Indeed it may not be too much to claim that active co-operation between Rome and the Votadini was now a tradition, for there is evidence that even in the first half of the C4 at least one Roman site, Cramond, was being used by people who built in a Roman military style and used imported Roman pottery. While it is by no means certain that such activity betokens a military occupation, it is not impossible that under Carausius or Constantius, or even Constans, Rome capitalized on the deep-rooted attitudes of the local *civitas* to promote the greater stability of the northern frontier. Certain it is, at any rate, that before another century had passed the descendants of the Votadini were making their own provisions for the security of the frontiers of sub-Roman Britain.

MEDIEVAL CHURCHES

BY CHRISTOPHER WILSON

THE earliest religious foundations in Lothian of which we have
any record belong to the period of Northumbrian rule, starting
about 650. The bishop's see and monastery at Abercorn WL were
established by 685 at the latest and the monastery at Tyninghame
EL was in existence by the mid C9, but may have been founded
during the lifetime of St Baldred, i.e. before 756. Although
no remains of such early buildings survive at either place,*
there are sizeable fragments of two C8 standing crosses at Abercorn
which, if not first-class works of art, do at least show that this
region of Northumbria was artistically one with the rest. The
earlier cross has much in common with the celebrated cross of
Bewcastle in Cumberland (c. 670 or soon after). Its main sides are
divided into short panels like Bewcastle's and most of the ornament is similar: vine scroll, interlace and the scroll inhabited by
beasts and birds – all motifs known to derive ultimately from
Mediterranean and Early Christian sources. But there is also a
panel of animal interlace quite unlike anything at Bewcastle. The
origin of this form must lie in barbarian metalwork, although
similar designs had already been used in the Lindisfarne Gospels.
The other Abercorn cross can be dated later in the C8 or possibly
into the C9, on account of the dryer and harsher quality of its carving and the presence of 'ribbon animal'. The human figure does
not appear on either cross, in marked contrast to Bewcastle and
the still earlier and finer cross at Ruthwell in Dumfries-shire. That
there were sculptors in C8 Lothian capable of satisfactory figure
carving is proved by the upper part of an angel preserved on a
cross fragment from Aberlady EL.‡ Yet the most impressive
feature of this piece is the panel with intertwined pairs of birds.
Its vigour and three-dimensionality are unparalleled by anything earlier than the fantastic C12 trumeaux at Moissac and
Beaulieu.

The architectural history of Lothian begins with the reign
of David I (1124–53). One of the key features of David's policy
was the systematic introduction of the MONASTIC ORDERS.
Benedictines had already been installed at Dunfermline in Fife
and Coldingham in Berwickshire, but David favoured the newer

* But for remains uncovered by excavation in 1963 *see* note on p. 70.

‡ Now in the National Museum of Antiquities, Edinburgh, together with
later cross fragments from Borthwick and Lasswade ML.

reformed orders. Pre-eminent among these were the Cistercians who colonized Newbattle Abbey ML, the one important monastic house in Lothian. Unfortunately, the visible remains of its mid C12 buildings consist of no more than some bases from the W range, but they are enough to indicate close ties with Kirkstall, one of the major Cistercian abbeys of Yorkshire. Cistercian also were three houses of nuns founded around the mid C12, at Haddington and North Berwick EL and Manuel WL, 2 km. WSW of Linlithgow. Nothing survives of Haddington or Manuel and only parts of much later and rather confusing buildings at North Berwick. Other monastic remains are for the most part minor. At the preceptory of Knights Hospitallers at Torphichen WL (founded around 1153 possibly by David I) there are late C12 transepts remodelled in the C15. At the Carmelite friary of Luffness, Aberlady EL only the lowest courses of a late C13 church remain, but the church of the South Queensferry Carmelites WL is intact except for the nave. At the Trinitarian monastery in Dunbar EL there is the plain C15 tower that stood between nave and choir; at Soutra EL the hospital founded by Malcolm IV c. 1164 is represented by the shell of a late and almost featureless oblong building.

Returning to the C12, it is PARISH CHURCHES rather than monastic buildings that stand out, for another of the achievements of David I's reign was the establishment of a regular parochial system at least in the Lowland dioceses. Dalmeny WL naturally takes pride of place, but Tyninghame EL must once have been as good. 6 The plan is the same at both places – apse, chancel, nave and w 7 tower – and so, nearly, are the dimensions – 30.5 m. total length at Dalmeny, 35 m. at Tyninghame. Stylistically both are very pure Anglo-Norman and obviously dependent on Dunfermline Abbey, Fife, the central monument of the Romanesque in Scotland. Apses and chancels are rib-vaulted, arches have chevron, and capitals are mostly either simple block and scallop types or one of the variants found at Dunfermline. The s door at Dalmeny is more elaborately 5 decorated than that of any other Scottish parish church of the C12. This was not always so, for until c. 1790 St Giles, Edinburgh, had a N door of three orders (Dalmeny has only two) with voussoirs devoted to the same varieties of masks, fantastic beasts and tangled interlace. So it appears that the Lothians possessed something of a local school of Romanesque carvers. Most of the motifs in their repertoire can be traced to Dunfermline, but others, like the small reliefs of warriors beside the door at Dalmeny, imply a wider range of artistic contacts. Other Romanesque survivals are more fragmentary: Kirkliston WL has a tall W tower plus a long rectangular

nave and so has Uphall WL, though here the sole original detail
is the S door, Norman work at its most blunt and businesslike.
The old church at Lasswade ML was, until it collapsed in 1866,
of the same type. St Martin at Haddington EL preserves a very
simple rectangular nave with two windows in the S wall and just
one in the N wall, a peculiarity repeated locally at Dalmeny WL
and Duddingston (*see Buildings of Scotland: Edinburgh*). Chancels
are far less often preserved than naves, but wherever one can still
check, as at Gullane or Haddington EL or Kinneil WL, they were
narrower and entered through a chancel arch. At Borthwick ML
there is a plain unvaulted apse, heavily restored but preserving
the original forms. Except at Dalmeny and Tyninghame carved
detail is minimal. The one C12 tympanum in Lothian, at Abercorn
WL, has only simple incised patterns. In the category of NON-
ARCHITECTURAL SCULPTURE comes the coffin in the churchyard at Dalmeny WL, its front carved with thirteen crude little
figures under arches and its foot with a winged beast. It is possibly
the work of the same carvers as the church. A unique but sadly
damaged piece is the large stone crucifix, now in Kinneil House,
that probably stood over the chancel arch of Kinneil church.

After the relative riches of the Romanesque period in Lothian
the TRANSITIONAL and EARLY GOTHIC styles are very poorly
represented. Undoubtedly the chief building of the late C12 and
early C13 was the church at Newbattle Abbey ML, but it has been
destroyed down to the foundations. The choir and nave were
aisled, of three and ten bays respectively, and the transepts had
E aisles. The plan made after excavation in the late C19 shows several later medieval changes, but the E end as first built seems to
have followed its fellow Cistercian abbey of Byland in Yorkshire
in having its choir aisles returned to form a straight ambulatory. Byland was begun *c.* 1177, so Newbattle was probably built
from the end of the century into the first third of the C13. The
transition from Norman to Gothic can be studied at Kirkliston
and Torphichen WL. At Kirkliston there are two fine doorways
of which the southern is the richer. It is still round-headed and
projects from the wall in the Romanesque way, but the details
are no longer Romanesque. The arch orders have chevron of the
deeply undercut varieties popular in the late C12, and the complicated arrangement of fully detached shafts on the jambs shows
a similar concern with effects of depth and recession. Capitals are
a mixture of waterleaf and crockets. At Torphichen the W crossing
arch is the most telling survival, with its keeled shafts and crisp
waterleaf capitals. Windows at both places are small narrow lan-

cets. The only really good example of the mature style of the early
C13 is the chancel at Prestonkirk, East Linton EL. The E wall is
a composition of sufficient finesse to be the work of a cathedral
or major abbey workshop. Contemporary with it are more or less
completely preserved churches at Cockpen ML, Bathgate WL and
Keith EL. Unlike the C12 churches, they have no chancel arch
and maintain the same width from end to end. These long un-
differentiated boxes were to remain the norm for parish churches
during the rest of the Middle Ages. That they were not restricted
to parish churches can be seen from the remains of the late C13
church at the Luffness Carmelite friary EL.

The FOURTEENTH CENTURY was a period of architectural
dearth in Scotland, a fact readily attributable to unfavourable
political and economic circumstances. Only two churches in
Lothian can be assigned to this century, and those to the second
rather than the first half. The parish church at Temple ML is of 18
the 'box' type already mentioned, its details careful reiterations
of C13 forms with only a few touches that give away the late date.
With its fine mouldings and generous use of ashlar, Temple is,
all in all, the best of the late medieval village churches. The other
C14 survival – it is hard to see it as anything more than that –
is the N chapel at Pencaitland EL. Here the details show much
less skill, but what there are deviate little from C13 precedents.

For the FIFTEENTH and early SIXTEENTH CENTURIES
Lothian has more to offer than any other area of the country.
First must come the two burgh churches at Linlithgow WL and 10–12
Haddington EL. Both buildings are on a very generous scale,* but
in general conception they are radically different. Haddington is
cruciform with a central tower, fully developed crossing, and aisles
to the choir as well as the nave. St Nicholas at Aberdeen (late
C12) is the oldest representative of this type which recurs at St
Giles, Edinburgh (second half of the C14), and St John, Perth
(c. 1440). Linlithgow approximates much more to the contemporary English pattern, with its W tower, S porch, and projecting
chapels resembling low transepts. The placing of the tower at the
W end is found of course at other Scottish burgh churches, notably
Dundee and Stirling, but there are enough Perpendicular details
on the Linlithgow tower to allow one to think in terms of direct
influences from south of the Border. In elevation the tall arcades
and low clearstory are nearer to English ideas than the more
evenly divided storeys at Haddington. However, in this case
English influence seems unlikely in view of the many similarities

* Linlithgow 55 m., Haddington 63 m. long.

to the French-looking work of the early C15 in the E and S wings of the adjacent palace. Both these great churches were built slowly, and discussion of their individual features must wait until the rest of the late medieval picture has been sketched in.

The burgh churches are untypical of their period not only architecturally but historically, for they reflect the wealth and civic pride of the towns, whereas the great bulk of C15 and early C16 churches were ordinary parish churches partly or wholly rebuilt by individuals rich enough to found colleges of chantry priests. Roslin ML was a private collegiate church with no parochial function; but then it stands outside the normal in its architecture too. Three churches that were not collegiate can, for architectural purposes, be considered as belonging to the same category: the Carmelite friars' church at South Queensferry WL, the 'pilgrimage church' at Whitekirk EL and the intended collegiate church at Midcalder ML.

PLANS show little inventiveness. Dunglass, Whitekirk, and Seton, all EL, and Crichton ML are aisleless and cruciform.* The last two preserve only slight traces of naves and it has often been asserted that none were ever built. At Seton this is demonstrably incorrect and at Crichton unlikely on the surviving evidence. At both places the naves were wooden-roofed and hence more prone to decay than the stone-vaulted parts; the shell of an unvaulted nave at South Queensferry could be cleared away as recently as the early C19. South Queensferry has also the curious feature of a single S transept with none to balance it on the N side. Evidently space for the cloister was at a premium. At Borthwick ML the chapel added to the S side produces a similarly lopsided plan, though there is here no misleading central tower. At first sight Dunglass and Seton seem perfectly homogeneous buildings, but neither was intended to be cruciform initially. At Dunglass the transepts were a revision made during or after building, at Seton they came sixty years after the choir and at least two centuries after the nave. Apart from Haddington and Linlithgow, the only aisled nave is at Dalkeith ML. The arcades are of three bays only, and the easternmost opens out into transeptal chapels in the Linlithgow manner. E ends are on the whole flat, but three churches have three-sided apses, a fashion that began c. 1440 at Crossraguel Priory, Ayrshire, and continued with Trinity College, Edinburgh, of c. 1460. The Lothian examples are: Seton (c. 1470), Dalkeith (c. 1500) and Linlithgow (c. 1500). Roslin ML is in plan, as in everything else, exceptional. A straight E ambulatory opens

* So was the destroyed church at Dunbar.

into a row of four chapels – a plan right out of the late C12, almost certainly via Newbattle Abbey only 7 km. away. The choir is aisled, as the unbuilt nave was meant to be. The transepts were to have had two bays each.

Stone VAULTING is used far more frequently over main spans than in English churches of the same period, although the modest heights and widths involved reduced technical problems to a minimum. By far the commonest form is the plain pointed tunnel-vault – something practically unknown in NW Europe since the late C12. The choir of Whitekirk is covered in this way, as are the choir and transepts at Seton and Crichton and all four arms of the cross at Dunglass. At Roslin there are tunnel-vaults over the main vessel and the aisles: in the latter they run transversely, an odd arrangement and unique in Scotland. What are the origins of the Scottish preference for tunnel-vaults? In military architecture such vaults had been used from the late C14 to achieve greater stability and fire-proofing in siege conditions, and in this violent period such considerations would not necessarily be out of place in a church context. Another, equally Scottish type of vault is the pointed tunnel with ribs applied as surface decoration. The examples in our region are in the E half of the choir at Seton, the choir at Dalkeith (collapsed) and the S porches at Dalkeith and Seton. Rib-vaulting of the conventional kind, i.e. with lateral as well as longitudinal cells, is comparatively rare in the Late Gothic period. Occasionally it covers the crossings of otherwise tunnel-vaulted churches, e.g. Whitekirk EI and Seton. At Roslin it appears only in the E chapels, which suggests that even when no expense was spared, rib-vaults were regarded as something special. No church in Lothian was completely rib-vaulted, but Haddington came closest to this ideal as only the central span of the nave had an open timber roof. The transepts there and the choir at Midcalder ML have had tierceron-vaults: otherwise simple quadripartite vaults with ridge ribs are general. Linlithgow WL has rib-vaulting in the aisles and transeptal chapels and under the W tower. The main span had until 1812 a wooden roof and ceiling with heraldic decoration. Other major examples of rib-vaulting are in the transepts at Torphichen WL and the E range at Newbattle Abbey ML. Rib profiles are usually plain chamfers.

The most impressive and enjoyable TRACERY is at Linlithgow WL, in the nave aisles and N and S chapels. It is flowing, though not specially similar either to French Flamboyant or English Curvilinear in its details. The spectacular S chapel window is 14

closer to German Late Gothic tracery, particularly in the way that
the bottom of the convex triangle enclosing the tracery rests
directly on the mullions, as if it were a sort of curved transom
(cf. the E window at Nördlingen in Bavaria). C15 windows are
generally very much less enterprising, mostly of two or three lights
and the tracery nominally flowing, i.e. with simple arrangements
of converging or diverging mouchettes. At Dunglass and South
Queensferry tracery is dispensed with, and ogee-headed lights are
grouped under segmental and straight heads respectively. The
transept windows at Torphichen and the N choir windows at
Crichton are still late C13 Geometrical. Generally speaking, tracery design becomes progressively simpler and coarser from the
mid C15 onwards, although it would be hard to find a slacker design than the transept windows of c. 1450 at Crichton. One of the
main indicators of late C15 or early C16 date is the omission of
cusping. Another is 'loop' tracery, i.e. tracery which is no longer
flowing but composed of round-ended mouchettes like loops of
cord. The best display of this tracery anywhere is at Midcalder,
in the choir of c. 1540. The choir at Linlithgow, the W front of
Haddington and the transepts of Seton have it also, the last two
examples divided by an excessively thick Y-shape. English Perpendicular tracery makes several appearances in Scotland around
1400 and again around 1500. Linlithgow church had this kind of
tracery in the W tower, the apse, and the W window on the N side
of the choir. Probably all these sections of the building are late
C15 to early C16. Simpler Perp windows were used in the rebuilding of the S range of the palace. This revival of interest in Perp
has often been linked with James IV's political *rapprochement* with
England.

The design of PIERS requires a brief mention. The simplest
are octagonal with moulded bases and capitals (Dalkeith, Newbattle Abbey E range, and formerly Torphichen S nave
aisle). Pier plans at Haddington EL and Linlithgow WL still
follow C13 precedent: bundles of eight shafts alternately with fillet
and without in the nave at Linlithgow, four shafts alternating with
chamfered strips at Haddington and the Linlithgow choir. Capitals and bases are often of the elided variety characteristic of Scottish Late Gothic. The ordinary piers at Roslin ML are an exaggera-
tion of the Linlithgow nave type to the point where they cease
to be groups of shafts and become convex fluting. The famous
'Prentice Pillar' in the ambulatory is essentially similar beneath
its lacy foliage spirals.

The TOWERS of medieval churches provide nothing like the

same element of continuity in the landscape as they do in England. The finest by far are at Haddington and Linlithgow, the one over the crossing, and the other at the W end. As things stand Haddington is probably the more impressive of the two, but both should be visualized with openwork crown spires of the St Giles 13 kind. That at Linlithgow was taken down c. 1821 and replaced in 1964 with a paraphrase of the original design clad in yellow anodized aluminium. At Haddington the preparations for a crown are obvious, but it is not known whether one was actually built. Neither is datable with any exactitude, although both must be later than the 1470s when the crown steeple at St Nicholas, Newcastle, was in building. Seton has an unfinished stone spire and Whitekirk EL a slated timber spire; Crichton and Torphichen have low towers under saddleback roofs.

The Late Gothic of Scotland is on the whole a blunt and unadorned style. Roslin Chapel is Lothian's one great exception. Interior and exterior are loaded with enough decorative SCULPTURE 20-2 for a building ten times as big. Most of it is foliage of the usual knobbly Late Gothic kinds, but some capitals in the ambulatory sprout strange celery-like shoots that it would be hard to parallel elsewhere. The figure sculpture occasionally represents important subjects, but it is squashed into the same shapes as the foliage and becomes almost indistinguishable texturally. Many churches have niches for full-length figures, but all are now empty. At Linlithgow there is a rather weathered figure of St Michael at the SW angle of the nave. The finest C15 sculpture is without doubt in Linlithgow Palace: the musical angel corbels in the chapel, the heraldic sculpture on the E range and the fireplace in the S range. Two stone panels from a late C15 Passion retable are preserved at Linlithgow. All figures are stocky with big heads, and the emphasis is on narrative clarity rather than refinement of detail. It is disgraceful that the larger and better preserved panel should have been recut recently. Nothing else that could come under the heading of FURNISHINGS has survived except for aumbries, piscinas and sedilia. The best example of the last is at Dunglass EL. Of funeral MONUMENTS the earliest are no doubt the hogback stones at Abercorn WL of the C11 or C12, but the first effigy is that to a C13 priest at Bathgate WL. The gentle grooved 9 folds and sprigs of stiff-leaf down the sides give a date of c. 1250. At Luffness EL there is a very battered knight of c. 1300, lying in the cross-legged pose normal for the period. Tomb recesses survive in considerable numbers from the late C14 on, but few effigies. The best aesthetically and also as regards preservation

16 are the mid C15 knight and lady at Borthwick. The couple
at Seton are similar but less well carved, and the architecture
of their tomb is less ambitious. At Dalkeith are the effigies
of James Douglas, Earl of Morton, † c. 1498 and his wife Princess
Joanna. He is shown wearing civilian dress. The lumpen quality
of carving is apparent despite the poor condition. This was a free-
standing tomb, and the sides of the sarcophagus are enriched with
heraldry and tabernacle work. Incised slabs survive here and
there, all with crosses except one at Roslin with a knight in full
23 plate armour. What is left of the monument at Torphichen WL
to Sir George Dundas († 1532) combines very pure and crisp
Renaissance forms with typically macabre Late Gothic iconography.

POST-REFORMATION CHURCHES

POST-REFORMATION CHURCHES play an important part in the Lothian scene. There was no sudden wave of church building in the late C16, for the old parish churches continued in use, gradually modified for the new forms in which the preaching and hearing of the Word and the sharing of the Lord's Supper had supplanted the east-facing worship of the Word made Flesh. The pulpit strategically sited half way along the main wall, the pews facing it from all directions, and the lofts or galleries providing a second tier of seating wherever possible; these were the basic furnishings of the Reformed Church, and often still are, though the long communion table in the body of the kirk (e.g. at Durisdeer in Dumfries-shire) cannot now be seen anywhere in Lothian.* Nor can any of the original lofts of the incorporated trades such as were formerly crammed into many an old church like St Nicholas at Dalkeith ML, though the idea persists in one or two Victorian churches, e.g. the 'Old Kirk' (a rebuild of 1885 on another site) at Bo'ness WL. Nevertheless many of the 'lairds' lofts' that were made for the local landowner have survived, the grandest the Hopetoun loft at Abercorn WL (1708): they some- [27] times (as here) incorporate a retiring room. A family burying-place annexed to a church, with or without a loft on top, is rather confusingly known as an aisle, a name inherited from the chantry chapels that filled many burgh churches before the Reformation.

The plain square tower of Prestonpans EL, the earliest post- [28] Reformation church in Lothian (1596), still stands; towers, and even belfries at gable-heads, tend to last longer than the main church building, and so do the bells, which are not included in this volume, e.g. the Burgerhuys bell of 1618 reinstalled in the new church at Bolton EL. The first and most important of the early rebuilds of churches was at Pencaitland‡ EL (late C16 or early C17), and this also has links with the Netherlands, both in its work and in a remarkable monument. Another pulpit of Dutch origin has been re-used in the 'Old Kirk' at Bo'ness WL.

A standard type of new church building appears at last in the early EIGHTEENTH CENTURY at Gifford EL and Carrington ML (1710) and Newbattle ML (1727). This is the T-plan kirk with the

---

* An alternative arrangement, a shelf in front of each pew, can be seen in a late and somewhat altered example at Torphichen WL.

‡ Pencaitland church may have been E-facing in the period before the building of the Saltoun aisle – a short-lived Laudian arrangement.

pulpit against the long wall and, in all these cases, a tower making a fourth limb to the back of it. Newton ML (1742) and Torphichen WL (1756) are good later examples of this arrangement, though without towers, and Livingston WL (1732) is one of many rebuilds of a simple rectangular plan on old foundations. All these are plain, dignified boxes, and even the elegant square church by the *Adam* firm at Lasswade ML (1793, demolished 1956) observed their traditional austerity. Only St Mungo at Penicuik ML (1771) has a portico; very plainly detailed, it looks down the main street. Later Georgian churches occasionally have pedimented fronts, e.g. at Roslin ML (1826). Steeples of Gibbsian pretension are equally rare, but the church at Inveresk ML (1805), notable for its unusually lofty interior, has a modest specimen.

The Gothic revival churches of the NINETEENTH CENTURY were more demonstrative from the start, and were often designed by architects of some note. The elaborate castellated Gothic church at East Saltoun EL (1805) with its landmark spire is probably by *Robert Burn*. Many of the late Georgian churches that pop up in the Lothian landscape like pieces of leggy rural furniture have tall, pinnacled towers, e.g. *James Gillespie*'s at Dunbar EL and *Archibald Elliot*'s at Cockpen ML (both 1818) or *William Burn*'s at Stenton EL (1829). Then *Burn* characteristically comes to the fore with a series of transitional Gothic revival churches, more conscientiously antiquarian but decidedly sluggish in detail although they maintain an overall picturesqueness, e.g. the Buccleuch Church at Dalkeith ML (1840). At Dalkeith we also see Burn's partner *David Bryce* casting out the accumulation of galleries and drastically restoring St Nicholas' church. The big churches that had been curtailed, subdivided and filled with lofts following the Reformation were to come in for similar treatment, e.g. St Mary, Haddington EL (*George Henderson*, 1891), and St Michael, Linlithgow WL (*John Honeyman*, 1894); in both cases the restoration process has continued in various ways, the Haddington church being more discreet in its acknowledgement of C20 ideas.

The history of the major denominations in Scotland must be briefly explained. The established Church is the Church of Scotland, a highly democratic organization run by its members through individual kirk sessions and governed by the consent of the General Assembly. Most church buildings belonged to their kirk sessions till 1925, when they became the property of the Church of Scotland Home Board. At the Disruption of 1843 a large section of the Church, i.e. a good part of almost every congregation, broke away to form the Free Church. In 1847 certain sects stemming from the Secession of 1733 were joined to form the United Presbyterian Church. This in turn was joined to most of the Free Church in 1900 to form the United Free Church, which joined the established Church of Scotland in 1929. The present Free Church consists of those congregations that did not come together in the union of 1900. Buildings erected for newly formed congregations (e.g. after the 1843 Disruption) have generally been renamed, but the denominations for which they were built have been mentioned, where known, in the gazetteer. It will be obvious that this highly confused history, in which the politics of establishment and questions of social purpose played a very large part, has created vast problems of redundancy in church buildings. As for the Episcopalians, only the 'jurors' who were prepared to recognize the royal house of Hanover were allowed to build churches in the C18 (e.g. the 'English Chapel' at Haddington in 1769) until the penal laws were repealed in 1792. In the following year the Roman Catholics were similarly emancipated.

The Church of Scotland in the Victorian age increasingly sought its identity in a medieval revival that was inconsistent with its character. Older churches, which certainly included medieval ones, were 'orientated' towards a communion table at one end, often in a chancel. After 1866 the table could be supplemented (e.g. at the Buccleuch Church, Dalkeith ML) by an organ, and often by the pulpit and elders' chairs on a platform, a formidable ensemble that has few admirers among church historians and restorers. The church at Stow ML (1873) by *Wardrop & Reid* is an ingenious compromise between the diversity of an old-Gothic exterior and a reformed internal arrangement. All the later Gothic revivalists, for whatever Church they were designing, were able to make some play with towers for stairs giving access to galleries, but Gothic aisles presented a problem for an auditorium church, most impressively solved at St David's, Bathgate WL by *J. Graham Fairley* (1904). Glencorse Church ML by *R. Rowand Anderson* 35 (1883) is the most perfect of 'high church' buildings designed for the Victorian Church of Scotland in Lothian.

The Free Church started, as far as its means permitted, with the spiky Gothic of its time, e.g. at *Thomas Hamilton*'s Abbey Church, Dunbar EL (1850). But its buildings were speedily eclipsed by those of the United Presbyterians; Lothian, at what is now called the South Church in Penicuik ML by *F. T. Pilkington* 34 (1862), has one of the finest expressions of their fervour. Gothic diversity is used in a new and even violent fashion to make a single overwhelming experience. This flair for enlisting architectural originality was inherited by the United Free Church and is seen 36 & 37 at *Sydney Mitchell*'s Arts-and-Crafts Church at Cockenzie EL (1904) and *Scott & Campbell*'s Art Nouveau St Andrew at Bo'ness WL in the following year.

In the Victorian Gothic revival the Episcopalians and Roman Catholics were on their own historical and liturgical ground. Two churches at Dalkeith ML were the first in Lothian to explore the 33 possibilities: first *Burn & Bryce*'s Episcopal chapel for the Duke of Buccleuch (1843) within its stolid exterior, then *Hansom*'s R.C. church of St David (1853) whose fine organic build-up gives an idea of the spatial and functional diversity within. No other Catholic church in Lothian, not even *Dunn & Hansom*'s Star of the Sea chapel at North Berwick EL, surpassed it in dramatic effect. The Episcopalians took a calmer and at the same time a more scholarly line, e.g. in *R. Rowand Anderson*'s church at Dunbar EL (1889), and many of their later buildings have the look of a modest country church in England. *Hippolyte Blanc*'s chapel at Lasswade ML (1890) is typical; the church at Penicuik ML by *H. O. Tarbolton* (1899) is much larger but no less modest, with a West of England vernacular charm. Tarbolton also designed the best C20 church in Lothian, the noble Romanesque chapel at Bangour Village Hospital WL (1924).

The TWENTIETH-CENTURY churches of all denominations may be discussed together. They fall into three main stylistic groups. The first is austerely historical, in the tradition of the plain Scots kirk and the unpretentious churches of the C19 Episcopalians; *Rowand Anderson*'s little chapel at Balerno ML (1869) is so important in this context that it may be mentioned here along with much later buildings, *W. J. Walker Todd* built the plain Episcopal churches at Bathgate WL (1916), Bo'ness WL (1921) and Linlithgow WL (1928), with an increasing interest in a round-arched Early Christian style that could be economically achieved with the use of tiles, and *B. N. H. Orphoot* developed this theme in his additions to the chapel at Haddington EL (1930). But the Church of Scotland took the same line in some of its 'extension' churches, e.g. in *Ian Lindsay*'s quite dateless kirk at Livingston Station WL (1949). The Roman Catholics did the same at Nunraw Abbey EL (1951–), but here *Peter Whiston* introduced some of the common elements of C20 practice into the time-honoured monastic layout. The second group consists of the churches which are obviously of their time but have the same traditional good sense. *Alan Reiach*'s parish church at Easthouses ML (1954), *Ian G. Lindsay & Partners*' chapel at Carberry Tower ML (1965) and 39 *Kenneth Graham*'s extension to Loretto School chapel, Mussel-burgh ML (1962) are the best examples in Lothian. The third group consists of expressionist churches, designed perhaps to startle the beholder into belief through disbelief. *Archibald Mac-pherson*'s R.C. church at Rosewell ML (1926) is the most successful 38 because it is built of a credible material, the common stock brick of industrial Lothian. The abstract white harl of *Gillespie, Kidd & Coia*'s church of St Mary at Bo'ness WL (1960) is more fre-quent, but this is an unusual building for its time, since it is orien-tated in conventional fashion. Centrally planned churches in eye-catching geometric shells are now favoured, if for slightly different reasons, by the Established and Catholic churches alike, e.g. at Brucefield Church of Scotland, Whitburn WL (1964) and St Andrew's R.C. church, Livingston WL (1968).

There are not many notable MONUMENTS – and still fewer of much sculptural quality – within the post-Reformation churches of Lothian. Incomparably the finest Renaissance monu-ment is that of George Home, Earl of Dunbar († 1611), in the 24 parish church, and there is little doubt that it was shipped from London; the sculptor, however, is still unknown. This, with the Earl kneeling in armour and attended by allegorical figures of the virtues of government, is very much an official monument. The slightly earlier one, commemorating Lord Thirlestane († 1595) and his wife Isabella Seton with separately placed effigies and a great display of heraldry, is more dynastic in intent; it is in the parish church at Haddington EL. The same church contains a much later work (1682) of almost equal grandeur in memory of a Provost of the burgh, William Seton. Its figures are old-fashioned for the time, but do not lack provincial charm. Best of this period, however, is the Anderson of Whitburn monument (*c.* 1695) attached to the ruin of Keith parish church, Keith Marischal EL. It is formed like an altar and reredos, with a large assembly of the characters and paraphernalia of death under a broken pediment.

The Reformed Church did not allow burials within the kirk building proper; hence the number of family 'aisles' with their own burial places that were either built on to churches or created in left-over areas within them, and hence also the general paucity of indoor monuments. From the C18 only two in Lothian need be mentioned. The wall-monument to Robert Dundas of Arnis-ton († 1787) in Borthwick church ML is a competent job signed

by *Bacon* of London. The lovely memorial to Lady Elibank
(† 1762) in Aberlady church EL is in quite another class. It is by
Canova, and its mourning figure personifies grace and sorrow with
a masterly lack of sentimentality. Also in the church is a notable
Victorian record of mortality, direct and awe-inspiring: the chilling effigy of the Countess of Wemyss († 1882) by *John Rhind*.
It is of high merit, and shows that still in the late C19 a Scots
sculptor was not averse to describing the reality of death. Ten
years later the effigy of the fifth Duke of Buccleuch in St Mary
Dalkeith ML, by *Edgar Boehm* and *Alfred Gilbert*, is a more conventional work altogether.

Out in the churchyards and burial grounds the story is quite
different. The outdoor memorials are a rich collection indeed, of
equal interest in their iconography, their spirited execution by
local schools of carvers and, of course, the abundance of historical
material in their inscriptions. In Lothian as in the rest of Scotland
their systematic recording and study – not to mention their conservation – are matters of urgency. Such articles as have been
published (e.g. in the *Proceedings of the Society of Antiquaries of
Scotland*) show how great have been the losses of the last hundred
years. Lasswade ML is one place where quantities of capsized
stones have simply been tidied into a heap. Nevertheless very few
churchyards (certainly not this one) are without a worthwhile
assembly of C17–18 monuments.

The clear and forceful symbolism of these monuments has two
purposes; to identify a man's trade if he had one, and to remind
the onlooker of his own impending death as an encouragement
to the godly life. Trade symbols are frequent: the shoemaker's
knife, the butcher's cleaver, the ship (South Queensferry, 1755)
or mermaids (Dirleton † 1746) for the sailor, and for the mason
his own tools. Then come the basic *memento mori* of skull and crossbones, the whole skeleton (often as death with a scythe), the hourglass, shroud and coffin. None is more frightening than the primitive skull on the weaver's tomb at Uphall WL (1710). But more
often, taking the grim message for granted, the carver makes the
best of it and indulges his enthusiasim and inventiveness. Usually
the emphasis is on the anonymity of death, but portraits are not
unknown and suddenly become popular in the middle of the C18,
e.g. in the farmers' monuments at Humbie EL († 1751) and
Temple ML († 1742). A road surveyor is shown in action at Lasswade ML (later C18). All these are headstones, mainly for lesser
folk. For grander people there was the tabernacle monument displaced, as it were, from the inside of the kirk and set up against

a wall; such is the late C17 monument at Dunbar EL with its lively scenes of the Last Judgement. But other types developed, and the most important was the table monument, usually on six legs. Tranent has the best collection, and the rollicking foliage carved on headstones and table-tops alike suggests that it was the centre of an East Lothian 'school'. A quite exceptional shape is the domed pillbox for a surgeon-apothecary at Haddington EL, with the very early date (of death) 1687. But individual talents can also be detected. A headstone at the Old Pentland Burying Ground, Loanhead ML († 1765), has the grace of the best contemporary plasterwork. Here also is *Thomas Hamilton*'s Gibsone Mausoleum (*c.* 1845), even more austere than his superb monument at the Valleyfield Mills, Penicuik ML, to the French prisoners who had died there in captivity. For the rest, churchyard monuments of the early C19 generally attained a decent mediocrity, with the old forms dying hard. One curiosity is the group of iron headstones at Crichton ML (1841).

Some history has already emerged; other examples may be given at random. There is the tablet at Pencaitland EL to the daughter of the 'Minister to the English Merchants Adventurers at Delf'; and the monument of Robert Burns's mother († 1820) at Bolton EL. Andrew Meikle (Prestonkirk, East Linton EL, † 1811) invented the threshing machine; William Mitchell (Ratho ML † 1809) was killed by it, and now occupies an outdoor stone coffin.

SECULAR BUILDINGS

THE account of the earlier CASTLES must begin with some mention of Lothian as a theatre of war and local conflict. First came the wars of independence against the three Edwards, Kings of England; in 1298 Dirleton Castle was captured for Edward I by the Bishop of Durham. Then followed the baronial plottings and rivalries of the later C14 and the C15, with powerful families establishing themselves in massive tower houses, a dozen of which may still be seen, although some are ruined. Of those that have been enlarged, Dalhousie, Hawthornden and Lennoxlove are still lived in, and Borthwick, the finest of all, is still inhabited in its original form. James IV of Scotland provides an important historical landmark. He married Margaret, daughter of Henry VII of England, and their great-grandson was to become James I of the United Kingdom. But Flodden (1513) was a battle against the English in support of France; James IV was killed, and so were many of the strongest Scots barons. Thenceforth the lesser barons, the lairds and (in the towns) the merchants were the principal builders. Scotland's civil institutions began to take shape despite her hazardous international position, torn between France and England. The blockhouse at Dunbar harbour EL, an early example of artillery fortification, was probably the work of the Duke of Albany's French faction (c. 1522–36). The sacking of Dunbar and of many other towns and castles (e.g. Roslin Castle and the town of Haddington) was due to the destructive invasion of Lothian by the Duke of Somerset (formerly Earl of Hertford) in 1544–7 on behalf of the English; known as the 'rough wooing', it ended with the defeat of the Scots at Pinkie. The later C16 saw the further development of the tower house. The fact that it remained the most important building type in Scotland well into the C17, with crooked ground plans and projecting turrets, and the surprising appearance of defensive shot-holes in the harled walls of some of the most (to us) charming examples, demonstrates the continuing uncertainty of life in Jacobean Scotland. Nor was Lothian yet free from major conflict. East Lothian, whose coastal plain forms the main approach to Edinburgh from the S, was to see two more battles of some importance: Cromwell's victory at Dunbar (1650) and Cope's defeat at Prestonpans (1745). But by the latter date Lothian, and especially East Lothian, had already become the scene of a peaceful revolution in the improvement of estates and the building of new villages and country houses.

With these operations the Lothian landowner fulfilled the ideals of the Act of Union (1707) between England and Scotland.

Lothian has three CASTLES OF ENCLOSURE from before the wars of independence: Dirleton, Hailes and Yester. The first two 42 & 2 are now Ancient Monuments in the guardianship of the Secretary of State (hereafter abbreviated to AM), and the third is an interesting fragment in private ownership. All are in East Lothian. Dirleton, built by the immigrant Norman family De Vaux, despite alteration retains its general appearance and its original donjon tower, complete with elaborate domestic arrangements and the use of much transverse rib-vaulting. The grandest use of these ribs, however, is in the Goblin Ha' (hall) at Yester. The Earl of Dunbar's castle at Hailes is far less complete. Tantallon EL, built 2 in the C14 by the Earl of Douglas, is also a castle of enclosure 40 although its fortification consists of a single prodigious curtain wall across a promontory; on the three other sides is a sharp drop into the Firth of Forth. Rooms and passages are buried in the wall, and the extensive later fore-works must have made this the most aggressive of Lothian castles.

Apart from the earliest rebuilding of the royal palace of Linlithgow (1425) the C14–15 present a picture of noble families consolidating their power on their own behalf in a notable series of TOWER HOUSES with corbelled parapet walls and corner bartizan turrets. The first tower at Crichton ML (AM), of the C14, is rec- 44 tangular in plan, and so are the mid-tower of Blackness WL (AM) and the old tower of Hawthornden ML, both C15. Some other C15 towers are more complex, but this was more for convenience than defence. Cairns ML and Lennoxlove EL are of L-plan. 43 Dundas WL very soon acquired an addition to the outer angle of its L. The Crichtons at their castle and the Halyburtons who now held Dirleton added ambitious new ranges to their old castles of enclosure. Here it must be remembered that the tower house, though it was a self-contained fortified dwelling, was not built in complete isolation; it had, and very often still has, the added protection of a barmkin wall with which it was usually connected. The C15 L-plan tower of the Ramsays at Dalhousie ML, however, used to stand free within its wall, to one of whose angles a round tower was added later in the century. Borthwick ML (1430), the most consummate of all these towers, was connected to its barm- 45 kin by an entrance bridge.

There had been many displays of brute strength, and considerable feats of that ingenuity which is necessary for the making of habitable towers and is indeed the main point of interest in the

Scots tower house. But Borthwick, whose double L-plan allows
a complete arrangement of hall, kitchen and solar on one storey
from the start, is an achievement of formal architecture. The C15
Elphinstone Tower EL (demolished 1955, a casualty of mining
subsidence) was a simple rectangle in plan but went even further
than Borthwick in using the thickness of its walls for staircases
and subsidiary rooms. The refined (and doubtless expensive) simplicity of these two master-works has no rival in Lothian or elsewhere in Scotland. For well over a century the tower house continued as before, and even variations in detail, e.g. the winged
heads that enrich the corbelling of Carberry Tower ML, are few
and far between. When change came, it was in the direction of
complication and diversity.

Unique in Lothian, and by far its most important secular building, is Linlithgow Palace WL (AM). Its huge square bulk, now
bereft of the skyline incidents of gables and turrets, gives it the
aspect of a grim tower house, vastly enlarged. Even the sculptural
47 display over the entrance of James I's E front (c. 1425) became
irrelevant a century later when James V made a new entry on the
S side. The courtyard is a different matter. Three of its phases
represent the royal moods of the last three Jameses: James IV
on the S side with an English Perp window grid (virtually unknown elsewhere in Scotland though it occasionally appears in
other contexts, e.g. at Huntly Castle in Aberdeenshire); James
V with his Gothic-Renaissance fountain; and James VI's
49 N elevation, Scots Renaissance of considerable refinement but
relatively prosaic design. The only other buildings in Lothian that
have aspired to the status of palaces are the quasi-symmetrical
52 house of Kinneil WL (AM), built in the mid C16 by James Hamilton, Earl of Arran, and the long-demolished Seton Palace EL. As
to the courtyard or 'palace' plan, Mark Kerr's C16 house at Newbattle ML has been rebuilt, and the quadrangular C17 house of
the Lauderdales at Hatton ML – built round an older tower house,
not a courtyard – is no more. Barnes Castle EL (before 1594) is
unique in its awareness of the sort of formal courtyard planning
that was by now familiar in England.

The development of the later tower house is merged with that
of the LAIRD'S HOUSE, i.e. the house of the lesser landowner,
from the late C16 to the mid C18. 'Gentlemen's houses built all
castle-wise' were noted by Sir William Brereton as he rode
through West Lothian in 1636, and right through the C17 the old
baronial style was undergoing a simultaneous process of refinement and elaboration in its new, almost entirely domestic role.

The needs of full-scale defence gave way to everyday security and a modest show of prestige. Walls are now manifestly thinner, and indeed lose all semblance of thickness with their coats of harling. The heavy wall-head apparatus of parapets and bartizans has disappeared, the latter replaced by boldly corbelled snuffer-roofed turrets with intermediate dormers along the eaves. Often the turrets, e.g. at Midhope Castle WL (late C16), are extended down- 46 wards to a corbel table nearer the ground, and often they contain turnpike stairs, thus giving outward expression to the vertical as well as the horizontal disposition of the rooms. Always an organic style as far as internal arrangements have been concerned, the Scots baronial is now pushing out of its shell and showing its anatomy on the outside too.

Roslin ML and Preston Tower EL provide two examples of a fancy C17 top on a plain C16 base; at Roslin this seems to have been a continuous operation. But nicely integrated houses were already being built in the late C16. Linhouse ML (1589) is one of the most ingenious, with the added bonus of rope and billet decoration on its stone dressings. Fountainhall FL at the same 56 time and then Pilmuir FL (1624) have a square projecting jamb for the stair – or at least for the first part of it, a corbelled turret stair taking over on the upper levels. Many such houses were extended in the same style quite early in the C17, losing their identity as towers but often gaining the indoor amenity of a broad new staircase, e.g. at Linhouse and at Northfield, a C16–17 house whose many-turreted exterior is easily visible from the road at 54 Preston EL. Duntarvie Castle WL and Roslin Castle ML (late C16) are exceptional in having had straight staircases from the start; the latter type, going from top to bottom, is not repeated until the late C17 at Calder House, Midcalder ML, where it ends with a roof-top platform.

By the early C17 the L-plan had established itself in Scotland, and most abundantly in Lothian, as the favoured type for the laird's house. Hamilton House at Preston EL is exceptional in having its main rooms on ground level. Over the vaulted ground floor the L is basically formed by one large and one small room on each level. Access is provided by a stair-turret in the internal angle, generally quasi-octagonal, with the main doorway at its base and a conical roof at its head. Out of a score of well preserved examples Haddington House EL and Ford House ML are two whose 57 exteriors are most easily seen. Symmetry is rare, but Duntarvie Castle WL has a precocious double-L plan seen again nearly a hundred years later, in 1676, at Philpstoun WL. Baberton House

ML (1622), also a double L until the middle was filled in, was almost certainly designed by its owner, *James Murray*, Master of the King's Works and one of the first men in Scotland to be called an architect. In 1620 *William Wallace*, the King's Master Mason, doubled the L-plan of the existing house of Winton EL but in a lopsided fashion, contenting himself with a roughly symmetrical Renaissance treatment of the elevation between the two jambs; the older L with its angle turret remained dominant. Monkton House ML was developed into a simple L about 1680, and its fretted 'Renaissance' quoins, as used at Baberton, were by then quite old-fashioned; its string courses, a much more frequent motif in C17 Scotland, go back as far as Duntarvie. Until quite late in the century the main, almost the only, use of the classical vocabulary was to accent and ornament the front doors and dormers of the laird's house; as an accessory, in short, to the native way of building. By the start of the C18 symmetry had at last gained the day, but with a continuing preference for functional elements, not merely architectural ones, to establish the character of a house. Bankton House near Preston EL (*c.* 1730) has a pedimented front door and curly end gables. The similar shaped gables above the wall head on each side were functionally justified not only by bullseyes to light the attic but by chimneys; the wall-head chimney was indeed to be a recurring motif in Scottish building, especially in towns, right through the C18 and 19.

Something must be said of the interior decoration of the nobleman's and laird's house in the C16–17. Fountainhall EL, where the removal of a lath-and-plaster wall revealed a tapestry *in situ*, shows that even a house of moderate importance might be clothed in this way. Compartmented plaster ceilings, flat or vaulted, were fairly frequent in the east of Scotland and there are three first-rate sets of them in Lothian, at Winton and Whittingehame EL and at The Binns WL, where the name of a plasterer is known – *Alexander White*. TEMPERA PAINTING (using a glue medium on a white ground) was a universal Scottish practice, drawing chiefly on woodcuts for its iconography. Kinneil WL has an excellent set in poor condition, including a room in which the mid C16 scheme has been overpainted in the early C17 with a more formal design of simulated plaster ribs. Northfield at Preston EL has the finest and best-preserved example, painted on the boards of walls as well as ceilings, and the nearby house of Prestongrange boasted one of the largest and earliest in Scotland (1581) until it was removed to Edinburgh for safety.

Dovecots, or rather DOOCOTS as we must here call them,

deserve a paragraph in view of their frequency in Lothian. Their external characteristic is the string course to prevent the entry of vermin, and their internal walls are lined from the top almost to the bottom with freestone nesting boxes whose considerable cost is evidence of the value of this source of food, even though it might be described as parasitical; the damage to grain crops must have been enormous, but doocots continued to be built right through the age of agricultural improvement and well into the C19. The earliest surviving are of the C16. Some are of 'beehive' 112 form, e.g. at Dirleton and Preston EL and at Linlithgow WL (*see* 110 p. 306), which allowed for a potence or ladder to reach the boxes, turning on a central pole; others rectangular, e.g. by the churches at Athelstaneford EL (1583) and Tranent EL (1587). The latter type, usually of two chambers with the flight-holed roof pitched towards the S, is called a 'lectern' and usually given an C18 date; 111 a few, for example that at Philpstoun WL (1725), are actually dated. It is hard to believe that the legislation of 1617 designed to limit the ownership of doocots actually prevented it for the rest of the century. The fine lectern doocot at Newliston WL is one of those to which one would like to give a date in the C17. The gable-doocot of Northfield House, Preston EL, almost certainly belongs to that century and is one of a number incorporated in larger buildings at various times, e.g. in the church tower at Aberlady EL, and in steadings of almost any date. Of cylindrical C18 examples the best are at Elvingstone House EL and in the village of Bolton EL. Some C18 doocots are dressed up as landscape ornaments: the one at Johnstounburn EL as a two-storey Gothic house (1730, but this treatment may have been later) and the one at Huntington EL (*c.* 1750) as the top of a tall summer house, 113 pilastered and pedimented. One of the latest doocots is an early C19 Gothic tower at Harburn WL.

CLASSICAL MANSION HOUSES must necessarily take up a considerable part of this introduction. Lothian is fairly well endowed with classical houses from before the Union of 1707, and was to be the very cradle of the house-building enthusiasm that followed it in lowland Scotland along with agricultural and other estate improvements. From the mid C18 the *Adam* brothers did much classical work in Lothian and more may be attributed to them, e.g. the library at Newhailes EL. Their skill in the ensemble of the country house was never quite equalled by their contemporaries. A certain weakness in late Georgian classicism is redeemed by an abundance of romantic houses, noted in a later section. Some of the gaps are man-made. Even before the local government reorganization of 1975 the Lothians had lost their claim to a number of houses within the spreading boundary of Edinburgh, e.g. Craigiehall by *Bruce*, The Drum by *William Adam* and Duddingston by *Sir William Chambers*, to name only the most important. There have also been demolitions, e.g. *Isaac Ware*'s Amisfield EL, the spectacular *Adam* interiors at Archerfield EL, *James Adam*'s elaborate classical composition at Balbardie WL, and *Richard Crichton*'s masterpiece of picturesque classicism at Dunglass EL; in each of these cases there is, or was at the time of writing, just enough left to warrant a mention in the gazetteer.

In a sense the basic type of classical house, with *corps de logis* and flanking pavilions, was a formalized, outward-looking version of the Scots arrangement of house-and-forecourt whose final de-
52 velopment can be seen at The Binns WL and Kinneil WL; indeed a feeling of enclosure, with the long sides of the pavilions facing inwards, is characteristic of Scots classical houses, especially in the second generation. Of the first generation very few belong in the C17, but Preston House ML must be mentioned – a ruin, but sufficiently entire to show that it was a curious hybrid, with square ogee-hatted pavilions like a pair of gazebos, joined to the main block by serpentine links. *James Smith* used pavilions with even
68 more curvaceous roofs at Yester, Gifford EL *c.* 1697, and characteristically they were a foil to a formidably austere and regular house – one which will reappear at each of the later stages of this
66 account. Smith's own house, Newhailes ML (built as Whitehill in 1686), is perfectly plain on the outside, but his design for the
69 ducal house or palace at Dalkeith ML, with its build-up of piend roofs from the staggered wings, is the finest of all houses in the Dutch Palladian manner in Britain. *Sir William Bruce*, who was actually Smith's senior and was succeeded by him as Overseer of the Royal Works in Scotland in 1683, designed two houses in the present Lothian Region. In the note on Hopetoun WL (1699) in *Vitruvius Britannicus* he is said to have been 'justly esteemed the best Architect of his time in that Kingdom' (the expression
72 & 74 by then an archaism for Scotland). Hopetoun as first built (though the pavilions and links intended by Bruce do not seem to have been carried out) was a house of sober grandeur and some originality; the E front has gone, but most of the panelled interiors
67 have survived. Auchindinny ML (1702) is a modest, practical house joined by curved screens to its dependencies; the Americanism is justified by some strikingly similar houses in the eastern States.

At the Union in 1707 *William Adam* was a young man of eighteen. He became Mastor Mason to the Board of Ordnance in 1730, and supplied the needs of Lothian's growing prosperity as the owner of a coal-mine (*see* p. 263), a brewery and a pantile factory. As a builder he won many large contracts, e.g. at Inveraray in Argyll in 1745. As an architect he now faces the critic at a disadvantage because he stands between the fastidious professionalism of Bruce and the brilliant achievement of his own sons. This is precisely his position at Hopetoun WL, where his vast aggrandizement of the E front was itself modifed by *John*, *Robert* and *James*. His own work is varied to an extreme degree. For anything like the restraint of his predecessors we must look to Dalmahoy ML (1725); for his grandest interior to the saloon at Arniston ML (after 1726) with its joyous plasterwork done by *Joseph Enzer*; for sensitive additions, to Yester, Gifford EL (1729). His best integrated design is the lovely shell of Mavisbank, Loanhead ML (1723), where Sir John Clerk was far from being an unquestioning patron. The conclusion is inescapable: that William Adam always did his best, but did his best architecture as a collaborator, when he was in touch not only with his source-books but with other lively minds. His architectural contemporaries are so few, e.g. *John Douglas* at Archerfield EL in 1745, that one wonders whether Scottish architecture at this period of sudden demand would have achieved very much without him. The same, for some years after his death in 1748, may be said of his sons. The eldest, *John Adam*, who comes into prominence with the splendid gates at Yester, Gifford EL (1753), was perhaps responsible for the sumptuous interiors at Newhailes ML. At Hopetoun WL (from 1752) the brothers developed their notion of interior design as a composite art form, and the culmination of their early period in Scotland is the saloon at Yester (1761). Of the unattributed houses of the mid C18 the most important are Gilmerton and Drummore EL (*c.* 1750 and 1760). Both of them have the jolly Rococo plasterwork that was by now established in Lothian and turns up in the modernization of numerous houses, e.g. Oxenfoord Castle ML, Colstoun EL and Calder House, Midcalder ML. The period culminates in *Sir James Clerk*'s own house at Penicuik ML (1761), which still, though now only a shell, represents the fullest realization of a Lothian landowner's dream: the Scots Palladian mansion at the centre of an improved estate in which Romano-Scottish history and C18 husbandry go hand in hand.

75 & 76
71
77
78
81–3

Robert and James Adam inevitably dominate the last quarter of the C18, but of their late classical houses only the modest example

79 at Newliston WL (1789) has survived inside and out, though with some tactful extensions. The other two have lost whatever interior quality they may have had. Lauderdale House EL (1790) is virtually an adjunct to Dunbar High Street, and sadly lacks its former parkland outlook on the other side. The great seaside pavilion of
80 Gosford EL (1790) is partly smothered by rhetorical C19 display, and even the abstract classicism of its rear elevation (cf. the back of Penicuik House) has been tampered with. For the grandest interiors of this time we must refer to *James Nisbet*'s brilliant drawing room at Leuchie EL (1779–85), *James Playfair*'s manifold ingenuity at Melville Castle ML (1786–91) and *Robert Mitchell*'s
84 graceful staircase at Preston Hall ML (c. 1794). This last, the most ambitious work of an architect who practised mainly in England, marks the final development of the pavilioned house, with entrance front and garden front stretched out to the utmost in two long and suave (but unrelated) elevations.

In his calmer moods (but not at Melville except in a few of the rooms) *James Playfair* was a true neo-classicist. The alliance of classicism with abstract geometry is tantalizingly represented
63 by *John Henderson*'s walled garden at Amisfield EL which has the early date of 1783, and possibly the pyramidal mausoleum at Gosford. But in Lothian we have to wait for *Sir Robert Smirke* to produce a wholly neo-classical house. Whittingehame EL (1817) is a design of the greatest severity, the exterior based on abstract geometry, the interior dominated on its two main axes by a large, simple order of columns and antae. Something like Smirke's crisp
85 geometry can be seen at *James Burn*'s house of Hopes EL (1823), particularly in the central saloon which has only an implication of classical orders. More directly derived from Smirke are the classical works of his sometime pupil *William Burn*. But St Joseph's Hospital at Tranent EL (1821), with temple steps leading up to a primitive Ionic portico, shows an interest in fundamental classicism which is very much Burn's own. His best Grecian interiors in Lothian, apart from those he added to Whittingehame, occur rather unexpectedly in the huge Gothic house of Saltoun Hall EL (after 1817) and the Tudor Gothic Ratho Park ML (1824).

Victorian classicism is a rarity in Lothian but the one outstanding example must be mentioned; the Marble Hall at Gosford EL by *William Young* (completed 1891). It is a huge apartment (the roof span made possible by steel beams) uniting a ceremonial staircase, open galleries and more intimate spaces within an opulent but disciplined whole. Comparable splendour can only be witnessed in municipal buildings, including Young's own City

Chambers in Glasgow (1883–8), but no such awkward thoughts arise here; it is unmistakably domestic, and in its detail entirely charming.

The ROMANTIC COUNTRY HOUSES of Lothian are a fairly comprehensive collection, starting with the CASTLE STYLE of *Robert Adam*. His recasting of Oxenfoord Castle ML (1780–2) is in his intermediate, still rather tentative manner, with corner turrets and intermediate bow windows. Seton House EL (1789) is the most perfect realization of the style: a 86 towered forecourt leading up to a strongly modelled block on whose outer sides the convex wall, pushed out in all directions as if by a central force, plays a dominant part. *John Paterson* was the inheritor of the Adam castle style and it was probably he who used it for the stable range (*c.* 1800) at Pinkie House, Musselburgh ML. At Melville Castle ML (1786–91) *James Playfair* used another castle manner, and in many respects a more primitive one, going back to the simple toy fort with corner towers which Roger Morris had pioneered at Inveraray in Argyll (1745). *William Burn* came even closer to the original at Saltoun Hall EL (begun 1817), for this has a central saloon and lantern with a dizzy Gothic vault, rising through the core of the house. So, until the recent fire, had *Archibald Elliot's* Newbyth EL. These last two, of course, are not 87 predominantly castellated houses, for all their battlements, but Gothic. For the pure fun of a Gothic Revival exterior we must look to the romantic extension of Newhall ML by its owner *Robert Brown* in the late C18, or to the stables at Vogrie ML (*c.* 1825) which may be attributed to *R. &. R. Dickson*.

The other Gothic partnership is with the English TUDOR style, which *William Wilkins* brought to Scotland at Dalmeny EL 88 (1814). The great merit of this house lies not in its flat elevations with their (literally) mechanical enrichment, but in the relaxed and masterly detail of its cloister-like Gothic galleries which – rather curiously – lead to simple Grecian rooms. Then of course *Burn* took a hand. Dundas Castle WL (1818) is spartan externally, intricate within. At Ratho Park ML (1824) he perfected the Tudor country house in late Georgian terms; the interiors, indeed, are treated in the plainest Grecian manner.

William Burn's leading part in this story is now becoming evident. 'For twenty-eight years, i.e. till he moved to London in 1844, he pursued a brilliant career in Edinburgh, patronized by the highest nobility and aristocracy, and devoting himself especially to domestic architecture. And so successfully did he study that class of building and mansion house architecture that he became almost the exclusive designer of the country houses for the nobility and gentry throughout Scotland.' But his solitary leadership must now be questioned. *David Bryce* entered his office *c.* 1825, becoming his chief clerk and then his associate in 1841, 'succeeding to a great extent eventually [i.e. after Burn's departure] to the Scottish connexion'.* Bryce's independent career was indeed to be a brilliant one, and it is clear that before 1844 he not only exercised a powerful influence in the office but carried on a considerable practice outside it. Contemporary attributions to Burn and recent, more speculative attributions to 'early' Bryce should be seen in this light.

JACOBEAN REVIVAL houses of any size are not common in Lothian. Shaped gables appear in Burn's extension to the old tower of Riccarton ML (1823, demolished 1956), and other Jaco-
90 bean details at Tyninghame EL (1829), at Spott EL (1830) and at Tyneholm near Pencaitland EL (1835). The Burn–Bryce part-
92 nership was responsible for the prodigious Whitehill ML (1844, now St Joseph's Hospital), despite recent indignities the finest surviving house of its kind in Scotland. What led up to this triumph? The best answer is at Bourhouse EL (1835) which is the work of Bryce on his own. But the highly original Jacobean house of Bonnytoun WL (*c.* 1840, attributed to *Thomas Hamilton* because of its extraordinary interior) must also be mentioned. Attempts to revive the Scots Jacobean style, i.e. that of Heriot's Hospital or Winton, are rare indeed; Bonnington ML (1858) is a solitary example.

When did the SCOTTISH BARONIAL REVIVAL really begin? Adam used corner bartizans at Oxenfoord, crowsteps at Seton, but merely as accessories to his own castle style. In the vernacular it is doubtful if crowstepped gables ever went out of use during the Georgian period. But the first conscious efforts – not all of them very well informed – to cultivate the old Scots style of castles and lairds' houses in Lothian were made in the 1820s. The little ruin of Murieston Castle ML was 'restored', Georgian fashion, in 1824. In the following year *Burn* added a pair of crowstepped gables to Pinkie House, Musselburgh ML, and in 1829 came his recasting and extension of Tyninghame EL, a bold asymmetrical composition which marks the beginning of the revival not only in Lothian but in Scotland. Spott House EL (1830) repeated the same performance on a smaller scale, and in the same year *W.H.*
91 *Playfair*, better known as a classical designer, extended Preston-grange EL in his own version of the style. All these jobs involved

* Memoir by T. L. Donaldson, *R.I.B.A. Transactions*, 1870.

existing buildings; for the baronial house *de novo* we must again turn to *Bryce*. Elvingstone EL (1837) may be attributed to *Burn* but Preston near Linlithgow WL (*c.* 1840) is almost certainly the work of *Bryce*. It introduces his favourite type of bay-window, canted below and corbelled out to a gabled upper storey. His Seacliff EL (1841) is unhappily a ruin. Clifton Hall ML (1850) and Ormiston ML (1851) show the full development of his baronial manner. It represents the transformation of a charming and rather wayward vernacular tradition into a tough and positive architectural style. Apart from the mere elements, what the two have in common is an organic quality, form always expressing function; this is the touchstone of the Scottish baronial.

R. W. Billings's *Baronial and Ecclesiastical Antiquities*, prepared with the assistance of Burn, was published in 1848. *Billings* himself was a wild architect, and his only work in Lothian, the huge gate at Gosford EL (1854), is not baronial whatever else it may be. His book, with its hard and super-accurate steel engravings, made the style common property. Nobody used it quite as well as Bryce, but *Peddie & Kinnear*, of whom the latter had been his pupil, went on building baronial houses till the end of the C19; Invereil EL is dated 1899. *John Henderson*'s Borthwick Hall ML (1852) and *Wardrop & Reid*'s Barnbougle WL (1881) are among those rare houses in which a more rugged interior style is tried out as an alternative to the civilized Jacobean of the Burn–Bryce manner. Carlowrie WL by *David Rhind* (1855) and Limplum EL by *Shiells & Thomson* (1884) are examples of inorganic, overblown baronial. The only architect who managed to develop and at the same time refine Bryce's achievement was another of his former pupils, *Andrew Heiton* of Perth; Vogrie House ML (1875), 93 with its extreme simplification of the stone surface and its complication of other detail, is the final statement of the baronial style, though chronologically by no means the last. *Scott & Campbell*'s Grange WL (1904) is a discreet postscript to the story; only a few insignificant doodles were to follow it.

Small houses designed with conscious aesthetic intent, and subsequently known as VILLAS in the debased sense of the word, have increasing importance from the mid C18 until today, when they represent the last preserve of private architecture. There is a temptation to include the roadside architecture of country-house LODGES. Newbattle ML has its grand Renaissance display, *Smirke* 60 provides a neo-classical series at Whittingehame EL, Balgone EL 62 has a baronial extravaganza; but these free-range architectural exhibitions are a bonus too numerous to describe in detail. The story really begins in the mid C18 when a villa was properly a *villa*, i.e. a superior farmhouse. East Fortune EL has a dated example built in 1768, and Gifford Vale EL with its symmetrical outbuildings (1786) is another little classical house more obviously self-sufficient than most of its contemporary neighbours. The tradition is carried on by Bankhead at Balerno ML in the late C18, and by the sophisticated early C19 farmhouses of Phantassie and Tynefield near East Linton EL. Bonnytoun farmhouse WL (*c.* 1840) is a classical *ferme ornée*; but by that time a simple form of English Tudor was practically the rule for the grander farm owner or manager, e.g. at Spittal near Aberlady EL. A few baronial farmhouses can be found, like Sunnyside near East Linton EL (1856), but *Sir James Gowans'* extraordinary country seat and farm buildings at Gowanbank WL (*c.* 1860) are the final spectacular example of the latter-day laird's house.

So now to the villa intended as a retreat to the attractive countryside or the gregarious suburb, or sometimes to both at once. Lothian, with its capital city and its industries to get away from, and its picturesque river valleys and its later discovered seaside to get away to, is indeed a region of villas. Sir Walter Scott lived at Lasswade Cottage ML at the turn of the C18, and was visited there by the Wordsworths. Here, as at Broomieknowe by Bonnyrigg ML, scores of villas still enjoy the rural solitude of the Esk valley, insulated from each other and from the wreckage of industrial exploitation by thick trees. Most of them are Victorian, the substantial, stone-built progeny of the great houses already mentioned, or of other stylistic families like the Italian which had first appeared at *Thomas Hamilton*'s Kirkhill ML (1828). As to the towns, each had its spacious residential suburb to westward. Dalkeith's satellite Eskbank ML, suddenly brought within easy reach of Edinburgh when it acquired its own (Tudor) railway station in 1846, is the best known example. In the eighties, however, the dominance of ponderous yellow sandstone began to weaken and the out-of-town villa, whether designed as a permanent home or as a retreat, took on a new colour and informality. *R. Rowand Anderson* at Currie ML and *G. Washington Browne* at Penicuik ML began to explore mixed styles and colours, with red Dumfries-shire sandstone and even (in the latter case) English half-timbering. Indeed by the end of the century the English cottage style had gained a firm hold, nowhere more than in the coast resorts of East Lothian. Norham, North Berwick EL (1897), by the sculptor-architect *Sir T. Duncan Rhind* is one of many villas thus classified at the time. Gullane, on the same coast, presents a row of half-timbered frontages to the unsuspecting visitor, who begins to wonder if he is in Scotland after all. It also boasts, towards the shore, a number of stone-built 'English' manor houses like *J. M. Dick Peddie*'s Coldstones (1912) with local Rattlebags rubble in place of Cotswold stone; the partnership of *Kinnear & Peddie* had already designed the adventurous Queen Anne mansion of Glasclune, North Berwick EL, in 1889. *Robert Lorimer* and the Scots revival now come to the fore. He has his fussy and his unfussy manner, and The Grange, North Berwick, begun in 1893, is a combination of both. Whiteholm at Gullane EL (1904) is one of the most perfectly comfortable and unpretentious 96 examples of his own cottage style, Scottish in its white-harled walls and the easy articulation of one form with another, rather than in the forms themselves, though a reference back to some C16–17 houses like Fountainhall EL shows that this relaxed, horizontal feeling was by no means new to Scotland. Lorimer was also, of course, a master of interior style. The Grange has some of the earliest of his serene cove-ceilinged bedrooms with their Anglo-Scots plasterwork, and his finest indoor ensemble, executed with great virtuosity of classical detail, is at Midfield MI. (1914). Comparisons with Sir Edwin Lutyens are hard to avoid; there is indeed one *Lutyens* house in Lothian and it is a masterpiece. Greywalls at Gullane EL (1901) is essentially small with 94 a minimum of formality, but artfully outspread to enjoy the separate but connected spaces of its approach and its gardens. But it is to Lorimer's simple cottages that one returns, possibly because of their link with the late C20. Opposite Whitcholm is the beautiful house by *Morris & Steedman* (1964) properly known as The 97 Quarry; improperly, by neighbours who like houses to fulfil concepts, as the slice of cheese. Such is the mild penalty awaiting the architect who seeks abstraction.

Something must be said about HOUSING, i.e. the houses provided as a public service by local authorities under the statutes that begin with the Housing Act of 1924, designed to counter Scotland's terrible deprivation in this field. Hardly a town in Lothian is without its quota of good houses built at this time, differing from the miners' brick rows of Newtongrange ML and the stone terraces of Bo'ness WL in that they are mostly semi-detached and their layout is circuitous in the tradition of the Victorian suburb. Much the best are those by *Dick Peddie & Walker Todd*, e.g. at Macmerry EL, gabled for individuality yet severely 95 disciplined in details. From before the second world war at Dalkeith ML, and after it also in other Lothian towns such as East

Calder ML, comes the rubble revival that was some authorities'
answer to the recognized failure in housing design and the need
to keep traditional crafts alive. They may have helped. The new
town of Livingston WL, which dropped its early experiments with
prefabrication in favour of easily produced *in-situ* terraces harled
overall (the universal Scots cover-story), provides a lot of agree-
able places to live in. The main complaint, against the absence
of the near-at-hand amenities of town life, applies to almost all
large housing schemes. It may disappear in course of time as the
established towns are sucked dry of their social and commercial
institutions. Of towns that have attempted to solve their housing
problems by central rather than peripheral redevelopment, Linlithgow WL is outstanding. Good old buildings have been lost,
but survival is possible. Dunbar EL has adopted a less drastic
policy, with excellent housing on sites just outside the historic
core. Dalkeith ML has attempted to follow a middle course with
curious results as far as architecture is concerned. Only Haddington EL has managed to follow the difficult but rewarding path
of Development through Conservation. Finally, a visitor to Lothian will be impressed, outside Edinburgh, by the complete
absence of multi-storey housing.

TOWNSCAPE and TOWN BUILDINGS can be discussed
together. Lothian townscape is mainly of the last two centuries,
but the key buildings are sometimes earlier, e.g. the burgh kirks
of Haddington EL, Linlithgow WL and Dalkeith ML, each differently related to its town. Musselburgh ML has a C16 bridge
and tolbooth, the latter one of the earliest surviving in Scotland.
The C17 tolbooths at Dunbar EL, with Dutch tower and spire,
and Dalkeith ML, with regular ashlar front, are equally notable.
Mercat crosses are virtually all of post-Reformation date with
heraldic finials, and the grandest is the drum-based C17 'cross'
at Preston EL. Ormiston EL has a cross in fact as well as in title,
but it probably came to John Cockburn's C18 village, which had
no formal status as a burgh, from somewhere else. Two of the
earliest town plans belong to Linlithgow WL and Haddington EL,
both royal burghs founded by David I in the C12 (even Edinburgh
only received this title in the C14, having started as a baronial
burgh). Linlithgow's high street coincides with the main traffic
route. Haddington's is a broad wedge shape, subsequently cleft
by a central island of buildings with the town house and steeple
(1831) at its apex. As to private buildings, constant renewal and
recent clearance (e.g. at Prestonpans EL) have resulted in the dis-
appearance of almost all the town lodgings and lesser houses of

the C17, but Linlithgow and South Queensferry WL offer some isolated exceptions. A few closes in Haddington and Dunbar EL still show how the original burgess riggs (gardens) were built up with parallel ranges of close-packed houses behind the street front. In the C18 Haddington produced a fine series of town lodgings – Kinloch House with its curved gable and then the palace-fronted houses that became its speciality. Later the town pro- 100 duced the most important of local Georgian architects, *James Burn*. The plain chimney-gabled tenements that were the basis of the Georgian streetscape in many Scottish towns are best seen in the broad high street of Dunbar. South Queensferry WL, with its well-defined entry and exit, and its split-level high street formalized with terraced shops in the early C19, is one of the most 103 distinctive townscapes in Lothian. Inveresk ML, a village transformed into a grand C18 suburb, is another. Its neighbour Musselburgh offers the extreme contrast between a noble street space well served by builders and architects until the end of the C19, and the trivial intrusions of the C20. The Victorian age left little mark on the established town scene; for one thing there are surprisingly few of the substantial palace-fronted banks which are an important Scottish type. But of course there are exceptions. Bathgate WL for instance was transformed, and hardly for the better, by Victorian prosperity. And apart from the churches which are described above, there was a huge programme of central area building for education and welfare. Until 1872 very few schools (e.g. the sombre Bathgate Academy WL, 1831) had been 104 of major architectural importance. Soon after the Education Act of that year, no town was without its board school, generally of symmetrical boys-and-girls pattern but seldom without architectural quality. Penicuik ML acquired its Renaissance-style Institute in 1893 (built of the red sandstone from Dumfries-shire that was now invading the whole of Scotland), Bo'ness WL its classical hall and library in 1901.

Good VILLAGES abound in East Lothian, thanks largely to C18 landowners and their successors but also to the recent control of development by the planning authority. There is little conscious prettiness, at least until the later C19, but an abundance of good materials, siting and planting. Gifford is the first and grandest 102 estate village, and what is left of Ormiston is worth seeing, mainly for its trees. Tyninghame is the most perfect example, only its later cottages venturing into the sort of conscious picturesqueness which is seen round the big green at Dirleton. Central greens of this kind are rare and a simple linear plan is much more frequent, but Stenton's main street is punctuated by green patches. Like most villages it has an adjoining farm steading; the one at Bolton, on a hilly site, makes a picturesque group with the church. There is a handful of decent villages in Midlothian (e.g. Ratho, Fala and Temple) and West Lothian (e.g. Ecclesmachan) which have not been swamped by the mushroom growth of industry. But with the decline of their cottages, or alternatively the uncontrolled 'improvements' of commuting settlers, they depend more than ever for their identity on the church and the old church-school building whose own futures are by no means assured.

FURTHER READING

NOT many books are devoted to Lothian and its buildings, and still fewer are in print. The *Inventories* of the Royal Commission on the Ancient and Historical Monuments of Scotland (RCAHMS) were published in 1924 (East Lothian) and 1929 (Mid and West Lothian combined). They are indispensable, but both were limited to the period 'from the earliest times to the year 1707'. Most of the Ancient Monuments under the guardianship of the Secretary of State have *Guidebooks* in print, and the National Trust for Scotland publish guides to their own properties, as do the owners of all country houses regularly open to visitors. *Country Life* articles, with their magnificent photographs and definitive accounts of architectural history, are referred to in the gazetteer. One of the few general books on country houses, and lacking in anti-Victorian prejudice, is *Castles and Mansions of the Lothians* by John Small (1883); it includes and illustrates many that have now been demolished or reduced. As to towns, the Victorian histories written by local men are often useful, e.g. John Martine's excellent *Reminiscences of Haddington* (1883). For general history, especially social and economic development, the *Statistical Account* edited by Sir John Sinclair (1791–9) is a splendid source; the sections on the Lothian counties were re-issued in 1975 in a volume which has a helpful introduction by T. C. Smout. The *New Statistical Account* performs a similar service for Scotland at the threshold of the Victorian age. Geology is well served. *The Rocks of West Lothian* by Henry M. Cadell of Grange (1925) is worth looking out for, and of publications in print the most useful are the maps of the Institute of Geological Sciences and the 'excursion guide' entitled *The Geology of the Lothians and South-East Scotland* by G. Y. Craig and P. McL. D. Duff.

Apart from the standard works, some good material is available in many libraries within the Lothian Region. These items, not generally published, include the Secretary of State's *Lists of Buildings of Architectural or Historic Interest*. Special Lothian studies include the East Lothian Planning Department's survey of *Farm Buildings* prepared in the sixties, Frank Tindall's inventory of *Water Mills in East Lothian* and Basil Skinner's *The Lime Industry in the Lothians* (1965).

Finally, and leaving aside the classics long out of print, some

currently available books on Scottish architecture must be
mentioned; John Dunbar's *Historic Architecture of Scotland*
(1966); Stewart Cruden's *The Scottish Castle* (1960); George
Hay's *Architecture of Scottish Post-Reformation Churches* (1957).
For general history Rosalind Mitchison's *A History of Scotland*
(1970) and for economic history T. C. Smout's *History of the
Scottish People 1560–1830* (1969) are recommended.

LOTHIAN

★

ABBEY MAINS *see* HADDINGTON

ABERCORN
4 km. WNW of South Queensferry

PARISH CHURCH. In origin a C12 church of the standard two-cell type, but the only feature certainly of that date is the blocked S door squeezed in between later burial aisles. Single order of shafts, block capitals and shallowly carved chevron on the arch. A hoodmould outside the arch must have been removed. The tympanum is one of two C12 decorated examples in Scotland. The other, at Linton in Roxburghshire, has a figural relief, but here is only a pattern of lozenges lightly scratched into the surface. The church was reconstructed in 1579 and three appendages were added later to the S side for local families. Starting from the W, the Philpstoun enclosure with the date 1727 and the Binns aisle of 1618 are built on to the nave. The former has a shaped pediment, the latter a pair of lancets, a frame for heraldry and the initials T D for Thomas Dalyell at the peak of the gable. The Duddingston aisle of 1603 abuts the (former) chancel which was fitted out in 1708 as the HOPETOUN AISLE. *Sir William Bruce* was the architect, *David Mather* the mason. On the N side they built a two-storey annexe for the retiring room with the burial vault underneath. It has a piend roof and is harled, with stone dressings. Long-and-short quoins, banded rustication to the margins of doors and windows. The little forecourt to the N has curved walls and rusticated gatepiers.

In 1893 the church was restored by *P. Macgregor Chalmers*. The old belfry on the skew between nave and chancel was rebuilt, and the W end, which had acquired a stumpy Georgian bellcote and a pair of strengthening buttresses, Normanized with clasping buttresses, a chevroned doorway and a round window in the gable. Along the N side an aisle was added, its W end set back but slightly taller, with a centre buttress and a belfry.

Between the old nave and new aisle Chalmers made a Norman arcade with scalloped capitals. He similarly restored the old chancel arch and resited the pews to face it – an odd effect, because the communion table is now overlooked from the rear by the HOPETOUN LOFT. This is a grand affair with panelling underneath, the opening bordered by a pierced pelmet of foliage and coronets under a moulded cornice, all of timber. The woodcarver was *William Eizat* who also made the panelling throughout, and *Richard Waitt* painted the armorial achievement of the Earl of Hopetoun on the back part of the coomb ceiling with the same mixture of verve and precision. The heraldic colours are original, but the sky-blue ground and the realistic colouring of the carved foliage are of 1964–5 by *Hubert W. Fenwick*, who also restored the RETIRING ROOM, panelled under a coomb ceiling, with Ionic pilasters flanking the fireplace and scrolled overmantel. An oval opening (not from the room itself) gives an oblique view of the PULPIT, much reduced from the C18 original. – STAINED GLASS. In the S wall, as a war memorial, two lights (Abraham sacrificing Isaac) by *Douglas Strachan*, 1921. – MONUMENTS, in the churchyard. A good number of C17–18 headstones, many with trade symbols, but much weathered. – HOPETOUN MAUSOLEUM, to the SE. Gothic, by *William Burn*, 1829.

In a room under the Hopetoun aisle are collected a number of SCULPTURAL FRAGMENTS. The most important are three pieces of two standing crosses dating from the time of Northumbrian rule in Lothian. That a monastery and episcopal see existed at Abercorn by the late C7 we know from Bede's account of how Bishop Trumwine and the monks were driven out by marauding Picts in 685 after their victory over the Northumbrians at Dunnichen.* A religious establishment of some sort must have survived, for the style of the crosses indicates a date considerably after 685. The earlier cross is represented by two long fragments that until 1934 were built into the parapet of Midhope bridge. The surviving main face is divided into a series of short panels each carved with a different type of ornament – a method first used on the minor faces of the cross at Bewcastle in Cumberland (shortly after 670). The vine scroll and the knot patterns are taken over from Bewcastle, but the scroll inhabited by birds and beasts, which features so prominently there and

---

* In 1963 excavation to the N of the church revealed traces of an oval enclosing *vallum* or bank, and two small, apparently rectangular structures which may have been cells within the enclosure. The source of this kind of plan is ultimately Ireland (cf. Nendrum, Co. Down), but it had already been used in Northumbrian monasteries (e.g. Whitby) and on Iona.

on the earlier Ruthwell cross, is here reduced to a single short panel. In addition to these motifs of ultimately Early Christian and Mediterranean extraction there is one panel of northern and barbaric animal interlace of a kind found in the Lindisfarne Gospels. But although the ornamental repertory is wider than those of Ruthwell or Bewcastle, there is no attempt to emulate the ambitious and remarkably accomplished figure sculpture that is the chief glory of the earlier crosses.* This shift of emphasis was to prove decisive, and in the great majority of c8 and later crosses the human figure plays a minor role beside ever more varied forms of zoomorphic and abstract pattern. Despite the poor preservation of surfaces, it can be said that the quality of carving here does not compare with the relaxed and convincing naturalism of Ruthwell and Bewcastle or the contemporary Jedburgh shrine fragment. A loose fragment of a cross head carved with a rosette has been associated with the one just discussed although it does not come from Midhope bridge. The complete cross must have stood about 14 ft high (cf. Bewcastle, 14½ ft). – The third fragment, standing 4½ ft high on a modern base, was found re-used as a lintel in the church in 1842. On one main face a very worn pattern of symmetrically entwined tendrils enlivened by smaller sprigs, on the other short panels with fret, interlace and a whorl-like 'ribbon animal'. The sides have a very open scroll and a vine scroll compressed into a series of lozenges. The surface of three sides is far better preserved than that of the other cross, yet the relief is perceptibly less controlled and varied. The loss of naturalism is evident in the way that the berries in the vine scroll are mechanically slotted into little triangular spaces whereas on the other cross the berries always have a convincing downward sag. The open scrolls on the other side, though competent, are dry and repetitious. This schematization of late c7 form with no admixture of new ideas suggests a date well into the c8. – Two HOGBACK STONES and a small fragment of a third. One has the usual fishscale pattern in imitation of roof tiles or shingles, and a steeply rounded back. The fragment comes from a very similar stone. The other, broken hogback has longer, almost oblong 'tiles', and hardly rises towards the centre. – Other fragments include a late c12 base cut in two (or is it two responds?) and two c13 coffin lids.

FREE CHURCH at Woodend, 1.5 km. SE on the A904. 1885 by *Hippolyte J. Blanc*, a lanceted church of Dalmeny stone with

* It is possible that the destroyed major face included figural subjects.

Abercorn church, cross, eighth century, front and side views (restored)
(*Proceedings of the Society of Antiquaries of Scotland*, vol. 72)

a belfry gable towards the road, an octagonal apse for the pulpit
at the other end, and a central flèche. – MANSE to match, and
a terrace of five COTTAGES with mullioned sash-windows and
bracketed porches. Two similar rows dated 1879 and 1881 are
on the road to Abercorn.

ABERLADY

EL 4070

PARISH CHURCH. A CI5 rubble-built square tower adjoins the
W end, with a set-in top storey and a slated pyramidal spire
behind a corbelled parapet. The storey above the string course
was later adapted as a doocot, with flight holes in the slit window
on the S side. Nothing can be seen of the Georgian kirk of 1773.
On the N side it incorporated two burial aisles of the early post-
Reformation period (both with simple tracery of lancets-and-
vesica type, one transomed) which *William Young* duplicated
on the S side when he completely recast the body of the church
in 1886 (*see* Gosford House). Young also added twin porches
to the N and S sides of the tower, and the session house at the
E end. His transformation of the inside was highly ingenious.
Pointed arches on Transitional capitals open into the four aisles.
Between, a lesser arch, repeated as a blind arcade all round the
chancel. Open timber roof. – FONT and PULPIT are both of
Caen stone inset with porphyry-like stone (supposed to be local)
which is also used in the chancel floor. – COMMUNION TABLE
by *Scott Morton & Co.*, 1961. – STAINED GLASS. The whole
scheme, progressively carried out, was by *Edward Frampton* of
London. At the E end three lights (Nativity, the Madonna
adapted from the Gosford Botticelli), and round the chancel
six lancets, an apostle in each. St Paul is signed E F 1889. –
In the S aisle two lights with the Sermon on the Mount and
Christ with little children and another two with the Raising of
Jairus' daughter. – In the N aisle two pairs of two lights (Christ
after the Resurrection). – CROSS SHAFT (*see* Introduction, p.
34). A replica of a C8 fragment. – MONUMENTS. On the W
wall, but formerly against the wall separating the church from
the N aisle, a wall-monument by *Canova* to the Belgian Maria
Margaretta de Yonge † 1762, wife of Lord Elibank, who apolo-
gizes for his lateness in setting it up. An angel weeps over an
urn beneath a Doric pediment, her hair falling forward in a disarmingly natural expression of grief. – In the SE aisle, but
formerly in the chancel, a deathbed effigy of Louisa Bingham
Countess of Wemyss † 1882, by *John Rhind*. It has a chilling but

[margin note: Certainly not, says Clifford]

pathetic nobility. – In the churchyard a fair collection of C18 table-tops and headstones. – At the entry to the churchyard a LOUPIN-ON STANE (i.e. mounting stone).

CARMELITE FRIARY, W of Luffness House (*see* p. 318). A pitiful remnant, no more than the lowest courses of a long narrow church, 27 m. by 6 m. From the buttresses of the E and W walls one can reconstruct three W windows and two E windows. At the E end of the N wall a segmental recess containing a battered effigy of a knight in late C13 armour. The position is that normal for a founder's tomb. W of this a plain pointed door into the cloister. Parts of the choir floor remain *in situ* with a TOMB SLAB of *c.* 1500 to Kentigern Hepburn. Slightly more than half way to the W are traces of the pulpitum between nave and choir. The earliest mention of the friary is in 1336, but the effigy proves a date for the foundation earlier by several decades. The long box-like proportions compare with late C13 mendicant churches outside Scotland (e.g. Alnwick Carmelites, Brecon Dominicans).

Aberlady is a feudal-looking village (the stump of the MERCAT CROSS marking its former status as a burgh of barony) and a golfing one. The HIGH STREET is on the main route from Edinburgh to North Berwick, but people still live there, glad of the front gardens which are a frequent but not a typically Scottish feature. It has a number of single-storey cottages of the C18, and three rows of red sandstone Gothic terraces built by the Wemyss Estate *c.* 1835. The longest has ten front doors, the one containing the Waggon Inn the extra pretension of a bracketed cornice and an upper floor behind Gothic dormers. Not many private villas, but THE LODGE of *c.* 1860, with its double driveway and central tower, makes a big show. At the W end, by the early C19 TOLL COTTAGE, is the village's quota of excellent semi-detached COUNCIL HOUSING, by *Dick Peddie & Walker Todd*, 1920. In HADDINGTON ROAD to the E a good block of mullioned and crowstepped Wemyss Estate housing dated 1884; presumably this is by *William Young*. Further on a stone-dressed house of *c.* 1770 with keystoned door lintel. The main road has now turned off down SEA WYND towards Aberlady Bay. On the W side is a long, rubble-walled warehouse, on the E the VILLAGE HALL by *William Young*, 1882, its only effort at display a thistle finial on one gable.

BALLENCRIEFF HOUSE. *See* p. 89.

FARMS

CRAIGIELAW, 1 km. w. The farmhouse and a row of cottages (originally six) are of Wemyss Estate type, *c.* 1835, with hood-moulded windows. The cattle courts of the steading, which is probably of the same date, have later curved roofs supported by lattice trusses and covered with tarred felt.

SPITTAL, 3 km. s. An unusually grand farmhouse of *c.* 1835 in the Wemyss Estate Tudor style. FOOTBRIDGE over the railway to the N of iron lattice type (*see* Drem).

ACREDALES *see* HADDINGTON

ADDIESTOUN HOUSE   ML *1060*
1.5 km. ESE of Ratho

1938 by *Charles G. Soutar*. A small L-plan baronial swan song, with a turret in the angle, well related to its garden walls, in one of which is a C17 arched doorway. The little LODGE is of similar type.

ADDIEWELL   ML *9060*

ST THOMAS (R.C.), West Calder Road. 1923 by *Reginald Fairlie*. A harled building on a raised site, quite simple except for the tall gable at the (liturgical) w end which is economical but effective Baroque, of two scrolled stages, with a niche for a statue at the head. Nave spanned by elliptical arches and lit by round-headed windows. w gallery. Priest's house adjoining.

By the church the red brick BOARD SCHOOL by *J. Graham Fairley*, 1896, and the R.C. SCHOOL, 1916.

LOGANLEA HOUSE, at the far w end. Dated 1798, but the roll-moulded doors look earlier. On what is now the garden front the central chimney-gable is oddly corbelled out over a Venetian window.

FACTORY, in the industrial estate. By *Christopher R. Dinnis*, 1975. The finned precast concrete gable is an advertisement for its own products.

The foundation of Addiewell in 1866 had much to do with the chemical manufacturing interests of James Young (*see* Mid-calder parish church). It has grown steadily, making almost nothing of a beautiful site; the nearest thing to a centre is the tumbledown FARM dated 1762. A few late C19 brick rows, a group of semi-detached houses of British Iron & Steel Federation type (architect, *Frederick Gibberd*), *c.* 1950 – otherwise just a straggle of nondescript housing with one or two vandalized 'amenities'.

AINVILLE *see* KIRKNEWTON

4070   ## ALDERSTON HOUSE   EL
2.5 km. NW of Haddington

A pedimented house of *c.* 1790 with three storeys above a sunk basement. Rusticated ground floor. Set-back pavilions with canted fronts, and a central kitchen block to the rear. Single-storey W wing added *c.* 1830. The porch with its pairs of Roman Doric columns seems to have been added *c.* 1820, a likely date for the graceful plasterwork and plain chimneypieces inside (in a bedroom is one more elaborate specimen, with sickles, grapes and corn in the centre panel). In one or two of the upper rooms woodwork of *c.* 1760 presumably from an earlier house.

STABLES. Also of *c.* 1760. A compact square without a court-yard, presenting to the N (formerly the main) approach a portico with bulging Tuscan columns. The bottom member of the architrave is of wood. Depressed archways with keystones on each side. The other elevations are of two storeys plus a dummy-windowed parapet. The older stalls inside have niched and keystoned mangers.

5070   ## AMISFIELD HOUSE   EL
1 km. ENE of Haddington

The house itself, the most important building of the orthodox Palladian school in Scotland but demolished in 1928, was designed *c.* 1755 by *Isaac Ware** 'for Francis Charteris Esq.'; his maternal grandfather had bought this estate of Newmilns and given it the name of the family seat in Dumfries-shire. Of the main block nothing remains *in situ* (*see* the Golf Club House, Longniddry), so only the shortest description can be given here: principal front of seven bays with a rusticated basement; *piano nobile* with pedimented windows, and small upper windows beneath a cornice and balustrade; central Ionic portico on the arcaded basement; advanced end bays with the basement blind-arcaded to match.

However there is still a good deal to see. The house faced

* Illustrated in the *Complete Body of Architecture*, 1756.

approximately N, and immediately to the E of its site is the
STABLE BLOCK by *John Henderson*, 1785. Five thermal windows to the front, the centre one enclosed in a rusticated arch
with a pediment. Ten blind arches to the E, six to the S. (The
inside of the courtyard is of earlier C18 character, possibly
before Ware's house.)

WALLED GARDEN near the E lodge. Also by *Henderson*,
dated 1783 over the segmental arch in the E wall, and the chief
monument of C18 neo-classicism in Lothian. It is very large,
with a slight slope to the S. Brown masonry, of smooth ashlar
inside the N wall only. At the corners four identical cylinder
towers built a little higher than the walls, whose coping con-   63
tinues round them as a string course. Above the cornices
stepped bases that may or may not have been surmounted by
domes. The towers swell from the external angles of the wall,
and have plain niches. To the inside they present Roman Doric
porticoes of six columns, more closely spaced at the ends, facing
each other diagonally across the garden.

To the S, and visible from the garden, a building whose main
function seems to be as a landscape ornament; castellated
Gothic of three bays with a higher centre, probably early C19.

ICE HOUSE across the river Tyne. C18, of very unusual design on a single-storey square plan. An oblong groin-vaulted
main chamber leads into a narrower one with a slabbed floor
on massive stone joists beneath which ran a lade from the river.

TEMPLE, presumably by *Ware*, overlooking the river Tyne
to the NE of the site of the house. Roman Doric prostyle portico
of four columns with rustic belts and a Rococo frame in the
pediment. Rustic base, rustic quoins, and mask keystones to
the blind arches on each side.

GATES. To the W (the Haddington side) twin two-storey
lodges with cushioned piers joined by quadrant walls to similar
(but fluted) piers with vases. They look earlier than Ware's
time, and so do the blocked outer piers of the E gates.

AMISFIELD MAINS *see* HADDINGTON

ARCHERFIELD HOUSE   EL *5080*
1 km. NE of Dirleton

A forlorn shell, but of the highest value and interest. Archerfield
was built at several dates, and the following are the principal
ones we have. Small (*Castles and Mansions of the Lothians*) says

that it was built for William Nisbet of Dirleton in the late C17. *William Tender* was paid for mason work in 1733, and in 1745–6 the architect *John Douglas* received £465. From 1754 *George Paterson*, another architect, worked at sundry houses belonging to Mr Nisbet. In 1790 *Robert Adam* was paid for extensive alterations – the only part of the work to be specified in the documents, which are supported by drawings in the Soane Museum; but even this is rather confused by the fact that repairs and additions are stated to have gone on from 1789 to 1795. Moreover the Adam interiors were stripped in 1962 when the house was made over into a grain store. The great carcase survives, Palladian in layout, Baroque in detail.

Without venturing to match this probably incomplete chronology exactly, the various stages can be put in order. The late C17 house probably formed three sides of a courtyard open to the E, where the end walls of the wings can still be seen. In the first half of the C18 the W side took its present form (which can be attributed to *John Douglas*), the two-storey wings and quadrant links were added, and the main block refaced. Most likely the starting point for the design was the central frontispiece, which appears to be of the late C17 and may even have been moved here from the courtyard. Doorpiece on the main storey with Ionic pilasters and a segmental pediment; over it a swagged coat of arms, and then a tall window with pilasters and supporting scrolls which combine very oddly to support broad capitals. This tall pile of grey stone (contrasting with the warmer colour of the rest) forms the front of a canted bay. It is set slightly forward, and its rusticated quoins are not continued on to the flanks. At the head, however, the side walls take up the rhythm of its blind semicircular arch, and the result is a Vanbrughian central feature, once crowned with rotund urns, standing up above the wall head. For the rest, the three bays on each side are treated with considerable power. Gibbsian windows on the main storey, their pediments alternately triangular and segmental, rest on massive brackets which link them strongly to the basement. Above them a conspicuously blank wall suggests lofty coved ceilings within. The top windows are close under the cornice. No pediments on the canted sides of the bay, but bullseye niches for busts.

It was probably rather later that the plain limb, with canted end, was pushed out to the E on the central axis. It already existed when *Robert Adam* recast the main rooms on a grand T-plan: drawing room and library on the W front, and between them a saloon opening to the E into the round top-lit anteroom and finally the dining room. 'Great stairs' were inserted into the N internal angle of the T, and the front door was resited on the ground-floor level. The C19 successor of Adam's new porch was itself removed in 1962 when a large opening was made to admit machines. The small pilastered extensions to drawing room and library were probably made before 1795.

The Adam rooms with their coves and dome were executed but are now no more. In a building of such importance it is proper to add that their makers are known. The plaster friezes were modelled by *Williams* (only the patera frieze of the drawing room survives), and so were the figures for the library ceiling. Of the statuary marble chimneypieces by *Richard Cooke* of London there is at the time of writing just one, in the NE room on the first floor. It has a centre panel of an elongated vase and finely carved grapes. Some of the latticed iron balconies by *Thomas Chalmers* are still in place.*

ARMADALE
WL 9060

A hamlet that mushroomed with the beginning of the mineral exploitation of West Lothian in the mid C19. Precious little to notice. Near the central crossing the Kerr Memorial Lamp Post of 1919 and the Mallace Memorial Clock Tower of 1924, with arcaded base attached to the street front and a curious louvred belfry. The only other buildings that do anything for the place are OCHILVIEW SQUARE, red brick and harling, *c.* 1970, and the COMMUNITY CENTRE, red brick and copper, which is by *William Nimmo & Partners*, 1971.

ARNISTON
ML 3050

2.5 km. SW of Gorebridge

The architect was *William Adam*, 1726. Robert Dundas was one of the half dozen of his patrons who were professionally involved with the law, and possibly the most important; he was to be Lord President of the Court of Session in 1748–53. The house has been given‡ as an example of the third category

* A rather different reading of this complicated house has been put forward by David Walker, who takes the position of a C17 stair as evidence that the old courtyard opened to the W rather than the E. He may well be right, as he certainly is when he points out that the surviving marble chimneypiece is not in the documented Adam addition; so it may not be of Cooke's making.

‡ A. A. Tait: *William Adam and Sir John Clerk: Arniston and the 'Country Seat'*.

specified in Sir John Clerk's *The Country Seat*, designed for 'convenience and use', but it is actually a compromise between that and the second type, the nobleman's residence. Thus in the nine-bay N (entrance) front the two end bays with their Gibbs surrounds are slightly advanced, and three bays of the recessed centre are signalized with a modest giant order of attached Ionic columns and a heraldic pediment. The rusticated triple arcade that formed the base and the straight temple stair that ascended through the basement stage have been obscured by a crudely ceremonious entrance hall with a rival pediment, by *Wardrop & Reid*, 1872. This main block is connected by canted links (originally simple corridors of one storey only) to twin pavilions presenting their long fronts to the forecourt, a Venetian window in the centre of each; kitchen to the E, stables to the W.

The other fronts of the main block are plainer. They do not continue the crowning balustrade – the two S corners have pedestals and vases only. They do, however, continue the entablature of the central order which on the S front is obliged to jump up under the centre pediment in order to allow for the arcaded windows of the three central bays of the first floor. On this front there can quite clearly be detected in the masonry, now unharled, the wall of an earlier house. The central projection on the 'ground' storey and the double stair to garden level are of *c.* 1800. On the W front there is a real contradiction in levels. The W third of the house was built later, completed by *John Adam* in 1753 (the interiors two years after). To the N and S it maintains the symmetry of the design with three storeys of false windows above the basement, but the genuine windows on the W front betray the fact that there are only two storeys within the same height, the lower windows with their pediments belonging to the two lofty rooms John Adam provided on the 'ground' floor.

The Victorian porch, deep and high, provides a stately ascent to the SALOON, the work of *William Adam*, with plasterwork by *Joseph Enzer*. Two storeys in height, three bays wide and two in depth, it is a happy invention in both senses and a remarkable example of collaboration between architect and craftsman. The basic system is of giant Corinthian pilasters, groin-vaults springing from them to support a heavily framed rectangular ceiling. The shallow pilasters are made credible by the arcaded wall on which they are planted (the arches open into the smaller scale of corridor and gallery), and the corners are nicely managed with quarter-columns on which are perched baskets of fruit in exaggerated relief. The architectural solemnity below, enlivened only by twin chimneypieces with scrolly broken pediments under open arches, continues right up to the gallery handrail; no balustrade, because of the peculiar changes of level on the first floor. At this point the plasterwork takes its cue from the Corinthian capitals, and the compartments of the vault are decorated with fat swags. Diagonally paved marble floor. The only restless detail is the form of the bustiferous doorheads to the ground-floor rooms, their broken segmental profile an awkward echo of the arches through which they are seen. The doors on the upper level are less formally treated, with fruit and flowers on ribbons.

Beyond the saloon, a pair of timber STAIRCASES side by side, to the l. the oval service stair, to the r. the main stair, surmounted by a heavy cornice and a deep cove enriched with large husks and then a monster egg-and-dart moulding below the lantern. This seen, it is easiest to take the rooms in chronological order. Most of the woodwork in the OAK ROOM on the s front seems to belong to the earlier house, e.g. the Corinthian pilasters flanking the two basket-arched fireplaces of figured marble, though the fireplaces themselves are apparently of William Adam date. The same applies to the one in the bedroom overhead, with its framed overmantel painting. Over the saloon, with windows facing N, the LIBRARY, of five bays by three. From the Ionic pilasters supporting an elaborate pulvinated frieze over the bookshelves spring groined plaster vaults with diverse lacy reliefs; spaces for busts between them. Recessed grey marble chimneypiece crowned with two eagles. More chimneypieces of the William Adam period in the bedrooms to the E.

The work of the brothers Adam is seen in the ground-floor rooms *en suite* to the W. The plasterwork, alas, has been dismantled* because of dry rot and can only be described from records. In the DINING ROOM a plain coved ceiling above a leafy pulvinated frieze and bracketed cornice. Very strange marble chimneypiece, both the moulded opening and the eccentric upper moulding running into a big cartouche panel in the middle. The SECOND PRESIDENT'S DRAWING ROOM, named after Robert Dundas's son who attained the same office, has a frieze of antique foliage and then a coved Rococo ceiling with pheasants among the fronds, all of the highest quality. Yellow marble chimneypiece with Ionic columns. In

---

* But it is stored for reinstatement.

the bedroom above, whose windows are at present bizarrely exposed on two different levels, a chimneypiece with pulvinated laurel frieze.

Apart from some evidence of later C18 work, there remains only the NEW LIBRARY on the ground floor, its refurnishing dated 1868. It has an elaborate cornice, and a Flemish chimneypiece with terms supporting the arcaded overmantel. The KITCHEN in the W pavilion is notable for the shelf-lined Roman Doric column in the middle, and for the Victorian food lift and railway communicating with the dining room.

ORANGERY to the W. Lit by Venetian windows, its interior divided by two transverse arches. It used to have a coomb ceiling.

In 1726 *William Adam* made a plan for the GROUNDS which was largely carried out: a bold semi-formal system of avenues with a formal parterre on the S side of the house. Some of the avenues remain, but the overall pattern was obscured by *Thomas White*'s new layout in the Capability Brown manner in 1791. To the S of the house is now a lawn, and the intimate little landscape beyond it was created in the early C19.

In the WALLED GARDEN of c. 1791 some fragments of the Renaissance frontage of the old Parliament Hall in Edinburgh (1631–40, destroyed in 1808): a semicircular pediment with the royal cypher, mounted on a columned loggia, and pilasters with nailhead rustication flanking an arched doorway under a strapwork lintel.

LODGES, etc. To the S a late C17 gateway with banded circular piers surmounted by playful lions, removed from Nicolson Street in Edinburgh. To the N, standing back from the A7, a pair of late C18 lodges, square in plan, with arched windows between coupled pilasters, one bearing a lion, the other an elephant, realistically modelled. The original GATES and GATE-PIERS are still *in situ* between the lodges.

PARISH CHURCH. 1868, but by no means the first on the site. It has transepts, a semi-octagonal chancel to the E and a bellcote on the W gable. – STAINED GLASS. Three windows by *C. E. Kempe*: at the E end Presentation of Christ in the Temple, 1906; on the S side Crucifixion and Resurrection, 1902, and Adoration of the Magi, 1909. – MONUMENTS, in the churchyard. On the W side the burial enclosure of Robert Blair † 1811, son of the manse, President of the Court of Session and author of 'The

Grave'. – MANSE, opposite the church. Possibly C18, but much altered.

Athelstaneford is a village on a ridge, whose name is supposed to commemorate the defeat and death of the Northumbrian Athelstane at the hand of Angus MacFergus the Pict. More important is its place in the history of Lothian improvement, owing to the special encouragement given to craftsman-smallholders by the feudal superior Sir David Kinloch of Gilmerton in the mid C18 (*see* Gilmerton House). Most of the single-storey cottages built continuously along the street are of the early C19, though some could be older: HOME HOUSE, of two storeys with scrolled skewputts, nicely sited at the E end of the village, is certainly of the mid C18. Good lectern DOOCOT, dated 1583.

GILMERTON HOUSE. *See* p. 215.

KILDUFF HOUSE. *See* p. 270.

FARMS

ATHELSTANEFORD MAINS, 1 km. SE. The steading has a depressed-arched entrance surmounted by a stone bull's head and a clock enriched with the fruits of the earth. The house plain Tudor, *c.* 1840.

WEST FORTUNE, 1 km. NNW. Steading of *c.* 1830 with crow-stepped centre and wings. Black pantiles. The showy Tudor farmhouse was built soon after 1844 in grey stone.

AUCHINDINNY HOUSE
2 km. NE by E of Penicuik

ML 2060

Auchindinny, built for John Inglis of Langbyres, Lanarkshire, on the estate which he bought in 1702, was finished in 1707. Traditionally the architect was *Sir William Bruce*. Henry Mackenzie the Man of Feeling, who lived there from 1795 to 1807, cited it as an example of Bruce's skill in designing non-smoking chimneys. A more obvious indication of his authorship is the easy handling of a Palladian villa layout even on the very small scale which the job required.

The main house, with a slightly bell-cast roof, is of five bays and three storeys including the basement. The long sides of the twin two-storey pavilions linked to it by quadrant screen walls face inwards, making a forecourt which slopes gently up to the house so that its basement is partly sunk. The masonry is coursed rubble keyed for harling, with smooth rybats and moulded wall-head cornices. Two of the similarly corniced chimney stalks mark the division of the house into the simplest form of double-pile. The front door with its pulvinated frieze and pediment, reached by a bridging stair (a Georgian replacement), looks down a grassed avenue to the road. The only other decoration is the lugged frame and scrolly bracketed sill of the first-floor window on each pavilion; the one to the N looks down the drive, a parallel avenue formed by a third line of trees. Large dormers and a bathroom block were added to the back of the house c. 1920, and the S screen wall has been built up behind with a communicating passage. Glazing is mainly of the mid c18 or later, but some twenty-four-pane windows with very small panes on the N end of the house seem to be original. Two parallel ranges of outbuildings to the N. Up-hill to the S a stone-vaulted land drain with a square rubble head built up above ground level at each end.

Inside, the centre and S part of the basement are vaulted, but the kitchen was probably in the N part; there are signs of a bakehouse in the N pavilion and the wide segmental doorway of the S one suggests that it housed the stable. On all three levels the house is divided by cross walls containing the flues. An easy-going scale-and-platt stone stair ascends between them, the nosings of the upper flights returned downwards at the ends. Some original panelling survives, but cornices are surprisingly absent, suggesting that the ceilings have been strengthened by lowering. The division of the N and S 'piles' into rooms has been altered with the shifting or removal of partitions, but the original plan can be inferred from the siting of the bolection-moulded stone fireplaces. The best rooms are on the top floor, entered through lugged pine doorways from the landing. The oak-lined drawing room to the S with its prettily lugged and corniced chimneypiece has been united with a little room at the back, the panelling made up in pine. In the bedroom to the N painted panelling, the overdoor and overmantel boards with romantic landscapes.

₁₀₆₀   BABERTON HOUSE   ML*
1 km. NW of Juniper Green

Built in 1622 for – and probably by – *James Murray*, Master of the King's Works, on land granted to him in that year by James VI, Baberton is a little three-storey house of traditional double-L-plan, formalized and trimmed in the Jacobean court style,

* Now Edinburgh.

with gabled and chimneyed wings projecting symmetrically forward to form a small courtyard with stair-turrets in the angles. The walls are of rubble (originally harled) with enrichments of uncommon delicacy: chamfered chimney stalks very different from the wild convolutions of Winton (see p. 472), fretted quoins and corbelled obelisks at the angles, pediments over many of the windows including the row of three dormers to the N. All the original windows were half-shuttered, with fixed glazing inserted in the check still visible in the upper half, and even those on the first floor were barred on the outside. No external change is visible until 1765, when the courtyard was filled in with a pile of rooms which breaks forward in a semi-octagon. Its parapet used to have a pair of central chimneys serving the two upper rooms. On ground-floor level the new front door with Gibbs surround and copious masons marks opens into the entrance hall. On its w wall is the moulded stone surround of the old entry; the strapwork pediment that once crowned it has been mounted face downward as a wall-head corbel in an angle of a new outbuilding to the N W. Behind the N wall the stair-turrets are buried. The w one survives, and at its head on the second floor is the finest of an original set of oak doors panelled and inlaid in the Dutch manner, still with its ornamental strap hinges. This stair was supplemented by another, ascending in a curve from ground to first floor in the w wing, also of stone, with wrought-iron balusters in a crisply intersecting pattern. The E stair was removed but replaced from first to second floor by another in wood, more amply curved, with twisted balusters.

The vaulted ground-floor rooms to the E may be earlier than 1622. In the N W room two niches, one with a mask keystone, probably of the early C18. The principal rooms are on the first floor. The huge stone fireplace in the dining room to the N W is Murray's, for of the three triglyph panels on the lintel, all strapworked in miniature, the centre one bears his initials. The room was pine panelled in the early C18, with a shell-headed display niche, but its fine detailed plaster cornice must be of c. 1765. En suite with it to the NE, the principal bedroom of Murray's house has a geometric plaster ceiling with the moulded attributes of the United Kingdom in the central compartments, stars in the outer ones. In the bay-fronted drawing room an ambitious cornice of 1765, but the chimneypiece on the E wall is of c. 1810. The flat-arched chimneypieces of the upper bedrooms belong to the early C18.

SUNDIAL BASE. The fretted baluster to the S is evidently
Murray's work, as is the little pediment with strapwork cartouche over the door into the walled garden to the SW.

PARISH CHURCH (former United Presbyterian). Gothic. By
James Fairley, 1888.

ST JOSEPH (R.C.) (former United Secession). A barn-like building of 1827 with windows indicating the position of the pulpit
in the middle of the S side. The interior was transformed for
its present use by *Peter Whiston*, 1965, a quiet, effective
treatment, with shallow-pitch ceiling.

ST MUNGO (Episcopal), Ladycroft. By *R. Rowand Anderson*,
1869. Economical but effective, with a very steep roof over low
walls, harled and lanceted. The W gable has a centre buttress
and bellcote. Interior of painted brick, with dark stained scissor
roof of light and therefore frequent timbers. – STAINED GLASS.
Two lights (St Mungo, the Virgin and Child) by *John Blyth*,
1957. – One light with a splendid mix-up of patterns and
colours (St Margaret) by *William Wilson*, 1959.

COCKBURN HOUSE, 2 km. WSW. Plain, L-plan, with a quasi-
octagonal stair-turret in the angle. Built for William Chiesley
in 1672, the date on one of the dormer pediments. Wall
sundials. (Inside, an C18 stair and early C19 rooms, quite plain.)

MALLENY HOUSE (property of the National Trust for Scotland), 0.5 km. E. A single range with two storeys and dormered
attic, front door on one side (E), turnpike stair on the other.
But when was it built? The up-to-date plan suggests the first
half of the C18, crowsteps and all, incorporating the big chimney
of an earlier house, which appears on the W side next to the
stair-turret. On the inside of it is a very wide kitchen fireplace
of the late C16 or early C17 with a reset fragment of an armorial
panel dated 1589 which probably comes from over the entrance
of an earlier house. The ground floor is not vaulted. The first
floor has a passage past the middle room giving access to the
end ones. All have panelling and chimneypieces of *c.* 1740 with
overmantel paintings of classical ruins in the manner of the
Nories, but the middle room is lined with oak, and round its
bolection-moulded fireplace is a double-lugged chimneypiece
like one at Auchindinny. A N extension of one grand storey was
added *c.* 1820 for General Thomas Scott. The architect is not

known. It has a bow to the E into which the drawing room fits
a half-dome, then a transverse oval dome on pendentives, then
a segmental vault; and another to the W for the dining room
with its massive black chimneypiece. A link between new and
old is formed by a fanlit front door and a groin-vaulted vestibule
from which a plain stone stair goes up to the old first-floor passage, unfortunately cutting off the end of a room in the process.
The castellated service wing to the S is probably a little later.

DOOCOT. With double-pitch crowstep gables, perhaps again
C18.

VILLAS

BANKHEAD, Johnsburn Road. A house of the later C18 with an
addition of *c.* 1810 to its front so that there is a pair of gables
at each end. The new front has rusticated quoins, a basement
area with iron railings, and tripartite ground-floor windows
flanking a bracketed doorpiece. Painted dressings on harled
walls. Inside, the staircase (of the later date) has wrought-iron
balusters, each pair nicely joined at top and bottom. The chimneypieces are mostly plain, but a late C18 specimen of pine
with composition ornament has a pretty oval plaque of children
playing – prototypes of Kate Greenaway. – WALLED GARDEN.
Probably of the earlier date, enjoying the steep S slope of a
beautiful site.

HARMENY HOUSE, Mansfield Road. A modest house by *R.
Rowand Anderson*, 1906, lengthened to E and W in the following
year by *Robert Lorimer* without any loss of character. It is informally but severely composed in crisp white harling, the only
exposed stonework being at the wall head and occasionally at
the openings, e.g. at the front door, which is entered through
a cavernous arch springing from a battered base. The other (S)
side is dominated by an ogee-roofed turret with an off-centre
Renaissance door leading into a garden porch. The bell-cast
roof with its solid dormers and careful slating has an altogether
heavier, more laborious look, perhaps due to Lorimer. A compact plan; no rooms of special note. The LODGE and STABLES
at the entrance from the road are entirely by Lorimer, equally
informal but much more complicated, especially in the
treatment of the roof.

JOHNSBURN, Johnsburn Road. Pale pink harling with sandstone
dressings; *c.* 1900. A cosier mixture of Scots vernacular and
Renaissance, with dormers and curly gabled, almost colonial,
porch. An octagonal turret is merged into the internal angle
of the L-plan on the garden side.

LARCH GROVE, to the W, entered from Johnsburn Road. Built
c. 1890, basically an L-plan house with a round turret in the angle,
it has finely dressed bays and bows, and Renaissance detail
grafted on to its stugged masonry walls with considerable taste.

LEASINGSIDE, Lanark Road. White harl and red sandstone and
tiles; *c.* 1910. A deep canted bay whose ground floor is a porch
with bulgy Roman Doric columns is jostled by a tall, plain
chimney with a battered edge.

NORTHFIELD, Lanark Road. Harled, with red sandstone dressings; by *G. Mackie Watson*, 1910. A tall house, casually composed, with swept skews on the gables. The approach and the
formal garden retain their original planting of trees and shrubs.

RAVELRIG, Lanark Road. DOOCOT of C18 lectern type, with
two storeys and 274 nesting boxes.

TREETOPS, Lanark Road. White harl and timber, the main rooms
clad in shallow courses of dark grey terrazzo.

DESCRIPTION

Balerno's other buildings are best noted in the course of a walk.
The POLICE STATION on the approach is a good geometric
composition of well laid (for Scotland) buff brick, by *S. Green*
and *C. Park* (*County Council*), 1974. Brick (but this time red
and yellow) is also the material of the sprawling SCHOOL and
adjacent schoolhouse by *Wardrop & Reid*, 1877. Next to the
two churches (*see* above) the ROYAL BANK OF SCOTLAND,
a jolly mixture of vernacular and grandiose, with dormers and
scrolled skewputts over a heavy cornice, by *David J. Chisholm*,
c. 1935. A nice view over to St Mungo's and two pairs of painted
steel prefabricated houses of *c.* 1920 in LADYCROFT. The entry
to MAIN STREET is marked by the dull blank walls and monopitch roofs of the SHOPPING CENTRE, *c.* 1970, and on the
other side by the usual Co-op. But the street itself climbs pleasantly between varied grey stone fronts of the later C19 (e.g.
the GREY HORSE INN of 1860) till it is firmly stopped by the
projecting front of No. 27. The traffic has been stopped here
too, and the place is now rediscovering itself. Beyond, at the
town-head, is the baronial turret of the PAPER WORKS, in red
sandstone, 1916. This is in BAVELAW ROAD, which also has
two good housing developments in closely grouped harled
blocks. The first, by *S. Green* (*County Council*), 1974, connects
with Main Street; the second, LENNOX TOWER GARDENS,
was built for the Lennox Tower Housing Association by *Henry
Wylie & Partners*, 1975.

BALGONE HOUSE   EL 5080
2.5 km. SSE of North Berwick

An accumulation of the C17–19. It began with the L-shaped C17 part at the S end. This was lengthened c. 1700, and the polygonal stair-turret duplicated so that the main (W) front became symmetrical. At the same time it was given two-storey piend-roofed pavilions with quadrant links. Finally c. 1860 the wall between the turrets was pushed out flush with their faces on both levels, the turrets themselves were crowned with balustrades, and a baronial wing was added at the NE. The interior has little except for a pretty ceiling over the well stair of c. 1800 at the back, and the large dining room which was the reason for the new wing. Its cornice is deep and billeted, its ceiling divided into squares by double ribs made of four diamonds coming to a point at the bottom, and its chimneypiece is of brown marble: a ribbed segmental archway, the spandrels carved with high reliefs of retrievers persecuting birds and killing a badger in two roundels, the remainder with foliage of considerable delicacy. Mantelshelf with round corner brackets. The architect of this High Victorian work was probably *J. Anderson Hamilton*, who certainly designed the LODGES: the S one of 1859, a 62 baronial gatehouse at Brownrigg (now separated from the estate), with a wild string course and three crowstepped gables; the N one of 1863, more conventionally baronial, adjoining a ball-topped archway.

STEADING. Dated 1849, with an octagonal horse-walk converted to an engine house. The round brick chimney is still in place.

BALLENCRIEFF HOUSE   EL 4070
2 km. SE of Aberlady

A wreck, but its general lines are clear enough. The SW part of this long rectangular house was built in the late C16 and early C17 by John Murray, first Lord Elibank. The N front and E end were added c. 1730. The new N elevation had a centre block with a cornice and smooth dressings, and a tall chimneyed gable with scrolled skewputts set slightly back from it on each side. Much red brick was used for walling, but not exposed. The house was burnt out in 1868 and has since been deserted, but a two-storey outhouse of the later period, said to have been the laundry, still stands to the W and is inhabited. This is one of the two wings shown on a drawing of 1834.

To the SW of the house, BALLENCRIEFF GRANARY, an L-plan building of the C16 with crowstepped gables. On the underside of three skewputts shields carved with heraldic motifs. The RCAHMS suggests that it was part of the Hospital of St Cuthbert. There is no internal stair, and the high corbelled platform on the S side in the angle strengthens the traditional idea of its purpose; access to the upper levels would have been by ladder, and there could have been a winch on the platform.

0070   BANGOUR VILLAGE HOSPITAL   WL
4 km. WSW of Uphall

Bangour (the accent on the second syllable) was the estate of the Hamiltons of Bangour, of whom William Hamilton the C18 poet is the best known. On this large and hilly site a lunatic asylum for the City of Edinburgh was built in 1898–1906, the term 'village' referring not to any existing village, nor to the architectural character of the whole thing, which is neither small in scale nor close-knit in layout, but to the idea of a self-contained community in the country, its inmates usefully employed in the grounds, farm and workshops. The architect of the original buildings, which are remarkably intact, was *Hippolyte J. Blanc*. The general style is 'Queen Anne', in snecked rubble with red sandstone dressings, with much attention to the skyline. The patients are housed in villas, each well sited on a slope, like the residences of a sylvan university: the nurses' house and medical block would be its academic buildings, and the Physician Superintendent's house up the hill would be that of the principal. A church has pride of place at the centre; built some twenty years later, it completes the illusion.

VILLAGE CHURCH (dedicated to Our Lady, but inter-denominational from the start). An unexpectedly large building – by far the grandest C20 church in Lothian – in a simplifed Romanesque style, by *Harold O. Tarbolton*, 1924–30. The influence of contemporary churches in the Netherlands is strong, but the chief external material, snecked yellow-brown whinstone, is more lively than Dutch brick. Dressings, striped horizontal bands and arch stones are of paler sandstone, and the Caithness slates of the roofs have weathered to a matching colour. All the work, including the furnishings, was done by the hospital's building and maintenance staff under *William Livingstone*, clerk of works.

The long nave starts with a massive W gable. Clasping buttresses at the corners, diminishing into shallow gablets near the top, and whinstone piers carved with the dedicatory monogram M R, a formidable undertaking both in strength and skill. Between them the tall w window with slim mullions, the tracery very quirky to avoid any graceful impression. N and S porches, spurning enrichment except in their iron gates; then aisles, with small round-headed windows like those of the clerestory. There is no crossing and thus no real transepts, but on the S side the apsidal WAR MEMORIAL CHAPEL (oddly orientated to the S) is followed by the rectangular tower, stumpy and solid, pierced at the head by slits as if for a belfry. To the S the boldly projecting louvres are sheltered by a round arch, but on the longer E and W sides a lead roof runs down on top of them at a very steep pitch; runs down, that is, from the squat broach-spire, which is lead-covered (not copper as originally intended) with rolled joints, crowned with a lead cross. On the N side the composition is more elaborate, and smaller in scale; choir room and vestry and a small rectangular tower with saddle roof.

Internally the same idiom continues, but the snecked rubble is now of sandstone, graded to a smaller size at clearstory level, and fine smooth ashlar takes on a more important role (much of the stone came from the demolition of Hamilton Palace in Lanarkshire). Of ashlar the plain five-bay nave arcades (consecration crosses on the piers) and the taller arches of the two bays to the E with galleries on the N side, Memorial Chapel and organ case on the S. The largest arch, slightly stilted and resting on plain corbels between smooth piers, opens into the chancel. Of the expression of mass through plane surface, and the fault-less detailing of stonework, Tarbolton is here seen as a supreme master. The stonework is matched by the roofs, dark stained in the nave, with huge pairs of principals, hammerbeams on corbelled braces, and kingposts above. The chancel roof is de-rived from Lorimer (cf. those at St Peter, Edinburgh, or the chapel at Stowe), with a wooden tunnel-vault traversed by tie-beams and bracketed from the wall. – WOODWORK in the chancel of Perp character, PULPIT, FONT COVER, REREDOS CANOPY, and ORGAN CASE, all in oak, designed by *Tarbolton* and carved by the hospital's woodworkers. – ORGAN by *Jardine & Co.* of Old Trafford.

The rest of the hospital is best described in the course of a walk. All the buildings are by *Blanc* except when stated. After the entry from the A89 into the well planted central part the SHOP in the cottage style, with timbered gable and elaborate glazing.

To the E the BOILER HOUSE with red brick chimney, and the WORKSHOPS, much altered. The same applies to the LAUNDRY and KITCHEN straight ahead to the N, both still used for their original purposes. The original bakery is now the INDUSTRIAL UNIT. Further to the E the HALL, 1906, of grey stone with a Venetian window in the gable, buttressed flanks and a square fly-tower at the rear end. The installation of the CINEMA ORGAN from the Lonsdale Cinema, Carlisle, in 1972 has not interfered with the delicate internal furnishings. Next to the hall is the PHYSIOTHERAPY BUILDING, plain Italian with harled walls. Then on to the ADMINISTRATIVE CENTRE, plainer than the villas, with canted wings which formerly housed the male and female admission wards. The little SPORTS PAVILION in front of it was the hospital's railway station, built in 1914 and moved here when the line was closed. Behind it is the church, and overlooking this from the N are the two senior buildings of the whole layout: the NURSES' HOME with its two octagonal central turrets, ogee-roofed in lead, nicely extended by *E. J. MacRae*, Edinburgh City Architect, 1931; then the MEDICAL HOSPITAL, whose centre is baronial. In this area Blanc designed a number of later blocks in a less substantial style than the rest of the villas, e.g. No. 31, of red brick and pebbledash (probably the isolation hospital built in 1909), and No. 32, now the PSYCHOGERIATRIC UNIT, its appearance spoiled by a central lounge block. Additions to villas Nos. 7 and 32 by *Scott & McIntosh*, 1972, are more tactful and imaginative. The villas to the W suffer from lack of planting; they were economically supplemented in 1939 by Nos. 24 and 25, the *Edinburgh City Architect's Department* making no effort at architectural sympathy. To the N of them the original SCHOOL. At the extreme W end of the site is the FARM, made over to serve the hospital as part of the original works. There remains BANGOUR HOUSE, on a secluded eminence to the NW, at the time of writing unfortunately derelict. Designed by *Blanc* as the PHYSICIAN SUPERINTENDENT'S HOUSE, it is of cream-painted harl with red dressings and a S-facing verandah. The rocky WATER GARDEN behind it is still well maintained.

BANGOUR GENERAL HOSPITAL to the NW has a formal, hutted layout. Built in 1940, it is typical of its kind, devoid of any architectural interest.

In DECHMONT VILLAGE, to the SE of the Village Hospital, a number of single-storey staff cottages which were part of the original building programme.

BANKTON HOUSE
WL (ML) *0060*
2 km. sw of Midcalder

A broadly proportioned three-bay house of droved yellow ashlar by *Charles Black*, builder, 1812, for James Bruce who was Secretary to the Excise Board. Roman Doric doorpiece between tripartite ground-floor windows; single-storey wings with little Venetian windows.

BARNBOUGLE CASTLE
WL* *1070*
0.5 km. N of Dalmeny House, 2.5 km. NE of Dalmeny

A three-storey tower house of hungry-jointed rubble by *Wardrop & Reid*, 1881. Twin gables to the w. Small jamb to the E with a corbelled stair-turret in the angle. The old castle became a ruin after the building of Dalmeny House (*see* p. 170) in 1817, but a lot of the underground cellarage remains, and just enough of the masonry of the N and E walls to demonstrate what would have been the apex of *R. & J. Adam*'s scheme of 1774-93 for a huge triangular castle pointing NW into the Firth of Forth. The Victorian rebuild makes far less dramatic use of the site, but is interesting because it was designed as virtually a single-function building – a private library with modest living quarters for the fifth Earl of Rosebery. The result is far simpler and archaeologically more convincing as an imitation C16 tower house than a complete country house could ever be. At the SE a big turnpike stair of noble proportions serves a varied sequence of well detailed, brown stained library rooms. The two largest are to the NW – heavily beamed on the ground floor, loftily timber-vaulted on the first, a two-storey galleried hall with a clear view over the Forth to Fife through tall mullioned windows, one an externally treated oriel in the manner of May-bole, Ayrshire. A second oriel on the s lights the Parlour, whose husked chimneypiece is a faint intimation of the forthcoming Adam revival.

SUNDIAL, a little way to the s. C17 obelisk type, with polyhedron dials half way up.

BARNES CASTLE
EL *5070*
2 km. NE of Haddington

John Seton of Barnes, who died in 1594, 'made ane great building at the Barnes Voult height, before his death; intending that the

* Now Edinburgh.

building bound a court'.* It has a dominant site on the Garleton Hills, but building seems indeed to have stopped with the basement vaults which give it its current name. The square corner towers of the principal range, on the NE side, are repeated at the other angles of the courtyard. This formal layout is highly advanced for its date in Scotland.

BARNEY MAINS see HADDINGTON

Four islets stand off the N coast of the blunt North Berwick promontory. From W to E they are Fidra, the Lamb, Craigleith and the Bass which is the largest; a huge trachyte plug 105 m. high whose aspect on three sides is of sheer cliff, supporting a colony of 23,000 gannets. It is composed of giant laminations whose eccentric curves form a bizarre profile, and is pierced by a natural tunnel some 150 m long.

41 BASS CASTLE. The slope to the S is gentler and the long screen wall of the castle cuts it off from the lower promontory on which it is possible to scramble ashore. Only the E end of the castle is approachable because a battlemented wall projects from it at r. angles. This has an internal stair with gun ports covering the approach, and ends at the rock edge with a round battery whose ports command the landing place. At the N end a gateway leads past a bastion to a projection in the main screen where an entrance gives access to a long stair. On the S side the remains of a turnpike stair to the wall-head, on the N a single range of rooms. The screen wall continues, incorporating a little room known as Blackadder's Lodging (John Blackadder, minister of Traquair, was one of the Covenanters imprisoned here in the late C17), till its final bastion merges into the cliff. Underneath Blackadder's room is a well chamber. All this is built of the Bass's own brown rock, with occasional quoins and nosings of imported freestone, and the RCAHMS gives it a C16 date; at that time it still belonged to the Lauders of Bass, eventually passing to the Crown in 1671 and to Sir Hew Dalrymple of North Berwick in 1706. In 1902 the E part of the screen wall was pointed and given a flat-topped profile, and the lighthouse built above it; masked by the rock to the N, this is only of service to inshore shipping.

* *History of Seyton* (Maitland Club) quoted by the RCAHMS.

CHAPEL. The ruin of the castle chapel stands above the castle to the N, a small, simple rectangle with precisely wrought skew-putts. The dressings of the window in the W gable and the two arched windows of the S wall have disappeared, but the S door has a chamfered lintel and there is a holy water stoup just inside. In the E gable a piscina of crude ogival profile, formed of tufa. The plan of c. 1700, of which a transcript is published by the RCAHMS, shows this building as the magazine. It also shows a rectangular garden on the summit. Was this a ruin pressed into service as a sheltered vegetable patch, just as some of the old rooms of the castle are now used by the lighthouse staff for their potatoes? There is now only a rough enclosure of in-determinate plan. The fresh air of discovery, with a strong admixture of gannet and herring-gull, still hangs over the Bass. The birds are its custodians, and a guano-spattered cannon, visible from the foghorn platform to the NE, is part of their charge.

BATHGATE   WL 9060

OLD PARISH CHURCH, 2 km. E of the centre, on the A89. Roof-less and plain. Much of the masonry is no doubt medieval,* but of features there are only the N door jambs with worn capi-tals of c. 1200 (square abaci, elementary still-leaf) and one small N lancet near the E end. – Mid C13 EFFIGY of a priest. Of quite 9 good quality once, but badly weathered. Underneath the effigy several voussoirs apparently from the N door. – In the S wall an early C16 TOMBSTONE to Andrew Crichton of Drumcorse.
HIGH CHURCH, Jarvey Street. By *Wardrop & Reid*, 1882, re-placing the church built on this new and excellent site in 1737. Thinly Romanesque, assisted by a SW tower, buttresses and crocketed pinnacles. The S gable implies a non-existent trans-ept. The round-ended hall and session house make a good com-position at the NE. Inside the W porch a triple Romanesque arcade. The church has a flat, beamed ceiling, coombed and bracketed all round, with a coved top light in the middle, a horseshoe gallery, and a rib-vaulted semi-octagonal apse seen through a round arch. – ORGAN by *Bishop*. – MONUMENTS, in the churchyard. Wall-monument to the Rev. Walter Jardine † 1811 with laudatory panel, garlands and pediment, none the worse for being forty years behind the times. – Small loose stone 'in Memory of George Wilson Alias PUDDIN died 1853, the

---

* The walls were consolidated in 1846.

celebrated Gaberlunzie (beggar)', handsomely lettered, with a
Grecian wreath.

ST COLUMBA (Episcopal), 1 km. W of the centre, on the A89.
By *W. J. Walker Todd*, 1916, an economical harled church with
a dwarf tower set into the N side, in which the door jambs are
smooth dressed. The other stonework is rubble. Tiles are set
in the concrete lintels. Very simple interior with a rubble arch
leading into the semi-octagonal sanctuary. – ALTARPIECE
painting by *Mabel Dawson*, c. 1930.

ST DAVID, George Street. By *J. Graham Fairley*, 1904. 'Remarkable for originality of design in the tower,' said *The Architect*,
'but the author has scarcely escaped too close a resemblance
to the town hall type.' Even if true, this matters less since Fairley's own town hall of 1899 has now gone. The church is modernized E.E. in red sandstone, with a lanceted gable front to the
street. Linked to one side are the halls, well integrated with
the church on two levels, to the other the tower, its clasping
buttresses shooting up, with smooth continuous mullions
between, to eccentrically profiled battlements from behind
which springs a lanceted aedicule with a copper-roofed dome,
concave and then convex. It is the sole but fine signature of
Bathgate's skyline at the centre. The inside is equally original.
Through a porch with a welcoming fireplace opposite the door
one enters a big six-bay hall with open timber roof, the struts
of the last bay continuing down to the floor as tall posts. The
aisles are respectively of two storeys with a gallery, and of one
storey with clearstory lights above. – STAINED GLASS. Three
lights at the chancel end (SS. Columba, Andrew and Ninian,
with panels underneath showing Bathgate's three industries of
mining, steel and engineering) by *William Wilson*, 1954.

ST MARY (R.C.), Livery Street. Built in 1858, altered in 1908
by *Charles Menart* of Glasgow. The pinnacled Gothic W front
precedes a big aisled church of three bays with marbled arches,
the last higher to form transepts. Open timber roof. Richly
Gothic sanctuary with mosaic figure of Christ. – STAINED
GLASS. In the baptistery the Baptism of Christ by *William Wilson*, 1959. – His also are the two lights in the Lady Chapel,
the Annunciation and the Adoration of the Virgin, 1954, with
gorgeous reds. He called them 'small but exceedingly rich'.

BATHGATE ACADEMY (now the Teaching Development
Centre), Marjoribanks Street. By *R. & R. Dickson*, 1831. This
most sombre of neo-classical academies, and Bathgate's only
large public building, was endowed by the C18 carpenter turned

Jamaica planter, John Newlands. On its dominating site (not that there is much to dominate) it has a Baroque spread of twin pavilions on massive bases, the centre and links approached by the very wide stair between. Yet all movement is paralysed by the most static detail, mainly Grecian. The end temples are walled with channelled ashlar on the same plane as their corner antae. Deep balustrades weigh down on the thinly supported links. And the vast centre temple of two Doric columns *in antis* is surmounted, with what can only be deliberate awkwardness, first by a stepped base, then a clock stage, finally a tall square aedicule whose balustrade draws attention to its emptiness. Here and there a dreadful gusto gives a Baroque push to its stiffness, e.g. in the scrolled consoles at the base of the tower, in the curly ends of the stair walls, and in the empty niches of the pavilions. Goodridge's Lansdown Tower near Bath, six years earlier, is comparatively light-hearted. But the point is inescapable: this is visibly a memorial though functionally a school. The horror did not, or at least does not, extend inside.

DESCRIPTION

Bathgate spreads over an interesting site, a series of gentle humps to the sw of the Bathgate Hills, with few important buildings and only one large one. It was the centre of a medieval sheriff-dom (distinct from that of Linlithgow) and a market town, but the old centre is evident only in the street names. It was later a stage on the Georgian turnpike road from Edinburgh to Glasgow, and its early C19 expansion was partly due to a surprisingly late boom in handloom weaving. But only a few traces of Georgian order survive, for example in HOPETOUN STREET (the Earl of Hopetoun was hereditary sheriff) where the HOPE-TOUN ARMS has two doorpieces with fluted pilasters and the house opposite boasts an entrance with columns set back behind pilasters with a fluted lintel; such was Bathgate's version of the Georgian idiom, but most of it is fragmented beyond recall,* and the early C19 houses round the corner in Jarvey Street are mere shells. The railway arrived from Edinburgh in 1849, and the expansion of old industries like coal and new ones like shale mining (for the extraction of paraffin, the waste being dumped in huge bings over this part of West Lothian) made Bathgate an artisan town of makeshift character, its richer inhabitants resorting to villas like the High Victorian WELL PARK of

* Literally fragmented; demolition is in progress, October 1977.

c. 1860 (now the County Library) in Marjoribanks Street. Towards the turn of the century civic pride began to assert itself in a showy generation of public buildings. In JARVEY STREET *Peter Henderson* designed the three-gabled CO-OPERATIVE SOCIETY store in red and cream sandstone and the adjoining MASONIC LODGE, red stone Renaissance with a stained glass oriel over the entrance flanked by two tall shopfronts, both in 1902. *J. Graham Fairley* won many of the best jobs, like the baronial DREADNOUGHT HOTEL in Whitburn Road, and the Torphichen Street BOARD SCHOOL of 1904. His TOWN HALL, designed in 1899 and subsequently revised, was replaced in 1966. As usual the Edwardian POST OFFICE turned up trumps; it is a beautifully detailed Scots Renaissance building in George Place by *W. T. Oldrieve* for the *Office of Works*, 1913. To the E of the Bathgate Academy in Marjoribanks Street the COLLEGE OF FURTHER EDUCATION, built of smart red brick *c.* 1970. To the W of it in Balbardie Road two nice villas of the early C20, CLOISTERFIELD and GRANGE HILL; the first has a red tiled ogival roof on its corner turret, and both have Art Nouveau doorpieces and externally expressed ingles. Perhaps *J. Graham Fairley* was their architect.

NORTHBANK, Drumcross Road. An ordinary C20 suburban house with some old stonework facing the road: a window and an inscribed stone (Thomas Sharp and Marion Dalmahoy, 1599). These are fragments of Kirkton House, demolished in 1862.

GALA BRAES. *See* p. 206.

1060   BAVELAW CASTLE   ML*
4 km. SSE of Balerno

Bavelaw's present aspect is that of a C17 laird's house, but some of it could be earlier than 1628 when Laurence Scott of Harperrig, advocate, received the grant of the land 'with the town and manor place'. It consists of three blocks with two storeys and attic, each defined by its own crowstep gables: the main S range, a jamb to the N, and an oblong block at the external (SE) angle of the resulting L-plan. The door and stair are not in the internal angle but on the E side. Adjoining the NE corner a round turret with a pronounced batter, its roof swept into that of the jamb. Gun loops command the front door. High corbelled turret to improve circulation on the attic floor by *Robert Lorimer*,

* Now Edinburgh.

c. 1900. He also added the boat-shaped dormers, reconstructed the existing outhouses to the NE and W, joining them to the house with a balustraded screen, and laid out a small formal garden. Indoors he made the vaulted basement habitable, supplemented the existing woodwork, and added a thin-ribbed geometric ceiling in the drawing room.

BEANSTON   EI *5070*

1621 is the date on the roll-moulded doorway of this small house, with the initials of Patrick Hepburn and his wife, but little else survived the mid C19 alterations.

ORANGERY of *c.* 1760 by the high-walled garden. Four-bay arcaded ashlar front and rusticated quoins.

BEDLORMIE *see* BLACKRIDGE

BEESKNOWE *see* BIEL HOUSE

BEESLACK HOUSE   ML *2060*
1.5 km. NE of Penicuik

Dry castellated Gothic-survival, by *J. A. Bell*, a pupil of Rickman, 1855. 'Taste and correctness of study are everywhere apparent',* but also considerably out of date. Two-storey hall, its glass to Bell's design, with a bracketed ceiling on corbelled shafts. The well stair has traceried timber balusters and an arcaded landing. Lively vine cornices are the only other significant detail. The LODGE is also by *Bell*. The 'Swiss chalet' in the garden has disappeared.

BEGBIE *see* HADDINGTON

BELHAVEN   EL *6070*

PARISH CHURCH, on the main road approaching Dunbar from the W. Gable of dark red whin, tower and belfry in pale grey Catcraig stone; *c.* 1840.

BELHAVEN HOUSE. Five bays, two storeys and basement, of *c.* 1825, with later bracketed doorpiece. GARDEN of considerable interest, entered through a C20 arch which incorporates a sejant lion and two urns, all in red sandstone, of the earlier

* Small's *Castles and Mansions of the Lothians.*

C18. (*Vitruvius Scoticus* has a design for Belhaven House by *William Adam*.) LODGE with wrought-iron gates by *Robert Lorimer*, early C20.

BELHAVEN HILL SCHOOL. Red sandstone. The five-bay centre with its architraved windows and pedimented Roman Doric doorpiece belongs to the original house of *c.* 1760. The rusticated quoins and the two pavilions joined to it by quadrants were abolished *c.* 1920 and replaced by two pedimented end blocks built up against the main house, with Venetian windows over ground-floor bays. Internally there is something of everything. The entrance hall and the graceful stairwell ahead of it are of *c.* 1800. The room to the l., with its original finishings except for a late C18 chimneypiece, has been opened into a large well staircase apparently of the C20.

KNOCKENHAIR HOUSE, to the NE. A nicely sited house of 1907 by *R. Weir Schultz*, shaped to the ridge on which it stands, a square ogee-roofed turret marking the slight bend at the centre. The lower part of an C18 beehive-shaped WINDMILL forms an outrigger to the E.

BREWERY, s of the main road. A mainly rubble-built group with slated kilns, founded in 1719 and reconstructed after fires in 1814 and 1887. The brick chimney probably belongs to the latter date. The best interior is a large cellar of carefully cut masonry.

HOSPITAL, s of the brewery. An open layout of harled and gabled pavilions by *Sydney Mitchell & Wilson*, 1904, with straightforward harled additions by *Alan Reiach & Partners*, 1957.

Belhaven, a coastal village that used to have a harbour, is now virtually a suburb of Dunbar (*see* also Edinburgh Road in that town, p. 186), but worthy of note in its own right. From the main road, where a good C18 vernacular row includes the colour-washed MASONS' ARMS, runs DUKE STREET with its pretty mixture of C18–19 houses and garden walls, the C20 being self-consciously represented by Nos. 18–20, the work of *Ian Arnott*, 1974. Whin-chip pavements from end to end. Then NORTH STREET, where No. 1 on the corner is of L-plan, perhaps C17, with a stair-turret sunk in the angle and a second, red-roofed turret added in front of it as a porch in the early C20. Skewputt sundial. A good two-storey group, a row of cottages, and then the garden wall of the late C19 Manor House.

BELLWOOD HOUSE
ML *2060*
1.9 km. N of Penicuik

A two-storey, five-bay house of *c*. 1820, of fine ashlar, the three centre bays advanced and pedimented. Adjacent on the l. and cutting off its rusticated quoins, a bigger-scale addition with a deep bow and a Roman Doric doorpiece.

BELSYDE HOUSE
WL *9070*
2.5 km. SW of Linlithgow

A little harled house of 1788 on a spectacular hill-top site, Belsyde is distinguished by a moulded doorway (obscured by a later porch), two segmental-arched Venetian windows on the first floor and a pair of sundials at the corners; not to mention the Hamilton arms in a tablet now on the gable, in which there is a curious window with checked margin on attic level. The single-storey wings, probably added very soon after, repeat the Venetian motif both to front and rear. Their gable ends, curiously but logically, are pedimented, and both have their own Venetian windows – beautifully made with round tops, but blind. Late C18 pilastered sideboard recess in the dining room. Wood chimneypiece of the same period with thistle-and-rose enrichment upstairs.

BIEL HOUSE
EL *6070*
2 km. NE of Stenton

A complicated story. Embedded in the E end of the present block is an early tower house. About 1760 it was extended to the W, as is clear from the outlines of rusticated voussoirs (subsequently chopped off) over some of the windows on the N (entrance) front. By the end of the C18 the whole house had been battlemented, but in 1814–18 it became a mere appendage to vast monastic Gothic additions to the E by *William Atkinson*, who brought its harled exterior into conformity, adding hood-moulds over all the windows. At the W end was a large conservatory, rebuilt in 1883 by *R. Rowand Anderson* as an Episcopal chapel, with Gothic windows under Atkinson's battlements. Its floor is still *in situ*, and some fittings were retained when in 1952 the chapel and virtually the whole of Atkinson's house were demolished. Piscina, credence, sacrament house and bellcote, all in intricate late Gothic style, have been decently reset in the walls of what is now a terrace. At the E end a courtyard is entered through a pointed archway, giving access to Atkinson's office buildings, which still stand.

Thus reduced to something like its original size, the house is entered through Atkinson's porch, resited here in 1952. Immediately to the r. is the wooden staircase of c. 1760. On the ground floor the Brown Room has French-looking doorheads that may have been added in the early C19. The Tapestry Room was refitted by *Robert Lorimer* in the early C20.

On the s front a long and ancient TERRACED GARDEN steps down to the Biel Water. On the top level a Gothic PAVILION is linked to the house by a battlemented wall to the W. Down in the valley to the E the Biel is crossed by a two-arched BRIDGE of c. 1760, with a circular opening in the central spandrel. GATEPIERS to the N also of c. 1760, rusticated and vased, and probably moved here from the old office courtyard at the time of Atkinson's extension.

BEESKNOWE, 1 km. W. Red-tiled and half-timbered; by *R. Rowand Anderson*, 1886.

THE BINNS*
6 km. ENE of Linlithgow

C17, more interesting inside than out, and merged into early C19 additions in toy fort style, all harled except for the quoins and castellations. In 1621–30 the Edinburgh merchant Thomas Dalyell built the three-storey house, symmetrical with twin stair-turrets, which declares itself on the N (now the entrance) front. His son, General Sir Tam Dalyell, found time to adorn some of the rooms and to build the W range to match the earlier E one so that the house formed a U-shaped courtyard through which it was entered from the s. To the Devil, who threatened to blow down his walls and his house, he replied: 'I will build me a turret at every corner to pin down my walls.' This could refer to the two corner turrets which frame the view of the s side with its initialled and finialled dormers. There is to be sure no dearth of turrets in the enlargement and general remodelling from c. 1810; the architect is not known but it is in the style of *James Gillespie* [*Graham*]. At this time the E and W ranges were enlarged, all the major gables were decked with square dummy bartizans, and the whole thing (including a pair of steep new gables on each side) was battlemented. A single-storey range

* Property of the National Trust for Scotland.

was pushed out into the court from the old house, the battlements stepping clumsily down to preserve the view of the dormers overhead. The front door was resited on the outer face of the house.

The main early C19 interiors are the arcaded entrance hall (former LAIGH HALL), the new dining room and morning room to the S overlooking the courtyard, and the staircase to the W, its single flight and long landing parallel and with segmental ceilings separated by a colonnade. For the earliest work one goes to the E range with its vaulted kitchen or bakehouse. The important rooms of Thomas Dalyell's house, with their moulded plaster ceilings by *Alexander White*, are upstairs. In the HIGH HALL in the middle of the first floor a thickly ribbed ceiling and central pendant (dated 1630) of quirky geometry. The rose-and-thistle cornice survives only over the fireplace, which was replaced *c.* 1820, but there is an overmantel panel of the royal arms (with English motto) flanked by curious architectural trophies of Dalyell heraldry. To the E is the KING'S ROOM, the foliaged ribs of the ceiling enclosing in some compartments a rose, thistle, harp and fleur-de-lys, in others low relief heads of King Alexander or King David. In the frieze, swags of fruit in higher relief. Another royal coat of arms over the chimneypiece, which this time is of the late C18 but continues the Union theme of thistle and rose. The VAULT CHAMBER to the W has two median ribs only, enriched with foliage which incorporates roses and an unidentified species of flower; foliaged half-figures of caryatid type radiate from their intersection. These three state rooms embody the theory, if not the actual functions, of feudal loyalty. On the second floor is the small room known as the CHAPEL. The passage past this and its neighbours is an early C19 addition. At the W end it reaches the SEA ROOM (the view to the N is actually of the Firth of Forth). Three pendants hang from the crown of its plaster tunnel-vault, and the ribs are enriched with thistles, roses, and peacocks. As in the vault chamber below, the cornice line suggests more windows, and of a different height from the present ones. One further feature of Thomas Dalyell's house is the door in the base of the E staircase turret. That this is a bolt-hole, if not actually to Blackness Castle as is alleged, is confirmed by the provision for securing a door from inside the turret, whence a stair leads down.

General Tam's own contribution was made *c.* 1680 in the Laigh Hall and the two rooms to the E. All have stone chimneypieces of some originality, finely carved with classical mouldings and patterns. In the first are tributes of fruit on ribbons, with egg-and-dart border; in the BLUE ROOM a leafy ogee frieze; and in the LIBRARY, which has an overmantel portrait of the General in the Memel panelling, a bead-and-reel border and diaper enrichment. The basket-arched chimneypiece in the W range, with grotesque mask keystone, is of *c.* 1740.

The landmark TOWER on Binns Hill, round and crenellated, was built in 1826 to a specification by *Alexander Allan.*

BINNY HOUSE
1 km. W of Ecclesmachan

A most original house, built of Binny sandstone from the nearby quarry – fine and hard, and warm in colour. Main (S) front of two canted bays, between them a Roman Doric porch *in antis*, not projecting. This could all be *c.* 1840, but the tripartite windows in the bays, and the slim consoles supporting cornices overhead, have a much earlier character. The balustrades introduced into the parapet on the bay fronts are simply wilful. Yet the authority of the whole thing suggests an experienced designer. Only *Richard Crichton,* among known architects, could have done this, which would mean the second decade of the C19 at latest. Offices, with regular arcades, extend to E and N. Classical STABLES to the N, of even greater eccentricity.

BLACKBURN

CHURCH OF SCOTLAND, Main Street. 1908 by *Roberts & Paul* of Bathgate. A surprising amount of Gothic detail, but harled all over. Flanking tower and matching manse.

OUR LADY OF LOURDES (R.C.), Bathgate Road. 1965 by *Charles W. Gray.* Low-pitch copper roof on portal frames. The red brick cladding does not go well with the green copper or with the rubble porch.

PRIMARY SCHOOL (former Board School), at the E end. 1911. Red brick with red stone dressings. Two storeys, symmetrically gabled.

BRIDGES over the Almond, both at the W end. One is of 1774, with two arches and a big centre pier, the other early C19, with a single segmental arch.

Blackburn is an enlarged industrial village based on a main street which is also a main road. But it has a good TOWN CENTRE off Bathgate Road, a co-operative effort by County Council,

brewers and builders, all designed by *Wheeler & Sproson*, 1968.
The materials are blue-black bricks, 'Fyffestone' (split concrete) well used for once, and white-painted weatherboarding.
The canopied shopping walk leads past the supermarket and
under the Golden Hind Hotel to a tall harled block of maisonettes. On the s the circular PUBLIC LIBRARY. Community
and sports centre further on to the E.

BLACKBURN HOUSE, 1 km. E. Built *c.* 1760, of grey rubble with
grey dressings and rusticated quoins. The main (N) front has
a basement, two storeys and a deep but windowless attic behind
the parapet; five bays, the centre advanced and pedimented.
Longitudinally sited pavilions, hip-roofed, with quadrant links.
At the rear, two canted bays of full height enjoying the s prospect. The interior is complete as regards wood and plasterwork,
which is nearly all contemporary. Deep moulded cornices and
plain ceilings except in two bayed rooms to the rear, which have
Rococo enrichment of the utmost delicacy, the cornice bracketed in the E room, coved with a bold relief of birds and foliage
in the W room. Between them a stone stair with turned wood
balusters, alternate ones twisted. Fielded panel doors and shutters. The doorcases in the front hall have broken pediments
over pulvinated friezes. The upper room chimneypieces are of
the same character, but those of the main rooms have been removed.

BLACKNESS   WL* *0070*

BLACKNESS CASTLE on its headland sticks out into the Firth
of Forth like a ship. The two end towers are traditionally called
the stem and stern, and the curtain walls between them form
a deep, rock-bottomed hold in which stands the 'mainmast'
tower. It is almost all of brown whinstone with pale sandstone
dressings.

   The mainmast or MID TOWER, its orientation unrelated to
the rest, was probably built by the Crichtons in the mid C15.
The parapet is C20 but the original corbel course survives, with
bulges at the corners. The round stair-turret at the NE corner
supplanted the original wall-stair when it was adapted as a prison for Covenanters in 1667. Beside the turret is a well. Inside,
the basement vault has been removed and the tiny windows
with stepped in-goes have been restored. Mural chambers and
a fireplace on the upper level. The upper storeys are similarly
          * Now Central Region.

provided with rooms in the wall, and the crowning tunnel-vault seems to be a restoration, correct but tidy.

The ship-plan dates from the latter part of the C16. At the pointed bow or stem is the NORTH TOWER, two vaulted chambers with latrines, one over the other, with a pit prison below and gun platform (probably C18) on top. In the W curtain wall the original water-gate and a larger entry formed in 1870. The E curtain wall has stone corbels to support a wall-plate for lean-to roofs. The stern or SOUTH TOWER is the most important. A fragment of its original corbelling and parapet has been preserved in curious fashion above the door. Over the basement a good row of wide-mouthed gun loops for cannon (entry to the gun chambers is through a depressed-arch doorway from a raised terrace in the courtyard). The NW jamb and the present stair were added in the C17, and on the top floor is the vaulted HALL, entered by a moulded and round-arched doorway. Its roll-moulded fireplace was narrowed in the C18 and mezzanine rooms inserted (Blackness was one of the castles maintained for national defence after the Act of Union in 1707). To the W is the C17 SPUR whose segment-headed doorway, protected by an iron yett, opens into the courtyard through a pend. Later in the C17 the upper front was added, supported by corbels, with a corner bartizan and an additional tier of vantage points for small arms.

The last chapter in the military history of Blackness Castle was its conversion as the central ordnance depot and magazine for Scotland in 1870–4. The slim iron pier was built out into the Firth at that time, and so was the barrack block to the S. Rock-faced baronial officers' quarters to the W of the new forecourt.

MISSION CHURCH (formerly Episcopalian). Built c. 1914. Harled, with triangle-topped windows and slated broach-spire.

Blackness used to be the port of Linlithgow, and is still used by pleasure-boats on the Forth. Nothing of the old village survives. GUILDRY is a redevelopment of c. 1960 by the *County Council*, a single harl and rubble block, intelligently concentrated at a point of vantage in relation to both land and water. Cast-iron baluster PUMP with leafy base, dome and finial, 'the gift of Alexander McLeod Esq. of Nova Scotia to the inhabitants of his native village 1875'. Next to it a DRINKING FOUNTAIN with lion's head spout and similar top.

BLACKNESS HOUSE and BLACKNESS FARM, to the S. Early C19, but the farmhouse, though regular, is somewhat later.

BLACKRIDGE

WL *8060*

In 1838 a little brown whin box of a Gothic PARISH CHURCH was built as a Church of Scotland Mission Church. Its round-arched successor of 1901, designed by *J. Graham Fairley*, is not much grander despite its chancel, porch and belfry.

LIBRARY, across the road. A nice white-harled shape, top-lit, and supported on blue brick legs to bring it to the right level, by *Haswell-Smith & Partners*, 1974.

WESTERCRAIGS, at the E end. A big house of the late C18, built as a coaching inn in coursed grey rubble. The wide doorpiece has a segmental arch between Doric pilasters, and the centre windows over it are tripartite on first and second floors; then a blocked cornice, but only along the front. The coach entrance to the W has cylindrical gatepiers with dome tops.

BEDLORMIE, 1 km. W. A whitewashed farmhouse of mid C19 aspect which turns out to be a C17 L-plan house with a jamb to the rear and a truncated stair-turret in the angle.

HEIGHTS FARM, 2.5 km. NNE. A whinstone steading, probably C18. The byres have horizontal slit vents cut out of single pieces of red sandstone.

BOLTON

EL *5070*

PARISH CHURCH. Gothic, 1809.* The Second Statistical Account (1838) says: 'It is a handsome building in what has been called, whether properly or not, the modern gothic style, with a square tower at the west end.' This tower is angle-buttressed and pinnacled, and the stonework is variegated East Lothian rubble with yellowish Abbeymains dressings. Original diamond glazing at the W end. The inside is plain and unspoiled, complete with Carpenter's Gothic pulpit and gallery on clustered iron posts. – The MONUMENTS in the churchyard show that there was an earlier church on the site. To the E the square mausoleum of the Stuarts of Eaglescairnie, *c.* 1800, with an elliptical dome of smooth masonry. – To the S a headstone of historical interest, for it commemorates the mother († 1820) of Robert Burns, and his brother who was factor at Grants Braes. – C18 MANSE further along the road.

* The architect was probably *Archibald Elliot*. 'Mr Elliot, Archt., Edinburgh' was selected for the job but 'James Burns' (*sc. James Burn* of Haddington) asked for the specifications. Probably the latter was the builder of the church.

The village of Bolton boasts a pretty group of buildings near the top of a hump in the landscape. Most distinctive is the cylindrical C18 DOOCOT with a little lantern on its conical slated roof. It belongs to the adjoining STEADING whose early C19 house stands across the road, down the hill. Then the former SCHOOLROOM, built shortly before 1838 and unhappily altered to a garage, with the basically earlier schoolhouse behind it. Then the church.

EAGLESCAIRNIE. *See* p. 195.
PILMUIR HOUSE. *See* p. 388.

9080   BO'NESS   WL*

Bo'ness is short for Borrowstounness. Long established as a producer and exporter of coal and salt, towards the end of the C16 it acquired its own parish church (supplanting that of Kinneil to the W; *see* p. 270) and prospered increasingly as a port. Defoe credited it with 'the greatest trade to Holland and France of any [town] in Scotland, after Leith'. But the opening of the Forth and Clyde Canal in 1790, and the deepening of the upper part of the Clyde itself in the early C19, robbed it of its special role as an east coast port for Glasgow. It has now been entirely superseded by Grangemouth, and so much spoil has been dumped in the water that one would hardly guess that it had been a harbour town at all.

It is the landward terrain that gives Bo'ness its extraordinary character. The old town, merging into Bridgeness and Grangepans to the E, occupies a thin coastal strip. Villas and churches, Victorian and Edwardian, look down on it from the airy heights immediately to the S. Town hall and board school stand halfway down, and the slope is negotiated by steep pathways and hairpin roads, workers' houses pushing up-hill, villas gingerly down-hill. The strong personalities of two local architects, supplemented by others of national repute, provide still further interest. Post-1945 development has been concentrated, though that is not exactly the word, in Grangepans and on the plateau to the S; the centre has been neglected, which may be to its long-term advantage.

CHURCHES

OLD KIRK, Panbrae Road. By *Shiells & Thomson*, 1885. Gothic with a Normandy inflection; plain pinnacles at all the angles of an elaborate composition, dominated by the N (liturgical W)

* Now Central Region.

tower and spire. Additions to the orthodox cruciform plan are
explained by the provision of access stairs to the three lofts or
galleries: the Laird's Loft under the tower (the Duke of Hamilton subscribed to the building and his arms are carved over
the N door), the Mariners' in the W transept with a ship model
hanging overhead, Netherlands style, and the Miners' in the
E transept. Four-bay nave with alternate round and octagonal
columns, the timber roof springing from corbelled shafts.
Excellent masonry by *Russell* of Bo'ness, but the rubble walls
have unhappily been stripped and ribbon-pointed. – PULPIT.
Incorporating the pilasters and inlaid oak panels of a Dutch
pulpit imported in the C17 for the previous parish church. –
STAINED GLASS. Five-light N window in perfectly clear
colours (the Ascension, as a memorial to Queen Victoria) by
William Meikle & Sons, 1902. – In the N bay of the E aisle Solo-
mon and David by *William Meikle*, 1908. – In the S bay of the
E aisle Bartimaeus and Christ washing Peter's feet by *William
Wilson*, 1938. – Under the Miners' Loft, Resurrection subjects
as a memorial to James Thomson, architect, † 1949, designed by
J. Blyth.

CRAIGMAILEN UNITED FREE CHURCH, Braehead. By *Mc-
Kissack & Rowan*, 1883. Simple E.E., unadorned except for the
vine carving over the N (liturgical W) door and the eight-but-
tressed crown on the tall tower beside it. Three-bay arcaded
nave with galleries in the aisles and to the N. – STAINED GLASS.
Contemporary but ordinary; SS. Peter and Paul in the apse
windows are hidden behind the organ.

ST ANDREW (former United Free Church), Grange Terrace. By
J. N. Scott & A. Lorne Campbell, 1905, a cruciform church
in pale snecked rubble, its N (liturgical W) gable facing N over
the Forth and nicely related, on its corner site, to a square tower
which incorporates the main door. The tower has three stages:
the first solid; the second with angle buttresses that send up
Art Nouveau pedestals on to the clasping buttresses of the
third; finally a green copper flèche. The smooth octagonal stair-
tower at one corner ends with a concave, pointed roof whose
eaves are pierced by eight delicate stalks with pedestals. Internally the plan is ingeniously simple: a four-bay nave with N gallery over the vestibule, chamfered arcade without capitals, and
aisles merging into the transepts. Roof with concave principals
and triple kingposts with tracery between. – STAINED GLASS.
At the S end the Ascension in an Art Nouveau manner, 1908.
– At the N end the Sermon on the Mount, SS. Andrew and

Michael (war memorial), 1920 by *Oscar Paterson* of Glasgow.

ST CATHERINE (Episcopal), Cadzow Crescent. By *Dick Peddie & Walker Todd*, 1921. A fragment of a tiny church – sanctuary and chancel, crossing and transepts – stocky and solid, with clasping buttresses and slate-arched lancets. The N door has engaged shafts with unwrought block capitals, and so does the rubble arch between the groin-vaulted crossing and the chancel. Plain segmental arch before the sanctuary.

ST MARY (R.C.), Dean Road and Linlithgow Road. By *Gillespie, Kidd & Coia*, 1960. A neat white church like a cardboard model. Parallel louvres are stepped outwards so that it widens towards the altar; an inward-curved shell at each end.

PUBLIC BUILDINGS

TOWN HALL AND PUBLIC LIBRARY, to the N of Glebe Park. By *George Washington Browne*, 1901. On a difficult site and with only £10,000 to spend, Browne combined the two functions in one long block, symmetrical on its E–W axis but not the side; in fact it looks like a secular church. Hall to the W with a big lantern and an apsidal end, its upper windows of thermae type; library to the E with single-storey bows to N and S, its windows all domestic. The join is marked by a pair of little domed clock towers related to those at Adam's Register House, and sections of the parapet are relieved with a light Bramantesque balustrade. Rusticated underbuilding makes up for the steep slope to the N, and from here it presides not too pompously over a still sad town centre. From the S it is festive but informal, like the handsome contemporary BANDSTAND in the middle of the park.

MASONIC HALL, Stewart Avenue. By *Matthew Steele* of Bo'ness, 1909, and probably his best work. Piend roofs, the eaves supported by stumpy tapered columns without any detail at all; the four centre ones support a bell-profiled stone canopy with a simplified pediment over the door.

GRANGE SCHOOL, Grange Loan. By *H. & D. Barclay*, 1906. Longitudinally symmetrical on a towering site, with the two entrances (for boys and girls) at the end. A mixture of Art Nouveau and Queen Anne, boldly modelled in snecked rubble.

ST MARY'S R.C. SCHOOL, Gauze Road. A strong composition unimpaired by a diversity of materials in the Festival of Britain manner. 1954 by *Alison & Hutchison & Partners* who also designed the BO'NESS ACADEMY extension in 1971.

RECREATION CENTRE, Gauze Road. By *Alison & Hutchison & Partners*, 1972.

TOWN CENTRE

NORTH STREET, entered from the W, starts with a good gaunt early C19 warehouse. Further on, after it narrows into SCOTLAND'S CLOSE, is another and finer one dated 1772, and beyond it a house of 1711 with scrolled skewputts incorporating the former WEST PIER TAVERN. The view along North Street itself is dominated by two blackened corner towers: the JOURNAL office of 1887 with its tall candle-snuffer roof, and the ANCHOR TAVERN by *Arthur Colville* of Edinburgh, builder, 1891. Next door to it in HOPE STREET is the circular HIPPODROME THEATRE (now a bingo hall, with the gallery removed) by *Matthew Steele*, 1911; the ticket office was tacked on by *John Taylor* in 1926. SOUTH STREET has three C18 buildings. Nos. 15–18 are an early C18 block, sometimes called the tolbooth, with a bolection-moulded doorpiece. The original glazing is almost complete. No. 68 of *c.* 1760 has scrolled skewputts and a raised centrepiece formed by a chimney gable with Doric pilasters and pediment. And behind No. 41 is a tall tenement dated 1786 with scrolled skewputts once again. But most of the street is of late C19–early C20 character. *James Thomson* designed the showy Victorian-looking block at Nos. 54–58, with pediment and grouped windows, in 1900, and the ANDERSON BUILDING with central chimney dated 1902. His also is the CARRIERS' QUARTERS inn of 1904 at the junction with MAIN STREET; three bargeboarded gables, thistle corbels and recessed ground-floor bay-windows. Of public building on the waterfront there is little. The castellated tolbooth of *c.* 1780 in EAST PIER STREET was demolished about a century later, but *James Thomson*'s eccentric POST OFFICE of 1911 still stands on the corner. Along from it in UNION STREET is the ponderous CUSTOMS HOUSE by *William Simpson* of Stirling, *c.* 1880, with *Saracen* rustic iron lettering, and then the offices of the BO'NESS IRON CO. by *Matthew Steele*, 1908, in a sub-Mackintosh style with recessed bay-windows. The reader, it is hoped, will see these buildings presiding over something better than the present dismal scene.

In the E part of Bo'ness, at what used to be called Bridgeness, is the site of one of the WALL FORTS of the Antonine Wall (*see* Introduction, p. 30; also for the distance-slab).

OUTER AREAS

Away from the centre the picture is different. GRANGEPANS to
the E was completely rebuilt in 1958–69 by *Alison & Hutchison
& Partners*, a remarkably cogent layout of two-storey houses,
varied by four-storey flats over shops, all in grey brick and white
roughcast. Facing them is *James Thomson*'s other Art Nouveau
pub, the CROWN INN of 1909 (pretentiously refurnished in
1973). Even more interesting is the earlier C20 and late C19
housing which zigzags up the slope of the long ridge above the
town, only footpaths making the direct ascent. Most of it bears
the initials of the coalmaster Cadells of Grange, formerly the
town's largest employers: in PHILPINGSTONE ROAD, for
example, CORONATION COTTAGES on the S side by *G.
Wightman*, C.E., gabled and dormered, with rusticated quoins
and Gothic eaves, are inscribed 'HMC 1902'. On the N side
is PHILPINGSTONE TERRACE by *J. M. Dick Peddie, c.* 1905;
flatted cottages of the type pioneered in Edinburgh forty years
before, but prettily dressed up in harling, with curly cement
pediments over the double front doors, bullseye windows and
swept dormers. Round the back are the front doors of the upper
flats with their outside stairs; plumbing, despite the late date,
at the bottom of the yard. On a hillock at the E end of the road
stands the harled and battlemented shell of the round C18
BRIDGENESS TOWER. Built of Bo'ness brick as a windmill
to drive a Cadell pit pump, it became a vitriol factory, an
observatory, and finally a house. Besides the Cadell housing,
which deserves a detailed study before it begins to disappear,
a number of good peripheral schemes by the local authority are
worth seeing. GRAHAMSDYKE (the old name for the Antonine
Wall) to the E, of 1964, has a weatherboard finish between
roughcast spine walls, MINGLE to the S, of 1967, a slightly
more complicated pattern with tiled monopitch roofs. Both are
by *Alison & Hutchison & Partners*, who were also responsible
for part of another scheme on the S side at BORROWSTOUN,
1970, *James Gray* doing the rest, for the Scottish Special Housing Association.
KINNEIL HOUSE. *See* p. 271.

VILLAS

CAER-EDIN, Grahamsdyke Avenue. Probably by *W. G. Rowan*
of Glasgow, 1899, for the timber importer Sir Robert Murray.

All of stone, the blocked Ionic doorpiece oddly echoed in the courses of the window margins, alternately square and round. In the front hall, lit by stained glass painted with the heraldry of the European timber-exporting towns, a free-standing central fireplace. In the rooms to each side classical chimney-pieces of timber in deep ingles.

THE KNOWE, Erngarth Road. By *A. Porteous* of Edinburgh for George Cadell Stewart, 1879, extended upwards in 1907 by *Matthew Steele* with a rooftop billiard room and a wild corner tower, domed and columned.

ROSEMOUNT, Cadzow Crescent. By *James Dodds* of Bo'ness, 1910; bayed and battlemented, i.e. quite Victorian in character.

TIDINGS HILL, Cadzow Crescent. By *A. Hunter Crawford* of Edinburgh, finished in 1908. A relaxed composition in rough-cast with leaded windows, the gables kept pointedly separate from the chimney stalks.

Nos. 131–135 STEWART AVENUE are a strange group by *Matthew Steele*, 1909: bays and gables all in rough snecked rubble – even the projecting eaves course – but the chimney stalks end in smooth, tapered bells.

BONNINGTON HOUSE   ML* *1060*
3 km. WSW of Ratho

1858, in the Jacobean manner of Heriot's Hospital in Edinburgh, with fretted quoins, corner bartizans and strapwork; so *Alexander Black* is a candidate for its authorship. But this is not the whole story. A small house of 1622, which can still be discerned in the moulded front doorway now facing the garden, seems to have been doubled with another block of similar shape and size *c.* 1720, when the position of the front door was changed. The niches on each side of the new entrance may be of this date, but they now accommodate Victorian eagles. The panelled room just inside the old door is certainly of *c.* 1720, and a gay Jacobean fireplace has been contrived between the Corinthian pilasters of the chimneypiece. The rooms in the later E section have Grecian plasterwork of *c.* 1825.

SUNDIAL, in front of the old entry. C17, obelisk on poly-hedron on pedestal, all intricately dialled on every face, though the gnomons are missing.

* Now Edinburgh.

BONNYRIGG   ML

A crossroads mining village whose face and fortune were somewhat improved by a carpet factory and by the coming of holiday
visitors to enjoy the beauties of the river North Esk. In LOTH-
IAN STREET is the PARISH CHURCH, *c.* 1900, its lanceted
gable adjoined by a square tower with an octagonal clock stage
and a pointed copper roof. Then on the corners of DOUGLAS
CRESCENT two pleasantly varied buildings of harl and red
sandstone by *Greig, Fairbairn & McNiven*: the PUBLIC
LIBRARY, 1908, and PARISH COUNCIL OFFICES, 1909.
Local authority housing began in 1923 with MOORFOOT
VIEW by *James Gray* of Bonnyrigg, a harled terrace with little
gables, vestigially half-timbered, set diagonally at the corners.
More was to follow. In POLTON STREET *Gray* designed the
SCHOOL in 1910, with twin pavilions for boys and girls and
a central hall behind. By the intersection a decent long block
of *c.* 1960 with a tidy row of shops and shallow-gabled flats over-
head, spoiled only by the unnecessarily diverse wall treatment.
FACTORY (John Kelly & Son), Cockpen Road. Smart grey channelled cladding over a blue engineering brick base, by *Michael
Laird*, 1971.
BONNYRIGG PRIMARY SCHOOL AND YOUTH CENTRE,
Cockpen Road. Good warm-yellow facing bricks and unusually
natural-looking monopitch gables. Open-plan layout and good
finishes within. By *A. Ruffel* (Lothian Regional Council), 1974.
SHERWOOD COTTAGES, Cockpen Road. A neat gridiron layout
of late C19 miners' rows.
NAZARETH HOUSE, Hillhead. A large crowstepped baronial villa
of the mid C19 with institutional but decent roughcast additions
by *Reid & Forbes*, 1933.
BROOMIEKNOWE, towards Lasswade, begins with the baronial
THORNHILL and meanders past a whole gamut of C19 villas
too numerous and not quite distinguished enough to mention
separately.

BONNYTOUN HOUSE   WL
                      1.5 km. NE of Linlithgow

A gabled and bay-windowed Tudor house of modest size, built
of snecked sandstone (originally rendered) with smooth dressings. Its eclectic ingenuity and its predominantly Grecian interior strongly suggest that the architect was *Thomas Hamilton*,

c. 1840. The client was the local distiller Adam Dawson. At first sight it is pretty conventional: a tall gabled range facing w, a spiky dormered wing on the s (entrance) front, and the offices tucked in behind. But Hamilton's originality is shown in two ways. First in the detail, starting with a subtle variety of window treatment – some cornices, some hoodmoulds. The quoins of the main gables are bracketed outwards at the eaves, and this curve is repeated on the wall face so that there is a shield shape supporting the flat base of the skew. The oddest invention is the porch. This projects alongside the principal gable, and at its corners are panelled octagonal piers, their capitals formed by a cluster of scrolled brackets – a richly classical motif in a strange context. Heavy balustrade overhead, and tapering piers at the foot of the steps. Then there is the composition. The hierarchy of the three main elements is enhanced by descending window levels. Fiendish inconvenience in internal levels is the expected penalty of this external effect – but no; the height of the upper windows is quite naturally determined by the landings of the main staircase which give access to the rooms in these lower ranges.

The porch leads into a little marble-tiled hall, then into the central STAIRCASE HALL, square and lofty, with a stair of old-fashioned delicacy ascending on three sides, a landing on the fourth. Shaped steps of late C18 character, and serpentine cast-iron balusters; only the handrail is of weighty section. In the centre of the ceiling, carried on rows of simple consoles, a deeply moulded roundel of lotus leaves with key-pattern border. These Grecian details are not rivalled by heavy doorcases; the openings have plain arches and plain lintels, three open arches forming an arcade on the landing. In the w range, the (former) DINING ROOM is finished in highly unconventional fashion, with architraves of late C17 section. At the N end is a sideboard recess formed by a pair of columns with capitals of eight consoles under a plain abacus, their entablatures extending sideways to the walls, where they are carried by pilasters of the same strange order. The ceiling defers to this feature with a bowed gilt moulding; it is otherwise plain, but with a lotus centrepiece. The Rococo pelmets are in odd contrast. So is the chimney-piece, a late C18 pine-and-composition specimen with seashell decoration and the panels of the frieze moulded with tiny copperplate initials R and F, presumably those of its manufacturer. Everything else is original, but this was imported from Cowdenhill House, which has gone. Finally, this room has a west-

ward view over Linlithgow Loch to the palace ruins – a summa-
tion of the C18–19 idea of picturesque antiquity. The former
DRAWING ROOM, on an E–W axis, is typical of Hamilton's Grecian mode, at once strict and imaginative. The ingenious ceiling
is coffered eccentrically but logically, with rich mouldings and
a shaggy acanthus centrepiece. Conventionally Greek doors
with heavy bracketed cornerpieces. Bay-windows (originally
double-glazed casements) defined by panelled antae. Plain and
massive chimneypiece.

Technical thoroughness must also be mentioned: stone slab
water-tank in the basement, stone drain to the loch; a many-
arched wine cellar; the ventilation of every structural void to
the outside and sometimes also to the inside, e.g. in the drawing
room, where some of the inlaid floor can be raised to reveal
an iron grating.

WALLED GARDEN on the hill to the N. Over the entrance,
which has the date 1848 inscribed at the sides, a C17 broken
pediment with ball finial most likely from the Town House of
Linlithgow (see p. 290) whose reconstruction after a fire was
paid for by Adam Dawson. Bizarrely erected in the centre, as
an ornament, is a CHIMNEY, apparently concocted of left-overs
from Dalmeny House (see p. 170). It has a cusped head, and
the shaft consists alternately of rampant lions and coroneted
roses, cast in pairs and supplemented in places by cement sub-
stitutes.

BONNYTOUN FARM, 1 km. N. The farmhouse was built c. 1840
with certain details recalling Bonnytoun House and its attribution to *Thomas Hamilton*. It is a kind of Tuscan villa in Roman
cement, but with Tudor hoodmoulds over its big shuttered
windows. Two single-storey blocks – one hipped, the other
gabled – contain the two large rooms. The two-storey link, of
roughly the same height, has a simple colonnade below for the
porch, boldly detailed casement windows above. The construction seems to be of brick, with single-brick brackets along
the wall head. The interior has been altered and extended, but
the two large rooms remain. Heavy Greek detail in the drawing
room to the r. and in the annexe beyond it, which has a corner
chimneypiece with a lintel between pylons. These two rooms
were subsequently thrown into one with a bracketed arch. The
dining room to the l. has four columns standing free of the wall,
upright acanthus leaves on their shallow capitals; at the diameter of the bowed end are two more, not aligned with them,
carrying an entablature into the room from the corners, as at

the main house. Undercut foliage cornice. The upper room in the link block has some details of earlier character: the pine chimneypiece with thistles and roses in moulded composition, and the ceiling centrepiece, with fluted umbrella and husk garlands, in a square supported on three sides by a deep cove and then a flat soffit divided into squares, an archaeological motif in the centre of each. Thus the little room has two scales: lofty in the centre, intimate round the edges.

FARM BUILDINGS. Probably of earlier date, rubble-built, with both slates and pantiles on the roofs. Covered cattle-courts.

BORTHWICK

3 km. SE of Gorebridge

ML *3050*

PARISH CHURCH (ST KENTIGERN). Mostly mixed Gothic of 1862–4 by *Thomas Brown* of *Brown & Wardrop* whose best contribution is the W tower and broach-spire, a landmark and a nice foil to the castle. But the E part is substantially medieval. The apse is Norman and, though over-restored, its main features are vouched for by pre-1862 descriptions. Small plain windows, arch on half-shafts with cushion capitals. Part of the chancel S wall is also Norman. N of the apse is the Dundas of Arniston burial aisle converted *c.* 1606 from the medieval sacristy. The N door was put in in 1862 when access from the chancel was blocked. Some at least of its stones are C17. Inside, a PISCINA and traces of E and W windows. More attractive and authentic is the S transeptal chapel. On the S gable are the Borthwick arms, so it has been assumed that the first Lord Borthwick who built the castle also built the chapel. Stone-flagged roof, eaves cornice with foliage and grotesque heads, and buttresses to the E and W walls, though none at the corners. The tracery of both windows is restored, the S one probably not correctly. The E wall has always been blank. Sundial dated 1705 on the SW corner. Inside, a plain pointed tunnel-vault. The arch to the church was built up in 1862. Battered piscina in the S wall, and by the C19 W door a holy water stoup. In the S chapel, against the E wall, the splendid TOMB of *c.* 1450 ascribed to Lord 16 Borthwick and his wife. Its present position, the site of the medieval altar, is anomalous. Before the restoration it stood inside the apse, but this cannot have been its original place either. Segmental canopy with foliage trail, ogee hoodmould with crockets, flanking buttresses and fleuron cornice. Much of this looks recut. The effigies by contrast are quite exceptionally well preserved, even to traces of original colour (gold, green, black, etc.). His modish armour and her jewellery have been reproduced to the last detail. For the rest, *Brown*'s internal work is a perfunctory compromise between a medieval church and a reformed one, though the arcade detail is conscientious. A painted inscription over the chancel arch records that 'this site was occupied by a church destroyed by fire in 1775', referring no doubt to a post-Reformation church on the site of the nave. – MONUMENTS. Wall-monument to Robert Dundas of Arniston † 1787, an obelisk on a pedestal with book, sword and scales inscribed with the maker's name, *J. Bacon* of London. – In the churchyard, a good headstone of the late C17 with the attributes of death and the inscription on a book 'Verbum Domini manet in Aeternum'.

BORTHWICK CASTLE. Before he built the castle Sir William Borthwick had already figured in history as one of the hostages for the release of James I from York Castle in 1424, and then in the following year as a member of the assize court that saw to the judicial execution of Murdoch, Duke of Albany. He bought this estate from the Hays of Lochorwart (a nearby farmhouse is still called Loquhariot), and on 2 June 1430 was granted a royal charter to build a castle. Queen Mary was here with Bothwell in 1567, and in November 1650 Oliver Cromwell wrote to Lord Borthwick 'You have harboured such parties in your house as have basely unhumanely murdered our men; if you necessitate me to bend my cannon against you, you must expect what I doubt you will not be pleased with.' The huge scar on the E wall is generally attributed to Cromwell's guns.

No literary tourist has adequately described the character of Borthwick Castle, but Pennant (1772) said that it was 'seated on a knowl in the midst of a pretty vale, bounded by hills covered by corn and woods; a most picturesque scene'. This is still the case. The site is bounded on three sides by the confluence of the Gore Water and Middleton North Burn, and the barmkin wall is roughly triangular, with a round tower at the SW right angle. Most of the wall, with the upper part of the tower and the gateway just to the N of it, was rebuilt in 1892. But the base of the W wall with its wide mouthed gun ports is original, and so are the two massive understoreys of the tower with its own strategically placed gun loops, one of them canted to take in the fall of the ground. Downhill on the S side of the wall are the remains of a smaller tower of D-plan.

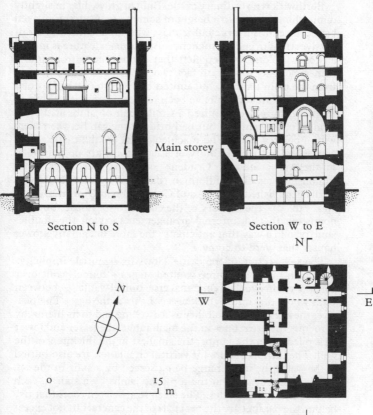

Section N to S

Section W to E

Main storey

0   15 m

Plan of main storey

Borthwick Castle, sections north-south and east-west and plan
(*RCAHMS*)

Borthwick is no ordinary castle. Built of grey ashlar in slightly diminishing courses to a height of some 24 m. from the splayed base course, it is a large cubic mass with an unequivocal air of passive strength and permanence. But its main feature is indeed
45 an equivocal one: a deep cleft that divides the W front into a pair of close-set towers, in fact two wings or jambs projecting from the main E range, but united by the external angles of a parapet that must once have been higher. Hermitage Castle in Roxburghshire had acquired a similar pair of jambs at the beginning of the century, but had bridged the gap between them with a pointed arch. The machicolations are the castle's only concession to the possibility of attack; there are no gun holes in the walls. Stewart Cruden* says that Borthwick, with Elphinstone also in Midlothian (damaged by subsidence and finally demolished in 1955) and Comlongon in Dumfries-shire, makes the C15 the century of the classic tower house, but also points out that its internal arrangements exploit the double-jamb plan in a way that anticipates the more imaginative tower houses that were to come.

The E–W section of the castle shows its essential simplicity. The main range has three vaulted stages – tunnel-vault over pointed vault over three transverse tunnel-vaults – between walls whose maximum thickness is 4.3 m. at the base. The plan gives the key to its workability as a dwelling and to its hierarchy of rooms: the great ones in the main range, the lesser and lower ones piled up in the jambs, the smallest in the thickness of the wall. The turnpike stairs for vertical circulation are also buried in the walls, the main range being served by a stair in the NE corner (now curtailed at the top), the jambs by a stair in each of their re-entrant angles. The steep stone-slated roofs that rise behind the parapet are the best part of the general but not excessive restoration that took place from 1892 to 1914.

Entrance is through a round-arched door on the level of the principal storey, formerly gained by a bridge from the barmkin walk; the remains of the connecting arch can be seen, and there are signs of an armorial panel overhead. But first the basement, entered by the round-arched doorway directly underneath, into which the splayed base course is returned. Inside, a turnpike immediately to the l. leads up to the main guardroom. Each of the three vaulted chambers of the basement was divided by a timber entresol and has a high set window with steeply inclined sill to supply light to both levels. In the S jamb is the

* *The Scottish Castle*, 1960.

well, with access to the main floor by way of a steward's room which has a fireplace. Like the prison in the N jamb, it has a garderobe in the thickness of the wall.

On the main floor the entrance leads into a short passage with the guardroom on one side and on the other the KITCHEN, which occupies the N jamb. Nearly half its area is taken up by the arched fireplace, lit by three windows. Then through the site of the screens into the HALL, the grandest medieval hall in Scotland, a princely apartment with a pointed vault finishing 9 m. above the floor – the height occupied by three storeys in each of the jambs. The words 'Ye tempil of honour' are just discernible in tempera-painted black letters along the W side of the ashlar vault, 'Ye tempil of religion' even less clearly along the E side (fragments of tangled foliage painting in black and white can be seen elsewhere in the principal rooms). At the S end a large fireplace.* Moulded lintel (restored in the centre) with a line of rather sluggish foliage. High windows on each side of the pyramidal hood. To the E two spacious embrasures with seats, vaulted inside but with flat lintels over the window apertures – a feature standard throughout the building, as is the hooded type of fireplace, though on a smaller scale than in the hall. In the SCREENS at the N end, a SINK on an engaged pedestal like a piscina, its canopy intricately ribbed on the underside. Beside it, a moulded doorway to the main stair, with a three-sided arch. Finally to the W, and handy to the deis, an ogee-arched buffet recess with crockets, coarsely restored. A door beside it opens into the solar, which has a garderobe in the wall, serviced by a hatch. The similar tunnel-vaulted space over the hall was divided by a timber mezzanine, and the lower part into two sections by means of a partition; the room to the S has a canopied fireplace, that to the N a large E-facing embrasure appointed as a chapel.

BORTHWICK HALL   ML‡ 3050
0.5 km. SE of Heriot

By *John Henderson*, 1852. Baronial with Tudor hoodmoulds, its complex composition dominated by a central tower and corner stair-turret, and tied together with a rope-moulded string

---

* Christopher Wilson points out that the arrangement of major and minor shafts under the hood of the fireplace follows long-established French usage, e.g. in the fireplaces of Charles V's donjon at Vincennes, completed *c.* 1373.

‡ Now Borders Region.

course. The entrance hall is effectively lofty. A corbelled stair-turret breaks into one corner, as do other turrets into bedrooms. One moulded ceiling in the Jacobean manner remains. The other rooms on the ground floor were discreetly remodelled *c.* 1930. In an alcove at the end of the now subdivided billiard room a chimneypiece with armorial tiles by *G. & H. Potts* of Edinburgh, designed by *de Hoenische.*

6070   BOURHOUSE   EL
                    2 km. s of Dunbar

A modest-sized Jacobethan mansion of two storeys by *David Bryce*** for Maj.-General J. Carfrae of the East India Company, dated 1835, of excellent pale ashlar probably from Cullalo in Fife, intricately and carefully detailed. Bay-windows and gables (straight Tudor, curly Jacobean) are the main elements in its dynamically balanced composition. The long front, surveying the N W view over a seated terrace, has unequal canted one-storey bays whose strapwork parapets are repeated over the porch at the N angle. This is adjoined by a five-sided bay crowned with scrolled gables and a pointed roof; the office wing beyond it, though sporting a massive chimney, is of junior scale. Square chimneys, set diagonally like the corner finials. All the windows have corner lugs with nailhead centres, and retain their original glazing in small panes. Any blank wall space is relieved by blind vertical slits. Most adventurous is the cornice, showing sawn-off profiles at all external angles on the N W front, doubling as erratic string course or continuous hoodmould on the end elevations; when interrupted by dormers it terminates in big square nailheads at the same angle as the roof pitch. The gutters are of the secret kind, with internal rain conductors.

The inside is simplicity itself. The five-windowed bay lights a long hall that penetrates the house; alongside it, the library and drawing room *en suite* with liver-coloured Louis chimneypieces, at the end the dining room (regulation black). All the ceilings are geometrically ribbed, but without too much structural continuity and even without enriched cornices – simply a thin cove. The main stair, in a self-contained well, has iron balusters like celery with flattened leaves at the head. Those of the service stair are round and spindly, of exceptional grace. Both in fact are Georgian – but one more solemn, the other prettier.

* The job was done through *Burn's* office, however.

STABLE COURT, adjoining the office wing. Entered between piers with obelisk heads.

LODGE. Bayed, with Bryce's characteristic scooped corbels at the head, and curvaceously bargeboarded under deep eaves.

DOOCOT. C18 double lectern type. This and the walled garden, and indeed some urns of early C18 date, suggest that there was a house here before. The tracery fragments lying in the grounds are said to be from the old parish church of Dunbar.

BOW
3 km. S of Stow

ML* 4040

The well preserved foundation of a broch. The inner courtyard was about 9.5 m. in diameter within a wall about 4.6 m. thick.

BOWLAND HOUSE
4 km. S of Stow

ML* 3040

Built c. 1810. Castellated Tudor Gothic on a spectacular hill-top site, coursed black whin giving a strange inflection to the characteristic cardboard shapes. But the dressings are in sandstone. The S front has a porte cochère, and over it the frontal pretence of a square tower. A smaller tower at the W end is balanced by two thin and quite purposeless octagonal turrets to the E. Canted square turret on corbels at the NE corner. All this is the work of *James Gillespie [Graham]*. The earlier house adjoining to the N was removed for additions by *George Henderson*, 1890, and further extensions were made to the E by the firm of *R. Rowand Anderson*, 1926, both in a congruous style. Plaster rib-vaults in the entrance hall and over the staircase with its delicate Gothic cast-iron balustrade. Otherwise only a few chimneypieces survive from the early C19 interior, and the character of the rest is late C19 with much panelling; not a very palatable mixture with the earlier Gothic.

NORTH LODGE. Arched and towered, c. 1810.

DOOCOT. Probably C18, of lectern type, to the W of the house.

STONES. Three sculptured slabs brought back from India by the builder of the house, Brigadier-General Alexander Walker, and set in the arcade of the retaining wall to the N.

---

* Now Borders Region.

1050   BRAIDWOOD   ML
                      2 km. SE of Currie

The remains of a two-period Iron Age settlement: (*one*) an area
of some 54 m. by 36 m., surrounded by a timber palisade with
a second palisade outside it (the palisade trenches can still be
detected in some places as slight grooves); (*two*) a pair of earth
banks to replace the timber enclosure. The sites of about twelve
houses can be seen in the interior.

9070   BRIDGE CASTLE   WL
                    3 km. WSW of Torphichen

The three-storey keep, built in the C16 and acquired by Lord Livingstone in 1588, has a cap-house enclosed by a corbelled parapet walk with open corner bartizans, a massive chimney on its
E gable. A second block on the N, with an arched link, is C17.
Brown & Wardrop designed the additions of 1876. These and
the crowstepped extensions of 1889 are pleasant enough, but
those of 1899, in yellow stone, spoil the effect of the main elevation.

0070   BROXBURN   WL

PARISH (formerly United Presbyterian) CHURCH, at the E end
of Main Street. Half-hearted French Gothic with tower (containing stair to gallery) and spire beside the rose-windowed entrance gable. By *Hippolyte J. Blanc*, 1880.
ST JOHN CANTIUS AND ST NICHOLAS (R.C.), at the W end
of Main Street. A lanceted church built in 1880 for the Dowager
Countess of Buchan. Bapistery to one side of the porched W
gable (actually the S, facing the street), staged tower and spire
of 1890 to the other. All by *Shiells & Thomson*. Aisles with sawtooth gables. Inside, tall iron shafts with florid caps support
the steep timber roof of the seven-bay nave and the transverse
roofs of the aisles. Gallery at the (liturgical) W end, semi-octagonal sanctuary at the E. Some furnishings survived the
modernizations of 1948 and 1961. – FONT. The octagonal stone
basin, C15 or early C16, from the medieval parish church at
Uphall, excavated from underneath it in the C18 and later found
in a field near Kirkhill. The Gothic inscription apparently reads
STA ECCLESIA NICHOLAI. M. IHS. Late C19 pedestal. – HIGH
ALTAR. Elaborate Gothic with reredos and canopied niche for
the Sacrament, all in Caen stone and marble inlays, by *Pugin
& Pugin*, who perhaps designed the Lady altar too. – PULPIT.

Canopied Gothic in dark stained timber, with carved figures of Faith, Hope and the evangelists, and painted panels; resited. – STAINED GLASS. Here again there was almost a clean sweep, but some of the new work is worth noting. Over the W gallery four lights (the evangelists) and four more saints in the aisles, by *Helen Turner*, executed in the 1950s.

CHURCH HALL by *Reginald Fairlie*, 1937.

To the E the CANON HOBAN MEMORIAL HALL by *Reginald Fairlie*, 1936, and a tiny Dec memorial chapel to the twelfth Earl of Buchan † 1857.

ST NICHOLAS FREE CHURCH, Station Road. Originally another United Presbyterian church, with plate-traceried entrance gable, staircase wings and conical pinnacles; by *J. Graham Fairley*, 1890.

WEST CHURCH (former Free Church), towards the W end of Main Street. Weird and wonderful Gothic, 1855.

KIRKHILL HOUSE, to the N of Main Street. A tall, plain house of the C17 at earliest,* remodelled probably in 1770, the date over a window of the stair-turret on the S side.

The burn of Broxburn's name is just to the S. Broxburn started as a village with a toll house and inn (the early C19 Buchan Arms) on the Edinburgh–Glasgow road. In 1821 the Union Canal skirted it closely to the W, passing under bridge No. 28 at Port Buchan, and in 1849 the railway passed near it to the S. So it was well equipped for the transport of the mineral resources discovered in 1858: iron, coal, and above all the oil extracted from shale, the residue being piled into the huge orange bings which still dominate the landscape. Shale accounts for the steady growth of the population from 660 in 1861 to 5,898 in 1891, and for the present aspect of the town, which mostly belongs to the end of this period, though a few earlier Victorian villas survive between the grey, shop-lined terraces of MAIN STREET. Three churches, all on the N side of the street, provide some feeling of welcome and expectancy in its 3 km. length, which runs into Uphall at the W end.

PUBLIC BATHS, at the E end of Main Street. Buff brick, by *G. R. M. Kennedy & Partners*, 1974.

HOUSING. To the S, in what is called the OLD TOWN, a good

---

* The C16 Renaissance dormer and C16 heraldic panel from an earlier house or castle, noted by the RCAHMS as being built into the farm steading immediately to the E, were removed into the care of the local authority when this building was demolished. The orrery erected by the eleventh Earl of Buchan on the lawn to the W has entirely disappeared.

scheme of flats and maisonettes, terrace houses and a few shops, harled with Scots slate roofs, by *Wheeler & Sproson*, 1967–70; a pity this genuine redevelopment plan (not just units of housing) was not completed. To the N a haphazard postwar growth on whose fringes any feeling of place (and along with it, any attempt at maintenance) has gone by the board. It includes a decent scheme at STEWARTFIELD by *Alison & Hutchison & Partners*, 1969.

SCHOOLS. BROXBURN ACADEMY by *Alison & Hutchison & Partners*, 1966. A large and highly competent building, mainly of exposed concrete, with good rubble walls offering some welcome intricacy on ground-floor level. KIRKHILL PRIMARY by *Lane, Bremner & Garnett*, 1965. Well composed, with continuous reeded fascias. The infant school to the rear is a simple geometric arrangement of glass and white harling.

6070   BROXMOUTH PARK   EL
                        2.5 km. ESE of Dunbar

Built for the Duke of Roxburghe, probably by *James Nisbet* shortly after 1774 when he gave an adverse report on the condition of the existing house, of which nothing remains. Main (S) front of two storeys, with three stone-dressed bays on each side of the pedimented centre of grey ashlar. Roman Doric porch added *c.* 1830. The ground falls away to the rear, so that the W elevation has a basement, as Queen Victoria noted; the iron stair to the balcony of the ashlar bow is said to have been made for her stay in August 1878, to give access from her room to 'Cromwell's Mount' and the grounds (the deer park was laid out in 1845). She planted the cedar to the SW of the house. The W and E sides are returned to form a U-plan, but some of the service buildings forming a courtyard to the N have been removed. The two main rooms have plain moulded cornices (the centrepieces added *c.* 1830) and white marble chimneypieces of the C18, rich and heavy, that in the dining room boasting a long fat garland of fruit and flowers tied through the end brackets with ribbons. In the bow-ended library to the W a Louis chimneypiece of *c.* 1850 (this was Queen Victoria's room); in the room to the N, as in its counterpart upstairs, an old-fashioned bolection-moulded one, again C18. In a well in the SW angle an (altered) C19 staircase with wooden balusters. Original service stair to the NE, its nosings returned down the edges in the old style.

GATEPIERS. Early C18, partly fluted with alternate cushion stones, partly panelled. LODGE of the same date with pyramidal roof.

TOWER, on a knoll towards the shore. Octagonal, of c. 1850, with battlements and a square turret.

WALLED GARDEN. Probably earlier than the house.

STABLES of red sandstone, dated 1841.

BRUNSTON CASTLE
3 km. SW of Penicuik

ML 2050

A ruin, but surprisingly full of interesting details. On the SE side of the courtyard the principal range. Attached to it, within the court, a square stair-tower whose upper storeys are corbelled out on a sort of cornice, its uppermost moulding a cavetto. In the base the entrance door, with a curiously moulded head. Over the cornice a panel with the Crichton arms and the date 1568 – the third figure differently cut and so very likely wrong. Two big fireplaces survive. One is in the kitchen at the NE end of the basement; the other, in the principal room on the first floor, has a wide roll-moulded opening and a mantelshelf cornice supported on brackets inscribed with a C and a Y. Three-storey tower at the N angle of the courtyard with oval gun loops under the windows. The main entry must have been in the NW barmkin wall, for the round-headed and moulded opening in the NE wall is too small and the SW side evidently housed outbuildings.

BURNHOUSE
5 km. NNW of Stow

ML* 4040

Early C19. Whin walls and stone dressings. Five bays, the centre advanced and pedimented. Columnar doorpiece at the head of a balustraded stair.

BUSH HOUSE
4 km. NNW of Penicuik

ML 2060

The main body of the house built c. 1750 by Archibald Trotter was probably entered on the S front between the advanced N bays. In 1791 alterations were carried out by R. & J. Adam. At this time probably the entrance was moved from the S front to the E end and the office court added to the N. The third trans-

* Now Borders Region.

formation was by *R. Rowand Anderson*, 1894–5. On the E front he Venetianized the ground-floor windows and added (or rebuilt) the centre bow between them, giving it a coupled Roman Doric order; its bulging frieze tactfully echoes the pulvinated string course of the 1750 house. He also extended the S front and provided the re-formed roof line with dormers with curly broken pediments. Indoors, the main Adam contributions are the elegant staircase in a square well to the l. of the front door, with a balustrade of trellis and beaded hoops, and the room to the r., though its chimneypiece is a bit later. Two pretty chimneypieces of *c.* 1800 were incorporated in Anderson's polite and comfortable reconstruction.

The specialized departments of the Edinburgh Centre of Rural Economy are housed in an informal group of buildings in the park. All are long and low, but their architects have used a variety of treatments. The most elegant in design is the IN-STITUTE OF TERRESTRIAL ECOLOGY by *Morris & Steedman*, 1969, but its dark timber beams and steel stanchions are weathering badly; this cannot all be intentional. The buildings of the UNIVERSITY OF EDINBURGH AGRICULTURE DE-PARTMENT are more orthodox in design, e.g. with unbroken curtain walling, and more exact in workmanship. The EASTER BUSH FIELD STATION is by *Alan Reiach & Partners*, 1962, the TROPICAL VETERINARY MEDICINE CENTRE by their successors, *Alan Reiach, Eric Hall & Partners*, 1969.

BYRES *see* HADDINGTON

9070   CAIRNPAPPLE HILL   WL
                        2 km. ESE of Torphichen

The remarkable view and the sequence of archaeological periods make this a particularly worthwhile site to visit. An important series of ritual sites clearly laid out by the Department of the Environment. Five archaeological periods are represented, the first four dating from about 2200–1500 B.C.: (*one*) a small cremation cemetery; (*two*) a henge monument, stone circle (later removed) and small burial cairn containing Beaker pottery; (*three*) a cairn (using some of the stones of the circle as kerbstones) containing two cist burials; (*four*) the cairn enlarged to cover two burials in cinerary urns; (*five*) four graves for extended burials, probably dating from the early first millennium A.D. (For extended remarks on this site *see* Introduction, pp. 22–3.)

CAIRNS CASTLE
7 km. SSE of Midcalder

The ruin of the C15 tower of the Crichtons of Cairns, overlooking Harperrig Reservoir. L-plan, with separate entries to vaulted basement and main storey.
CAIRNS CASTLE SCHOOLHOUSE (formerly the inn, now a house). 1822 by *James Gillespie* [*Graham*]. Single-storey with projecting centre. All the windows fronting the Lanark Road have slanting canopies integral with the lintel. Across the road a three-sided STABLE courtyard of the same period with gatepiers in the front wall.

CAKEMUIR CASTLE
6 km. SSE of Pathhead

ML *4050*

A rectangular, four-storey mid C16 tower probably built by Adam Wauchope, advocate, whose arms are carved on a resited stone. The entry on the N adjoins the semicircular projection of the stair-turret, which supports a crowstepped cap-house. Behind the corbelled parapet a walk runs all round the garret, blocked only by the chimney of its W gable with two flag-roofed refuges. The Georgian W extension was baronialized in the later part of the C19.

CALDER HOUSE *see* MIDCALDER

CAMPEND *see* DALKEITH

CARBERRY TOWER
3.5 km. SE of Musselburgh

ML *3060*

A baronial agglomeration, U-shaped in plan, with N at the top. Building progressed anti-clockwise, beginning at the NW corner with the early C16 Tower itself. Its architectural character and strategic function are concentrated at the head, where in place of a corbel course there is a cavetto-moulded cornice lined continuously with winged heads and interrupted by large gargoyles of human form, much weathered. The central solid on each side of the massively crenellated parapet has a gun loop; in another

solid on the W side, a shelter with stone seats (cf. Cakemuir
Castle, p. 129). There is no cap-house. The RCAHMS suggests
that the flat roof may have been meant as a gun platform. At
its NW corner a circular wrought-iron fire basket is mounted
on the parapet. Next came a late C16 crowstepped extension
to the S, turning along the bottom of the U where it has a corbelled stair-turret. The rest of the S range, two blocks side by
side, is basically Georgian. One is probably late C18; the early
C19 saw the building of the second and the crenellation of both,
along with the addition of hood-moulds to the C16 part and
a porch to the old Tower. Just where the latter was originally
entered remains a puzzle. The U was completed c. 1860 by
David Bryce's E range, with two good strong pepperpots at the
NE, linked by a stepped string course. His also is the single-
storey billiard room to the N of the Tower, and the bay-window
and balcony of the W range. In 1909 *Thomas Ross* baronialized
one of the Georgian S blocks with crowsteps and pepperpots
(weaker in detail and position than their Victorian equivalents
to the E), and four years later he did the same to the other one,
with a tall bay-window; all this for the Elphinstones who owned
Carberry from 1801 to 1961.

The inside is not distinguished. In the Tower, two rooms with
solid vaulted ceilings. Timber galleries show the level at which
both were originally divided by intermediate floors. The finishings are early C20 except for the more vigorous panelling in the
ground-floor hall. In the upper (Beacon Room) fireplace are
some good Persian tiles. In the entirely refinished billiard room
two old fragments, both probably resited: a gun-looped stone
in the SW corner, and a stone fireplace with a delicate palmette
moulding which could be of the late C17. Quiet Jacobean oak
staircase by *Bryce*, lit from the central well by C20 armorial
glass. On the first floor a pair (formerly a trio) of identical late
C18 marble chimneypieces in the drawing room to the W, with
brown inlay and oval centre panels of Cupid asleep. The N
library has another, of white marble with pairs of dolphins at
the top corners. Its compartmented ceiling is good enough to
be Victorian, but most of the other rooms are half-hearted
classical of 1909–13. The S library however is enlivened by a
giant oak mantelpiece with grotesque beast capitals – an elaborate mounting for a little carved panel (early C17 Flemish?)
of the Garden of Eden – and the organ by *Hill* of Edinburgh,
1910.

In the grounds two SUNDIALS. The shaft and finial of the

first, in the early C20 Italian garden to the S of the house, are new, but between them is a C17 polyhedral dial stone, pierced in unusual fashion. The second, entirely C17, with two Ionic-capitalled caryatids supporting thirteen dials on their heads and shoulders, is stranded beyond the WALLED GARDEN, where nothing of interest survives except a skittle alley of the late C19. Mid C19 STABLES (by *Bryce?*), symmetrical and crow-stepped. The central copper-spired clock tower on the W front looks towards the CHAPEL by *Ian G. Lindsay & Partners*, built in 1965 after the Church of Scotland acquired Carberry as a conference centre. Boldly stepped rubble walls, one prolonged to enclose a quiet lawn, and a single-pitch copper roof carried by compound timber purlins. The porch is entered through a double bronze-framed screen, and a further screen of turned balusters divides it in more traditional style (as in Falkland Palace) from the chapel itself. Over the porch, at the high end of the sloping timber ceiling, is a gallery. The use of 'period' detail in the painted screen and pews as a foil to straightforward C20 construction is highly successful; but the main idea of the interior is its concentration on the view past the communion 39 table, through the fully glazed E wall at the lower end of the roof, to the wooden rood which stands on the lawn.

CARFRAE *see* GARVALD

CARLEKEMP   EL *5080*
1 km. W of North Berwick

A long two-storey house like a Tudor manor in the Cotswolds, designed in 1898 by *John Kinross* for the papermaker James Craig. Walls of finely snecked Rattlebags stone with freestone mullions and other dressings. Simple composition, with a gable breaking up from the parapet at each end (the lower E section housing the servants) and another over the projecting entrance bay. Gentle in fact, but far from genteel; the little canted bay that forms an alcove in the library has lively stone dolphins curling down its roof, and the front doorpiece is vigorous Jacobean, crowned with a strapworked cartouche and obelisks.

The same balance is observed inside, where the woodwork is of the finest quality: random-width floorboards, the doors gaily Jacobean throughout, and likewise the fireplaces, to whose ingenuity the flat insets of different marbles are a foil. Roses are a recurring motif. Along the W end the sequence is as follows. To the s the LIBRARY, whose ceiling and cross beams have a Tudor rose cornice in low relief. The shelves and panelling are warm unvarnished oak, with arcaded niches for porcelain at the head. Fireplace with two splendid lion heads. Then the HALL, two storeys high, the lower oak-panelled. It is overlooked from the E by a gallery over the entry from the front door, from the N by an oak-framed oriel opening off the upper corridor on the male side of the house. The oriel has flanking obelisks, and a similar pair crown a vast overmantel with Gothic niches and stone strapwork fireplace. In the DRAWING ROOM at the NW corner, now the school chapel, a rose cornice, a fireplace with exceptionally rich marble inset (variegated purple and white), and two canted alcoves; the one overlooking the sea includes a cunningly contrived door for walking out, as does the window of the smaller drawing room to the E. After this comes the DINING ROOM, its panelling and fireplace relatively flat. The other notable ground-floor room is the BILLIARD ROOM, which has a bay-window and a row of cusped windows on the s front, a beamed ceiling and a fretted Gothic cornice, and a stone fireplace with Gothic niches. To the E of the hall the STAIRCASE in a square well, with square oak newels. Its ceiling is coombed, with cartouches on each face, and so is that of the master bedroom to the NW. Its mate to the SW has one of the most spectacular of the Jacobean bedroom fireplaces, which altogether show amazing resource. Equally varied are their cast-iron grates, some enriched with brass.

STABLES and LODGE to the s are *en suite* with the house; both are basically symmetrical but artfully sited for the oblique view.

1070

CARLOWRIE   WL*

1 km. E of Kirkliston

This middle-sized and very baronial house by *David Rhind* for the Leith merchant Thomas Hutchison, 1855, is part of a fine contemporary ensemble. In itself, raised on a terrace amid a variety of mature ornamental trees, it is striking but decidedly awkward. First, in the s front, a rather formal entry at the base of a fat round tower. A subsidiary turret with candle-snuffer roof gives access to the second floor and to the platform top which has an arched balustrade in the manner of Winton Castle, big and top-heavy. The house on each side of this is laboriously

* Now Edinburgh.

asymmetrical: the main windows are all eight-pane sashes, but everything is purposely at odds, e.g. on one side a corner barti-zan which is very little use to the adjoining room within (it happens to be the billiard room), and on the other an extraordi-nary pedimented turret half-way along the wall head. Wildly jumping string courses and heavy rows of corbels are every-where. In short it is 'applied baronial', lacking the functional guts of the original style, and is described here because it is the exception, not the rule. The other elevations are more con-vincing, with single-storey offices to the N and W and a con-servatory (much simplified in the course of repairs) to the E.

The interior is another matter. It has a splendid progress from the round, mosaic-floored entry, through a narrow vesti-bule into the central SALOON, galleried on first-floor level, with a coved structural ceiling with top lighting. From floor level it rises to a wide ceremonial landing, and thence on the N side a stair ascends to the first floor, another on the S side to the second floor. Stairs and landings have twisted iron balusters. The principal rooms on the ground floor – dining room to the W, drawing room and library to the E – have structural ceilings with pendants midway along the enriched beams. All the chim-neypieces are plain marble, the one in the drawing room with a spectacular brass tabernacle grate of c. 1880 with brown tiles.

From a distance the house appears to be surrounded by large forest trees apparently of greater age and including avenues that run up to it from three directions; there was certainly an older house on or near the site. But within them, adjoining the house, is a long rectangular GARDEN bounded by a wall to the N. Its progression is as follows. Semi-formal lawns to the E by the conservatory; an arboretum with cypresses and a monkey-puzzle, a little Gothic shelter – possibly Georgian – looking into it from the wall; a lawn for games; a laundry-green adjoining the laundry; and finally the main walled garden, which has glass-houses on the N side, a crowstepped stable range to the W and a tool house in a round tower to the S.

LODGES to S and W. Contemporary, but much plainer.
CARLOWRIE FARM, 1.5 km. NE. Baronial, by *Robert Bell*, 1858.

CARRIDEN

CARRIDEN PARISH CHURCH, at the E entry to Bo'ness. By *P. Macgregor Chalmers*, 1908. Simple Romanesque in snecked

* Now Central Region.

rubble, with attached w tower and pyramidal stone spire. Incised 'consecration crosses' show the extent to which the Reformed Church was willing to defer to antiquarian precedent; more specifically Scottish is the baronial stair-turret attached to the session house, which is the s 'transept'. Within, the tower forms a tall narthex, followed by an aisled, clearstoried six-bay nave with a half-round timber ceiling. The N aisle widens half-way along to form a baptistery chapel with a mosaic half-dome apse, entered under a chevroned arch. A higher but plainer arch leads from the nave directly into an E apse with eleven arcaded sedilia at its base. – FURNISHINGS. Oak pulpit, lectern, precentor's box and communion table, all in genteel Romanesque, as is the circular arcaded stone font. – STAINED GLASS. In the apse St George, Christ in Glory, St James, all good work of 1912. – On the w side of the tower, Elijah.

In the churchyard the ruin of the OLD CHURCH of 1766, a T-plan galleried kirk of simple Georgian Gothic to which were added c. 1850 an innocent Gothic tower and lucarned spire to the E, a session house to the w and a nice aedicule to the N to protect the wall MONUMENT to Sir William Maxwell of Carriden † 1771 with its pretty Ionic order and pulvinated laurel frieze. In a corner, the burial plot of Sir James Hope, R.N., † 1881, with an edging of iron anchor chain. Cast-iron DRINKING FOUNTAIN with dish and cup-hooks bearing the mark of *Saracen*, Glasgow.

CARRIDEN HOUSE. Liberally sprinkled with dates from 1602 to 1863, which represent the broad span of the building's history even though most were inscribed about the latter date. It looks as if a C17 E range was enlarged c. 1800 with a w wing which was given a sawtooth profile c. 1850; then also came the s porch with its corner bartizan, and finally (except for some later functional additions) the more convincingly baronial pepperpots on all the corners of the older work. The main floor of the w wing has a long, low room with finishings of c. 1800; graceful plaster ceiling and chimneypiece.* – LODGES. 1818 (hoodmoulded) and 1894.

Near Carriden House is the site of the Roman Castellum Velunia(s), a WALL FORT of the Antonine Wall (*see* Introduction, p. 30).

HOPE COTTAGES, Muirhouses, by Carriden. An informal group of seven single-storey cottages dated 1864–74, all with snecked masonry and half-hipped overhanging slated roofs; one of them

* The rest of the inside could not be seen; C17 ceilings are reported.

is the Library House, with a corner column supporting the library porch. They were built for Admiral Hope of Carriden. The former Girls' School in the centre (1865) with adjoining two-storey staff house was a benefaction by his sister.

CARRINGTON

ML *3060*

PARISH CHURCH. Dated 1710. A plain kirk of plum-coloured rubble with paler quoinstones, on a T-plan with a square tower against the cross-bar as at Gifford or Newbattle, but un-staged. Ogee Gothic window above the door, round-headed belfry windows near the top, and small square vents below the eaves of a slightly bell-cast pyramidal roof. Sundials mounted on each corner of the exactly symmetrical front. The tall Y-traceried windows with darker margins are by *Thomas Brown*, 1838; the little Gothic gatehouse was built about that time. The interior was gone over by *Brown & Wardrop* in 1858, and panes of glass in vivid colours were inserted round the edges of the windows. But a tablet records that the N jamb contained the Rosebery loft, and the PULPIT facing it, with a hexagonal sounding-board, is of composite Georgian date.

RAMSAY MAUSOLEUM, to the NE, on a path from the Edinburgh road. Early C18, built for the Ramsays of Whitehill on the site of the old parish church.

CARRINGTON HILL (former Manse), to the E. A plain two-storey house built in 1756, repaired in 1790, and altered since.

CARRINGTON BRIDGE, to the W, across the Redside Burn. A single arch, late C18, with its name carved on a tablet on the outer N side.

FARMS

CARRINGTON MAINS. C18–19, rubble and pantiles, presenting a long blank wall towards the church.

PARDUVINE, 1.5 km. WNW. An early C19 slated farmhouse with wings, fronting a good pantiled group which includes an octagonal horse-mill.

CASTLE GREG

ML *0050*

4.5 km. SE of West Calder

FORTLET. One of the best preserved earthworks of the Roman period in Scotland. Defended by a turf rampart and two ditches,

it measures *c.* 58 m. by 50 m. and may be compared to the late
CI A.D. fortlet of Gatehouse-of-Fleet.

2060   CASTLE LAW   ML
3 km. N of Penicuik

Excavation has revealed the sequence of construction of the (*one*)
Age fort and souterrain: (*one*) a palisaded settlement; (*two*) univallate fort with timber-lacing at the entrance; (*three*) multivallate fort; (*four*) a souterrain built about the C2 A.D. in the ditch
between two ramparts (19.8 m. in length, a corbelled cell to one
side). The site is in the care of the Department of the Environment.

9070   CATHLAW HOUSE   WL
1.5 km. E of Torphichen

The modest and much altered early C18 house (the lugged doorpiece survives outside and the scale-and-platt stair inside) of
the Hamiltons of Cathlaw and West Port, Linlithgow. Attached
to the front, several late medieval ARCHITECTURAL
FRAGMENTS of high quality. Three vault bosses, one with swirling foliage and a central hole for a lamp chain, two with stylized
castles, different in their details. Above the front door a niche
canopy with dainty flowing tracery. Lying on the ground, half
a richly carved capital and two more bosses with holes, doing
duty as flower pots. There seems to be no record of the source
of all this. The strongest candidate is the S part of St Giles,
Edinburgh, demolished *c.* 1829. The castles must be the arms
of the burgh of Edinburgh, and the plan of the capital almost
matches the arcades between the two S aisles at St Giles.
It is probably from the pier of the third S aisle, the Lauder Aisle
of 1513.

1070   CHAMPFLEURIE   WL
3.5 km . ESE of Linlithgow

Champfleurie is the C18 name for Kingscavil (*see* p. 270). *R. &*
J. Adam designed a house for Alexander Johnston in 1790 but
the present house, as seen from outside, bears no relation to
it, being a late C19 tower-house of L plan with a turret in the
angle, of beef-red sandstone and forbiddingly plain. STABLES,
near the gates. Hoodmoulded Tudor, *c.* 1830.

CLIFTON HALL
4 km. ssw of Kirkliston

ML *1070*

A baronial mansion by *David Bryce*, 1850, middle sized but powerfully composed. The entrance (E) front builds up from l. to r.: first a porch tower with pepperpots and attendant stair-turret, then a taller gable pushing into a four-storey round tower which echoes the tower at Castle Fraser, Aberdeenshire. On the w front the main part is symmetrical; pepperpots at the ends, and two canted bays with gables, linked at the principal-floor level by a balustraded terrace. This anticipates Bryce's Craigends, Renfrewshire (demolished 1966). Within Clifton Hall is the shell of an earlier house. A Tudor-style reconstruction scheme by *Wardrop*, 1848, seems not to have been carried out.

The entrance, squeezing between two internally expressed turrets, leads straight upstairs to the long hall whose windows are seen to the l. of the porch. Grandly organized oak staircase at the s end, and a Peterhead granite chimneypiece. The drawing room is lit by one of the bay-windows of the w front, the dining room by the other. The shelves of the library between are topped with masks in typical Bryce fashion and the chimneypiece is of the same Peterhead granite. Ceilings are uneventful and cornices polite, so the early C19 white marble chimneypiece in the drawing room (with reeded piers and a centre panel of Galataea with dolphins, salvaged from a demolition in Leith *c.* 1930) looks quite at ease. More romantic and feudal is the Gothic hall added to the s end allegedly *c.* 1930. It has heraldic glass, a ribbed ceiling and a timber chimneypiece with two tiers of columns.

STABLES. Close to the s end, and more like a farm steading, with a number of separate cottages in Bryce's manner and an older range dated 1812 with the shell of an octagonal DOOCOT over a low-arched pend.

COCKBURN HOUSE *see* BALERNO

COCKENZIE AND PORT SETON

EL *4070*

CHALMERS MEMORIAL CHURCH (formerly Free Church), Gosford Road. The highly original work of *Sydney Mitchell & Wilson*, 1904, though its debt to the Arts and Crafts movement is obvious. A saddleback tower with formalized Scots skews 36 stands broadside to the road, carrying on its ridge a tall lantern with a slated spirelet, bulbous and then pointed, Swiss-style. Its walls are raked, and so are the heavy buttresses of the church to whose gable it is attached. Flush-pointed rubble masonry, beautifully variegated, as also is the slated and dormered roof which rises from very low eaves. Gothic detail is tellingly limited to the N end (and the S windows of the chancel if one goes back to see them) and the wooden tracery of the dormers, which is Perp, except in so far as it leans slightly backwards. The twin doors into the porch have boldly curved iron hinges. Broad interior spanned by an open roof of seven bays, gloriously light, stencilled in pale blue on cream and vice versa. At the N end the porch and the gallery landing (the staircase is in the tower), screened off with diamond panes. Then comes the gallery, on two oak posts which continue upwards as twisted columns till they meet the roof struts. The next four bays form the body of the church, with wooden arcades jumping up from tie-beams to purlins and matching the arched braces which jump across. Similar arcades below the wall plate. The last bay is cut off by tall posts and canopied in the centre to form a chancel. Semicircular vault stencilled red on cream, the reredos in two shades of red. On each side a delicate veil of loop tracery, red and cream and gold. The W aisle, or in English terms transept, is roofed with a structure of similar ingenuity about a central post.

FURNISHINGS. The oak pews are possibly (a number of monuments obviously) reinstated from the earlier Free Church building. The remainder were specially made and are of high quality but unattributed: seven-legged communion table, stalls, pulpit and font pedestal all of oak, the basin of bright pewter. A few gas-light fittings survive, with iron back plates swept over as smoke guards. A green glass lantern with a lacy gilt crown hangs over the communion table. Model fishing boat on the tie-beam overhead. – STAINED GLASS. Except for one window whose glass seems to be from the earlier church, to the design of *Margaret Chilton*; to the W (Except the Lord build the house) 1922 by *Marjorie Kemp*, and in a dormer to the E (Christ as a carpenter, St Matthew) 1949 by *John Blyth*.

COCKENZIE POWER STATION, at the E end. 1962, by *Kennedy & Donkin* and *Strain & Robertson*, consulting engineers, and *Robert Matthew, Johnson-Marshall & Partners*, consulting architects and wholly responsible for the service buildings to the E. This building and its two chimneys dominate the town and are the chief feature, natural or man-made, of this whole stretch of coast. Old spoil-heaps eliminated, coal dumps concealed, the coal carried across the road to the steel and glass generating hall whose simplicity abstracts it altogether from human scale – it is all organization, but the final product is architecture. Except for the five-storey administration block, the colours are soft black and white. There is a public promenade along the sea wall to the N, the more complicated side of the station. To the S of the road the single block of the switching station, from which the lines erupt on to a mess of divergent pylons.

COCKENZIE HOUSE, at the W end of the High Street. Basically of the late C17, a long, shallow house of two storeys, basement and attic, with a scale-and-platt staircase in the centre. It was built by the Winton estate,* presumably as a residential base for the manager of their harbour and salt pan. The best view is from the garden to the S: a long, harled elevation of two storeys over a basement, with nine tall windows on the principal floor and a deep wall-head allowing for a spacious attic. The slightly bell-cast roof has scalloped lead flashings at the piends. Many of the original roll-moulded fireplaces are *in situ*, and there is mid C18 panelling. Late C18 chimneypieces with applied ornament. Ill-considered additions to the N front in 1845 and 1902 made the house more manageable but gave it the look of a pair of town tenements; the nice cobbling of the forecourt is dated 1845.

The GARDEN WALLS AND BUILDINGS belong to the period when the house was occupied by the Cadells. The perimeter wall is topped with dark brown Icelandic lava, said to have been brought back as ballast. At the S corners two circular conical-roofed gazebos. In the middle of the garden a lava GROTTO facing the house, with three pinnacles and the word HECLA (an Icelandic volcano) in raised letters over a Gothic arch formed by a pair of whale jawbones. Interior lined with shellwork. Shellwork panel on the E garden wall. The whole effect is of a green, axially planned forecourt entered by a gateway from the main road.

---

* Patrick Cadell has collected this and other information on the ownership of Cockenzie House. In 1715 it was forfeited and passed, like many such houses, to the York Building Company. In the mid C18 it was sold to the Cadells of Haddington, who were responsible for the pilastered porch and the other additions. Since the house was visited many internal and external finishings, including window-glass, have been destroyed or removed.

WAREHOUSE to the W, adjoining the house. This is called the 'Great Custom' in documents antedating the house, but in its present form it appears to be of the early C18. It is of three storeys, the wide span of floors and roof supported by massive central stanchions. Ties on four levels at a regular interval of some 2 m., the last two bracing the roof, which has diagonal struts. S gable with scrolled skewputts and a round flight hole for pigeons. On the W side a large crowstepped gable marks the entry into the High Street.

The two names of Cockenzie and Port Seton were already combined in the Statistical Account report of 1794, and in fact the second is little more than a straggling continuation of the first. Their harbours, however, are quite separate; to the W Cockenzie, improved in 1835 by *Robert Stevenson* for Messrs Cadell the coal shippers, to the E Port Seton, reopened and enlarged by *D. & T. Stevenson* of Edinburgh from 1880, with the aid of Lord Wemyss. The salt panning industry declined in the mid C19, but fishing and coal mining are still important. Summer holiday accommodation is provided by the shanty development to the E. At the W end is the real if not very lively HIGH STREET, terminated by the early C19 terrace of MARSHALL STREET, pantiled, as are a sprinkling of older houses such as No. 111, whose curvilinear brick gables are unfortunately cemented over. The OLD PARISH CHURCH was built in 1838. The rest is decent late Victorian and Edwardian. The lead given in housing standards in 1882 when the Wemyss Estate built the substantial crowstepped terraces of WEMYSS PLACE and ELCHO PLACE to the E was followed after 1914 by local authority housing to the S. Facing the green in front of EAST LORIMER PLACE is the former Cockenzie SCHOOL by *Peddie & Kinnear*, 1865.

9070   COCKLEROY   WL
                        2.5 km. SSW of Linlithgow

The denuded remains of an Iron Age fort; the line of the main wall can be seen as well as an additional wall on the NW. The situation, however, is superb, and the fort is accessible by way of a forestry path from the SE.

3060   COCKPEN   ML

OLD PARISH CHURCH. An overgrown ruin screened from the

main road by large trees. E wall with clasping buttresses and
two small lancets, the N one intact except that its head has been
cut into to allow shutters. The other walls are probably also
C13 in their masonry, even if there are no features to prove it.
All openings square-headed except a round-arched door into
a burial aisle at the SW corner. Of two more burial aisles, only
that of the Dalhousies in the centre of the N wall is still roofed.
Stairs to galleries against the E and W walls. Birdcage bellcote
on the W gable.

PARISH CHURCH. Perp, by *Archibald Elliot*,* 1818. Cruciform, 32
with diagonal buttresses. The tower, half engaged with the W
end where it forms a porch, starts with diagonal buttresses and
continues with slim octagonal turrets – the cornerposts of the
fretted parapet – terminating in flat knobs. Inside, a minimal
ribbed plaster vault, springing from the four shafts at the
corners. The galleries still have their Gothic fronts. The matching PULPIT was incorporated in the coarser Gothic ORGAN
CASE in 1886 by *Kinnear & Peddie*, who also renewed the
PEWS. – ORGAN. Presumably of that date, by *Wadsworth*; unaltered.

BRIXWOLD HOUSE, 0.5 km. NW. Mainly *c.* 1880 by the builder
John Dennis, a Newcastle man, for himself. He enlarged the
existing house of *c.* 1790, adding a bargeboarded jamb, a four-
storey Italian tower in the angle and a baronial turret to one
side, plus an elaborate conservatory. The show front is Roman-
cemented, the window mullions lined internally with mirror
glass. To the rear a coach house with loft overhead, adjoining
an octagonal doocot tower, battered and buttressed; all in red
brick.

COLSTOUN HOUSE
2.5 km. S of Haddington

EL 5070

Externally severe, hiding a good deal of antiquity and mystery
under a drab overcoat of harling. From the E (entrance) side
it is a long three-storey block with asymmetrical wings. The
W side, looking over the Colstoun Water, is a little clearer. Corbelled turret at the NW corner of the centre block. The dormer
head incorporated in the upper wall (subsequently re-exposed)

---

* The Edinburgh Magazine wrongly attributes this church to Richard
Crichton, and calls it 'uncommonly fine'. R. & R. Dickson seem to have agreed,
for they designed an identical church at Kilconquhar in Fife two years later,
thus adding to the confusion.

bears the initials PB.ER (Patrick Broun and Elizabeth Ramsay), indicating a date *c.* 1574. S wing added as a dining room *c.* 1750 by the Judge Lord Colstoun. N wing of 1875. The pedimented dormers belong to a reconstruction by *J. M. Dick Peddie* following a fire in 1907.

The solid porch is of 1875, its doorway redesigned after the fire. Fragments of the original door with an C18 armorial panel are preserved inside, and so is the pit prison on the W side. Interior mainly of 1875, modified in 1903 and 1907. At the S end of the principal storey the SMOKING ROOM, subdivided from the old dining room in 1903 by *Robert S. Lorimer*, with a lugged mid C18 chimneypiece of which the parts are more convincing than the whole. The outside doorway and the wrought-iron balustrade are characteristic of Lorimer. Then a central corridor runs straight up the spine of the house from wing to wing. Some of the rooms along the W side have been opened into it through Tuscan columned screens (again by *Lorimer*), and owing to a discrepancy of levels there is a ramp where it penetrates the old N wall. At the N end are the two main Victorian rooms. The main ceiling of the DRAWING ROOM to the W and the ceilings of two out of the three interesting digressions at the corners are enriched with some quite lively Rococo plasterwork. The chimneypiece, of built-up pine in the spindly Gothic-classic taste of *c.* 1810, with shells and weeds and a mourning figure with an anchor, is the finest of those brought in after 1907 (a similar one is in the main bedroom on the upper floor). To the E the DINING ROOM whose bay was added in 1907. Its refurnishing is no less idiosyncratic than that of the drawing room: ceiling with radiating leaves in a thick oval ring of vine with large grapes, chimneypiece of white marble with strange low reliefs – grapes and animals and a female mask in the centre. It was brought in like the others.

GARDENS. A formal yew garden, reached by a bridge, was made *c.* 1910 on the other side of the Colstoun Water which also bounds the N side of the early C19 walled garden.

STABLES. The carriage-shed section is early C19, probably built by *Patrick Brown* in 1808, the rest later C19, incorporating a cylindrical C18 DOOCOT.

LODGE, with rustic timber pillars, built by *John Swinton* in 1827.

CRAIGIELAW *see* ABERLADY

CRANSTON   ML *3060*

PARISH CHURCH, off the A68 in the policies of Oxenfoord
Castle. 1824, a crisp little Gothic kirk in the manner of
Cockpen, with a tower at the E end. The diagonal buttresses
of the tower end in battlemented turrets, but those of the church
itself have serious Gothic pinnacles and crockets in the spirit
of 1861, when it was rebuilt by *Wardrop* after a fire. On one
of the S buttresses a sundial of 1797, when the original parish
church on this site was restored. Charming, flat-vaulted interior. The Dalrymple aisle to the N, facing the pulpit between
two galleries, has been enlarged; probably in 1875 by *Wardrop
& Reid*. But one would not guess that the interior had been
altered in any way since 1824.

CRICHTON   ML *3060*

PARISH CHURCH (ST MARY AND ST KENTIGERN). Sir
William Crichton, James II's Chancellor, established a college
here in 1449, and the existing church is presumably the more
or less immediate result of this. It is a typical building of its
class, cruciform, aisleless and plainly tunnel-vaulted. It is typical even in having no nave, although it will be seen that there
are good grounds for thinking that one was built. Choir of three
bays divided by buttresses with stubby pinnacles. Round-
headed priest's door in the central S bay. The N windows have
convex-sided lozenges over two lights, the S ones C19 flowing
tracery. The tracery of the E window is of 1898 by *Hardy &
Wight*, as is the N porch on the site of the medieval sacristy.
Below the eaves cornice runs a second cornice, presumably to
mitigate the big expanses of plain wall over the windows caused
by the tunnel-vaults within. The transepts have similar vaults
but lack the buttresses and extra cornices of the choir, so the
former must be no less decorative in intention than the latter.
The tracery of the big end windows is of 1898, apparently to
the original design.* The crude, tensionless curves and the lack
of cusping suggest the early C16 rather than the C15. The original transept roof lines appear on the tower, which is low, with

* But the engraving dated 1847 in Billing's *Baronial and Ecclesiastical Antiquities* seems to show a different and more accomplished design.

a recessed saddleback roof and later mullioned windows. It
extends further W than the transepts – a piece of illogic not without parallel in the crossings of late medieval collegiate churches.
In the blocking of the W crossing arch a small round-headed
door and a panel with unidentified arms. There is no sign of
a vault over the nave, although the raggle for the roof is clear.
It has always been said that no nave was ever built, but if this
were the case would the stair to the tower have been set where
it is now, in a length of wall some feet away from the tower?
It would surely make more sense to suppose that the nave was
pulled down after the Reformation as being superfluous and,
with its wooden roof, more liable to decay than the stone-
vaulted parts. The fragment of the N wall would have to be
kept as it contained the only means of access to the tower. Why
the turret should be so placed is another question. Was it to
avoid a screen? The turret is externally three-sided, with a
pointed roof and a worn figure as a finial.

The interior of the church is impressively cavernous. The
vaults grow directly from the walls with nothing to mark the
springing. Steep, low-springing crossing arches with single
shafts and some foliage capitals. – SEDILIA. Triple, with ogee
tops flush with the wall, the seats broken away. – SACRAMENT
HOUSE. Ogee-headed and cusped. – PISCINA in the S transept,
again ogee-headed. The bowl is intact. – The furnishings of
1899 are unremarkable but complete. – WOODWORK by *Jones
& Willis*. – ORGAN. By *Joseph Brook & Co.* of Glasgow. –
STAINED GLASS. Four lights at the E end (the Agony in the
Garden) by *Ballantine & Gardiner*. – MONUMENTS in the
churchyard. A group of three cast-iron 'headstones' of ogee
Gothic profile, the first erected by *George Douglas* of the
Broughton Foundry, Edinburgh, 1841.

CRICHTON CASTLE. Crichton's courtyard is surrounded by
buildings of three centuries, late C14 to late C16, finishing with
a Renaissance elevation of extraordinary virtuosity. But from
the outside only the N front gives any hint of this. Grim and
forlorn, the shell of the castle stands on a plateau among small,
gentle hills, its best natural defence the steep drop to the river
Tyne on the W side. The earliest part is the keep in the middle
of the E side, probably built by John de Crichton, who received
the barony charter from Robert III in the late C14. The original
doorways at the N end are hidden by later work. The C15 saw
the building of three ranges to form a courtyard, all in the same
sort of masonry as the keep: roughly squared and coursed

rubble with big smooth quoins. First came the three-storey s range, which was also a gatehouse, with a round-headed entry (now blocked) to a pend leading into the courtyard. Its bold machicolations are interrupted by the s e corner tower with its higher wall head. A lower n service range was then added. The enclosure was completed by a w range which, like its neighbour to the s, has a splayed base course and one corner tower. The re-entrant angle between them is left open. In the late c16 a corbelled balcony of semicircular plan was made in the end wall of the s range. But this is to anticipate. The Crichtons were implicated in the conspiracy against James III and forfeited the estate in 1483.

The land passed to the King's favourite Sir John Ramsay, later Lord Bothwell, who in turn lost the estate in similar circumstances. James IV granted it to Patrick Hepburn, Lord Hailes, along with the title Earl of Bothwell. It was the fifth Earl, nephew of Queen Mary's consort, who gave Crichton its special architectural quality. On the w front the vertical joint to the l. of the postern shows where the gable of the service wing began. The work above it is Bothwell's; a tall gable, with windows directly beneath the chimney, suddenly brings life to the whole ensemble. A corbelled bartizan at the angle is the beginning of the band of five corbel courses that crown the new n front. A break in these, and a segmental arch in the deep parapet above, acknowledge the staircase that we are to see later. The main windows are high above the falling ground. Gun loops on the lower levels. Further to the e, and to the n of the old keep, Bothwell added a bakehouse. He also made a new round-arched gateway, probably crowned with a pediment, between the keep and the s range; a hole-in-corner approach to his internal show front, far inferior to the old entry through the pend, which he blocked up. Defence was the motive.

Time has made the courtyard into a large cutaway model, 44 tidied up by H.M. Office of Works and its successors. To the e the keep is torn open to reveal, within vastly thick walls, two longitudinally tunnel-vaulted spaces, one over the other. Each was separately entered from the n end, and there was no internal communication between the two. The lower, used no doubt for storage and servants, was divided by a wooden entresol whose joist-holes remain, reached by a stair in the thickness of the wall. A pit prison, reached by the same stair, steals a corner of the space. Over it is the kitchen, which had its own stair to the screens. The hall, which fills the upper space, has a fireplace on the outer side and a turnpike stair in the corner to an upper floor no longer existing.

The SOUTH RANGE is more elaborate. At its w end a high segmental arch forms a recessed canopy for a forestair to hall level. The stair was subsequently remade for wider and easier going, and this angle of the courtyard is overlaid by the ruin of a turnpike stair added by Bothwell. The C15 round-headed doorway at the top, with two orders of roll moulding on bell bases and a pretty hoodmould carved with leaves, leads into a lobby with adjoining service room, and thence through an ogee-arched doorway into the hall, later divided. End fireplace with shafts and foliated capitals supporting a heavily moulded lintel and canopy. Just to the S, a turnpike ascends to a tiny round room complete with shot-holes, virtually a turret, commanding an awkward internal angle. This is another defensive precaution by Lord Bothwell, and above the hall are more of the pleasant surroundings he wanted to defend: his alterations made this space into a single, south-facing room with an informally placed flat-arched fireplace and an enriched stone cornice.

Bothwell's work in the NORTH RANGE is roughly dated by his monogram FSMD (for Francis Stewart and his wife Margaret Douglas), with an anchor, above the two central columns of the arcade. He came back from Italy in 1581 and was Lord High Admiral till 1591. Who was his master mason and what was the source of this remarkable design? The Palazzo dei Diamanti at Ferrara has often been mentioned, and Dr Rowan* has pointed out that the Palazzo Carnesali in Verona was under construction in 1580–1, the very time when Bothwell was in Italy. The arcade or *piazza* was not unknown in Scotland, e.g. at the Montrose Lodging in Glasgow (demolished in the mid C19), but neither this theme nor that of diamond rustication was widely used in Scotland for another hundred years – and the latter only for pilasters, e.g. at Norrie's House in Stirling, never a whole façade. Whatever the answer, the remarkable thing about this work is not its classical detail, which is minimal and crude, but its discipline. The arcade is seven bays long, with a return bay to the W. The windows above it, though far from regular on account of their differing function, are precisely related to its intervals. The overall nailhead rustication, like a huge bar of chocolate, is in admirable contrast to the smooth flow of its arches and to the smooth window margins; and the

* Alistair Rowan, *Country Life* 7 January 1971.

cornice, or what is left of it, effectively introduces a still finer texture. The scale-and-platt staircase, with an inviting projection of steps into the court, the landings lit on both sides, is taller than the rest of the range. With columns attached to the ends of its median wall, it once again anticipates Scottish practice of a century later, e.g. at Prestonfield, Edinburgh. The soffits of each flight are moulded, not in plaster but in stone. At first-floor level a lobby on one hand leads into the kitchen, partly stolen out of the C15 W range, with a large twin-arched fireplace; above it, Bothwell's replanning involved the construction of a balcony whose corbels remain on the W courtyard wall. On the other hand the dining room, with a fireplace to the E and a buffet recess between the windows to the N. Beyond it, in Bothwell's new extension, is the withdrawing room. It has a little chamber in the corner turret above the bakehouse oven. The draw-well which served the castle from the first can be seen behind the arcade, at the entry to one of the old cellars on which Bothwell based his new range.

STABLE, to the S. Bothwell's work again, the lower part entered by a horseshoe arch with thong enrichment, the upper part a hayloft. Crowstepped gables. Later buttresses.

SOUTERRAIN, 1.5 km. E of the church. Access is through a short passage to a gallery 15 m. long and 1.8 m. wide, the flat roof lintels original but the arched roof modern. Dressed blocks of Roman masonry are incorporated in the structure and a lintel is carved with an animal sometimes described as a Pegasus.

CRICHTON HOUSE
2 km. S of Pathhead

ML 3060

A plain, upstanding, whitewashed L-plan house. Three storeys below the wall head. Crowstepped gables. Octagonal stair-turret merged into the angle and standing up proud of it, with a pointed roof. Many of the chamfered openings are built up, including the door at the foot of the turret, whose classical mouldings confirm the late C17 date of the building. Empty armorial panel above it.

CROOKSTON OLD HOUSE (SOUTH MAINS) ML*
8 km. NNW of Stow

4050

A two-storey C17 house with crowstepped gables and piended
* Now Borders Region.

dormers. s side altered *c.* 1860 with a bay-window and a project-ing central jamb which incorporates and conceals the turnpike stair-turret. The stair ascends anticlockwise. The ground-floor room at the E end, traditionally part of the tower built after 1446 by John Borthwick, second son of the builder of Borthwick Castle, has an arched fireplace at the end gable, and its thick walls evidently supported a longitudinal masonry vault. C18 panelling in the W room on the same floor.

4050 CROOKSTON HOUSE ML*
7.5 km NNW of Stow

The house of 1816–19, five bays and two storeys on a basement, can still be seen on the s front. In 1860–4 it was heavily Jaco-beanized by *Brown & Wardrop* for John Borthwick of Crook-ston. They added a large porch, three curly gables with a balu-strade between, and corner bartizan turrets which originally had ogee roofs. But they used the same materials (grey whin with sandstone dressings) and left the rusticated quoins on ground-floor level, even repeating them under the turrets of the new work at the rear. To the W they built a big classical con-servatory with a Jacobean gabled ballroom behind, both linked to the house by a glazed passage; a strange composition, but successful with the aid of a cast-iron balustrade across the whole affair, forming a terrace to the W. Some Georgian interiors sur-vive. The staircase was recast with Jacobean woodwork and an armorial window of 1873. A modest Roman Doric chimney-piece was re-used in the large drawing room, which has a curious hybrid ceiling: heavy square compartments (with tiny pendants) at the corners only, the deep members not crossing the whole span. The ballroom ceiling is quite classical, com-partmented and coved.

STONES. Two Celtic fragments with interlaced carving built into the rear of the house are said to have come from the ancient church of Borthwick. There is also a stone inscribed ... IESUS FOR MY PORTIOUN. AS AL SUFICIENT TO CONTENT 161 (?).

To the N and S of the house two octagonal SUMMER HOUSES have been improvised, the former with four slim Roman Doric columns (formerly attached – to what?) and low relief marble jambs of *c.* 1800 used most unsuitably as lintels, the latter with four full columns of the same height.

* Now Borders Region.

CROOKSTON MAINS *see* STOW

CROWHILL FARM *see* INNERWICK

CURRIE

ML *1060*

PARISH CHURCH. 1784 by *James Thompson* of Leith. Oblong classical, but with Gothic glazed windows in the N front whose centre, accommodating the gallery staircases, is advanced and pedimented; over it a square clock stage, then an octagonal belfry and stumpy spire. The interior was carefully recast by *David Bryce* in 1835, and *David Cousin* enlarged the windows in 1848. The PULPIT in the middle of the S side still has its original shell-moulded niche flanked by engaged Corinthian columns. The other three sides are galleried, the ceiling coved. To the E are fragments of the choir of the old church. – STONES. The three crudely carved slabs noted by the RCAHMS are still here. Each has a circled cross, two of them a sword.

GLENBURN HOTEL (formerly Braeburn House), over Kinleith Bridge, on a Pentland foothill. Scots Renaissance by *R. Rowand Anderson*, 1887, in red sandstone. Galleried hall and staircase panelled in oak. To the E an observatory, probably a later extension.

CURRIEHILL HOUSE, to the NW. Large fragment of a plain but idiosyncratic house by *David Cousin*, 1856. One of the external angles is rounded off to accommodate a staircase, and the skew above it is correspondingly swept round. Strangely panelled chimneys.

LENNOX TOWER, to the SW. Virtually a garden ornament in front of the mid C19 *cottage orné* of LYMPHOY, the ruin of a C15 rectangular tower traditionally built by the Lennox family, with a door at the NE corner and a stair in the thickness of the wall just inside.

Currie, once known as Kinleith, is a long parade of villas (the lesser kind, with a few from *c.* 1840) lining the A70 to the W of Juniper Green, which is in Edinburgh. The RICCARTON ARMS is plain late Georgian. Two public buildings betray their date with red sandstone: *J. MacIntyre Henry*'s GIBSON CRAIG MEMORIAL HALL, 1901, and *William Baillie*'s single-storey BOARD SCHOOL, 1903. The huge CURRIE HIGH SCHOOL by *Eric Hall & Partners*, 1960, is visible only from the N. Immediately to the S of the road is the valley of the Water of Leith, to whose benefits industry has staked a large claim; quite re-

cently all but the office buildings of *R. Rowand Anderson*'s
KINLEETH HOUSE was demolished for a factory. KINLEITH
BRIDGE, built in 1831 for General Scott (*see* Malleny, Balerno),
leads to BLINKBONNY, where opposite the farm is a pair of
red brick cottages with fancy black-and-white gables and mutual
dormer by *Charles Hay*, 1891. Across the next bridge is the
church, the crowstepped SCHOOLHOUSE by *David Bryce*,
1830, and the MANSE which he enlarged in 1837, the original
building being by *Charles Smith* and *Andrew Denholm*. To the
W ROSEBERY COTTAGES, the old parish school designed by
William Burn and executed by *David Bryce* in 1828–9, single-
storey with diagonal chimneyshafts.

3060

DALHOUSIE CASTLE   ML
3.5 km. SSW of Dalkeith

Built by the Ramsays of Dalhousie, who owned the barony from
1150, a tower of *c.* 1450 complete with its curtain wall in which
most of the later additions are contained; all of the hard pinkish
sandstone which apparently came from the quarry to the SE.
On the S side, downhill towards the river South Esk, the main
slab of the tower can still be seen standing back from the curtain, though both of course are somewhat altered, and the curtain in fact conceals a range of vaulted cellars probably of the
C17. But the projection at the SE corner had a vaulted chamber
from the first, standing half astride a drum-shaped ravelin. On
the E side the curtain has a battered base, numerous vertical
slits, and a secondary entrance doorway, round-headed, under
which is one of a pair of corbels that supported a timber ramp
or drawbridge. On the N it is obscured by C19 offices. Here and
to the W the original dry moat has been filled in. The W front
itself is now a curious meeting of three rival elements. First
the main entrance of the mid C15, a tall projecting archway
whose wider N jamb allows for small internal chambers, surmounted by twin machicolated bartizans; under the arch, the
carved corbels mark the approximate level of the pivot from
which the drawbridge arms swung up into their housings; over
these is an ogival-headed and cusped frame of the same period,
in which a C17 panel displays the Ramsay eagle. The NW drum
tower which covers the entry was evidently an afterthought,
though an early one. Finally in 1633 William, first Earl of Dalhousie, built out to the curtain from the old tower, inscribing
his own title on one of the window-head pediments, those of

his countess Margaret on the other. But not quite finally, for some time in the early C19 this range was enlarged and heightened by a storey, with hoodmoulds over the windows and new corner turrets, battlemented overall. Also facing this way, but set back in the angle of the old L-plan tower, is the new frontage of the staircase built *c.* 1600 by the first Earl's father, Sir George Ramsay, with three roundels – two initialled, one heraldic.

The Georgian additions are a riddle. Those of the C18 concerned only internal work, which has disappeared. *William Burn*'s drawings of 1825 show no additions except to the N of the entrance, and most of the elevational designs are missing. The considerable range of style suggests that at least some of the castle's scenic castellations date from before Burn's time.*

Inside, the picture is unusually clear, thanks partly to the work of *Mottram, Patrick, Whitehorn, Dalgleish & Partners* in 1972 when the castle was replanned as a hotel; antiquarian and commercial interests have coincided, and much relevant masonry has been exposed. But Burn's work is respected, most notably in the ENTRANCE HALL, a double square. In the first part is a miniature imperial staircase with brass balusters rising over to a mezzanine landing which occupies the second, a canopied Gothic niche on its further wall. Both parts are fan-vaulted in plaster, gilt ribs on green, the central half-fans 89 springing from free-standing shafts. Over each is a lantern with a tiny ribbed and pendanted roof. From the lower level one enters Burn's large dining room, which has a very flat Gothic timber ceiling, or, through the original external door, the basement of the C15 tower, which has three parallel vaulted rooms forming the S side of its L-plan. In its N jamb is the vaulted PRISON, which formerly had no access on this level, but was approached by a winding stair from above. The door was secured by an external draw-bar. Ventilated latrine recess, but no lighting. A timber floor separated it from the pit underneath.

Beyond Burn's entrance hall is his STAIRCASE with Gothic iron balustrade in the same position as Sir George's stair of *c.* 1600. The masonry of the old external wall has been exposed

---

* Sir Walter Scott's *Journal* for 23 December 1827 has a relevant record of a visit. 'The old Castle of Dalhousie ... was mangled by a fellow called, I believe, Douglas, who destroyed, as far as in him lay, its military and baronial character, and roofed it after the fashion of a poor's-house. Burn is now restoring and repairing in the old taste, and, I think, creditably to his own feeling.'

on the E side, that of his addition on the W. On the first floor, filling the S side of the tower, Burn's LONG ROOM, with a Jacobean ribbed ceiling (a similar one downstairs has small pendants) and at each end a white marble chimneypiece; the two are identical, strange hybrids from the whole of Burn's stylistic repertoire. But no odder than the LIBRARY, which has a pinnacled Gothic substructure of shelving right round (even into the windows, except for the largest, and over the plain dovegrey chimneypiece), and then a coved Rococo ceiling – albeit rather thick as to scrollwork. The only other room of note is the ARMOURY, where a ceremonious Jacobean staircase, by Burn again, descends into a tall space with a pointed tunnelvault, unlit except through the Gothic doorway which emerges on ground level to the S.

DALKEITH

CHURCHES

EAST CHURCH (ST NICHOLAS). An important late medieval church spoiled by extremes of restoration and neglect. The nave and transepts are externally all by *David Bryce*, 1851–4, and their smooth stonework contrasts painfully with the eroded and blackened details of the unroofed choir. But the W parts are still medieval in their basic structure and form part of a rebuilding to which Sir James Douglas contributed at various dates between 1390 and 1420. The church became collegiate in 1406, though it was only in 1467 that it ceased to be a chapel dependent on Lasswade and became a parish church in its own right. In 1477 the college was expanded by James Douglas, first Earl of Morton. His tomb is in the choir, and there is a good chance that he was responsible for the choir itself. Its westernmost bay, still roofed, seems to belong structurally with the nave. The main part of the choir would, if it were better preserved, be a prime monument of the Scottish Late Gothic. It has two bays and a three-sided apse. The only earlier Gothic apses in Scotland are at Crossraguel Priory, Ayrshire (c. 1440), and Trinity College, Edinburgh (begun 1460). The exterior is dominated by bold and richly detailed buttresses whose design can best be studied from the restored SW buttress. Windows of three lights with uncusped loop tracery, which points to a date near c. 1500. The SW window differs from the others in some details, e.g. the omission of capitals. There are no windows in the N wall,

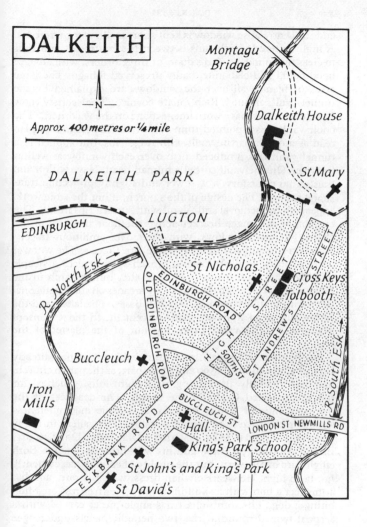

DALKEITH

N

Approx. 400 metres or ¼ mile

Montagu Bridge

Dalkeith House

St Mary

DALKEITH PARK

LUGTON

EDINBURGH

R. North Esk

St Nicholas

Cross Keys
Tolbooth

STREET

CROSS STREET

ST ANDREW'S STREET

HIGH STREET

SOUTH ST

EDINBURGH ROAD

OLD EDINBURGH ROAD

Buccleuch

Iron Mills

R. South Esk

BUCCLEUCH ST

ESKBANK ROAD

Hall

King's Park School

LONDON ST NEWMILLS RD

St John's and King's Park

St David's

and the centre apse window is kept short to allow for a reredos. A high battered plinth runs between the buttresses and rises to clear the round-headed s door, of three orders, with an ogee hoodmould and elaborate, badly preserved foliage. The large areas of blank wall over the windows are explained by the tunnel-vaults inside.* Rich foliate cornice. The sacristy (now Buccleuch vault) has a worn image niche on the w corner.‡ The choir vault was a pointed tunnel with surface ribs. The plan read as a quadripartite vault with ridge ribs, but applied to a tunnel-vault this produced a rib over each window as well as between. On one vault corbel a human head. Nave with N and s aisles, no clearstory, a w tower and slightly projecting transeptal chapels. The design of the s porch, if not the stonework, appears to be medieval still. Vault with surface ribs inside. The original of the image bracket above the door now lies in the choir. The aisle windows, with their over-ambitious tracery based on Lincluden, Dumfries-shire, are *Bryce*'s. The w tower and its meaty, English-looking broach-spire replace a steeple of 1762. The vault inside is of 1851 etc., but the arch to the nave is medieval, as are the three-bay arcades on short octagonal piers with moulded capitals and bell bases. The labels and the rather silly head stops are made of cement. In the N transept a simple PISCINA has been dug out of the plaster of the wall.

At the time of Bryce's 'restoration' the E part had already been abandoned since 1590 and the w part, as the parish church, had been radically altered, e.g. with eight lofts (galleries) for the Incorporated Crafts of the burgh. The deadness of the recreated interior is due both to its organic incompleteness and its irrelevance to reformed worship. The gallery in the w tower was formed in 1885. – MONUMENT. James Douglas, first Earl of Morton, † *c.* 1498 and his wife Princess Joanna. Both effigies are badly worn, but the quality of carving has evidently not been high. He wears civilian dress, which is rare, and has at his feet a lion with a skull in its jaws. Her feet rest on a lion biting a dog. The tomb-chest has angle pieces carved with a serpent twined round a tree, two heraldic panels under ogee arches on the long sides, and three blank spaces with projecting gabled canopies presumably for sculpture. – ORGAN. By *Foster*

* At Seton this was avoided by making the windows cut into the vault.
‡ The inside was not examined. The upper storey has an original pointed tunnel-vault, and over the lower storey a segmental vault replacing the original wooden floor.

& Andrews of Hull, 1884. – STAINED GLASS. At the E end two lights with the Good Shepherd and St Nicholas, after 1957. – In the E wall of the S transept two more (the procession to Calvary), after 1918. – BANNER of the Dalkeith Hammermen's Society, dated 1665. – MONUMENT, at the W end. A tabernacle with mortuary trimmings, to William Calderwood Minister of Dalkeith † 1680.

BUCCLEUCH (formerly West) PARISH CHURCH, Old Edinburgh Road. Gothic of a lean but hardly muscular variety, by *William Burn*, 1840. It is T-planned, with chancel to the E, tower and spire to the W, pinnacled buttresses standing up like ramrods between regular, hoodmoulded lancets: altogether trim rather than exciting. However the tower comes to life with traceried windows at the second stage, and its dry spike of a spire, attended by thin pinnacles, has inestimable value on the town's skyline. In the W porch under the tower a rib-vault and a handsome hanging lantern; in the SE porch a laborious flat arch between heavy buttresses, on which griffons wait to pounce. Inside, the timber ceiling is slightly coombed, the 'nave' exceptionally wide. – PULPIT. Lively Jacobean, with sounding-board, in the middle of the short E limb, which is unhappily blocked by the organ case added later to each side of it. – Most of the lancets have their original geometric glazing with tinted edges, but there is also STAINED GLASS: two lights in the S transept (I am the Way, and I am the Good Shepherd) by *William Wilson*, 1962. – MANSE, probably contemporary, with a good build-up of gables.

CHURCH HALL, Buccleuch Street. Built in 1879 as the Buccleuch Street Church by *R. Thornton Shiells*. Large, elaborate frontage in an Italian Romanesque manner.

ST DAVID (R.C.), Eskbank Road. 1853–4 (presbytery 1860) by *J. A. Hansom*, endowed by Lord Lothian and other members of the Kerr family. Simple early Dec style without a tower (open belfry on the E gable of the nave), but all its parts clearly distinguished – a lively group on a conspicuous site. Steep roof with bands of fish-scale slating over the five-bay nave, shallower roof over the aisles. Separate gables for chancel, NE Lady Chapel and SW chapels. The priest's house has been rebuilt. The interior is basically plain, with alternate round and octagonal piers supporting the nave arcade and the clearstory, which has trefoil windows set over the piers. The quicker rhythm of a half-size arcade separates the S aisle from the two chapels. St Aloysius' Chapel towards the E is rib-vaulted; the rest of the church is roofed in timber, with eccentric trusses over the aisles. Another unorthodox device is the considerable slope of the nave floor, so that you find yourself hurrying towards the E end. Of *C. H. Goldie*'s original decorative scheme not much has survived the repainting and liturgical reorganization of 1971–2 by *Sean Cullen* except for the panelled and painted roofs of chancel and Lady Chapel, the latter with elaborate gilt bosses; the same chapel also retains its dado of glazed tiles with fleurs-de-lys in relief.

The furnishings were given or approved throughout by Victorian and Edwardian Kerrs. The HIGH ALTAR (since modified), carved by *Earp* in Caen stone with marble insets, with quatrefoil reliefs of Our Lady and SS. Margaret and David, is not badly obscured by *Cullen*'s new altar in front. – STAINED GLASS. In the chancel E windows the figures of Our Lady and SS. John and Paul were brought 'from Wardour Street', restored and made up to fit. – PAINTING over the chancel arch by Miss *Gibsone*: Coronation of the Virgin in a central vesica and attendant saints, fringed by a little of the original blue and gold diaper background. – STATIONS OF THE CROSS. Brought from Paris in 1854 by Lady Lothian. – STATUE of the Sacred Heart, 1880 by *Mayer* of Munich, with pedestal and canopy by *C. Anderson*. – ORGAN, at the W end. 1864 by Dr *Monk* of York Minster, built by *Hamilton* of Edinburgh, Gothic over a timber arcade. – The LADY CHAPEL ALTAR by *Goldie*, enclosing a relic of S. Vitale, has five carved figures of saints in an arcaded reredos. – STAINED GLASS in the Lady Chapel: SS. Mary and Joseph in two lancets by *Morris & Co.* – The HOLY SOULS (SW) CHAPEL ALTAR is of 1883 by *Mayer* of Munich, with a realistic figure of the dead Christ beneath. It incorporates an altarpiece PAINTING of Our Lady of Perpetual Succour, imported in 1868. – In ST ALOYSIUS' (S) CHAPEL the ALTAR corbelled from the wall is surmounted by a STATUE of St Aloysius by *Pollen*.

ST JOHN'S AND KING'S PARK (formerly King's Park United Presbyterian), Eskbank Road. By *R. Thornton Shiells*, 1871. The lanceted tower, which has a broach-spire with two tiers of lucarnes, is attached to one side of the street-facing gable, a staircase turret to the other; both are quite ordinary, but the gable itself is more dramatic – boldly modelled below, and its traceried roundel bursting up from a level sill with two flanking shafts. The drama is sustained inside: massive roof with big wooden ties, the round window glaring in over the back gallery.

– STAINED GLASS. Two pairs of lancets, one each side (the four Evangelists with appropriate New Testament subjects and texts), by *William Wilson*, 1939.

ST MARY (Episcopal), just inside the gates of Dalkeith Palace at the N end of the High Street. Built in 1843 by *William Burn & David Bryce* as the palace chapel, which it remained until 1958. *Benjamin Ferrey* had in the previous year made a design on the instructions of the Rev. Lord John Thynne, who had specified an E.E building to cost under £2,000. There is an unsigned paper entitled 'A Few Hints respecting the Construction of a Church of England Chapel', and this may well be Thynne's brief for him. Ferrey's design was not used and the cost limit was to be forgotten, but Burn and Bryce generally followed the 'Hints' both in style, which is mostly E.E., and in proportion: it is an aisleless church, tall and long. Yet from the outside it is decidedly earthbound; the paired lancets with their thin shafts and stiff-leaf capitals are delicate enough, but massive gableted buttresses weigh it down on each side. Cusped E.E. arcade at the W end, its arches blind except for that of the central door which has elaborate iron hinges by *Potter* of London. In the gable overhead a wheel window and a crowning bellcote. The chancel, N transept and S vestry are original, but the memorial chapel to the fifth Duke of Buccleuch was added by *Sir Arthur W. Blomfield* in 1890, in a watered-down version of the same style. 33

The Burn–Bryce interior is impressive indeed. Over the five-bay nave a ten-bay double-hammerbeam roof of steep pitch. Heraldic tiles by *Minton* lead up between poppyhead PEW ENDS, then spread across at the foot of the chancel steps and into the rib-vaulted choir and sanctuary. – The octagonal FONT with marble-shafted base was designed by *Ferrey*. – *Burn & Bryce* were responsible for the stone PULPIT in the SE corner of the nave, reached by a vaulted stair through the chancel wall. It rests on a big leafy corbel and is derived from that at Beaulieu. – The large hydraulically blown ORGAN by *Hamilton & Miller* of Edinburgh, 1846, occupies a Gothic case by *Bryce* over the arcading at the W end. – The brass eagle LECTERN is notable but unattributed. – Oak CHOIR STALLS, with carved figures inset in the ends, designed by *William Butterfield* and made in 1846 by *F. & W. Vigers*. – The gilt CANDLESTICKS on the altar with angels sitting on lion feet were supplied by *Thomas Potter* in the following year. – STAINED GLASS. The mosaic glass of the W wheel window and the glass in the three E lancets

(New Testament scenes in Gothic frames) are by *Ward & Nixon* of London, 1845.

Blomfield opened up the MEMORIAL CHAPEL to the choir and N transept with two iron-screened arches which add dramatic perspective to the older work. *S. Gambier Parry* was in charge of the decoration and fittings, which were carried out in 1913, including the marble pavement over the burial vault and the deep marble dado. – MONUMENT. The recumbent marble figure of the fifth Duke was begun by *Sir Edgar Boehm* and finished by *Sir Alfred Gilbert* in 1892. – STAINED GLASS. By *James Powell & Sons*, 1913–15; three lights to the E ('Now is Christ risen from the Dead ...' with figures in architectural Gothic frames), and two more triplets to the N ('As in Adam all die ...' and 'The Lord is my Shepherd'), each united by a leafy tree structure springing from a central stem. – In the N transept a pair of lancets in memory of the sixth Duke by *A. K. Nicolson*, 1927. – Beside them a memorial TABLET to the seventh Duke designed by *A. F. Balfour Paul*, 1936.

BAPTIST CHAPEL. *See* p. 164.

PUBLIC BUILDINGS

OLD TOLBOOTH, on the N side of the High Street. A C17 building as we are told, with cells in the subterranean basement, weigh-house on the ground floor and courtroom upstairs. But the ashlar frontage with its rusticated quoins has a polite look. Even so, there is no reason to doubt that the pediment over the doorway, the Buccleuch arms and the date, 1648, all belong to the original building. The rest has probably been altered. For other public buildings *see* Description, pp. 162–6.

DALKEITH HOUSE

69 An old castle virtually rebuilt by *James Smith* in 1702–11, Dalkeith in its main aspect is the grandest of all early classical houses in Lothian and for that matter in Scotland; Smith's earlier work at Hamilton Palace with its somewhat similar frontage is now no more. The estate was bought from the Earl of Morton in 1642 by Francis, second Earl of Buccleuch, and the reconstruction of the old castle was carried out for his younger daughter Anne; her husband was the Duke of Monmouth, and these two were created Duke and Duchess of Buccleuch in 1663.

Built of fine sandstone, warm and slightly variegated in colour, the house is perched on the steep bank of the North

Esk, and its cluster of chimneys can be seen over the trees on the approach from Edinburgh. It faces roughly SE, but for clarity this will be taken as S. Smith demolished part of the existing castle in 1702 but incorporated most of it in the new house, so that the N wall is substantially of the C16. So is the slightly splayed W wall, except where it was brought into line for the windows of the new staircase; some original masonry was left on each side of these windows, including that of the SW tower, but the remainder was refaced in rubble to suit the new fenestration. The E range is largely C17, but the bow window on its splayed-arch basement, lighting the library, was added by *James Playfair* in 1786; *Alex. Young* was the mason. So Smith worked on the basis of a big lopsided courtyard, open to the S. He lined it with another room-thickness that entirely conceals its irregularity. Each bay of the main façade and its projecting wings has the same pattern of three windows diminishing towards the top. The crowning cornice and piend roof are also continuous, interrupted only by the central pediment, richly bracketed but with plain tympanum, over a giant order of Corinthian pilasters. Between these the windows have cornices; outside them they do not. The walls are of rubble, once rendered, the storeys defined by moulded string courses that continue on to the outer pavilions, whose roofs are similarly bell-cast. This ensemble, like the later version at Althorp, Northants, is the fullest realization of the Dutch Palladian courtyard theme (e.g. at the Cloth Hall at Leyden) and its possibilities for inward and upward movement towards the centre. Something of the detailed richness of Dalkeith may be due to repair and refacing by *John Adam* in 1762–3, but the design is assuredly Smith's. Contemporary records give the names of the original masons, puzzlingly, as '*James Smith, James Smith* and *Gilbert Smith*' as 'partners' (does one of them refer to the architect himself?). *William Walker* was the joiner. *Peter Sympson*, the slater, did his work in 1705 and then re-slated the altered N side (this could refer to what is here called the E) in 1707. As to the interior, sums were paid to *John Sampson*, plasterer, *William Morgan* and *Isaac Sylverstyn*, carvers, and to the marble-cutter *Richard Neale* from London. Some 'patterns of marble' were brought from Holland. In 1831 *William Burn* was responsible for some additions, which may have included the blocking of the front door and the building of a new porch on the W side of the courtyard; it is said that George IV on his visit in 1822 had caught cold from the draughts. The original entry was reinstated and internal restoration meticulously carried out by *W. Schomberg Scott* in 1973.

The bolection-moulded panelling and sober detail of the entrance hall establish the basic mood of the interior. To the E is the service stair, to the W the MARBLE HALL of which the main stair is an extension, the marble floor running through from one to the other. First a panelled room under the landing, with marble doorcases. At its open end two depressed arches with coffered soffits spring from a central Corinthian column and wall pilasters – all of white marble, grey veined. Entered through one arch, the cantilevered marble stair with panelled risers ascends the three sides of the well. Its handrail and delicate wrought-iron balustrade are evidently late C18 replacements. Overhead, stair and landing are united by a continuous cornice and plain ceiling. To the S of the stair, in the base of the old SW tower, is the one room that survives in anything like its pre-C18 form. It has a vaulted ceiling. To the N of it is the DINING ROOM: huge doorpieces and bolection-moulded fireplace, all of dove-grey marble, and matched in scale by oak wall panels that reach from the dado to the lofty coved cornice and are repeated in the deep window embrasures. Two rooms of similar but slightly more modest character follow *en suite*. The finest are the set of three small rooms at the NE corner: the ANTEROOM, with oak panelling and cove, a bolection-moulded marble fireplace and similar overmantel surmounted by pulvinated frieze and cornice; the BOUDOIR, whose fireplace has a heavily garlanded border round its bolection mould and an enriched overmantel frame surmounted by a carved monogram; and DUCHESS ANNE'S ROOM, with oak-panelled walls with geometric inlay between enriched mouldings, and a foliage cove to match. Fireplace and overmantel are of red marble figured with white, and in the latter is the white marble panel of 'The Story of Neptune and Gallatea (*sic*)' for which *Grinling Gibbons* rendered his account in July 1701; the figures are of small scale in varied relief. Over it, a silver monogram set in blue glass. In this room a tripartite window was formed *c*. 1800, with access to the grounds by way of an outside stair. Next is the bow-windowed LIBRARY. *James Blaikie* made the bookshelves in 1769–70, *Alex. Govan* the old-fashioned chimneypiece in 1771, but the classical cornice evidently dates from 1786, when *James Playfair* added the bow. Two chimneypieces at the end of this E range are of later date. One is conventionally late C18 classical in white marble; the other, of Louis type in liver-coloured marble, is of *c.* 1830, so perhaps *William Burn* was here too. The bedroom storey has some original fireplaces, e.g. the one in the room over the anteroom, a delicately moulded two-stager of white marble veined with grey.

STABLES and COACH HOUSE to the NE. 1740 by *William Adam*. The two opposing ranges of two storeys forming a long courtyard entered at each end between rusticated piers remained quite plain until *c.* 1840, when a clock and belfry were added to the middle of one side, possibly by *William Burn*.

LAUNDRY. Probably early C19 and definitely before 1852. Nine bays, with projecting quoins and advanced centre, a recessed wall-head course under the cornice. Quite plain, the window panes curiously small.

CONSERVATORY. Fiercely detailed Jacobean by *William Burn*, 1832–4, at the time of writing an unglazed skeleton. Twelve-sided, with twelve Roman Doric columns on a stepped base supporting an entablature and spiked vases with strapwork between; the lower part of the columns, the wall beneath the windows, and even the central chimney are likewise strapped. Radial iron trusses of geometric design to support the glazing. The building formed part of an elaborate parterre laid out by *W. S. Gilpin*.

BRIDGES. MONTAGU BRIDGE. 1792 by *Robert Adam*. One semicircular arch carrying the W drive high above the North Esk between massive parapets of droved ashlar, the abutments treated as piers, with deep niches and panelled heads. This is a notable feat of C18 engineering. – OLD COW BRIDGE (South Esk). Originally medieval but frequently repaired. Major and minor arch; brick parapet with refuges. – LAUNDRY BRIDGE (South Esk). C18, with two keystoned arches, the parapets splayed outwards at the approaches and the refuge over the central cutwater.

LODGES and GATES. TOWN LODGE, at the N end of Dalkeith High Street. The piers with fluted tops and iron tripods and the arch-in-grid gates are by *James Playfair*, 1784, but the lodge has been replaced. – DARK WALK GATES, to the E. C18, with wrought-iron arch, scrolled and coroneted. – DUKE'S GATES or King's Gates, to the W on the A68. 1848 by *William Burn & David Bryce*. A huge drive-in with four rusticated piers and florid vases; flamboyant ironwork to match. Steeply gabled lodge.

HOME FARM, to the N. The (former) farmhouse is a remnant of SMEATON HOUSE, built *c.* 1710 on the basis of an earlier fortified house and credited in *Vitruvius Scoticus* to *William Adam* under the name of EAST PARK. It was a long, plain building with projecting wings to the front, corner towers to the rear; one of these, with its middle window subdivided and a shallow conical roof of Italian aspect in place of the original ogival one, is virtually all that remains, together with the stump of the other. It has a gun loop near the ground, and the attached square jamb contains a stair. Both tower and jamb are crowned with a cornice of ogee section. – LODGE. Late C19 rock-faced baronial, but the gatepiers are early C18, the inner pair blocked and fluted, the outer polyhedral.

DESCRIPTION

Dalkeith, a small country town that grew up as a baronial burgh under the Douglases and then under the Buccleuchs, occupies a wedge-shaped plateau between the rivers North and South Esk – the confluence is to the NE beyond Dalkeith House. The first section of the High Street, which runs from the gates of the house (previously the castle), provides a broad market area. It was never a main route, but its narrower second section, after St Nicholas' church, goes on till it meets the Old Edinburgh Road and its continuation, Buccleuch Street and London Road. The present Edinburgh Road, formed *c.* 1840, did little to improve access to the town and created an awkward dog leg in the main road (A68) to the S. The horse-drawn 'innocent railway' from Edinburgh was opened in 1831 and mechanized in 1846, when another station was built at Eskbank (*see* below) on the main North British line. Dalkeith today has kept its shape rather than its buildings, but the C19 churches are still notable. Many lesser buildings have been replaced in accordance with the policy of an enterprising town council, some in rubbly 'traditional' style, others by an amazing mixture of new architecture which emulates the diversity of private enterprise work.

The approach from Edinburgh passes the Duke's Gates (*see* above) and descends to BRIDGEND. This, a pleasant early C19 row of cottages featuring a round turret of 1852 and a sundial dated 1759 on its older E end, overlooks LUGTON BRIDGE, a single arch with the inscription 'Built 1757 Widened and Improved 1816'. For Lugton *see* Addenda, p. 525.

The main walk through the town begins with ESKBANK which lies to the SW, its original suburban character belied by a roundabout at the principal road junction. It started with ESKBANK

Lugton   Su Addmda

HOUSE, built in 1794 as the manse for Newbattle. Five bays, with rusticated ground floor over the basement, and a Roman Doric porch. Intact contemporary plasterwork. A Victorian conservatory opens out of the Venetian window halfway up the stair. Subsequent feuing of sites for villas began c. 1846, when the symmetrical Tudor STATION was opened (it is open no longer). WESTFIELD PARK in Bonnyrigg Road, of c. 1845, has a low-pitch piend roof, a bracketed doorpiece and advanced ends. GLENESK, Avenue Road, also of c. 1845, is severely detailed with the masonry vertically emphasized on each side of the tripartite windows, and banks of chimneys with mutual cornices over the shallow-pitch piend roof. The porch is reportedly later. About the same time a more fanciful but still solid type of villa appears in Eskbank Road, and some sites to the rear were later feued for terraces, e.g. GLENESK CRESCENT, c. 1880, with bay-windows and cast-iron cresting. LAMP POSTS dated 1878 and 1899. The most spectacular house is LINSANDEL (formerly NETHERBY), Melville Road, richly Italian, with elaborate bargeboards and a tower in the angle. It is by *Knox & Hutton* of Edinburgh, 1884, of Gunnerton stone, with mullions and balusters of red Dumfries-shire. The bargeboards and finials were painted olive green; the roof was of green slates with red ridge-tiles.

HARDENGREEN, 1 km. to the s. A substantial farmhouse, finished by 1796. Squared and stugged masonry; smooth quoins and other dressings. The front door cornice was removed c. 1830, when an extension with a new door was built to one end. Each part has its staircase and other details complete. In the dining room a pilastered sideboard recess, and a geometric chimney-piece of suitable date imported from Crichton Street, Edinburgh. Late C18/early C19 STEADING with a red brick chimney.

After Eskbank itself, the first incident in ESKBANK ROAD is the polychrome brick octagonal WATER TOWER with lucarned tank-house by *James Leslie*, 1878. Here a path leads down over the North Esk. In a bend of the river the IRON MILLS, a metalworks of c. 1820 whose tall build-up is enhanced by Gothic windows. The New Statistical Account commends the enterprise of its owner, Mr Gray, whose own house nearby has a separate stable block of similar more elaborate Gothic detail with lancets and trefoils as well as four-centred arches, but is itself plain late Georgian.

Here also Dalkeith begins spaciously enough with St David's and St John's and King's Park Churches to the r., and the park itself

between them, backed with poplars. Beyond it appears the
KING'S PARK SCHOOL by *T. T. Paterson*, 1903, in cream
and red sandstone Queen Anne. Jolly skyline with curvaceous
gables and a tall centre lantern. To the l. the railway station
has been replaced by a shopfronted bus station. The ROYAL
BANK on the other side, a latterday palace front from discreet
sources with a red tile roof, is by *Sydney Mitchell & Wilson*,
1911; after it, the miniature baronial BURGH CHAMBERS of
1882, enlarged by *Tarbolton & Ochterlony* in 1908. To the r.
the view down BUCCLEUCH STREET is nicely closed by Nos.
1–3 LONDON ROAD, connected houses of *c.* 1770. It is worth
going along to see the charming rudimentary Gothic front of
the BAPTIST CHAPEL, 1871, opposite them, and the detached
mid C18 house at No. 6 which as well as a consoled doorhead
pediment has the unusual combination of scrolled skewputts
and corner pedestals – the latter probably for urns that have
now gone. On the way, to the l. the BLACK BULL, a highly
original and organic pub with columned corner entry and half-
timbered gables by *Charles H. Greig* (built as the GOTHEN-
BURG for the Public House Improvement Co., 1906), and to
the r. traditional housing at the sweep round into Lothian Road,
by *T. Aikman Swan* for the town council, *c.* 1935.

HIGH STREET has an entry effectively narrowed by the double-
gabled C18 BUCK'S HEAD, but it then falls into disorder until
the pavement opens out to the r. into the new TOWN CENTRE
by the Burgh Architect, *R. J. Naismith*. This is in three main
parts. The COUNCIL CHAMBERS of 1960 are four-square and
heavily framed, with stone panel infill. The block behind is of
the same date, a convex arc of canopied shops, the three storeys
of flats overhead camouflaged from outside and given some pri-
vacy inside by continuous concrete 'bressumers' between
rubble spine walls. A second free-standing, slab-walled block
of 1964 acts as a curtain-raiser. It makes an effective group,
and its addiction to variety is redeemed to some extent by the
one factor common to each part: the pink aggregate units which
pop up in a different shape and role each time. Paving and planting are well handled, and the survival of the pool and sculpture
is witness to its public acceptance. For the fourth phase of 1969,
off South Street, *Naismith* used a more relaxed brick treatment,
and his LIBRARY AND ARTS CENTRE of 1973 are quite at
ease, in plain white harl.

Past the Town Centre goes SOUTH STREET, whose remaining side is early C19, starting with a slim flatiron block. The

ground floor of Nos. 21–23 is rusticated, with a double Ionic columned porch to the shop. The OLD MEAL MARKET INN is C18, twin-gabled again, and then the A68 takes the l. fork past the startling Flemish clock tower of the CO-OPERATIVE SOCIETY building by *J. W. Maclean*, 1887. After the LODGE of Newbattle Abbey (*see* p. 345) the road leaves Dalkeith by way of NEWMILLS BRIDGE over the South Esk. Three arches, 1756, widened in 1814 and reconstructed in 1839 by *James Jardine*, engineer, *James Lees*, builder.

High Street now widens out, granite-causewayed from end to end. One of its few distinguished early C19 fronts, No. 75 with a windowed pediment, happily faces the entry from South Street. On the corner of the Edinburgh Road junction (formed in the C18) the baronial ROYAL BANK by *Peddie & Kinnear*, 1870. A key C18 building in the curve of the E side is No. 160, which has a windowed chimney-gable; another on the W is the little gable end just before St Nicholas' church. This forms one side of BRUNTON'S CLOSE, and its long flank is now exposed by demolition which in 1973 made possible a meaningless rubbly garden. After the church in its unusually prominent position, the broadened street which is now rather pointless was once the busiest part of the market centre. However it is still faced by the tolbooth (*see* p. 158) and the CROSS KEYS HOTEL built *c.* 1800 by the Duke of Buccleuch. Five-bay front on a channelled base with a Doric pilastered doorpiece and an arched stable pend. Delicate blind balustrades to the first-floor windows. From here onwards High Street has largely been rebuilt, first on the E side with the early gabled tenements of exemplary snecked masonry by *T. Aikman Swan*, *c.* 1935, and then with the midly Scots block by *Forrester*, 1937, on the far W side. Opposite it, the tenement with tall rubbly chimney which suddenly narrows the street is by *R. J. Naismith*, 1956; in 1959 and 1963 he also did the group on the W side, at HUNT CLOSE, which leads back pleasantly to what must have been a gazebo at the foot of a garden, probably early C19 but now truncated, with a view along the valley to Dalkeith Palace. The VOLUNTEER ARMS by *Peter Whiston*, 1956, is odd, combining Naismith's random rubble with shutters and other intimations of Mediterranean sunlight and gaiety. United only by being so demonstratively stone built, what all this needs is a dominant feature. The gabled Tudor CORN EXCHANGE by *David Cousin*, 1853, would play the part if it did not stand back from the line of Forrester's housing. Seen from the N end the church

apse is still something of a focus. But more than these it is the
negative presence of the disused bus station on the W side that
sets the tone. Northwards the early C18 block at Nos. 228–230,
with scrolled skewputts on both end and wall-head gables, was
piously 'restored' to the rubbly norm *c.* 1935, and reality returns
only in the last stage before the palace gate: to one side No.
175 with its octagon turret and harl-pointing (blessed relief
after all those hungry joints), and then DALKEITH PARK
HOUSE, sober Jacobean baronial in stugged ashlar, *c.* 1840
(*William Burn* did a drawing that probably refers to this). Both
stand behind walls, and the wall opposite is an interesting compound of the fronts of the C17 houses which once crowded up
towards the palace gate.

Parallel with High Street to the E runs ST ANDREW STREET,
formerly Back Street, its redevelopment by *R. J. Naismith*,
1954–73, roughly centred on Duke Street. Behind its front
gardens is a variety of character, from the big-drawn, petrified
vernacular we have seen in High Street through a considerable
repertoire of more recent fashion; all dignified and made more
permanent, if not more lively, by the use of stone.

To the NE of Dalkeith, on the r. bank of the Esk, is the site of
a ROMAN CAMP (*see* Introduction, p. 29).

MELVILLE CASTLE. *See* p. 320.

FARM

CAMPEND, 2 km. NW, on the A68. A symmetrical crowstepped
steading of *c.* 1850. Cottages were built in that year and some
had already been erected in 1829. Farmhouse *c.* 1840.

See p. 525

Sherifhall   Sa Aldmde

1060   DALMAHOY HOUSE   ML*
                      2 km. SSE of Ratho

Dalmahoy was built by *William Adam* for George Dalrymple,
youngest son of the Earl of Stair, finished in 1725, and sold
c. 1750 to the Earl of Morton. It is an austere three-storey
double-pile house with a projecting base and a heavy intermediate string course, crowned by a deep cornice, square balustrade
and spindly urns. Both fronts have seven bays, the first and
last two advanced. Quoins and other dressings are of yellow
sandstone against harled walls, but the W (entrance) front has

* Now Edinburgh.

been stripped to reveal coursed masonry. The central projection added to it in the early C19 matches the rest in its mouldings etc. but has octagonal turrets at the two corners, their pointed roofs rising oddly from blind balustrades. On main-storey level and rebuilt on the new frontage, the original segmental-headed front doorway, its cornice supporting a scrolly coat of arms, was left high and dry when a new front door with a Gothic porte cochère was formed underneath it, on basement level, in 1830. The E front, much less altered, with a similar doorway still in place and a finely carved heraldic cartouche interrupting the string course, is reached by a curved double stair whose inner balustrade is of plain stone, the outer of wrought iron; at the top, a stone bench with a stone cushion. Office wing at the N end of 1787 by *Alexander Laing*, who also made numerous small alterations inside the house. *William Burn* made drawings that probably refer to the 1830 work, and *Brown & Wardrop* carried out some alterations in 1851.

On main-storey level the centre room on the E side has its original cornice and basket-arch chimneypiece with an unusual swept-up centre. A more orthodox type, but of striking brown-veined marble, is in the SE corner room which, like its next neighbour, has simple original panelling in pine. The room in the new entrance block has plain finishings of 1830. What used to be a well staircase to the S of the centre has been a good deal altered, first in the early C19 when it was opened up into the axially placed vestibule through an awkward Roman Doric screen, then in the early C20 when the vestibule was united with the upper landing by cutting an oval hole in the ceiling. All the balusters are of the same design as those on the E front, and at least some of them are contemporary with the William Adam house.

GATES, to the A71. Broad rusticated piers, with applied pilasters fluted and grotty in alternate courses, bearing armorial pedestals with the snake supporters of the Dalrymples. The ball finials are missing. Quadrant flanking walls, one of which meets a two-storey house with crowstepped gables and moulded chimney heads. All *c.* 1725. The disused E gates have solid Greek piers with key-patterned tops.

BRIDGE over the Gogar Burn. 1786, probably by *Alexander Laing*. One semicircular arch on tall piers splayed outwards at the approaches. Parapets decorated with fluting and paterae and earlier coats of arms.

STABLES. Built *c.* 1750, but only a fragment remains,

embedded in later farm buildings: two segmental arches with a Dalrymple armorial panel (probably moved here) in between. CHAPEL. *See* Ratho.

1070   DALMENY   WL*

6 ST CUTHBERT. Dalmeny is famous as the best preserved Norman parish church in the country. It is also richly ornamented and highly finished, though what survives at Tyninghame and at Leuchars in Fife shows that it was not unique in this. Nothing is recorded of the circumstances of its construction, but it has been plausibly suggested that the initiative came from the wealthy lords of Dalmeny, either Earl Gospatric who died *c.* 1147 or his successor of the same name who died in 1166. The components of the design are a W tower, a nave, a narrower and lower chancel and a still narrower and lower apse. The total length is 30.5 m. The only extension of the original plan is the N (Rosebery) aisle built in 1671 and remodelled piecemeal in the first half of the C19; the arms of Archibald Primrose, who bought Dalmeny in 1662, survive on its W wall. The new W tower, on the foundations of the original one which disappeared at some unrecorded date, was designed in 1937 by *Alfred Greig*, who took over in 1927 the restoration begun by *P. Macgregor Chalmers* in 1922. The church is built of a fine greyish-white limestone, possibly quarried at South Queensferry.‡

5 The S door of the nave is the decorative showpiece of the church, although it has only two orders. The voussoirs have one motif each, reliefs in the inner order, reliefs alternating with masks in the outer. The subjects are not all recognizable and it is evident that they are not arranged to any system. One or two are signs of the zodiac, and there is an Agnus Dei, relegated to the bottom inner voussoir on the r. Two of the capitals have volutes and rows of primitive concave leaves; one has interlace and the other a defaced figure subject. Abaci, hoodmoulds and string courses with scroll and leaf patterns as elsewhere in the church. Polygonal inner shafts. To l. and r. of the arch are small single figures, the better-preserved with a sword, spear and shield. The whole door stands in a projection with a band of intersecting arcading over. The nearest Scottish parallel for this

* Now Edinburgh.
‡ The numerous masons' marks were recorded by the late A. J. Turner who noted identical marks at Dunfermline Abbey and Leuchars in Fife (RCAHMS Library).

arrangement is the N door at Dunfermline – indeed the Dalmeny door can be seen as a compilation of ideas from all three of the nave doors at Dunfermline. The W door there has the polygonal shafts and voussoirs with alternate masks and reliefs, the E processional door decorated abaci and an angle mask capital. However, this still leaves a residue of motifs which must come from farther afield. Exact parallels for the Dalmeny strain of volute capitals existed on the destroyed N door of St Giles, Edinburgh, and something very like their short, concave leaves can be seen on a capital from St Helen-on-the-Walls, York (in the Yorkshire Museum). But where should one look for similar small-scale figures flanking the doorhead? Yorkshire again?

Almost all the nave corbel table was destroyed in a re-roofing of 1766, the date on the skewputt at the SW corner. But those of the chancel and apse remain, and repay study. The walls are divided by a string course into a dado and a window zone. Windows with nook-shafts and decorated capitals and hoodmoulds. Some were widened in the C18 or C19, but they have been reduced again to their original size. In the N wall of the nave one centrally placed window as against the three in the S wall (cf. e.g. St Martin at Haddington; Duddingston). The Rosebery aisle has elaborate but inaccurate neo-Norman details. The W tower tries to avoid competing with the original work by drastically simplifying details. It is undoubtedly much too low (cf. Kirkliston). The tower arch, with its half-shafts and plain cushion capitals, is only partly old. The arches of chancel and apse are infinitely more splendid. Both have voussoirs decorated with chevron of slightly varying patterns, chip-carved hoodmoulds, groups of three shafts with scalloped capitals, and plain outer orders to the E. The chancel arch has an extra order of voussoirs with no corresponding shafts. Chancel and apse are covered by rib-vaults similar in construction to the aisle vaults at Dunfermline: the domical profile is the same, and so is the infilling of rubble embedded in mortar with the stones meeting at r. angles at the ridges. This remained for long the usual English procedure, whereas in the C12 in the Île-de-France it was *de rigueur* to make the infilling of coursed ashlar running parallel with the ridge. Only by this more rational and economical approach was progress made towards the dissolution of the immense massiveness of the walls and the sense of enclosure which one enjoys at Dalmeny. The rib profile is a roll between chevron. In place of wall shafts there are corbels carved as heads, some of them monsters, others just about human, and one a muzzled bear (chancel s side). The abaci have a pattern recognizable as an abstraction of the acanthus on the s door abaci at Dunfermline.

FURNISHINGS. STOOLS. Two of three wooden ones bought in 1709 to support collection bowls. – PULPIT. Of timber, in a style sympathetic with the church, the capitals formed as the evangelistic beasts, by *H. O. Tarbolton*, 1928. – FONT. Equally effective in stone, by *Ian G. Lindsay*, 1950. – STAINED GLASS. Three lights in the apse (the Madonna and Child, ss. Margaret 5 and Teresa) by *Lalia Dickson*, 1942. – MONUMENTS, in the churchyard. Opposite the s door a stone coffin decorated on three sides; at the foot a fantastic beast, on the front thirteen doll-like figures under arches, possibly intended as Christ and the apostles. Can it be the coffin of the builder of the church? The absence of carving on the N side suggests that it stood originally against a wall, and burial N of the altar was usually reserved for founders or specially important benefactors. – For the rest, a good collection of C17–18 table-tops and headstones, e.g. to the s of the chancel a table tomb with three skulls on square baluster legs, dated 1699, and a headstone with inverted harp and curlicue top. Some of the C18 stones bear masons' tools.

DALMENY HOUSE, 2 km. ENE. Tudor Gothic, on a gentle rise overlooking the Forth, by *William Wilkins*, 1814–17, and the finest of his houses in this style (Dunmore, 1820, is now a ruin anyway). Sir Archibald Primrose of Carrington acquired the estate in 1662, but the family continued to live in the old tower house of Barnbougle on the shore, resisting Adam's ambitious plans for its romantic enlargement (*see* p. 93), until the third Earl of Rosebery was finally persuaded (it is said, when he got up from dinner and was drenched by a huge wave) to move house a little inland. Wilkins suggested a Corinthian temple, Jeffry Wyatt a Tudor house rather like what was built, but larger, with a tall saloon and staircase in the middle of an H-plan. Wilkins's final solution took better note of the site with its views to N and E, and concentrated on two ranges that would enjoy them; an L-plan with the offices filling in the angle. The commission seems to have been complicated by the particular needs of the family at this time. The fourth Earl succeeded in 1814 and probably occupied the 'private apartments' at the SE corner, his four children being accommodated at the NW and the dowager Countess presiding over the main part of the house.

Turreted and battlemented entrance (E) elevation, with a tall projecting porch flanked by dissimilar bay-windows. The one to the l., eccentrically mullioned and elaborately decorated and turreted, belongs to the Earl's apartments, which have their own s entrance. Long, symmetrical N side with projecting end blocks and central tower. The triangular gables standing up in between have no roofs behind them, and their job is to enliven the skyline of a composition which, like the main corner turrets, is otherwise flat and heavy. But it is very well calculated; the richness of carved panels and battlements is projected upwards into groups of elaborately moulded chimneys, and their prickly topknotted outlines dissolve the bulk of the house romantically into the sky. At this point it must also be mentioned that the NW block, built over a basement storey of wine cellars, is of three floors and not two as it seems. There were servants' rooms on ground level, and then at transom height a mezzanine which, with the floor above, provided rooms for the children. The w side is not systematically composed. The kitchen is in the middle, a charming bay-fronted dairy to the r., the laundry round the corner facing s. The house and its continuous moulded courses are of fine yellow-grey stone, the panels, chimneys and other enrichments of *Coade* synthetic stone shipped from London at a total cost of £5,000.

The interior is Gothic for communicating spaces, mainly Grecian for the rooms. Taking the first, it is rather startling to find, after the two rib-vaulted bays of the entrance hall, the large STAIRWELL of which the outside gave no hint at all. It adjoins the private suite to the s and the main house to the N. The stair ascends round three sides (not symmetrically as first intended) under a three-bay hammerbeam roof with battlemented pendants. The branched Gothic LAMPS in the corners may be mentioned as they are fixtures. The effect of the GALLERY, sidestepping to the s, is not of a romantic infinity of vaulting but of a sequence of fan-vaulted anterooms, each one corresponding to the room alongside, and separated from the next by a four-centred archway. The vaulting, of small cloister scale, springs from simple ribbed shafts without capitals. In the windows on the s side stained glass which may possibly include some old fragments. The principal rooms which open off the gallery have one distinctive detail in common: a slim shaft with reeded head and elongated lotus capital, set back into the grooved uprights of the doorcases. In the LIBRARY at the E end these features punctuate the bookcases; otherwise the room has been altered, partly for structural reasons – the cove deep-

ened and the original cornice and antefixae removed. The
pretty white and yellow Rococo chimneypiece with a head of
Diana in the centre came from No. 36 Berkeley Square, London, to replace a plain Grecian one. In the canted bay to the
E the difficulty of stacking the centre shutters against thin mullions has been solved by sliding them downwards as a sash. In
the DRAWING ROOM a cornice of late C18 character with
quoins and paterae has been substituted for the Grecian original, but the NAPOLEON ROOM is untouched. Designed as the
billiard room, and corresponding with the central tower on the
N front, it is entered beneath a depressed arch with coffering,
and has heavy Greek plasterwork and a neo-classical chimneypiece of white marble with a long frieze of figures. The pelmet,
also Grecian, matches those of the DINING ROOM, where the
ceiling has a huge fretted centrepiece and a bracketed cornice.
The PRIVATE APARTMENTS are on a much smaller scale, with
plain chimneypieces, some with panelled and some with reeded
jambs. One of them has curious flourishes of Grecian Rococo
in the corners of the ceiling cove.

The seven LODGES, all nicely inscribed with their names, explore the romantic vocabulary with occasional classical touches
and are presumably also by *Wilkins*. With the exception of
Barnbougle Castle (*see* p. 93) the other buildings in the park
are not particularly distinguished. Some are probably the work
of the Edinburgh architect *John Chesser* who superintended the
estate works from the death of his father until 1858.

Dalmeny is a spacious feudal village at a T-junction. The WAR
MEMORIAL in the middle, of *c*. 1920, with a heraldic lion on
top, looks like a mercat cross. Cottages look over the broad
green to the main road. There is only one two-storey house, in
front of the church, harled, with stone dressings, and dated
1772(?) on the SE skewputt. The rest are of the first half of
the C19, loosely connected with each other, the earlier of rubble,
the later of snecked ashlar with deep eaves. To each end a delightful prospect between mature trees. The few public buildings are scattered to the SW of the village.

STATION. Built *c*. 1885, probably by *McLaren*, general superintendent, and *Bell*, engineer, a monumental block of rock-faced
yellow sandstone laid in straight courses. Steel lattice bridge
and footbridge.

SCHOOLS. Two single-storey schools in Burgess Road are worth
noticing: the stugged ashlar BOARD SCHOOL with a hint of
Art Nouveau by *William Campbell*, clerk of works at the Dal-

meny Estate, 1909; and the yellow brick PRIMARY SCHOOL with cast concrete window units, *c.* 1970.

FACTORY (Hewlett Packard), Station Road. A good, disciplined block by *Marshall & Morrison*, 1966 and 1969; aluminium-framed curtain walls over a base of concrete blocks which are also used for the partly separated stair tower.

ASHBURNHAM HOUSE. 1899. Roughcast with red stone dressings and red tiles, quite large but prettily detailed, with gabled bay-windows and an octagonal ogee roof over the stair-turret.

ROSSHILL HOUSE. A sentinel at the s end of the Forth Railway Bridge. 1806. Droved ashlar frontage with a pedimented centre and a fanlit door in an arched recess. Later dormers and w wing.

DECHMONT *see* BANGOUR VILLAGE HOSPITAL

DIRLETON
EL 5080

PARISH CHURCH. The parish was officially transferred in 1612 from Gullane to Dirleton, and the new church must have been built soon afterwards. It is long and wide, with round-headed windows under the low eaves. W tower. The s side and roof are interrupted by the pedimented aisle built of ashlar in 1664 by James Maxwell, Earl of Dirleton. It has a stone roof nicely supported along the eaves by stone brackets, and between the rusticated corner piers a loop-traceried window. On the E side a pedimented doorway. The spiky Gothic parapet of the tower, which was redesigned in 1836, stands on a corbel course whose horizontal line accords charmingly with that of the rest of the church. The lowest storey is stone-vaulted inside. Plain interior with a w gallery and a thin Gothic 'chancel' arch. – STAINED GLASS. In the aisle three lights (St Francis and the Animals) by *Margaret Chilton*, *c.* 1935. – On the s side the best is a very naturalistic window (Christ and the Children), after 1893. – MONUMENTS, in the churchyard. An obelisk well sited in front, and to the sw a stone of the scrolly Tranent type, with two stern-faced mermaid caryatids, to George Seton † 1746. – MANSE of 1708, with mid C19 SCHOOL attached.

DIRLETON CASTLE. The site – a rocky outcrop at the E end of a gentle ridge which overlooks the coastal route from Edinburgh – was chosen by the de Vaux who was given the barony of Dirleton in the C12. Stewart Cruden notes that the castle was already described as a *castellum* in 1225, and attributes the earliest and most important stage of the present building to John de Vaux, seneschal to Marie de Coucy who married Alex-

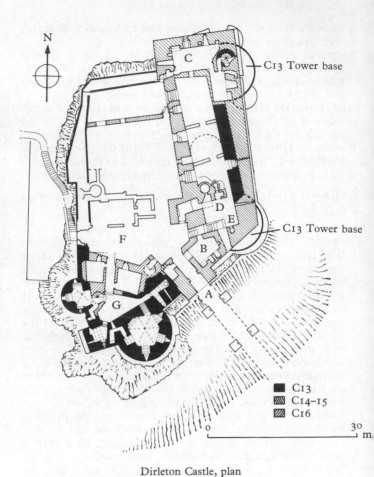

C13 Tower base

C13 Tower base

0   30 m

Dirleton Castle, plan

A Drawbridge   B Guard Room   C Chapel (Prison under)   D Bakery
E Well   F Close   G Inner Close

ander II of Scotland in 1239. Its original perimeter was hardly affected by subsequent work, and its square ashlar is easly distinguished from the rubble walling of the Halyburtons (C14–15) and that of the Ruthvens (C16) with its fancy string courses.

The site was naturally steep to the w, and the other sides were protected by a ditch (now filled in except to the s) whose formation seems to have involved the removal of some of the rock itself. The de Vaux castle of enclosure was built on the resulting eminence, its fronts facing the cardinal points, except that on the s, which actually faces SE. At the sharp sw corner a cluster of C13 towers whose bases spread out to merge into the rock. The largest is the drum tower of the donjon. A square tower adjoins it, splayed into an octagon above basement level; then a short length of wall with a pair of corbelled garderobes, and a smaller drum. The SE side begins with a short length of C13 wall incorporating the pointed arch of a postern gate, but it is interrupted by the forework added to the original main entry by the Halyburtons. Here two massive piers, the l. one with a corbelled garderobe to the side, are united at the head by a pointed arch. Turret corbels at their outer angles. The drawbridge came up between them, and its inner end, when it was raised, fell into a pit. A later version was pivoted further out and its movement was allowed by a splay in the wall under the archway. To the r. of the entry a C14 crosslet window from the guard room. The E face is Halyburton work, built against the original curtain wall to take the strain of their new tunnel-vaulted range and blocking a small doorway in the process. At the ends are the stumps of two more drum towers, with a subsidiary tower attached to the N one. Their projection would originally have been greater, and indeed the N tower has lost its position of vantage at the corner because a second stage of the Halyburton work extended this range beyond the old curtain. The N face of the new work has two windows boldly framed, one quarter-round within another. The curtain on the N and W sides has disappeared. The steps to the w curtain seem to have been formed in the C16.

The entry, with guard room to the r. just beyond the portcullis housing, is Halyburton work of the C14. Once inside the close it is best to turn l. into what was the original inner close, although its N range, with stair-turret, arched pend and jumping string courses, is a C16 rebuild by the Ruthvens on the old plan. The further sides of the triangular inner close contain the de Vaux apartments within the s w group of towers. Their characteristic feature is the solid pointed vault with chamfered false ribs: it appears on the ground floor in the hexagonal room of the donjon and the squarish rooms within the two other towers, one ribbed transversely, the other diagonally, and on the first floor, where the donjon contains the seven-sided LORD'S CHAMBER with seats in three of the window embrasures and a fireplace whose recessed shafts and bell capitals support the corbels, enriched with nailhead, for a canopy. This room connects with its neighbour past one of the numerous garderobe closets, but the other rooms are not interconnected and the original pattern of access is far from clear. A separate passage from the inner close leads past the well to the postern.

The E range was built by the Halyburtons within the old wall of enclosure. Its continuously tunnel-vaulted basement is divided into storerooms, each with its own entry from the close. In the C15 bakery at the S end two ovens and a well. An extension of this range to the N, marked by the change from the shuttermarks of the old vault to the exposed random stones of the new, ends with the CHAPEL, its tunnel-vault running E to W. One of the windows on the N side is seated. In the W wall a book cupboard and water stoup, at the SE corner a credence and piscina; between them a door leads to a small room in the thickness of the wall, with its own stair down to the cellars. Under the chapel a PRISON, reached from the close, with a low vault, and a PIT PRISON with hatch access underneath, its floor the solid rock. On the level of the close this range contained the HALL of the Halyburton period. Only the base of its walls now stand, but on the S end wall within the screens area there is still a C15 buffet with a segmental arch with highly stylized leaf-and-stem carving on the voussoirs, and three stiffly carved finials, the centre one carried on an ogee arch with a shield. From the screens a trans leads past a large service hatch to the KITCHEN, the crown of its vault, some 9 m. high, pierced by a circular vent. Arched fireplaces in the N and E walls, and floor hatches to the bakery and the well below. The additions to the N of the hall provided a dais chamber. Other items of interest are all from the C16 Ruthven period. The four-stage DOOCOT is of beehive type, with billet-moulded wall head. GATEWAY nearby, with moulded semicircular arch. The yews in the GARTH to the W are a relic of its original formal planting, but it was subsequently cleared as a bowling green. Embossed floor TILES from the Ruthven building are exhibited in the pavilion.

The W approach leads down past the SCHOOL by *J. A. Carfrae*, 1910, picturesquely composed with 'colonial' gables, and two early C19 cottage rows with crowstepped ends. Overlooked by three substantial houses of the C17–18, the road then descends to the long triangular green, whose short W side has a good show of estate architecture. The CASTLE INN by *William Burn*, *c.* 1820, stands strategically on the corner. Its dormers with bracketed heads are echoed in a two-storey block with a single-storey wing further on. The deep-eaved SWISS COTTAGE (actually one cottage over another) and the LODGE of Archerfield House (*see* p. 77) with its scrolled bargeboards are of the next generation of C19 picturesque. Further to the N lies the church. The long S side of the green is filled mostly by the early C19 wall of the castle grounds, with a little drum-tower pavilion at the angle and the castle itself looming behind. The N side is at no pains to present a continuously built face; numerous cottages, and even the considerable early C19 house of OATFIELD, lurk to the rear. Apart from the trim but nondescript OPEN ARMS HOTEL, the only real frontages are the little Tudor gable of ROSE COTTAGE (again related to the Castle Inn) and the double C18 cottage with rubble walls and pantile roof. Of the same architectural family are IVY COTTAGE with its long three-gabled front, and at the point of the triangle VINE COTTAGE, with wild Gothic dormers breaking up through the eaves, which marks the end of this rather loose enclosure. There is also a second-generation row of five cottages with slate roofs swept down to make porches, and bargeboarded, finialled dormers. The round-headed C16 GATEWAY, formerly an entrance to the castle, now serves DIRLETON MAINS, whose barns were built by *Hurd*, mason, in 1703. Beyond the green some good inter-war housing.

INVEREIL HOUSE. *See* p. 263.

DOON HILL
3 km. S of Dunbar

EL 6070

On a sheltered plateau just below the summit of the hill excavation has revealed the remains of two timber halls set within a substantial palisade. The trenches in which upright timbers have been set have now been filled in with different coloured concrete to indicate the successive phases: (*one*) a C6 A.D. British timber hall set within the surrounding palisade; (*two*) a C7 Anglo-Saxon hall, closely comparable to those at Yeavering, Northumberland, built within the refurbished palisade after a disastrous fire (Department of the Environment).

DREM

Dominated in a friendly way by the STATION, *c.* 1845, which has twin low-pitch gables and a station cottage in similar style beside the forecourt. Iron lattice FOOTBRIDGE by *George Smith*, founder, and a wall-mounted DRINKING FOUNTAIN with a chained cup inscribed NBR [North British Railway] Keep the Platform Dry. The rest is a little farm hamlet with a U-shaped range of single-storey cottages of *c.* 1830. Past them and along the lane is first a row of earlier (possibly C18) cottages and then the mid C19 smithy, much altered. At the end, the STEADING. Its massive archway suggests a date no earlier than 1840, and it has pigeon boxes on one side. The farmhouse, with its own entrance lodge in a later and jollier version of the station cottage style, forms part of the village group.

THE CHESTERS, 1 km. S. A well preserved Iron Age multivallate fort; its low-lying and vulnerable position is unusual (Department of the Environment).

DRUMMORE HOUSE
2 km. WSW of Prestonpans

A house of *c.* 1760 in warm, coursed sandstone with grey dressings, whose stark simplicity makes it look newer. It is three bays long and three storeys high, the pedimented centre, which bears three vases, supported by plain pilasters from top to bottom. The rusticated quoins likewise, and on the back (N) elevation the centre bay is quoined instead of pilastered. No horizontal lines between base course and cornice. Other details are characteristic of their time. All the windows are lugged, the tall ones of the main storey pedimented. The window over the front door has a broken pediment with a shell in the middle, for this was the house of Lord (formerly Sir Hew) Dalrymple of Drummore, who became a Lord of Session in 1726. In the front pediment, between crisp, high relief foliage, is the inscription from James Thomson's poem 'The Seasons':

DEO PATRIAE AMICIS – SEISE THE PLOW AND GREATLY INDEPENDANT LIVE;

In the back one, under the motto STEDDY,

ALL IS THE GIFT OF INDUSTRY, WHATEVER
EXALTS, EMBELLISHES AND RENDERS LIFE
DELIGHTFULL. PENSIVE WINTER CHEARD BY HIM
SITS AT THE SOCIAL FIRE, AND HAPPY HEARS
THE EXCLUDED TEMPEST IDLY RAVE ALONG.

At the E end a semicircular bow, strangely corbelled out on
top (presumably later). To the W an early CI9 two-storey pedimented wing. A CI9 porch covers the lugged front door. The
bracketed segmental pediment that used to crown it, now built
into the garden wall to the E, is inscribed

HOME IS THE RESORT
OF LOVE, OF JOY, OF PEACE, OF PLENTY, WHERE
SUPPORTING AND SUPPORTED, POLISHED FRIENDS
AND DEAR RELATIONS MINGLE INTO BLISS.

The same words have been recut in the new porch, which leads
directly into the hall, lit by a shell-niched bullseye window on
each side. In the room to the l. a late CI8 pine chimneypiece
decorated with thistles. The hall is also the staircase well, unaltered except for some early CI9 infill, with twisty balustered
stair and landing round all four sides. Deeply coved ceiling with
floppy fronds in the corners and a key pattern centre panel.

On the first floor the DRAWING ROOM fills the whole E end.
Rococo ceiling on a bracketed cornice, the conventional foliage
here and there sprouting naturalistic tendrils. From each end
of the central motif two ribbons charged with fruit run out towards the corners, where there are oval framed portrait heads
of the Four Seasons in low relief (one has fallen, and been replaced in flat plaster). The woodwork is elaborately carved.
Window architraves start from the chair rail, and so do two pairs
of Ionic pilasters, those on the E side flanking a little alcove
or canted bay lit by a bent Venetian window, those to the W
supporting the overmantel with trophies (hung on ribbons) of
Law and Government ('Suum Cuique') and Letters ('Plinius'),
of Husbandry and of Music, all meticulously detailed; at the
top, a head of Diana with bows and arrows.* The chimneypiece
is Rococo, of veined white marble, so well carved that it merits
the full title Louis XV, though it is most unlikely that it was
part of the original scheme. The smaller room to the W has
similar woodwork and a lugged overmantel with broken pediment, the chimneypiece missing; otherwise it is plainer, with
a simple cornice and a coved ceiling. On the N side, adjoining

* These exquisite reliefs have now (1977) been coated with gloss paint.

the drawing room, a small lofty room whose chimneypiece has a centre panel of fruit and vegetables pouring from a cornucopia.

GARDEN WALLS of warm stone with red brick tops, and, most unusually, very close to the house on the W side and actually adjoining it to the E. To the W again are FARM BUILDINGS of the original mid C18 date but much altered. The GATEPIERS at the E lodge are alternately blocked and fluted.

1070

DUDDINGSTON HOUSE   WL
2 km. WSW of South Queensferry

Castellated Gothic of c. 1820, attributed to *William Burn*. Excellent construction of droved grey ashlar from Black Quarry, between Newton and Winchburgh, but a very odd design which looks like an early attempt to break away from symmetry. It is all machicolated and battlemented, with hood-moulded rectangular windows bisected by mullions and tracery, those on the upper floor distinctly taller. Nothing could be more symmetrical than the W front, of five bays, with a tall dummy turret at each end. But this is only one limb of an L-plan; there is another and not very useful round turret in the angle, the traditional position for the stair tower. The front door is to one side of it. The E gable has two more elements from the romantic building set – a dummy bartizan on one corner and a couple of Tudor chimneys on the other. On the S side the staircase bow forms a more functional turret over the little office court. On the S wall a triangular dormer head with the initials of the builder of an earlier house, David Dundas, and the date 1585. The interior is very plain, with rudimentary Gothic chimneypieces.

STEADING. Dated 1822 on the back of the entrance arch. It faces the W front of the house. No hesitation about symmetry here. E front with a row of three five-centred arches for cartsheds on each side of the entry, and plain sash-windows on the first floor, except for the hoodmoulded one in the middle. The other show front has wooden Gothic frames to its ground-floor windows. Both fronts are machicolated and battlemented overall, with pint-size corner bartizans. Both the centre sections have thick cable moulding towards the wall head.

ICE HOUSE. Dated 1825.

Asymmetrical Gothic GATEPIERS.

DUNBAR   EL 6070

PARISH CHURCH, at the far S end of the town. 1818–21 by *James Gillespie [Graham]*, in Dunbar Red sandstone from the Boorhouses quarry. It replaced a large and rich collegiate church built by the Earls Patrick and George in 1342, which had become the town kirk in 1560 and received a new tower in 1739. On this raised site the new church, like its predecessor, is a prestigious landmark; boxy late Gothic with battlements and square corner towers, the tall W tower providing a porch. Pinnacled buttresses at every angle, but not bonded into the walls. In 1897 *W. & J. Hay* of Liverpool added the five-sided chancel. Inside, they renewed practically everything. Square overall, it formerly had galleries on all sides, reached by stairs in the corner towers. The reconstruction gave it a W to E axis, with aisles. Five-bay arcade of pink sandstone with round piers and moulded capitals. The shallow roof trusses were exposed and gothicized. The one remaining gallery, occupying the W bay, is fronted with some of the original traceried panelling. The abolition of the others resulted in a superfluity of light, so the unstained windows were filled with amber glass quarries which cast a strange glow.

FURNISHINGS. PULPIT of 1918 and COMMUNION TABLE of 1934. Both good-quality Perp, in oak, but they do not enliven the general effect. – The LECTERN of 1926 does so: a bronze angel supporting the bible with upraised arms. – ORGAN. By *Foster & Andrews* of Hull, 1901. – STAINED GLASS. In the centre of the apse or 'chancel' two tiers of three lights (the Nativity and the Ascension) in dark blue, drab green and gold, by *Edward Frampton*. – On each side an earlier set of glass was re-used in the new tracery; to the l. scenes of Faith and Resurrection, 1865, to the r. the Sermon on the Mount and other New Testament scenes, 1871. Both are by *James Ballantine & Sons*, very crude and wooden with gaudy colours. – On the S side of the church three lights by *Arthur L.* and *Charles E. Moore*, after 1926. – MONUMENTS. At the E end of the N aisle a triumphal-arch wall-monument in polychrome marble and alabaster to George Home, High Treasurer of Scotland and then Chancellor of the Exchequer in England to James VI and I, who created him Earl of Dunbar in 1605. He died in 1611 at Whitehall and his body was brought from London, whence probably his monument followed. He is realistically and sensitively portrayed kneeling at a desk under the arch, the Garter 24

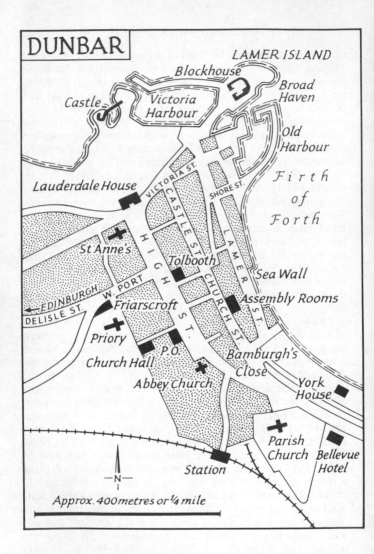

robes worn over his armour. Inscription in a strapwork panel overhead. On each side are knights armoured cap-a-pie, supporting figures of Justice and Wisdom who stand on the upper stage. Fame and Peace appear as low reliefs in the tympana. Heraldic panel overall – nearly 8 m. high altogether. The monument was restored, and its position apparently altered, by *W. Grant Stevenson* in 1897. – On the wall nearby a marble WATER STOUP (two putti holding a shell) is a surprising memorial to the Rev. Robert Buchanan † 1901; it could be of earlier date. – Of the monuments in the churchyard, the older are weathered, the newer undistinguished. The best is a late C17 wall tabernacle to the w, with bulgy Ionic columns and an angel blowing the last trump in the arch. – Early C19 Gothic TOOL-HOUSE. – In the churchyard wall a roll-moulded C17 DOORWAY. – WAR MEMORIAL at the main gate, a red Corsehill sandstone obelisk in memory of the Lothians and Berwickshire Yeomanry who fell in South Africa, by *C. S. S. Johnston*, executed by *W. Grant Stevenson*, 1902.

CHURCH HALL, off the High Street behind the Post Office. 1910. Inside, STAINED GLASS (the Good Samaritan) by *A. Ballantine & Son*, removed from St Giles in Edinburgh for the building of the Thistle Chapel.

ABBEY (former Free) CHURCH. 1850 by *Thomas Hamilton*. E.E. frontage in white Catcraig stone, lanceted gable between blind arcaded wings, a pinnacled turret giving perfunctory asymmetry. Earns all its marks for townscape, closing the s end of the High Street.

ST ANNE (Episcopal), just off the N end of the High Street. 1889–90 by *R. Rowand Anderson*, 'adhering closely to the original ideas of the late Mr Wardrop' his partner. Dec with some Scots detail, in the same Dunbar Red stone as the parish church, but stugged, with smooth dressings. One roof from end to end, clad in bright red tiles which are also used for the makeshift pyramidal roof of the unfinished tower attached to the N side. The N porch near the W end is also unfinished as to bosses and corner crockets. The townward E end has four buttresses, windows in the outer intervals, and a canopied Dec niche (for a figure of St Anne?) in the middle one. Rose window above. The space inside is divided into a nave five windows long whose massive open roof has double ties, the upper one arched and the lower expressively tapered, and a wagon-roof chancel. Tiny St Margaret's Chapel on the s side opposite the porch. The external arrangement of the E end is now explained; it makes possible a reredos (sadly missing, for Lorimer's design of 1893 was not carried out) *and* three E lights finely related to those on the N and S walls. – Oak ROOD SCREEN with figures. 1896 by *Willis*. – STAINED GLASS. The three windows at the E end (the Crucifixion, Resurrection, and Christ in Glory in the rose) are contemporary with the church, by *A. Ballantine & Gardiner*; theirs also are two of the nave windows (Christ and St Peter), 1904. – Then a pair (the Nativity) from the *Abbey Studio*, 1945–6. – In St Margaret's Chapel two lights (the Virgin and St Margaret) by *Heaton, Butler & Bayne*, *c.* 1920.

RECTORY dated 1912, a small but impressive symmetrical Anglo-Scots composition, with harled walls, hipped gables and deep roof, by *W. J. Walker Todd*.

TRINITARIAN PRIORY, Friarscroft, on the W approach. Founded *c.* 1240–8 by Christiana de Brus, Countess of Dunbar. All that survives is the late medieval steeple of the church, converted into a DOOCOT. The tower itself is square and short and stands over a passage between the gables of the former choir and nave. This odd arrangement was usual in English friars' churches and existed also at the Glasgow Blackfriars (see Slezer's engraving of the Old College). Of course there must once have been arches to choir and nave, but the insertion of nesting boxes has obliterated all trace of them. Inside, plain round arches on moulded imposts carry the N and S walls of the tower.

DUNBAR CASTLE, by the harbour. The castle of the Earls of Dunbar. Ruined by order of Parliament in 1567 after Queen Mary's visit to the town, it consisted of a courtyard castle on the rocky peninsula, covered by the S battery on the landward hillock, with an enclosed link crossing the natural bridge between the two. It is now even more dilapidated than in Grose's and Scott's engravings.

BLOCKHOUSE, on Lamer Island. Polygonal, with deep embrasures, probably built by the Duke of Albany *c.* 1522–36. One of the most important survivals of early artillery fortification in Scotland.

THE TOLBOOTH, High Street, is of two storeys and dormered attic, with a pseudo-hexagonal (actually five-sided) stair-tower capped by a slated piend roof and then a lead-covered, oval-vented spire. Wood-framed spires even of this modest ambition are a rarity in Scotland, and so are the multi-course gableted crowsteps of the S gable which acknowledge Dutch practice (e.g. at Delft). The projecting base and two string courses of the tower suggest a date after 1650. The lower (original) window on the first floor is heavily barred and the top storey of the tower has a sundial on the s w face, a c19 clock facing s and n. Stripped of its harling c. 1920, all the stonework is now badly weathered. Vaulted ground floor. The first floor probably included a strong room. Coomb ceiling under the roof of the Council Chamber above. Bolection-moulded fireplace at each end, both with c18 overmantel panels of the royal arms.

MERCAT CROSS. The pedestal and shaft of the cross have been moved from the centre of the town (where?) and parked in a flowerbed just in front of the tolbooth. Four skewputts carved with human heads salvaged from a demolition have been cemented to the top; an effective oddity.

ASSEMBLY ROOMS (former), in Church Street. A very plain block of 1822, of ironstone rubble with Catcraig dressings. Two storeys over a deep basement and five bays, the first the kitchen with supper-room over, then the entrance and staircase, then the ballroom, which has three big windows looking seaward, three niches on the street side. Bowed balcony entered from the stair landing at one end, wood chimneypiece with thin columns at the other, with a coved ceiling over a heavy moulded cornice. Most other furnishings have gone and the Rooms are at the time of writing a furniture store.

LAUDERDALE HOUSE. 1790–2 by *R. & J. Adam*. About 1740 Captain James Fall M.P. built himself the original house on this privileged site at the head of the High Street. His son Provost Robert Fall was obliged to sell it in 1788, but its carcass still forms the centre block (with different masonry treatment) of the enlarged house whose elevations were drawn in October 1792, that is, after the death of Robert Adam in January the same year. Adamized with fluted and patera frieze, balustrade and sphinx, it became a centrepiece between pedimented end blocks a storey higher, the enlarged elevation filling the whole n end of the street without undue grandeur, and still deferring to its scale. Apart from its townscape merit, this pavilion treatment recalls Croome Court, Worcestershire, but here their strong lateral emphasis, going right back to similar pediments on the n elevation, anticipates Soane's Chillington Hall, Staffordshire. At the e end this continuity was lost when a well was cut into it during its conversion in 1859 to military quarters. On the n* front too this pavilion suffered by the insertion of new windows, but the w pavilion still shows the intended relationship of central Venetian between two smaller lights. The half-round portico with four giant Ionic columns in the middle of this front was poorly executed, but would be more at home overlooking the parkland of the Adam sketch than the asphalt of today's disused barrack square. Of the interior furnishings, one plain stone chimneypiece remains in the centre block. The neighbouring two-storey BARRACKS were built in 1911.

STATION. 1845, with a T-plan Tudor station house in ironstone with Catcraig dressings. Ground-floor windows hoodmoulded, first-floor windows gabled. Modernizations of 1963 removed the arched public entrance (and the date stone, now in the garden) but creditably slipped plain steel joists over the track to support the original fretted canopies. One of a pair of matching cottages survives. The iron footbridge by *Macfarlane* of Glasgow was moved from Ayton, Berwickshire.

DESCRIPTION

Strategically placed on the coastal strip between Berwick and Edinburgh, Dunbar owes its name (Gaelic: the fort on the point) to the castle which belonged to the Earls of Dunbar until its forfeiture, together with the town, to James I in 1434. A royal burgh from 1445, Dunbar was twice sacked by Hertford: in 1544 and again (when he was Duke of Somerset) in 1547. Fynes Morrison noted that it 'lay ruined' (1598), and there are few signs of recovery (though the present High Street seems to have been formed in the early C17) until after Cromwell's victory against the covenanters at the battle of Dunbar (1650), when he spent £300 on works at the E pier. To a prosperous market town, port, and fishing harbour the late C18 added importance as a garrison town which only ceased after 1945, replaced to some extent by C20 tourism. The population of 4,500 is below the C19 level, though more widely spread. The town's own building stones range from deep Dunbar Red to pink sandstone, fine Catcraig limestone, and orange ironstone. Villas of the early C20 are surprisingly few, but a small group in MARINE ROAD includes ST RULES by *T. Duncan Rhind*, 1903, in rock-faced red sandstone, with a strong composition of green-slated roofs, the smaller gables half-timbered, the larger tilehung.

In 1768 three gates or rather ports were standing: at the W end of West Port, at the S end of the High Street, and at its E entry (possibly the W entry to the older town).

The W entry (*see* Belhaven) begins with the EDINBURGH ROAD. Local authority housing on both sides: to the S by *George Simp-*

son of Edinburgh in the 1920s; to the N by *Wheeler & Sproson*, 1965–70, harled and pantiled, a well-calculated series of gables to the road, a diversity of house types including patios and maisonettes on the rising ground to the rear. Then after a garish interlude the first outlying villa, EDEN HOUSE of *c.* 1820, with Dunbar's standard Ionic doorpiece. At the foot of the dip the C18 FRIARSCROFT STEADING with octagonal horsemill and the priory DOOCOT in the field behind. On the other side CASTELLAU HOUSE, with an Ionic doorpiece and a big bow at the W end, all in imported yellow ashlar much overcleaned on restoration in 1972 as a public library. In DELISLE STREET a good sequence of closer-packed late Georgian villas, the biggest, No. 3, of five bays plus flanking block and stable archway keeping up the continuity to each side. Up on the level the town really begins with WEST PORT and a continuous row of houses of *c.* 1750. Nos. 15 and 17 have coarse metal canopies over shops. Nos. 7 and 13 are still houses, and the latter still has an anta doorcase and scrolled skewputts.

Entry from the S. This is the direction in which later C19 Dunbar expanded, but first on the r. comes KIRKHILL HOUSE, a villa of *c.* 1800 with an Ionic doorpiece. Its address is ROXBURGHE TERRACE, but this properly applies to an ambitious group of bay-fronted houses of *c.* 1880, in blocks of 2–1–4 with linking walls. NEWHOUSE on the l. is thin Tudor of *c.* 1840 added to an C18 farmhouse, with a tower of *c.* 1870. NEWHOUSE STEADING, with an octagonal horsemill, is now a discreetly restored adjunct to a filling station. ROXBURGHE LODGE on the r., polychrome Renaissance of *c.* 1885, was extended soon after in less sumptuous fashion as the Roxburghe Hotel. QUEEN'S ROAD begins with a gay Regency villa on the r. with a seaward bow, puritanized with grey cement. Then BOWMONT (dated 1884), a powerful trio of terraces wilfully diverse in gable treatment but unified by huge segmental pedimented dormers throughout; probably a speculation by the farmer J. H. Bowe, who lived in No. 1. (His monogram also appears on YORK HOUSE (Cottage Hospital since 1927) of *c.* 1900 downhill towards the sea, elaborately half-timbered, pargetted and red-tiled.) On high ground to the l. is the BELLEVUE HOTEL, *c.* 1900 by *James B. Dunn*, Queen Anne Baronial, splendidly entered between bridged turrets, if a bit thin on the other elevations.

The HIGH STREET, a quarter of a mile long, was observed by Cobbett in 1832: 'So wide as to be worthy of being called an

oblong square instead of a street.' He deplored what he
regarded as the rapacious system behind its market function,
which is now supplanted by parked cars. Otherwise its present
aspect is still intensively developed C18 vernacular, or rather
redeveloped, for many backlands survive from the early C17,
when the street was probably laid out; e.g. at No. 23, BAM-
BURGH'S CLOSE runs back between low-rise houses till it
meets a C17 one, which it penetrates by a pend under the forestair, then threads its way down to Church Street. The short
length of wall to the r. of the house represents the S limit of
the C17 town and may thus be part of the wall noted by Defoe
in 1769; a peripheral wall built and maintained by individual
proprietors rather than a town wall proper, though the town
would have closed it with the South Port across this end of the
High Street. (A similar close is entered at No. 73.) But the
Georgian High Street begins well to the S, with on the r. TEM-
PLELANDS, a short terrace of c. 1820 with Ionic doorpieces. ST
GEORGE'S HOTEL is inscribed 'Aedificata 1625, Renovata [i.e.
completely rebuilt] 1828' and has a spirited sign, with a dragon,
curiously placed on the ceiling of the Roman Doric porch. The
lane at the side leads down past former coach houses to the old
Assembly Rooms building (*see* p. 185). On the l. is the POST
OFFICE dated 1904, by *H.M. Office of Works*, as urbanely
Baroque as its single storey of fine yellow sandstone allows, but
just as much out of scale with the street as its too tall contemporaries, which are luckily few. The countryfied POST-
MASTER'S HOUSE behind is equally accomplished and equally
inappropriate. The NEW INN (now Eventide Home) is late
C18, with a Roman Doric porch (but no bases) and a side archway leading to a coach house. For the rest the street consists
largely of three- and occasionally four-storey Georgian tenements, often distinguished by wall-head chimney gables (No.
58, a key frontage, has the finest with a pair of bullseye lights),
with pends (some, e.g. No. 63, with rusticated and pedimented
C18 entrances) leading to the backlands. No. 99, a regular six-
bay C18 front, is important at the end of the view along West
Port. No. 65 has one of the very few decent shopfronts (c. 1850),
but the painting of most frontages is correct and effective; not
so the false cement masonry imposed on too many of them in
the 'Dunbar Improvement Scheme' commemorated on a
plaque at No. 123.

In VICTORIA STREET (formerly Cat's Row) Nos. 1–9 form a
Tudor terrace of c. 1840 with big carriage pends in each house.

Then come three C20 housing redevelopments. The first, of
1935, is in a terrace of staggered pairs, with roofs and porch-
archways of black pantiles. The second, of 1953 by *Basil Spence*,
goes right down to the harbour, a brave combination of old and
new practice in rubble, colour wash, and slimly detailed concrete, stepping deftly downhill but self-conscious behind its
fussy boundary walls. This, like the third development, of 1962
by *Sir Robert Matthew, Johnson-Marshall & Partners*, received
a Saltire Society Housing Award, but the two could hardly be
more different. The last mentioned, in plain white harl and
weatherboard with no pitched gables, is simpler in its use of
the site and presents fewer maintenance problems. In the midst
is the early C19 VOLUNTEER ARMS, restored as part of the
second scheme; a well-head is marked in front of the first. At
the foot of Victoria Street (site of the old mercat cross?) are
two barely surviving blocks of old Dunbar, including a large
four-by-ten-bay warehouse. The rest is domestic, of little individual but much townscape value, like the corbelled corner
of Shore Street, and at the time of writing still hangs in the
balance. The C18 Customs House stood (until 1954) beyond.
LAMER STREET runs s between tall early C19 rubble industrial
buildings with two good domestic interludes. It is finely split
by the forestaired gable of the MALTINGS, with two kilns on
the further street front.

The OLD HARBOUR has two dates, 1574 and Cromwell's grant
in 1650. The wall has indeed two types of masonry – large random rubble, and the stratified kind with vertical joints. Two
wall walks, the lower recessed for mooring posts. Traces of a
cantilever stair down to the water, now silted up and boatless.
Excellent cobbles. Opposite the Old Harbour is the three-by-
five-bay CROMWELL HOUSE; the twin iron lamp posts in
front ('*Dunbar Foundry* 1836') supply an acceptable date for
its exterior (the doorpiece is missing and it has an odd crowning
string course with pendant guttae) and for the quirky geometrical wood and plasterwork within. But the staircase has twisted
balusters and a heavy kinked handrail of *c.* 1770 at latest. Then
four good C17–18 houses at the SHORE; beyond them and the
maltings an impressive length of sea wall possibly built after
the parliamentary order for coast town walls in 1503. In front
of the Old Harbour a MEMORIAL as a pedestal for a barometer
(now missing), with the inscription 'Presented to the Fishermen
of Dunbar to whose Perilous Industry the Burgh owes much
of its Prosperity' on a sail looped from spar and oars with a

swag of shells in relief, and a fisherman leaving his family; by
A. Handyside Ritchie, dated 1861. BROAD HAVEN, the
smallest of three harbours, is formed by the causeway to
Lamer Island with its C16 blockhouse. VICTORIA HARBOUR,
begun in 1844, with granite harbour wall, is entered from the
W past the castle ruins, which were further damaged in its building.

BOURHOUSE. *See* p. 122.

1070 DUNDAS CASTLE WL*
1.5 km. S of South Queensferry

The new castle designed by *William Burn* in 1818 is plain Tudor
Gothic, of two storeys with battlements; a quietly efficient
rather than a lively composition. To the W is the pointed archway of the stable court, in a long blank wall at r. angles to the
S front. This begins with the family rooms (in two sections, the
second with a canted bay-window), and then builds up to the
slightly bigger scale of the main block whose l. half is compassed
by a porch, wide-arched and corner-turreted; the other half
accommodates the canted bay of the drawing room. Round the
corner (a thin round turret providing the undramatic hinge),
the E front has the big hoodmoulded windows of the principal
rooms, overlooking from this eminence the distant city of Edinburgh – three windows for the drawing room, then for the
library the turreted centrepiece with armorial gable, three more
windows for the dining room, and finally a dead stop with a
square tower. The pattern of glazing that must have added a
modicum of intricacy to this sternly functional progress has
been replaced by blank plate glass. Plain symmetrical office
block to the N. The visual relationship of the old castle (*see*
below), standing in the yard, with the new one is merely accidental.

Shallow porch rib-vaulted in plaster with feudal-looking
heads as corbels. Its great width embraces the flanking windows
that light the square ENTRANCE HALL with its ingenious ceiling (narrow arches all round, their heads linked by diagonal
and transverse ribs to the flattened grid of the centre). An oak
chimneypiece with primitive Ionic columns was added by
C. H. Greig in 1900 – a direct affront to its crisp Gothic. Twin
archways lead on to the staircase and to the GALLERY, which
runs past the three main rooms (originally *en suite*), ribbed and

* Now Edinburgh.

bossy like the hall, but admirably varied in its vaulting system. Of the first three bays, the middle one has canopied niches. In the DRAWING ROOM what must be one of the first of Burn's lacy Jacobean ceilings, with pendants, over a deep-cut foliage cornice. Doorcases of later C19 French character, with putti representing Painting and Architecture in overdoor roundels. In the LIBRARY a ceiling of nine rectangular compartments over a bracketed cornice. Round Burn's stone Tudor fireplace the woodwork has been Jacobeanized, probably by Greig. The room is given its character by mellow plum-coloured damask, hung curtain-wise on the walls. The DINING ROOM has a similar ceiling, but Burn's chimneypiece has been replaced with a delicately moulded and fretted specimen of C17 workmanship, in stone.

The STAIRCASE was reclothed in thin Jacobean by *Greig*, with hollow tapering balusters and newels. Burn's general plan was retained, but of his Gothic treatment only the big window survives. The last feature of the interior is a mystery: three rooms with mid C18 finishings apparently imported – perhaps from London *c.* 1930, but in any case with great skill and care. In one of the bedrooms on the E side fretted doorcases crowned with vases in concave broken pediments, a lugged chimneypiece with yellow marble slip, and even a matching cornice. On the ground floor of the family part two more rooms complete with their Rococo ceilings. The first has a central sunburst with an interesting combination of free modelling and regular garlands around it. The second has bold ribbon modelling and figures of eight at each end of a central oval which has been filled with a poor imitation of the same kind of work. The cornice is equally uninspired.

FOUNTAIN AND SUNDIAL to the E. A tremendous Renaissance affair with three square basins on each elevation, a bulging frieze over each with a mask waterspout, and then a full-dress entablature. All this makes a platform, reached by a flying stair, for a baluster sundial on winged terms. The Latin inscription says that it was built by Sir Walter Dundas in 1623.

The OLD CASTLE is presumed to have been built soon after the licence was granted in 1424 'to build a tower or fortalice of Dundas in the manner of a castle with the kernels [crenellations] etc. usual in a fortalice of this sort according to the manner of the Kingdom of Scotland'. L-plan with the open angle and entrance to the SE, soon enlarged by a supplementary jamb at the NW corner. This seems to foreshadow the defensive Z-plan in which all the main walls are overlooked by shot-holes, but there is no such provision here, nor any defensive arrangements, except possibly the diamond-shaped plan of the extra jamb. The whole thing is rubble-built with large smooth quoins and a slight chamfer on one corner of the jamb. At the head of the wall C16 corbels carry a battlemented parapet with, on the external angles, bartizans bearing Dundas shields on their outer faces. Most of the windows have been enlarged, and the main door, formerly round-headed, has been squared up. It has an iron yett. From here the main turnpike, buried in the angle of the wall, ascends to the first floor, where the hall has a large fireplace with a segmental arch between attached columns, presumably original. The ceiling, formerly of timber, is now brick-vaulted. The kitchen has been moved from the original s jamb to the new N w one. The stair, at some time re-routed with a straight flight overlooked by a hatch in the ceiling, now arrives on a landing adjoining the screens. C16 moulded fireplaces in the rooms on the second floor. The former service stair, rib-vaulted at the head, has been adapted to give access to the new jamb with its tunnel-vaulted rooms, and a further stair leads up to a circular lookout tower on the roof.

COLLEGIATE CHURCH (ST MARY). In the grounds of the now demolished Dunglass House, within sight of the sea. Of long low outline with a stocky little tower at the crossing. Externally it is the fine coursed ashlar and the slab roofs that tell, for carved and moulded details are few and most windows have lost their tracery. The side windows of the choir are still complete, all with two ogee-topped lights under a segmental head. Their nearest parallel is the s transept window at the South Queensferry Carmelite church, which dates from soon after 1441. Dunglass church is almost certainly of this period too, for a college was founded here some time before 1450, probably in 1443. The E window of the choir has a pointed head, but the tracery as well as the wall beneath was ripped out to let in carts when the church became a barn. On the N side is a sacristy-cum-burial aisle with one detraceried N window and no buttresses. The choir has buttresses only at the outer angles of the E wall. In the s wall a priest's door. Round head continuous with the jambs, the mouldings a roll with fillet flanked by hollows. Bell bases and hoodmould with big carved terminations. Over the arch a canted shield and mantled helm and over that an image niche. The E gable like the others has skews with cusped and crocketed gablets and heads. In the end walls of the transepts windows formerly of two lights beneath which the wall projects as a sort of continuous set-off. The tower has in each face a single cusped lancet, and must once have carried a timber spire. The corners of the N and S faces are connected to the transepts by sloping pieces of wall. Those on the W have to be canted out to reach the transept walls, an awkwardness due to the addition of the tower and transepts to an existing nave, as will become clearer inside. The nave is taller than the choir and transepts. N and S walls are identical, each with two buttresses (the W ones set back from the angles), a window in the E bay and a round-headed door in the W bay.

Internally, every division except the crossing has a pointed tunnel-vault. In the choir, very pretty triple SEDILIA with cusped and crocketed ogee canopies, pinnacles and angel corbels, one holding a shield, the other playing a lute. To the r. of the site of the altar a big corbel with a blank shield projects from the wall. In the choir and N sacristy several CONSECRATION CROSSES. The vaults have large numbers of beam holes presumably for floors put in when the church was a barn. The E arch of the crossing is the only arch which has foliage capitals and proper Late Gothic mouldings, and is also the only one that fits happily against the adjacent walls. The explanation is that it originally formed the chancel arch of a church consisting of chancel and nave only. The foundations of nave walls on the line of the N and S crossing arches have been found. The other crossing arches are clearly insertions, and the E walls of the transept have been cut back to receive them. The plan of the crossing is extraordinary, for the tower stands within rather than above it. The builders obviously wanted to have transepts of a decent width (i.e. wider than the existing chancel arch) and a square as opposed to an oblong tower. A complicating factor was the slightly greater width of the nave compared to the choir, but even so it would have been possible to contrive solid corners taking up the difference in width between the arches and the sides of the tower. As it is, the crossing works as a barrier between the four arms of the cross instead of linking them spatially. – MONUMENTS. In the N wall of the sacristy a segmental tomb recess with fine mouldings. On each jamb a female head, one, specially nicely carved, showing a lady dressed in the fashions of the mid C15. To l. and r. small corbels, the W one with a lute-playing angel. – Tomb recesses also in the end walls of the N and S transepts. The one in the N transept has the arms of Sir Thomas Home and his wife, the grandparents of Sir Alexander Home, founder of the college at Dunglass.

Of DUNGLASS HOUSE itself (*see* Introduction, p. 56) nothing survives. It was designed by *Richard Crichton* for the antiquary Sir James Hall in 1807, gutted by fire in 1947 and subsequently demolished. There Crichton's classicism was picturesque; at the STABLES (converted to a house) it is monumental. Two parallel ranges with pedimented ends, forming a square. Centrepiece with a pediment over a thermal window. Hexagonal GAZEBO, dated 1718. Rusticated angles. Each face has Roman Doric pilasters flanking a depressed arch that pushes up into the architrave. The C17 SUNDIAL, on a mound to the E of the church, has four antae supporting a sharply profiled and disproportionately large cornice, then a little cube for the dials. LODGE with shallow-pitch roof and deep eaves, GATE-PIERS with paterae and ball finials, both contemporary with the house.

BRIDGES. Four in all, crossing Dunglass Dean. The 'new bridge' designed by *George Burn* in 1797 for the old post road promptly collapsed but was rebuilt in much the same form, with two rustic arches and battlemented parapets. The similar single-span bridge to the E was opened in 1798. The railway viaduct, of c. 1840, has battered piers and a main span of 40m. It is the spectacular work of *Grainger & Miller*. The A1 now crosses a reinforced concrete bridge by *Blyth & Blyth*, 1932.

0070   DUNTARVIE CASTLE   WL
3.5 km. WSW of South Queensferry

Now a ruin, the interior inaccessible, Duntarvie was built in the late C16 by the Durham family. The S front of the long main block is treated with impressive and (for the house of a middling Scottish landowner) precocious symmetry: five bays with a modest entry in the middle, a heavily rolled string course under the big windows of the *piano nobile*, and then much smaller windows immediately under the straight eaves course or cornice. The rhythm is broken only at the centre, with a panel for a coat of arms, and little windows overhead which light the staircase running from front to back of the building. Two square towers are attached to the ends of the N side, with turnpikes corbelled out at first-floor level in the re-entrant angles. So this front is symmetrical too – indeed more so, for in the C17 the main block was lengthened to the W, and the S front thus knocked off balance.

EAGLESCAIRNIE   EL 5060
2 km. ESE of Bolton

Built c. 1760, with a canted bay on the S front. E extension of c. 1830. The RCAHMS suggestion of a C17 date for the stair-turret at the back is rather dubious, for it contains a distinctively C18 stair. Detection is difficult because the whole thing was burned out in the C20, and the thinly restored interior has only one attraction, a large mid C18 white marble chimneypiece in the E drawing room. Caryatid terms on flared pedestals support a rich cornice. Between them a frieze carved with a very informal gathering of gods and goddesses. The chimneypiece is said to have come from the Senate Room of Edinburgh University's Old Quad, but its original home is unknown.

STABLES. Of c. 1800. Centrepiece with a simple pediment and a pair of Gothic windows, one either side of a flight-holed bullseye opening and a stone panel dated 1595 from an earlier house.

EAST CALDER   ML 006c

OLD PARISH CHURCH, at the W end. C16. A simple rectangle of rubble, now a ruin. In the E gable a pair of chamfered lancets; the W gable is carried up in stages to a C17 bellcote. Disused since 1750, when the parish was joined with that of Kirknewton, the church has been divided by thick spine walls into three plain burial enclosures. – MONUMENTS, in the churchyard. The C17 and 18 stones are distinguished for their crudity; an exception is the Rococo headstone of 1731 to the W of the church. – To the S a much earlier stone, shaped like a small coffin, carved with a sword on top and various attributes, including shears and a huge key, in high relief on the chamfered edge.

PARISH CHURCH (former United Presbyterian). 1886, Gothic, with a spirelet and a stair-wing flanking the traceried gable.

Although the smallest of the Calders, this one has a long main street mainly of the later C19 and continuous with the A71. To the W the REGISTRAR'S OFFICE, a little single-storey villa with a Roman Doric doorpiece, nicely set back. Near the middle, two pleasingly conservative housing developments of the C20: on the N side a row of dormered cottages built in rubble by the Scottish Veterans Garden City Association, 1924; on the s, Nos. 79–121, designed by *D. Dewar* (Midlothian County Council), *c.* 1970, two-storey houses and flats and a few shops combining rubble with rendering, the centre set back to form a landscaped square.

ALMONDELL COUNTRY PARK. The entrance is at the E end of the village. The GATEWAY, a segmental arch between two piers which have rusticated vertical bands, belonged to Almondell House, built by Henry Erskine *c.* 1791 but demolished in 1969. The BRIDGE over the river Almond, of *c.* 1800 and attributed to *Alexander Nasmyth*, with two rocky arches and a crenellated parapet, is now tree-grown and half ruined. FOOT-BRIDGE of 1966 by *Morris & Steedman*, a long, slender beam hung on cables from a single pylon.

EASTER BROOMHOUSE *see* SPOTT

EAST FORTUNE   EL

EAST FORTUNE HOUSE. Dated 1768 on the keystone over the front door. Three bays, two storeys and ventilated cellars, with rusticated quoins and neat stone margins, the stone strip under the eaves punctuated inexplicably by four inset wood blocks showing their end grain. The interior is much altered, but the half-round stair (not centrally placed) is original. So apparently is the kitchen fireplace in the E wing. DOOCOT of lectern type, of the same period, with three fancy finials and a blind Venetian window towards the house. It is in the s wall of what seems to have been an C18 steading. Cartsheds are suggested by the row of round piers on the N side, where the house stands on a natural terrace. The STEADING, a long range with parallel sheds behind, is dated 1882.

EASTHOUSES   ML
3 km. SSE of Dalkeith

PARISH CHURCH, Bogwood Road. 1954 by *Alan Reiach & Partners*. A plain white harled church on a hilly site, with hall attached and a rubble bell-tower, all roofed with pantiles; agreeably related to the surrounding local authority houses, and especially to the neighbouring square of BOGWOOD COURT (two storeys over shops) and the pub opposite, which were all built about the same time.

EAST LINTON

EL 5070

PRESTONKIRK PARISH CHURCH (ST BALDRED), on a hillock to the E of the town. The chancel is by far the most worthwhile piece of C13 church architecture in Lothian. What survives is the E wall and the much truncated side walls attached to a plain late Georgian church of 1770.* There has evidently been some restoration (the hoodmoulds in particular look suspicious), but the flavour is still Early Gothic at its purest. In the E wall three slender lancets of equal height separated by narrow chamfered buttresses. Angle buttresses at the corners, to the E with gabled tops. Plain single lancets in the side walls. The very high unmoulded plinth is unusual and may be a later alteration.

The Georgian church was recast by *James Jerdan* in 1891–2. He opened new windows (though sticking to the same round-headed type), abolished the galleries, and concentrated the interest of the interior at the W end with an arcaded Renaissance SCREEN, one half housing the ORGAN by *H. S. Vincent* of Sutherland, the other opening grandly into the vestry. – STAINED GLASS. On the S side St Baldred by *William Wilson*, after 1955. – MONUMENTS, in the churchyard. The front of a burial enclosure, *c.* 1770, attached to the E end of the church. – To the SW the very informative headstone of Andrew Meikle, inventor of the threshing machine, † 1811 *aet.* 92.

ST ANDREW (former Free Church), The Square. German Romanesque, mainly of 1879, with a slated helm spire; this is the town's chief landmark.

BRIDGE over the Tyne. The two four-ribbed arches and huge stepped cutwater are of the C16, the upper parts 1763 and later.

RAILWAY BRIDGE. Of *c.* 1845.

'East' distinguishes the town from West Linton in Peebles-shire, and the name Linton refers to the rocky falls of the river Tyne. A small town of red whin and sandstone (plus grey, pink and yellow in the course of the C19) – some of the older buildings are pantiled – it makes the most of an up-and-down site, and its spaces are well defined. The A1 by-passes the town. On the approach from the W is the octagonal MARKET HALL, mid C19 with pointed slate roof, of the cattle market.

* The chancel was the burial place of the Smeaton family, and this no doubt ensured its survival.

The approach from the N is past BROWN'S PLACE, a semi-formal early C19 development in which single-storey terraces alternate with two-storey houses with columned doorpieces. Then to the E, secluded from the road, PRESTONKIRK HOUSE (formerly the East Lothian Combination Poorhouse) by *Peddie & Kinnear*, 1864. PARK END, a red-tiled and white-painted villa of 1910, looks up to the HIGH STREET, which is quite narrow in the middle as it climbs the slope. No. 30 has a circular stair-turret against its N gable, but spreads out into a triangular space at each end. At the N end a good group of plain C18 houses to close the view, but the space to the S is larger – a real town centre whose focus is the cast-iron FOUNTAIN presented by John Drysdale of Buenos Ayres in 1882, with three lamps and four urn-carrying boys pouring water into the basin. The row that closes the view is called THE SQUARE. Of its three C18 houses the end one has become a shop, with an extra storey. At the other end, behind a weeping ash, is the surprising St Andrew's church (*see* above).

There are two exits from the triangle, one down MILL WYND, which has pantiled cottages and former mill and kiln buildings, mainly C18, the other into BRIDGE STREET past a red stone terrace of *c.* 1800 whose return end is another excellent vista-stopper. The harled C18 house at No. 4 BRIDGEND does the same job at the bottom of the winding street, by the bridge. A different and more obtrusive bridge is that of the railway, but its effect is lightened by the lattice construction characteristic of this part of the former North British Railway (*see* Drem). The STATION HOUSE of *c.* 1845, now disused, has an advanced centre carried up to a battlemented parapet with dummy bartizans, and a hoodmoulded window over an octagonal columned doorpiece. Across the road is the HARVESTERS HOTEL of *c.* 1800, with a pedimented centre and a Roman Doric doorpiece.

HAILES CASTLE. *See* p. 246.
PENCRAIG HILL. *See* p. 379.

FARMS ETC.

KIRKLANDHILL, 2.5 km. ENE. Crowstepped steading and farm-house of *c.* 1830. To the SW a STANDING STONE, 3.35 m. high.
KNOWES, 1.5 km. ENE. The pantiled steading, of varicoloured red rubble, is by *James Hannan*, mason, and *Adam Dickson*, wright, 1819. In 1854 the same tradesmen built a large exten-

sion to the Georgian farmhouse. *J. Farquharson* designed additions to the steading in 1893.

LUGGATE, 2 km. s. A very complete steading of *c*. 1820, of coursed red rubble with freestone dressings, the roofs pantiled. Cartsheds on both sides of the road, their roofs inclined with the slope. Cattle courts entered between massive square piers, the intermediate troughs with pantile roofs supported by bold timber cantilevers. To the N the turnip shed has a roof like an inverted pyramid, with similarly solid timbers. The threshing mill to the W has a later round chimney of red brick. FARM-HOUSE to the s of the same period, remodelled *c*. 1840.

OVERHAILES, 2.5 km. WSW. A handsome white-harled farmhouse of *c*. 1760 looking across the river at Hailes Castle. Stone dressings, including a Gibbs-surround front door and four bullseye windows. Adjacent steading of *c*.1830 with a stumpy square tower. To the N a range of cottages of 1857.

PHANTASSIE, immediately to the E of the town. John Rennie the engineer was born here in 1761. About 1820 his elder brother George added a new wing to one end of the C18 farmhouse, suppressing the ground floor into a basement and placing the new front door in a plain fanlit arch under a pediment. The canted bays were added *c*. 1840.

  STEADING. A long two-storey front built in ashlar with gabled centre and ends, *c*. 1840.

  COTTAGES. A single-storey half-square of the same period.

  DOOCOT, to the N, approached between garden walls. Bee- 112 hive type, with three string courses and a horseshoe-shaped parapet tilted up to the N side to shelter the flight holes in the roof. It belongs to the National Trust for Scotland, and its 544 nest boxes and fixed ladders are in good repair.

  LIME KILN. Late C18.

PRESTON MILL (The National Trust for Scotland). A beautiful 106 and still functional group, probably of the C18, of variegated orange sandstone with red pantile roofs; that of the polygonal kiln, with oast-house ventilator at the peak, is the dominant feature. Undershot wheel and wooden machinery.

SUNNYSIDE, 1.5 km. s. A steading with a real baronial air by *Peddie & Kinnear*, dated 1856. Pointed dormers, a corbelled loft over the entrance arch, crowstep gables at the ends; all in orange rubble with grey dressings. Slate roofs on the main fronts, pantiled behind. Towards the road the engine house with round yellow brick chimney. On the other side a baronial farmhouse, with a stair-turret in the angle of the L-plan.

TYNEFIELD, 3 km. ENE. A sophisticated farmhouse built *c.* 1820 of black whin with fine cut grey dressings, very much in the manner of *James Burn*. The single-storey pavilion frontage has a segmental opening for the elaborately fanlit door. False Venetian window on each side of it. The central jamb to the rear is of the same height but two-storeyed, with hoodmoulded windows.

4060   EAST SALTOUN   EL

31 PARISH CHURCH. A gaily castellated T-plan Gothic kirk built in 1805 on the site of an older church by John Fletcher Campbell 'as a monument to the virtues of his ancestors'. s tower attached to its flat side to form a session house, then a clock stage, and finally a spire pierced by quatrefoil openings and pointing up over the gentle ridge on which the village is built. Lancets grouped in threes and hoodmoulded. Behind the corbelled battlemented parapet each gable has a chimney (indicating a fireplace in each gallery). Little square bartizans, pinnacled and crocketed, at every angle. Under the N jamb (presumably the Saltoun aisle and gallery) is the Fletcher family vault, with a cusped fleur-de-lys parapet on its N projection. The purpose of the capital letters from A to M, running anticlockwise, incised 1 m. up the walls all round is to provide a key to the location of burial plots in the churchyard. The interior was glumly recast, without galleries, in 1885. The architect was probably *John Lessels*, who presented plans for the work in 1879. In plan and in spirit, but not in all its detail, the church is related to an untitled sketch by *James Adam*; it is certainly the country cousin of his St George's Chapel in York Place, Edinburgh, but the actual designer is most likely to have been *Robert Burn*, the architect of the manse (*see* below). – MONUMENTS. Some good stones in the churchyard, notably one to the SW (John Broun, Farmer, to his wife Margaret Nimmo † 1754) with gingerbread figures and foliage.

The well-treed village straggles up-hill from N to S, beginning with the early C19 former SCHOOL HOUSE; then the late C18 OLD CASTLE and East Saltoun Farm. At the road junction a modest focus is provided by the angel-topped FOUNTAIN (for people and dogs) in granite and Portland stone, a memorial to John Fletcher of Saltoun † 1903. Here a row of three early C19 cottages (bearing Fletcher's initials and the date 1892, when apparently he improved them) looks down the road to West

Saltoun. Further up the main street on the E side the
MANSE, by *Robert Burn*, 1802. The former smithy stands at
the junction with the Gifford road. On the opposite side the
C18 GARAGE HOUSE, much altered, but still with a large ingle
at its N end.

SALTOUN HALL. *See* p. 423.

HERDMANSTOUN, 2 km. N. The house, which was mainly C17,
has now entirely disappeared. The surviving early C19
STABLES have a good S front facing the site. Arched pavilions
at centre and ends. To the W the burial CHAPEL of the St Clairs,
rebuilt *c.* 1840, and across the river a large but ruined lectern-
type DOOCOT. The gatepiers of Herdmanstoun Mains incorporate rusticated stones which may have come from the
house gates.

ECCLESMACHAN

WL *0070*

PARISH CHURCH. The medieval church of St Machan has been
almost entirely rebuilt, but two arched doorways of *c.* 1200 on
the S side have segmental hoodmoulds with serrated undersides.
The l. one has a moulded opening. The date 1710, curiously
incised between the rustications of the lintel over the door of
the session house to the NW, may also apply to the N jamb,
with a two-storey bellcote on its gable, which made the church
into a T-plan. All three gables have little scrolled skewputts.
Round-headed windows on the S front. The windows on the
N and E gables (thermal and Venetian respectively) are later C18.
The final stage, dated 1908 on a sundial mounted on a buttress
to the S, added a W 'chancel', re-using the stones of the earlier
gable, and made the church roughly into a square with a new
porch to the NE. The architect was *John Honeyman*. Inside, the
church became a long nave and N aisle, separated by two piers
formed by quadruple clusters of Roman Doric columns, the
old T-plan defined by segmental plaster vaults, the square completed with two shallow domed compartments. In the session
house an early C18 stone chimneypiece with moulded surround,
pulvinated frieze and cornice shelf, the opening lined with
Dutch tiles of biblical subjects. – STAINED GLASS. On the S
side one light (He is not here, He is risen) by *A. Ballantine
& Son*, 1905. – At the E end three lights (David and SS. Francis
and John) by *William Wilson*, after 1954. – In the N gable one
light (He hath exalted the humble and meek) also by *Wilson*,
but in more modish vein, 1964. – MONUMENTS, in the church-

yard. Some boldly carved C18 headstones to the s of the church, including one to James Mickel † 1728, and one bearing an accurate relief of a plough, dated 1737 on the voluted top. – MANSE. Mostly 1800, enlarged and enriched by *Brown & Wardrop* in 1858, with a triangular carved panel over the porch.

A nice row of C18 cottages faces the church. SCHOOLHOUSE of *c.* 1840, with deep eaves. The large square schoolroom, its pyramidal roof crowned by a lantern, was added *c.* 1910.

OATRIDGE AGRICULTURAL COLLEGE, to the w. A complicated building on the hillside overlooking the village, by *Colin Webster*, 1972. Concrete block construction, the important rooms cantilevered outwards in shuttered concrete. Monopitch roofs. Further to the w a FARMHOUSE of *c.* 1800, with rusticated quoins and a fluted frieze over the door. Contemporary steading, much altered.

BINNY HOUSE. *See* p. 104.

₄₀₇₀   ELVINGSTONE   EL
                    1.5 km. N of Gladsmuir

A tall, plain Jacobean-baronial house of 1837. The architect is unknown; *William Burn* is a possibility. Entrance (s) front with three well organized gables. The most prominent contains the depressed-arch front doorway with a strapwork balustrade. The E section, on a distinctive L-plan with a stair-turret in the angle, has a shaped dormer head and candle-snuffer roof, but what we miss in this early intimation of the baronial revival is a door at the bottom. Square chimneys, set diagonally. Within, two drawing rooms *en suite* to the w with geometric ribbed ceilings. In one is a Louis chimneypiece, in the other a plain Grecian one with winged female heads, looking down the vista. The dining-room ceiling is also ribbed, but squarely.

STABLES. Turning obstinately to the N, away from the drive, the stable range, flanked by gabled dormers, has a strange turreted centrepiece with a steep gable. What it is looking at is the cylindrical DOOCOT, probably of the C18, with one string course and, behind a battlemented parapet, a little stone lid on legs between which the birds can enter. The inside, lit by two bullseye windows, has seven hundred and sixty four nesting boxes of fine ashlar and a potence with bars right across the diameter – all in perfect order.

LODGE with bowed ends, *c.* 1800.

ESKBANK *see* DALKEITH

FALA AND SOUTRA

PARISH CHURCH. A long C18 kirk economically Gothicized *c.* 1860. A 'new church' designed by *David Bryce* in 1863 was 'being built' in the following year, but the description hardly fits. – MANSE of 1792.

SCHOOL and connected schoolhouse of *c.* 1840, extended 1875 and later.

FAIRSHIELS (till 1880 the Blackshiels Inn). C17, with swept dormers on the S side and crowstepped additions of *c.* 1850. The adjacent STEADING has a blind-arched front to the road with simple bullseyed pediment.

TOLL HOUSE, 2 km. SE, at the junction of the A68 and A6137. T-plan with diamond glazing; built *c.* 1834, when the turnpike road to Lauder was opened.

SOUTRA AISLE on Soutra Hill, 3 km. SE. This is the name of the fragment of the church and hospital of the Holy Trinity which was founded by Malcolm IV *c.* 1164 for use by travellers. It survives because it was used by the Pringles of Soutra as their burying-place. It is *c.* 8m. long, with a stone roof and a roll-moulded doorway; over this the inscription DP AP 1686 and a pair of lancets, each arch made of a single stone.

ROMAN ROAD. A section to the SW of the A68.

FALSIDE CASTLE

4 km. SW of Tranent

The ruin of the four-storey C15 tower of the Fawside family with a C16 L-plan addition to the S. (MacGibbon and Ross in their *Castellated and Domestic Architecture of Scotland* give a detailed account of the interior arrangements.)

FAULDHOUSE

ST JOHN (R.C.). 1873 by *W. & R. Ingram* of Glasgow. In the W gable a spirelet and a round window with wooden star tracery. – STAINED GLASS. On the E side of the sanctuary and at the foot of the stair to the W gallery, two imported lights (Ascension and Annunciation respectively) by *Hardman*. – On the N and S sides of the sanctuary two lights (SS. Margaret and Patrick) by *E. M. Dinkel*, 1956. – Eight lights in the nave etc. (various saints) by *John Blyth*, 1951–6.

Fauldhouse is a C19 village based on coal, iron and paraffin, and its buildings do not entirely spoil an attractive site. There is a good row of stone houses of *c.*1830, and the CHURCH OF SCOTLAND, 1866 by *Angus Kennedy*, is quite an ambitious Gothic composition of traceried gable and pinnacled tower. A hundred decent houses by *William Baillie* of Glasgow were built in prompt response to the Housing Act of 1924.

5080   FENTON TOWER   EL
                     3 km. SSW of North Berwick

A ruin of the late C16 with three storeys of stone-vaulted rooms. A square tower at the SW corner and a half-round turret on the N side provide turnpike stairs to the first floor only; the rooms on the upper levels are reached by little subsidiary turrets tucked into the angles.

2060   FIRTH HOUSE   ML
                     1.5 km. SE of Glencorse

Built *c.* 1770, of good ashlar, but over-cleaned. SW front of three wide bays, the centre bay advanced and pedimented, the entablature of the Roman Doric doorpiece grotesquely restored. Similar extension to the l. with a recessed link. Moulded architraves to all the windows, plus cornices on the first floor; rusticated quoins. An oval room in the bow to the rear.

3060   FORD   ML

The DOWERY HOUSE. A C17 tower with a circular stair-turret, enlarged in the late C18 and early C19. Tall bowed end with round-headed Georgian windows on three storeys. With its roughcast walls and battlemented profile the whole thing has the aspect of a cardboard castle. The panelled interiors and the present name date from *c.* 1910, when it became a dower house of Vogrie (*see* p. 462).

57 FORD HOUSE. A trim little L-plan house, some 13 m. each way, with crowstep gables and stone margins, built in 1680 for Col. Fraser, one of the Frasers of Lovat, Inverness-shire. An octagonal stair-turret, entered on one of the straight sides, rises in the angle to serve the first floor and the attic with its sweptroof dormer overlooking the courtyard. Harled walls, colourwashed rusty orange. Inside, the original fittings are remarkably

complete, undisturbed in the sensible adaptation by *Mary Tindall*, 1961. The most distinctive feature is the moulding of the backs of the shutters so as to be seen when they are folded across the windows; the best room the one on the first floor in the N jamb, with a moulded stone fireplace with panelled pilasters above and below the deep moulded shelf. The rest of the pine panelling is divided by a bold dado rail which is neatly returned into the flat surface before it meets the upstanding mouldings of fireplace and door frames – all in the best practice of the time.

LOTHIAN BRIDGE, carrying the A68 across the Tyne. By 3 *Thomas Telford*, dated 1831, and thus contemporary with the Dean Bridge, Edinburgh, which is of the same type. Five segmental arches, each with an inset arch describing a deeper arc. *James Lees* was the builder.

FOUNTAINHALL
2 km. SW of Pencaitland

EL 4060

A little mansion of the late C16 prolonged in the early C17 on the 56 same intimate scale and with the same materials, the fine-grained harl matching the pale yellow sandstone of chimneys, crowstep gables and other dressings. The W end, one room thick with a projecting stair-turret, was probably built soon after 1685; the ridge chimney and crowsteps show where it once stopped. The turret was afterwards widened, filling in the small re-entrant angle to the W and becoming quite a grand affair in its own right, with a corbel course above the first floor, then another storey and a dormered attic. The sundial on the corner of the new work is canted to face due S. In the E angle a round stair-turret is corbelled out over the front door to provide access to the attic storey. Its roof and the adjacent gable have evidently been modified. The next principal stage of the building was the much lower range to the E, originally separate, with gables to N and S, and access to the dormered upper floor by an outside stair. This was the work of John Pringle who had bought the estate in 1635. His initials appear on one of the dormers with the date 1638. He subsequently continued the original building to join up with it, providing a round stair-turret at the back of the link and probably adding the fine display of pedimented dormers all round. He may well have been responsible for the enhancement of the W end as well. Piecemeal as it is, the whole house builds up calmly and beautifully from E to W. In 1685 the estate was bought by John Lauder of Newington, in Edinburgh, and the house, previously known as Woodhead, became the seat of the barony of Fountainhall. The drawing room on the first floor of the original building still has a wide, roll-moulded fireplace, but most of the internal finishings are the work of the Lauders in the early C18, with fielded pine panelling and plain plaster cornices, though the cornice in the main first-floor bedroom is of timber. (For a reference to the tapestries in the room beyond it, *see* Introduction, p. 54.) The W part of the basement is paved with red brick. Much of the lesser door furniture and hinges is thin wrought ironwork of the early C18 with delicate, varied profiles. The JOUGS attached to the S wall recall the judicial functions of the head of the barony and reinforce the tradition that the building to the E was a courtroom. But the barony was created later, so it is more likely to have been a woman house or guest house.

C17 WALLED GARDEN adjoining the E of the house. Moulded doorway with a pediment flanked by obelisks in relief.

The ruined C17 lectern DOOCOT to the S of the house is worth mentioning because it was later provided with an identical twin. The RCAHMS suggest that the two buildings flanked an C18 approach to the house – presumably a pedestrian one, in view of the gradient. They also note the four classical cast-iron ovals on the ball-finialled GATEPIERS to the W; for the time (1924) a unique display of interest in the later C18.

6060   FRIAR'S NOSE   EL
                    13.5 km. ESE of Gifford

A multivallate fort in the angle of Whiteadder Water and Kilmade Burn. Entrance on the NE. Hut circles inside.

9070   GALA BRAES   WL
                    1.5 km. NE of Bathgate

An impressive standing stone on a ridge. The stump of a second stone is visible about 70 m. to the W.

5070   GARLETON CASTLE   EL
                 3 km. WSW of Athelstaneford

Very far gone, but apparently the C16 castle built by Sir John Seton of Garleton. A round tower remains, with some gun loops. The forecourt had two little houses at the corners. The shell of the s one is complete, with a kitchen fireplace in the centre partitition of one of the vaulted ground-floor rooms, a canopied fireplace in the corner of the other. Round stair-turret on the outer side.

GARVALD

EL 5070

PARISH CHURCH. Four Gothic windows and the w belfry betray the complete remodelling of 1829; *John Swinton* of Haddington was the contractor and possibly the designer. But there is a chip-carved string course from the C12 church at the NW corner, and the N aisle is of 1677. The interior has been reconstructed to face towards the E. – JOUGS attached to the w gable. – SUNDIAL on the s wall dated 1633. – MANSE. 1820, with a pretty fanlight.

The name means Rough Burn; the main street of the village runs along the N side of the Papana Water. Nearly all the earlier buildings are of deep red sandstone, pleasantly varied by the cream-washed harling of pre-1939 County Council cottages which have not been sited in a single lump but sensibly mixed into the townscape. Pantile roofs are the general rule for both old and new houses. Starting at the w (Gifford) end, on the N side of the street are the gabled (former) SCHOOL and schoolhouse of c. 1845, and behind them a plain kirk of about the same date (also converted to a house) with a later tower and slated spire. The street line then retreats to form a small village green. On the s side a good sequence: three single-storey cottages of varying scale, and then the inn of c. 1830 with a slightly later hoodmoulded extension and a fancy chimney on the gable. A gap reveals two ranges of single-storey houses of c. 1970, whiteharled and pantiled, with good simple fenestration. Next, after a picturesquely angled corner, a rarity in the shape of a single-storey house of c. 1750 with ashlar quoins and panelled pilasters supporting a flat arch over the door. Another single-storey house acquired c. 1830 both an upper floor and a staircase tower to the rear. The vista ahead is well closed by a two-storey house with snecked masonry and an arched porch. This deflects the street, which makes its way to the r. towards the church which is still out of sight. A dip in the middle aids the admirable grouping of houses on each side. The two-storey ASHLEY LODGE is dated 1834.

MORHAM. *See* p. 331.

FARMS ETC.

CARFRAE, 2 km. SW. Early C19 farmhouse of red sandstone with
pilastered doorpiece. The contemporary steading has timber-
lintelled cartsheds.

SNAWDON, 3 km. S. Early C19 steading, the roof pantiled, with
slated eaves courses. Shallow loft windows above the timber-
lintelled cartsheds, four on each side, the one in the middle included in a tall pointed arch flanked by ornamental slits and
crowned with battlements.

For the STONE CIRCLE on Kingside Hill near Mayshiel, 7.5 km.
SE, and the CAIRN on Spartleton Hill, 7 km. SE, see Introduction, p. 23.

NUNRAW. See p. 369.

STONEYPATH TOWER. See p. 442.

PARISH CHURCH. By *James Smith*, finished in 1710. T-plan,
white-harled. In the centre of the long side, facing down the
street, a square staged tower with a slated spire rising from
within the parapet. On each side of it a pair of tall round-headed
windows, the shorter ones at the ends betraying the galleries
within. Gothic-glazed windows of 1830 in the plain-skewed
gables. The family aisle at the back, the stem of the T, is entered
through a lug-framed door up a few steps. The chimney in its
gable used to serve a fireplace in the retiring room on the ground
floor. Inside, the loft on top has two hatchments and a panelled
front with the coroneted monogram IHS for John Hay and
Jean Scott. – PULPIT, possibly moved from the old parish
church. C17, with bowed front and oak panels enriched in
Dutch style (*see* Pencaitland). Bracket for a baptismal basin.
The cantilevered sounding-board was apparently made up to
match it *c.* 1710. More panelling was added to the sides in 1895,
the date of the pierced oak RAIL of Renaissance character round
the communion table.

YESTER HOUSE and the OLD PARISH CHURCH are described below at the end of the entry on Gifford, and YESTER
CASTLE is noted after them.

The old barony of Yester belonged to the Norman family of Gifford who built the castle. In 1418 it passed by marriage to the
Hays. The village of Bothans (i.e. bothies or workers' cottages)
lay somewhere near the old parish church which still stands

close to Yester House, but by the end of the C17 it had been resited, under the name of Gifford, on the present line parallel with the avenue to the house and separated from it by the green or bleaching ground. On the other side of the avenue, towards the Gifford Water, is another green once used as a sheep pound, now as a recreation ground. The AVENUE itself consists of hybrid limes of the Dutch species *Tilia europaea*. It is at r. angles to the main road, but the latter soon became part of the layout, with the bridge (1704, rebuilt in the early C19) at one end, the new parish church at the other. At the junction of the resulting L-shape are the MERCAT CROSS of 1780 with a heraldically topped shaft and ball finial on an older steeped base, and the public WELL whose stone cistern was rebuilt in 1850. 102

The layout was always regular, but although the original small-holdings formed a continuous line, the houses along their fronts (of one or two storeys) did not do so until the C19; this is the main reason for the alternation of older and newer houses, e.g. in the trio at the start of the avenue on the river side, of which only the outer ones are of the C18. The other side is now built up along its whole length, and three C18 buildings are of particular interest. The TWEEDDALE ARMS with its arched entry to the coachyard still has the same sort of post and beam sign that it had in the late C17, and the far end house, BEECH-WOOD, has a square projecting stair-turret with a pair of stone balls on the parapet. Both probably incorporate some C17 work, but one intermediate house, with rusticated quoins and a Gibbs-surround doorpiece, seems entirely of *c.* 1770. At the cross, and facing up the avenue, two early C18 houses stand back from the street line to form a little square. The spired TOWN HALL of 1887, with steps up to the door, is squeezed into the space between them. The main street begins with the GOBLIN HA' HOTEL at a point of vantage on the corner, but few of its individual houses are of much quality until it forks off to the r., past the church, towards Duns. More good ones in the wynd that links the main street diagonally to the avenue. Right out of the village in the Duns Road are the single-storey (former) SCHOOL and dormered schoolhouse of 1843.

MANSION HOUSES

For its size, Gifford is surrounded by an unusual number of small Georgian mansions, some of them built or subsequently occupied by the Hay family (*see* also Hopes, separately noted because it

is some distance away). There is also the expected sprinkling of
good C20 houses.

On the road from East Saltoun and Edinburgh the first house is
BOLTON MUIR by *P. D. Hepworth*, 1930. Of whitewashed
brick and stone, with rough-edge timber and a long roof of Norfolk reed thatch sweeping over the dormers, it snakes forward
to the roadside to which it presents, without shame or indeed
any need for it, an oak-doored garage.

On the approach to the village, BROADWOOD by *Mervyn Noad*,
1938, the whole upper storey a pantiled mansard.

GIFFORD BANK, on the opposite side. Built *c.* 1820. Two storeys
and three bays with an advanced centre, the broad pilastered
doorpiece flanked by tripartite windows with segmental heads
and a hint of Gothic in the fine detail of the entablature. The
windows are repeated in the single-storey wings.

FORBES LODGE is next. Late C18. Three bays with dressed
quoins and oval bullseye in the centre pediment all in pink sandstone; single-storey wings added later. The twin bay-windows
and hoodmoulded doorpiece seem to have been put on *c.* 1841–
2, when the interior was remodelled. Corner-block doorcases,
Grecian plasterwork, and chimneypieces by *David Ness* of
Leith Walk, Edinburgh, including one of grey marble with flattened half-columns in the drawing room to the l., and another
in iron, with fully closing shutters, in a bedroom to the rear.
The house is deep in plan. Staircase to the l. with Grecian iron
balusters.

On the Haddington Road is the MANSE, *c.* 1830, two storeys and
three bays with single-storey wings, all the windows hoodmoulded. In its garden THE RINK by *Ian Arnott*, 1963,
single-storey, with whitened brick walls boldly distinguished
from plate-glass voids, and upstanding monopitch roof lights;
remarkably sympathetic with the church nearby.

GIFFORD VALE follows. 1786 according to the date over a garden
door. Two storeys and three bays, with a vase over the pedimented centre, and a corniced doorpiece. Dressings of grey
stone. Inside, the entry to the stair at the back has a double-
arch divide. The chimneypiece in the ground-floor room to the
l., of pine, with sea-pinks, thistles and roses in composition,
was brought from Heriot Row, Edinburgh. To the rear a nice
axial layout of four pavilions for the offices.

On the Duns Road, BARO HOUSE by *Reginald Fairlie*, 1939,
a harled house on a 'butterfly' plan.

FARMS ETC.

TOWNHEAD, 1.5km. ENE. C18 rubble steading with hipped roofs. Additions dated 1836 have five segmental cartshed arches facing the road. Contemporary farmhouse with vernacular canopied door.

KIDLAW LIME KILN 5km. SW. C18. Mentioned in the New Statistical Account.

YESTER HOUSE

Yester* is basically the large, austere box of a house built to the design of *James Smith* and *Alexander MacGill* in 1699–1728. As soon as it was finished, *William Adam Sen.* set about enlivening it, and in 1789 *Robert Adam* wanted to bring it up to date, but neither of them (at least on the outside) was allowed to go very far. Finally, *c.*1830 the longsuffering N front lost its *raison d'être* completely when the entrance was moved to the W end. But it is still a majestic place, with sufficient authority for these later tamperings to be seen as mere eccentricities. Inside, there is no Smith work to be seen, but that of the *Adams*, father and sons, is of outstanding quality, and the early C19 architect *Robert Brown* produced something sufficiently different to be acceptable in this company. *R. Rowand Anderson* worked at Yester in 1877.

The old Yester had consisted of a tower, probably C16, with the usual agglomeration of gabled ranges round a courtyard. In 1670 John Hay, second Earl of Tweeddale, had consulted Sir William Bruce about a new house; he was created Marquess in 1692 and died in 1697. His son, already in his fifties, immediately instructed *James Smith* to start work, and the result is the plainest of geometrical statements, a great pinkish block six bays deep and nine bays wide (the end windows more widely spaced). Its solidity is emphasized by horizontal channelling, barely interrupted at quoins and window margins, applied to basement and two upper storeys alike; this was a favourite motif of Bruce (cf. Hopetoun House). It is complemented by an (originally) uncluttered roof of bell-cast profile, and by the ogee roof, with lacy flashings cut out of lead, of the E pavilion (the balancing W pavilion has unhappily gone). The old house was cleared away in 1699. The woman house to the N, still surviving, was being built in 1701, the pavilions (as temporary accommodation) in 1704–5.

* Alistair Rowan, *Country Life*, 9, 16 and 23 August, 1973.

William Adam was called on in 1729 by the fourth Marquess over a purely practical matter: the roof of this deep house had a centre valley which filled up with rain and snow. Adam duly made it into a platform roof, but also proposed new centre-pieces: a portico for the N front, pilasters for the S. What he was allowed to build was a row of four Ionic pilasters to mark the entrance, with a pedimented attic overhead; and on the S front just an attic, more successful because it does not break the lines of horizontal channelling (that of course was precisely what he had wanted to do). This front indeed was enhanced, its whole interest being focused on the round-headed window that breaks up into the pediment. *Robert Adam*, less than usually perceptive, wrote to the seventh Marquess in 1789. After paying tribute to the internal arrangements to which he himself had already contributed, he returned to his father's old complaint: 'those lines of flat ashlers running from end to end and from top to bottom of both fronts of the House dazzle the eye and render them a mass of confusion'. The result was an attempt at a further face-lift, but only the N centrepiece was touched; William Adam's order of pilasters was pushed up into the attic, right under the pediment, and the windows between them were enlivened with round tops. This is elegant enough in itself, but mean in relation to the rest, for Adam's plan to reface the whole thing and add a crowning balustrade to keep the attic company was not carried out. On balance this seems fortunate. In 1797 the W pavilion was burnt, but immediately repaired. Its destruction dates from *c.* 1830, when *Robert Brown* reorientated the house. In 1838 he added the reasonably suitable porte cochère on the W front. Both father and son had the same name; which of them did the work we do not know.

Smith's room-plan (MacGill is not mentioned in the accounts till 1710) – a sort of triple-pile with two staircases in the middle – is largely intact, but taken in cross-section the house has been rearranged. Over the vaulted basement, still unaltered, a two-storey entrance hall and saloon originally occupied the central N–S axis. *William Adam* reduced the entrance hall to single-storey height. It later became the dining room, and so the first architect we meet inside is now *Robert Brown*. He made a long corridor from the new front door to the main staircase, chopping off the end bay of the old entrance hall to form a narrow vaulted passage and re-using Adam's two Ionic columns, with new capitals, to articulate the broader first section. His competent Grecian treatment was also applied to the two S rooms with coffered ceilings which were formed *en suite*. The plain chimneypieces were pretentiously replaced *c.* 1970. The NW corner room is of *William Adam* vintage, with a flat-arched chimneypiece and a leafy key-block over the doorway. The present DINING ROOM is his best interior at Yester, or for that matter anywhere, for its spacious square shape justifies a fairly heavy cornice, and the superimposed Ionic pilasters that support it are quite unportentous. The Rococo chimneypiece with overmantel and supporting figures is crisp and charming, and so is the fastidious Rococo relief at the corners and centre of the flat ceiling, the latter coming down in a swirling pendant. *Joseph Enzer*, who came to Yester in 1736, may have been the plasterer; he was certainly responsible for the STAIRCASE, a much more characteristic work, its surprisingly small well framed at the corners by vestigial Ionic pilasters rising from masked consoles at first-floor level and supporting a substantial entablature above. In the deep cove overhead wildly exotic trophies of earth, air and water, with Venus tended by cupids; then an oval dome, probably later, with light garlands and swags.

The SALOON is the finest room in Lothian, if not in Scotland. 78 Typically of Yester, it is a collaboration, in this instance between the Adams, father and sons. The basic idea of the coved ceiling and the tabernacle doors belongs to *William Adam*, but it was carried out, after much discussion, by his sons, *John* the business manager and *Robert* the executant. The huge cove is relieved by diminishing octagonal coffers (cf. the Basilica of Maxentius) and by long foliage tendrils in the corners. Chimneypiece and overmantel in an updated version of the Rococo work downstairs. The pedimented tabernacles, Palladian without pomposity, and their wall reliefs foreshadow Robert Adam's later treatment of state rooms in great English houses. Finally there are the paintings beneath them, by *William Delacour*, completed in 1761, classical fantasies whose lovely colour opens the room to far horizons outside. Or almost finally; for it was only in 1789 that *Robert Adam* was at last able to adjust the windows at the N end to a form and stature to suit the room, albeit with some awkwardness at the corners. This adjustment, reconciling the interior with the elevation, was the justification for his otherwise unnecessary changes outside.

The CHAPEL, close to the house, consists of the choir and transepts of the collegiate church of St Cuthbert, which continued

as the family burial place after the building of the new parish
church in Gifford. Transepts with a C15 base course. Their
stone roofs abut the side wall of the crossing. No evidence of
a central tower, or of the building of a nave. There has been
much refacing. Reticulated E window dated 1635. In the S skew
an older grotesque carving of a shepherd and two sheep.
30 Externally, of course, the main feature is the Rococo Gothic
frontage applied by the *Adam Brothers* in 1753 which represents
(with the garden buildings at Alnwick, Northumberland) the
best realization of Robert Adam's early Gothic fantasies. It is
the icing on a venerable cake, all the more effective because
there is genuine antiquity underneath. The transept wall heads
are extravagantly corbelled, with a fretwork parapet, the crossing has been given a steep gable with a cusped and crocketed
skew, and all the corners have angle buttresses, now sadly lacking their pinnacles. In the central arch an ogee-topped doorway,
a large coat of arms, and a bullseye window with wild, loopy
tracery.

Inside there is much more of the old church to be seen. Each
limb has a solid pointed vault. Transepts entered through
slightly depressed arches in two chamfered orders. The choir
arch, altered probably in the late C17, is now pointed, springing
from leafy consoles. A clue to the date is the engagement, and
the payment in 1688, of *Alexander Eizat* to make a panelled
balustrade above the family burial place in the choir, and 'to
plaster the roof ... after the gothic manner'. The shadow of
the ribs can still be seen on the vault; diagonal and transverse,
meeting at a single point on the ridge. – MONUMENTS, in the
S transept. In the floor two tablets dated 1566 and 1613. – Wall-
monument with pilasters and a pointed arch; in the tympanum
a shield with the initials WH HC for William Hay and Helen
Cockburn † 1614 and 1627. – C18 headstone with *memento mori*.

Most of the documents about the GROUNDS refer to the C17,
when the second Earl was laying out a park for the new house
which he never started; he had already enclosed it by 1676,
when Lauderdale finished his wall round the park at Lennoxlove. The WALLED GARDEN, whose hump-topped walls are
lined with red brick, is later. Cardboard-Tudor STABLES of the
early C19. The KIOSK to the S of the house is the clock-case
from the Caledonian Station, Edinburgh, moved here *c.* 1970.
The GATES at the end of the village avenue, by *John Adam*,
1753, grand square piers with coupled Ionic columns attached,
and the pair of piend-roofed LODGES are all in red sandstone.

Splendid contemporary ironwork. DANSKINE GATE to the E
is early C18, with channelled piers and contemporary gates.
(YESTER CASTLE, 1.5 km. SE of the house. The barely accessible
remains of the castle built by Hugo Gifford of Yester † 1267
occupy a promontory between the Hopes Water and a little
tributary. To the N is one side of a high curtain wall with an
offset base. Beneath it, a stair descends to the subterranean
GOBLIN HA' (Goblin Hall) which Gifford was said to have constructed by magic. It is some 12 by 34 m. in size, lined with
ashlar in massive courses. Pointed vault with chamfered ribs
set close together. The space seems to have been floored across
at the level of their springing. At the N end are two holes for
corbels, apparently for a vanished canopy. The recessed flue
slopes backwards and upwards to emerge in a square hole outside the curtain.)

GILMERTON HOUSE
2 km. ENE of Athelstaneford

EL 5070

A handsome three-storey house of yellow-grey stone built for Sir
David Kinloch of Gilmerton in the 1750s. *John Aitken* was the
mason. The windows are Gibbsian and generously tall on the
ground floor, corniced on the main storey, and lugged at all
four corners on the top one. Rusticated quoins. Seven bays,
the three in the middle slightly advanced and carrying a pediment with an armorial flourish in red sandstone. Three urns
of the same material above. The deep cornice running all round
the house is nicely reduced under the pediment, with a distinctly cheerful result. Side and back walls were originally
rendered. Although no wings are visible from the front, when
the body of the house was built an existing smaller-scale two-
storey N range was extended further to the N. The canted bay
belonging to the Music Room, with a round-arched centre window and flat side windows surmounted by blind ovals, is of grey
ashlar, but the slightly bulkier ground-floor wall and the whole
of the junction with the old work are of red brick, formerly
rendered.

The only later additions are by *William Burn*, 1828. He
designed the porch with its coupled pilasters and balcony on
each side, bracketed and balustraded, the single-storey bow on
the E side, and the offices to the N. On the W side he gave a
twin brother to the original bay, identical save in its thinner
astragals.

After the porch, the ENTRANCE HALL seems to confirm the idea of a modest standard of finish (plain lugged doors and windows) early superseded by a more showy one. It is likely however that the chimneypiece, with coupled Ionic columns with diagonal volutes and an inset brown marble fireplace of rather sluggish Rococo form, was moved here from another, less austere apartment during Burn's alterations. The cornice of the hall, with rosettes on the soffit between the modillions, keeps cropping up in the rest of the house, and red pine is the timber used throughout, large-grained but dense enough for the finest carving.

The rooms on each side of the hall are modestly Grecian, for they were re-finished by *Burn*, but the dining room to the E has panelling of the C20, when the imported chimneypiece supplanted Burn's black marble one. To the NE the STONE PARLOUR, its walls painted (as they may have been from the first) to imitate masonry, its woodwork of the austerer type. Along the house from E to W runs an arched corridor, and to the N of it are the two STAIRCASES. The main stair to the W is of timber, the platts consummately detailed and inlaid from end to end of their treads, the balusters of wrought iron, alternately plain and serpentine, with shaped leaves. Ceiling with a cornice of uncommon richness, Rococo decoration in the corners, and a rather naturalistic eagle hanging on to a chain carrying a central light. A basket arch upon Corinthian pilasters leads on to the landing. To the E is a more old-fashioned staircase, with straight flights and a semicircle of winders. But for the ascent from first to second floor it changes from stone to wood and is hardly less refined than the main stair, each platt having a panelled soffit. Twisted balusters also of wood.

On the first floor the main rooms, by *Burn*, are the two DRAWING ROOMS *en suite*, higher on the W, with yellow marble chimneypieces facing each other from the ends. But the finest thing in the house is the MUSIC ROOM in the N wing, probably designed as the library. It is a long room with a spacious bay opening off one side, and its ceiling combines rigid cruciform motifs with Rococo swirls which are happily intertwined in the bay. The woodwork seems never to have been painted. Its principal motif is the coupled Ionic order already seen in the hall, based on the chair rail and used in pilaster form to flank the pedimented display niche at the S end, but as columns to celebrate the bay and its Venetian window. It is otherwise a little undisciplined; the work of a craftsman showing what he could do.

LODGE. Basket-arched and shallow-pitched, presumably by *Burn*.

The HOME FARM is unremarkable except for the high screen wall on the N side, probably of *c.* 1800, with battlemented ends and blind windows in cloddish Gothic, apparently intended to give it an architectural front towards the house.

GLADSMUIR

PARISH CHURCH. A solid affair, but not without charm, by *William Burn*, 1838. Tall round-arched windows. Fussy s front with a sort of vestigial tower rising flatly from porch to top-knotted bellcote. Very shallow 'chancel', and transepts two gables wide. Inside (the church was burnt in 1886 but faithfully restored by *John Farquharson* of Haddington) the transepts have twin segmental ceilings with plaster ribs running happily into a similar vault on the main axis. Horseshoe gallery, with pine panelling stripped to match the excellent WOODWORK and furniture (including a two-part organ case), by *Scott Morton & Co.*, directed by *M. Ingram*, from *c.* 1920. – STAINED GLASS. Three lights at the s end (the Ascension) by *Ballantine & Gardiner*, after 1892; above their average.

OLD PARISH CHURCH. Directly to the N, but not quite on the same axis, the ruin, lacking much of the s wall, of a long kirk of 1695 with a rather grand bellcote on the crowstepped w gable, a rose carved on the crowning stone of the other. The windows are small, with checks and hinge-pins for outside shutters. Joist holes show that there was a gallery at each end. On the N side a semicircular arch leads into a N aisle with a thistle finial on its skew which may have been the aisle of the Baillies of Lamington who built the church and owned Hoprig nearby. Burial enclosures are attached to the exterior. – MONUMENTS. The best are a small collection from the C18, e.g. a squirly table-tomb in the N aisle; to the E a wall-monument lacking a wall, its pilasters enriched with mortuary trophies of primitive delicacy, to Robert Hogg † (?)1768. – Also in the w limb of the church, a life-size relief of Col. James Ainslie † 1876 in Dragoons uniform. – MANSE, to the E. Large and bargeboarded; of 1871.

The name means 'moor of kites', and the village, such as it is, stands on a long ridge with a view of the Forth at its back. The

A1 tears past its front, and to this it presents a trim face: the kirk with its symmetrical approach between twin hollies, a string of pantiled cottages on each side, a little steading to the E, and the schoolhouse of c. 1840 to the W.

LIME KILNS. To the E of the village, by the next road N from the A1, are the Landridge Kilns, a splendid pair reported in 1853 as 'long disused'.

ELVINGSTONE. *See* p. 202.

FARMS

108 GREENDYKES, 3 km. W. A symmetrical steading of 1832, noticed at length in Loudon's *Cottage, Farm and Villa Architecture* (second ed., 1839), and described in the New Statistical Account as 'more like the offices you might expect to find connected with a Ducal palace than the house of a tenant'. It was planned by Mr *Swinton* for David Anderson of St Germains. Baronial crowstepped gables, a little flat in pitch, are crowned with stone balls and spikes. The middle one, with twin coats of arms over a triangular flight hole for pigeons, is the centre bay of the main front, which has nine segmental cart openings in a row and the granary windows overhead; so it faces SW to catch the prevailing wind. Calling this the S side for convenience, the straw barn lies along the N and the workhorse stables along the W; riding horses were kept at the SE corner, nearest the house. The courtyard (now roofed) was divided into four open courts with access from the W side, and cattle sheds along the E side of each. Most of the massive stone piers that marked the corners of the courts are still *in situ*, and so is the cobbled floor. On the W side the engine house (for threshing, now without its chimney) and a subsidiary court with cowsheds and piggeries. Contemporary farmhouse.

TRABROUN, 2 km. NE. A square farm steading of c. 1830. Stumpy tower over the arched entry, its upper stage octagonal with Gothic windows. Flight holes under the eaves of the slated pyramidal roof.

OLD PARISH CHURCH. The sad hilltop ruin, on the other side of the road and now hidden by trees, of the long kirk of 1665 made cruciform by the addition of two family aisles in the late C17. Both have outside stairs to their lofts, moulded string courses, and roll-edged doors, windows and heraldic panels.

But the Glencorse aisle to the N has a moulded skew to its gable and a tunnel-vault underneath its loft; the Woodhouselee aisle (the house is demolished) to the S has a crowstepped gable with a round window with Gothic Survival tracery. W tower and weatherboarded spire of 1811. – MONUMENTS. A good collection of headstones from the late C17 and the C18, with many trade symbols.

PARISH CHURCH. 1883 by *R. Rowand Anderson*, in pale stugged sandstone which shows off its refined modelling, with paler dressings. Its layout is of the 'High' Church of Scotland persuasion, with a distinct chancel and nave (indeed the original design was turned right round on its site for the proper orientation), and a saddle-roofed tower, housing the vestry, in the angle between the two. The whole composition is confirmed within. Communion table in the chancel, with the pulpit to one side. The triple N arcade opens into an aisle, the double S arcade into what had better be called a transept, leaving one bay for a big window to light the back of the church, which has a W gallery. Internally the structure is of stone, the walling of hard red brick. – FONT. Cubical, with roll-moulded edges, from the old church. – STAINED GLASS. In the N aisle, by *Moore* of London (Christ blessing the children), 1895, and by *Douglas Strachan* (St Patrick contemplating a ruined castle), after 1918; neither set is distinguished. – Outside the church is a large BOULDER with twenty-two cup marks and five cup-and-ring marks.

GLENCORSE HOUSE. A three-bay house of *c.* 1810 with advanced centre, columnar doorpiece and lower wings. The LODGES were picturesquely extended at the end of the C19 in the half-timbered manner also seen in the village of MILTON BRIDGE on the A701. This has on the E side a continuous row including the post office, on the W side some detached cottages and a steading of *c.* 1840 to which half-timbering has been added.

GLENCORSE MAINS. A much altered Georgian steading. On the approach road a terrace of three-storey houses of *c.* 1800, with harled walls and pilastered doorpieces.

GLENCORSE BARRACKS, on the A701. The nucleus, possibly including the octagonal tower, is said to be Greenlaw House; a dry sort of Tudor, 1803. It was a barracks soon after, and for some time a military prison. MEMORIAL GATES, rock-faced, with ogee-roofed pavilions, by *John A. McWilliam*, 1934.

FIRTH HOUSE. *See* p. 204.

LOGANBANK HOUSE. *See* p. 316.

GOGARBANK HOUSE   ML*
1070   3.5 km. E of Ratho

Early C19. Whin and sandstone. Twin bow-fronted wings, the one
to the E with a pediment. The body of the house, of two storeys
and basement, may be a little earlier. Immediately to the S it
overlooks a walled garden enlivened by the Gogar Burn which
flows through the middle, under an arch in the wall.

3060   GOREBRIDGE   ML

PARISH CHURCH (former Stobhill Parish Church), Hunterfield
    Road. Almost a complete reconstruction by *Hardy & Wight*,
    1884–5. Saddle-roofed stair-tower on one side of the main
    gable, on the other a turret with a sharp spire which is a land-
    mark from the A7.
ST PAUL'S CHURCH OF SCOTLAND (former Free Church),
    Hunterfield Road. Again a gable between stair-towers, this one
    symmetrical, with a prettily detailed E.E. bellcote at the head,
    by *MacGibbon & Ross*, c. 1885. The bellcote is truncated, and
    the church sadly disused.
Gorebridge is a Victorian mining village with a wide spread of
    C20 rehousing and expansion, the earliest on the approach from
    Edinburgh by the B704: fifty-two houses in roughcast blocks
    of four each (two up, two down) by *James D. Cairns*, 1927. The
    DUNDAS HALL with a red brick arch front is by *J. M. Aitken*
    of Airdrie, 1925. But the nucleus is older, making good use of
    a hillside position. The N side of HUNTER SQUARE, an in-
    formal road junction, is weakly overlooked by the mid C20 Bowl-
    ing Club and endless houses, but the stepped terrace housing
    on the E side by the *Midlothian County Architect's Department*,
    1972, is simple enough.
In two other directions there is plenty to notice. First MAIN
    STREET, entered past the GOREBRIDGE INN and its
    neighbour, of the 1840s, with horizontal glazing. The earliest
    house, heavily altered, is No. 20, with the date 1806 on the plain
    skewputt. The rest presents a picture of solid Victorian pros-
    perity: stone houses, rather sooty, stepping downhill on a slight
    curve, the shops kept going by the big population which the
    C20 has accumulated round about. One building presents a

                            * Now Edinburgh.

gable to the street – the crowstepped POST OFFICE, dated
1879. Next to it the DAIRY (No. 45) with a gabled porch.
Otherwise (though as usual the supermarket steps out of line)
the fronts are continuous. Many blocks are initialled and/or
dated, e.g. Nos. 22–26, 1880, and Nos. 32–34, inscribed JP (for
Pearson, the developer) 1889, with the same heavily arched
windows as the next block of houses. Finally the block inscribed
JMcN 1894 makes a clean end to the street – or nearly so; there
is an older cottage, GLENCAIRN, beyond. Its chimney must
have given trouble, cured by a flying brick flue built against the
gable of its new neighbour. The steep slope brings the street
to a halt. Along it can be seen the little Gothic R.C. Church
of 1904 and then the disused line of the railway with the abandoned station, two-storeyed with shallow-pitch roofs. The railway was the source of Gorebridge's prosperity from the 1840s,
and the town continued to grow across the valley where GORE
COTTAGE, with its centre gable in the same style as the station,
is the best of a number of small villas.

The other exit from the Square is HUNTERFIELD ROAD, which
also has a strong Victorian character, this time a feudal one with
a more open layout. Many of the buildings take their name from
Newbyres Castle, demolished in 1963, and were built by the
Dundas Estate (see Arniston). First NEWBYRES COTTAGE
and its nicely projecting stable of c. 1830. Next to it St Paul
(see above). NEWBYRES HALL, facing it, of thin ecclesiastical
character, dated 1882, now offers a cement-faced addition to
the main view. Then the MEDICAL CENTRE, built as the
Public Library, a cottagey building with a lot of gables and
Gothic trimmings inscribed RD (for Dundas) 1886 in the foils
of a carved panel on the chimney. A row of three cottages with
gabled porches also bears the RD monogram. Then comes a
single cottage inscribed RD 1888 with the motto TIME FLIES
and a youthful figure of Time in a panel. NEWBYRES ROW
has crowstepped porches and the inscription RD 1885. Behind
the parish church the SCHOOL. Extension, with red sandstone
dressings, by *A. Murray Hardie*, 1908.

GREENHALL HIGH SCHOOL, to the N, 1973 by *David Harvey,
Alex Scott & Partners*. Large and rather disjointed. Built of
red brick and a good deal else.

HARVIESTOUN MAINS, to the W. Yellow sandstone with a
square red brick chimney. Inscribed RD (for Dundas) 1874.

HARVIESTON HOUSE. *See* p. 247.

KIRKHILL HOUSE. *See* p. 273.

GOSFORD HOUSE   EL
                      2.5 km. NNE of Longniddry

80 Gosford was the work of *Robert Adam*, 1790, the Earl of Wemyss
   having bought the estate (together with Old Gosford House)
   in 1784. It was altered and extended, the wings being replaced
   with much larger ones, by *William Young* of Glasgow and London, who finished his work in 1891.

   The date 1800 in the pediment shows that the Adam house
   was not completed till that year. Lady Louisa Stuart gives a
   lively but unsophisticated description of it in the early years
   of the C19: 'There is a *corps de logis* and two pavilions, all with
   domes, so at a distance it looks like three great ovens, but the
   front is really a very pretty one. They say the plan is absurd;
   three rooms in the middle, of fifty feet long each lighted with
   one huge Venetian window and unconnected with the rest.'
   Assuming that the Adam scheme was followed, the pavilions
   were of Greek-cross plan, joined by colonnaded quadrant links
   to the *corps de logis*. The latter however was altered in execution,
   and possibly thereafter. The drawing shows the present
   arrangement of twin pilasters at the ends, twin engaged
   columns flanking the centre. It also shows Lady Louisa's 'huge
   Venetians', but the side ones were flanked by square-topped
   niches. In the event these were left out, and the fluted Corinthian order was reinforced with a further single pilaster on
   each side of the centre bay. This arrangement, or rearrange-
   ment, is quite worthy of Adam, and the simplicity of this elevation is awe-inspiring, splendidly enhanced by the nonchalant,
   snarling lions at each end of the parapet.

   What Young did to this front is not unsuccessful. He put
   a rusticated arcade right across the basement, where the Adam
   drawing shows merely an artificial mound rising to a door in
   the centre. His pavilions are very elaborately composed, late
   Victorian versions of the Adam wings that had been demolished
   some time before. Opposite the Venetian-windowed bays that
   link them to the main block wide-branching staircases offer four
   different ways of descending from the terrace to the Italian
   garden, whose further (W) wall is well adjusted to the view
   across the Firth of Forth. All in all it works, though with some
   reservations. The Doddington stone of Young's work is yellower
   than the older stonework. The balustrade along the terrace
   hides the bases of Adam's Corinthian order, and the fluted
   drum of Adam's serene central dome (with a large number of

chimneys) is clamped into a huge iron contrivance supporting a flagstaff.

On the E side Young's transformation was unfortunate. This was Adam's entrance front, by no means conventional, but conceived and executed with throwaway elegance. The advanced ends of the main block have shaped, sphinx-bearing parapets over the cornice, panels with Doric guttae underneath it. The porch, with a joyous heraldic display on the skyline overhead, used to mark the centre of a symmetrical carriage-sweep. Young's instructions were to make the former front hall into a billiard room. So the front door lost its function and became a garden access by way of a new and very formal flight of steps. Some of the windows were likewise formalized with pediments and moulded surrounds.

Young's pair of N pavilions unites quite cleverly into a service block which has a central well lighting the kitchen from above. ~~many-gated forecourt to initiate the new longitudinal~~ form advanced ends for an entrance front of five bays, with five Venetian windows of two different orders, crowned with a Netherlandish shell-in-niche over Adamesque swags. A single-storey porch advances with maximum ceremony into the many-gated forecourt to initiate the new longitudinal progress through the house. All the best rooms are now by Young.

The low porch interior, its ceiling divided into low-relief foliaged compartments, opens into the MARBLE HALL, a great space three Venetian windows wide (matching those of the outside) on *piano nobile* level, plus side galleries with niches for classical statuary at the near end. It is four Venetian bays long, plus the gallery along the front. Coved and compartmented ceiling with a central dome. Polished Caen stone is used for the greater part of the wall surfaces, pink and white Derbyshire alabaster for the orders, for insets in the ceiling and for the balustrade of the double stair that curves up past fat alabaster urns to gallery level. It is a *coup de théâtre* of considerable skill as well as complexity. Centred under the curve of the stair, for example, a focus is provided by a *Cinquecento* marble chimneypiece imported from Italy. And through the Venetian screen straight ahead is a long transverse GALLERY, lit from the ends, its domestic use asserted by a pair of modest Renaissance-style chimneypieces, its palatial scale by a slightly larger order than that of the main hall. Dado and frieze are of the same pink alabaster. *Kirkwood* of Edinburgh were the builders, with structural steelwork by *Sir William Arrol* of Glasgow; stone and marble by *Farmer & Brindley*, plaster by *Jackson*, both of London. The rooms on both levels to E and W are consciously in an Adam manner, but hardly of Adam elegance, and the same may be said of most of the rooms in the main block. Here only the staircases, one on each side of the original entrance (their elegant balusters part cast- and part wrought-iron), survive from the Georgian interior. The large rooms on the W front, possibly recast in the mid C19, have groined ceilings and reeded gilt ribs, not Gothic, but tied together with rings and ribbons like some sort of tent. The intermediate wall has no cornice, which suggests that the rooms were once continuous, forming one long picture gallery. Some of the rooms were gutted by the fire in 1940. The important collection of paintings is outside the scope of this account.

STABLES. Said to be by *Adam*, *c.* 1790. Classical on a small scale, they are built of variegated yellow-brown rubble with grey dressings, with a show front facing the house. Pedimented centrepiece with two carriage doorways, a stone panel of griffons, and a clock by *Veitch* of Haddington, 1792. Single-storey wings jut forward to form a semi-courtyard with more griffon reliefs and larger ones representing agriculture and painting, sculpture and geometry. The face of each wing has a screen wall, vased like the pediment, with panels of classical scenes between profile heads of antique appearance.

MAUSOLEUM, on a raised eminence in the woods. A pyramid on a square base with four Roman Doric porticoes, only one of them serving a door.

ICE HOUSE. Entered from a pretty three-arched grotto with benches inside.

LODGES and GATES. The WEST LODGE, built on the Long-niddry side for access to and from the station, monogrammed and dated on the back RWB (for *R. W. Billings*, architect), 1854, is put together from a giant building set, approximately Flemish Baroque, in the form of a Venetian arch which is cruelly thrown off balance by the heavy blank wall of the lodge on one side. A string course jumps up it to enclose the Wemyss coat of arms, and over the arch are the mottoes JE PENSE and FORWARD. Nine polyhedral sundials on the skyline. To the front a large forecourt, to the rear colossal fluted basins bracketed from the wall, for horses. The NORTH LODGE is also by *Billings*, 1857. Spiked gatepiers flanked by twin octagonal lodges with elaborately pierced parapets and dummy dormers. EAST LODGE, towards Aberlady, of *c.* 1890, with bracketed eaves and pilastered bay.

GOWANBANK   WL 9070
3 km. N W of Armadale

An oddity, but a perfectly serious one, and at the time of writing in a serious state of decay. Basically the plain gabled house of the mason *Walter Gowans*, *c.*1840, it was enlarged by his son (later Sir) *James Gowans* as his country place, with whin walling and typically quirky freestone dressings, of structural or quasi-structural character, from the nearby quarry. The ground floor is conventional enough, but the skyline is wild, with the bracketed eaves interrupted by hooded dormers, an oriel dormer, and even by diagonal dormers at the angles – some boldly chamfered below, some on triangular sills with triglyphs. The gateposts on the main road are complicated octagonal pedestals with big incised spheres resting on their points. One has fallen over. Inside the house only part of the staircase, with fretted square balusters, is original. Here it may be remarked that the strangeness of Gowanbank, and indeed of everything designed by this engineer-builder-architect, is not a matter of anarchy but of a thoroughly worked out personal system. Geology and mason work were an obsession, expressing itself most characteristically at the corners of buildings and on the skyline.

The STEADING downhill to the S is in the same manner. All but the N wall of the byre has been replaced, but the following survive (W to E). The barn and engine house (chimney removed) dated 1842, which is the earliest date recorded for the whole group. A cottage with bracketed eaves, porch and dormers, the brackets on the dormer cheeks of both wood and stone to the same profile; on its S gable white quartz pins in the cyclopean whin and walling, variegated stones on the ingles framed out from ground floor and first floor. The cottage also includes a stable. A house over the E end of the byre, with Gowans' favourite clustered shaft chimneys and the inscription

HEB III 4
FOR EVERY HOUSE IS BUILDED BY SOME MAN
BUT HE THAT BUILT ALL THINGS IS GOD
ECCLES II.4, XI, XII. I AUGUST 1862.

Finally a combined coach house (its dormer gable removed) and dairy. There is also a shed to the S.

GRANGE   WL
2 km. N of Linlithgow

Baronial, by *J. N. Scott & A. Lorne Campbell*, from 1904. A
dramatic group dominated by a square tower of four storeys,
visible from miles around on its hilly platform; at a closer view
admirably austere, with harled walls and Anglo-Scots Renaissance detail. The tower, with its corner turret changing
abruptly from harl to ashlar and thus vertically emphasized,
makes a tense climax to an otherwise comfortable Edwardian
spread. The earliest plans show a taller house with main rooms
on the first instead of the ground floor, and the front door on
the higher level to the W. Another change of mind was the introduction of corbelling from Old Grange House (demolished
1905) to support the internal-angle turret on the E side.

Owing to this change of plan the hall in the base of the tower
is of one storey only, rising through an arcade to a slightly
higher landing beyond which an old-fashioned dog-leg stair
pushes out a bowed turret into the rear courtyard. Along the
W side are the anteroom with fitted settles and overmantel *en
suite*, and to the S of it the drawing room with a ribbed segmental
ceiling and a Connemara marble fireplace, the two separated
by Ionically capitalled piers and miniature arcade, cream-
painted. To the N the continuous cornice of the library tops
the bookshelves and then breaks forward over the fireplace supported by Ionic columns without benefit of frieze or architrave.
This and all the other woodwork is oak, the doors with two
laminated vertical panels and the remainder to match. Along
the S side the rooms have beamed ceilings: in the centre the
billiard room with a deep bay-window, and at the SE corner
the turreted dining room. Its overmantel, whose cornice jumps
up over Ionic pilasters in two sizes, sums up the whole compromise between Edwardian pomp and Art Nouveau circumstance, all the luscious marble fireplaces subscribing to the
former. Overlooking the courtyard is a 'private kitchen' for the
ladies of the house, a prophetic facility. The two main bedrooms
are on the first floor to the W, both with segmental ceilings.
At the top of the tower the plank-lined geological museum of
Henry Moubray Cadell Sen., the builder of the house.

At the head of the garden to the W is GREENCLOAKS, by
Stanley Ross-Smith, 1956. In its vicinity a collection of CARVED
STONES including a steeply pedimented dormer head with a
castle, thistles and roses and the date 1619, and a later C17 lion

bearing a shield with the initials S G M K (probably Sir George
Mackenzie of Rosehaugh). STABLES COTTAGE by *Tait & Wilson, c.* 1910.

GRANGEPANS *see* BO'NESS

GREENDYKES *see* GLADSMUIR

GULLANE   EL 4080

FORMER PARISH CHURCH (ST ANDREW). Abandoned in
1612 on account of its remoteness from Dirleton and because
the churchyard was being 'continewallie overblawin' with sand.
The ruins were subsequently turned into burial enclosures.
Surprisingly much medieval work remains, but the blocked
Norman chancel arch is the only worthwhile feature. The outer
order has chevron and shows from the W, but one has to enter
the E burial enclosure to see the half-shafts and capitals with
hollowed-out scallops *à la* Tyninghame. The side walls of the
chancel exist, the S one with two small lancets. Late medieval
N nave chapel with a semicircular arch, broken PISCINA, and
signs of a W window. Outside, the N walls of nave and chancel
have pieces of C12 string course.
ST ANDREW (PARISH CHURCH), East Links Road. By *John
Honeyman*, 1887. Simple Norman with E apse. The zigzagged
chancel arch is derived from that of the old parish church, and
so is the S doorway, whose tympanum has a low relief of St
Andrew.
PARISH CHURCH HALL (former United Free Church), Main
Street. By *Sydney Mitchell & Wilson*, 1908. An ingenious enlargement of the slightly earlier United Free Church. It consists
of a large, squat tower in the same pink rubble attached to the
S end, the parapet stepped up at the corners, and a ladder of
projecting blocks making a diagonal on the W face. The slated
spire is craftily broached into a hexagon whose points are on
the axis of the composite church. Within the tower the great
lofty space has small clearstory windows and a flat panelled ceiling of stained pine with painted ribs and flat painted discs, the
Lamb of God at the central intersection, the evangelistic beasts
at the cardinal points, the twelve apostles on the cornice of overlapping scalloped boards. Plain semicircular archways open
into the older church (now blocked) and W transept, and a triple
arcade into the S chancel, with cylindrical piers and cushion

capitals; on the soffit of the stilted centre arch an incised vine pattern, drawn in charcoal on the red Dumfries-shire sandstone and then carved direct, by *Herbert W. Palliser*. In the grille of the wood screen enclosing the two side bays, roses and singing birds carved and painted by *Joseph Armitage*. – STAINED GLASS. Four loop-traceried lights in the transept (the Evangelists), disarmingly primitive, in memory of the father † 1909 of Sydney Mitchell; three lights in the chancel with a star overhead (the Three Kings) in memory of his mother † 1904, simple and assured; and two windows of more complex but spirited drawing on the E side, not named, but incorporating parts of a paraphrase of Psalm 124 which was a favourite of the architect himself († 1930); the words appear in full on two carved and coloured panels.

ST ADRIAN (Episcopal), Sandy Loan. A plain aisleless church in beautiful flush pointed rubble by *Reginald Fairlie*, 1926. The five nave windows on each side are round-headed, the two chancel ones pointed, and the whole thing is enlivened by the bell-cast of the roof, which gives a slight projection at the eaves. The low tower attached to the N side of the nave, their E walls continuous, has a shallow inset upper stage and the same sort of sweep to its slated pyramidal spire. Inside, plaster arches spring from rubble buttresses with a coombed timber roof between. Rubble chancel arch. – PULPIT. Norman, probably from an earlier Episcopal church. The workmanship of the wrought-iron rail resembles that of the LECTERN. – STAINED GLASS. Three lights at the E end of the chancel (Love, Courage and Humility) by *Douglas Strachan*, after 1924.

ROYAL SCOTTISH NATIONAL HOSPITAL, MUIRFIELD HOUSE, at the E end. 1909 by *Robert Lorimer*. A two-storey administrative block with a single-storey ward canted forwards on each side.

94 GREYWALLS, to the N of the above. A house and garden of the highest importance designed for Alfred Lyttleton in 1901 by *Edwin L. Lutyens* and *Gertrude Jekyll* respectively. Their effect, however, is inseparable. The house is of very modest size and spreads horizontally into walls of the same warm, flush-pointed rubble which define the compartments of the garden and assist in the stage-management of the approach. Here, and here only, the house makes an impression. The forecourt is entered between footmen's bothies, and its walls converge upon a frontage of impressive simplicity. It is of two storeys, detailed so as to offer the minimum distraction from its wide, slightly con-

cave plane; small casements set almost flush with the wall, lintels camouflaged with tile ends, the parapet very slightly battered over each section between the windows. The only ceremony on the central axis is in the scrolled pediment over the front door and the simple lantern (lighting the staircase) breaking the skyline. The interior is very small-scale, but broad and relaxed in detail. The main feature is the continuous suite of rooms forming a T. The cross-bar is the library, with a bolection-moulded grey marble fireplace. In the middle of the upright the rotunda, with a fireplace on the inner side, French windows opening into the garden on the outer. Beyond the semi-formalities of the garden lie the undisturbed ridges of East Lothian hills. *Robert Lorimer* added a kitchen and dining room to the N in 1910.

SALTCOATS CASTLE. *See* p. 422.

VILLAS

HILL ROAD. The first two villas to exploit this seaside strip were both designed by *Charles Hay* of Edinburgh. First PURVESHOLM, 1898, whose address is really in Sandy Loan. It is redtiled Franco-Scots, with gableted crowsteps and two kinds of dormers (François I and Queen Anne) plus English Tudor chimneys formerly all of plum-coloured Portobello brick. Then SEA HOUSE, 1899, in pink snecked sandstone on an L-plan; somewhat Scots, with a silly turret to prove it. Next, as the road slopes upward, come two villas by *James B. Dunn*: THE WARREN, 1909, in stone-dressed harling with a crowstepped gable to each side (the mansard in the middle is an addition), and WHATTON LODGE, *c.* 1910, which shows what he could really do – in a gabled and mullioned Cotswold style translated into the local Rattlebags rubble. COLDSTONES by *J. M. Dick Peddie*, 1912, uses the same style and material to greater effect, building up an impressive composition from the hipped gable of COLDSTONES COTTAGE. At the top of the row is the CORNER HOUSE by *Robert Lorimer*, also built in 1912. Like its two neighbours it is stone-slated, but roofs and dormers are cosily hipped, and the rubble walling is of warmer colour, its flush pointing studded with dark, washed gravel. Across the road BELTON by *Richardson & McKay*, 1924. Its main outlook is downhill and its complex roof is pantiled, the harled walls relieved by the curious but effective mannerism of stones suddenly exposed, e.g. in a tall masonry buttress near one corner

and a similar band, with black whinstone pins, round the wall
head of the tall bow.

NISBET ROAD. THE DUNES. Roughcast and red tiles, by *James
B. Dunn*, c. 1910. MANSE (of the former United Free Church),
harled, with red brick and tiles, by *Sydney Mitchell*, c. 1908.

96 WHIM ROAD. WHITEHOLM by *Robert Lorimer*, 1904,
white-harled and very simple, with one projecting wing, informally approached from the road. MARGRIE (former parish
church manse) is by *James B. Dunn*, 1910. THE QUARRY by
97 *Morris & Steedman*, 1964, has two overlapping monopitch
gables, rendered white, over a brick and glass ground floor, the
larger one sloping down to shelter a verandah overlooking the
little glen.

ERSKINE ROAD. MIRAMICHI by *Robert Lorimer*, 1905,
roughcast with hipped roof, almost symmetrical. WHITE
LODGE (formerly WHITE HOUSE) by *John Jerdan*, 1933,
Colonial, with a curly gable canted across between the wings
of an L-plan. DALBRECK, by *Sir Frank Mears*, 1923–34,
half-timbered and perverse, is on the corner of Hopetoun Terrace, in which a group of twelve semi-detached houses by *Dick
Peddie & Walker Todd* for the County Council, 1920, put much
of Gullane's private housing to shame. They are of Rattlebags
rubble with much emphasis on their Welsh slated gables. The
doors are not on the front but at the ends.

Others of known authorship include GROSVENOR COTTAGE
and CRAIGLEA, a complicated double villa in MAIN STREET
by *James B. Dunn*, 1910; and MUIRFIELD GATE (formerly
THE PLEASANCE), designed by *Sydney Mitchell* for himself
in 1902, an intimate house, harled and tilehung, behind a single-
storey cottage range with a pretty gatehouse.

5070   HADDINGTON   EL

CHURCHES

15 PARISH CHURCH (ST MARY). Arguably the most impressive
of the late medieval Scottish burgh kirks. It is 62·8 m. long, i.e.
0·7 m. longer than St Giles, Edinburgh. But whereas St Giles
is the product of several centuries' fairly haphazard growth,
Haddington possesses a measure of uniformity that suggests
either a rapid rate of building or an unusually conscientious
adherence to original plans. This ideal quality of the building
is emphasized by its situation in a big open churchyard well

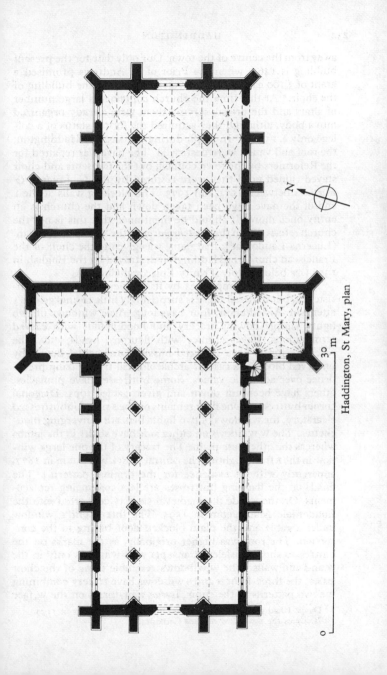

Haddington, St Mary, plan

away from the centre of the town. Our only date for the present building is 1462, when the Prior of St Andrews promised a grant of £100 each year for five years towards the building of the choir.* At this time the church contained a large number of altars and the priests serving them were already organized into a body, although they acquired the formal status of a college only c. 1540–6. In 1548, during the siege of Haddington, the roof and vaults were destroyed. The nave was repaired for the Reformers by the town council, but the transepts and choir stayed ruined until they were restored by *Ian G. Lindsay & Partners* between 1971 and 1973. The blocking walls at the E end of the nave have been taken down and the church is an entity once more. It should be mentioned that this is not the church referred to in the *Scotchronicon* as the 'Lamp of Lothian' (Lucerna Laudoniae): that name was given to the choir of the Franciscan church in Haddington destroyed by the English in 1356 (*see* below, Holy Trinity Episcopal Church).

The EXTERIOR impresses by its ample scale and its consistency, but in detail there is surprisingly little to engage one's attention. Aisled choir, four bays long. Aisle windows of two lights, simple flowing tracery and hoodmoulds with carved terminations. Eaves cornice with fleurons, heads, etc. The recent restorers have replaced missing ornamental details by uncarved blocks – a case of archaeological truth taking precedence over aesthetic values. Some buttresses have pinnacles, others have been cut down and given gabled tops. Diagonal corner buttresses. One flyer remains on the S side. Unbuttressed clearstory, the windows of two lights beneath converging mouchettes. The W windows on either side have shafts in the jambs whereas the others are plain. The tracery of the one large window in the E front, lighting the central vessel, was put in in 1877, apparently without evidence for the original pattern.‡ The finials on the flanking buttresses are less convincing replacements. On the N side the medieval sacristy converted into the Lauderdale Mausoleum in 1595. The three-light E window under a gable and the plain blocked door belong to the conversion. The roof was higher originally, as the marks on the buttresses show. Aisleless transepts with windows only in the W and end walls. The W windows resemble those of the choir aisles; the three-light N and S windows have tracery combining the two patterns of the choir. Large stair-turret on the W face

* David I had granted Haddington church to St Andrews in 1139.
‡ It copies the E window of Iona Cathedral.

of the s transept. The w corner of the N transept is of 1971–3. The crossing tower is a fine, severe design, almost a perfect cube in proportion. To each face three tall, closely spaced lancets with round heads, transoms and roll mouldings separated by hollows. Large stretches of plain wall either side of the openings are broken only by single image niches. This obviously incomplete design finishes abruptly with a fleuron cornice and gargoyles. The usual assumption is that it carried an open crown of the St Giles variety, and certainly the corbelled projections in the centre of each side make sense only as supports for this kind of termination. Yet is it not rather odd that there should be no provision for diagonal arches rising from the corners? If the intention to raise a crown is beyond reasonable doubt, there appears to be no positive evidence that one was ever actually built.

The nave is of yellowish-grey stone as against the red of the choir and transepts. The system is much the same as in the choir except that in four bays the aisle windows are like the end windows of the transepts. They are still two-light in the easternmost bay because the transept buttresses reduce the wall space. In 1811 *James Burn** raised the aisle walls by several feet and gave them English-looking parapets and pinnacles. The old cornice was re-used, but a small piece remains at the original level in the E bay on the s side. The easternmost window of the N clearstory has been blocked, presumably to stabilize the tower. The w front has one large window of six lights divided into two groups of three by a thick Y (cf. Seton). Capitals to the centre mullion and the jambs. Round-headed w door with several orders of filleted shafts, bushy foliage capitals and bell bases, both elided. Hoodmould with a foliage trail. One arch order with lumpy undercut leaves. The door is divided by a trumeau carrying semicircular arches. On the trumeau capital the Arma Christi. The whole design comes very close to the former s door (now E door) of St Giles, Edinburgh. The parapets and pinnacles are of 1811, as are the angle buttresses. Originally they were diagonal.

The most impressive thing about the INTERIOR was the [10] extensive use of stone vaulting. There are vaults still, but those in the choir and transepts are of fibreglass and belong to the 1971–3 restoration, those in the nave are plaster and part of the restoration of 1811. In the choir and transepts one can treat them as part of the original design, as they reproduce what

* The Heritors' Records show that he worked to *Archibald Elliot*'s design.

was there before. In the central vessel of the nave they utterly
alter the original conception, being replacements for an open
timber roof.

The choir arcades are tall but top-heavy in their proportions.
The fault lies with the piers, which are too short in relation
both to their own girth and to the height of the arches they
carry. They have four shafts alternating with four chamfered
projections, elided bases and mostly foliage capitals. The arch
mouldings are a sequence of flattened rolls with wide fillets.
Clearstory windows isolated by big areas of blank wall. The
vault shafts start directly above the piers as triplets and, most
perversely, turn single above the string course. High vault with
ridge ribs in both directions. Plain aisle vaults, quadripartite
and carried on corbels. The crossing piers follow the system
of the choir piers except for the introduction of fillet and extra,
slimmer shafts for the high vaults. Blank E walls in both transepts, presumably to allow for high reredoses (cf. Roslin). Very
steep arches into the nave and choir aisles. S transept vault with
two sets of tiercerons and two of ridge ribs. The N transept vault
has no tiercerons but was evidently meant to have them initially
(see the SE springers).

The nave gives a much less authentic impression, thanks to
James Burn. Originally it continued the system of the choir
almost without change. The most conspicuous feature of Burn's
work is the spindly plaster vaulting, four-centred and very flat
over the aisles to allow for galleries now removed. The other
main alteration – the raising of the arcades – was for the same
purpose. It is hard to believe that the result is not an improvement on the rather phlegmatic proportions of the choir. The
old capitals and arches were re-used. The position of the original aisle vaults is still clear from the chopped-back wall ribs
and corbels.* The plaster vault over the main span springs from
capitals that originally carried the wall post of a wooden roof
(cf. Holy Rude, Stirling). – PULPIT, FONT and WEST GAL-
LERY all by *George Henderson*, 1891, the first two of pink Corn-
cockle stone carved by *Birnie Rhind*. Expensively and dully
Late Gothic. – In the N transept a large new GALLERY of light
unvarnished wood by *Ian G. Lindsay & Partners*, a refreshingly
straightforward design, not without elegance. In time it will
carry an organ. – SCULPTURE. In the N choir aisle a stone panel
with the Haddington burgh arms (a goat) supported by angels.
It was discovered in the foundations of the N transept during

* Two original corbels remain in the W corners.

the 1971–3 restoration. – STAINED GLASS. S transept S window by *Morris & Co.*, late 1870s. Brought from St Michael, Torquay. The drawing has deteriorated, particularly the faces. Cleverly extended at the top to fit the present taller format. – In the S nave aisle three lights with simply and strongly drawn panels (Christ and the woman of Samaria *et al.*) against a background of pale green squares with flowering plants, by *Edward Burne-Jones*, executed by *Morris & Co.*, 1895; three lights (the vision of St John at Patmos) by *A. Ballantine & Gardiner*, 1893, the colours effectively graded towards the pale centre. – In the N aisle three lights (Christ preaching) by the same firm about the same time. – At the S end of the W gallery three lights (the Transfiguration) by *Heaton, Butler & Bayne* after 1931. – MONUMENTS. Against the N wall of the former sacristy, the Lauderdale monument, of marble, to Chancellor John Maitland Lord Thirlestane † 1595 with his wife Jane Fleming, and to their son John first Earl of Lauderdale (who erected it) with his countess Isabella Seton, both † 1638. Their effigies of alabaster lie in twin archways with three advanced Corinthian columns surmounted by tall consoles which support a thin cornice and broken pediment. Within the arches are busts, with inscribed black tablets beneath. A display of the combined heraldry of all these families culminates in the (possibly later) Maitland achievement. – Against the E wall of the S transept a stone tabernacle to William Seton, provost of Haddington, erected by his wife Agnes Black, 1682. Ionic capped caryatids, life-size, support an entablature with a pulvinated frieze and a scrolled broken pediment; between the scrolls a swag of fruit and a coat of arms with two boy supporters. – In the churchyard, a few older monuments are scattered between the newer. – Two C18 table-tops of red and cream sandstone respectively, to Galloway and Aitchison. – A square panelled pillar with cornice and domed top, beautifully inscribed to 'John Eliot Chyrugian Apothicary Burges in Haddington' † 1687 *aet.* 37. – War memorial at the entry. A cross of red sandstone by *G. Washington Browne*, 1919.

HOLY TRINITY (Episcopal), Church Street (on the site of the Franciscan friars' church known as the Lamp of Lothian, destroyed by the English in 1356). Built in 1769–70 as the English Chapel, i.e. for those who accepted King George; Lord Wemyss paid half the cost. The churchyard is entered between clustered shaft piers of the late C18, now clad in cement. Originally the church had windows to the S only, galleries to the W

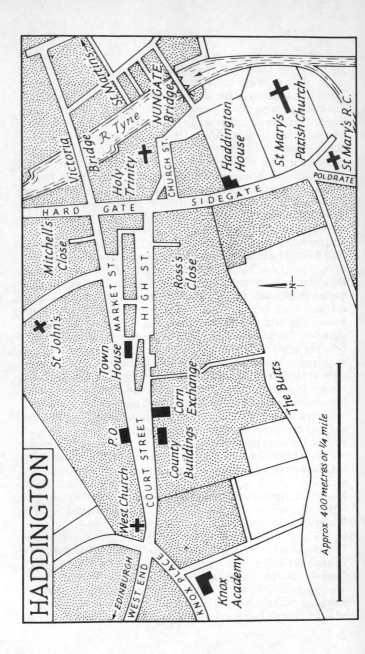

and N. The Wemyss room (now blocked off) was entered from the N gallery. In 1843 the building was overhauled and gothicized with tall lancets to the S and N, the open porch was added to the W entrance and a new three-sided gallery installed. In 1930 the shallow apse of 1843 was replaced by *B. N. H. Orphoot*'s Romano-Byzantine chancel with interlaced-arch windows and a red-tiled roof, and the whole interior is now his skilfully adaptive creation. Only the curved W section of the gallery remains, cutting into the rectangular space so as to suggest a cruciform church. The white-walled, groin-vaulted chancel, its grey-pink marble dado trimmed with mosaic, is seen through a triple arcade with white Byzantine columns and gilt capitals. (The adjacent round-arcaded church hall of 1892 gives its naïve sanction to the fashion of thirty years later.) – PULPIT. By *Birnie Rhind*, 1893. Of pink Corsehill stone, hexagonal, with relief panels of the four evangelists and the Good Samaritan, supported by Devonshire marble shafts, grey veined with pink and white. – ALTAR. Late C19 with alabaster reliefs, re-used in the new chancel by Orphoot, who added a reredos by *C. d'O. Pilkington Jackson* showing the Crucifixion and attendant angels in bas-relief. – STAINED GLASS. A late C19 memorial window (Feed My Lambs) has been artfully reset in a colourless glass surround on the N side of the chancel.

ST JOHN'S CHURCH OF SCOTLAND, Newton Port. Disused. A square Gothic box built in 1838 as a chapel of ease (i.e. for an overflow congregation) by *David Bryce*. Ashlar front projecting elaborately with a depressed-arch doorway, triple lancets and finally a delicate belfry of interlaced arches. Inside this projection is a gallery.

ST MARTIN. On the outskirts of the town by the Whittingehame road, with a few mature trees for company. The church came into the possession of the Cistercian nunnery at Haddington in the late C12, and what there is of detail would fit that date. Only the nave exists, ruined but fairly complete. Irregularly coursed red stone with lighter ashlar dressings. Round chancel arch with a hoodmould and plain imposts. Two windows in the S wall and one in the N wall, all round-headed with broad internal splays. The deep buttresses are no doubt connected with the addition of the pointed tunnel-vault. Of the same late date the N and S doors of the nave and possibly the plain openings in the W wall. A peculiar feature is the large number of square holes which go right through the walls. The RCAHMS discounts any connection with scaffolding, but offers no alternative explanation. To the s stands a mysterious square pillar with a worn fluted cornice and looking like a stranded gatepier. Is it a sundial?

St Mary's R.C. Chapel, Poldrate. 1862 by *E. W. Pugin*. An aisleless, lanceted church of yellow sandstone with paler horizontal bands and dressings. The wheel window in the w gable lights an openwork timber gallery whose dark stain matches the pulpit and scissor roof. Apsidal sanctuary and two flanking chapels.

West Church of Scotland (former Free Church), Court Street. 1890 by *Sydney Mitchell & Wilson* in red Loch sandstone. Mixed Gothic, the gables of church and hall building up towards the corner turret of the square tower, which has a gently baronial top. The interior is detailed with equal care: square chamfered piers between clearstory-lit nave and narrow aisles, the roof principals springing from attached shafts. Gallery at the s end.

PUBLIC BUILDINGS

Town House, e end of Court Street. *William Adam* produced elevations for work to be done in 1742, but nothing remains from that period. In 1788 the courtroom was built to the w over a segmentally arcaded basement. Pedimented gable with coupled pilasters, Venetian window in the centre. Slightly later s wing with panelled pilasters in the manner of *James Burn*. The steeple, replacing an earlier one of Dutch type and echoing the detail of the courtroom gable with suitable austerity, is by *James Gillespie* [*Graham*], 1831. The courtroom itself was repaired, and a good neo-Georgian vestibule formed underneath, by *Peter Whiston*, 1952.

Knox Academy, Knox Place. The original building is by *John Starforth*, 1877, very Gothic, with a statue of Knox in a niche on the central tower; portraits of other reformers in the panels between the windows were never carried out. 'Hardly appropriate for a memorial to the great leveller of Mediaeval observances', says the *Builder*. Extension by *J. A. Carfrae*, 1909. A quite separate school built *c.* 1930 was extended by *Alan Reiach & Partners* in 1959. It is an excellent building, but the same firm did better, and with fewer materials, at the Primary School round the corner in Meadowpark: buff brick and horizontal boarding, beautifully matched in line and colour. Its date is 1970.

County Buildings, Court Street. Mullioned and hood-

moulded Tudor by *William Burn*, 1832, with a depressed arch
over the entrance (cf. St John, above). Snecked rubble extension along Court Street by *Dick Peddie & Walker Todd*, 1931.
The further extension to the s by *Peter Whiston*, 1956, is equally
well judged.

CORN EXCHANGE, Court Street. Freely classical, with pedimented 'nave' and aisles, by *Francis Farquharson* of Haddington, 1853; *Bailie Durward*, builder. Massive timber roof
with top lighting over the central hall by *Dickson*, joiner, with
Robertson & Lister of Glasgow.

FACTORY (Tandberg), on the w approach. 1976 by *A. Campbell
Mars*. An organic plan is expressed by a variety of treatments
from the monumental to the pseudo-vernacular, but the colours
are disciplined and the landscaping excellent.

HERDMANFLAT HOSPITAL, Aberlady Road. The Admission
Unit, of panel construction with the male and female wards projecting on cantilevers, is by *Peter Womersley*, 1965.

DESCRIPTION

Leaving the A1 by-pass, which has saved Haddington from
through traffic, the approach from Edinburgh is along WEST
END, lined to the l. with Victorian and then early C19 villas
of which BELLEVUE is unusual; its single-storey wings, common features in this wealthy town, have been built up *c.* 1840
like corner towers and topped with ogee roofs. After an interlude of well maintained traditional housing of the C20 on a decisive cross axis, the MONUMENT to Robert Ferguson M.P.
of Raith marks the real beginning of the town. It is dated 1843.
The figure on its Greek Doric column and the four mourners
at the foot are by *Robert Forrest*. KNOX PLACE leads off to
the r. past Knox Academy (*see* above) and eventually the former
HADDINGTON FOUNDRY, a three-aisled early C19 shed now
used as a garage, its pantiled roofs supported by cast-iron
columns. A pantiled cottage nicely sited on the splayed corner
of Knox Place welcomes you into town. Here stood the West
Port, and COURT STREET forms the apex of what was until
the C16 the long open triangle of the medieval High Street.
After the West Church (*see* p. 238) it continues rather unexpectedly in the character of a Georgian suburb with spaciously laid out villas. HILTON LODGE, in fine red brick,
shelters behind a high wall with round gatepiers, but the rest
are open to the street and have been politely urbanized by
change of use. The grandest is No. 44, now the BANK OF

SCOTLAND, with tripartite windows under segmental arches on the ground floor, relief panels on the wings and a sphinx crowning the centre. It was built in 1802–3, possibly by *James Burn*. Like the single-storey WESTON on the other side (built before 1819 and now the POLICE STATION) it has a lamp-holder of virtuoso ironwork bridging its gatepiers. Beside the police station the good straightforward FIRE STATION of 1964 by *Reiach & Hall*; glazed doors with heavy transoms reveal but protect the engines inside. Amid the villas the classical POST OFFICE by *W. T. Oldrieve* of *H.M. Office of Works*, 1908, is quite at home. To the r. a row of limes cuts off a quiet sliver of street from the traffic. The crown-topped MONUMENT in red sandstone, 1880 by *David Rhind* (modelled on the well head at Pinkie, *see* p. 336), commemorates the eighth Marquess of Tweeddale with a portrait bust signed and dated *G. B. Amendola* 1880. Behind the trees are the County Buildings and Corn Exchange (*see* p. 238). At this end the central island blocks the old High Street triangle with the plain VICTORIA INN, but Court Street pushes past it to the l. and (with closer-packed frontages which are ordinary except for the mid C19 GRANARY to the r.) forms a little square in front of the Town House (*see* p. 238) whose spire has presided over the street from the start.

Past the Town House is MARKET STREET. In the wider first part the oldest building is the crowstepped back gable of No. 78 High Street (the mercat cross is glimpsed down the slit beyond it) and the grandest Nos. 60–62, a quoined three-storey block with a pedimented doorpiece and scrolled skewputts. Market Street, its end almost blocked by two more early C19 pubs, then squeezes past them into Hardgate, with a major incident on the way: the Palladian palace front of Nos. 7–8, of *c.* 1760, five bays with a pedimented centrepiece of giant Ionic pilasters over a rusticated ground floor, the three first-floor windows lugged and pedimented – triangle, segment, triangle; altogether a flattened version of *Isaac Ware*'s house as executed for Lord Wemyss' son (*see* Amisfield), omitting the outer bays and parapet. On the same side are two closes, the first with a paved cart track threading its way past the C18 manse of John Brown, the secessionist minister to the former BURGHER KIRK of 1806 (now used by the British Legion), a rectangular meeting house whose countrified pantile roof and orange rubble walls are set off by the elaborate contemporary glazing of the four tall round-headed windows. Further to the rear a slightly later house and its garden occupy the rest of the original burgess plot. The second is MITCHELL'S CLOSE, with an early C18 polygonal stair-tower to the l. and a pleasant clutter of later backland development of the sort that rulebound restorations usually sweep away, preserved entire in 1964–7 by *Campbell & Arnott* for the County Council, one side being kept as housing, the other as craft workshops, in a perfect blend of archaeological and adaptive restoration. The same architects, as part of the same Comprehensive Development Area Scheme, designed the sensible modern CLINIC, thus adding large plate-glass windows to the vocabulary and yet another use to this little close, which now runs out into HARDGATE. This (the road to Dunbar) has lost much by widening as part of the same C.D.A. programme, but the corner is well reorganized to form a small square in front of the white-harled early C18 KINLOCH HOUSE, of three storeys with crowstepped gables and a central curvilinear chimney gable, restored by *Campbell & Arnott*, 1962.

Parallel to Market Street is High Street, which begins to the r. of the Victoria Inn with the short LODGE STREET. The former MASONIC LODGE itself has a pend arch supported on the l. by a stumpy C17 or earlier half-column, but its main feature is now the late C18 Venetian window on the upper floor. Then the mid C18 façade of what is misleadingly called CARLYLE HOUSE,* a tiny five-bay palace with channelled quoins which decide to form piers after an indeterminate start to the l. A rusticated ground-floor centrepiece (altered) supports giant Corinthian pilasters which just qualify for that name because over the elaborately keystoned *piano nobile* windows are panels (enriched at the centre) concealing the lower part of an attic. The dormer windows, chastely abolished in the Town Council restoration of 1960, were camouflaged by a balustrade. Vases overall. The house projects, with its less pretentious end elevation, inconsequentially into the HIGH STREET, a neat rectangle with a slight bow on the s side and only one obvious exit, down a narrow extension into Hardgate. To all appearances a mixed Georgian street of three and four storeys, it nonetheless hides some earlier work. The s side has frequent variations in roof pitch. Nos. 43–45 (until 1855 the Bluebell Inn) have a bulging stair-turret, and No. 31 still has fragments of late C17 moulded ceilings. Of early Georgian work the most obvious is betrayed by the flat arch of No. 11 and the thick astragals and piended dormers of Nos. 15–18. ROSS'S CLOSE at No. 34 also

---

* Dr Welsh's house where Carlyle's wife was born is the late C18 house immediately behind it, with a tall pedimented s front to the garden.

has big astragals. (Behind it the new housing by *Campbell &
Arnott*, 1963, is a misfire, an up-to-date exploitation of some
supposedly traditional principle of caprice in the placing of windows.) No. 32 has a horizontally channelled first floor (and formerly second floor too) with scrolled skewputts to the dormer.
Of later Georgian the most suave example is at Nos. 35–36,
with a patera string course and simplified giant pilasters at the
ends – the trademark of *James Burn*, who rebuilt much of the
N side in 1803–7. Here Nos. 82–84 are outstanding, with angle-
voluted Ionic columns along two shopfronts and the central
common-stair entry between them. Of Victorian shopfronts the
finest are at Nos. 19–20, with cast-iron cresting. As if eager to
eliminate street-front gables, the COMMERCIAL HOTEL at
No. 73 has joined two narrow gables to form one wide one. Of
the C19 commercial palace style there are only No. 47, *c.* 1830,
with its horizontal glazing and eccentrically placed ground-
floor openings, and the palace-fronted BANK OF SCOTLAND
(formerly British Linen Bank) at No. 48, *c.* 1850. The vista ends
at the E with the C18 CASTLE HOTEL, to which the early C19
added a tower and battlements and the early C20 some deplor-
able false stonework; only the S end round the corner is un-
affected, with an elegant tripartite ballroom window. The ballroom and its anteroom are designed *en suite*, with plain Grecian
plasterwork of *c.* 1820. In 1962 the whole High Street was the
subject of an improvement scheme (the first in Scotland) by
Eric Hall, and an unaffectedly high standard in paint colour
and street furniture is now established throughout the town.
HARDGATE, starting from the N, has some detached houses of
which the best is the OLD BANK, probably by *James Burn*,
c. 1800; it has another curly iron lampholder between its
gatepiers. The junctions with Market Street and High Street
are both rather untidy despite the green plots that have replaced
buildings demolished to improve the sight lines. But the former
has a block of rubble-faced FLATS by *John Grant*, 1957, well
enough related to Kinloch House (*see* above), and the latter the
single block of the medieval CUSTOM STONE resited in the
middle of the grass. On the E side No. 14, a detached Georgian
house standing back from the rest, is followed by a nice pair
of Victorian shopfronts and then by No. 1, whose standard
Georgian frontage closes the High Street vista. SIDEGATE
begins with a decisive corner building of 1874 incorporating
a FLOOD MARK of 1775 and continues with bread-and-butter
Georgian and also a good selection of cake. On the N side SUM-

MERFIELD HOUSE, early C19, with a painted front and a Roman Doric doorpiece, two little pedimented pavilions to the front. Then the pedimented MANSE of the same period, up its own drive at r. angles to the street, and NEWBURN LODGE with three grey stone gables, 1875. On the S side HADDINGTON HOUSE. The balustraded stair and canopied doorway bear the initials of Alexander Maitland and his wife Katherine Cunninghame with the date 1680, but the rear view shows that this is a somewhat earlier C17 house on a L-plan with an octagonal stair-turret in the angle. About 1800 a bowed fillet was inserted between the turret and the S jamb, and the street front extended with a single-storey wing with a Venetian window to the garden. On the N side three late C17 rooms, all with pilastered fireplaces. Incorporated into the overmantel of the first-floor fireplace a tempera-painted panel, apparently of the earlier C17 date. Elsewhere are good finishings of the early C19. The house was restored by *W. Schomberg Scott* in 1969 as the headquarters of the Lamp of Lothian Collegiate Centre. Sidegate continues past the entrance to the parish church and is well terminated, albeit by a nondescript house, before it continues into POLDRATE. Here is St Mary's R.C. church (for both churches *see* above) and POLDRATE MILL (or East Mill) on the site of the medieval Kirk Mill. The present group of buildings is mainly of the C18, including the mill itself at the roadside, reconstructed in 1842, the granary, maltings and a range of workers' houses to the rear. Their conversion for use by the Lamp of Lothian Trust was begun in 1968, and the C19 iron wheel and some of the machinery have been preserved *in situ*. WATERLOO BRIDGE was built across the Tyne in 1815 with stone from the Colstoun estate.

CHURCH STREET has a splayed entry at the point where Hardgate becomes Sidegate. Its S side begins with the freely remodelled local authority houses of ST ANNE'S GATE, the work of *John Grant* in 1955, in which a relief panel of the Haddington goat has been reinstated. Then No. 19 of *c.* 1830, with a heavily pilastered doorpiece, followed by an outstanding C18 group: the mid-century block of Nos. 14–16 (built as the Burgh School) with a central chimney gable and quoins and other dressings in red sandstone, followed by the lower, whitewashed row with two chimney gables. Both blocks were restored as housing for the Town Council by *John Grant* in 1960. They face Holy Trinity (*see* above). The end of the street is nicely contained by ELM HOUSE, built in 1785, but it continues into

THE SANDS, a good row in which No. 1 has a pedimented porch. Further on on the r. is LADY KITTY'S (i.e. Lady Catherine Charteris's) GARDEN. In the wall a gateway with ball finials and a castellated Gothic cylindrical DOOCOT on a square base. The doocot is on the line of NUNGATE BRIDGE with its three ribless arches, basically a red sandstone construction of the C16, repaired in the C18 when the steep gradient of the E side was modified by further arches and an ingenious pair of stairways to the road along the further bank. Here was the Barony of NUNGATE, some of whose character has survived thanks in the first place to the restoration of No. 1 with its Gothic fanlight, just after the bridge, by *Mary Tindall* in 1953. A good row still stands along the river Tyne to the s of the bridge, but the future of this little place rests equally with the new housing that is just beginning to fill the gaps.

The other way over the Tyne is in the direct line of Market Street by way of VICTORIA BRIDGE, two spans in cast iron by *Belfrage & Carfrae*, engineers, 1898. To the N on the further side the BERMALINE MILL of *c.* 1900 in red rock-faced sandstone, and beyond it, to the N again, the rubble and pantile GIMMER'S MILL which had the only double undershot wheel in the county.

AMISFIELD HOUSE. *See* p. 76.

BARNES CASTLE. *See* p. 93

LENNOXLOVE. *See* p. 279.

LETHAM HOUSE. *See* p. 281.

STEVENSON HOUSE. *See* p. 441.

VILLA

(GREENKNOWE, near the A1. A villa of *c.* 1820, single storey and basement. Pilastered five-bay front of fine ashlar. The wreathed frieze breaks forward over the Doric-columned doorpiece. Garden house with brushwood eaves.)

FARMS

ABBEY MAINS, 3 km. ENE. The farmhouse has the distinctive horizontal glazing of *c.* 1830. The single-storey cottages were built at the same time – originally as a continuous row of eight one-room dwellings. In 1845 they were split into three blocks, each containing a pair of two-room dwellings, and two more blocks were added to the E. They were altered once again *c.* 1956, each block into a single house.

ACREDALES, 1 km. S. The steading, much altered, is adjoined by a neat row of six early C19 single-storey cottages. A smart white paling to the road.

AMISFIELD MAINS, 2 km. NE. The castellated Gothic lodge with pink sandstone frontage to the A1, and also the range up the hill with similar end gables, were, according to tradition, put up by Lord Wemyss as useful ornaments to the park of Amisfield House (*see* p. 76), apparently in the early C19. The former is now supported by cottages of *c.* 1830 and the latter, which lay along the old road, is part of a steading. The white-harled early C19 farmhouse owes its distinctive look to the blanking-out of the front door under the centre pediment.

BARNEY MAINS, 2.5 km. NNE. A complete early C19 group, almost a village, consisting of a farmhouse (heavily altered), steading and numerous rows of cottages.

BEGBIE, 4 km. SW. An early C19 farm steading. Large central shed with four parallel pantiled roofs. Facing their gables a six-doored cartshed. – BRIDGE over the Tyne. Probably late C18, with rustic piers and segmental arch over which the parapet comes to a point.

BYRES, 3 km. NNW. Farm and farmhouse of *c.* 1800 with arcaded cartshed and cottage rows, all built of variegated rubble with sandstone dressings, the roofs mainly pantiled. A compact group and still a picturesque one, despite modernization.

MONKRIGG, 1.5 km. SSE. A modest dormered house by *William Burn*, 1834, to which was added *c.* 1863 (to judge from the steading) a square orielled tower of formidable profile and a single-storey porch to one side. To the other was appended a baronial water tower, and a two-storey wing now demolished. The centrepiece of the steading, dated 1863, has scrolled supports and a slated octagonal spirelet. The whole building was made into flats in 1975. Bargeboarded farmhouse, presumably of 1863 as well.

SAMUELSTON, 4 km. SW. A long string of single-storey cottages, some now missing, linking three farm steadings. The house of EAST MAINS is largely of 1828. Its mill and farm were built in 1835. It has a chimney, as does MID MAINS, rebuilt after a fire in 1896–7 (the farmhouse 1900). Further to the W a mill and farmhouse of 1819, and finally the early C19 WEST END FARM. At some distance is SOUTH MAINS, whose cottages are of 1835.

WEST BEARFORD, 3 km. ESE. A picturesque group on a sloping site, probably C18. Granaries and cartshed of rubble with pantile roofs; yellow brick chimney.

5070   HAILES CASTLE   EL
                      2 km. SW of East Linton

2 A C13–14 castle of enclosure, well viewed from the A1 which runs
   along the ridge to the N. The first part, probably built by one
   of the Earls of Dunbar, has an oblong tower and a curtain wall
   extending to the E, perched on the rocky S bank of the river
   Tyne. The curtain is penetrated by a stair with chamfered cross
   ribs descending to the well, and possibly by way of a ladder
   to the river itself. In the C14 the Hepburns extended the curtain
   to the W, ending with a salient square tower on the promontory
   between the Tyne and a small tributary stream. The rest of
   the curtain is of the C14, and the surviving parts include a main
   gateway on the S side and a little postern at the E end.
      Both the towers have pit prisons, entered through a hole in
   the tunnel-vault. The earlier tower has pointed openings in its
   cubical masonry. Upper parts rebuilt. To the E a vaulted cellar.
   The W tower is a little clearer in its arrangements: a turnpike
   stair at the NE corner, with two windows in the form of an I
   with serifs, for crossbow firing. On the S wall are traces of a
   big fireplace at an upper level. The range between the towers
   is puzzling. It seems to have been formed behind the curtain
   in the C15, and it has a tunnel-vaulted basement which Dr
   James Richardson in the DOE guidebook does not hesitate to
   call a bakehouse. But where are the flues? The next floor is
   entered through an external doorway built into the middle of
   a big depressed-arch opening, chamfered all round, with
   corbels underneath for an external wooden landing. Dr
   Richardson quite plausibly calls this a chapel, and takes at its
   face value the ogee-topped piscina to the E of it, but the
   RCAHMS insists that the latter is not in its original place. Why
   would anyone bother to move it? The old tower which provides
   the W wall of this upper room (whatever it may have been) has
   had its stepped string course chopped off on this side. If the
   upper part was indeed a chapel, it was certainly much altered
   later on by the introduction of a normal storey height for ordinary rooms.

0060   HARBURN HOUSE   ML
                      3.5 km. SE of West Calder

   A largish house in droved yellow ashlar, its plainness accentuated
   both inside and out by the stiff detail characteristic of its date,

1804. Five bays, two storeys plus a basement which is sunk on the entrance front. Roman Doric doorpiece. Two bow windows at the back. The entrance hall leads between fluted Roman Doric columns to the stairwell, the graceful balusters with lion's head medallions a concession to prettiness. In the library and drawing room to the l., both with shallow bowed ends, chimneypieces respectively of black marble with corner blocks, white marble with a head of Apollo in the centre panel.

SUMMER HOUSE. Late C19, a finicky and delectable specimen in painted wood, facing the front door at an angle. – STABLES to the s, a square with arched pend, possibly earlier than the house. – WALLED GARDEN. – DOOCOT of c. 1830, a tall crenallated Gothic tower. – MONUMENT. A column with ball finial commemorating the visit of Charles X of France to Harburn in 1832.

HARDENGREEN see DALKEITH

HARELAW
5 km. SSE of Gifford

EL *5060*

An Iron Age timber-laced fort with traces of vitrifaction, originally about 60 m. by 30 m. Outworks are also visible.

HARESTONE HILL see HOPES

HARVIESTON HOUSE
0.5 km. S of Gorebridge

ML *3060*

Probably C17 in the first place, enlarged with a modest bow c. 1800, almost obscured by a baronial porch and dummy turrets (the work of *James Brown*) in 1869, and further by battlemented bays in 1901. In the bow is the first-floor drawing room of 1869 with a coved ceiling and pretty roundels of putti. LODGE, also bowed, and GATEPIERS of c. 1800.

HATTON HOUSE
4 km. E of East Calder

ML *1060*

Built in the late C17 by Charles Maitland, subsequently Earl of Lauderdale, Hatton was a near-quadrangular composition, with circular corner turrets, round a C15 L-plan tower. Later used as a farmhouse and store, it was burnt out in 1952 and demolished in 1955. Only a few accessories remain. TERRACE along the S side of the house site, with a two-storey pavilion at each end, formerly ogee-roofed. Behind its bowed centre a BATH HOUSE built into the higher ground. Segmental-vaulted and lined with a bench on each side, it ends with a round bath under a rusticated arch. LION GATES on the E (entrance) side, a pair of rusticated piers bearing lions, dated 1665. SUMMER HOUSE dated 1704. The SOUTH GATES, standing back from the A71, are inscribed on the keystone ANNO DOM 1692–1829 (1829 is the date when they were resited here). Tall central arch with fluted Roman Doric pilasters bearing deep cornices (the finials are missing). Between them an inverted arch. The rhythm is kept up by scrolls over the smaller side archways.

HAWTHORNDEN CASTLE   ML
0.5 km. NW of Rosewell

The castle stands on the precipitous rocks that here form the E bank of the river North Esk. It is triangular overall. At the SE corner a ruined C15 tower faced with ashlar blocks like the contemporary work at Roslin 2 km. upstream, but of red sandstone. In the N wall a very uncomfortable stone seat for a doorman. A hatch to the S gives access to a pit prison of the same period, partly cut out of the rock, and vaulted with chamfered buttress-ribs; in its S wall a window and pointed-arch garderobe, complete with drain. The round-headed windows along the S side of the courtyard must have lit a hall of later date. The buildings to the N are basically the work of the poet Sir William Drummond who, according to a Latin inscription on a tablet on the N range, restored the house 'for himself and his successors' in 1638. The E range has a handsome doorpiece to the outside of the pend, with a square heraldic panel breaking into a crowning pediment. Studded timber door with an iron knocker, its plate cut out with the initials of Sir William's son and daughter-in-law. One of the slots for draw-bars at the back is said to have its original oak lining. Oval gun loops overlook the entry from the pink rubble wall, stripped of its harling. In the N range a rather more refined Renaissance doorway with the graceful heraldic plaque of Bishop Abernethy, dated 1795, set over it. The windows in the red-harled wall are of various dates, including some from the early C18 with thick astragals, and a row of late C19 dormers on the third (attic) floor. At the W end of this range a single-storey extension with a large grotesque head carved in red sandstone. Finally a bench carved out of the rock on the brink of the cliff.

The internal layout of Sir William's L-shaped building has been altered, but a first-floor bedroom to the E still has a moulded ceiling of effective crudity formed of a central panel and radiating plaques, only one with enough space to be complete. In the adjacent bedroom at the NE angle an early C18 flat-arched and panelled sandstone fireplace carved with three shells. Also early C18 the little round-arched fireplace at the foot of the staircase, and most of the finishings in the ground-floor LIBRARY: fielded panelling, lugged doorcases, and a flat-arched fireplace with a late C18 iron hob with a half-circular hanging grate. The bracketed cornice and the informal but elegant main staircase are of the same period.

MEMORIAL at the base of the old tower. To Sir L. Abernethy (C14) and to the poet Sir William Drummond, erected by Dr William Abernethy Drummond, spouse to Mrs Drummond of Hawthornden. It is also inscribed:

O SACRED SOLITUDE, DIVINE RETREAT
CHOICE OF THE PRUDENT, ENVY OF THE GREAT . . .

WELL, in the courtyard. The shaft is cut through the rock into the floor of the cave below.

FOUNTAINS, to the E of the tower. C17, with pediments and finials.

The CAVES below the former S range, pronounced by Dr Stukely to be Pictish, go back at least as far as Alexander de Ramsay in 1341. Largely man-made, they bear narrow chisel marks on the rock walls. Two converging galleries, with a flight of worn steps leading up to cave-rooms of more natural and highly romantic contour at the cliff face, where there are openings. In one of them a COLUMBARIUM of about 370 compartments, cut from the rock. The RCAHMS also notes a cave in the rocks to the NE of the castle.

HEDDERWICK HILL
4km. W of Dunbar

EL 6070

The red brick WALLED GARDEN of the demolished house, probably late C18, can be seen on the slope to the N of the A1.

HERDMANSTOUN see EAST SALTOUN

3050

HERIOT   ML*

PARISH CHURCH. Quite solitary, near the Heriot Water. Rebuilt in pink rubble by *Wardrop & Reid*, 1875, in a highly fancy Gothic style with a bellcote and crosses on the gables. One harled gable is an odd survival from the old kirk of 1804.

HERMAND HOUSE see WEST CALDER

HERMISTON see RICCARTON

HILTY see LINLITHGOW

5060

HOPES   EL
Longyester, 5 km. SE of Gifford

Secluded between the Hope Hills, a square house built *c.*1823 for the Hays of Yester by *James Burn* of Haddington, who probably designed it too, to judge from the abundance of plain piers, triple openings and segmental arches. Two storeys plus a basement whose windows are clear of the ground except on the smooth white ashlar entrance front, where a carriage-sweep mounts to the door. The semicircular porch (*see* Dunbar, Lauderdale House), with two rather squat Ionic columns and a balcony balustrade, and the advanced side bays are out to impress, but the other walls are harled except for string course and cornice.

The real impression is made inside, by lucid plan and telling detail. Square entrance hall with a round ceiling on pendentives (thin ribs coming down to near-Gothic brackets). Wide, shallow niches on each side. A finely glazed screen repeating the external openings leads into the central saloon-cum-staircase, again square, with a black marble chimneypiece (plain lintel between pylons) in one corner. The stair ascends round three sides. From each end of the landing on the fourth, a gallery runs round behind antae – three bays on each side. The antae are simplified Doric with beaded edges and no base. Over them on all four sides are segmental arches containing big foliated paterae, then pendentives, and a shallow dome with a conical light. The rooms, except for the little apsed boudoir over the

85

* Now Borders Region.

hall, are large and simple (the tripartite windows are a sham), with Grecian cornices of egg-and-dart variously supplemented, and woodwork that is by no means up-to-date. Of the original chimneypieces the finest is in the small dining room; white statuary marble with reeded columns supporting graceful reliefs of Justice with sword and scales, Education with birch, and at the centre Music with tambourine, in airborne posture. Those in the drawing rooms on the S side (both c. 1840) were introduced from outside c. 1962.

On Harestone Hill, 1·5 km. SE, is a CAIRN (see Introduction, p. 23).

HOPETOUN HOUSE
3 km. WNW of South Queensferry

WL 0070

A veritable palace, whose inconsistencies may be easily recognized and as easily forgotten. The E (entrance) front is seen first, a work of resounding splendour by *William Adam* from 1721 until his death in 1748 when *John Adam* and his other sons took over, slightly modifying his design and fitting out the new rooms. On the W side the body of the earlier house by *Sir William Bruce*, 1699–1701, survives as a reluctant centrepiece. The Adam additions and alterations do not come to terms with it, but internally the relationship between old and new is much more satisfactory.

The Hopes bought the estate in the C17. Charles Hope was sixteen years old when his mother Lady Margaret Hope signed the contract with Bruce on 28 September 1698. The mason was *Tobias Bachope* of Alloa (his name is variously spelt), the plumber and glazier *John Forster* of Berwick. The main block, three sides of which can still be seen on the W front, has much of the three-dimensional quality of James Smith's Melville House in Fife, then still under construction. It is a double-pile with pedimented centrepieces on its deep flanks to N and S, and a big segmental pediment over the recessed centre to the W. Except for the quoins, only the basement is rusticated. The remainder, supplanted by Adam's work, is illustrated in *Vitruvius Britannicus* (second volume, 1717). Two flanking blocks were attached to the E corners. Their main effect was on the E front 74 where, with the pedimented centre, they formed a majestic trio, united by horizontal rustication; thus the change of scale from one front to the other was already explicit in Bruce's design. On the E front the median cornice ran right along the top of

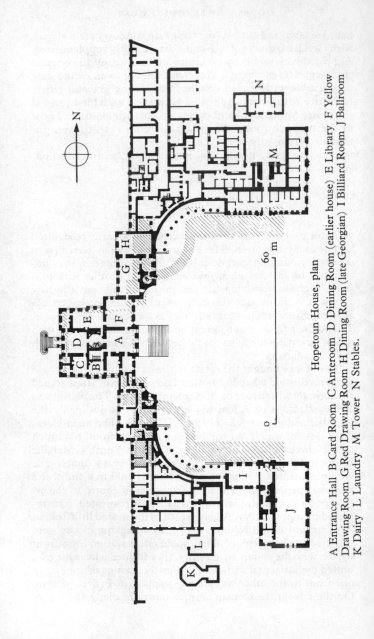

Hopetoun House, plan

A Entrance Hall B Card Room C Anteroom D Dining Room (earlier house) E Library F Yellow Drawing Room G Red Drawing Room (late Georgian) H Dining Room I Billiard Room J Ballroom K Dairy L Laundry M Tower N Stables.

the main storey and then continued over the giant flanking colonnades which, if they were built, were of convex plan, bulging into the forecourt. The apex of the whole composition was the 'stone Cupola over the great staircase'.

William Adam's work took shape in a rather piecemeal fashion. The documentation* begins in 1721 with a bill to Charles Hope, now first Earl of Hopetoun, for demolition at the S end of the 'old' house. Here Adam built a new flanking block, further from the centre than Bruce's and of greater projection; the account for the mason work for this block, which forms the S end of Adam's frontage, was presented in 1725. In the following year prices were agreed for 'Pillars of the Collonnade' at the S end, which suggests that Bruce's colonnades were never built. 1729 saw an 'Agreement on new E front to conform to the new south Building'. Adam was to 'take off the old Cornish and Pediment with all the work‡ above the lintels' and 'to build the new designed north addition ... which is 2 ft longer than the S building'. In May 1736 prices were agreed on the 'N Collonade stables and other buildings or offices on that side as also the addition to the S Collonade, Library and Billiard Room ... commenced the beginning of the year 1735 when the N Collonade was begun'. The 'Measurings of ye Steeple' (presumably the cupola over the N pavilion) were submitted in 1724. After sundry other business Adam received his general discharge for £4,443 on 30 May 1746; he was the contractor as well as the architect in the modern sense.

Although William Adam may have started his work without a clear idea of how it was going to finish, his aim was obvious: to provide the Earl with a House of State, the term used in Sir John Clerk's poem *The Country Seat* (*see* Mavisbank, Loanhead). Bruce's E front was long (thirteen bays) but characteristically modest, with an entrance that was merely the centre arch of a triple arcade. *Vitruvius Britannicus*, in which it was illustrated, also furnished Adam with ideas for its transformation. His giant order of Corinthian pilasters with attic and balustrade recall many of the designs in the book, e.g. the London house of the Duke of Powis. At Hopetoun they unite a complicated front from end to end, not only in the regular rhythm of the centre but in the two forward breaks, one with a concave curve, as if the plan of the entrance front at Blenheim had been raised to a uniform height. The round-headed windows with

74

76

* I am grateful to Dr Alistair Rowan for these particulars.
‡ Some of the carving may be at Luffness House EL.

mask keystones resemble those at Castle Howard. The result
is by no means up-to-date, but judged on its own merits it is
highly successful. Perhaps the whole front is over-articulated
– e.g. by the string courses that lash it together horizontally –
but the detail is sensitive in its projection from the grey ashlar
front, and beyond praise in execution. Over the three centre
bays Adam intended, and apparently provided for, a huge portico. The *Vitruvius Scoticus* engraving shows how it would have
looked: tetrastyle, of distyle projection, its pediment overlapping the attic storey, its basement flanked by a perron staircase.

The weakest features – exactly those in which Bruce had
excelled – are the colonnades, which William Adam designed
in the more orthodox concave quadrant form. They are uneasily
related to the frontage and carelessly joined to it. Spatially they
give no sense of enclosure, only of sideways spread; here the
central portico would undoubtedly have helped. Architecturally they are much better related to the PAVILIONS, which,
though on the available evidence apparently built by William
Adam, are very different from those in the *Vitruvius Scoticus*
plate. Their classical elegance is surely more characteristic of
the sons than the father, but John was only fifteen and Robert
eight years old when the library (S) pavilion was started in 1736.
Tall pedimental windows have been substituted for the two
storeys previously intended, and coupled pilasters have taken
the place of single ones, with coupled columns supporting the
central pediments whose heraldic carving is executed with great
virtuosity, tenuously undercut but still perfectly preserved.
The 'steeples' that rise from the pavilions are by William Adam
as we have seen: square base, octagonal cupola with gadrooned
roof, and a little crowning lantern. The one to the N forms a
grand entrance feature, with scrolled supports, to the STABLES.
A pend at the base, diagonally rib-vaulted, leads to the mouth
of the straw-chute (the loft is overhead) and thence to the stalls
with their arched and niched mangers. The S pavilion is identical from the front but very different behind, concealing miscellaneous offices to the rear of a N-facing billiard room and an
E-facing ballroom. Although some of the woodwork, e.g. in the
vestibule, is C18, the remainder has more of the character of
c. 1900. The ballroom in particular (this was the position of the
library) is expert but perfunctory. It is impossible to say
whether it would have been within the capability of *Andrew
Dickson*, the estate clerk of works from 1878 to 1913 and 'architect for improvements to Hopetoun House'. *R. Rowand Ander-*

son, who designed the main gates (*see* below), is a possibility, but no record has come to light.

On the WEST FRONT William Adam can hardly be said to have respected the surviving body of Bruce's house. He faithfully reproduced the detail and the levels, but the wings have nudged forwards and robbed the pediments of their central position. An even greater difficulty is the attic, a proud feature of the new E elevation; it is returned along the ends and then comes to a sudden stop – a regular Yukon front with an impossible false window. The workaday single-storey extensions and the outlying wall with yew trees in its blank arcade are much happier.

John Adam and his brothers, of whom *Robert* commanded respect at Hopetoun even before their father's death in 1748, were responsible for the third stage in the development of the house. They did not build the portico, but Lord Hopetoun was put to considerable expense in 1754 for the rebuilding and recutting of what had already been done. The result was the barest advance of the three middle bays, and the plainest of temple staircases leading up to them without a balustrade. Whether it was the second Earl, who succeeded in 1742, or his architects who inspired the decision, the effect is one of sober magnificence; a neo-classical centrepiece to the rough-and-tumble of William Adam's Baroque façade.*

OLD ROOMS. Most of the rooms in *Bruce*'s main block remain intact, with their plain coved ceilings, sparingly enriched panelling with lugged doorways, and moulded chimneypieces of speckled marble. The almost square plan is neatly divided by cross-walls into nine sections, i.e. eight rooms *en suite* round a central staircase. The position of each room is here indicated by a compass bearing. Bruce's entrance hall (E) was recast by the Adam brothers (*see* below). Octagonal STAIRCASE with cantilevered stone steps that are all winders. The plaster soffit is plain, but the moulded string and handrail conform to the octagon with considerable skill, as do the balusters with richly foliated middles – square-section on the landing, rectangular on the ascent. The timber is oak, the lining of the well enriched at the angles by long garlands of fruit, shortening as the stair climbs. *Alexander Eizat* was the carver. The bolection-

---

* William Adam's mausoleum in the Greyfriars Churchyard, Edinburgh, was designed by John and Robert in 1753. A low relief on the sarcophagus shows the E front of Hopetoun, the portico ruined and the drums of its columns scattered.

moulded panels between them are just as nicely related
to the ascent; one of them opens over a slim balustrade into
a lobby, the rest were prettily painted in classical *trompe l'œil*
by *William McLaren*, 1970. At the head, the landing is spa-
72 ciously rectangular, with a central door and pedimented overdoor, neatly joined by triangular fillets to the octagonal lantern
overhead. Scale-and-platt SERVICE STAIR to the S, eccentrically supported, with a joyous serpentine balustrade of wrought
iron by *William Aitken*. In the CARD ROOM(S) on the ground
floor a corner fireplace with a domed ogee top. The ANTEROOM
(SW) is specially elaborate. The gilded *trompe-l'œil* enrichments
and trophies, probably painted by one of the *Norie* family, include a warlike trophy above the overmantel mirror. Marble
chimneypiece, unusually modern for its time, with pilasters and
a foliage frieze as well as the standard inner moulding. The
overdoor paintings by *Philip Tideman*, representing the Re-
wards of Learning, the Patronage of Music, and the Choice
between Virtue and Vice, belong to a set of thirty-seven (including perhaps the original staircase panels) for which he was paid
in 1703. In typical Bruce fashion there are two tiny adjoining
rooms: the WRITING CLOSET, which shares the same decorative scheme and has a corner fireplace, and a vaulted STRONG-
ROOM. The DINING ROOM (W) has Ionic pilasters flanking
the fireplace, and a matching pair on the opposite side. In the
SMALL LIBRARY (NW) a fireplace of the same green and red
marble, and a two-stage overmantel. The LIBRARY (N), two
rooms thrown into one, was fitted out *c.* 1830. Of the bedrooms
on the first floor, the WEST WAINSCOT ROOM with its Brussels
tapestries is the finest, but all have a share of *Tideman* overdoors
and overmantels – classical and allegorical.

NEW ROOMS. The 'Great Rooms' were fitted out by the
Adam Brothers after 1752. But first, in that year, they started
to refit the ENTRANCE HALL. The original Bruce design may
be imagined from his surviving interiors; that intended by
William Adam senior was elaborately architectural, of two
storeys with a swagged cove ceiling. The brothers' answer is
austere, clearing the decks not only as a prelude to Bruce's rich
staircase to the W, but for their own splendid progress to the
N – and indeed in the world beyond. The cubic space is fastidiously divided by a modillioned cornice, deep cove above, bare
wall below relieved by bracketed doorpieces to front and rear,
simpler versions to the sides. Marble plaques and a bust, family
souvenirs of the grand tour, are too small to supply much

Bo'ness (near), the Bridgeness distance-slab, second century, from the west end of the Antonine Wall

2. Traprain Law and Hailes Castle, thirteenth–fourteenth century, from Overhailes

3. Ford, Lothian Bridge, by Thomas Telford, 1831

4. South Queensferry, the Forth Rail Bridge, by John Fowler and Benjam
Baker, 1882–9, and the Forth Road Bridge, by Mott, Hay & Anderso
1958–64

5. Dalmeny, St Cuthbert, south doorway and sculptured coffin, mid-twelfth century

7. Tyninghame, Old Parish Church (St Baldred), mid twelfth century

8. East Linton, Prestonkirk Parish Church (St

9. Bathgate, Old Parish Church, effigy of a priest,

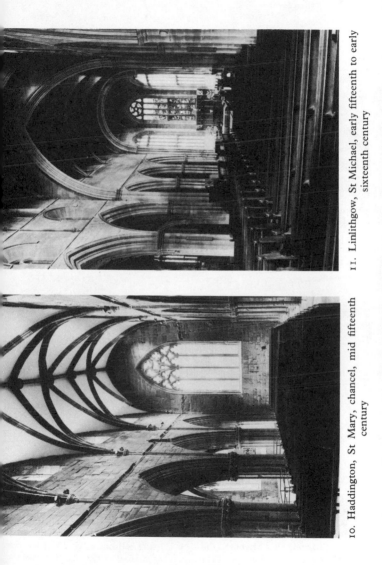

10. Haddington, St Mary, chancel, mid fifteenth century

11. Linlithgow, St Michael, early fifteenth to early sixteenth century

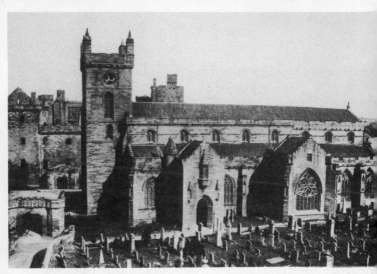

12. Linlithgow, St Michael, early fifteenth to early sixteenth century (before the addition of the new spire in 1964)

13. Linlithgow, St Michael, the crown spire, taken down *c.* 1821 (from Sir Walter Scott's *Provincial Antiquities*)

14. Linlithgow, St Michael, window of the south chapel

15. Haddington, St Mary, west front, *c.* 1500

16. Borthwick, St Kentigern, tomb, probably of Lord Borthwick, *c.* 1450

17. Dalkeith, East Church (St Nicholas), east end, c. 1500

18. Temple Old Parish Church, late fourteenth century

19. Seton, St Mary and Holy Cross, choir, c. 1470–8

20. Roslin, St Matthew, *c.* 1450, north side of choir

21. Roslin, St Matthew, *c.* 1450, south side of choir

22. Roslin, St Matthew, *c.* 1450, lintel in the south aisle; a bishop; Pride;
Drunkenness; Giving Drink to the Thirsty

23. Torphichen Preceptory Church, monument to Sir George Dundas
†1538 (fragment)

24. Dunbar Parish Church, monument to George Home
†1611 (*Copyright Country Life*)

25. Tranent Parish Church, headstones, early eighteenth century

26. Temple Old Parish Church, headstone of John Craig, farmer, †1742

27. Abercorn Parish Church, Hopetoun Loft, installed in the former chancel by
Sir William Bruce, 1708

28. Prestonpans Parish Church, tower, 1596

29. Carrington Parish Church, 1710

30. Gifford, St Cuthbert (former) near Yester House, west front,

31. East Saltoun Parish Church, 1805

32. Cockpen Parish Church, by Archibald Elliot, 1818

33. Dalkeith, St Mary, by William Burn & David Bryce, 1843

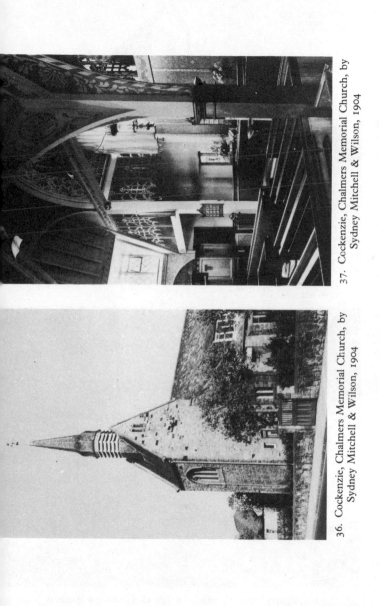

36. Cockenzie, Chalmers Memorial Church, by Sydney Mitchell & Wilson, 1904

37. Cockenzie, Chalmers Memorial Church, by Sydney Mitchell & Wilson, 1904

38. Rosewell, St Matthew, by Archibald Macpherson, finished in 1926

39. Carberry Tower, chapel, by Ian G. Lindsay & Partners, 1965

40. Tantallon Castle, c. 1370

41. Bass Castle on the Bass Rock, sixteenth century, the lighthouse 1902

43. Lennoxlove, fifteenth century

44. Crichton Castle, keep, late fourteenth century

45. Borthwick Castle, *c.* 1430

46. Midhope Castle, late sixteenth century

47. Linlithgow Palace, east side of the courtyard, early fifteenth century

48. Linlithgow Palace, chapel, late fifteenth century

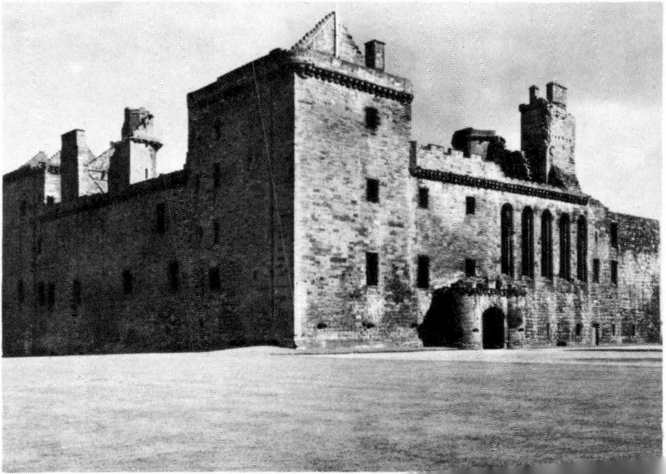

LINLITHGOW

DIRLETON CASTLE (left top)

This ancient stronghold of the de Vaux, in the lovely hamlet of Dirleton, is one of the most picturesque ruins in Scotland. The oldest buildings, a group of thirteenth-century towers, are probably among the earliest examples of a 'clustered donjon'. Other fine remains range from the fourteenth to the sixteenth centuries. The castle was besieged by Edward I in 1298; and its history was a lively one until it was dismantled by Lambert in 1650. The garden has a seventeenth-century bowling green. There is a sixteenth-century dovecote.

Situation – in village of Dirleton on Edinburgh–North Berwick road (A198). Hours – standard. Admission – 10p. OS 1-in. map, sheet 63, NT 516839.

CAIRNPAPPLE HILL (left centre)

Excavations show that this site probably goes back to 2000 BC. The first two phases of its construction – marked by an irregular 300 ft (60.9 m) across –

49. Linlithgow Palace, fountain, 1530s, and the north side of the courtyard, 1618-20

50. Musselburgh, Pinkie House, east range, *c.* 1613

51. Musselburgh, Pinkie House, tempera painted ceiling of the gallery on the second floor of the east range

52. Kinneil House, sixteenth century, recast *c.* 1677

53. Kinneil House, tempera painting on plaster (the Priest and the Levite), mid sixteenth century

54. Preston, Northfield House, early seventeenth century

55. Preston, Northfield House, tempera painting on wood partition, early seventeenth century

56. Fountainhall, late sixteenth to early seventeenth century

57. Ford House, 1680

58. Winton House, recast by William Wallace, 1620–7

59. The Binns, ceiling of the High Hall, by Alexander White, 1630

60. Newbattle Abbey, lodge gates, early eighteenth century

61. Arniston, lodge, late eighteenth century

62. Balgone House, lodge, by J. Anderson Hamilton, 1859

Amisfield House, one of four pavilions at the corners of the walled garden,
by John Henderson, 1783

64. Lennoxlove, sundial, 1679

65. Newhall, central vista in the
walled garden, late eighteenth century

66. Newhailes, by James Smith, 1686, centre

67. Auchindinny House, traditionally by Sir William Bruce, finished in 1707

58. Gifford, Yester House, south front, by James Smith and Alexander MacGill, 1699–1728

69. Dalkeith House, by James Smith, 1702–11

70. Loanhead, Mavisbank, by Sir John Clerk and William Adam, from 1723

71. Arniston, by William Adam, 1726, saloon, with plasterwork by
Joseph Enzer

72. Hopetoun House, staircase landing in the earliest part by Sir William Bruce, 1699–1701, Alexander Eizat, carver

73. Hopetoun House, Red Drawing Room, by the Adam Brothers, c. 1755

74. Hopetoun House, east elevation by Sir William Bruce (from *Vitruvius Britannicus*)

75. Hopetoun House, east elevation as intended by William Adam (from *Vitruvius Scoticus*)

76. Hopetoun House, east elevation as executed by William Adam and his sons from 1721

77. Newhailes, dining-room overmantel, *c.* 1760, detail

78. Gifford, Yester House, saloon, by Robert Adam, finished 1789

79. Newliston, by Robert Adam, 1789

80. Gosford House, by Robert Adam, 1790, altered by William Young, 1891

81. Penicuik House, by Sir James Clerk and John Baxter Senior, from 1761, entrance front (*Copyright Country Life*)

82. Penicuik House, garden front (*Copyright Country Life*)

83. Penicuik House, the stable block from the portico of the house (*Copyright Country Life*)

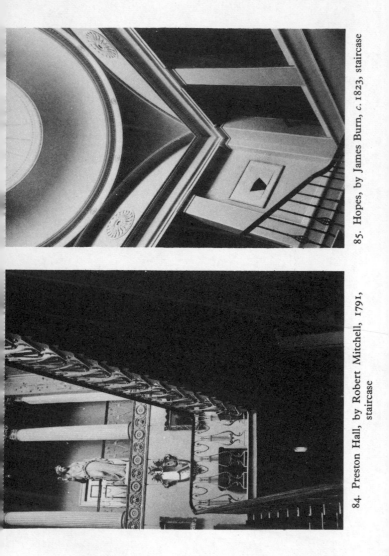

84. Preston Hall, by Robert Mitchell, 1791, staircase

85. Hopes, by James Burn, c. 1823, staircase

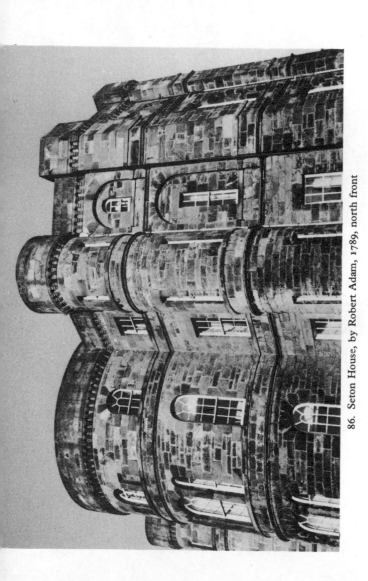

86. Seton House, by Robert Adam, 1789, north front

87. Newbyth House, by Archibald Elliot, 1817

88. Dalmeny House, by William Wilkins, 1814–17

89. Dalhousie Castle, entrance hall, by William Burn, 1825, vault

90. Tyninghame House, by William Burn, 1829

91. Prestongrange, recast by W. H. Playfair from 1830

92. St Joseph's Hospital (formerly Whitehill),
by William Burn & David Bryce, 1844

93. Vogrie House, by Andrew Heiton Jun., 1875

94. Gullane, Greywalls, by Edwin L. Lutyens and Gertrude Jekyll, 190

95. Macmerry, local authority housing, by Dick Peddie & Walker Todd,

96. Gullane, Whiteholm, by Robert Lorimer, 1904

97. Gullane, The Quarry, by Morris & Steedman, 1964

98. Musselburgh Tolbooth, 1590, with courtroom wing, 1762

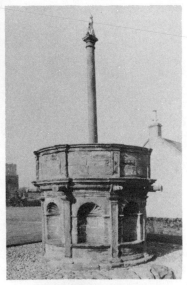

99. Preston, Mercat Cross, c. 1617

100. Haddington, Nos. 7–8 Mark
Street, c. 1760

101. Haddington Town House, with spire by James Gillespie Graham, 1831

102. Gifford, early eighteenth century

103. South Queensferry, an early-nineteenth-century rationalization of an earlie
layout

104. Bathgate Academy, by R. & R. Dickson, 1831

105. Riccarton, Heriot-Watt University, by Alan Reiach, Eric Hall & Partners, 1968, lounge of Hugh Nisbet building

106. East Linton, Preston Mill, eighteenth century (?)

107. Rosebery House, steading, early nineteenth
century (?)

108. Gladsmuir, Greendykes Farm, 1832

109. Gowanbank, steading, by James Gowans, from 1842

110. Dirleton Castle, 'beehive' doocot, sixteenth century

111. Pencaitland, 'lectern' doocot, eighteenth century

112. East Linton, Phantassie, 'beehive' doocot, eighteenth century

113. Huntington House, doocot, c. 1750

114. Prestonpans, beam engine at Prestongrange colliery, 1874

5. Cockenzie Power Station, by Robert Matthew, Johnson-Marshall & Partners, consulting architects, 1962

116. Kirkliston, aqueduct carrying the Union Canal over the Almond valley
c. 1820

character to the room. Its focus is the white marble chimney-piece, traditional in its lugged corners, modern in the classicism of its central panel – Apollo's head in a sunburst – supplied in 1755.* In the room to the s a contemporary chimneypiece of entirely classical character: Roman Doric columns with inlaid flutes, a grape-hung head in the centre. Each of the two rooms to the N was planned as an ensemble, with furnishings selected or commissioned by the brothers. The furnishings are outside the scope of this account, but the rooms are remarkable enough. The YELLOW DRAWING ROOM, formerly the dining room, takes its name from the yellow silk damask, procured in 1768, stretched between the dado and the foliage frieze. Above the cornice the deep cove is relieved at the corners by Rococo cartouches matched by a central cartouche of solemn gilt plaster, fringed by more charming and naturalistic flourishes. White finishings – a bracketed marble chimneypiece and pedimented doorcases with palmette friezes – are set against the yellow silk and answer the white of the ceiling. This room was enlarged from the original one in the NE angle of Bruce's block, but the RED DRAWING ROOM was part of the *William Adam* 73 additions. It is also in some ways a reversion to his style; not in the sober doorcases set on the red silk, but certainly in the crowded and magnificent Rococo ceiling, which may be attributed to *Clayton*. It is a long room. In the ceiling above the cove a large oval, tangential with the long sides, with plenty of space beyond it for further Rococo twiddles at the N end, a Chinese hut with pendant umbrellas at the s. It is also in its general lines a solemn room, but the only solemnity in the plaster detail is in the pair of swags in the cove over the chimneybreast. The chimneypiece itself is grave indeed; of white marble, with caryatid terms facing diagonally outwards and a central plaque of sporting cherubs, it was carved by *J. M. Rysbrack* and installed in 1756. The next room is designated as the STATE BEDROOM in the *Vitruvius Scoticus* engraving. The doorcases are Adam work, but the other finishings, with the possible exception of the palmette frieze, are blatantly of the early C19, when this became a dining room. Sunburst centrepiece and undercut vine cornice, plain chimneypiece and elaborate pelmets; none of these, though adequate in their kind, is a match for the absolute taste of the firm of Adam.

The layout of the PARK, basically that of a plan drawn by

* In the same year John Adam furnished a similar chimneypiece to Banff Castle.

William Adam c. 1725, combines a tentative informality with carefully planned sight-lines, some already implicit in Bruce's placing of the house, e.g. the line from its E front to the isle of Inchgarvie (now the centre pier of the Forth Rail Bridge, *see* p. 435) and North Berwick Law. In Adam's drawing a parterre is shown to the S of the house.

The SERVICE BUILDINGS to the S form a group. On the STEADING, a single range with lofts over arched cartshed openings, a keystone inscribed 'John Earl of Hopetoun 1774'. Beyond it the former SLAUGHTERHOUSE (now a squash court) of about the same date. Two-storey fenestration and pedimented ends. WORKSHOP of *c.* 1740, with rusticated quoins and big cornice. ESTATE OFFICE of *c.* 1840.

WALLED GARDEN to the SW. Late C18 rusticated piers with stone balls. Early C18 SUMMERHOUSES with deep segmental pediments. MAIN ENTRANCE to the E. Pomp and circumstance by *R. Rowand Anderson,* 1893. Two piers with coupled Ionic orders attached to them, diagonally voluted, and showy wrought-iron gates between. Flanking quadrant screens of Tuscan columns, single to the N, double to the S. Crowning vases of the William Adam period, re-used. LODGE to match. BUTLAW LODGE, on the older (but not original) E approach, is early C19, prettily bow-fronted, with a conical roof set in front of a piended one. Its abstract quality is nicely matched by a geometric, white-rendered extension to the rear by *Michael Shepley,* 1972. The mid C18 OBELISK GATE consists of obelisks with ball finials on rusticated piers. Thatched LODGE, with round boulders used for the quoins and the margins of the arched windows, related to STANEYHILL TOWER, to the SE, the hill-top ruin of a C17 L-plan house with a chamfered stair-turret in the angle. ABERCORN CASTLE. An C18 mound in the park was excavated in 1963 to reveal one wall of a medieval tower and remains of a C15–16 manor house on the same site. SOCIETY HOUSE to the E is L-plan again, with an angle turret.

HOUSTOUN HOUSE *see* UPHALL

HUMBIE

PARISH CHURCH. A T-plan kirk of 1800 (the date on a stone in the family aisle, crisply carved with a thistle) gothicized in 1866 by *David Bryce.* The 'chancel' was added in 1930. – MONUMENTS, in the churchyard. At the entry a heraldic tablet

to one of the Borthwicks of Whitburgh, early C17, with concave
pointed top and the inscription

> HERE LYS INTERD WITHIN THIS PLP OF STONE
> A BORTHICK BOLD SCARCE LEFT HE SUCH A ONE
> TRUE TO HIS GOD AND LOYAL TO HIS KING
> A GALEAND MAN AND IUST IN EVERITHING

This is in fine grey stone, the others are in red. – To the E a
broad monument to James Scriven of Ploulandhill † 1668,
erected in 1682, the inscription on drapery held by two cherubs
under a heraldic pediment crested with skulls and an urn. –
Further from the church a group of early C18 table-tops even
bolder than those of Tranent, mostly supported on baluster
legs, but one on two slabs whose ends are carved with four
gingerbread men. – To the E a tabernacle to James Baillie
'Farmer in Begbie' † 1751, with the attributes of death on Ionic
pilasters and a half-length high-relief portrait in deep-sleeved
coat and wig, holding a skull. – DOOCOT. C18, converted to
a house by *Morris & Steedman*, 1971.

Humbie is the result of the union of Keith Marischal and Keith
Hundeby in 1618. There is not much of a village. HAZY HILL
at the road junction is a red sandstone house of *c.* 1830, spiky
symmetrical Tudor.

CHILDREN'S VILLAGE, to the SE. Scattered cottages on an open
site. The honorary architect of the original settlement was
J. H. Cooper, 1905.

HUMBIE HOUSE, 1.5 km. NE. Late C18. In the C19 it was
extended sideways in unexciting fashion and reversed, so that
the front became the back.

SCADLAW HOUSE, to the W. L-plan, with a shingled monopitch
roof mitred at the angle like a picture frame, its gutter concealed
in a long slit just above the eaves. By *Morris & Steedman*, 1967.

JOHNSTOUNBURN. *See* p. 268.

KEITH MARISCHAL. *See* p. 269.

FARMS

LEASTON, 3 km. ENE. A pale-orange-harled house of *c.* 1710,
with five windows along two storeys. Curly chimney gable on
each front, with scrolled skewputts resembling those of the
main gables, those on the entrance front obscured by early C19
wings that form the two sides of a paved forecourt. The front
doorpiece is a restoration. STEADING dated 1858.

POGBIE, 2 km. SSE. Plain symmetrical Tudor of *c.* 1840, with
ground-floor bay-windows.

HUNTINGTON HOUSE
3 km. 🐖 of Haddington

Late C17, with rusticated quoins and a lugged and pedimented doorpiece, enlarged *c.* 1830 by the addition of a parallel block to the rear. A steep gable was then substituted for the central pediment.

DOOCOT. Of *c.* 1750; the grandest in the whole region. Square in plan, and all of stone-dressed harling except for the pilastered frontispiece, which has flight holes in the pediment. Three crowning vases at the front, a square vase-shaped chimney at the back serving the little basement room.

STABLES. Probably of the same date; a long block with a depressed-arch opening and a C19 wooden spirelet.

INGLISTON HOUSE   WL
2 km. SE of Kirkliston

Dated 1846, by *Brown & Wardrop*, and now the headquarters of the Highland and Agricultural Society and home of the annual Highland Show. Eccentric baronial, uncluttered by out-buildings, the basement-level offices contrived in the fall of the ground with their windows unseen on the main frontage. Built of pale grey ashlar, clean-cut and lightly stugged, it indulges in triangular dormer-heads, corner bartizans round and square and both equally useless, and flues strangely corbelled across gables – all for effect, especially in silhouette. Lofty interior with sparely-ribbed Jacobean ceilings. In the drawing room a Louis chimneypiece of white marble, steel-grated. Effective small stained-glass panels, one in the entrance hall, three more (Ceres, Pomona and Flora) on the staircase. Painted glass roundels of C17 Dutch character in the library to the l. of the front door (Elizabeth and Essex) and the morning room to the r. (Queen Mary and Darnley).

STABLE BLOCK with rib-vaulted pend, and turreted baronial cottage adjoining, by *John Kinross*, 1904.

Here was discovered an inscribed ROMAN MILESTONE* (*see* Introduction, p. 30).

′   INNERWICK   EL

PARISH CHURCH. A plain kirk of 1784 with a bellcote on the w gable. Inside, the w gallery on Roman Doric columns

* Now in the National Museum of Antiquities in Edinburgh.

remains, but the rest was reorganized in 1870. Most of the furnishings are C20. – STAINED GLASS. Two windows by *William Wilson* (the Good Samaritan, Christ with Martha and Mary), after 1939. – MONUMENTS, in the churchyard. A fair collection of early C18 table-tops and headstones with many a *memento mori*. – MANSE. 1726, repaired in 1788 and thickened in 1830 by the addition of a single-storey range on the higher ground, with a pretty front to the N.

Innerwick is a pink East Lothian village, out of the ordinary because of its high position and because it is built along two adjacent ridges. The line of the new road runs slightly to the s of the old one, with a little burn between them. In the cleft at the W end. TEMPLE MAINS, a splendidly complete farm group of the early C19 with a good buildup of roofs both gabled and piended, mostly pantiled, and cobble floors still *in situ*. The threshing mill got its round red-brick chimney in mid century. INNERWICK FARM at the E end, on the new road, is slightly later. A few C18 houses stand by the old road. The cottages built in 1834 by *James Cunningham & Co.*, masons, and *William Belsillie*, wright, could be any of those scattered along the new road between the farms, or the short row at its W junction near the gate of the big house, THURSTON (by *John Kinross*, 1895, demolished in 1952). Signs of feudal patronage appear at the POST OFFICE, dated 1893, with a nicely rounded corner and a cantilevered gable for shelter, and at the JUBILEE HORSE TROUGH on the W approach, a stone gable with a projecting iron trough and an inset niche, dated 1887, by *Macfarlane* of Glasgow. Above them a slate tablet as at the Post Office. This one reads

A MAN OF KINDNESS TO HIS BEAST IS KIND
BUT BRUTAL ACTIONS SHOW A BRUTAL MIND.
REMEMBER HE WHO MADE THEE MADE THE BRUTE.
WHO GAVE THEE SPEECH AND REASON MADE HIM MUTE.
HE CANT COMPLAIN BUT GODS ALL SEEING EYE
BEHOLDS THY CRUELTY AND HEARS HIS CRY.
HE WAS DESIGNED THY SERVANT NOT THY DRUDGE.
REMEMBER HIS CREATOR IS THY JUDGE.

In the dip in the middle of the village the long block of the mid C19 SCHOOL adjoins a two-storey schoolhouse with fancy gables. To this pleasant ensemble the C20 added a corrugated iron CONCERT HALL in 1909, six harled cottages with stepped chimneys by *Dick Peddie & Walker Todd* in 1920, and the well disciplined BARNS NESS TERRACE.

(INNERWICK CASTLE, 1 km. E. The ruin of a castle built by successive Hamiltons of Innerwick, protected by a ditch (with access presumably over a timber bridge) on the W side and by a bend of the Thornton Burn on the other three. The original building, which the RCAHMS dates no earlier than the C15, comprised a wall of enceinte with a keep on the S side of the enclosure. Subsequent infilling included a tunnel-vaulted hall to the E.)

FARMS

CROWHILL FARM, 1 km. E. *James Nisbet* did mason work here in 1722, and the long pantiled range impressively seen from the inland heights could be as early as this. On the E side is an iron-pillared cartshed continuous with a row of cottages. To the S of the road the farmhouse of 1748, much altered, and the remains of an early C19 mill which stole the water of the Thornton Burn by way of a tunnelled lade.

The burn reaches the sea at THORNTONLOCH, where there is a steading and a group of early C19 cottages and sheds, one of which adjoins the base of a large chimney. SKATERAW, 2.5 km. NE of Innerwick, was its harbour, probably formed in the late C18 for the export of lime and the import of coal to burn it. The fine round arch of a LIME KILN can be seen by the shore a little way to the W.

THURSTON MAINS, 1.5 km. SW. An early C19 farmhouse and steading where the Second Statistical Account reports a steam threshing mill. It owes its spiky architectural pretensions and a number of cottages to *Robert Bell*, 1857.

BRIDGE, carrying the B904 into Stirlingshire. C18, with five arches and rounded cutwaters.

TOWER. A circular ruin in coursed rubble, vaulted on the first floor, all that is left of the Hamilton castle razed in 1455 by James II.

Inveravon was the site of one of the WALL FORTS of the Antonine Wall (*see* Introduction, p.30).

* Now Central Region.

INVEREIL HOUSE
2 km. NE of Dirleton

EL 5080

A deep red sandstone baronial house by *Kinnear & Peddie*, 1899, with a mildly asymmetrical front – the front door at one end, a stair-turret at the other, a bracketed balcony under a crow-stepped gable in the middle. The same architects designed the rustic LODGE in 1898.

INVERESK *

ML (now EL) 3070

The name implies a position at the mouth of the Esk, and properly belongs to the whole parish or (going further back) to the manor, 'comprehending the town of Musselburgh and port of Fisherrow' etc., which David I granted to the abbey of Dunfermline. But with the rise of Musselburgh, where the Esk actually flows out into the Forth, the old centre gradually assumed the character of 'the Montpelier of Scotland' with which it is credited by the New Statistical Account. However apt it may seem, this description is misleading. Inveresk today certainly looks like an antique suburb, with houses of the C17 and haughty mansions of the C18 looking over the long walls that stretch almost continuously for 1 km. on each side, the church standing on its hill at the w end and the cluster of humbler dwellings pulling their forelocks at the E. But a closer look at the garden walls shows numerous built-up cottage fronts incorporated in them, and historically it is more realistic to see Inveresk as a loose ribbon development of roadside cottages and houses, the grander ones occupying the backlands and latterly claiming a direct view on to the road, though even these have subsequently cut themselves off with more wall. It is a small town, in short, in which the great houses have prevailed. The New Statistical Account also sheds some light on the C18 industrial history of the parish, reporting that *William Adam* the elder erected a coal works at Pinkie in 1739 and drained it by means of a water pump driven by a diversion from the Esk which runs along the valley to the s. It is not easy to see how the tunnel at Eskgrove, traditionally associated with this, could have helped, unless there was another pump to get the water over the ridge.

ST MICHAEL'S PARISH CHURCH. By *Robert Nisbet*, 1805. A startlingly tall box of a church on a raised site at the w end of the village, traditionally occupied by a church since the C6; tall because it had a second-floor gallery (the Fishermen's Loft) and

* For a plan of Inveresk *see* Musselburgh.

thus appears a three-storey building. All the windows have low
segmental arches. Evenly rusticated quoins. Entrance was by
way of a Tuscan-columned doorpiece on the N side (blocked
in 1893). To the S is the projecting session house, with a
pilastered first stage and thermae windows in the second, which
brings it up to the level of the church's own wall-head cornice.
Then come three more stages and a pierced spire, altogether
a slightly simpler version of that of St Andrew in George Street,
Edinburgh, and a landmark from the firth and the surrounding
country. In 1893 *J. MacIntyre Henry* remodelled the interior
on high church lines so as to face the communion table at the
E end instead of the pulpit on the S side. On the outside this
is seen in yellow stone additions, to the W for a staircase well
with two interlocking flights (it is not clear how the galleries
were reached in the 1805 layout), to the E for the organ. The
main gallery goes round all sides except the E, and the new Fishermen's Loft is overhead to the W. But the whole is still dominated by the high ceiling, which appears to be original, not least
because its central circle and the oddly stretched fan inside it
would have suited the old arrangement rather better; the lack
of an adequate cornice (and of any frieze underneath) may also
be due to the original designer. In this context Henry's work
is a good synthesis. He put the organ in a pilastered archway.
Its case is a conscientious effort in pale stained oak, given extra
weight by large brackets. The PEW ENDS are enlivened with
little undulating pediments. – PULPIT. Oak, with bracketed
Corinthian columns, matching the ORGAN CASE (both by
Taylor & Son of Edinburgh). – ORGAN. Enlarged in 1897 by
Lewis & Co. of Brixton. – COMMUNION TABLE. Made up by
Adams of Edinburgh 'from a C16 carved communion rail taken
from a church in Antwerp';* a relief of the Last Supper on
the front. – STAINED GLASS. In the S wall the four Evangelists
below scenes from the life of Christ, *c.* 1893. – In the E wall,
to the N, Dorcas, a bold architectural treatment on a blue
ground, *c.* 1900; to the S St Michael by *Douglas Strachan*, 1923.
– At the foot of the stair a small light (SS. Bride and Modwenna,
foundress of the first church here) by *Margaret Chilton*. –
MONUMENTS. A gravestone discovered during the new work
and resited indoors at the W end, carved as a tabernacle with
strapwork top, commemorates a Town Clerk of Musselburgh
† 1676. On one side it is inscribed '... WILLIAM SMITH ANAGR

* This is in a contemporary newspaper account, but the work is actually
of the early C18.

ALL MY WILL'S TO HIM ...'; on the other is his portrait in
relief, with a quill pen. – Another salvaged stone is a small black
oval to the Duke of Lauderdale † 1682, set in a marble relief
of c. 1790, on the s wall. – On the N wall a shallow wall-monument to John Fullerton † 1775, with slim diagonally voluted
Ionic pilasters, their bases inscribed '*Craig* ARCHT' and '*Gowan*
Carver'. – On the w wall outside a tablet to the Rev. Alexander
Carlyle † 1805, minister of St Michael's, for whom the church
was built. – On the s wall of the session house a pair of C18
SUNDIALS, one by *Archibald Handasyde* of Fisherrow, 1785.
ROMAN CAVALRY FORT, civil settlement and temporary
camps, and Romano-British field-system, on the r. bank of the
River Esk and largely overlain by the village. Little is to be seen
above ground, but a visit to the churchyard is worthwhile, if
only to appreciate the type of ground chosen for the fort. A
fragment of one of the hypocausted buildings of the civil settlement survives in the garden of Inveresk House. Most of the
finds have been deposited in the National Museum of Antiquities of Scotland, Edinburgh.

DESCRIPTION

The E end of Inveresk can be approached from CROOKSTON
ROAD. First to the r. a row of C19 single-storey cottages, and
then a house and two cottages of c. 1840. Between them, on the
other side, is Pinkiehill Farm. Then EASTER WHITEHOUSE,
externally unremarkable but with a large upper room (now subdivided) which has a nice *trompe l'œil* overmantel PAINTING
of heraldry in a neo-Gothic arch of c. 1800. Over it is an imaginative shorescape, and part of another survives at what was
the other end of the room. The signature of *William Kirk* has
been reported, with the first half of a C19 date. Outdoors again,
after the constriction at Easter Whitehouse comes the LAIGH
HOUSE at the corner, restored in 1972. As you come out into
the main street, the C18 WHITEHOUSE is seen to be the wicket-
keeper, the early C18 SHEPHERD HOUSE (with a curly gable
and a handsome pair of sycamores) the long-stop at its E end.
The street begins with a very good sequence: after the Laigh
House a smaller-scale row, and then two adjoining C18 houses,
the two-storey ROSECOURT and the three-storey ROSEHILL
which stands back from it so as to carry up the same skew-line;
it has scrolled skewputts and a nice single-storey adjunct as
termination. The architectural grandees of the village stand
back from the street (or road, as it seems) and are now given

in order from E to W, with an indication of the side of the road
on which they are situated.

INVERESK LODGE(S).* An L-plan house with an octagonal stair-
turret in the angle, one of the windows dated 1683. The dormers
of a slightly later wing which extends one of the jambs to the
W have swept roofs in the Halkerston manner. Large panelled
drawing room on the E side, basically of the early C18.

HALKERSTON (S). An unusual house of the late C17, its square
plan and pyramidal roof recalling one type of contemporary
farmhouse in the Netherlands. But it has two tiers of swept
dormers and a central chimney; the other chimneys, multi-
staged, are round the outside. Tunnel-vaulted cellars. In the
upper rooms, served by a turnpike stair which lies within the
house but shows its presence by a crowstepped gable, some
bolection-moulded fireplaces and slightly later panelling.

THE MANOR HOUSE (S). This was built for Archibald
Shiells, whose florid monogram and the date 1748 are carved
in the pediment. The ogee-roofed pavilions, probably of the
C17, stand forward on the road line, and one of the curved link
walls remains despite C19 additions. The gatepiers are early
C19, but the big stone vases on top of them are original. The
house is of three storeys and basement, with rusticated quoins,
keystoned windows and a pedimented Gibbs-surround door on
the main storey. Seven bays, the central three advanced to carry
the vased and chimneyed pediment, whose cornice is higher
than that of the main block. To the rear the six windows on
each level are grouped in pairs. The plan is simple: on each
floor a passage behind the central range serves the whole width
of the house, and a scale-and-platt stair‡ fills one room space
on the r. of the entrance hall – a modest affair until one gets
to the top, where the L-shaped ceiling is grandly coved and stuc-
coed with an eagle, foliage and shells. Most of the panelling
and other finishings are original too, with occasional unorthodox details such as coved angles to the window recesses. But
once again the top floor provides surprises. The end bedroom
on the r. has painted panels over the doors and chimneypiece
– classical-romantic landscapes featuring round towers – and
shallow panels of garlands over the windows. Probably rather
later is the painting of the entire passage wall with scenes of
hunting. *Trompe l'œil* dado rail and overdoor panels with
groups of game. The drawing room at the r. end of the main

* Property of the National Trust for Scotland; the garden is open to visitors.
‡ This may well have belonged to a C17 house.

floor was refinished (like its neighbour) *c.* 1820, leaving the original shell-headed display niche and its curved shelves. – ICE HOUSE in the garden; mid C18. – The DOOCOT at the S corner, with a pyramidal roof, is probably earlier. It has been converted into a garden house.

CATHERINE LODGE (N). Named after Catherine Fergusson of Kilkerran, Ayrshire. Three storeys and five bays, the centre one crowned with a chimney gable and inscribed AC (Alexander Christie) 1709. The internal finishings are of various C18 dates, the most distinctive *c.* 1790, including a stair with a curved handrail of extraordinary delicacy supported by wrought-iron balusters of similar design to those at Baberton House.

ESKHILL (N). Three storeys and seven bays, the first and last three a little apart from the centre. All openings hoodmoulded except for the ground-floor front door, which has a pediment on plain brackets with guttae. Two-storey wing to the W, with pedimented door. *Thomas Mylne* owned Eskhill in 1710, and whether or not he designed it, one's first question is about the hoodmoulds: are they original, or were they added *c.* 1790? Today under its smart paint and harling the frontage seems all of a piece. Original roll-edged doorpieces in the front hall, but the carved overdoors with cornucopias are from a house in George Square, Edinburgh. Late C18 stair and first-floor finishings, enhanced by two imported marble chimneypieces: in the centre room from Fordell House, Fife (demolished *c.* 1960), of *c.* 1760, with bowl-of-flowers centrepiece and yellow slip, and in the E room from Lord Aberconway's South Audley House, now demolished, in Mayfair, London. The second-floor rooms are largely original. – In the NW corner of the WALLED GARDEN a crowstepped lectern DOOCOT of *c.* 1700. Later baluster SUNDIAL at the centre. The splendid stone urns are from Tredegar Park in Wales. – The LODGE by *David Brown,* 1972, adjoins a little round tower which was formerly a reservoir. – CHEESE PRESS dated 1796.

OAK LODGE (S). Early C18. T-shaped, the staircase incorporated in the advanced centre whose pediment, like that of the Manor House, stands proud of the main cornice. Pedimented Gibbs-surround doorpiece. W wing of *c.* 1820. Awkward C20 insertion in the angle of the T. The main entrance was moved away from the axis *c.* 1970 to serve a garage.

ESKGROVE HOUSE (N). A harled early C18 five-bay house of two storeys and basement with rusticated quoins. The wall on each side of the moulded and pedimented doorpiece is canted for-

wards to make a little more room inside. Much of the interior
is quite recent, but the well staircase is original: stone steps
with a bullnose moulding following the edges of both treads
and risers, a scrolled bracket under each r. angle (but the
wrong way round, larger scroll outwards), and a wrought-iron
balustrade of scrolled stalks and flowers between twisted
newels. – LODGE. A low-pitch cottage of *c.* 1830 with hoodmoulded windows. – Ruinous lectern DOOCOT with stepped
skews.

INVERESK GATE(S). 1774. Three bays on the main s front (away
from the road), two storeys and basement. Rubble with dressed
margins. A large bowed room was added at each end in 1821,
the NW wing in 1885. Other depredations to front and back.
– DOOCOT of lectern type, ruinous.

INVERESK HOUSE (N). Two parallel ranges, both altered. The
C17 E range is partly concealed by a large bow of the mid C19.
Pediment dated 1643, apparently resited, over the fanlit front
door of *c.* 1800. In the mid C18 the w range was added alongside,
and the two contiguous N gables were given rusticated quoins.
1757 is the date inscribed on the frame of an earlier (1682)
armorial stone reset between the two keystoned windows which
light the well staircase with its stone steps and handrail and
turned balusters of oak. – STABLES of *c.* 1840, with gatepiers
and arch of 1851.

JOHNSTOUNBURN
                       1 km. SSE of Humbie

About 1730 the original modest house, possibly of the C17, was
given a two-storey jamb with rusticated quoins. In 1863 it was
extended towards the burn with a turreted and battlemented
block like a tower house, dominating the rest. *Leadbetter &*
Fairley improved the old garden front in 1895.

GARDEN, adjoining the house. Yew-hedged and walled,
probably of the early C18, the period of the square GAZEBO
with urns at the corners of its pyramidal slated roof.

DOOCOT. 1730. Lectern type, but unusual first because of
the internal arrangement, with floors on each level and a central
round pillar lined with nest boxes like the walls (some 2,000
in all); then for its curly gables and diamond-paned dormers.
The gables at least are of early C18 type, but it is more likely
that this romantic trim was added a century later. There is
similar detail at the GATEWAY with its romantic profile, and

at the STABLE COURT or steading some distance from the house.

KEITH MARISCHAL
2 km. NNW of Humbie

EL 4060

A long house with a vaulted ground floor, built in 1589 by the Keiths, who were Grand Marischals of Scotland. The N front was baronialized in 1889 by *Kinnear & Peddie*, but the jamb at the E end is original, and the upper part of a stair-turret in the angle can still be seen from outside. The balancing jamb at the W end is pre-Victorian but it is hard to say by how much. The S front is undisturbed, the top floor of the taller tower at its E end served by a little corbelled turret in the angle. In the first-floor room in the E jamb a moulded fireplace (as in the room overhead) plus panelling and cornice of *c*. 1740. The garden room is similarly panelled. Comfortable finishings of 1869. Plain marble chimneypieces of *c*. 1820. Not so plain is the stone chimneypiece of *c*. 1800 in the entrance hall, Gothick,* with clustered shafts and a traceried lintel. – STEADING of *c*. 1800, a plain classical front to its stables and hayloft and a semi-octagonal bay behind – just as if it were a house. On the same axis and in the centre of the court an octagonal DOO-COT. Domed lantern with flight holes between the tiny columns.

KEITH PARISH CHURCH. A ruin, embedded in a clump of trees opposite the N front of Keith Marischal. E wall of *c*. 1200 with two plain lancets beneath a vesica. At the E end of the S wall, between two incised discs with geometrical ornament, a late medieval lancet with an obtusely pointed cusped head. Another lancet in the W wall. – Against the S wall a sumptuous MONU-MENT to five children of the family of Anderson of Whitburn † 1685 to 1695. 'Reredos' with Corinthian columns framing the inscription and a broken scrolly pediment. Many small figures, forgivably morbid in theme. Flanking the columns and perched on fancy consoles are putti with an hourglass and a skull. Over the inscription a child with a horn, a skeleton, Old Father Time and a child with scales. On the 'altar' more skulls and a car-touche with crossed thighbones and spades.

* The similar treatment of the N front was replaced by the Victorian altera-tions.

KIDLAW see GIFFORD

5070
KILDUFF HOUSE   EL
2 km. W of Athelstaneford

A little house of the mid C18 so much altered and extended that it would not earn a mention had it not been built by John Home, author of the tragedy of *Douglas*. It is crisply whitewashed, as is the early C19 farmhouse nearby.

0070
KINGSCAVIL   WL
3 km. E of Linlithgow

A steep-roofed, bargeboarded group including a SCHOOL with Gothic windows and flèche, and a schoolhouse, all in the manner of *James Gowans*, *c.* 1870. The walls are of pale brown rubble laid with calculated disorder, separated by horizontal bands at regular intervals.

5080
KINGSTON   EL

A pleasant hamlet of sufficient importance to merit a BOARD SCHOOL of 1878. STEADING dated 1848 over the entry arch, with plain skewed ends; slated, the cattle court divisions pantiled. Four pairs of contemporary semi-detached cottages with big gabled dormers ventilating (but hardly lighting) the upper floors. Plain early C19 farmhouse.

9080
KINNEIL   WL*

KINNEIL CHURCH. Kinneil village declined rapidly in the early C17 and was superseded by Bo'ness. The church was disused from *c.* 1670 and fell into ruin after *c.* 1730. It was given to Holyrood Abbey between 1130 and *c.* 1163 and to this period belong the existing remains. The W gable stands to its full height, recognizably Romanesque in its masonry but featureless‡ except for the bellcote with twin corbelled-out arches. The footings of the other walls were exposed in 1951. The nave and chancel were two short rectangles in plan (cf. e.g. Duddingston) and the chancel arch was narrow. An aisle was added on the

---

* Now Central Region.
‡ The rows of putlog holes are paralleled in Lothian at St Martin, Haddington.

S – after the Reformation, as the Romanesque cross now in Kinneil House (*see* below) was found under one of its walls.

KINNEIL HOUSE. Two distinct C16 sections, impressively
united and systematized in the C17, almost completely gutted
in the C20 and now a guardianship monument in a municipal
park. The block which now forms the centre was built by James
Hamilton, second Earl of Arran, at the beginning of his protec-
torate, which lasted from 1542 to 1554. The only distinctive
features remaining are the wide gun loops on the W side (the
back of the house). In 1553 Arran began the 'palace' to the N.
It has large windows whose external bars have been dragged
from their holes. Corner garderobe on the W, its shallow projection supported on corbels. Having taken refuge in France,
Arran returned in 1569 to find the older block ruined by the
Earl of Morton; and so it remained till 1677 when Anne
Duchess of Hamilton began to rebuild it, giving the main E front
a regular pattern of sash-windows five high and three wide. On
ground level a modest central door with a lugged architrave and
a primitive bracketed segmental pediment. Equally crude but
immensely effective are the massive cornice and balustrade
crowning the frontage. Of the square four-storey towers
attached to each end (they used to have pyramidal roofs), the
S one has a frame for a big armorial panel now indoors, the N
one links up with Arran's 'palace'. Tuskings in the masonry
show that a balancing block was intended to the S, and two piers
with attached columns mark the near side of the forecourt.
Behind the towers, in the angles they form with the central
block, are square stair-turrets; the triple stone promontory is
impressive indeed.

Internally, the centre block shows complicated signs of the
rebuilding, but the only late C17 features are three bolection-
moulded fireplaces, the largest suggesting a big room filling the
first floor. The N and S towers however still have plaster cornices
at first-floor level with amorini developed into foliage in which
appear the heads of crocodiles. In the S tower this crowned a
stone staircase, once balustraded, with thickly bullnosed steps
and corner landings. Of the 'palace' interior there is more. Its
plan is interesting: a central turnpike stair serves all four rooms
on each level, windowed with borrowed lights whose recent
external glazing looks odd today in the middle of a semi-ruin.
In the course of the intended demolition of the whole of Kinneil
in 1941 the two E rooms on the first floor were found to have
a complete scheme of tempera decoration on the plaster beneath

the C17 panelling. The PARABLE ROOM, under a compartmented timber ceiling of that date, has walls divided by a Corinthian flat arcade of columns with roundels and heads in the
spandrels, set out without much regard to the available wall
spaces. The Good Samaritan's story from which the room's
present name is derived takes up six panels, St Jerome, the
Magdalen and (allegedly) Lucretia having one each; all are in
simple black line with few traces of colour, their primitive zest
diminished by retouching. The tunnel-vaulted ARBOUR ROOM
takes its name from the decoration of the same period, *c.* 1554.
Above the foliaged dado band big curvaceous wreaths of foliage
with birds and beasts and lettered ribbons encircle well placed
roundels (Samson and Delilah, David and Bathsheba, the
Sacrifice of Isaac and Temptation of St Anthony) and the arms
of Arran and his wife on the crown of the vault. A joyous scheme
and edifying too, but it was overlaid in 1621–4 by a painted
simulation of panelled dado and compartmented ribbed vault,
wood and plaster being the new signs of status. Parts of both
stages of the decoration have been exposed and the channels
formed for late C17 wood grounds have been made good.

The massive stone CROSS in a basement room comes from
Kinneil church. As nothing very like it survives in Scotland
or England there can be no certainty as to its date. The hand
of God above the head and the stiffly outstretched pose recall
such late Anglo-Saxon roods as that at Romsey in Hampshire.
The format of the cross, in particular the oblong ends and the
disc behind, appears to be unique, at least in large-scale stone
sculpture. It is not easy to know for what sort of setting the
cross was designed. It was not free-standing because the back
is rough, and the finished sides mean that it was never let into
a wall. The most likely answer is that it was supported on a
corbel above the chancel arch.

KINNEIL COTTAGES. To the NE of the house is a good group
of C18 farm buildings and cottages, the latter partly restored
as a museum by *W. A. Cadell* in 1974. To the SW the ruin of
the cottage where James Watt devised his improved steam
engine in 1765.

At Kinneil was one of the WALL FORTS of the Antonine Wall
(*see* Introduction, p. 30).

KIRKHILL HOUSE

ML *3060*

2 km. NW of Gorebridge

1828 by *Thomas Hamilton*. He seems to have retained an existing
Georgian house to the N and built a new block at r. angles to
it, with a continuous cast-iron balcony along its S elevation. The
shallow-pitch piended roofs with deep eaves have the same calm
simplicity. Linking the two blocks is a strange tower with
round-headed lancets. Chimneys act as finials. It is expressed
to the rear with a low-pitch gable, to the front with a Tuscan
doorpiece. Internally it acts as a miniature atrium, small square
apertures giving clearstory lighting. Original liver-coloured
marble chimneypiece (entablature between pylons). Everything to the N has been altered at various times, but the two
rooms to the S, now connected, still have coffered ceilings and
plain Grecian doorpieces. In the larger room, which has a bay-
window at the end, an C18 carved wood chimneypiece (centre
panel of nesting birds) of the first quality. Did this, and the
overdoor friezes which are plainly an addition, come from an
C18 house such as Arniston?

KIRKLANDHILL *see* EAST LINTON

KIRKLISTON

WL* *1070*

PARISH CHURCH. In a dramatically elevated position with the
ground falling away sharply on three sides. From the churchyard impressive views to the Pentlands. The church is Transitional Norman and slightly larger in scale than Dalmeny,
though not nearly so well preserved. What we have is most of
the nave, rewindowed and much added to, plus the curtailed
W tower, a bold composition of few elements which perhaps
helps us visualize the demolished tower at Dalmeny. Its details
establish a very late C12 date: battered plinth, clasping buttresses, tiny lancets. Two and a bit storeys, the third cut down
to make a saddleback roof. The belfry and weathercock add a
nice jaunty note. Broad stair-turret at the SE corner. The nave
is preserved for its full length, apart from what has been cut
away to the S for the burial aisle of the Earls of Stair, 1629,
and to the N for a sympathetic addition by *R. Rowand Anderson*,
1883 (there are records of previous alterations and the building
of the manse by *Brown & Wardrop*, 1865). The walls are

* Now Edinburgh.

divided by a string course into dado and window zone much as at Dalmeny. None of the later openings respects this system. The corbel table is complete on the S side, the corbels unsculptured and no longer of a Romanesque type.

The S door is the showpiece of the church although its value is reduced by its poor condition. Four arch orders alternate between mouldings and deeply undercut chevron typical of the late C12. Chevron also on the big hoodmould. Free-standing jamb shafts in a complex alternating rhythm. Foliage capitals, including some large crockets. The door stands proud of the wall, and originally there would have been more projecting masonry above it. The E wall bears no trace of the chancel arch, but one can judge the width of the chancel by the string courses continued from the N and S walls. In a line with the E wall is the original N door of the nave, removed here when the N extension was built. It is much better preserved than the S door, but plainer. It too stands away from the wall. The gable above is still preserved, though restored. Both arch orders are moulded, capitals are of the S door types, and bases are waterholding. This last reinforces a date shortly before 1200. – Nothing of note inside save a Romanesque PULPIT by *David Rhind*, 1860 (and in the session house a MODEL of the church showing the seating plan in 1822–84). – MONUMENTS, in the churchyard. Some gingerbread headstones of various C18 dates.

FREE CHURCH. Lanceted, and bearing the date of the Disruption, 1843. Spire added by *Hippolyte J. Blanc*, 1880.

The only other building of any note in the village is CASTLE HOUSE, which has a round stair-turret and a 'marriage lintel' with the date 1683.

FOXHALL, to the E. Five-bay house of *c.* 1810. Central pediment, tripartite doorway with a fanlight. Rusticated quoins.

PRIEST MILL (or Breast Mill), to the SW. The mill of the barony of Liston from 1672, it worked until *c.* 1920. Three storeys with crowstep gables. Converted to a house in 1967.

LIN'S MILL, 5 km. SW. Converted to a house by *Morris & Steedman*, 1971. SLAB nearby with a crude coat of arms, *memento mori* and the inscription HERE LYETH THE DUST OF WILLIAM LIN RIGHT HERITOR OF LINSMILN WHO DIED IN THE YEAR OF OUR LORD 1645.

BRIDGES, etc. Four bridges over the Union Canal numbered 19 to 22. – AQUEDUCT carrying the canal over the river Almond at Lin's Mill. Of the same date, *c.* 1820. Five arches with battered rock-faced piers plunging into the valley. – RAILWAY

VIADUCT, flanking and then crossing the Almond to the w, with thirty-two rock-faced arches and dressed parapet, by *Grainger & Miller* for the Edinburgh & Glasgow Railway, 1842.

CARLOWRIE. *See* p. 132.

INGLISTON HOUSE. *See* p. 260.

NEWLISTON. *See* p. 355.

KIRKNEWTON

ML *1060*

PARISH CHURCH, on the East Calder Road. Originally built in 1750 when the parish was united with that of East Calder, transformed into a Gothic church with a short saddleback tower by *Brown & Wardrop*, 1872. – MANSE to the rear of 1750. In 1835 a broad-gabled wing was added to the front in an old-fashioned classical manner, with projecting quoins.

CHURCHYARD (of the old parish church), in the village. Some good C17–18 monuments, mainly defaced, but the early C18 headstone of James Smith, Smith, Kirknewton, bears the tools of his trade. – Wall-monument to William Cullen † 1790, Senator of the Royal College of Justice, with Ionic pilasters and an urn. It stands in an enclosure of 1764 with a low-relief portrait head in bronze over the entrance.

The village is notable only for the unusual narrowness of the winding main street. The houses are mainly of the C19. Of those with two storeys, DUNALLAN (derelict and empty at the time of writing) has the odd combination of a bracketed Georgian doorpiece and Tudor hoodmoulds over the windows. It is named over the door and dated 1840.

KIRKNEWTON HOUSE, to the SE. Originally built in the C17 and repeatedly extended. Known as Meadowbank until it was drastically reduced *c.* 1950. What survives is one wing, possibly C17 but overlaid with work by *W. H. Playfair*, 1835, and later baronial detail, and a fragment of C18 wall with rusticated quoins. Playfair's screen wall to the office courtyard is punctuated by square piers and crowned with a miniature arched balustrade. – VASES from the C18 house have been re-used in the garden. – SUNDIAL. Late C17; a plain column, the deep cornice interrupted by deep fascias for the dials. – LODGES, by the village. A blunt square tower probably by *Playfair*, and a later one with crowsteps.

HILL HOUSE, to the E. A two-storey, five-bay house with plain dressings, built in the second half of the C18. Attic with a

Venetian-windowed chimney-gable in the middle, the centre light blank to allow for the flue.

AINVILLE, on the A70, 3·5km. SSW. A late C18 farm. Two parallel ranges with keystoned arches in their front gables, small round ventilators along the sides. Contemporary farmhouse with bracketed doorpiece, block cornice, round-headed attic windows in the gables.

ORMISTON HALL. *See* p. 374.

KNOWES *see* EAST LINTON

3060   LASSWADE   ML

OLD PARISH CHURCH. The medieval church was abandoned in 1793 and its ruins collapsed in 1866. It was a late Norman to Transitional building, aisleless, with a large W tower rather like that at Kirkliston. The most individual feature was a large tribune or gallery opening into the nave immediately above the tower arch. Fragments of two pre-Romanesque crosses recovered from the ruins were presented to the National Museum of Antiquities. Three burial aisles attached to the N wall remain. The W aisle was the burial place of the Drummonds of Hawthornden, including William Drummond the poet † 1649; it was restored in his honour in 1892, with a bronze relief portrait over the door. Inside, a graceful pedimented tablet to Jean Drummond † 1777. The aisle E of this belonged to the Clerks of Eldin. Rubble with raised dressings. In the end wall a Gothic survival window with a vesica in plate tracery. Also the corniced early C19 Melville enclosure, and that of the Prestons of Valleyfield with a C15 EFFIGY of a knight, carved in high relief rather than in the round. – MONUMENTS, in the churchyard. First a large heap of about ten tons of them, but a few of interest remain upright *in situ*. The best are of the early C18, when the mason or masons had a fine and grisly grasp of the *memento mori* idea, e.g. one to the NE inscribed 'Hear Layes Jain Laidlaw ...' † 1739, with the customary trappings on the reverse. Against the N wall a later C18 stone, otherwise weathered away, shows two gentlemen with the instruments of road survey and construction.

The old churchyard is reached through the r. of a neat trio of early C19 gateways. The middle one leads to the MANSE of the same period, the l. one to the site of the square church by the firm of *R. & J. Adam*, 1793 (damaged by dry rot after closure, and demolished in 1956), of which not a trace remains.

Lasswade church, west tower, south and east elevations (MacGibbon and Ross, *Ecclesiastical Architecture of Scotland*)

Across the road a C20 gateway with rusticated piers and a pair of lodges leads into a third burial ground.

PARISH CHURCH (originally United Secession). A plain square box in a nice position with a pediment dated 1830 in the middle of its ashlar front. Porch, bellcote and new woodwork (including pulpit) by *Hardy & Wight*, 1894. – STAINED GLASS. To the l. of the pulpit Moses: Christ's preaching and miracles, and to the r. John the Baptist: Martha, Mary and Dorcas, by *A. Ballantine & Gardiner*, 1894. – The original MANSE is a pretty Georgian house at No. 45 Polton Road.

ST LEONARD (Episcopal), Low Broomieknowe, off Polton Road. By *Hippolyte J. Blanc*, 1890. Nave and chancel only; simplest E.E., modulated to a round-arch style inside. In the chancel a ribbed timber tunnel-vault seen through a concentric arch. – STAINED GLASS. At the w end three gorgeous lights (Come

Unto Me . . .) by *Mayer & Co.* of Munich and London, 1890.
– To the s one light (Samuel) by *William Wilson*, 1961.

ELGINHAUGH BRIDGE (A7 over the North Esk). 1797. A wide segmental arch between two smaller ones. The four piers have battered and rusticated buttresses.

PITTENDREICH HOUSE. *See* p. 389.

In the early C19 Lasswade was the head of a very large parish. Now vastly outgrown by its neighbours, it is a battered village in the still recognizably lovely setting of the valley of the North Esk, across which it carries the A768 by means of a two-arched C18 bridge, brutally widened. The ugly withdrawal of the paper industry has left its mark, and traffic has blighted many of the houses that made a tight pattern along the roadside. But the ghost of a townscape can still be seen in the long descent from Eskbank, and even at the river crossing, where a house of *c.* 1840 pushed out a friendly bow but has now blocked up its door in self-defence. Next to it the colour-washed early C19 LAIRD AND DOG is one of the few buildings still glad of its intimacy with the road. The E side of the river is a disaster area, but it is worth going on to the Jenny Lass Wade Hotel, formerly ST LEONARDS, of *c.* 1840, a Greco-Italian villa of some originality. It has a smooth projecting bay with bracketed balcony and bellcote, and a very simple Greek porch beside it, similarly finished. Along the w bank are the early C19 RIVERSIDE and ESKVIEW (both heavily altered) and the OLD BANK BUILDING, bow-fronted, of three storeys. From here the way is uphill past the very dominant three-gabled BOARD SCHOOL of 1875 to the sites of the two old parish churches on the summit.

VILLAS

To the NW of Lasswade, across the river, is an interesting variety of C19 villas and a few of the C20, some bordering the Loanhead road at Wadingburn, others enjoying the view from the wooded ridge above the village, and still others looking over into the little glen supervised by Mavisbank (*see* Loanhead).

LASSWADE COTTAGE, Wadingburn. The r. (earliest) part of the garden (s) front is late C18–early C19 with a single bow of droved ashlar, a dormer window buried in its thatched roof. Then comes a prosaic baronial extension of the later C19, incorporating an earlier rustic arcade, and finally a more romantic wing dated 1914. A row of vernacular Georgian cottages leads up to the gateway whose brick piers have *putti* on ball finials. Sir

= Barony House

Walter Scott lived here in the late C18, but the earliest interior finishings are of *c.* 1810, and minimal at that.

THORNHILL HOUSE, Wadingburn. Showy baronial of *c.* 1860. In the first-floor drawing room a Greco-Egyptian cornice and a fanciful Rococo painted ceiling in which pale blue predominates.

KEVOCK ROAD. A merry assortment, the following worthy of notice. The OLD LODGE (reputedly by Mavisbank) is of *c.* 1810 with later horizontal glazing. Square centre with a shallow pyramidal roof and a central chimney. Clustered gatepiers, with Gothic gates and railings, of *c.* 1830. ESK TOWER is Italianate, of *c.* 1850, in yellow sandstone. A broad anta-porch projects between the advanced sides, which have bracketed canopies-cum-balconies. No. 16, by *Robert Steedman* of *Morris & Steedman*, 1958–9, has a two-storey central block, quite blank to the road but glazed to the N view. No. 14 by *Ian G. Lindsay & Partners*, 1971, is white-harled with weatherboarded gables to its monopitch roof. Its slope, and the change from one storey to two, is well expressed in the open-planned interior.

LAWHEAD *see* TYNINGHAME

LEASTON *see* HUMBIE

LENNOXLOVE   EL 5070
1.5 km. S of Haddington

The estate was called Lethington when the Maitlands acquired it in 1385. In the C15 they built the large L-plan tower, whose 43 long sides, of three full storeys, face S and W. Within the parapet, with its continuous rope-and-billet corbelling, is an L-plan penthouse. The parapet walk, drained by crudely masked gargoyles, bulges out into open bartizans at the corners. The one at the SW merges above the stair into a cap-house of the early C17, the date of the curved platform above the internal angle, on a squinch arch, its parapet pierced with observation holes. The doorways are concealed from the outside by later buildings. The first, on the E side of the main block, has the Maitland arms and motto overhead, the second enters the jamb just before it joins the main block. The latter was built by John Maitland Earl of Lauderdale in 1626, and a Roman-lettered tablet over the cornice tells how he enlarged the windows of the tower and provided an easier stairway (*faciliorem ascensum*) in that year. He had already built the long E wing (originally of two storeys plus dormers, one of whose pediments is built into the E wall), but the tower at the SE end is an addition, dated 1644 on one of a pair of wall sundials.

The new name of Lennoxlove was decreed in the will of the Duchess of Lennox who died in 1703. Of a mid C18 scheme for Palladianizing the whole building, the only executed part was the long range to the NW and the twin-arcaded coach house, both with busily rusticated windows and quoins.* The coach house was given a cheeky round turret by *Sydney Mitchell & Wilson* in 1914. The early C19 contribution was the raising of the E wing wall head to a prosaic parapet with false machicolations, and the remodelling of the SE tower as a rather feeble version of the old one. Major W. A. Baird bought the property in 1900, and the front door of the E wing is part of the work done for him by *Robert Lorimer* in 1912; so are the cherub-topped piers, with wrought-iron gates in Scots style, leading to the formal garden. The Duke of Hamilton purchased Lennoxlove in 1947.

It will be easiest to take the inside, like the outside, in roughly chronological order. The old tower is entered on ground level by John Maitland's doorway, protected by an iron yett. At the SE corner of the tunnel-vaulted CELLAR in the main block, now used as a chapel, is the well, reached from above by a shaft. The turnpike stair in the internal angle leads up past the guard room to the principal floor, where the whole of the main block is filled by the HALL. *Lorimer* stripped this down to the rubble, exposing the vents in the stone vault above. He did not attempt to restore the gallery at the S end, but he did contrive a vast stone fireplace, grand with four clusters of shafts but homely with four comical heraldic beasts, along the whole length of the N wall. A defaced Maitland tablet has been inserted above the door that leads into a lobby, formerly the kitchen, with the fireplace in the E gable. Above it is the room now called the LADY'S BOWER, square in plan and owing its extraordinary character to the deep embrasures of entry and window. The whole space is enriched by a geometric ceiling of square and star pattern with little pendants. The fireplace casually shoved into one corner has a panelled overmantel with the initials I M S for

---

* John Dunbar (*Sir William Bruce*, Scottish Arts Council, 1970) tells how Bruce drew up a scheme for remodelling Lennoxlove in 1673. The existing work, however, is mainly of later character.

John Maitland and his wife Isabel Seton, and the date 1632. Still further up, above the s half of the hall, Lorimer provided a bedroom called the DUCHESS OF LENNOX'S ROOM, with a coved ceiling (diagonally opposed thistles and roses) and heraldic panels over the embrasured windows. On the same level, in the jamb, is the TOWER LIBRARY whose lugged chimneypiece, with overmantel and coroneted pediment, is from one of the pavilions at the Hamiltons' eye-catching 'dog kennel' of Chatelherault in Lanarkshire.

The E wing interiors are still more mixed in character. The earliest work is the plaster ceiling of the ground-floor SITTING ROOM, of similar type to the ceiling in the tower. The date 1618 over the old fireplace has been left amid the C20 panelling above the new one. The prettily carved wooden chimneypiece in the ENTRANCE HALL*, with cherub terms on the flanking brackets, is mid C18, and so apparently is the cantilevered timber STAIR in the oblong well straight ahead. Its levitation was formerly enhanced by an oval window, now blocked and visible on the outside only, directly behind the main flight. The stair has had to be propped up at the corners. Plasterwork at the head of c. 1800. The white marble Louis chimneypiece in the DINING ROOM was installed c. 1960, but two late C18 ones on the first floor have always been in the house. That in the DRAWING ROOM, which has a C19 moulded Rococo ceiling, is of white marble carved in low relief with a long frieze of cherubs at a vintage. The other, in the adjacent bedroom, is of timber and composition.

SUNDIAL, in the C20 formal garden to the E. A saucy lady 64 in stiff court dress, a fan in one hand, in the other a rose against her bosom, standing on an octagonal stepped platform and balancing on her head a polygonal block with seventeen dials. She comes from North Barr in Renfrewshire and bears the initials of Donald MacGilchrist, who built that house, with the date 1679.

STEADING, at Lennoxlove Mains. C18, with round piers between the cartshed arches, and a circular brick chimney.

LETHAM HOUSE
1.5 km. WSW of Haddington

EL 4070

The centrepiece was originally a C17 house with a projecting stair-tower at the E end. An ambitious rebuilding was planned

---

* The entrance hall and the adjacent room have been opened into each other through an arcaded Ionic screen, probably soon after 1900.

c. 1735, the date on a lintel of the E pavilion which is, like its fellow, of two storeys in fine style with rusticated quoins and quadrant links. But the old house remained. Later in the C18 it was given an E extension with its own projecting stair-tower, *c.* 1800 its windows were enlarged, and then *c.* 1835 it was half-heartedly baronialized, with a little porch adjoining its recast tower. House and pavilions were separately modernized by different architects in the early 1970s without significant alteration of their exteriors. In 1971 the STEADING to the W, originally of the early C18 and now known as West Letham, was given a semi-octagonal tower with a pointed roof as part of its improvement by *Mary Tindall*.

GATEPIERS. Rusticated; of *c.* 1735.

DOOCOT. Ruinous. C18 double lectern type.

5080   LEUCHIE HOUSE   EL
                  2 km. s of North Berwick

Leuchie, built for Sir Hew Dalrymple in 1779–85, is an eclectic house both within and without, and unusually innocent of the urge to be consistently fashionable. Of warm rubble with free-stone dressings, it has two storeys over a high ground floor, and then a parapet pierced over the windows by a heavy balustrade. Full-height canted bay on the s (garden) front, and bows at the ends. The entrance front had the only elaboration (three Venetian openings on the ground floor and a four-columned doorpiece in the middle), but it was covered up *c.* 1855 by the addition of one room-thickness to this side.

The Victorian front door is off-centre, and the plain, decent rooms do not conform to the strong axial plan of the Georgian house. But the STAIRCASE is entered on the N side, just as it was through the old front door. The stair, ascending round three sides of the well, has a Victorian mahogany balustrade, but the architectural treatment is concentrated on the landing (s) side; or rather on the plasterwork, which like all the rest is by *James Nisbet* of Edinburgh. On the ground floor low-relief figures in ovals over the side doors, on the first floor crossed palms. The central door is pedimented in both cases. The side rooms are served by pairs of arched doorways at the angles. The whole of the stair soffit has thin husk garlands meeting tangentially in the middle. Finally, the deep cove under the roof light, with large-scale antique foliage and pendant strings of vines at the corners, in bold modelling which recalls that of the stair at Yester some forty years before.

The three main rooms are equally showy, with certain features in common, like full-height orders and window soffits that are tilted, giving a hint of false perspective. First the DINING ROOM, which with the staircase occupies the central third of the original ground floor. Slim Corinthian pilasters at the junctions with the bowed ends. The ceiling was treated by *Nisbet* as a pure oval, though he put rectangular tablets at the centre and cardinal points. Otherwise it is busily curvilinear; two ranks of arcs striking into each other within the oval, circles chasing round outside it. Chimneypiece with white marble columns against a pinkish background, its white centre panel, a relief of Bacchus and Ariadne by *John Flaxman*, repeated by *Nisbet* on the plaster frieze above. The w third of the house was filled by the DRAWING ROOM (now a chapel), in which the order is a pair of Corinthian columns checked into the angles where the room meets the bow. The ceiling is much more disciplined than others in the house, its curved ornament kept between rectilinear limits. In the plaster frieze another classical group alternates with pairs of griffons, again repeating the design of the chimneypiece. Finally the UPPER DRAWING ROOM, over the dining room and of the same shape, its walls similarly articulated. But the pilasters are of a novel order – tall leafy capitals with an eagle between grotesque masks at the top. The oval ceiling is of calmer elegance. In the white marble chimneypiece, almost the equal of its fellow downstairs, a panel of bacchantes set on an urn-and-husk frieze.

STABLES. A plain gabled range dated 1859, which is the only clue to the date of the enlargement of the house.

Large WALLED GARDEN in two parts, the walls lined with red brick. In one corner of it an excellently simple HOUSE by *Law & Dunbar-Nasmith*, 1962.

LIMPLUM
EL 507
3 km. w of Garvald

A strongly modelled baronial house with a dominating central drum tower, by *Shiells & Thomson*, 1884. Lodge to match.

LINHOUSE   ML (now WL)
4.5 km. SSW of Midcalder

C16–17. The older part, to the r. of the main (NW) front, consists
of two square towers of one-room size, attached to each other
by one corner. So there are two internal angles, each with a
bulging turnpike stair, the one on the main front corbelled out
to contain the last stage of the ascent. It is carved with billets
and rope at the bottom, more billets at the top; then, all in stone,
a ball-finialled conical roof with four gablets, one of them leading out on to the battlemented roof-top platform. The excitement is not, however, restricted to the upper parts. The SW
end is cunningly splayed and corbelled, all the original windows
are roll-moulded, and the old front door by the angle (now a
window) is inscribed with the date 1589 and the legend NISI
DOMINUS FRUSTRA (Except the Lord build the house). The
Muirheads, who acquired Linhouse in 1631 (WM is lightly
carved in the roof-top gablet), lengthened the house to the NE,
the extension breaking forward at the end so that the whole
frontage forms a shallow U. The front door is now in this projection. In its lower part, leading up to the main storey, a fine
scale-and-platt stair whose bottle nosings have been chopped
off, though the end returns survive. The spine wall between
the flights is not carried right up, but is heavily moulded as
a handrail, and the whole stair-space is united by a deep plaster
frieze with a sinuous vine in shallow relief. The rooms on the
main floor have pine panelling of the early C18, but a few of
the original moulded fireplaces remain. Two pine and composition chimneypieces were imported in the C20.

LAKE, to the SE. Profiting from the steep fall of the Linhouse
Water (hence indeed the name), the present owner excavated
in 1975 a lake with an islet in the middle; by 1985 it will be
fully acceptable as a pleasing quirk of nature.

DOOCOT, to the N. C18 lectern type, with an elliptical window over the doorway to each of the two compartments.

LINLITHGOW   WL

CHURCHES

12 ST MICHAEL'S PARISH CHURCH. Spectacularly sited at the
top of the promontory between the town and the loch, and big
enough to hold its own against the great mass of the palace,

though this comes out better in distant views than from close to. The actual measurements, inside the walls, are: length 182 ft; breadth across the transepts 102 ft. In Lothian only Haddington is larger, but compared to Haddington Linlithgow is less compact and more varied in grouping, a distinction largely due to the placing of the tower at the w end instead of over a crossing. One factor common to both churches is the adherence to a single plan throughout a long building campaign, with only minor modifications. The earlier church was burned in 1424, but its destruction cannot have been total, for Queen Joan is recorded as worshipping there in 1429.* Rebuilding began with the nave, but our only firm date for the w parts is the *terminus ante quem* provided by the burial in 1489 in the N nave aisle of the mason *John Frenssh*. Possibly he was the designer or builder or both. The choir was begun around 1497 and must have been nearly complete in 1532, when an agreement about its battlements was made between the town council and the master of the 'kirk werk', *Thomas Frenssh*, son of John. There have been two major restorations, one in 1812 and one between 1894 and 1896. In the first the chancel arch was demolished, a solid wall was built across the choir, and the medieval roofs were replaced by plaster vaults. The second, under the direction of *John Keppie* and *John Honeyman*, involved the removal of pews and galleries, the rebuilding of the chancel arch and the addition of a choir vestry on medieval foundations.

Inevitably the most eye-catching feature of the exterior is the spire added to the w tower in 1964 by *Geoffrey Clarke*. The material is bronze-tinted aluminium; the shape resembles a wigwam without its cover, giving no impression, as with medieval spires, of growth upwards from the tower. The openwork form derives from the medieval crown steeple taken down *c.* 1821 but [13] recorded in sufficient detail to have made it feasible to build a replica. The tower is narrower than the nave and generally smaller in relation to the church than the w towers of most comparable English churches would be. It is in fact a rather quiet design with no buttresses, only a polygonal stair-turret at the NW angle. The w door has a trumeau, and in the tympanum an image niche flanked by glazed vertical lights. The w window is of three lights with simple Perp panel tracery. Above this a small lancet, then a larger lancet for the bell stage, and lastly a round window with interlocked mouchettes. One window only in the E face, none in the N face. Battlemented parapet

* A C12 scalloped capital is lying loose in the s choir aisle.

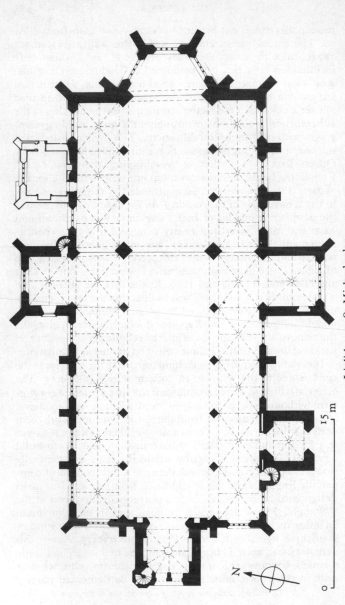

Linlithgow, St Michael, plan

with corner pinnacles. No dates are recorded for the tower, but the untidy junction with the nave plinth on the N side proves it is later than the nave. The nave aisles have tall windows and buttresses with pretty image niches. On the SW buttress a worn figure of St Michael, later C15 to judge by the armour. Low clearstory with small windows and much plain wall between. Wide battlements to both sets of parapets. The tracery of the aisle windows is mostly of two designs, one a heart shape composed of two trefoils and a soufflet, the other a circle with mouchettes enclosing a trefoil. The exceptions are the W window of the N aisle, with a simpler arrangement of mouchettes, and the E window of the S aisle, which is larger in format and cuts into the cornice. Its tracery is nominally flowing, but the intersections of the mouchettes produce something devoid of fluency and closer to loop tracery. There has at some stage been a low chapel or vestry abutting the W wall of the S aisle. Roof corbels and two panels of blind reticulated tracery remain.*

The S porch is two-storeyed. Arch of three orders, the outermost with boldly undercut foliage (cf. the original entrance to the great hall in the palace). Above is a pretty oriel with a pointed roof, very like one formerly in the same position at St Giles, Edinburgh. At an intermediate level two image niches. The porch front as a whole derives its effect from the contrast between crisply carved and moulded forms and sheer ashlar background. The roof is divided from the main body of the church by an inner gable which, like the outer one, is crow-stepped. In the W angle a round stair-turret with a conical cap. Inside a simple rib-vault, and on the E wall a niche, daintily carved, or perhaps just better preserved than usual. S doorway of five orders with mouldings like the porch arch, and above, a bracket with an angel holding a scroll (or a napkin?). Plain round-headed N doorway. The N and S transeptal chapels, roofed like the porch, differ in nearly all details. The N one is shallower and has a N window of one of the nave types plus a small window in the W wall. The S chapel has only one window, but it is the 14 *pièce de résistance* of the church, and indeed the most beautiful Late Gothic window in Scotland.‡ Its singular distinction is that the tracery is divided from the lights by a kind of curved transom which combines with the head of the window to form

* The piece of string course on the l. may mean that the window sill had been started at the normal level before this annexe was decided on.

‡ But the W window of Dunkeld Cathedral was practically identical.

a convex equilateral triangle. Within this figure three circles alternate with three big dagger forms, all elegantly subdivided. The heads of the lights simply follow the 'transom'.

The choir reveals its later date only in details. Buttresses are deeper and statue niches simpler. Windows have loop tracery,* except for the westernmost window on the N side, which has Perp tracery deprived of some uprights. This window is also exceptional in having concave jambs, so it may be older than the rest of the choir. A w to E sequence for the construction of the choir is in any case evident from the partial continuation eastwards of the nave type of plinth. No E windows to the aisles. The apse is substantially lower than the choir. In this and in its plan (three sides of a hexagon) it is a pendant to the contemporary apse at the Holy Rude, Stirling. The craggy buttresses and the great expanses of window make an impressive show. Two windows have what might be termed sub-Perp tracery; the other has a circle with five whirling mouchettes. An interesting detail is the diminutive reproduction of these two patterns on the niche canopy of the NE buttress. The apse is sometimes described as an addition to the choir, but there is no evidence for this in the masonry, and, moreover, the window embrasures have fairly elaborate mouldings identical to those of the choir.

The interior is spacious and largely devoid of furniture, though this was not always the case. In 1787 Robert Burns was filled with disgust at the sight of galleries and pews crammed into the nave: 'What a poor pimping business is a Presbyterian place of worship! – dirty narrow and squalid, stuck in a corner of old popish grandeur . . .'. Nave and choir are consistent in the essentials of their elevations, except that the nave has a triforium of sorts where the choir has blank wall. The stone-vaulted aisles, together with the tall arcades, are the greatest asset of the interior. Unfortunately the main span has early C19 plaster vaulting, absurdly shallow in profile. Turning to details, we start under the w tower. Quadripartite vault with ridge ribs interrupted by the big bell-hole and the doubling of ribs to take account of the stair-turret in the NW corner. In the N and S walls two large and unexplained recesses with cusped heads. The arch to the nave is tall and narrow but still leaves room for another round-headed opening at clearstorey level. The nave piers are a cluster of eight shafts with fillets carried into the capitals and bases. Blank shields on the intermediate shafts.

* The w window of the s aisle has been extended downwards at some time, destroying in the process the top of a blocked priest's door.

The arch mouldings are different on the N and S sides, and there are many further small variations in the aisles that suggest an extended building period. Only a few can be mentioned here. In the S aisle the capitals of the vault shafts have foliage and the bosses are plain. In the N aisle the capitals are plain but the bosses are decorated, some with shields (Hamilton and ?Seton). The arch between the nave and choir aisles is much simpler on the N than on the S. The NW vault shaft of the last N compartment is corbelled out just above the floor – it must have been forgotten when the lowest courses were being laid. Returning to the elevation, the clearstorey and triforium are about equal in height and in width. Triforium with deep splays, a hoodmould and meagre tracery. Original wall shafts. These upper storeys appear weak and unresolved above the bold striding arcade. The chancel arch of 1894 etc. occupies the position of the original arch. The choir piers have chamfered projections in place of intermediate shafts. Capitals and bases are all elided, but none is exactly the same as another in its mouldings; so again one suspects a slow rate of building. There is no middle storey as such, just blank wall bounded by string courses. No wall shafts, only corbels. The apse arch is semicircular.

FURNISHINGS. Few, considering the size of the church, and none requiring special comment. – PULPIT and FONT by *Honeyman*. – STAINED GLASS. In the apse, four sets of four lights (the Creation) by *Clayton & Bell*, 1885. – In the S chancel aisle four lights (St Ninian and three others, with four monarchs) by *Alfred Webster* of *Adams, Glasgow*, 1914, and three lights (the Women at the Sepulchre), drab and vapid, by *Cottier* of London, 1885. – In the S transept six lights (Christ and the little children) by *Clayton & Bell*, after 1892. – In the S nave aisle four lights (the Evangelists) by *Morris & Co.* from *Burne Jones's* design, 1899, and at its W end four lights (Adoration of the Magi and scenes of Christ with children) by *Herbert Hendrie*, 1936; he avoids both the mechanical and the sentimental look of much work done at that time. – In the W window three lights (the Transfiguration) by *Ballantine* of Edinburgh, 1898. – In the N nave aisle four lights (Christ and the little children) by *Mayer* of Munich, after 1909. – In the N transept one light (the infant Samuel) by *Meikle* of Glasgow. – MEMORIAL SLAB in the S choir aisle to Provost John Forrest † 1589. – SCULPTURE. In the vestry two high-relief slabs from a C15 Passion retable. The larger, over the fireplace, has scenes of the Agony in the Garden and the Betrayal divided by a thin column.

Ogee canopies, much made up in cement. The figures are close-packed and stocky, with big heads and bulky robes, but further discussion of their sculptural qualities is pointless because of the recent thorough retooling of all surfaces, following a fire. – On the opposite wall the Mocking of Christ, less complete but at least unrestored. The costume details indicate the end of the C15. – Elsewhere in the church two scraps from the same sequence: parts of a soldier holding a scourge and of the fainting Virgin from a Crucifixion.

ST MICHAEL (R.C.), Blackness Road. 1887 by *Pugin & Pugin*, enlarged in 1893, a long, aisleless Gothic church of snecked rubble, with adjoining presbytery and school in a similar style. Seven-bay nave with scissor-beam roof, two-bay sanctuary and N chapel. – STAINED GLASS. One light in the chapel (St John) by *John Blyth*, 1957. – The internal modernization by *J. A. Coia*, 1952, includes a panelled REREDOS.

ST MILDRED (Episcopal), High Street. A tiny church by *Dick Peddie & Todd*, 1928, filling the gap between two houses. Simply a door in an archway, the capitals carved as a lion and a bull; in the tympanum a vesica containing a St Andrew's cross, supported by two angels. Thermal window with tile arch overhead.

ST NINIAN'S CRAIGMAILEN, Falkirk Road. Built as a United Free church in 1874. Lanceted Gothic with a wide nave and an attached tower whose lucarned broach-spire is a landmark to the W of the town. In 1901 the S aisle was added and the semi-octagonal hall at one end incorporated in the church, making a somewhat unfulfilled climax to the very spare interior. – ORGAN. Of the same date, by *Abbot & Smith* of Leeds, to one side of it. – STAINED GLASS. Three grouped lancets at the E end (the six Christian Acts of Mercy) by *James Ballantine & Son*, 1885, in memory of the papermaker Thomas Chalmers who lived at Longcroft House. – Five single lancets along the sides with large figures set in white glass (Christ, Mary, Martha; Phoebe, Christ with children) by *W. Meikle & Sons*, early C20. – In the S aisle a double light (I am the Way, the Valley of the Shadow), well drawn and painted in seductive, satiny colours by *J. T. Stewart*.

PUBLIC BUILDINGS

TOWN HALL, on the upper (N) side of the Cross. A single massive block on a tall basement with a square six-stage tower behind, built by the master mason *John Smith* in 1668–70 to replace the old town-house demolished by Cromwell in 1650. Damaged by fire in 1847 and restored in the following year by *Thomas Brown*; the inscription on the frieze records that Provost Adam Dawson of Bonnytoun (*see* p. 114) paid for the work. Smith's design was generally followed: a main front of seven bays with triangular pediments over the windows of the two upper storeys and a slightly larger one over the door; the calcined stonework of some of the old windows can be seen at the back. But the crowning balustrade of the original was omitted, and so was the metal-clad belfry on the tower, which received its clock in 1858. Brown's design was modified in its turn, for in 1905–6 *William Scott* of Linlithgow removed the iron-framed loggia that stood in front of the basement, replacing it with a monumental stair. At the same time he designed the MASONIC HALL to the E. No town in Lothian, perhaps not even Edinburgh, has a grander civic focus. The interior was drastically recast in 1962–3 as a set of public halls by *Rowand Anderson, Kininmonth & Paul*.

For other public buildings *see* Description, below.

LINLITHGOW PALACE[*]

A royal manor house existed at Linlithgow in the reign of David I, but nothing is known about its appearance or its exact position. In 1301–2 it was converted by Edward I of England into a base for his siege of Stirling. This involved the construction of earthworks, water-filled ditches and a wooden palisade or 'peel' ‡ all designed by the Savoyard *James of St George*, architect of the great Edwardian castles in North Wales. The site is eminently defensible – a promontory jutting into the S side of Linlithgow Loch and raised well above the valley which shelters the High Street. The great building now occupying this position is dominant in any view across the water, but down in the High Street it is invisible behind the Town House and the parish church. It consists of four high ranges about a square courtyard with square towers at each corner. This simple plan, unique in Scotland in the Middle Ages§, was probably derived from such northern English fortified manor houses as Bolton and Sheriff Hutton (North Yorkshire) and Lumley (Co.

[*] The account of Linlithgow Palace is by Christopher Wilson.
‡ The name is now applied to the low-lying garden to the E, but this is unlikely to have been part of the fortified enclosure. It is possible that the terracing around the palace is a survival of *James of St George*'s earthworks.
§ But followed in the early C17 at Heriot's Hospital, Edinburgh.

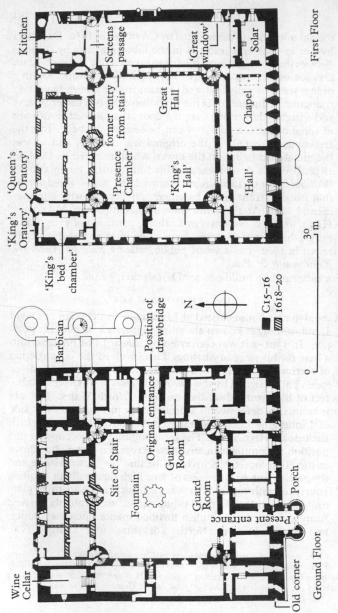

Linlithgow Palace, plans of ground and first floors

First Floor

Kitchen

'Queen's Oratory'

'King's Oratory'

Screens passage

former entry from stair

'Presence Chamber'

'King's Hall'

'King's bed chamber'

'Great window'

Solar

Great Hall

Chapel

'Hall'

N

0   30
|_____|
m

C15–16
1618–20

Ground Floor

Barbican

Position of drawbridge

Original entrance

Site of Stair

Fountain

Wine Cellar

Old corner

Guard Room

Guard Room

Porch

Present entrance

Durham), all of the last quarter of the C14. Linlithgow may also be classified as a fortified manor house, for it combines sophisticated domestic planning with defensibility against anything short of a concerted siege.

Despite its compact plan, the palace is far from homogeneous in structure or style: it is in fact the product of four major building campaigns spanning two centuries. The first began in 1425 and was apparently a total rebuilding of the 'manner' burnt in the preceding year: by 1437 over £4,500 Scots had been spent. Around 1470 some further work was being done, but the next important campaign started in 1490 and ended only in 1513, the year of Flodden. From 1502 the master mason was *Nichol Jackson*, who had worked on the royal collegiate church at Ladykirk, Berwickshire. He was succeeded in 1512 by *Stephen Balty* or *Bawte*. In the third phase, lasting from *c.* 1534 to 1541, Thomas *Fransh* or *Frenssh* was in charge (*see* St Michael), and the scale of operations must have been large, judging by the quantities of stone bought. The final phase consisted of the rebuilding of the N range by *William Wallace* in 1618–20, the earlier range having collapsed in 1605. The main builders of Linlithgow were thus the first, fourth, fifth and sixth Jameses.

All these facts are known from the records of the Royal Works, but unfortunately the accounts for the first three building periods hardly ever specify what work was being done. As a result, any attempt to assign C15 and C16 features to documented periods of work has to be based entirely on stylistic and archaeological evidence, and it is only fair to say that the interpretations offered here differ widely from those already published. The documents are also unhelpful in the matter of identifying the functions of individual apartments. Most of the present names derive from late C16 and early C17 sources and so do not necessarily reflect the original uses. The palace was last used as such in 1633 and, after a century of neglect, was burned out in 1746, during occupation by the Duke of Cumberland's troops. The Office of Works took it over in 1874, and many wall heads, floors and lintels were renewed in the 1890s.

The block-like compactness of the EXTERIOR is perhaps its most memorable quality, for individually the outer fronts are severe almost to the point of blankness. Partly this is due to the smallness of the windows, but more important is the fact that the corner towers do not project beyond the intervening ranges and so break up their flatness.

The present approach to the palace is by way of the steep Kirkgait and the outer gate built by James V to serve his new s entrance. However, the circuit makes more chronological sense if it begins not on the s but with the EAST FRONT, the original entrance front.* The declivity at its N end accommodates what can only have been a barbican protecting the approach to the entrance, but its detailed arrangement is no longer clear. The remains comprise three round ashlar towers linked by a rubble wall and joined to the front by flying buttresses. In the middle tower was a spiral stair which could be entered from outside. Only the lowest parts of the s flyer are old, and they show that the original pitch was lower than at present. Whatever the drawbridge rested on has been destroyed. The entrance itself is a plain round arch, but above it is a splendidly large relief of the royal arms supported by two angels with a third hovering above. All this has its own basket-arched frame, and a further frame with pendant cusps encloses both the slots for the drawbridge mechanism and the recess housing the drawbridge itself. Flanking the whole are two big niches which may have held statues of St Andrew and St James. The similarity of their details to those on the nave buttresses of the church must indicate that this is James I's work. Moreover, the use of large-scale sculpture and heraldry to garnish an otherwise plain front compares with early C15 French castles, e.g. La Ferté-Milon or Pierrefonds. Near the top of the wall six small and regularly spaced rectangular windows light the great hall, and to their l., at the dais end, where in England one would expect a bay-window, is a much larger rectangular window. It has moulded jambs and originally was divided into two lights. The ingenious arrangement of the cusping should be noted. ‡ This is almost certainly the 'great window' for which *Nichol Jackson* was paid in 1502–3.

Some imaginative effort is needed to visualize the original skyline of the E front. The s w tower was taken down and rebuilt behind machicolated parapets in the late C16 or early C17 (see the projecting window margins). Before then its walls continued upwards in the same plane as the fronts below. The original limit of the machicolation is fixed by the canted corner corbel a few feet to the r. of the northernmost hall window.

---

* The old line of approach followed the present Kirkgait, branched r. above the Town House and continued round the E end of the churchyard.

‡ A reconstruction is in F. T. Dollman's *Ancient Domestic Architecture* (plate 3).

The SE tower has almost completely disappeared except for its N wall and that of two extra storeys added c. 1600.

Before proceeding to the S front, the 'OUTER ENTRY' at the head of the Kirkgate must be described. It is broad, of one storey, and has a plain depressed pointed arch flanked by polygonal turrets with gun loops. The impression is not at all formidable. A cable moulding runs below the parapet, which has panels (replacements of 1845) carved with the insignia of the four Orders of Chivalry to which James V belonged: the Garter, the Thistle, the Golden Fleece and St Michael. Slezer's engraving of c. 1678 shows a steeply pitched roof rising behind the parapet. Segmental tunnel-vault with closely spaced transverse ribs and a ridge rib. On the three pendant bosses nicely carved reliefs of a unicorn, a lion and a winged stag.

The SOUTH FRONT is the outcome of at least three periods of work. The oldest, recognizable by its rougher masonry, includes the SE tower and the lower half of the centre between the tower and the porch. The five tall cusped lancets belong to the chapel, probably built in the early 1490s.* That the chapel is later than the wall below is suggested by its superior ashlar but proved conclusively by the presence of a blocked garderobe shoot at the foot of the wall. The closely set lancets are not unique in Scottish Late Gothic architecture (cf. e.g. Melrose Abbey N transept and Aberdeen Cathedral W front). The porch and everything else W of the chapel belong to James V's work of the 1530s. Everything else, that is, in terms of surface masonry; for the straight joint about six feet round the corner on the W front reveals that James V thickened the W half of the S front. Two further alterations to the tower whose purpose can only have been to make it balance the SE tower are its widening eastwards and the blocking of all windows near the outer corner. These are visible only from inside and so will be discussed with the interior; but it should be mentioned here that this is a very early example, possibly the earliest in Scotland, of the superimposition of symmetry or near-symmetry on irregular older work. The porch stands in line with the outer gate and resembles it in being low and equipped with gun loops. The flagged roof was originally hidden behind a parapet with

* The timbers of the chapel roof were bought in 1492 (accounts of the Lord High Treasurer). There are no references to the stonework, but the 'pendin of thre voutis' was done in 1491 and, as there are three vaulted cellars below, the chapel was probably under way by 1492.

the royal arms. Tunnel-vault inside with surface ribs in a quasi-sexpartite arrangement.

The WEST FRONT has few architectural pretensions. The windows are all rectangular, of various dates. Near the middle is a relieving arch. Some projecting feature below it, entered from adjacent rooms on the first floor, has been removed. The machicolations are presumably those documented as being built by *Nichol Jackson* in 1504.

The cliff-like appearance of the NORTH FRONT is due to the 1618–20 rebuilding of the centre nearly to the same height as the towers. The regular rows of windows all originally had mullions and transoms. The small loops lit privies serving each set of chambers. The transomed and mullioned window in the SE tower lacks projecting margins and so is probably earlier than the rest. The most remarkable feature of the front is a group of oriel windows projecting from the NW tower at first-floor level. The best preserved is an enlarged version of the S porch oriel at St Michael's, with the addition of a sort of pedestal reaching to the ground. This feature and the tall pointed roof indicate French influence. To the l. the pedestal remains from a similar window, and to the r. is most of a shallow rectangular oriel which was lit by ogee-headed lights grouped under a square hoodmould. Beside this was yet another oriel, again three-sided, judging from the stumps of ribs on its outer vault boss. This window and the well preserved one are generally called, on inadequate evidence, the King's and the Queen's Oratories respectively. Remains of similar oriels are on the E front of the royal lodgings in Edinburgh Castle.

The COURTYARD is entered through James V's S porch and a barrel-vaulted passage formed out of an earlier cellar. In the
49 centre stands the FOUNTAIN, wedding-cake-like in its dense decoration and its shape. It is octagonal, with a tank on each of three tiers, in the tradition of monastic lavatoria, e.g. at Wenlock Priory, Shropshire. The architectural parts are straightforward Late Gothic: clustered shafts at the angles, much-cusped parapets, cusped and crocketed flyers linking the tiers, and at the top a lantern with a crown exactly like that on the tower at King's College, Aberdeen. Only the sculpture betrays Renaissance influence. On the pinnacles at the bottom level are heads in roundels, a favourite early C16 motif, here very close in detail to those beside the W door of Holyrood Abbey. Alternating with the pinnacles are pedestals whose details are more explicitly Renaissance in character, e.g. sphinxes, candelabra

and nude figures (their identifying scrolls are unfortunately illegible). Only one lion survives of the heraldic beasts that sat on the pedestals. Round the middle stage are standing figures, some of them recent. The four original ones include a mermaid and a drummer. One side of the middle tank has foliage in relief, as presumably the others once did. The building of the fountain is not mentioned in any document, but there can be no doubt that it belongs to the 1530s. On one of the pedestals is a courtier wearing costume of that date and looking very similar to the figures on the Palace wing of 1540 at Stirling Castle. Moreover the cusping over the Stirling figures is almost identical to that of the flying buttresses on the fountain. We may even know the exact date, for the lead pipe feeding the fountain was dug up in the Kirkgait in 1894 and found to be inscribed with the date 1538. The relatively complete appearance of the fountain is due to its recent reconstruction to designs made by *J. S. Richardson* in 1930. There is no reason to think that the arrangement is incorrect. Some fragments not re-used are in a cellar at the E end of the N range.

The examination of the COURTYARD FRONTS will follow the clockwise order used for the outer fronts. Over the inner door of the original entrance in the centre of the EAST FRONT are three niches formerly housing figures of the Three Estates. Only one pair of feet remain. Sumptuous but poorly preserved canopies. Overhead are three magnificently conceived angels with outstretched wings. The whole composition is tied together by a huge bracket-like hoodmould with cusps ending in animal heads. Between the arches and to their r. runs a series of small windows lighting the passage for operating the portcullis. In the NE corner is the original door to the great hall. The roll mouldings of its deep jambs once continued into the head as undercut foliage like that on the S door of St Michael. The arch is a cross between an ogee and a basket arch. When the newel stairs in the angles of the courtyard were built the door was blocked and all trace of the stairs up to it removed. The W clearstorey of the hall is a later rebuilding, one of the windows being placed awkwardly in relation to the statue pedestal on the hoodmould over the entrance. The plain round heads and wide proportions suggest an approach to Renaissance canons and a date in the 1530s.

The SOUTH FRONT is given over to grid-like fenestration reminiscent of English Perpendicular. As James IV is the likely builder and his queen was Henry VII's daughter, direct influence is possible. The rows of straight-headed windows are interrupted only by the arch of James V's s entrance, not part of the original design, as traces of blocked windows prove. The image niches and the spectacularly wayward strings over the door are also later. A lily pot and Virgin remain from an Annunciation group, the quality of their carving greatly inferior to the sculpture on the E range. The windows light no major apartment, just corridors on three levels. The upper two became necessary once communication within the range had been interrupted by the building of the chapel *c.* 1491–2, so a date around then or soon after 1500 seems likely for the front. The newel stairs in the corners are of the same build, but slight traces remain of an older stair in the s w corner. Lumley Castle near Durham, built *c.* 1380, has newel stairs in each corner of the courtyard, but they project less than the Linlithgow stairs and lack their impressive array of narrow lights.

The WEST FRONT is not a unified composition. To the r., round-headed windows similar to those of the hall. Above the lower pair a long, low window of fourteen lights whose function was presumably to give extra illumination to a richly decorated ceiling. It is a spectacular piece of flat-arch construction, far wider than any fireplace lintel. Similarly placed windows occur in the Watching Chamber or Guard Room of 1535–6 at Hampton Court. Near the middle of the front are large windows of the same workmanship as the N range, then more plain windows including three small ones at the same level as the fourteen-lighter at the N end.

A few traces remain of the pre-C17 NORTH FRONT. Against the N W stair are traces of windows like those in the adjacent part of the N side. At the E corner the jamb and part of the flat arch of a door,* proving that the ground floor was more important here than in the other ranges. *Wallace*'s N front has five storeys and is smaller in scale than the other fronts. The repetitive effect is not lessened by the gradual reduction in the height of the storeys. There are no orders, only string courses which originally formed a linear grid with the downpipes. The thin pediments sprout finials in the form of roses, thistles, etc. and are filled with initials and the emblems of the newly united Kingdom. The flatness of all this is offset by a centrally projecting newel stair.

The description of the INTERIORS will deal largely with their few surviving decorative features, since little research has

* It was converted later into a window, see the glazing groove.

been done on the functional reasons for their often complex planning. The W, S and E ranges all stand on barrel-vaulted undercrofts, no doubt used mostly for storage. In the guard room E of the S entrance passage a reset C15 fireplace with foliage trails on the jambs, ending in seated figures, one with a lap-dog, the other dandling a child. The basement of the NE tower and the room adjoining on the S have enormous kitchen fireplaces, probably of the C16. The WINE CELLAR under the NW tower goes beyond the functional character of the other basements. Pointed tunnel-vault with surface ribs arranged as two quadripartite bays. Two of the corbels have small boozing figures. This room and that to the S can be overlooked from a tiny mezzanine within the wall which separates them.

The tour of the main floors starts with the KITCHEN in the NE tower. Its domical vault with ribs springing from the corners and the centres of the walls was demolished when the upper part of the tower was rebuilt. The fireplace and ovens are later. In the S wall, serving hatches open into the vaulted screens passage at the N end of the GREAT HALL. This was normally entered from the NE newel stair, but when the large W entrance was still used the screens must have stood further S to divide it from the hall. Over the present passage is a minstrels' gallery, also barrel-vaulted. The internal elevation is of the clearstorey type which became almost universal in England after the rebuilding of Westminster Hall in the 1390s. The only other Scottish examples are at Stirling and Bothwell Castles. The main form of decoration was tapestry, for which some hooks remain, but between the windows are brackets for statues. The difference in date between the E and W windows shows in the details of their masonry and their lack of alignment. The W windows were evidently rebuilt to include a wall passage linking the two newel stairs. The fireplace at the dais end is truly regal in scale (6.9 m. wide). The parts restored c. 1907 are easily recognized. Clustered shafts with foliage capitals and tall bases divide the hearth into three, and above them are brackets which carried statues standing free in front of the enormous hood. The purpose of the shallow tunnel-vault over the fireplace seems to be to carry an eastward extension of the SE tower, probably made in the 1530s. Beside the large window a small door leads S to the SOLAR, whose poor lighting belies the name.*

From here the CHAPEL is reached via a lobby at the E end.

* In C17 documents this room is referred to as the 'Chalmer of Dease', presumably meaning *chambre d'aise*.

Between its two doors was set a high reredos. On the w wall are indications of a wooden gallery, the roof raggle of the much lower buildings which preceded the chapel, the gable end of the higher buildings farther w, and the masonry added to raise the gable to the height of the chapel walls. Between the deep splays of the s windows are image niches with delicate canopies and excellent corbels carved as angel musicians. Traces of steeply sloping sills below the windows. The next room westwards is called by the RCAHM the HALL, but if the king's suite began here it would be the guard room. It is possible that the queen's suite was on the second floor, because from here round to the NW corner the first- and second-floor rooms are very similar in their arrangement and details. Most of the details are in fact not closely datable. In the 'hall' two fireplaces, apparently of different periods. A s window has been partly blocked by the porch roof. One of the means by which James V made the s front more symmetrical – the second E gable of the sw tower – can be seen from here. It is carried on an arch over the second floor and therefore has no effect on the plan. The s windows of the small room in the tower have been blocked for the same purpose. Tunnel-vaulted corridors in the s range, that on the first floor housing various SCULPTURAL FRAGMENTS including two corbels from the N range, a C16(?) head in three-quarter profile and a very large frontal relief of a king's head whose date and original position are unknown.

In the s apartment of the w range, called the KING'S HALL in the C17, a fireplace of C15 type with a hood and paired shafts. Similar fireplace in the room above, much renewed recently. The fireplace in the PRESENCE CHAMBER, with a tall hood, capitals with foliage and masks, and provision for square shafts, is of the same workmanship as those in James V's royal lodgings at Stirling. Traces of black and orange paint were reported in the C19. The N wall of the KING'S BEDCHAMBER, with its plain fireplace of c. 1600(?), opens into the oriels identified as the KING'S ORATORY. Both compartments of this are vaulted, the bosses finely carved with unicorns and mottoes. The larger QUEEN'S ORATORY has a similar vault. Where one would look for a piscina there is a later fireplace. If the identification as the queen's oratory is correct, it must follow that the queen's suite was in the N range. The oriel is now entered from a corridor connecting with the NW newel stair. At the top of the stair a pretty vault on corbels with entwined I's and M's (the latter on their sides). The use of Roman capitals makes the

1530s the most likely date. On top of the vault is QUEEN MAR-GARET'S BOWER, a small octagonal vaulted room where tradi-tionally James IV's queen received the news of Flodden. More steps led up to a look-out on the roof. The N range is for the date relatively primitive in its planning. The rooms, *en suite* to N and S of a chimneyed spine wall, were reached by corridors running N from the central newel stair. The best interiors were the two N rooms on the first floor. Their fireplaces are chastely classical and no longer in the C16 tradition. The smaller rooms on the upper floors were sets of chambers. At ground-floor level in the NW corner is the only trace of the medieval interior of the N range: a door jamb whose very finely moulded C15 base is further confirmation of the original importance of the ground floor here.

DESCRIPTION

The High Street, the only important street in Linlithgow, extends for 2 km. along the erratic line of the Edinburgh–Stirling road, by-passed by the motorway only in 1973. To the N is Linlith-gow Loch, with the royal residence that formed the focus of the first settlement; to the S the high ridge occupied by the Union Canal (1818–22) (*see* below) and the railway (1838–42). These two natural bounds have emphasized the longitudinal growth which is typical of the initial shape of most Scots burghs, but not of their subsequent expansion. As a town for courtiers and ambassadors Linlithgow is disappointing.* The palace is still the chief building, but few of its attendant town houses had much distinction and the majority have disappeared – some quite recently. Of Linlithgow as a mercantile centre there is more to see. It was made a royal burgh by David I in the early C12, built a splendid Town House in the C17 (more than adequately replaced two centuries later), and specialized in leather work till the end of the C19, by which time it had also acquired two distilleries and some paper-mills. In the 1960s its future planning was made the subject of a combined working party of Burgh Council, Scottish Development Department and the architectural firm who subsequently designed most of the central redevelopment. The outcome was a negative, or at least highly selective, preservation policy, but the results have been better than might have been expected.

* The finest recorded medieval town house in Scotland, the House of the Hospitallers, stood on the S side of the High Street at the E end (MacGibbon and Ross, *Castellated & Domestic Architecture*, vol. I). It was demolished in 1885.

LINLITHGOW

Edinburgh

Stirling

Boness Road

M9 Motorway

Linlithgow Loch

N

Palace

St Michael's R.C.

Longcroft House

St Michael's Parish Church

Academy

Town Hall

Blackness Rd

St Ninian

Cross Street

Edinburgh

St Mildred

High

Doocot

Falkirk Rd

W. Port Ho.

Royal Terr.

Union Canal

Canal House

Clarendon House

Approx. 800 metres or ½ mile

The High Street is entered from the E past ST MICHAEL'S HOS-
PITAL (1854, formerly the poorhouse), under the canal and
then under the railway, and finally past the huge, sombre warehouse built in 1880 for the ST MAGDALENE DISTILLERY.
On the other side a dreary bonded warehouse was permitted,
c. 1960, to blot out the preview of the loch.

The A803 comes in from the motorway past the LINLITHGOW
ACADEMY, 1900 by *J. Graham Fairley*, symmetrical, with
Scots gables and central hall, the round turrets over boys' and
girls' entrances a quotation from Holyrood and Falkland. In
the fork the former Nobel Explosives Company's REGENT
FACTORY, an arcaded front with Italianate towers in red-and-
yellow brick designed in 1908 by *William Scott*. The HIGH
STREET itself begins with a broad splay dominated by the
three-storey STAR AND GARTER of c. 1760, with rusticated quoins and a lugged doorpiece, followed by the ST
MICHAEL'S HOTEL, 1886, with early Scots Renaissance
dormers. In front of it on the pavement a WELL HEAD surmounted by a figure of the archangel with the town's arms and
inscribed '1720. SAINT MICHAEL IS KINDE TO STRAIN-
GERS'. The narrowing street focuses nicely on the baronial
turrets of No. 23 (1885) and No. 55, the ROYAL BANK OF
SCOTLAND, 1859 by *Peddie & Kinnear*. Between the two is
the Scots Renaissance POST OFFICE, 1903 by *W. W. Robertson*
of the *Office of Works*, and then a good Georgian build-up to
the pedimented front of Nos. 43–47. Behind No. 59 an armorial
panel dated 1527 from the town house of the Cornwalls of Bon-
hard.

Meanwhile the convex curve of the N side of the High Street is
good average Georgian in manners if not in date, but the triple
grouping of Nos. 20–24, of c. 1840, with a continuous ground-
floor cornice breaking forward over the arched centre door and
bracketed side doors, is exceptionally pretty. Then a diverse
group of three, conscientiously if incorrectly restored by strip-
ping down to the rubble. No. 36 (Town Council), of the C18,
has a round stair-turret at the back from which it is now entered.
Nos. 40–42 and 44–48 (the National Trust for Scotland), of the
C17, have crowstepped and chimneyed gables to the front (the
latter with flight holes for a pigeon loft) built forward from the
main roof. The first is stone-slated and has a round-arched pend
leading to its built-up backlands, the second is pantiled, a narrower pend leading to back quarters demolished except for a
bread oven. Between the two a neat stair with its own pantiled

roof. From here on the N side is largely Georgian, starting with
the three-storey RED LION at No. 50, but with baronial inter-
jections at No. 62 and then at the VICTORIA HALL (now Ritz
cinema), 1886 by *J. Russell Walker*, in Pardovan stone (which
was Linlithgow's staple material), the turrets on each side of
its tremendous balcony sadly truncated. Finally No. 114, the
LINLITHGOWSHIRE JOURNAL office of *c.* 1910, has a fine
show of cast-iron rainwater heads with grotesque dragons.

THE CROSS is the name of the northward annexe to the High
Street, but the mercat cross itself has gone. In the centre is the
octagonal CROSS WELL, carved by *Robert Gray* in 1807, which
convincingly claims to be a replica of its predecessor by *John
Ritchie*, 1628, and betrays its date only in the pretty oval bas
relief of Diana over the inscription. It is of three stages, the
two upper ones with clustered columns. The waterspouts of
the new version do not function. To the S a contemporary
pedestal with a draped head as a gargoyle, the town's arms, and
the date. There is an effective slope up to the Town House (*see
above*), and to the W the CROSS HOUSE, its main crowstepped
block C17 but altered *c.* 1760 with a Gibbs-surround doorway
and a bowed W extension containing a large upper room with
a Rococo ceiling. Between the two buildings KIRKGATE runs
up to the church and palace (*see above*) by way of the PEEL
GARDEN. Here is the MONUMENT to the first Marquess of
Lothian, a large bronze figure in the robes of the Governor
General of Australia, by *Sir George Frampton*, 1911.

The W side of The Cross introduces the large central redevelopment by *Rowand Anderson, Kininmonth & Paul*, begun in 1967.
A pediment from the old Golden Cross Inn with thistle and
strapwork and the date 1674, reset in the new wall, is the only
souvenir of the good group which was demolished. The replacement is just as distinguished in its way. The whole layout is
of three blocks: this one and another running N and S, and a
third, which links them, standing up on spine walls to reveal
the loch beyond. All this consists of flats over shops, but there
are also a range of public service buildings and some well hidden
car parking. The layout, like the white dry-dash walls and set-
back timber window heads, is severe and admirably consistent,
with a proper urban scale.

The S side of the High Street continues with the former BRITISH
LINEN BANK by *G. Washington Browne*, *c.* 1890. Then the
COUNTY BUILDINGS by *Dick Peddie, Todd & Jamieson* from
1936, a decent neo-Georgian front in snecked rubble which

proves to be just one end of a monumental block set at r. angles
to the street. Next to it the COURT HOUSE by *Wardrop &
Reid*, 1861, not quite symmetrical Tudor, gabled and hoodmoulded. To the r. of the door a MEMORIAL PLAQUE to the
Regent Murray † 1570, with a relief bust by Mrs *D. O. Hill*,
1875. Houses then resume on a concave curve, many with pends
and all Georgian, including No. 123, built in the late C18 by
the Incorporation of Shoemakers and restored in 1973 by
Rowand Anderson, Kininmonth & Paul; only the frontage now
remains.

From here onwards the buildings of the S side are still old, those
of the N side almost all new. But the relationship, at least at
the time of writing, has not yet been happily established. With
the exception of the tiny Episcopal church (*see* above) which
looks down the Vennel to the loch, none of the C19 buildings
is individually very distinguished, but they have diversity (as
at No. 137 with its big carriage pend), group value, and an
excellent relation to the line and contour of the street. What
they have unfortunately lost is continuity. The WEST PORT
WELL, C18 with a pyramidal top, is a good piece of street furniture taking its place in a line of trees. The frontages behind
it are effectively set back, but the miserable gap at the W end
will require some well judged infill. They face a supermarket
called PEEL HOUSE; this and the VENNEL housing development by *Rowand Anderson, Kininmonth & Paul*, 1974, are the
least successful part of this firm's contribution to the town,
especially in the complicated treatment of pavement levels.
Their adjoining WEST PORT development of 1963 is relatively
assured and now well established, its white rendering relieved
by brown weatherboard. Both sides of the street are well terminated, the N by the spire of St Ninian's Craigmailen Church,
the S by the early C17 WEST PORT HOUSE, L-plan, with a
stair-turret in the angle. To the street it presents a three-storey
frontage with swept dormers, and along with its supporting
group of single-storey houses it is perched on a terrace formed
when the gradient of the street was eased *c.* 1800.

S of the HIGH STREET a series of WELL WYNDS climbs up the
steep slope, each named after one of the wells in the High Street
itself. The best, with bowed walls at the head, is LION WELL
WYND which was opened in 1750. At the head of NEW WELL
WYND are LINDISFARNE, a prim early C19 Georgian villa,
and St John's Evangelical Church. The upper terraces are also
worth exploring. No. 6 ROYAL TERRACE is a late Georgian

villa, ashlar-faced, with horizontal glazing. Pedimented centre with concentric arches round the fanlight and a little oval window above. No. 14, a whin-built bungalow, has a pilaster doorpiece and Gothic glazing. Nos. 2–5 STRAWBERRY BANK are a late C19 terrace with bay-windows moulded in cement like knobbly logs. DOOCOT in the public garden at the summit, of C16 beehive type, built at the tail of the garden of the Ross of Halkhead town house. To the S the former canal port. On the near side CANAL TERRACE, late C19, excellently improved, with severe timber porches, and on the far bank the late Georgian villa of CANAL HOUSE with another concentrically arched doorway, good outbuildings and mature planting; an idyllic scene of the first technological revolution and its accompanying benefits.

CLARENDON HOUSE, to the SE. A solid affair of c. 1845 with a recessed doorpiece of plain Greek Doric columns *in antis*. Bay-windows and Italian tower added later.

LONGCROFT HOUSE, off Falkirk Road. A villa ornée of c. 1840 and later, with many deep-eaved gables; a little Italian tower at one end, a corbelled bay-window intimating the baronial fashion at the other. Two subsidiary groups in the same style: LONGCROFT GARDENS, and a pair of connected cottages (now the offices of LOCH MILL) formerly owned by Thomas Chalmers the master of Longcroft. The mill, in several stages, some disused, has a notable juxtaposition of brick gables, the first red and yellow, dated 1870, the second a more vivid red and alarmingly steep, with a high loading door. The dignified stone mill beyond them is dated 1898.

MONUMENT, 2 km. N of the town, a conspicuous landmark on the ridge to the E of the Grange (*see* p. 226). A staged Gothic cross on an octagonal base in memory of the Hon. Adrian Hope, killed in India in 1858.

FARMS

CAULDHAME, 2 km. SE. C18 barn and octagonal horsemill; coursed sandstone and pantiles.

HILTY, 1.5 km. S. A late C17 house of rubble with freestone quoins and chamfered window margins. Bowed stair-turret to the rear. One rusticated gatepier with a ball finial; the other has been used for various purposes. The house is a mere annexe to the C18 STEADING and the whole group is at the time of writing in a sorry state.

BONNYTOUN HOUSE. *See* p. 114.

GRANGE. *See* p. 226.
PRESTON HOUSE. *See* p. 398.
WILLIAMSCRAIGS. *See* p. 471.

LIN'S MILL *see* KIRKLISTON

LIVINGSTON NEW TOWN   ML AND WL*   0060

In the case of Livingston the historical and planning background
is of such importance that it must come before the descriptions
of individual buildings, which are given by districts. The
initials *L.D.C.* refer to the Livingston Development Corporation; *Peter Daniel* was their Chief Architect and Planning
Officer in the initial stages, and his successor is *W. Newman
Brown*. Livingston Village and Livingston Station, although
within the new town boundary, are in some ways separate places
and thus have their own entries in this gazetteer.

Livingston is the only c20 new town in Lothian, but the fourth
in Scotland, coming after East Kilbride, Glenrothes and Cumbernauld. Founded in 1962, it was the first in Britain to be
designed from the start as the principal town of a sub-region,
i.e. the 345 square km. of 'Greater Livingston' which embraces
Bathgate and Armadale in West Lothian, the Calders in
Midlothian, and a number of declining industrial villages in
both. To turn this decline into growth was the main object of
the sub-regional plan drawn up in 1962 by Professors *Robert
Matthew* of Edinburgh and *J. O. Robertson* of Glasgow, confirmed by the Lothians Regional Plan of 1966. The designation
order provided for a population of 70,000 for the new town
itself, four-fifths of it moving in from Glasgow and the rest of
west central Scotland. The target has now been raised to
100,000 by 1990. Manufacturing industries, attracted by Livingston's position at the centre of the national motorway system, now provide about half the employment; the old primary
industries are still on the down grade.

   This is a third-generation new town, its layout based neither
on the self-contained neighbourhoods of the earlier towns nor
on the centralized plan of the newer ones like Cumbernauld,
but on the principle of interdependence – first between its
adjoining districts, then between the town and the sub-region.
Also it is flexible; the whole place or any part of it can grow
more or less than intended, or in unexpected ways. The plan

* Now WL.

is a simple linear one with a N to S dual carriageway (Livingston Road) punctuated by the interchanges that serve the peripheral roads of the districts. These in turn serve the houses and most of the public buildings by means of cul-de-sac lanes – a good example, in fact, of Professor Buchanan's principle of the hierarchy of roads and, thanks to the basic grid, one of the easier new towns to find your way about in.

The site is a splendid one, but the only real drama is in the outward view to the S, across the Lothian plain with its huge red shale-bings to the not far distant Pentland Hills. Within the town such excitement as exists is of a more prosaic kind, e.g. the uninterrupted sweep of the dual carriageway over the river Almond by way of the 310 m. concrete BRIDGE designed by the *L.D.C.* in 1972, or the long green-roofed terraces of the Ladywell District massed along the contours. Likewise there is little spectacular architecture, but rather buildings that are impressive in a straightforward way; these unfortunately do not include the district health centres, whose design is disappointing. As to housing, low-rise harled terraces are almost the rule, with allowance for one car-place to each house. There is sufficient variation in house design without undue straining after effect, and the layouts are mostly intimate (unlike the example of Ladywell mentioned above) without being self-consciously picturesque.

CRAIGSHILL

ST ANDREW (R.C.). A really dramatic gesture, and thus untypical of Livingston, by *Alison & Hutchison & Partners*, 1968. Thin concentric walls of grainy shuttered concrete coming to a steep point, their curves turned outwards for the occasional surreptitious window and for the entrance, which is guarded by a concrete stockade; a church militant perhaps, but manifestly defensive too along with its sculptural quality. Fine top-lit interior trivialized by fluorescent tubes screwed to the ceiling.

ST COLUMBA (Ecumenical). By *Graham Law* of *Law & Dunbar-Nasmith*, 1966. A harled box on a good site, as simple as can be, with a bell-tower of black brick and a timber canopy bumping into it; much more typical of the no-nonsense Livingston style.

LETHAM PRIMARY SCHOOL. By *J. D. Robertson* (Midlothian County Council), 1969. White harl on black trim on stilts, but quite relaxed.

PUBLIC BUILDINGS COMPLEX. Not complicated, and that is to its credit, but a very mixed bag. The best site on the uphill terrace is occupied by the car park. At its w end the TOWERS PUBLIC HOUSE rises from a lower level, a welcome piece of commercial show based on precast concrete units of H-form, by *Matthew Smith & Partners*, 1967. At the other (E) end the HIGH SCHOOL, its long horizontal windows alternating with white mosaic, by *J. D. Robertson* (Midlothian County Council), 1967. s front of deep red brick exceptionally well laid for Scotland. The same material was used for the nearby HEALTH CENTRE, built at the same time. To the s of the car park the splendid view is interrupted by the gables of the SHOPPING MALL designed by the *L.D.C.*, 1967. Its two almost continuous indoor lanes, joined by a glazed ramp, are lit from above by gabled roof lights which slope from a two-storey height on one side to a single-storey on the other; the idea better than the detailing. To the s of the ramp, which also provides an entrance, the ALMONDBANK LIBRARY and PRIMARY SCHOOL, a nice humane group of yellow brick with black trim, by *S. Robertson* (Midlothian County Council), 1969.

FIRE STATION. By *Bamber, Hall & Partners*, 1967. Ribbed concrete tower with black cantilevered balconies. The roof over the engine shed is of moulded sections like a water tank.

ROAD RESEARCH LABORATORY. An awkward combination of dry concrete units and dark red brickwork by the *Architectural Research Unit, University of Edinburgh, c.* 1967.

The first housing in Craigshill, and thus the first in the new town, was designed by the *L.D.C.* in 1964 and built of large pre-cast concrete units made in Livingston by the Laing-Jespersen system. It consists mainly of stepped four-storey terraces with superimposed flats underneath, maisonettes on top; the steps provide balconies on three levels. These were not a great success, and later housing is of more conventional appearance, much of it in harled no-fines *in situ* concrete. Subsequent work in Craigshill includes the COURTS area, with harled bases, timber tops and monopitch roofs, by the *L.D.C.*, 1966; the GROVES area with its white-harled terraces relieved by the odd colour-washed house, by *James Parr & Partners*, 1966; CORSTON PARK, etc., long terraces with some of the windows framed in colour, by *Philip Cocker*, 1968; and probably the pleasantest at BEAULY DRIVE, etc., by the *Scottish Special Housing Association*, 1969, an ingenious semi-formal layout of semi-detached houses connected by garages.

DEANS INDUSTRIAL ESTATE

The M8 passes through it from E to W. On the N side, two simple and effective industrial 'sheds': the SCOTTISH GAS SUPPLIES DEPARTMENT clad in grey, and GILBY VINTNERS in white with black uprights by *Westminster Design Associates*, 1970.

MOTEC, on the S side of the M8. This stands for Multi-Occupational Training and Education Centre (for the motor transport and other industries). Seen by many people who never go into Livingston itself, it is the new town's showpiece – a brash and in places spectacular group of buildings by *Newman Levinson & Partners* from 1970. Most remarkable are the BOILER HOUSE, a display case for the heating plant like a glass doughnut with the chimney sprouting from the centre; three practice OIL RIG PLATFORMS; the HEAVY GOODS VEHICLE BUILDING with white concrete block walls over which the backward-slanted glazing is complemented by inverted pyramids of bright orange fibreglass; and the RESIDENTIAL BUILDING, last to be completed, its predominantly vertical block walls unnecessarily fussed by moulded horizontal courses. Yet the entry to this building is simple and impressive, even tempting to the student or visitor. Of how much post-1945 architecture can this be said?

SCHLUMBERGER TRAINING SCHOOL, to the W of Motec. By *S.G.A. Buildings*, 1974. Another simulated oil rig.

The DEANS district to the S of the industrial estate is still (1977) quite a small place, with the older-established village of Livingston Station (*see* p. 312) as its centre. Vast expansion is planned, along with schools and so on; but so far the new town's best achievement here has been the complete removal of a large shale bing.

WOODLANDS PARK, to the NE. An orgy of owner-occupied executive housing built in the 1960s and 70s in all available styles and materials, and a contrast indeed to the tasteful paternalism of the new town proper. On the summit of the site is DECHMONT HOUSE, in the white-harl and red-tile cottage style, 1914.

DEDRIDGE

Two SCHOOLS, both by *Midlothian C.C. Architect's Department*, make good use of two main elements – monopitch roof and boiler-house chimney: No. 1 PRIMARY, of two buff brick ranges, by *J. D. Robertson*, 1971, and the R. C. PRIMARY of 1972, with harled walls and green-tile roofs, not quite so well detailed, by *B. McDowall*.

LANTHORN COMMUNITY COMPLEX. By *G. R. M. Kennedy & Partners*, started 1976.

LIVINGSTON CENTRE. By *Hay, Steel & Macfarlane*, 1974. The first phase was finished in 1976. A fully enclosed and air-conditioned shopping centre, the exterior noncommittal, but well built of mulberry-coloured bricks.

HOUSTOUN INDUSTRIAL ESTATE

Two industrial buildings by *W. Newman Brown*. CAMERON IRONWORKS of 1963 is a fine build-up of white boxes with black tops, on a very large scale. GEORGE WHILEY LTD is of 1975, the main shed, clad in buff-coloured steel channelling, separate from the brown glass box of the office block.

HOWDEN

HOWDEN HOUSE. Harled, with stone dressings and a Roman Doric porch, *c.* 1770. Three storeys, with two-storey wings. Very handsome in its green surroundings. No very interesting interiors were sacrificed when it was institutionalized as meeting rooms by the *L.D.C.* in 1966, as the surviving late C19 features show.

HOWDEN PARK CENTRE. The S front of the early C19 stable block remains, of brown whinstone with sandstone dressings and two little pediments with flight holes for pigeons. At the rear a hall, theatre, studios and dining room by the *L.D.C.*, 1970. Only the last has a calculated relationship with the old work.

TORONTO PRIMARY SCHOOL (the name is the result of the helpful habit of giving a family title to the roads and buildings of each district; Howden is 'Canadian'). A distinguished building by *J. Lyall* (Midlothian County Council), 1967, in buff brick, with a copper fascia uniting the whole of the ground floor and crowning the less extensive upper floor.

ST ANDREW'S PRIMARY SCHOOL. By *J. D. Robertson* (Midlothian County Council), 1970. Three square blocks with tiled pyramidal roofs, diversely treated.

HOUSING. In ALBERTA AVENUE, etc., white-harled patio houses surrounded by long red-roofed terraces whose end gables are exposed by halves to give a monopitch look; by *James Parr & Partners*, 1967. Dreary garage-scape behind. NELSON

AVENUE, etc., a cosy layout of stepped and staggered terraces with orange brick bases to some of the walls, is by *L.D.C.*, 1973.

KNIGHTSRIDGE

PRIMARY SCHOOL. By *Lane, Bremner & Garnett*, 1971. To the E an uneasy mixture of exposed aggregate panels and pink brickwork; simpler and more effective to the W.

NURSERY SCHOOL. By *West Lothian C.C. Architect's Department*, 1974. Two white-harled blocks with monopitch gables opposed to each other so that the taller one has clearstory windows.

0060   LIVINGSTON STATION   WL

CHURCH OF SCOTLAND. A very simple 'hall church', harled and slated, by *Ian G. Lindsay*, 1949. The tower with pyramidal roof attached to the N gable provides internally a 'chancel' that can be screened off. It is lit by three round-headed lancets containing older stained glass. All the other windows are plain domestic sashes. Gabled jamb on the E side for the porch.

SCHOOL. 1906. Red brick with Art Nouveau detail. Symmetrical board-school arrangement with girls' and boys' entrances.

The village of Livingston Station was named after a station that no longer exists, and is now absorbed into the Deans district of Livingston (*see* p. 310), but the name sticks, and so does a certain village character which has somehow eluded the designers of the new town.

0060   LIVINGSTON VILLAGE   WL

PARISH CHURCH. 1732, on the site of an earlier church; a plain, long kirk with a louvred bellcote on the W gable. The 'rebuilding' of 1837 did not alter it very much, for the fielded-panel PEWS are of the late C18; perhaps a gallery along the N side, uniting those at the ends, was removed at that time. – The PULPIT on the S side also seems earlier. Hexagonal Gothic sounding-board with pinnacles and a pretty stair with delicate iron balusters. – MONUMENTS, in the churchyard. Some spirited examples from the late C17 and C18, specializing in phoenixes and leafy cartouches. – S of the church a plain tabletop to Patrick Mil † 1676, and a broad headstone to Thomas Graham, farmer of Seafield, † 1769, the inscribed cartouche flanked by a sower and a reaper. – To the E of the church the headstone of Patrick Clarkson's children † c. 1799 with trophies of bones, scythes and spades on ribbons. – MANSE. 1803.

The church and churchyard stand in curious isolation on a but-tressed retaining wall, but from the N they make a good group with a row of C18 two-storey harled houses. In the main street, which used to be part of the Edinburgh to Glasgow toll road, a pleasantly irregular early C19 row faces the white-harled LIVINGSTONE INN, probably built in the C18. Both the inn and the adjacent coachyard were ingeniously adapted and enlarged by *Stanley P. Ross-Smith*, 1965. The C18 steading of BLOOM FARM, now in industrial use, has a gabled farmhouse of c. 1850. BRIDGE over the river Almond to the S, single-arch, of c. 1800.

LIVINGSTON DEVELOPMENT CORPORATION OFFICE, to the N. 1971 by *Baxter, Clark & Paul*. The vertical piers and certain functional elements are black-harled, with horizontal white quartz panels between them, or cantilevered out.

LOANHEAD

EAST (formerly Free) CHURCH, Polton Road. Plain, small-scale Gothic of c. 1850, with a break-front entrance in the gable, diminishing by buttresses into a stumpy, zinc-capped turret.

REFORMED PRESBYTERIAN CHURCH, Fountain Place. 1875 by *Donald Bruce* of Glasgow. Naïvely detailed, with plate tra-cery in the street gable and a four-stage pinnacled clock tower. The church is said to be built of shuttered concrete.

ST MARGARET (R.C.), Clerk Street. 1878 by *Charles Goldie*, lan-ceted and aisleless, behind a priest's house of the same date that fronts the street. – The HALL still further back, by *Reginald Fairlie*, 1924, is of pink stock brick, its genteel and extensive glazing protected in a wire compound. – The adjoining SCHOOL with half-hipped gables is by *R. M. Cameron*, 1891; the infants' gallery occupies the stem of its T-plan.

WEST CHURCH, The Loan. By *Hardy & Wight*, 1882. Tran-septs, an octagonal vestry, and a wheel window over the pulpit, but otherwise an economical version of what *the Builder* calls C13.

Loanhead is not a prepossessing town, but light grey Straiton stone still predominates. The churches do something to enliven its long T-junction plan. Nothing is left of the colliers' houses built in 1736 by the Clerks of Penicuik, but there are two good two-storey houses of this period in Linden Place, No. 43 harled, with a curved wall-head chimney gable and bullseye window,

No. 44, one of the lodges of Sir John Clerk's house of Mavis-bank (*see* below), in coursed rubble with a Gibbs-surround doorpiece. The Victorian coal industry flourished, joined for a time by shale, which has given Loanhead its bing (spoil heap), and by paper-making. Its situation above the North Esk attracted villa-dwellers in the late C19, and there has been a steady growth of post-war local authority housing.

OLD PENTLAND BURYING GROUND, 1.5 km. NW. A survival of a parish that lost its separate identity some time after the Reformation. Two monuments are of interest: the GIBSONE MAUSOLEUM by *Thomas Hamilton*, c. 1845, austerely pedimented, and the graceful Rococo headstone of George Brown, Portioner, † 1765.

MAVISBANK, to the SE. A beautiful house, though at the time of writing only a precarious shell, by *Sir John Clerk* and *William Adam* from 1723. *John Baxter Sen.* was the mason contractor. Sir John Clerk of Penicuik, second Baronet, writes that in May 1723 'I not only finished my design for the House of Mavisbank, under the correction of Mr Adams, a skilful architect, but laid the foundation'. The site commands a NE view down a little glen, and is plainly that to which he refers towards the end of his long poem 'The Country Seat':

On Esca's flowry Bank there is a Grove
Where the harmonious Thrush [mavis] repeats its Love,
There Ile observe the Precepts you [the Muse] indite
But never any more attempt to write.

Sir John's father had planned a house here, and a drawing of 1698 shows a plain square box with coupled chimneystacks perched on top of a tall piend roof. This is the basis, enriched and Palladianized, of the present house; the elements firmly specified by Clerk, their execution entrusted to Adam and his craftsmen. Their collaboration produced a highly original result.

The main house is of five bays like the original project, with a basement and two storeys (Adam wanted another, but had to give way in the end), and of solid though not actually square plan. The coupled chimney idea was retained and developed, with a domical piend roof rising behind a balustrade to support a long, panelled battery of flues. So the roof is (or was, until the fire of 1973) distinctly French, and so are the rusticated piers on basement pedestals. Similar piers support the pediment on each side of the three central bays. Bracketed mai▸

cornice with rosettes between. *William Silverstyne* was the stone carver, and Adam gained his point on the design of the pediment filling, with a central bullseye window and an allowance of six inches' thickness of stone for the 'large pieces of foliage on each side'. Sir John, following the letter of Palladio, had suggested that the coat of arms should go there, but Adam wanted it in the traditional place 'above the door', and that is where it is, carved in more perishable stone than the rest. But the door itself is significant, for it is really a porch, anticipating a need that was answered by later appendages to hundreds of Georgian houses. Although not shown in the *Vitruvius Scoticus* engraving which credits Adam with the design of the house, it was clearly executed at the time. Its scrolled roof is boldly three-dimensional. The bay design is that of the Mauritshuis at The Hague: the top-floor windows are as big as those of the *piano nobile* and have alternate triangular and segmental pediments, so that a Dutch house seems to be lifting its eyes to view the landscape of the Esk valley, which is very un-Dutch except in its miniature scale. Silverstyne carved the swags, still echoing the Mauritshuis, between first and second floors. At the back and sides, within the frame of piers and cornice, the early c18 vernacular prevails. Harled walls. Sills and lintels are prolonged into string courses to form a structural grid with the window jambs. To the rear the Tuscan porch added in the later c18, with a larger interval in the centre, leads out on to the level of the rising ground. Large symmetrical extensions of *c.* 1840, including a segmental-ceilinged ballroom, were demolished in 1954.

Now for the pavilions. Their quadrant links are of a single-arcaded storey over a basement, but *Vitruvius Scoticus* shows the basement without windows and the arcade (topped with vases like the house) quite open, with a view of the trees beyond, though the balustrade within the openings implies a forward prospect. The pavilions themselves, whose purpose is unspecified, appear to have been dependencies in the tradition of the Veneto; they are carefully demoted by a downward kink of the connecting cornice. Yet they have their own status, and this again is Dutch. Not only do they extend forwards to emphasize the enclosure of the space in front, but their ends are gabled in the manner of Vingboons. Curly scrolls to front and rear (the former more elaborate) support the obviously Scots chimneys. William Adam's characteristic basket arches allow the entrance of carts on the basement level. Their mouldings, and those of the Venetian windows overhead, were chopped off when the house was used and extended as an asylum in the C19.

The internal plan, a double-pile divided laterally by the big chimney wall, was altered *c.* 1840, when the plasterwork by *Samuel Calderwood* was removed, and the staircase, on whose treatment Sir John had urged an unwonted restraint, and which had occupied the corner of the house on the r. of the entrance, was destroyed. It was resited in the central body of the house. So only a few fragments of interior finishing, plus those of a confused remodelling, were lost in the fire.

BLAIRESK HALL (formerly Bilston Lodge), 1 km. to the s. An odd little house of one storey and basement, built *c.* 1800, probably in connection with Mavisbank. The very deep eaves cornice, the veranda and two oriels were added *c.* 1840; the three curvaceous dormers somewhat later. Inside, simple Gothic ceilings and doorcases of the earlier date. Then came the cast-iron chimneypieces (not just inset grates) and the incredibly ceremonious staircase leading up to the attic.

2060

LOGANBANK HOUSE
Glencorse

ML

The thatched cottage built in 1810 by the Rev. John Inglis of Greyfriars Church, Edinburgh, was transformed by his Lord President son, first with timbered gables and then with a tall, uncompromising tower at the E end. *David Bryce* was the architect; no date is known, but Bryce worked at Inglis's Edinburgh house in 1857. In front of the door are six mid C18 stone finials – four pineapples and a couple of urns (can they have come from Dryden, demolished *c.* 1890?). The indoor surprises begin with a set of mid C18 finishings in the ground-floor rooms to the w – doors and Rococo overmantelled chimneypieces of the finest quality. The entrance hall is lined with trophies of wood, including some C17 and earlier panels, and Dutch bed-ends. The tower includes a drawing room at the bottom, a billiard room at the top, with much C19 wallpaper. In the small N wing the late C19 owner-collector contrived a little Empire Room and lined it with grisaille wallpaper panels of Cupid and Psyche by *Dufour* of Paris. They have been rather unskilfully tinted in watercolour.

LONGNIDDRY

EL 4070

By 1836 (the date of the report in the New Statistical Account)
the old weaving village of Longniddry had already shrunk to
a mere 200 inhabitants, i.e. not much larger than the string of
cottages along the N side of the main road. Some of them were
joined up and converted into the LONGNIDDRY INN in 1974.
LONGNIDDRY HOUSE, a couple of small adjoining early C18
blocks with scrolled skewputts, is now buried in new houses,
but a steading of 1867 still abuts the road. Even after the building of the station (*c.* 1845 and still open) this handy and desir-
able spot remained undeveloped until in 1916 the Scottish
Veterans' Garden Cities Association were allowed to build
twenty harled cottages, mostly semi-detached, with two shops,
grouped round KITCHENER CRESCENT next to the road and
the circular 'Laird's Garden' to the N, in front of the school.
Their architects were *Henry & MacLenan*. *Dick Peddie &
Walker Todd* designed the semi-detached houses in ELCHO
ROAD (and possibly the little PARISH CHURCH as well) in
1920–1. The GOLF CLUB HOUSE at the foot of LINKS ROAD
was built *c.* 1929 with rusticated quoins and other stonework
salvaged from the demolition of Amisfield House (*see* under that
name).

Of the subsequent villa development two good examples are in
GOSFORD ROAD, both harled, with an effective touch of stone.
HARMONY, by *Tarbolton & Ochterlony*, 1933, has a pretty
stone doorpiece between shallow pitched twin gables. THE
COTTAGE, by *Basil Spence*, *c.* 1955, has a rubble cross wall for
the chimney and the walls are slightly canted back on each side
of it, producing a curious slope in the eaves.

EVENTYR. A house within the walls of Gosford (*see* p. 222)
designed in economical fashion* by *Ian G. Lindsay* of *Orphoot,
Whiting & Lindsay* in 1936, the date in pebbles stuck into the
pediment. It is white-harled, and its basic Scots Palladianism
is timid but at the same time rather wilful. The lesser windows
are placed at random. One of the side pavilions and its shallow
quadrant are built up to the same two-storey height as the main
block.

HARELAW FARM, 0.5 km. NE. An early C19 steading with a
square central tower whose pyramidal slated roof is stepped to

---

* John Reid, of Ian G. Lindsay and Partners, says that the client set a firm
cost-limit but was mightily shocked – indeed offended – when the actual work
fell within it.

form a doocot. Cartshed openings in the wings, whose roofs slope with the ground.

LONGRIDGE see WHITBURN

LOTH STONE see TRAPRAIN LAW

LUCHIE HOUSE see LEUCHIE HOUSE

4080

LUFFNESS HOUSE   EL
1 km. E of Aberlady

The present tower house of three storeys and attic, built in the late C16 by Sir Patrick Hepburn, forms a T whose short stem is a square turret, its first two storeys occupied by a turnpike stair. Over the original roll-moulded front door, with two pairs of hinge pins, on the turret's W side was probably set the stone fancily inscribed S P H . I H . 1584, now on the S W bartizan turret. This is corbelled out on a rope and double billet moulding, its fellow at the NE corner being much plainer. A small stair-turret on a squinch arch in the SE angle serves the two upper levels.

This is all there was until the end of the C18 when the Hopes, who had bought Luffness in 1739, were seized with architectural ambition. Robert Reid's project of 1802 for enlargement in the Adam castle style was not adopted, but a row of rooms with a canted bay at the E end was added soon after. In 1822 *William Burn* filled in the S W angle of the T with a small block whose balcony is supported on curly Jacobean brackets. In its crow-stepped W gable are the arms of the first Earl of Hopetoun, the purchaser of this property, and pasted into sundry other gables, like Victorian scraps, are bits and pieces of vegetable carving from about 1700. Can they be from Bruce's supplanted work at Hopetoun itself? In 1825 *Thomas Brown* added the round-arched, bellcoted kitchen to the NE, linked to the house by a strangely rustic segmental archway with a quatrefoil opening overhead. Then in 1841 he extended the W front with a baronial wing (demolished 1959). *David Bryce* went to Luffness in 1846, and over the next three years he licked the house into full-blooded baronial shape, closely instructed by its owner. The main evidence surviving on the outside is the massive stone benches on each side of the new front door in the original E gable, and the triangular gables on the canted bay. His next contribution was in 1874 – an elaborate gun-room wing, arcaded,

dormered and turreted, to form something like a forecourt, and
a stable court with arched and battlemented screen wall standing slightly back from it. The saloon behind the gun room was
designed in the same office (by now *D. & J. Bryce*) in 1891.
Billiard-room extension of 1907.

Inside, the main architectural interest is in small features like
Bryce's fireplace for the entrance hall (1849), and his glazed
doors formed like wooden yetts. The only grand sequence is
in the library, a double room with a geometric ceiling whose
W part is in Burn's extension.

OUTBUILDINGS. First of these is necessarily the fragment
of the Carmelite church (*see* Aberlady). Then a problem. The
house stands towards the NW angle of a square fortification
defined by a ditch, partly filled in. It is hard to say whether
this might be the work of the French commander de Thermes
in 1549 (as tentatively suggested by the RCAHMS) or whether
it shows the outline of an earlier castle or enclosure as Mr
Tranter asserts, but the former seems more likely. – DOOCOT.
Visible from the road; a three-stage beehive type of the late
C16, with billet moulding at the wall head and a top lantern
for the entry of the birds. – GATEWAY. The arch on the main
road (its faceted stonework repeated on the stables), probably
of the C19, opens into a tunnelled pend from whose W side is
the entry to a long, possibly earlier tunnel-vaulted chamber.
– Rectangular WALLED GARDEN to the W of the house, formed
in 1822, with a diamond-shaped inner wall, pantiled at the head.
The extra shelter was enjoyed by four beds of 'French pear
trees' with greengages at the centre of the geometric pattern
and hardier fruits in the remaining triangles of the main space.
Outer wall with brick-arched flying buttresses along the S side.
– The WATER TOWER, still further E, could be by *Thomas
Brown*. Tall and square, with diagonal buttresses, it once had
an arcaded top storey Italian fashion, with a shallow pyramidal
roof.

LUGGATE *see* EAST LINTON

MACMERRY   EL 4070

Twenty-four good semi-detached houses, 1925 by *Dick Peddie &* 95
Walker Todd, like those at Gullane, form a half-square to the
N of the A1. At the E end the SCHOOLHOUSE of *c.* 1840 and

its successor of 1889 by *J. & R. Farquharson* of Haddington,
extended nicely in 1927 and horribly thereafter.

MALLENY HOUSE *see* BALERNO

MARTYR'S CROSS *see* PENICUIK

3060 ## MASTERTON HOUSE   ML
5 km. SSE of Dalkeith

(The C17 L-plan house built for William Meggatt. The jamb is
slightly later than the main block, which has a C19 buttress imitating the stair-turret in the angle. The stair-turret is round
below, square above, and crowned with a doocot.) Thus the
RCAHMS. The author was directed to it but could not find it.

2060 ## MAURICEWOOD HOUSE   ML
1 km. N of Penicuik

A little L-plan house of *c.* 1840 with spiked gables, a turret in the
angle, and a big bay-window on the jamb. Turreted extension
dated 1897.

MAVISBANK *see* LOANHEAD

3060 ## MELVILLE CASTLE   ML
2 km. WSW of Dalkeith

Designed by *James Playfair* in 1786–91 for Henry Dundas, subsequently Viscount Melville. At first sight the exterior could not
be simpler – a three-storey toy fort with round, Gothic-win-
dowed corner turrets and two-storey wings, plus a single-storey
office court to the r. But hoodmoulds and battlements drive a
close bargain with other features whose neo-classicism echoes
the work of Soane. The entrance front has nine large tripartite
openings; or rather eight since the late C19, when a small Gothic
porch was added to the front door, impairing the effect of the
central mass – and indecisively too. This is just what Playfair
avoided in his treatment of the wings, which incorporate the
library to the l., the kitchen to the r. To these he gave their
own separate identity, marking their corners with crisp square
piers (half-piers at the junctions with the main block). On top
of the end piers are channelled drums like those on Soane's
Langley Park gateway design, and the same square grooves are

cut into the block-ended wall that emerges from the roof as a blunt finial to the main building (chimneys emerge from them, and also at odd points along the battlements). Fastidious detailing is also evident in the cutting of the light grey masonry, so that on the battered basement stage, for example, it is hard to say where design ends and virtuoso tooling takes over; judging by Playfair's drawings he was always in command, and it can only have been on his instructions that the crown glass panes of the windows in the middle block are set, contrary to normal practice, with their concave faces outwards, emphasizing the voids. Four bays between the corner stair-turrets on the garden front, the hoodmoulded windows lighting the principal rooms (dining room on the ground floor, drawing room on the first), with one window for the anteroom of each, all looking across the lawn to the North Esk.

The square ENTRANCE HALL is basically plain, with the thin gutta-and-taenia cornice which is also used in the library. All elaborate finishings are set within segmental-headed openings. Sober grey marble chimneypiece opposite the door, possibly not designed for this position. Fluted Roman Doric order to the r. (pilasters on a blank wall) and also to the l., where there are columns between pilasters. Through them is seen the astonishing STAIRCASE. Square well of three stages with landings opening off each, the first two under a broad segmental arch and coffered vault (Playfair's favourite disc-in-square form), the top one through a small-scale screen of columns between pilasters once again – only this time absurdly because the order is Greek Ionic, and the capitals face different ways. On the other three sides of the square, and thus off-centre, the thin cantilevered stair makes its way up in interrupted flights. Plain iron balusters are linked by beaded hoops which spring from opening leaves at the top and bottom of each, and surmounted by a kinked handrail. A frieze of Dundas lion-heads carries round the line of the first landing, fans and cornshoots the second, and at the head the cornice brackets have miniature fan-vaults on either side, each opposing pair leaving a semi-circular tympanum for the incised palmettes that form the frieze. On the ceiling, in a circular moulded frame, a delicate polychrome painting of putti chasing the clouds away, their realism heightened by four sepia corner roundels of more putti representing the seasons. All this is lit by the large tripartite window that breaks rather awkwardly downwards from the top storey.

The DINING ROOM on the ground floor and the DRAWING ROOM on the first floor are of matching shape, with bowed ends. The former has lost its cornice and the latter its chimneypiece, both replaced *c.* 1840, and their charm is now concentrated in their anterooms. That of the dining room picks up the bow-end theme, with wood and plasterwork of extraordinary refinement and a segmental vault overhead. The anteroom of the drawing room was planned with possible use as a bedchamber in mind, and this is in character with the grace of its plasterwork – a floral banded dome between more segmental vaults. What would have been a bed recess is flanked by cabinets with inter-secting oval glazing. The drawing room itself still has its frieze of what Playfair calls 'antique foliage', but the doors in the bow (their panels inset with coloured engravings of Raphael's Hours of the Night) are misleading; there were niches here, with a concealed door to the stair-turret so that you could go down to the garden. All the original chimneypieces, in varicoloured marble or (in some bedrooms) in painted wood, repeat the play-ful neo-classical theme, with the same hints of a highly domesti-cated Gothic in the vestigial fan-vault motif which again recalls Soane. 'Marbel and wood dressings' came 'from London' to Playfair's designs.

Sir Walter Scott wrote of 'Melville's beechy grove', but it is an impressive plantation of Wellingtonias that does most to confine the forward prospect from the castle, leading on over a hump to Playfair's U-plan STABLE BLOCK. The courtyard is entered between round piers matched by bullseye windows in the end gables. Quoins with curiously tapered square channelling are the only intimation of the delicate, painstaking Gothicism on the other three faces, with hoodmoulds running into string courses. The majority of the pointed windows, regu-larly spaced on both storeys, are blind.

MIDCALDER   ML (now WL)

PARISH CHURCH. A large T-plan church comprising a C16 choir and a transept by *Brown & Wardrop*, 1863. The choir was started some time before 1542 by the rector of Midcalder, Master Peter Sandilands, and in a deed of that year his nephew Sir John Sandilands undertook to complete the choir and build a nave, steeple and porch within three years.* In the event only

* This document, which includes a very full specification of the work to be done, is one of the chief sources of Scottish medieval building terminology.

the choir was built. It has two bays and a half-hexagonal apse plus a sacristy projecting from the E wall. Impressively large four-light windows with various kinds of loop tracery, double-chamfered splays and hoodmoulds ending in shields. Buttresses with many set-offs but no pinnacles. The E window is curtailed by the sacristy, a simple lean-to that also covers part of the NE side of the apse. Two-light window in the s wall, busily carved pinnacles on the E corners.* The placing of the sacristy is explained when one examines the N wall of the choir. Except for a few feet at the top it is rubble-built, and there are no windows. A row of corbels proves that there was to be a cloister here. The deed of 1542 specifically mentions a 'cloister', but why should a parish church have needed one? It must be assumed that the intention was to make the church collegiate. Cloisters in this position existed at St Salvator's College, St Andrews, and King's College, Aberdeen. The N door of the choir is blocked by an C18 monument. Everything to the w of the choir dates from 1863. Saddleback bell-turret on the thick W wall. The 'transept' has Gothic details of a period earlier than the choir, including a large W rose.

Inside, the choir is covered with a plaster tierceron-vault starting from the original springers but flatter in section than the medieval one, which was never finished. The deed of 1542 specifies that the vault was to resemble that of St Antony's Aisle in St Giles, Edinburgh, i.e. the outer part of the s transept. For no very obvious reason the SE springer in the apse is at a higher level than the others. On one of the W vault corbels a cowled figure with PETRS FECIT on a scroll, presumably intended for Peter Sandilands. Three-sided rear arch to the N door. The sacristy, now the vestry, has a segmental rubble vault. Traces of an original door in the N wall, and in the W wall a reset piece of interlace. Beneath it is the Sandilands burial vault. – TOMB RECESS. In the N wall. Plain segmental arch. – PEW BACK. Of pine, dated 1595. Simplified linenfold flanking the Sandilands of Torphichen arms. – STAINED GLASS. In the SW choir window four lights (SS. Andrew, Peter, Luke and an angel) by *Hardman & Co.*, 1895. – In the W wall of the transept two lights (Martha and Mary) in memory of James Young, F.R.S., 1883, of shale and paraffin fame. – MONUMENT, out-

---

* On the SE pinnacle the arms of Sir James Sandilands, Baron of Calder († 1559), on the NE the achievement of Sir James Sandilands, Lord St John († 1579).

side the s door. A table-top with moulded edge to Joseph
Douglas of Budds † 1636.

CALDER HOUSE, to the sw. The Sandilands family was given
the barony of Calder in the C14 and the title of Lord Torphichen
in 1579. The thick walls of the basic L-plan house indicate that
it was built somewhat before that date. The main (SE) range
has a row of tunnel-vaulted basement rooms, and one of the
second-floor windows is dated 1666, suggesting modifications
at that time. Towards the end of the C17 the short jamb of the
L was extended by three long bays, but a balustraded platform
directly above the new staircase interrupts the roof-line. Probably at the same time the whole house was slightly updated
with rusticated quoins and bullseye gable windows. But
this could have been done as late as c. 1760, when the front
door in the jamb, still on first-floor level and reached by an
outside stair, was given a handsome Venetian opening
which was covered c. 1820 by a big two-storey bow. A new
corridor and stair-tower attached to the main range at the same
time were later increased in height, with a shaped gable dated
1880.

The early C19 bow contains a stair rising to the earlier Georgian front door which is now (except for its round-headed
centre) an internal feature. It leads into a fine cubic VESTIBULE
with a bracketed cornice and a rather spindly Rococo plaster
centrepiece. Alongside it in the main range an oak STAIRCASE
of c. 1700 in a square well rising through one storey, with corner
landings. Heavy turned balusters with cotton-reel bases. Two
large rooms fill the rest of this range, lit by tall windows (the
sills lowered in the early C19) with very deep splays. In the DIN-
ING ROOM the cornice and the arched marble chimneypiece
are of the early C19. The fielded pine panelling is somewhat
older. The DRAWING ROOM *en suite* with it has a basket-arch
marble fireplace of c. 1740 but was otherwise recast, with a
heavy compartmented ceiling, in 1880. In the other wing the
C17 scale-and-platt stair runs from top to bottom of the house.
Here the basement is lower because of the falling ground, and
has a kitchen with a wide-arched fireplace.

As an exception to the general rule of this series, two notable
visitors to the house should be mentioned: John Knox to celebrate the reformed communion in 1556, and Chopin on his
Scottish visit in 1848.

GATEWAY from the main street beyond the parish church.
Dated 1670. Moulded piers with alternate rustic blocks, each

supporting half of a heavy broken pediment and then a ball finial.

BRIDGE HOUSE, to the E. 1908 by *Hippolyte J. Blanc*. White harl, red brick and tile. Twin gables over canted bay-windows; an arched porch under the dormered eaves between them.

BRIDGE, to the E (Linhouse Water). 1794, with two rustic arches and central oculus.

WILLIAMSTON BRIDGE (Murieston Water), 2 km. SSW. Single arch of 1647, since rebuilt.

WESTER CAUSEWAYEND, 7.5 km. S. Farmhouse dated 1802, with moulded doorway and block cornice. Contemporary farm buildings.

Midcalder was a post-village on the old Edinburgh–Glasgow road, with a number of inns and the gates of two big houses. Victorian mining activity to the N only added a few strings of nondescript grey stone frontages, and the C20 has not yet contributed much except for dereliction. The entry from the E lies over the Linhouse Water, then up-hill into BANK STREET. On the S side the TORPHICHEN ARMS of *c.* 1760, with scrolled skewputts. Inside, the original staircase with turned balusters. Then the bargeboarded lodge of Calder Hall (demolished in 1970). On the other side a decent Georgian row with the Venetian-windowed CLYDESDALE BANK and also a hopeful, but now disappointed, palace-fronted Victorian bank of *c.* 1860. The intervening wedge-shaped block of *c.* 1820, Midcalder's best townscape asset, now abandoned, is terminated by MAIN POINT HOUSE, with a tripartite window in the upper storey of its bowed end. In MARKET STREET the BLACK BULL and a matching corner house of *c.* 1830. MAIN STREET begins badly with a terrace of suburban character by *D. Dewar* (Midlothian County Council), *c.* 1955, but it rallies by the church, whose prospect is flanked by the C18 BREWERY HOUSE on one side (scrolled skewputts again) and by the gate of Calder House (*see* above) on the other.

BANKTON HOUSE. *See* p. 93.

MIDDLETON HALL

ML 3050

3.5 km. SE of Gorebridge

The main body of the house of 1710 is still there, its centre bays advanced and raised on both fronts to carry a comfortable segmental pediment. Quadrant wings would have suited it better than those added *c.* 1800 in line with the front and greatly prolonging it; each of the two pavilions has a Venetian window. But at least the stone-dressed harling of the original was continued (with square-channelled instead of V-jointed quoins). The linking sections, originally only one storey high, were raised to two in 1898 by *J. MacIntyre Henry*. The effect of the long continuous frontage is better on the garden side, where the links are recessed and the pavilions less formal, in spite of the bow pushed out *c.* 1800 under the centre pediment. Entering through the front doorpiece which was too emphatically added before 1898, you find a panelled interior of that date which combines entrance hall, galleried staircase, and ballroom; the two Ionic columns can be removed for dances. The assembly hall, for this is now a conference centre, has an original corner chimneypiece of *c.* 1710 with carved ogee-section frieze, in timber, but the 'Adam' ceiling is spurious. The green and white Ionic chimneypiece in the library is a more successful imitation.

STABLE COURT. Still in line with the house, and probably added in 1898. *Stanley Ross-Smith* adapted it as a bedroom block, and the house for conference use, in 1962. His work is positive but unobtrusive, as is the link from the house and the dining and kitchen block which he placed between the two.

3070   MIDFIELD HOUSE   ML
                    1.5 km. N of Rosewell

The coal-owner J. A. Hood lost his daughter in the fire which gutted his C18 house, and this influenced his wishes for the reconstruction carried out by *Robert Lorimer* from 1914. Children are a recurring theme in the design, and the very open layout is devised for escape from any future fire; Midfield is now a children's home. The blankness of the entrance front may be part of the same story. Except for the parapet which he put round the whole house (with little vases at intervals), Lorimer made no attempt to add interest to the dull Georgian fenestration, and the front door is marked almost apologetically by a shallow Gibbs surround in a blank new wall. The SW front is more eventful, with a Georgian bow, and on the SE the house comes to life. Here the garden (in fact the original walled garden) is viewed from a French-windowed bay, and then from a triple-arcaded loggia with Ionic columns. In a niche over the loggia a piece of sculpture in bronze of a woman and children.

The interior stands high in Lorimer's work. Grandeur is

tempered by considerable charm – partly that of the late C17–
early C18 tradition, and partly that of the folksy shallow-relief
plasterwork, which Lorimer took from the earlier English vernacular. The ENTRANCE HALL is immediately festive, with its
marble floor in big slabs, gaily profiled panelling, and moulded
fireplace of dark green marble. The rest of the floors on this
level are of beautiful random-width boarding. The heart of the
house is the STAIRCASE. It climbs round three sides of a well
to a two-sided landing which has no compunction in carrying
square piers, so that the nine-compartment ceiling is supported
all round. Domed skylight in the centre. The brass rail to stair
and landing is supported by wrought iron in the best Scots
tradition (e.g. at Hopetoun), and the lovely stained-glass windows illustrate childish themes.* Children also appear in the
centre plaques of two main rooms on the ground floor. It is
hard to say what were the exact finishes of panelling and plaster,
but the little library on the SW front and the large dining room
to the N are panelled with 'natural' timber. Upstairs at the S
corner a chimneypiece of c. 1820. The finest bedrooms are to
the N. One has a coved ceiling whose oval dome has the signs
of the zodiac in low relief. In the next room and the corridor
tunnel-vaulted ceilings with bands of low relief. The best
materials and workmanship are everywhere, their focus always
the chimneypieces of choice or exotic marbles. Woodwork
throughout by *Scott Morton & Co.*

LODGE on the Rosewell Road. 1891 by *J. MacIntyre Henry*,
with half-timbered gables.

MIDHOPE CASTLE   WL 0070
5 km. W of South Queensferry

The melancholy shell of the tower built in the late C16 by Alex- 46
ander Drummond. The tall ashlar turrets corbelled out at three
of the corners used to rise proud of the roof. The corbelling
of the fourth, at the NW corner, is all that is left: it rose above
the main turnpike stair, and housed a small turnpike serving
the attic. The tower is entered by a moulded and lugged doorway of the late C17 which formerly had the coronet and initials
of the Earl of Linlithgow in its segmental pediment. Extension

---

* The name of the artist is not known. But at Balmanno Castle, Perthshire
(also restored by Lorimer), the windows on the stairs are decorated with the
same exquisite technique and jewelled colours. One is prominently signed
'Florence Camm for T. W. Camm, The Studio, Strathurie'.

to the E of *c.* 1600 – two storeys and a basement with a moulded doorway inscribed on the lintel in Latin 'May Jesus help our undertakings', evidently resited and leading into the vaulted kitchen. In the later C17 the extension was raised and lengthened, and an oak staircase, of which only the structural timbers now remain, was put in next to the old tower.

GATEWAY into the courtyard to the S. Late C17, but under the ivy may be the resited lintel mentioned by the RCAHMS inscribed with Drummond's initials and the date 1582.

GATEPIER. One of a former late C19 pair, the rusticated stones incised with flowers and stars.

DOOCOT to the E. Late C17, of lectern form, with two chambers reached through moulded doorways.

1070

MILLBURN TOWER   ML*
4 km. ENE of Ratho

The miniature two-storey keep was built in 1806 and the single-storey Gothic extension to the S finished by 1815, both by *William Atkinson* for Robert Liston, who was British Ambassador in several countries, including the U.S.A., and lived at Millburn in 1821–36, after his retirement. The last part to the N is of *c.* 1821, in character but dull, replacing the late C18 cottage that had formed the original nucleus. The inside is workaday, *c.* 1970, but beyond reproach because the whole exterior was saved from dereliction.‡

STABLES. An arcaded court of the early C19.

LODGE. Circular, with a conical roof and a central chimney; an even smaller offspring, also circular, to one side. This may or may not have some connection with the fact that *B. H. Latrobe* designed a round house for Liston's estate near Edinburgh in 1800.

MILTON BRIDGE *see* GLENCORSE

MONKRIGG *see* HADDINGTON

MONKTONHALL COLLIERY *see* NEWTON

3070

MONKTON HOUSE   ML (now EL)
3 km. SW of Musselburgh

A venerable and distinctive mixture of three centuries. 'Monk'

* Now Edinburgh.
* Dr Alan Tait records an American Garden designed by *George Parkyns*.

refers to the monks of Newbattle Abbey, which owned the farm property till it came to a branch of the Hays of Yester. The Hays probably built the C16 tower, the earliest part of the group, of rubble with big quoin stones, gun loops (now blocked) in the vaulted basement, and an entrance door near one corner which led straight into a turnpike stair whose windows are also blocked; so are those that lit the upper rooms on this side, which have roll surrounds and traces of panel mouldings on their wide jambs. Some time in the C17 the Hays added two ranges forming an L. Only a part of the one on the NW side remains, but it is exceptionally grand despite its two quite low storeys. Over a continuous moulded string course are two large dormer windows, each divided by two mullions and a transom, flanked by panelled jambs and crowned with a tall pediment. In the three-faced stair-turret a moulded doorway to which the C20 contributed a new lintel and a coat of arms from Carberry Tower (*see* p. 129). Upstairs, in a room later cut off by a new end gable, is an original ogee-moulded fireplace with a high mantel, similar to one at Pinkie House (*see* Musselburgh). The stair is quite plausibly roofed with pantiles which continue the main roof pitch. It is used to go higher (how far and with what purpose is an open question), but on its way up to the existing range it also stepped off into the NE range which has now disappeared, and of which the only other trace is the roof raggle where it used to join the old tower. A barmkin wall must have completed the C17 courtyard layout.

The next step was the C16 SE range, in line with the tower and connected to it. It seems to have been built with basement, main storey and dormered attic, and recent excavations by the owner have shown that there was a tower at the external S corner; the door which he found in the corresponding angle of the cellar gave access to it from inside on that level. The SW jamb and adjoining gateway may possibly have been added later, but the whole SW frontage and that facing the courtyard were treated in the same way with a moulded string course at main-storey sill level, now chiselled off except on the gateway. The quoins of these elevations and the arch-stones of the gateway, which has the decayed head of a cherub on the keystone, are lacily fretted like those of Baberton House (*see* p. 84), whose date is 1622. The final change came in the mid C18, by which time the Hays, as Jacobites, had forfeited Monkton and it was a Falconer property. The S tower was pulled down, and so presumably was the stair-turret that must have existed to serve

the internal angle of the L. In place of the latter a range of passages was added to the main courtyard front, with a projecting
semi-octagonal stair-turret. The string course was chopped off,
the main-storey windows were all blocked or recast save one,
and the dormer storey was raised to full height, with a wall-
head cornice and a bell-cast roof. As a concession to the earlier
style the ornamental quoins were repeated (but in a redder
stone) up to the new height. Now or a little later the Gibbs-
surround pedimented doorways were built on the new passage
range (as the main door) and on the garden front to the SE,
the latter reached by a bridging stair whose arched support incorporates more fretted quoins; the ball finials at the foot of
it were salvaged from alterations at the Western General Hospital, Edinburgh. Down to the l., on what is now half-sunk
basement level, is a C17 shelved recess for beehives, now built
up.

The entrance passage boasts two of the many features
brought in since 1954 by the present owner, with pleasing but
bewildering effect: old oak panelling from the S.S. Franconia
(its previous home unknown), and a wooden armorial panel
from Gordon Castle, Fochabers. The ground floor is entirely
vaulted. The room nearest the tower has the jambs of a large
fireplace against the tower wall, and provision for a door to be
bolted from the inside; it also has wooden shutter-marking on
the lime of the vault. At the opposite end of the building, on
the end wall of the jamb, a segmental-arched kitchen fireplace
nearly 4 m. wide. The upper floors are reached by the C18 stair,
a nice combination of semicircular spiral and straight back-and-
forth flights. The intervening wall supplies one jamb of a highly
effective entry to the principal storey – mason's architecture
at its best. On this level is the drawing room – the C17 hall –
and next to it the library whose pine finishings are all of the
late C17: crude classical chimneypiece, cornice, and plain panelling of the type found in most of the rooms, here supplemented
with bolection-moulded panels suggesting that there were once
paintings. In the two tower rooms the styles and rails are
planted directly on the plaster, presumably to save space. In
the upper room a moulded stone fireplace of the early C17. Each
has a little corner room taking in the space formerly filled by
the old turnpike stair; the rest of the end wall is occupied by
a bed recess with a lugged flat-arch frame of the mid C18. The
lugged doorcases throughout the house are of the same period,
and so probably, for all its clumsiness, is the basket-arch stone

fireplace in the second-floor room of the w jamb. The drawing room has an enriched plaster cornice of that time and then unexpectedly a French Empire-style fireplace of marble and ormolu; it came from the liner L'Atlantique.

CURIOSA: in the courtyard the head, now paved, of the Roaring Well described in Maitland's History of Edinburgh; and in the garden a stone sink with a waterspout which may have belonged in the tower, plus a pointed-arch gateway moved from Hammer House at Prestonpans after its demolition in 1961.

MORHAM

EL 5070

PARISH CHURCH. A little kirk of 1724 with round-headed and keystoned windows and door in the s wall.* The bellcote with ogee stone roof on the w gable is a survival from the previous building of 1685. The DALRYMPLE LOFT of c. 1730 (not now opening into the church) forms a N jamb and has a grand showfront of white stone. Under the moulded skew is a two-stage artisan-classical composition three bays wide. A finely cut doorway of Gibbs-surround type leading into the vault is flanked by plain bays. On the upper stage two windows of the same kind flank a plain central bay; above this, in the triangle of the gable, an armorial tabernacle is supported on each side by drooped mouldings and crowned with a segmental pediment. The windows light the loft, which is reached by an outside stair to the E. – MONUMENTS, in the churchyard. A number of very stark *memento mori* headstones in red sandstone. – MANSE. 1827, with a smart fanlit doorpiece. Its walled garden is by the church.

The tiny parish of Morham was united with Garvald in 1957; there is nothing that can be called a village.

MURIESTON HOUSE

ML (now WL) 0060

3 km. SW of Midcalder

A five-bay house of c. 1800 added to the front of a smaller and slightly older farmhouse. Ground-floor windows with cornices overhead. Doorpiece in the advanced and pedimented centre bay of c. 1830, very flat with twin pilasters. Inside, the whole of this bay is filled by a cantilever staircase of the same date, with wrought-iron balusters; over the narrow rectangle an

* Also on the s side a re-used strip of C12 carving.

elongated dome on pendentives with peculiar lotus-flower corbels.

STABLES AND OFFICES. An assortment to the rear, including an earlier court of *c.* 1800 with a continuously arcaded main elevation, and a separate range with tall candle-snuffer turret dated 1855.

MURIESTON CASTLE, at Murieston Castle Farm, 1 km. SW. An artificial ruin made out of a real one. A fragment of the C16 tower has been left *in situ* and the odd stones have been used to make it into a neat little set-piece of two storeys. Pedimented door reached by a crazy outside stair; climbing up it you have to duck to avoid the corbelling (genuine) that supports a round turret. Lots of blind cross-loops and pointed openings; between two of the openings a medallion with the initials and arms of John Keir for whom the work was done, and the date 1824. The wall is irregularly finished above the crowning string course, and the turret sticks up in a diminished, cross-looped stage.

3070   MUSSELBURGH   ML (now EL)

CHURCHES

MUSSELBURGH HIGH CHURCH, at the SE end of the bridge. Built as a Free Church in 1843, it was recast in 1889 by *R. Thornton Shiells*, who added the tower and pinnacles. Broad symmetrical front with details from E.E. to Scots Renaissance.

NORTHESK CHURCH, Bridge Street. 1838 by *William Burn*. Flat Gothic. Porch between two level-topped and buttressed stair-towers in front of a gable supporting an arcaded octagonal bell-cote. The interior tunnel-vaulted in plaster with diagonal ribs, and with transverse ribs which continue on flat-ceilinged aisles above the wings of a horseshoe gallery. – STAINED GLASS. On each side of the flat arch into the apse, a pair of windows in architectural borders by *A. Ballantine & Gardiner*; to the r. after 1892 (the Good Samaritan), to the l. after 1907 (David and Jonathan). – MacGill memorial windows of 1907 at the back of the gallery, and a complete assembly of tinted glass in the remainder.

OUR LADY OF LORETTO AND ST MICHAEL (R.C.), Newbigging. 1903 by *A. E. Purdie* of Canterbury and *Archibald Mac-Pherson*. Ecclesiastical character is concentrated at the (liturgical) W front, with a lean-to porch and an apsidal baptistery at the centre. Both the nave and the dormered presbytery which extends to the N beyond the gabled sacristy have deep eaves

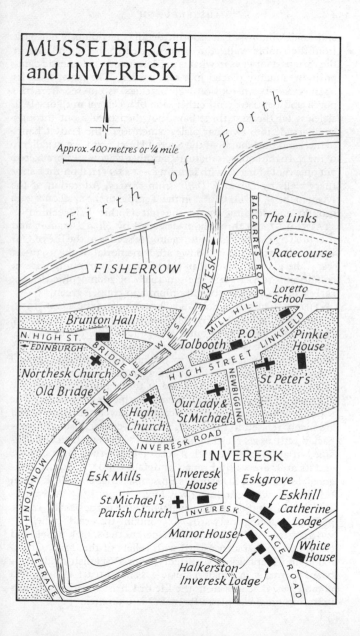

MUSSELBURGH
and INVERESK

N

Approx. 400 metres or ¼ mile

F i r t h   o f   F o r t h

FISHERROW

The Links

Racecourse

BALCARRES ROAD

R. Esk

WEST BRIDGE ST.

MILL HILL

Loretto School

Brunton Hall

N. HIGH ST.

← EDINBURGH

Tolbooth

P.O.

LINKFIELD

Pinkie House

HIGH STREET

NEWBIGGING

St Peter's

Northesk Church

Old Bridge

ESK ST.

High Church

Our Lady & St Michael

INVERESK ROAD

INVERESK

MONKTONHALL TERRACE

Esk Mills

Inveresk House

Eskgrove

Eskhill

St Michael's Parish Church

INVERESK ROAD

VILLAGE ROAD

Catherine Lodge

Manor House

White House

Halkerston

Inveresk Lodge

and small windows. Late Gothic detail is fastidiously cut back from the rubble walls and concentrated at the w end and at the various doorways in what is predominantly a domestic composition, suitably placed in a rose garden. The nave, with its open scissor-beam roof on wall brackets, is entered from the porch and baptistery on either side of a central mullion. It is aisleless for the first three bays, but then breaks out through a tall arcade into two-bay aisles which form the Lady Chapel to the s and the Chapel of the Sacred Heart, with organ gallery, to the N. In the square sanctuary a timber wagon roof bracketed out on a canted frieze with lettering. – PAINTING on the sanctuary walls by *David J. Duffy* from *c.* 1945, Adoration of the Magi to the N, Child Christ in the Temple to the s, all on a gold ground and leading up to the gilt Gothic baldacchino. – STAINED GLASS throughout designed by *Nina Davidson* and executed by *Guthrie & Wells*, mainly of scenes in the life of Our Lady. The latest (w) windows are a memorial of the 1939–45 war. The glass is devoted in spirit, and uncommonly sure in colouring. – CARPET in the sanctuary of zoomorphic design, early C20, its positive colours plum and copper green.

ST NINIAN (Church of Scotland), Levenhall, at the E exit. 1955. A successful effort by *Peter Whiston* as architect, *T. Harley Haddow* as engineer, to build a large hall- (i.e. dual-purpose) church at low cost. White rendered walls and low-pitch roofs make it an easy companion to the nearby housing of Pinkie Braes, and the accommodation now seems princely.

ST PETER (Episcopal), at the E end of the High Street. 1865 by *Paterson & Shiells*; cheerful mixed Gothic in grey ashlar. The N porch forms the base of an octagonal tower and spire which are nicely related to the street. Octagon-ended apse with pinnacled buttresses recalling those of St Nicholas, Dalkeith. Inside, an aisleless nave with a scissor-beam roof. The chancel and its arch are stiffly French in detail. – FONT. Stone, octagonal, formerly in St George's Episcopal Chapel in York Place, Edinburgh, whose architect was *James Adam*, 1793. A remarkably good imitation of medieval work, the corner shafts of the pedestal curving outwards to contain traceried panels. – WOODWORK in St Michael's Chapel, to the s. Oak panels and doors of C17 character carved with reliefs of the Trial, Crucifixion and Deposition, reportedly from a Spanish-made cupboard formerly in Pinkie House. – STAINED GLASS. Quite a notable set of scenes from the life of Christ in bright colours imitating medieval glass. Its maker is unknown.

PUBLIC BUILDINGS

TOLBOOTH (former), High Street. Like the Canongate Tolbooth 98
in Edinburgh, virtually a castle come to town. Built in 1590,
traditionally of stone taken from the chapel of Our Lady of
Loretto. The corbelled parapet above the first storey stops half-
way along the E end, so that the second floor, which looks like
a large cap-house, emerges into the main gable wall. The
ground floor, pierced by a pend, has no internal connection with
the first floor, which is reached by an outside stair of contemporary form. All three floors are tunnel-vaulted. The tower to
the W is more of a mystery. The New Statistical Account says
that it survived Hertford's invasion of 1544. A clock (still in
the building) was given to the burgh by the Dutch States in
1496. The belfry, resting on the chamfered corners of the tower,
is like a slated and static model of a Dutch windmill. Unfortunately there is no clear evidence to bring all these facts together,
and the only internal clue is rather discouraging – an early C17
fireplace on first-floor level. In 1762 a new wing was added to
the E end, with Gibbs-surround windows on the upper floor,
in which the courtroom of 1773 still exists, though subdivided.
Over its bell-cast roof appears the gable of the hall designed
in 1900 by *William Constable* of Musselburgh, who also made
some economical adaptations of the old tolbooth building and
put a new clock in the tower.

PINKIE HOUSE, to the E end of the High Street, S side. The
earliest part of Pinkie is the tower house built by a C16 Abbot
of Dunfermline. In 1597 it was acquired by Alexander Seton
(† 1622), the builder of Fyvie Castle, Aberdeenshire. He
became first Earl of Dunfermline in 1605 and married Margaret
Hay of Yester in 1607; the initials AS.ED and AS.MH appear
frequently in and around the house, which he extended on a
grand scale *c.* 1613. On the death of the fourth and last Earl
in 1694 the estate passed to the Hays, and three years later the
second Marquess of Tweeddale built the arched doorway on
the E (garden) front, with his initials IH (John Hay). In 1778
Pinkie was sold to the Hopes of Craighall, who built the bow
on the S front and for whom *John Paterson* designed the stables
c. 1800 and *William Burn* the twin crowstepped gables of 1825.
In 1951 Pinkie became a part of Loretto School.

Seton's manifesto on the E wall of the garden (*see* below) dedi-
cates his works at Pinkie to the cause of peace and the arts.
Another Latin inscription (over his front door, but now con-

cealed) relates that 'Alexander Seton built this house not to the measure [modum] of his desire, but of his fortunes and estate'. He retained the tower, adding a pair of square pepperpots at the N end and a parapet-walk between them. The projecting jamb he raised by two storeys, with battlements and ogee-roofed corner turrets, to form the centrepiece of his W elevation, for he built a long new wing to the S, with a short return to the W; here the tusked masonry shows that a full-height S range was intended, but even in its two-storey form it was probably not completed until the late C17. The pend which had penetrated it was later blocked and a corridor added to the N front.

It seems likely that Seton's regrets (assuming that he composed the inscription himself) refer not to the incomplete state of the work, nor even to the unpeaceful-looking turrets he added to the old tower (common enough as symbols of status in early C17 Scotland), but to the stylistic compromise which the tower's retention imposed; even here however it is noticeable that the new crowstepped gables are up-dated with rolled edges. To the outside indeed the house presents a different image. The E range has regular windows, straight string courses and a row of seven tall wall-head chimneys recalling those at Dunnottar Castle, Kincardineshire. At its S end is a bay-window, a revolutionary import from England and thus an architectural token of the Union of the Crowns. The triple lights on the second floor indicate the end of the long gallery. Even more remarkable are the rusticated columns attached as buttresses to what is left of the W courtyard wall. Had Seton or his master mason, whom John Dunbar tentatively identifies as *William Wallace*, seen Sir William Cavendish's belted columns at that very time under construction on the W front of Bolsover? The vestigial capitals that poke out of the wall like rolled paper are remarkably like those which act as finials, with equally brutal success, at Pinkie.

Before the front door is a well head, Seton's work, in the finest Scots Renaissance manner, a square-arched tabernacle carrying a crown of four diagonal buttresses, with corner columns and obelisk finials.

Inside, *Burn*'s contribution may be disposed of first. The ENTRANCE HALL and two-storey STAIRWELL have plain compartmented ceilings. The stair balustrade is a puzzle; perhaps these bold iron cut-outs of serpentine profile came from an earlier staircase. (There is a short section of similar work, possibly early C18, in the garden.) Burn's only other distinctive interior is at the SE corner on the first floor, where there is a ribbed geometric ceiling with four bosses bearing the anchor of the Hopes.

The most important rooms are Seton's, of the early C17. He left the lower part of the old tower, with its tunnel-vaulted basement, much as it was, but the rooms in the upper extension have his monogram over the doors, and moulded fireplaces with high stone shelves. The upper floors he remodelled and re-decorated. Only the far N room on the first floor still has its moulded plaster ceiling, but the three rooms above are a good series, reached along a passage whose inner wall is arcaded in low-relief modelling. First is the SETON ROOM, whose ceiling has a pattern of sinuous, leafy ribs without any continuous edge-moulding: of the reliefs between them, the lion and unicorn are particularly delicate. Seton arms over the fireplace. In the next room a ceiling with similar ribs forming circles. The KING'S ROOM at the N end has an extremely accomplished arrangement of moulded and foliated ribs with four pendants over a deep cove whose enrichment is partly of the late C18. In his S extension Seton used painted decoration. On first-floor level above a C20 staircase is part of a board-and-beam ceiling painted in tempera, the beams conventionally patterned, strings of 'grotesque' subjects on the boards between. Their colours are fresh and bright on a grey ground, and it is just as well to prepare for a less excellent state of preservation in the painting of the second-floor GALLERY. It probably included the walls, but what remains on the flat vaulted timber ceiling is remark- 51 able enough. The length of 23 m. is divided into a central square, with three large bays and a small one to N and to S. Each bay is painted with an arch on each side, its point towards the centre. Hung on a nail in every arch is a panel, with suitable motto, illustrating a moral precept. The square in the middle purports to show an octagonal lantern open to the sky in crazy perspective, with cherub musicians sitting on the edge, beneath an openwork dome. The whole square is linked to smaller end domes by a band of multi-coloured grotesques. The flat S compartment by the oriel shows a stork with the Greek motto 'Do not sleep all night', and part of an architectural frieze survives at the other end. But alas for this once gay triumph of morality over gravity. Burn's addition blocked the windows which probably lit it from the W. The RCAHMS reported in 1929 that it was 'singularly bright and well preserved', but restoration has robbed the whole thing of its fine spontaneity, making all the faces like potatoes and grossly darkening the fresh colours with wax. In short, this is now something to wonder at, but hardly to enjoy.

The Hays made their own improvements, starting with what seems to have been a new front door to the E, and a single-flight stair just to the S of it (now disused) with a coved ceiling of c. 1700. They then c. 1740 refitted the first-floor rooms of the tower, and gave the LIBRARY its twin overmantels with trophies of fruit. The N wall is lined with C18 architectural paper, printed in grisaille. A *Burn* ceiling in the room to the S, but he left the original Corinthian-columned bay-window. Most of the late Georgian work of the Hopes is in the S range, but none is important.

The WALLED GARDEN to the E is Seton's again. In the E wall a pretty strapwork-headed shelter, not quite in line with the Hays' front door, two Renaissance doorways which reveal the age of Seton (57) and his wife (21), and a moulded coping with an obelisk SUNDIAL. Of the two Latin INSCRIPTIONS the longer begins as follows:

'D.O.M. (to God most holy and most high). For himself, for his descendants, for all civilized (*urbanis*) men, Alexander Seton, lover of mankind and civilization, founded, built and adorned his house (*villam*) and gardens and these out-of-town (*suburbana*) buildings. Here is nothing warlike, even for defence; no ditch, no rampart. But for the kind welcome and hospitable entertainment of guests a fountain of pure water, lawns, ponds and aviaries.'

DOOCOT, to the E. Double-chambered lectern type.

STABLES, to the N. By *John Paterson, c.* 1800, with canted wings, the S side in the Adam castellated style, the N (concave) side plain Georgian.

GATEPIERS. Four obelisks of Seton's period reset on early C19 piers.

Pinkie is one of the boarding houses of Loretto School. In 1971 *David Carr* somewhat extended the S range and built two more houses, SETON HOUSE and HOPE HOUSE. They have a slightly Scottish, rather temporary look which is not altogether unsuitable. The other buildings of the school are on the other side of the A1, with a linking tunnel. Some of them are noted below.

LORETTO SCHOOL, E end of the High Street, N side. Loretto takes its name from the C16 chapel (demolished *c.* 1590) whose site is marked by a mound in front of the SCHOOL HOUSE. This is a conglomeration of orange-harled blocks which started with a house of the mid C18 facing E, with canted bay-windows to N and S. In the early C19 an elliptical porch was added to the S end. The lodge with its twin bows and segmental-arched centrepiece is probably contemporary. Known hitherto as Loretto Villa, the house first became a school in 1829. About 1870 a three-storey annexe was added bang in the middle of the old front. The interior is still quite rewarding. On the W side of the first floor a noble mid C18 room with a coved ceiling, diagonally voluted pilasters and an unusually modelled later C18 chimneypiece. The stair, also original, is of uncommon type – curved and cantilevered but retaining the old-fashioned detail of downward returned nosings. Scrolled wrought-iron balustrade. Two good rooms, refitted in the late C18, are lit by the S bay-window.

The CHAPEL is by *Honeyman & Keppie* of Glasgow, 1891. Four of its lanceted bays were retained to the W when it was brilliantly enlarged in 1962–5 by *Kenneth Graham* of *Sir Robert Matthew, Johnson-Marshall & Partners*. He accepted the existing structural module and also the roof pitch, but carried the eaves further down to a rubble wall with a triangular gable on each face. Inside, the commemorative woodwork by *Robert Lorimer*, 1922, remains, but the collegiate seating has been renewed. Here and in the roof structure colour and form are well matched, and the light level is admirable though unfashionably low. – STAINED GLASS. By *John Lawrie*.

GYMNASIUM by *Robert Lorimer*, 1912, a lovely hall with dark planked walls. A false ceiling unfortunately obscures the roof on the inside. COLIN THOMSON HALL is Baronial-Colonial by *Lorimer & Matthew*, 1936, with a tall interior of elliptical section.

DESCRIPTION

Musselburgh got its name from a mussel bank at the mouth of the river Esk on which it lies. As part of Inveresk it was granted to the abbey of Dunfermline by David I and gained importance as a bridge town and because of the shrines of Our Lady of Loretto* and St Mary Magdalen which stood at the E and W ends respectively. Its great house is Pinkie (*see* above), which gave its name to the battle in which Hertford, as Duke of Somerset, defeated the Scots army in 1547.

* I.e. of the Italian shrine at Loreto.

Musselburgh's elevation to a royal burgh in 1632 was successfully challenged by Edinburgh, but it continued as a burgh of barony and retains its distinctive market-town shape and its importance as a river crossing (and therefore a bottleneck for traffic) on the main coast road to the capital. Fishing was its first industry, but the little harbour at Fisherrow on the w side of the Esk, built in its present form *c.* 1850, is now used only by pleasure boats. Nothing remains of the earlier, partly cottage-based, textile industry, but between the High Street and the river there are still two red brick tanning sheds with timber louvres, probably of the C18. In the mid C19 came the Esk Mill for fishing nets (*see* below) and the Inveresk Mill for paper, followed by Brunton's Wireworks, all occupying a loop of the Esk on its E bank. Their workers' housing, mainly provided by the town council in the C20, covers a large area on the w bank and extends as far s as Monktonhall.

HIGH STREET. At its E end it has one of the most decisive entries in any town in Scotland. It is flanked by the PINKIE PILLARS, two rusticated piers of 1770 bearing urns carved with the burgh arms. Then on the N side a good group: Nos. 1–3 of *c.* 1760, with a Tuscan porch and twin pends (one blocked), Nos. 5–7 early C17 and called the FRENCH AMBASSADOR'S HOUSE, unpretentious except for the finials on the triangular dormer heads, and No. 13 of *c.* 1790, quite grand, with pilastered quoins and windows on ground level, elaborate fanlight and blocked cornice. After the contemporary cylindrical piers of its side entrance, No. 15 (PARSONAGE HOUSE, early C19) stands back behind a wall formed partly from an old cottage front. The POST OFFICE of 1903 is a congruous interlude in the piecemeal Georgian fronts that build up to a high point at No. 47 but are happily small at the Town House end. Here stands the MERCAT CROSS, a Tuscan shaft of the late C18 supporting a dilapidated lion and the burgh arms.

On the w side the street widens out after St Peter's church to make a spacious market place (no longer used as such). Here the Georgian norm is broken by, *inter alia*, the BRITISH LEGION CLUB by *Ronald W. Gardiner*, 1969, a complicated mixture of C17 and C20 ideas; *Douglas Sanderson*'s rubbly-modern corner block of the same date with ground-floor shops and a single-storey glazed rotunda intended as a pub; and the NAG'S HEAD on the other side of Newbigging (leading to Inveresk), *c.* 1910, its ogee-hatted corner turret remotely derived from Mackintosh's Glasgow Herald tower in that city. Th

sudden constriction caused by the Town House is matched c
this side by a gradual squeeze of early C19 fronts more or le
interfered with, as we enter the more heavily modernized h
of the street. Here the big names predominate, starting w
the BANK OF SCOTLAND by *Esmé Gordon*, 1969; solidly stone
faced with recessed slate dressings, it uses a pleasant bow-
fronted early C19 block as its annexe and leaves it blank with
amazement. Odd survivals like the fish sign at No. 136 and the
bollard in its pend made out of an inverted lamp post, the
quoins and scrolled skewputts of No. 123 and the excellent
chemists' shops at Nos. 121 and 165 do something to relieve
the shanty-town feeling whose climax is COOPERS FINE FARE
at No. 176, in Art-déco garage revival. Two good MONUMENTS
end the street: straight ahead the statute of Dr David ('Delta')
Moir on a pedestal like a truncated obelisk, by *A. Handyside
Ritchie*, 1853, and on the pavement at the bridge corner a yellow
sandstone fountain, sadly eroded, with an ogival top and
François I detail.

The NEW BRIDGE over the Esk, designed in 1806 by *John Rennie*,
with five arches and niched piers over rounded cutwaters, was
greatly widened in 1924 by *Blyth & Blyth*, without altering
its appearance from either side. From it can be seen to the SW
the early C16 OLD BRIDGE with three arches, refuges over the
cutwaters and a stair at each end; and to the NE two more
bridges. The first is the SHORTHOPE STREET BRIDGE (reinforced concrete) by *Bierrum & Partners*, 1968, the second the
ELECTRICITY BRIDGE (steel with concrete deck) by *Fairhurst
& Partners*, 1963. They are well related to the river scene.

BRIDGE STREET is unsatisfactory. On the N side a good long terrace at Nos. 13–45, the lower storey partly used as shops and
offices, and the free Palladian front of ST ANDREW'S CHURCH
HALL, 1889. On the S no continuity; Northesk Church (*see*
above) and the ROYAL BANK OF SCOTLAND by *W. J. Walker
Todd*, 1936 (masonry finely built and detailed), are isolated incidents. But at the end a more compact group, if a strange one:
the prim Georgian row at Nos. 18–26, the rendered front of
the former Hayweights Cinema, clamped on to a house in
c. 1935, and No. 34 of *c*. 1820, with three pediments, surviving
above a new shopfront.

Here NORTH HIGH STREET is joined. The BRUNTON MEM-
ORIAL HALL (Bruntons are the wireworks) and MUNI-
CIPAL OFFICES are by *Sir William Kininmonth*, 1971, with
gilded relief sculpture by *Tom Whalen* facing down the street.

They form a major civic group, well composed in white aggregate slabs, sufficiently human on ground level, sufficiently imposing above. To the rear a flat-section boiler-house chimney successfully doubling as a clock tower. In the street itself precious little except in details, e.g. the excellent Victorian shopfront of the FISHERROW POST OFFICE with a central segmental pediment at No. 92, and the double-faced SUNDIAL supported by a cherub's head, probably C18, above the shop at No. 177. Fisherrow Harbour, rebuilt in the C19 and now used by private pleasureboats, lies just to the N.

The second part of this description starts once again at the E end; this time with the LINKS, whose long oval has been enclosed by the racecourse* since 1816. They are overlooked from the S by LINKFIELD ROAD, whose older houses were built by the Musselburgh Heritages Company, ‡ 1878, and whose new ones were designed by *John A. W. Grant* in 1939. Then BALCARRES ROAD, where golf is the thing. First GOLF PLACE, a terrace with crossed clubs and the date 1886 over one of the doors. Second, the former clubhouse of the EDINBURGH BURGESS GOLFING SOCIETY by *John C. Hay*, 1875, snecked and stugged ashlar with elaborate gables, chip-carved detail and lotus chimneys, in the manner of Alexander 'Greek' Thomson of Glasgow. Finally the BRUNTSFIELD GOLF CLUB HOUSE by *Hippolyte J. Blanc*, 1885, of red Corsehill stone, with nice Flemish detail and a complicated wooden porch to the keeper's residence to one side. The *Building News* calls it 'Old Scotch', which is far-fetched as a description. Now back to MILL HILL, which is actually quite level, and past the pedimented TRAFALGAR LODGE of *c.* 1830, to finish with RED HOUSE, once the town mansion of the Edmonstones, a tall house of three wide bays and three storeys, all of red sandstone, with long and short quoins, a pedimented doorpiece, and a pedimented Venetian feature breaking up through the eaves. Intelligent additions for use as a school in 1895. The town's riverfront is grassed and planted with admirable simplicity on both sides, and the good houses of ESKSIDE WEST enjoy the sunnier bank. Starting at the NE (downstream) end, Nos. 1–6, three pairs of semi-detached cottages of *c.* 1840, followed by an elaborately gabled and strapworked Jacobean mansion with finialled gatepiers

* The racecourse stands are the work of *McDurment & Murdoch*, 1886.
‡ The centre of this development is to the E, where Victoria Terrace and Albert Terrace lead into Windsor Gardens, handsomely gabled and we' planted in the middle, with St Ann's Convent to the S.

round the corner in North High Street. ESKSIDE HOUSE was built *c.* 1810 on the site of Professor George Stuart's Eskside Villa, but the octagonal pavilion with Gothic glazing and a slated dome topped with an urn, supposed to have been the study of his son Gilbert, is of *c.* 1770. Then at the end of a continuous Georgian row a neat office block at No. 21 by *Alan Reiach & Partners*, 1964, awkwardly set back from the old building line but otherwise, with its domestic scale and its horizontal bands of white wall and black window, perfectly at home. This sets a good standard for the vital site, at the time of writing empty, on the corner. Eskside West continues on the other flank of the bridge with a straight, mainly Georgian row. Then towards Monktonhall a number of two-storey red sandstone terraces designed for the town council by *William Constable*. WEST HOLMES GARDENS are cottagey, MONKTONHALL TERRACE, 1922, is rather Victorian-looking, with a picturesque roof-line awkwardly crammed down over the bay-windows. The later housing to the N includes the STONEYHILL development by the burgh surveyor *John Barclay* in 1931, and more by *John Logan* who was his successor from *c.* 1935. Finally MONKTONHALL itself, i.e. a late Georgian mansion, a FARM STEADING with a pretty gabled frontage and a red brick chimney added to an earlier rubble-and-pantile group in the mid C19, and the MUSSELBURGH GOLF CLUB by *John Logan*, 1937, with stark white harling, horizontal metal glazing, and a symmetrical frontage to the course. The railings on the approach are made like inverted golf clubs.

A girder footbridge by *John Barclay*, 1923, crosses to the W bank of the Esk. The former STATION is Tudor, *c.* 1832. Up-river are the ESK MILLS, uncommonly interesting and well preserved. The jolly red sandstone turret, with ogee roof and wind-vane fish, was designed by *Robert Lorimer* in 1916; so was the wrought ironwork over the main gateway to the works, a large netting factory whose earlier, vaguely Gothic frontage was built in 1854. Two arcades in the splendid courtyard are dated 1857. The rest was built ten years later. One enters past massively simple iron arches for service bays. The long sides of the court are lined with Roman arcading, the near end hugely Grecian with a pedimented entry, the far end built up to four storeys with a rustic base, giant order and twin-pedimented attic with four allegorical figures (the iron-crested brick clock tower is an afterthought of *c.* 1890). In the middle of the court the central office, domed and cruciform, of one Greco-Egyptian storey with recumbent lions at the door like those at the Hamilton Mausoleum – and ultimately from Canova. Vigorous and eclectic plaster detail inside. The quality of the external stonework and sculpture is variable, but the picture of industrial prestige is established beyond doubt.

NEWHAILES. *See* p. 351.

3060   NEWBATTLE   ML

PARISH CHURCH. 1727-9 by *Alexander McGill*. A T-plan kirk with a strong resemblance to that of Carrington (*see* p. 135), its stem formed by the aisle of the Lothian family (but their patronage has not been limited to the Church of Scotland – *see* St David's R.C. church at Dalkeith). The tower on the opposite side has a slated pyramidal roof. Its lowest stage was originally the session house. Access to the church was through doors on each side (built up in 1750) and to the galleries by outside stairs, as is shown by the rybats and hinge-pins at the end next to the manse. In 1875-7 the opposite end was pushed further out, and both gables were given skews in place of the original piend roof; the windows were altered too. Piecemeal change is still more evident inside. The former Lothian loft was deepened in 1859 to include their retiring-room, but the upper part of its framed wooden opening into the church is still of *c.* 1770. The single gallery is of 1851 (the other was displaced at a later date by the organ). In 1895 the second stage of the tower was opened up to form the Ancram aisle, revealing McGill's bullseye window. – PULPIT. Of timber, hexagonal. There is no reason to doubt, as far as the Corinthian angle pilasters and arcaded panels are concerned, that this is the pulpit of Robert Leighton, minister of Newbattle in 1641–53 and subsequently Bishop of Glasgow, from an earlier church. – FONT. A small and battered seven-sided stone basin with a gargoyled drain, allegedly from Newbattle Abbey. – STAINED GLASS. A thin collection except for two windows flanking the pulpit (Teaching the Young; Feeding the Hungry) by *Mayer* of Munich, 1885. With more sense of unity than prevails elsewhere, these are set over arcaded tablets forming part of the same memorial. – The rose window is by *William Wilson*, 1961.

NEWBATTLE HOUSE (former Manse). The part towards the road, with its steeply crowstepped jamb and roll-moulded windows which formerly bore Latin inscriptions, was built *c.* 1625. It is joined to a plain house of 1812–20 whose main front faces the garden.

SUN INN, opposite the main gate of Newbattle Abbey. 1697, with a little oval window in the middle, by *James Chirnsyde*, wright.

NEWBATTLE ABBEY. The former mansion of the Kerrs occupies the site of a Cistercian abbey founded in 1140 by David I and colonized from Melrose. It was the most important medieval monastic house in the Lothians, but its buildings have been almost totally destroyed. There are no documentary references to the first buildings on the site, but a date *c.* 1160 is indicated by fragments from the W range – often the first part to be built in a Cistercian monastery. The plan of the CHURCH as excavated looks later in the century. A dedication took place in 1233 and Marie de Coucy, wife of Alexander II, was buried in the choir in 1241. The only remains above ground are the S half of the dorter undercroft, and this is very much later, late C14 at the earliest. It was incorporated into the mansion built immediately after the Reformation by Mark Kerr, the last commendator abbot. What had been a long narrow block of building (even when reduced by half) was thickened into a broad rectangle by building on to E and W. The foundations of the abbey church are exposed in the grass N of the recent extensions. The choir had aisles and the straight E end preferred by the Cistercians. Ten-bay nave, transepts of two bays each with E chapel aisles. The total length was 94 m. The choir and transepts had shallower buttresses than the nave, which suggests that the E parts were late C12 and the nave of *c.* 1200 or later. Big diagonal buttresses were added to the N transept, probably after 1385, when the church was partly destroyed by the English. The claustral buildings have been excavated and turfed over again.* Lying around in the grounds are four bases from the undercroft of the W range, i.e. the lay brothers' quarters. Two are circular, the third is octagonal, and the fourth quadrilobed with small triangular spurs between the lobes – a highly unusual section but identical in principle to some of the nave piers at Kirkstall Abbey, Yorkshire. This gives an approximate date of *c.* 1150–60.

Inside the house a long hall on ground level, reached from the main stair, represents the S half of the undercroft of the monastic E range, rediscovered, excavated and restored in the late C19. Five of its nine bays are still medieval, two at the N end, three at the S. With their plain quadripartite vaults carried on piers

* MacGibbon and Ross (*Ecclesiastical Architecture*) illustrate numerous mouldings recovered in the late C19 excavations, none of which is in evidence now. Most of the profiles were Late Gothic, but a few were C12 Transitional.

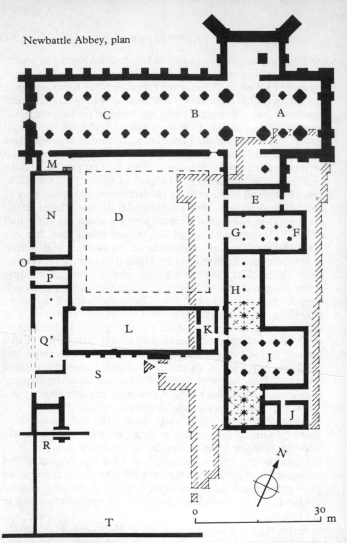

Newbattle Abbey, plan

A Presbytery B Monks' Choir C Lay Brothers' Choir D Cloister
E Sacristy F Chapter House G Vestibule to Chapter House H Under-
croft (Dormitory over) I Function unknown (Abbot's Quarters over?)
J Reredorter K Calefactory L Refectory M Lay Brothers' Night
Stair N Cellars O Entrance to Cloister P Parlour Q Lay Brothers'
Refectory? R Reredorter S Probable site of Kitchens T Southern
Boundary Wall

with moulded capitals and bases they could pass as C13 work
except for the Late Gothic swelling profile of the capitals. Probably all this belongs to the post-1385 rebuilding, to which
bequests were being made as late as 1419. In the w wall of the
s bays two original lancets and a pointed door leading to a room
with a C16 segmental tunnel-vault. To the l. of the large C19
fireplace in the E wall a converted lancet window leads into
a series of three tunnel-vaulted chambers below the library.
The centre of the undercroft, opposite the staircase, formerly
opened eastwards into a vaulted hall of five bays by four. The
bases of two massive piers remain and the positions of the rest
are marked in the floor. N of this a square bay with a late C19
segmental rib-vault. A door in its w wall gives access to a narrow
tunnel-vaulted room occupying the E end of the s monastic
range, usually identified as the calefactory, but possibly part
of the C16 house. It was furnished as a chapel in the late C19.
The wood block floor by *John Ramsay*, master of works, reproduces the pattern of the former tiled floor in variegated timber
from the estate. The FONT is an early C16 hexagonal bowl on
a C19 stem, the faces carved with the arms of James V and both
his queens, Ramsey of Dalhousie, and James Haswell, Abbot
of Newbattle from 1529.* In the medieval bays at the N end
of the undercroft a restored C17 fireplace with a large achievement of the Kerr arms on the hood.

Scot of Scotstarvet says that the commendator and his eldest
son 'did so metamorphose the building that it cannot be known
that ever it did belong to the Church, by reason of the fair new
fabrick and stately edifices thereon'. What were the new buildings like? The only clue is in a wall in the heart of the present
house on first-floor level: two C16 moulded window surrounds,
and between them a panel with the initials MK.LN with the date
1580 and a baron's coronet – odd, because it was Mark Kerr's
son of the same name who became Lord Newbattle in 1591 (and
in 1606 first Earl of Lothian). Architecturally, the panel shows
that Mark Kerr built a new E range parallel to the old dorter,
and that here, underneath, was the main entry to it. Panel and
windows became indoor features when a corridor was formed
in 1836. The only other possible C16 survival inside the house
is the turnpike stair further to the s. Outside, there is a fragment
of a C16 window surround on the w front, to the l. of the new
porch. But what of the buttresses on the N front? They have
a C19 look, but perhaps they were merely renewed or refaced

* It was brought from Mavisbank House after being dug up there in 1873.

at that time; if so, the original buttresses may have been designed to support the thrust not only of the undercroft vault, which still survives, but also the dormitory above, replaced in the early C17 by what is now the library.

The C17 documentation produces a tantalizing item: work to be done in 1650 by *John Mylne* for £9,200 Scots. It appears to have been a new show-front to the W, with orders, and we may well wonder why it was subsequently obliterated, for the present front is largely of the late C18. At that time also a double stair to the principal storey was built on the main axis (later replaced) and a well stair to the N of it. A full storey, crowned with battlements, was added all round. Windows were modernized, with a tripartite arrangement at each end of the E front, and all were given hoodmoulds, supported on leafy brackets to the W. Wings were also thrown out to the N and S. In 1836 *William Burn* added yet another storey to the E range, complete with curving gables to the sides (and another pair at the S end) and fancy dormers between. The crowsteps ending in masked corbels, despite the low pitch, are particularly effective. Burn treated the N side in the same way, stopping the extra storey against a square turret with a pointed roof. In 1858 *David Bryce* added the two-storey family wing with its oriel, and in 1875, the year of his death, he built another room at the end. Its battlemented top storey is of 1886.

Bryce's unknown successor added the single-storey classical porch in 1887, and was evidently responsible for the present finishings of the hall with its beamed ceiling and the complex double stair which gives you the option of going down to the undercroft. At the first landing it incorporates an C18 marble tondo of putti and a goat. The thin supporting posts are a legacy from Burn's hall treatment of 1836, and so is the French-style marble chimneypiece further in, on main-storey level. The rooms are now seen in sequence, giving them the names which appear on the 1858 plans and starting at the SW with the DRAWING ROOM of *c.* 1770. Such at least is the date when it was formed, four windows long and two storeys high, and of its cornice, dado and shutters. But the two Ionic marble chimneypieces, the doors and their marble doorcases, the deep pelmets and crested pier glasses are all of the later C19, as indeed is the whole spirit of the room, which was decorated by *Thomas Bonnar c.* 1890. All is brown with gilt relief, with a stencilled pattern of darker brown on the walls. The ceiling cove is divided into a pointed arcade, maroon at the corners, blue between, with grisaille medallions of putti variously occupied. The gold-framed soffit is more luminous in the colour of its grotesque ornament, and finally becomes realistic in the centre round – full-colour cherubs and clouds. But unhappily it is the drab khaki background which wins. In a small DRAWING ROOM to the E a bracketed marble chimneypiece of *c.* 1770 with ochre inlaid panels. The cornice, apparently of the early C18, is unorthodox, with modillions extending downwards instead of outwards. Then the panelled DINING ROOM, whose Corinthian pilasters and monogrammed overmantel are of the early C18, the rest made up later.

The next three rooms along the E front, all of *c.* 1770, are entitled BEDROOM, BATHROOM, and (after the stair) LORD LOTHIAN'S ROOM. Then comes the continuation of the suite into *Bryce*'s family wing of 1858. First the BOUDOIR, lit by the oriel, with a trellised plaster vault and a cornice monogrammed in thin rope – all gold on palest green, set off by a red marble chimneypiece carved with ivy and clover leaves; bold but delicate. The DRESSING ROOM and BEDROOM beyond are in conformity with the late C18 idea which Bryce knew how to imitate, but the later bedroom at the end confesses its date of 1887 on a dreary Ionic chimneypiece. Across the passage is a room surviving from the C18 range with the genuine article in marble. The oak-lined LIBRARY consists of two connected rooms at the NW corner, each with a ribbed and moulded ceiling of the early C17, one with pendants, both featuring the lion and dragon, diagonally opposed. Otherwise they are the work of *W. E. Nesfield*, 1878. Twisted shafts between the shelves. The elaborate twin overmantels incorporate a pair of C18 marble fireplaces with diagonally cut-off corners, alternately moulded and blocked.

SUNDIALS in the formal garden to the E. A fine C17 pair, both a good deal restored. Octagonal, with panelled steps and a pedestal on which four big-headed female chimeras stand to support a hefty octagonal block whose panels have dials in their lower parts, heraldry and curious shadow-casting profiles of mouldings above. CAL stands for Ann, Countess of Lothian, EWL for William, Earl of Lothian. Finally an obelisk carried by scrolls with male masks.

The subsidiary buildings are as varied as the house itself. To the S across a stream is a late C17 archway with fluted pilasters and a segmental arch. Behind it an egg-shaped brick ICE HOUSE. Early C18 main LODGE GATES near the church, their rusticated piers, bearing huge rotund vases, linked to the lodges by curved colonnades, a crouched lion on each. The KING'S GATE on the A7, a semicircular arch flanked by smaller ones, was built in 1822 for George IV's visit. The late C19 WEST GATE on the A68 just outside Dalkeith is combined with an attenuated baronial lodge, picturesquely composed. To the N the ruin of a seven-bay CONSERVATORY of the late C18. Tall windows with depressed arches. The two blind end bays are occupied by a niche and an archway, both built grotto-wise with large rocks, the latter attended by a hermit's cell. Nearby COTTAGE of the early C18 with later dormers. The L-plan STABLES were recast by *David Bryce* with a clock tower and a louvred broach-spire about 1875, the date of the gabled COACHMAN'S COTTAGE adjacent.

MAIDEN BRIDGE to the N, over the South Esk. Late C15, the ribbed arch not quite pointed.

5080

NEWBYTH HOUSE

EL

2 km. SW of Whitekirk

A nearly square four-poster (i.e. corner-towered) house in battlemented Gothic by *Archibald Elliot*, 1817. Each front is differently treated. Those to the S and W have a taller centre between thin octagonal turrets. On the W (entrance) front, however, the centre bays are recessed behind Gothic arches to form a porch below and a balcony above. All the windows are hoodmoulded and probably all used to have pointed glazing in the top lights. To the SE the billiard-room wing, joined to the main house by a curving, flat-arched link with service corridor below. The offices are cunningly concealed in a fold of the ground at this lower level. A new range was added *c.* 1900.

The porch opens into a vestibule with a delicate plaster vault, and before the entry into the central saloon it must be explained that in 1972 the house was almost entirely gutted by fire in the course of its conversion into separate flats. In the saloon there were slender shafts, paired across the corners, with plaster ribs dividing the upper walls and springing up to the octagonal lantern. It is now an open courtyard with harled walls. One room in the SE corner has its original woodwork and the balcony bedrooms still have simple Gothic chimneypieces and grates. Other fittings have been imported, e.g. the handrail and balusters of the stair from a house in Picardy Place, Edinburgh, and the dining room panelling from Clerkington House, Haddington, demolished in 1962.

NEWHAILES   ML (now EL) 3070
1 km. w of Musselburgh

A deceptively plain exterior. The centre block is by *James Smith*, 66 1686. The second stage was a partial refit by *William Adam* from *c.* 1720, and the third contributed the flanking blocks and more interiors which were completed by 1760. Smith's house was built for himself and he called it Whitehill. Its entrance (sw) front is seven bays long with channelled quoins, two storeys and basement, the centre advanced and lightly pedimented. A Roman Doric porch shelters the basement entrance, and over it a double stair mounts to the front door. The wrought-iron balusters and moulded wood handrail are of *c.* 1720 but the doorpiece seems to be Smith's work; tapered pilasters supporting a pediment in which a Janus is carved in low relief with the double head of an old and a young man and the inscription 'Laudo Manentem', 'I honour the stayer' – what better start to a house? In 1709 Whitehill was bought by Sir David Dalrymple and renamed after his East Lothian estate of Hailes, but no significant addition was made to the exterior till *c.* 1750, and even then the new blocks continued the unpretentious stone-dressed harling of the original. The only enrichments are the small keystones over the tall arched windows at the se end.

Inside, Adam designed a new staircase and hall with *Samuel Calderwood* as plasterer. The staircase has disappeared, but in the ENTRANCE HALL Calderwood's jolly stucco is at its best. He put elaborate Roman Doric doorpieces before and behind, but otherwise did not bother with formal structure and concentrated on enlivening the squareness of things. Draperies are thrown over the lugged doorcases for laden vases to be put on top of them; windows are similarly interrupted. Swags of greengrocery are everywhere, and shells stick up in the angles of the cornice. They will appear again and again in the house, sometimes as real shells attached to the stiles of panelling and gilded, as in the CHINESE DRAWING ROOM to the r. which Adam seems to have refitted a little later, for the marble chimneypiece is of his characteristic basket-arch type. The room is perfectly symmetrical, with windows at one end to the front and at the other to the back of the house. The shelved walls may have given temporary space for books and then been used for the display of porcelain. Pier-cases at the ends with gaily moulded tops with oval picture frames and painted floral swags above. The vast two-storey LIBRARY beyond, with a coved ceiling, fills the whole of one flanking block. Its tall windows are not on the main front, which has dummy ones to match the rest. The walls are books,* ten shelves high with a heavy cornice above. Over the two shell-enriched lugged doorways large PAINTINGS of Tantallon Castle and of Hailes Castle whence the family came, by *John Thomson* of Duddingston; they are thus later than the room. The chimneypiece between them is of white and coloured marbles, masks and husk garlands on red, with inner slips of dark green and then yellow. Over it on a foliaged base a gilt wood overmantel with diagonally voluted Ionic pilasters, a lion mask and shell in its broken pediment. Within its frame is a portrait of the son and grandson of Sir David Dalrymple, lawyer, antiquary and historian, who took the title of Lord Hailes when he became a judge in 1766. It was apparently for him that the library, and indeed the whole of the important third stage of the interior, was carried out. But who did the work? It may well have been *John Adam.* It would also be interesting to discover the name of the woodcarver who provided so much and such splendid decoration. Apart from the shells, its constant motifs are quarter-rolls enriched in a Chippendale manner, the larger ones with alternate ribbons and diamond-shaped flowers, lugged frames and Greek-key frets – all as a foil to monumental marble chimneypieces of the first quality. On this circuit of the house they are first seen in the little BUSINESS ROOM between the two rooms already visited, which was subsequently fitted up for the display of china. They appear at their grandest in the DINING ROOM, which balances the Chinese Drawing Room on the other side of the hall, but breaks out through a paired Ionic screen (diagonal volutes) into the newer part. In the overdoors PAINTINGS of four prospects from the house. Chimneypiece with a lion's mask and paws on the lintel. On the far wall a magnificent mirror of bevelled Vauxhall plates repeats the room as if seen through a window. What actually lies beyond is the SITTING ROOM, whose special features are the carved and gilded love-

77

---

* The walls *were* (lined with) books. Since this account was written the books have been removed by the National Library of Scotland on the instructions of H.M. Treasury, despite protests by the Historic Buildings Council for Scotland.

knots over the doors and the front halves of eagles projecting over the windows. Marble chimneypiece with bearded terms supporting the shelf, a garlanded frieze between them.

The upper floor is gained by turnpike stairways at the back of the house, one of them with a wrought-iron balustrade of spiral stalks and tendrils repeated on the curved landing at the head. The stalks are bunched rather than continuous (cf. Hopetoun, p. 255) and the work obviously belongs to Smith's original house. Adam's staircase must have been removed in the mid C18 to make way for grand new rooms. Of the BEDROOMS, three are notable. The puzzle is to say to which periods of the house each one belongs. The principal one is on the main floor at the N end. Its chimneypiece is another in the splendid marble series of c. 1750, this time with a draped female head, the drapery disappearing behind the corner lugs and re-emerging from their centres. The window surround is an arched mirror, glazed like the window itself with bevelled Vauxhall plate. But its DRESSING ROOM shows more of Smith's period, with a corner chimneypiece in which are set an octagonal portrait and an oval marble relief of SS. Mary and Elizabeth. Tiered top with display shelves for china, ending with a gilt finial. To the front (first floor) the ALCOVE BEDROOM with a coved ceiling and a solemnly pedimented bed recess is also of the Smith period, but the palm chimneypiece and painted decoration belong to that of Adam. The GREEN ROOM at the back is also alcoved between Corinthian pilasters, and Smith may have imported the paintings: panels of antique busts over the doors, their shape requiring a coomb ceiling, and a highly mannered wall panel in a lugged frame.

STABLES. 1790 by *John Craig*. Two-storey front with coupled columns supporting a pediment. Pilastered end bays. In the WALLED GARDEN an C18 DOOCOT of lectern type, with stepped gables. (Elsewhere in the grounds a SHELL GROTTO and an OBELISK, 1746, in memory of John, second Earl of Stair.) GATEPIERS in front of the house, plain blocks, pedimented, on piers with vermiculated quoins. The MAIN GATE has flanking arches and a rustic LODGE with lattice windows.

NEWHALL
6.5 km. SW of Penicuik

ML *1050*

A romantic house, frequented and subsequently inspired by the memory of the poet Allan Ramsay, beside a sinuous ravine of the North Esk. The harled s end conveniently shows the front of the old house, with a wall-head chimney gable over what used to be the front door, reached through a forecourt between two projecting ranges. At least part of this dates from the time of Dr Alexander Pennicuik, physician and poet, rather than that of the lawyer Sir David Forbes who acquired the estate in 1703. In 1783 it was bought by the Glasgow merchant Hugh Brown, founder of the weaving village of Carlops, and the house was thereafter transformed by *Robert Brown*, presumably his son, acting as his own architect. He removed the forecourt, refaced the twin w gables of the old house, and added a front porch with a new block jutting out on one side, thus discovering on his own the idea of romantic asymmetry. The style was equally original – crowstepped gables between buttresses with obelisk finials, and some derring-do features like the arrow-slit on the w side of the porch. To the new extension he gave a semi-hexagonal end with pointed first-floor windows. All this is in fine pale stone from Upsykehead, contrasting with the yellow, probably from Marfield, of *David Bryce*'s additions of c. 1850. Bryce did his work with customary tact. Adding an extra storey to Brown's extension, he squared off the first-floor windows but gave the new attic a craggy profile of acute-angled dormers. To the NW he built a round tower containing a new front door, resiting beside it a late C18 panel of pipe and crook, the insignia of the Gentle Shepherd. At the N end he made a square bay with a baronial pepperpot on each side, calmly corbelled out from Brown's angle-buttresses. He also designed the offices to the NE.

Bryce refitted most of the interior, from the dining room at the N end, to which he gave a big thistle cornice, along the gallery which was a feature of Brown's replanning, to the drawing room at the s where he installed a French chimneypiece of brown marble. Two rooms, however, he touched very little – the late C17 LAWYER'S ROOM on the first floor, heavily panelled and corniced, with a bolection-moulded fireplace; and the LIBRARY on the ground floor. On the library ceiling a painting on canvas by *William Aikman* shows a meeting in a Leith tavern of the Worthies Club, including Allan Ramsay, the poet, John Forbes of Newhall and Aikman himself. Round this centrepiece Brown's plasterer made a pretty frame of grapes, crossed pipes and crooks, and corner paterae. The late C18 timber chimneypiece, suitably pastoral in subject, was brought c. 1950 from Buccleuch Place, Edinburgh. Two good chimneypieces of the same date elsewhere in the house are original.

The house is surrounded by minor buildings and statuary. – The RAMSAY MEMORIAL, directly in front of the old entrance, is an obelisk with slightly concave faces, on one of which is inscribed 'Here ALLAN RAMSAY recited to his distinguished and literary Patrons, as he proceeded with the Scenes of his unequalled PASTORAL COMEDY amid the Objects and Characters introduced into it. R.B. 1810'. At its head a vegetable finial surrounded by eight octagonal dials. – DUNMORE MEMORIAL. A graceful obelisk to Robert Brown's grandfather Thomas Dunmore † 1794 of Kelvinside, Glasgow. – MARY CRICHTON'S BOWER. A round stone shelter above the glen, with a thatched roof and pointed windows. Like the monuments, this is presumably to *Brown*'s design. – The present owners have continued the tradition of allusive ornament with a pair of C18 lead STATUES of shepherd and shepherdess at the N end of the house, and have branched out into natural history with two stone horses of oriental character flanking a short ha-ha, and two C19 elephants in artificial stone to the W.

At some distance from the house is the WALLED GARDEN 65 with its main gate to the S, and some of *Brown*'s characteristic obelisks (the cloverleaf pierced stones and another dated 1796 were, however, brought here from one of his outlying properties). It has a perfectly maintained cruciform Scots layout, with two of the original vines in a newer house against the N wall, and a heated melon pit with an iron chimney. – STATUARY. Twin busts of Pan and his mother on the S gatepiers, probably early C18. – The SUNDIAL is composite, a round early C18 table dial with a scrolled stone gnomon on what is probably a late C17 pedestal of four figures of the seasons and their attributes, with foliage above and below.

The STEADING, uphill to the N, is again by *Brown*. Courtyard with walled midden in the centre, barn with flailing floor on the E side.

NEWLISTON
2 km. WSW of Kirkliston

The spectacular landscape garden was laid out by *William Adam* c. 1730 for the second Earl of Stair. The house was designed in 1789 by *Robert Adam* for Thomas Hog, whose father, a

London merchant, had bought the estate in 1747. *David Bryce* added the wings in 1845.

The N part of the LANDSCAPE is virtually entire. It follows the plan of 1759 (probably a survey drawing), still at Newliston, which shows a bastioned rectangle, bisected by a canal fed from the river Almond which cuts across it from W to E – but obliquely so; in fact the whole layout is like a formal one – with compartments, vistas and *ronds points* – which has been deliberately varied and knocked off balance. The resulting disorientation of the spectator is further assisted by such devices as serpentine walks. There is at least one external point of reference, for the central vista of the Union Jack layout at the SE corner is aligned (as noted on the drawing) with Craigiehall some 6 km. to the E. At the intersection is an C18 statue of Atlas supporting an openwork globe. The most contained part of the plan is of course the WALLED GARDEN to the SW, its two long walls pierced by gateways aligned with two of the main N–S avenues. Here is a jolly SUNDIAL, probably of the early C18, a complicated stone prism, the gnomon on each side provided by the bulbous nose of a grotesque mask, carved in profile. The large DOOCOT of lectern type to the SE of the house is probably of that period. The forecourt to the S, defined by a horseshoe-shaped ha-ha, was meant to lead up to a very grand house, though perhaps not such a grand one as *William Adam* designed *c.* 1723 (illustrated in *Vitruvius Scoticus*) with Corinthian portico, attic and wings. The 1759 drawing shows the old C17 house a little to the W of the intended site. It was to survive another thirty years. Only the pedimented STABLE BLOCK to the SW was built in the William Adam manner, and it might date from 1723, when Lord Stair paid Adam himself £150. In the mid C19 a little campanile was added to one side, and a baronial courtyard to the rear. Twin LODGES by *William Adam* flank the main axis to the S of the house. The baronial EAST LODGE was built in 1848.

79   The HOUSE designed by *Robert Adam* is much smaller and more austere – a villa in the late classical manner which he often adopted in Scotland. It is a tall box of the finest grey masonry, droved on basement level, rusticated at the ground floor, and polished at the first and second with their polite giant order of coupled half-columns which combine with the wall of the advanced centre, but carry a pedimented entablature that breaks forward once again. The capitals, in the same fastidious compromise between structure and decoration, are fringed with

upright leaves at the bottom only. Likewise the first-floor balustrade is blind under the side windows but stands free from
the tripartite window at the centre, with its segmental arch. The
drawings in the Soane Museum show an office courtyard immediately to the W of the house and sharing its E–W axis, but this
was not built. The house itself is very slightly out of line with
the garden layout, and perhaps it is not a coincidence that the
rear elevation with its bowed centre faces NNW in a direct line
with Hopetoun House, which can be seen from the top windows
on a clear day.

David Bryce's wings, though they obviously exaggerate the
symmetry which Adam had intended to qualify with his single
outrigger, are as sympathetic as they could be, standing back
from the frontage before they come forward with pediments
and tripartite windows. He raised the ground in front, and
further concealed the basement behind a balustraded area. He
also introduced two lateral balustrades to focus attention on the
main block, and was presumably responsible for the placing of
the twin facsimiles of the Florentine boar.

The plan of the house is simple: a double-pile divided
by a longitudinal passage on each level. On the ground floor
the square ENTRANCE HALL leads into it through Roman
Doric columns *in antis*, their austerity tempered by little
upright leaves under the capitals, their structural purpose by
the fact that they stand not under the triglyphs but the trophied
metopes of the entablature that runs all round. Doric chimneypiece of stone, with ox-skulls and paterae. Domesticity is re-
asserted by the fan centrepiece of the ceiling. In the bowed
(former) DINING ROOM to the rear a frieze whose archaeological trophies alternate with garlands, and a large marble chimneypiece of great refinement in shell pink blotched with grey,
dressed with white panels and low relief vases. Indeed the
variety of the chimneypieces is one of the chief pleasures of this
house: Piranesian, for example, in what is now the dining room,
white marble in the drawing room, with Orpheus between two
tripods. Here also were fitted the needlework panels worked
by Mrs Hog to Adam's design.* From here extends the
L-shaped BALLROOM of 1845, with a predictable Louis XV
chimneypiece in yellow marble, and a coved ceiling with
bracketed cornice.

* These deteriorated, and apparently no longer exist, but are illustrated in
Arthur T. Bolton's *Architecture of R. & J. Adam*, 1922.

PARISH CHURCH. 1742, T-plan, with long-and-short rusticated quoins and moulded cornice, a bellcote on one of the arms, and an outside stair serving the gallery in the stem of the T. Opposite this is a lower session house with a chimneyed gable with two Gothic lancets, scrolled skewputts and a wall sundial dated 1742. Plastered segmental groin-vault. – WOODWORK. Under the centre gallery, two resited fragments of panelling, pilastered and heavily corniced, painted with the crowned attributes of the colliers and dated 1732 and 1747. – LAMPS. A pair of Grecian ormulu pendants of c. 1830, with reservoirs. – MONU-MENT, in the churchyard. 1799. A table-top tomb on balusters for the Somerville family of whom Thomas † 1775, a school-master, is seen with pupils on the end relief panel.

NEWTON HOUSE. Late C17, of three storeys and seven bays. Pilastered doorpiece of c. 1820 on first-floor level reached by a spreading stair. Extension of 1835 to the rear (originally the front) with traces of a doorway on ground level. The vaulted ground-floor rooms and the first flight of the original staircase remain, but the rest of the interior was remodelled c. 1820, with delicate, unusual cornices. – DOOCOT nearby. C16, circular, with newer conical roof, surprisingly gun-looped round the bottom.

Newton is a scattered village on top of coal-miners' rows tied together with steel bands, and farmlands dominated by spoil heaps and the glazed pit-head tower of MONKTONHALL COL-LIERY, 1953 by *Egon Riss*. Of the OLD CHURCH only the C17 tower still stands, 1 km. to the S of the mansion house, pre-served in the C18 with a crenellated parapet so that it would continue to be enjoyed from the grounds of Dalkeith Palace. SCHOOL by *J. A. Carfrae*, before 1914. The FARM STEAD-INGS of Longthorn and Newton itself, of c. 1840, have sym-metrical courts and low-pitch crowstep gables.

PARISH CHURCH. 1942 by *A. Murray Hardie*, a broad, harled church with dormer windows, miniature flying buttresses and a saddleback tower.

The public buildings, such as they are, can be included in a general description. Groome's Gazetteer notes the Marquess of Lothian's collieries and brickworks, and remarks on '... a

painfully unpicturesque appearance, the houses, like most mining villages in Scotland, being built in rows nearly all of a uniform height and elevation ... and of the very cheapest character'. This Victorian fault is a modern virtue. The regular rows
of single-storey brick cottages (the streets called First Street,
Second Street, and so on up to seven) are sufficiently varied
by being stepped up the slope by a large green square occupied
by a large single monkey-puzzle tree, and by minimal oddities
such as the curved entry to LINGERWOOD ROAD. Here, at
the S end, are LINGERWOOD COTTAGES, laid out *c.* 1850 on
an L-plan, with rubble walls and canted bay-windows. The
gabled building nearby, dated 1873 with the Lothian initial and
coronet, appears to have been the colliery school. MAIN
STREET varies the cottage theme with dormer windows and
a few two-storey semi-detached houses of the early C20. The
DEAN TAVERN, which used to be the Newtongrange
Institute, of harl and red sandstone, 1911, and the
PICTURE HOUSE of 1914 at the S end were both designed by
A. Murray Hardie. Towards the N end MONKS' WOOD, a two-
storey terrace of deep red brick ornamentally diapered and
banded with yellow, the date 1871 carved over each of the front
doors. Most of the village would seem to be earlier in date.
NEWBATTLE HOME FARM, to the N. Brick steading and farm-
house.

NORTH BERWICK   EL *5080*

OLD PARISH CHURCH,* Law Road. A plain rectangular kirk, now
only a shell. The sundial at the SE angle bears two dates: 1680
(actually the church seems to have been started in 1659) and
1770. It is all of purple-brown rubble, but the more regular
block-and-pin work and all the white stone dressings belong
to the latter date, when the building was evidently remodelled.
The pattern of tall round-headed windows (keystoned to the
S) and small square ones shows that there were galleries at the
ends, and the pulpit was on the N side. The tower attached to
the W gable, of two stages and three storeys, crowned with a
cornice and ogival slated roof, belongs to the second phase too.
– MONUMENTS, in the churchyard. To the SE a table-top slab
with square baluster legs to John Crawford portioner of Coldingham † 1706 and his family; also a headstone (to Allison Meek

---

* The original C12 parish church near the harbour (*see* below) is now reduced
to the foundations of the W tower.

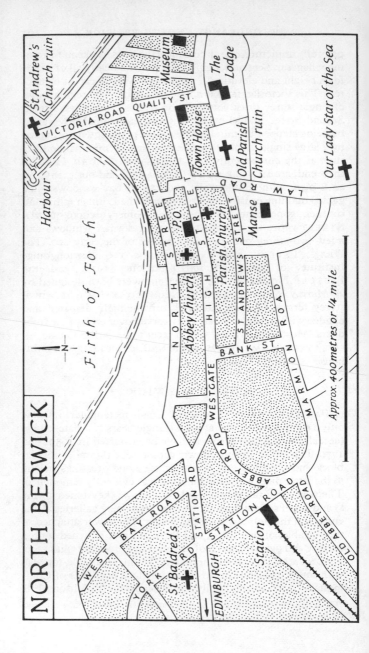

NORTH BERWICK

Firth of Forth

Harbour

St Andrew's Church ruin

VICTORIA ROAD   QUALITY ST.

Museum

The Lodge

Town House

Old Parish Church ruin

Our Lady Star of the Sea

LAW ROAD

Manse

ST ANDREW'S STREET

P.O.

HIGH STREET

NORTH STREET

Parish Church

Abbey Church

BANK ST.

WESTGATE

MARMION ROAD

OLD ABBEY ROAD

ABBEY ROAD

WEST BAY ROAD

YORK RD

STATION RD

St Baldred's

EDINBURGH

STATION ROAD

Station

Approx. 400 metres or ¼ mile

† 1714) whose crude scrolls-on-columns form is seen here and there in the rest of the churchyard.

ST ANDREW'S PARISH CHURCH, High Street. By *R. Rowand Anderson*, 1882. Cruciform E.E. in creamy snecked rubble, quite plain till 1907, when *Henry & MacLennan* added in a yellower stone the heavily buttressed porch with a figure of St Andrew by *Birnie Rhind* on the N (apparently W) front facing the street, and beside it the attached tower which is a North Berwick landmark, with smooth angle buttresses against the rubble, tall pairs of lancets, a blind arcaded top storey with clock faces in the middle, and battlements overall; an admirably confident effect. The inside is plain, with a boarded roof. On three sides a gallery which is deeper in the transepts. To the S a pointed chancel. – STAINED GLASS. A panorama of late C19 and the more conservative C20 modes, but few of the artists are known. Two pairs of lancets under the gallery are signed: to the NE Faith, Hope and Charity, after 1932, and in the next bay 'Worship the Lord' by *J. Ballantine*, 1912. – Likewise two of the round windows over the gallery on the W side, one of 1960 ('Thou shalt guide me'), and one by *William Wilson* ('Him declare I unto you'), 1962. – ORGAN. By *Foster & Andrews*, Hull, 1886, rebuilt and enlarged by *Ingram & Co.*, Edinburgh, 1914.

ABBEY CHURCH OF SCOTLAND (former United Presbyterian), High Street. 1868 by *Robert R. Raeburn* in a sort of E.E. style. Broad gable to the street, restrained by gableted pinnacles at the corners. – STAINED GLASS. A complete if not distinguished early C20 scheme. Superimposed on one window, without disturbing the ensemble, a highly original arrangement of freely suspended panes representing an ascent of doves, by *Sax Shaw*, 1972.

OUR LADY STAR OF THE SEA (R.C.), Law Road. By *Dunn & Hansom* of Newcastle, consecrated in 1879. Facing the road, a Gothic gable with diagonal buttresses and a round window in which the tracery is triangular. The presbytery is set back on the S side. Little wooden belfry on the N. The squared masonry shows that only the nave, sanctuary and presbytery were built in the first stage, but the two chapels to the N by *Basil Champneys*, 1889, seem to follow the original idea. Inside, the little nave looks through the chancel arch into a taller sanctuary with arcaded beam-filling. An arched gallery on the S side is answered by the lower openings into Champneys' chapels on the N side, the LADY CHAPEL with ribbed wagon roof opening

off the nave, the adjacent chapel off the sanctuary itself. Alas
for Champneys' altar, apparently removed under the influence
of the second Vatican Conference and replaced by good taste
in travertine marble. Some vestiges remain of the wall and ceiling decoration that may have been sacrificed to the same cause.
However, a good deal of painted woodwork was spared. –
STAINED GLASS. In the Lady Chapel one beautiful light, unattributed, representing Mary, Star of the Sea.

ST BALDRED (Episcopal), Dirleton Road. Neo-Norman, with
arched and shafted windows in rock-faced walling, the roofs
red-tiled; a puzzling design which despite its apparent uniformity was built up piecemeal to keep pace with the expanding
congregation of residents and visitors in the late C19 and (rather
more cautiously) with liturgical fashion. The original church
by *John Henderson*, 1861, included the three E bays of the
present building, with a lower semicircular apse for the chancel.
It was lengthened to the W in 1863, and an aisle was added to
the N. In 1884 *Seymour & Kinross* lengthened the apse, and
in 1890 added the aisle to the S. For these operations they re-
used the old masonry, and faithfully reproduced it for the apse
at the end of the new aisle. Both apses were raised so that their
roofs were higher than those of the rest of the church, and there
is an uncomfortable feeling of competition between them, even
though Henderson's little belfry was moved to the ridge of the
main one from its original position on the W gable. In 1917
Robert Lorimer added the S porch whose low profile does something to help this curious composition.

The redecoration of the interior *c.* 1954 did not soften the
stark lines of the red sandstone arcades with scalloped capitals
and the open timber roof with its dormer lighting. But it is still
redeemed by its furnishings. – ALTAR. Red Dumfries-shire
sandstone to match the rest, by *Seymour & Kinross*, carved by
Beveridge of Edinburgh. – PULPIT and wall before the chancel
en suite, with Gothic tracery, 1903. – WOODWORK. Choir stalls
and panels over the pulpit by *H. O. Tarbolton*, carved by *Scott
Morton & Co.*, 1910. – ANGEL SCREEN of the S apse by *James
S. Richardson*, 1912. – The ALTAR in this apse, which was
turned into the Lady Chapel by *F. E. Howard* in 1921, is by
the *Warham Guild*. – ALTAR PIECE in the N aisle, with carved
panels of the finest, probably earlier, workmanship, depicting
Resurrection subjects, installed when this became All Souls'
Chapel in 1921. – SCREEN. Very delicate woodwork, fitted at
the same date. – PORCH DOORS. Oak, with low-relief panels

by *Mrs Meredith-Williams*, carved by *W. & A. Clow*, *c.* 1926. STAINED GLASS. The glass in the original apse (Nativity, Crucifixion and Ascension) and S windows (Seventy-first Highland Division War Memorial *et al.*) was piously resited by *Seymour & Kinross* along with the stonework; all by *Ballantine & Son*, with figures in colourful geometric frames, some badly deteriorated. – MONUMENT, in the N aisle. Wall panel of 1843, surprisingly pre-dating the church.

In the grounds of an old people's home in Old Abbey Road the remains of a CISTERCIAN NUNNERY founded before 1177. They consist of a ruined late medieval range running E and W and built of rubble with dressings of a yellowish-white stone. The W part has been a hall, raised on a series of four barrel-vaulted rooms running N and S which can be entered only from the S. The N side is featureless apart from a row of corbels for a wooden lean-to. The upper floor is mostly gone, but its arrangements can be traced. The S wall was lit by small oblong windows wider than high. The W gable had a fireplace and the E gable a large door giving access to another apartment of which only the N wall stands. The line of its roof is preserved on the E gable of the first room, but its main feature is a large fireplace that projects outwards from the face of the N wall, presumably to leave more floor-space inside. Externally it has a series of set-offs like a buttress. In the inside wall of the fireplace a small lancet built up when the fireplace was made. Another fireplace of the same type and date adjoined immediately to the E, and the arched opening between the two is still there, blocked and pierced with a gun loop. A square tower projects from the N wall at the junction of the two rooms. In its W face is a round stair-turret, and at the NE angle a circular turret corbelled out. The tower may have been built around 1587, when the site was granted to Alexander Hume. By 1586 'the place quhair the Albany Kirk and Closter of Northberwick stuid' was ruinous, so what can the extant buildings have been? The most likely answer is that they formed the N range of the claustral buildings, refectory to the W, kitchen to the E. The cloister garth would then be represented by the present garden and the church would lie to the S. The extent of the monastic buildings can be gauged from the segmental-arched gateway on the W side of the garden and the continuation of the N wall for 17 m. E of the kitchen before it turns S.

DESCRIPTION

North Berwick (the prefix distinguishes it from Berwick on Tweed) was the name of a medieval barony belonging to the Earls of Fife from the C12. The settlement associated with the nunnery was also important as the ferry terminal for pilgrims to St Andrews in Fife via the port of Earlsferry. Its status as the mercantile centre of an agricultural area was confirmed when it was made a royal burgh, probably in 1425. By the mid C19 it was a fishing port of some note. The decline in this and other export trades, including wool, was matched by the rise of the burgh as a resort. In 1839 the New Statistical Account was already saying that 'the geniality of the summer and autumn is amply attested in the crowded influx of strangers for the enjoyment of sea bathing and perambulation among the beautiful scenery around'. The topography is certainly enticing. From S to N there are the volcanic cone of Berwick Law, the natural spit ending in the harbour, and out at sea the gull-whitened bulk of the Bass Rock. To the W of the headland are bland beaches, to the E a shoreline of immensely complicated rocks and the historic, lonely enterprise of Tantallon (*see* p. 444).

THE HARBOUR took its present shape in 1887. The adjacent open-air SWIMMING POOL, one of the earliest of its kind, was designed in 1929 by *Henry & MacLennan*. The longer of the two C18 WAREHOUSES, built of deep purply red rubble, was converted to flats in 1970 by *Mary Tindall*. The other (East Lothian Yacht Club) is of variegated rubble with arched doorways. Both have outside stairs. FISHERMEN'S HALL of 1883. By the ruined fragment of St Andrew's church, a Celtic CROSS of red granite by *S. McGlashen*, 1890, a memorial to Catherine Watson drowned in 1889 in a rescue attempt, with a low relief portrait panel of bronze inscribed 'A loving tribute from her fellow students of the Glasgow School of Art, the work of one of their number'.

After the narrow headland, VICTORIA ROAD closes in to an intimate two-storey scale, the E side mainly colour-washed. Opposite Blackadder Church at the junction with Forth Street is a block of HOUSING by *Frank White* for the Town Council, 1973, harled, with stair-turrets to the street, breaking the old building line, but constructively and with uncommon discipline.

QUALITY STREET is admirably regular on the W side, with a late C19 terrace of flats over shops. It is fragmented on the E side, but then come two hotels firmly on the street line: the three-storey DALRYMPLE ARMS, reconstructed in the early C20 but with old crowsteps poking through the roof, and then another in red sandstone dated 1893, converted to flats in 1973. It looks down High Street past the Town House, and after the junction Quality Street broadens out and is lined with trees. Two excellent houses of the C18, possibly as early as the improvement initiated in 1755, are No. 2 (the Beehive), built as a Dalrymple town house, with three tall Gothic windows above, tripartites below, and Nos. 15–17 opposite. Both are of deep red blocks from Berwick Law, alternating with smaller pins. At the end another important town house, THE LODGE, whose two main sections now look on to a grassed forecourt. That to the s has a piend roof, that to the E a chimney gable. Both are C18, but with later *ad hoc* extensions, e.g. in 1883 by *Kinnear & Peddie*. The whole group was renovated as flats for resale in 1964 by *W. Schomberg Scott* for the National Trust for Scotland. Square C18 DOOCOT in the gardens to the rear. WAR MEMORIAL of 1920 at the central intersection, in the form of a tall mercat cross, elaborately carved by *Carrick* to the design of *James S. Richardson*.

HIGH STREET. The first part is very narrow, with the Town House and its ground-floor shops on the s side, but an unfortunate gap on the opposite corner to improve sight lines for traffic. There is a still bigger hole in the street for a garage, but the COUNTY HOTEL, with good Edwardian bar fronts, makes up for it. The next good building on the s side is No. 25, of *c.* 1800, a three-storey tenement of block-and-pin masonry with a pretty fanlight; then a pantiled C18 house whose openings have escaped enlargement. Facing it, the pompous setback frontage of the thick classical POLICE STATION, the wall head kept down under an elaborate deference of dormers; *W. J. Walker Todd* trying very hard in 1933. Then Nos. 58–60, *c.* 1800, with wall-head chimney gable, valuable for its small scale and its adherence to the narrow street line. After it, at the junction with Law Road, a sudden widening. The s side has gone on with a nice Victorian shop (its bracketed lintel detail is a North Berwick feature, repeated at Nos. 120 and 126, on the other side at No. 67, and with a slight difference at Nos. 63–65). It then reaches the corner with a basic early C19 shopfront at No. 57. On the N side the widening is celebrated by the arcaded shopfront of No. 66 (Victoria House), with twirly columns under the gable. Bigger scale and wider frontages now begin to take over. On the N side Nos. 70–80 are a red sandstone terrace with half-timbered gables, early C20, and Nos. 88–100 a grey late Victorian adventure, the corner feature sadly truncated. On the S side the parish church, and the PLAYHOUSE CINEMA, pink sandstone (or synthetic) Art Déco by *J. R. McKay, c.* 1930. Nos. 93 and 125 are small-scale survivals, the former with an ingeniously modernized pilaster shopfront, but the big buildings are now taking over, notably the GOLFERS' REST, the red sandstone pub of 1904 looking down Church Road past the abbey church. On the N side the POST OFFICE with the still unfailing tact of *H. M. Office of Works,* 1906, and then the street changes its name to WESTGATE and its character to that of a road lined with trees and villas. Of these the best are No. 12 (Royal Bank of Scotland) with its rustic gables, *c.* 1840, and also on the N side BLENHEIM HOUSE, a stolid Italian villa of *c.* 1860, originally symmetrical but later enlarged sideways.

LEUCHIE HOUSE. *See* p. 282.

VILLAS ETC.

ABBOTSFORD ROAD. WESTERDUNES. 1909 by *J. M. Dick Peddie.* A mullioned Cotswold mansion of snecked Rattlebags rubble with smooth dressings and pilastered centre doorpiece. Rusticated gatepiers with ball finials. TEVIOTDALE (formerly GREYHOME). 1898 by *Robert Lorimer,* in his cosiest and almost his simplest style. Two storeys, harled and slated, with a far corner turret. BUNKERHILL. 1904, also by *Lorimer* but on a grander scale. A sophisticated Tudor mansion in uncoursed rubble, stone-slated. Masterly contrast of swept-out roofs with battlemented parapets. Round-turreted lodge. CARLEKEMP is noted under its own name. MILTON LODGE. 1896 by *J. M. Dick Peddie* and *G. Washington Browne,* with alterations of 1924–9. White-harled and red-slated, with a dentilled cornice at the eaves, the gables forming steep pediments. Dome-topped bow window to the drawing room. The chimney stalks have been prolonged upwards intricately in red brick.

WEST DIRLETON ROAD. CHEYLESMORE LODGE, up a drive on the S side. Three half-timbered gables united by an arcaded timber veranda, by *George Washington Browne,* 1899.

CROMWELL ROAD. MARINE HOTEL. The centre with its festive four-columned porch, embossed parapet and crowstepped central chimney appears to be the Hydropathic Institution by *Frederick T. Pilkington, c.* 1870. *W. Hamilton Beattie* made a design for the hotel in 1875, and the E end with its bluff round turrets is probably his.

WEST BAY ROAD. Two houses were altered by *Robert Lorimer*: CRANSTON, to which he added a dormered attic in 1925, and ANCHOR VILLA, internally changed in 1911. He also altered PARK END, No. 18 Westgate, in 1923.

MARMION ROAD. No. 28, NORHAM. 1897 by *T. Duncan Rhind* in the 'English cottage style'. Harled and half-timbered, with red dressings including a delicately enriched archway to the porch, and red tiles. In the main gable a plaster strapwork relief. No. 30 is by *Basil Champneys*, 1896. Two harled storeys and a slated mansard, enlivened by a canted stair-turret with Dutch crowsteps on the entrance (S) front, and an ogee-roofed turret enjoying the seaward view from the NE corner.

GLENORCHY ROAD. GLENORCHY. Again by *Rhind* in 1897, but very different from Norham. A hipped red roof is bizarrely enlisted to aid a violent and austere composition of gable and drum tower in snecked red sandstone. It is all tied together with a smooth band of yellow ashlar, but unfortunately the red colour has run down into it.

OLD ABBEY ROAD. MARLY KNOWE. 1902 by *Robert Lorimer*. Entrance (S) front with three bell-cast gables in a line and a gabled service wing. The slate-hung link has a boat-profiled dormer. N front likewise harled and slated, with a pair of gables in the centre. From its E end a harled screen wall with an arched entry joins the main house to the gabled coach house. THE ABBEY. A rambling manor by *Leadbetter & Fairley*, 1909. WINDYGATES. By *Kinnear & Peddie*, 1893, harled and red-tiled, with bracketed and gabled bays and red sandstone dormers.

BEECH ROAD. CEDAR GROVE by *W. J. Walker Todd*, 1914. Harled and red-tiled, with twin bay-windows.

ST BALDRED'S ROAD. EDDINGTON HOSPITAL by *W. Ross Young*, Burgh Surveyor, 1911. A cottagey building, quite at home among the contemporary villas.

WISHART AVENUE. A sensible row of houses by *Richard & B. L. C. Moira*, 1962, won a Saltire Society Design Award. THE GRANGE, on the N side, is of 1893 and 1904 by *Robert Lorimer*. The earlier (E) part, built for Lord Traynor and dated on a wall sundial, is harled and red-tiled, with a Renaissance porch and three gables in a row. The W section, designed for a new owner, Captain Armitage, is on a larger scale, with a rubble base. Strange butterfly-shaped heads to the upper windows.

Loggia to the W, and an outside stair to the garden with iron-work by *Thomas Hadden*. To the N W a strange baronial tower with heavy machicolations, built, it is said, against Lorimer's wishes. It is joined to the house by a crowstepped flying buttress containing a flue. Both sections of the house have examples of Lorimer's characteristic high rooms with deeply coved ceilings. The STABLES and WALLED GARDEN are part of the first stage; the DYNAMO HOUSE, with its boat-shaped gable, belongs to the second.

GREENHEADS ROAD. Three large houses of the late C19. GLAS-CLUNE was designed for J. B. Balfour by *Kinnear & Peddie* in 1889 and built by *Whitecross & Sons* of North Berwick. Interior work by *Scott Morton & Co*. Symmetrical Queen Anne, with four pedimented dormers, the outer ones over two-storey bays, the inner ones carried down to take in the first floor. Roman Doric doorpiece with curly broken pediment. The eclectic interiors foreshadow what Lorimer was soon to be doing. Jacobean timber stair with an arcaded gallery at the head. The ceilings have a touch of Rococo but a good deal more of Tudor; grapes downstairs, roses upstairs. Chimneypieces of *c.* 1750–90 are evidently part of the original scheme. RED-HOLM is by *Kinnear & Peddie*, 1892, the stables 1893 by the same firm, enlarged in 1903 by *Peddie & Washington Browne* who did the gates at the same time. All in a kind of Tudor, of fine-jointed red rubble, with mullioned windows, a Renais-sance porch and brick chimneys. Much altered and extended on its conversion into flats in 1973. ST BALDRED'S TOWER, Jacobean with a castellated Gothic tower, appears to be earlier than the others. Its architect is not known.

FARMS

BASS ROCK FARM (THE HEUGH), 1 km. SE, on the E spur of Berwick Law. Variegated rubble and pantiles. Octagonal horse-mill. Gable to the road with a blind Y-traceried Gothic arch.

BLACKDYKES, 2·5 km. ESE. Red rubble steading with smooth pink dressings and pantile roofs. Cartshed arcade facing the road. Octagonal horse-mill.

NORTH BERWICK MAINS, Law Road. An altered C18 steading. *James Hogg*, mason, built a stable and byre here in 1727.

ROCKVILLE, 3 km. S. In the steading a circular DOOCOT of the C18–19, its upper stage tapering towards a corbel course with a gargoyled and battlemented parapet.

NORTON HOUSE
1 km. N of Ratho

ML* *1070*

Built in 1840, and on the outside only the elaborate Renaissance porch betrays its transformation for the brewing family of Usher *c.* 1890. The inside is eclectic indeed. Entered between liver-coloured marble columns, the staircase hall is finished in oak, with a gallery on the half landing. Oak chimneypieces and pedimented doorpieces throughout the ground floor. Details range from Jacobean to neo-Adam. Dining room with oak dado and chimneypiece *en suite*. The chimneypiece has brass lions and *William de Morgan* tiles. In the drawing room a compartmented and delicately moulded ceiling still nicely painted in its original green and gold.

NUNRAW
1 km. E of Garvald

EL *5070*

The name denotes the nuns' row or hamlet; in the C16 the interest of the last three prioresses of the convent of Haddington in this property was variously combined with that of their kinsmen the Hepburns of Beanston. Nunraw is now a baronial mansion of 1860 incorporating the Hepburns' C16 tower house, all in deep red sandstone. The older work consists of a long block running E to W, with square towers to NE and SW and round stair-turrets in the two NW angles. The RCAHMS notes the similar Z-plan layout of Hatton Castle in Angus, built in 1575. Only the NE tower is externally unaltered; rubble walls and a parapet supported by a billeted corbel course of shallow projection, with the addition of a rope moulding under the open bartizans at the corners. Big gargoyles drain the wall walk, and there is a cap-house in the middle. Everything to the S of this tower follows the C17 building in general outline, though all is refaced in ashlar with new mouldings except the fancy corbelled parapet of the SW tower. To the E, a Georgian OFFICE COURT with depressed arches, entered through a turreted C19 pend, leads to what must have been the main door, from which passages go past vaulted cellars to the two turnpike stairs. The inscribed lintel and canopied niche above the door were added after 1880, when Walter Wingate Gray made the painted room into a chapel.

---

* Now Edinburgh.

The alterations and additions carried out by Robert Hay in 1860–4 are decidedly antiquarian in intent: the new staircase is a turnpike in the angle of the NW extension, the parapet is clumsily derived from the old design, and there are curious balconies like open-topped oriels. But it is very dull, and the interior no less so, though the restoration of huge Spartan apartments only to be pedantically subdivided into bedrooms suggests a remarkable zeal for a kind of authenticity. Much linenfold panelling in oak was installed after 1880.

During alterations in 1864 to the first-floor room at the E end of the main block a tempera painted board-and-joist ceiling was discovered. It bears the joint monogram of Patrick Hepburn and his wife Helen Cockburn, and the crowned thistle with lion and unicorn supporters suggests a date after the Union of 1603. Each compartment (two to the S are missing*) contains the arms of a European king held up by putti and supplemented by trophies and exotic beasts which include an elephant. The under-sides of the beams, which are nicely treated with a guilloche pattern of ribbons, have escaped the adzing that was so often the prelude to plastering. The white ground has gone, but a good deal of red and yellow survive, and the black line drawing is still unrestored and lively.

DOOCOT, N of the house. Beehive type, of six diminishing stages, with a sort of belfry added to the top in the C19.

SUNDIAL, to the S. Polyhedral, with cupped dials.

LODGE and GATE, to the W. Red sandstone, arched and turreted.

SANCTA MARIA ABBEY. By *Peter Whiston* from 1951, built mainly by the Cistercian monks who came to Nunraw in 1946. A startling apparition over the smooth fields on the hilltop, whence it can see as far as the Highlands, and not at pains to be different from a factory or a disciplinary institution. But at closer quarters the quality of siting, materials and detail is evident. The stone, from the reopened Rattlebags quarry near Dirleton, is of a yellow colour sufficiently variegated to be interesting in itself. For its period, the design is an uncommon feat of discipline. Basically it is a large square divided into four, with a cloister to the NE, a sheltered garden to the NW. The refectory, which separates the garden from the 'work cloister' in the SW quarter, has the one large chimney of the whole establishment (serving the boiler house) at the far end. The remaining quarter to the SE, when built, will have to do with visitors. All

* They are in the National Museum of Antiquities in Edinburgh.

the buildings of the s half will be rendered with plain cement.
The CLOISTER has obtuse triangular arches, all glazed, with
heavy timber frames. Along its E side will be the church, housed
for the time being in the N range. From the SW corner a flight
of steps ascends to the hexagonal anteroom and then the
REFECTORY, in which big stone piers and a timber ceiling are
the dominant features. The cantilevered lectern is one of the
very few period mannerisms. On the w wall a head of Christ
with four hands receiving the Sacrament, by *Anne Henderson*,
in Rattlebags stone.

OCHILTREE CASTLE
4 km. SE of Linlithgow

WL *0070*

A three-storey house of some pretension, L-plan, with the internal
angle to the NE. The RCAHMS quotes an account of the date
1610 inscribed on one of the wall-head dormers taken down
in the early C20. The other details are complete and unrestored:
rounded window margins, cavetto-moulded eaves, crowstepped gables and splayed chimney-heads. Round turrets at
the SE and NW corners carried on moulded corbels, the latter
more elaborate. The original entry was presumably at the foot
of the round stair-turret in the angle. The present doorway,
on the W side, with a big quirked edge-roll frame, is curiously
planted against the wall. Mounted on top of it what might be
a large dormer-head: three finialled gablets, two with heraldry
and the initials of Dame Grizel Ross and Sir Archibald Stirling
of Keir, the third rising between them. The door probably has
been moved, as the RCAHMS suggests, but its position makes
sense in relation to the internal remodelling that probably took
place in the late C17, with a straight stair to the first floor just
inside, and a new kitchen in the extended N jamb. Apparently
there was a courtyard to the W, for some C17 fragments can
be seen in the buildings on the N side.

OLDHAMSTOCKS

EL *7070*

PARISH CHURCH. Signs of an older church include the spreading
base of the E end wall to which the Hepburn aisle was added
in 1581; it has a stone roof, an elaborate moulded cope with
heavy corner finials, and a thistle at the apex of the gable, in
which a window with pleasantly crude tracery (some of it
merely sketched into the stone) is flanked by two splendid

armorial panels. The building was recast in 1701, a N jamb with a family aisle, entered through a pedimented doorway, making it into a T-plan. On the S side are two roll-moulded openings of this date, and the S door of the Hepburn aisle with its alternately blocked courses is probably contemporary. The pointed windows are newer in workmanship if not in form, and although the staged W tower may be original (or even basically medieval), the belfry, its pyramidal finial set diagonally above the cornice, is of the later C18. A SUNDIAL of intriguing geometric profile, evidently of 1701, is bracketed from the SW corner. Inside, the Hepburn aisle was developed as a 'chancel' in successive C20 alterations including that of 1930, which supplied the woodwork. It has its original ashlar vault. The arch opening into the family aisle has been renewed in segmental form, making the old half-round jambs look foolish. – MONUMENTS, in the churchyard. The C17 and C18 specimens are weathered and broken, but two later ones are worth a mention: a headstone with ball finial to John Dods † 1782 and his son Peter, cabinetmaker in London † 1781; and a stone to James Broadwood, wright, † 1774, and William Broadwood, wright and feuar in Oldhamstocks, † 1820 (this is the piano-making family). – WATCH HOUSE, to the S. 1824, neatly pedimented.

'Old Dwelling Place' is well named, because its prosperity came to an end with the large-scale agricultural improvements of the C18. Along the N side of the road a pretty row of pinky-purple rubble interspersed with black whin. Then the green, with an C18 pyramidal-topped PUMP and the MERCAT CROSS (the village was given the right to a weekly market in 1627), its ball finial repeated at the apex of the wide-gabled house, with hoodmoulded windows, to the S; its neighbour HILLCREST is a little later – c. 1840. The road goes on to the church between the miniature C18 steading and the walled garden of the manse to the S, the mid C19 school to the N.

ORMISTON HALL, 1.5 km. SSE. Only some fragments of the two successive houses. First the Hall, built for John Cockburn of Ormiston by *John Baxter*, mason, in 1745–8, extended by *Alexander Steven* and *George Tod* for the Earl of Hopetoun in 1772, and further enlarged in the early C19. Of this there is only a doorpiece and three ground-floor bays, with a projecting section of five bays to the r. Beside it, a zigzag wall with slits at

the angles, probably a screen to a laundry yard in which clothes
were dried. Then the old ORMISTON HOUSE of which a part
has been incorporated in the office courtyard nearby. This includes vaulted cellars and an arched and roll-moulded doorway. – DOOCOT to the SW. C18, cylindrical, with plinth and
parapet. Wooden nesting boxes.

ST GILES PARISH CHURCH, to the S. Another fragment, this
time medieval, with a pointed window in its E wall, a pointed
door to the S. In the N wall an arched recess for an effigy. Over
it, in a moulded frame, was the brass* commemorating Alexander Cockburn † 1535 *aet.* 28 in Latin elegiacs that recite
the details of his continental education.

NEW PARISH CHURCH. *See* below.

GREAT YEW, by the ruin of Ormiston Hall. An idiosyncratic
house, but architecturally conservative, by *Ian G. Lindsay &*
Partners, 1972.

The shape and history of Ormiston are now more interesting than
its buildings. About 1735 John Cockburn started to plan a new
village on his estate, to the E of the then existing mill hamlet.
It was to accommodate not only craftsmen for local needs
(blacksmith, shoemaker, and so on) but also a considerable cottage industry of spinning and weaving. Plots were feued off on
both sides of the wide High Street where markets were to be
held, and Cockburn provided building materials, but insisted
on certain standards. 'I can give my consent to no houses being
built in the Main Street of the town but what are two storeys
high.' Yet the return from these and other investments was not
sufficient, and in 1747 Cockburn had to sell the village to the
Earl of Hopetoun. The Statistical Account calls it a farming
village and refers to the failure of the linen trade; the distillery
closed down in 1811. What survives is the street line with closed
ends, and in the middle the C15 MERCAT CROSS, paradoxically
(for this new village) one of the very few pre-Reformation and
actually cruciform examples in Scotland. A tall monolith with
a filleted cross at the head of a shaft, it may have been connected
with a chapel that stood athwart the present High Street, and
made over for a new role in Cockburn's village. The street is
nobly lined with trees.

From E to W, HILLVIEW with its canted centre bay is of the mid
C18. The house on the corner of Cross Loan is probably of
Cockburn's time, though only its scrolled skewputts escaped
a dreadful recasting of *c.* 1930. The early C18 MANSE on the

* This is now in the National Museum of Antiquities in Edinburgh.

other side is set back from the street front. Dormered attic storey of *c.* 1840. Further to the w a continuous row with a pend giving access to backland buildings, ending in the POST OFFICE, which used to be the inn. It could have been built in 1736, the date of a sundial at the head of the wall, and so could a similar row on the s side. Past the corner shop which has another scrolled skewputt (No. 5 The Wynd) the High Street narrows. On the N side an early C18 house with a bullseye window, drastically altered. Change first set in when John Clark founded the Ormiston Coal Company in 1903. His contribution included the oriel-windowed house on the s side of the street. The PARISH CHURCH is by *T. Aikman Swan*, 1936. WAR MEMORIAL by *Fanindra Bose*, 1925. OBELISK in Peterhead Granite to Dr Robert Moffat by *D. W. Stevenson*, 1884.

Ormiston is now a sizeable mining village of respectable inter-war housing, with Cockburn's High Street as its pleasance.

0060   ORMISTON HALL   ML

1 km. SW of Kirknewton

A compact house of medium size built in 1851 of stugged and snecked ashlar for Sir Alexander Wilkie by *David Bryce*, with all his baronial trademarks. The entrance front enjoys the N view. Tall gable over the door, crowned with an eagle and flanked by a corbelled stair-turret. In the w front a canted bay, corbelled out to square, with a crowstepped gable. A square bartizan marks the NW angle. Dormered service wing to the E.

OVERHAILES *see* EAST LINTON

3060   OXENFOORD CASTLE   ML

5 km. ESE of Dalkeith

The core of Oxenfoord is the old tower of the MacGills, who were given the title of Viscount Oxfurd in 1657. The direct line came to an end in 1755, and thus it was that Lady Dalrymple, de-scended from the first Viscount's daughter, inherited the prop-erty in 1779. In the following year her husband, the lawyer and polymath Sir John Dalrymple of Cousland, engaged *Robert Adam* to enlarge the tower. In 1840 the fifth Baronet became the eighth Earl of Stair, and took on *William Burn* to bring the house up to date, so Adam's E (entrance) front is now half sub-

merged in Burn's weighty yet pedestrian additions; a great pity
as far as the outside is concerned, for the sloping ground on
this side provided the necessary dramatic setting for Adam's
castle manner.

The old tower, of course, is completely lost except for the
thick walls within the new castle. So it was at Culzean in Ayrshire, which Adam had similarly enlarged in 1777: tall turrets
at the corners of the central block, little dummy bartizans on
the corners of the wings. But at Oxenfoord the whole thing was
enlivened by full-height bows at the centre of the s and w
fronts. Still better was the E front; the porch has been engulfed,
but even without it the square and solemn upper half, relieved
by a recessed arch, clearly looks forward to the maturity of
Adam's castle style. On its blunt top recline two beasts chewing
the cud, a pun on the castle's name.

Burn had to provide more accommodation, and although he
respected Adam's work in some ways he seriously weakened
it in others. Under Adam's patently symmetrical entrance his
long new E front, of one storey and basement, is tiresomely near
to symmetry, but its fearsome entrance portal is not on the same
axis. The staircase tower behind it is the only decisive new element. The s front is doubled in width, the tall bow cut down
to one storey and given a more pretentious brother in the shape
of a canted bay. To the w it is reasonable to have given the
centrepiece an extra storey, understandable to have stuck out
another canted bay on one wing, but very odd to have added
a vertical – positively Tudor – bay through the full height of
the other. Solid worth, and undoubtedly the convenience of the
times, have taken precedence over c18 clarity.

Inside, Burn's ideas and those of his client excite more sympathy. The entrance hall is admirably accessible to the N service
wing and servants' stair. For visitors there is an impressive zigzag ascent through one lobby after another, with the MORNING
ROOM on the E side, a passable imitation of c18 work with a
(possibly resited) marble chimneypiece with wheatsheaf centre,
not of the best quality. On the s side the LIBRARY and DRAW-
ING ROOM *en suite*, of the utmost magnificence, with white
marble Louis chimneypieces, high white ceilings with gilt Jacobean ribs flowing into the bay-windows that looked so mean
from the outside, lacy gilt cornices and pelmets, all against
brown shelves and deep red wallpaper. Adam's modest cantilever STAIRCASE remains, filling out the original L-plan to a
rectangle. The ground floor of its well was also the hall, and

it opens into the DINING ROOM in the middle of the W side. The pretty woodwork here is of *c.* 1750, with carved swags and landscape paintings in panels all round. The ceiling is less happy. It has quite a delicate garland of grapes round the centrepiece, but the Rococo fronds and large thistle suggest that the whole thing may be an uninformed effort dating from soon after the formation of the bow window.

BRIDGE across the glen near the castle. Castellated, with three semicircular arches, by *Alexander Stevens*, 1773.

STABLES, 1 km. WNW. Courtyard with crowstep gables.

NORTH LODGE. Castellated drum with lattice windows, cast-iron gates between octagonal piers. These are both probably by *Burn c.* 1842.

OXENFOORD HOME FARM, 1 km. W, across the A68. A pair of two-storey C18 ranges with piended roofs, linked by a segmental archway.

CRANSTON PARISH CHURCH. *See* p. 143.

PARDUVINE *see* CARRINGTON

3060   PATHHEAD   ML

A single wide street on the A68, 1 km. long and curving up-hill, lined almost continuously with one- and two-storey houses of the mid C18 and after. The earlier roofs are pantiled and of steeper pitch. A monogrammed stone at No. 101 bears the royal warrant mark of the leather-workers.

CRICHTON HOUSE. *See* p. 147.

VOGRIE HOUSE. *See* p. 462.

To the S of Pathhead by the A68 is the site of a ROMAN CAMP (*see* Introduction, p. 29).

4060   PENCAITLAND   EL

PARISH CHURCH. The main body of the church is a long buttressed box apparently of the C16 or early C17, but probably standing on medieval foundations. Y-tracery in the E wall, lean lancets in the S wall. Round-headed doors converted into windows at the W end and another (blocked) farther E in the S wall. Sundial on the E gable. Of greater appeal are the three adjuncts to this basic structure, i.e. the W tower, the N (Saltoun) aisle and the N chapel. The W tower is square for most of its height, but at the top it turns octagonal and apparently serve

as a combined belfry and dovecot. In each face a small lancet.
Pointed slated spire. All this is presumably of 1631, the date
on the lintel of the w door. In the angle with the w wall a gallery
stair. The Saltoun aisle was formerly entered through a fine
mid C17 door in the w wall. Pilasters, broken semicircular pediment with a shield among strapwork. Above this a cartouche
with the initials S.I.S. (Sir John? Sinclair). To the r. a blocked
window of two lights. Immediately E of the Saltoun aisle a two-
bay chapel, normally dated to the late C13. But is it not rather
a case of Late Gothic conservatism? True, the gabled buttresses
and the tiny corbels used as label stops look C13, but the placing
of the buttresses away from the corners and the absence of any
on the end walls seem too arbitrary for the C13; and the tracery
of the w window is surely too crude. The other windows were
blocked and a square-headed door below a round window put
in when the chapel became a pew in the C17. The E window
tracery dates from 1882. The wall head has been raised and
the corbel table reset at a higher level. The individual corbels
have nicely carved heads. Rough buttresses with set-offs have
been slapped up against the original buttresses.

Inside, the thickening of the wall E of the N aisle may
indicate the position of a former chancel arch. The plain wide
arch to the N chapel was put in to accommodate a C17 loft which
still existed in 1880. It replaced a two-bay arcade of which the
coarse E respond partly remains. The mouldings to the rear-
arches of the windows cannot be C13. – PULPIT. Polygonal,
made up on a new base in the C19 with earlier chip-carved
panels of rosettes and symmetrical foliage. Attached to it a
wrought-iron bracket for a baptismal basin. – PEWS. The front
row in the Saltoun aisle is of Dutch character in oak, c. 1600,
with an arcade supported alternately by fretted corbels and by
reeded pilasters sprouting up into crude Corinthian capitals.
The front of the w gallery is treated in the same way, but heavily
grained and varnished. – ORGAN, opposite the pulpit. A happy
intrusion into the middle of the church, by *Peter Connacher* of
Huddersfield, 1889; the pipes stencilled in colour. – STAINED
GLASS. At the E end of the N chapel, three lights and a roundel
(Faith, Hope and Charity, and 'A New Commandment') by
C. E. Kempe, 1883. – At the E end two lights (Motherhood, the
Sower) by *Guthrie & Wells*, after 1924. – MONUMENTS, in the
churchyard. E of the church a fine table-top of the early C18.
– On the s wall, a crude but ambitious tabernacle to D. Pringle,
farmer, † 1733. – On the w wall a Renaissance tablet to 'Ka(th-

erine) Forbes, Daughter to Mr Jo(hn) Forbes Minister to the English Merchants Adventurers at Delf' † 1639. She was the wife of the minister John Oswald whose initials are carved over the w door. – JOUGS. On the NW buttress, by the outside stair, is fixed the ring and chain for the delinquents' collar. – OFFERTORY HOUSES, in the churchyard. With pantiled roofs, probably C18. – MANSE, to the s. Early C19; pretty Gothic with canted bays.

Pencaitland is divided into two by the river Tyne, and united by a BRIDGE whose main arch is supported on five ribs, the lowest at the centre. A shield on the s side bears the engrailed cross of the Sinclairs and the date 151(0?).

EASTER PENCAITLAND has the parish church. On the other side of the road is a row of pantiled cottages of the late C18 with privies quite acceptably attached to their fronts. Beside them are two gateways. One is to Winton House (see p. 472), the other to PENCAITLAND HOUSE, built in the late C17 by James Hamilton, Lord Pencaitland, or possibly just enlarged, for it had an old-fashioned centre block with a chimneyed gable at each end. This was burnt in 1878, but Hamilton's pavilions still stand as two separate houses with their curved link walls, of two storeys, handsomely dressed, with deep cornices and bell-cast roofs. ST MICHAEL'S is a Tudor villa of c. 1840, but the remainder reflects the picturesque taste of Lady Ruthven, 'patroness of every beneficent scheme, donor of every useful gift', who was mistress of Winton from 1846 to 1883. Her largest contribution was the SCHOOL, built in 1870 with an arcaded and inscribed porch supporting an ornamental turret (now truncated), and enlarged for the School Board in 1887 with three little spires and a plaque commemorating the Queen's jubilee. All quite dotty, but for fun of the lighter kind it is the best thing in Lothian.

WESTER PENCAITLAND has a MERCAT CROSS which may date from 1695, when the village became a burgh of barony under Lord Pencaitland. Stepped pedestal, octagonal shaft and sun-dialled crowning block. The lectern DOOCOT may be of the same period, but the single row of older pantiled cottages and the STEADING with five cartshed arches seem to be of c. 1800. BELFRY COTTAGES, probably converted from an early C19 school, have a bellcote and the stone figure of a pupil over one of the porches. The rest is largely the work of the Trevelyans of Tyneholm (see below); one pair of cottages is inscribed A T 1881 on its timber dormers. Further to the w, four single-storey terraces dated 1907 and 1910, still intended for miners. The SCHOOL by the church is the work of *Stanley Ross-Smith*, 1974.

TYNEHOLM, 0.5 km. SE. A Jacobean mansion by *William Burn*, 1835. Modest in size, but the entrance front spreads effectively from the main w block, with a strapwork doorpiece, to the E office wing dominated by a little square tower. The two principal rooms are *en suite* to the w, the further one with a Louis chimneypiece. Grecian balusters on the well staircase.

FOUNTAINHALL. *See* p. 205.

WINTON HOUSE. *See* p. 472.

PENCRAIG HILL   EL *5070*

1 km. w of East Linton

On the hill, an impressive standing stone, 3 m. in height.

PENICUIK   ML *2060*

PENICUIK HOUSE is described below, at the end of the entry on the town. p 385

ST MUNGO'S PARISH CHURCH. Possibly by *Sir James Clerk* of Penicuik, dated 1771. Between the round-headed windows of the w front a sturdy Roman Doric portico of bold projection. The rear part is a porch, well defined by angle pilasters, its cornice the same height as that of the piend-roofed body of the church. Flaming urns on the corners of the pediment, and a cross in the middle which was considered Popish according to the Statistical Account. The other elevations are spoiled by dull additions dated 1880, and even this one has been trivialized by a sort of suburban front garden. Interior devoid of interest. – ORGAN by *Casson & Miller* of Perth, 1887. – HEARSE HOUSE, to the N. A plain rubble shed, but elegantly dated 1800. – MANSE. Of *c.* 1820. The twin blocks to the w, with niched elevations to the street, are the wings of the old manse which was contemporary with the church.

OLD PARISH CHURCH. A tidy ruin in the churchyard to the E of the new one. Of the tower the first two stages are late C17, the belfry stage with round-headed arches of 1731–2 by *William Thomson* and *James Alexander*, masons. Pyramidal roof with ball finial. The tower is attached to the surviving w gable. In place of the church itself, a neat line of MONUMENTS and burial enclosures. In a fragment of the old s wall a moulded recess with an early c17 tablet with a Crichton-and-Adam shield. The enclosures of the Hays of Newhall and the Clerks of Penicuik face each other with identical late c18 doorways. Adjoining the latter is the MAUSOLEUM built by Sir John Clerk for his wife, dated 1684, square, with tiny, heavily moulded apertures. The base moulding and cornice and the ogee base of the crowning pyramid are all effectively massive. Elsewhere in the churchyard some excellently crude stones including a number in memory of departed stonemasons. Built into the e wall of the church, a pedimented headstone dated 1737 to 'Annabel Millar spouse to Thomas Rutherford Papermaker at Pennycuik'. Near it a free-standing stone dated 1709 to Janet Melrose, spouse to John Hodge. Inscription on drapery between two disarmingly paraphrased Ionic columns. On the reverse, three standing figures, a full-length skeleton between two babies.

SACRED HEART (R.C.), John Street. 1882. Plain Gothic with chancel and n aisle.

ST JAMES THE LESS (Episcopal), Broomhill Road. The original lanceted church of 1882, which now forms the nave, was designed by *R. T. N. Speir* of Culdees, the plans being drawn under his direction by *Henry Seymour* of *Seymour & Kinross*. It is of coursed rock-faced masonry with a w bellcote and a later n door and w porch. The rest, by Kinross's later partner, *H. O. Tarbolton*, 1899, built as a memorial to Sir James Clerk, eighth baronet, consists of a chancel (over a vestry built into the fall of the ground) continuing the roof-line of the nave, but with Perp windows. A very simple tower against the s side, slightly battered, is crowned with a low pyramidal roof behind the stepped battlements. The projecting stones on its n side were to have been carved with the Clerk of Penicuik arms and a cuckoo perched on the hoodmould. The additions are in snecked rubble with smooth quoins to match those of the older work. Inside, the nave has an open roof of four bays. The chancel roof, seen through the arch, is compartmented. To the s a pair of arches opens into the base of the tower. – REREDOS. Eight carved and painted panels, as a war memorial, by *Mrs Meredith & Williams*, 1921. – ALTAR RAIL made by *Scott Morton & Co.*, 1911, and ROOD SCREEN, 1912, with figures carved by *Thomas Good*, both designed by *Tarbolton*. – PULPIT formerly in St Mary, Soho, London. – STAINED GLASS. An excellent lot, including one light at the se end of the nave (St Patrick), 1903 by *Shrigley & Hunt* of Lancaster, who seem to have done most of the pre-1914 glass, and four magnificent lights at the w end (angels on a blue ground) by *Kempe*.

SOUTH (former United Free) CHURCH, Bridge Street. A master work by *Frederick T. Pilkington*, 1862, sadly frustrated by the absence of the spire. It is not a large building, but the effect is of such prodigious complication – even for Pilkington – that the underlying simplicity is not at first easy to grasp. In fact it is basically symmetrical on the E–W axis, though this is masked by the snuffer-roofed session house lying low against the s side, the tower against the N. And it is basically square in plan, despite the apparently mad combination of hipped and jerkin-headed gables and glissading, snow-boarded roofs. The purpose of them all, starting with the little gabled apses to NW and SW, is to build up to the huge E gable facing the street. This, with the tower beside it, is the final triumph of the stone-work that has elsewhere had a hard struggle to push the roofs up from the ground.

The E gable displays Pilkington's whole repertoire of virtuoso 34 modelling and texture (though not of the polychromy seen at Irvine at the same date). Its lower part is a porch; its upper windows light the back of the gallery. The porch is of four rock-faced arches each bearing on four shafts with leafy capitals of suitable vigour (this is shared by all the stone carving, and it is a pity the name of the sculptor is not known). Above them, three *œils-de-bœuf* as a pretext for narrowing the interest to the centre part of the gable. This corresponds with the break in the main roof and is framed by big pilasters supporting a cusped arch with rock-faced, radial voussoirs under the skew. Within it, a glazed colonnade, its narrow stilted arches lower in the middle to allow for the plate-traceried rose window. The outer sections, a parody of transept ends, have clasping buttresses that send up their own cusping, rock-faced against ashlar, from diminutive shafts. Meantime the tower, starting massively square in plan, has turned into an octagon, with tabernacles (unfinished) against the diagonal faces. Corbelled shafts at each angle, their capitals merging into a sculptured belt which includes a lovely angel over the N clock face, prepare to support the tall spire that was never built. It would apparently have been slated, its tallness emphasized by tri-angular lucarnes.

The explanation and the fulfilment of all this enthusiasm is inside, though it must be admitted that the detail is of a lesser order. Not so the carpentry, however. The square shape is fully expressed by an open pyramidal roof of brown stained timber,* set on spirally foliated shafts at the corners, the principals nicely distinguished from the common rafters. At the centre a chief kingpost; three more over the three apses to N, W and S. To the E the floor and pews are raked. Gallery on barley-sugar columns. Over it the roof is held together with wrought-iron ties. – FURNISHINGS. Not notable in themselves, but the ensemble of the whole religious auditorium, its family intimacy, and the pride of place and comfort given to pulpit and communion table, its jewelled glass in mesmerizing patterns, are disarming beyond all praise. – ORGAN. 1901 by *Hamilton* of Edinburgh. – MANSE (former) in Bog Road. Two baronially gabled blocks in snecked masonry, the canted bay to the front corbelled out in the Bryce manner, by *John Kinross*, 1896.

UTTERSHILL CASTLE, 1 km. S, on the road to Howgate. The ruined late C16 house of the Prestons of Gorton, with a moulded doorway in the middle of one side. It had a straight scale stair ascending from it, and a big segmental-arched kitchen fireplace at one end of the basement. It now has very little except a remarkable panorama of the town.

COWAN INSTITUTE, High Street. 1893 by *Campbell Douglas* of Glasgow, built by *James Tait* of pink freestone from the Moat quarry near Carlisle. Scots Renaissance, with a crowstepped gable over the grandly balconied triple window on one side of the street front, a dormered profile on the other. Between them a tower with an octagonal ogee-roofed belfry and a big bracketed clock.

VALLEYFIELD MILLS. What survives of the older mills, including the range in which French prisoners were housed in the Napoleonic War, is of archaeological interest only. But by the river is the MONUMENT of 1830 by *Thomas Hamilton*. It is in the form of a large sarcophagus with acroteria, supported on a massive swept-in base, and bears the inscription in English and French 'The mortal remains of 309 prisoners of war who died 1811–14 in this neighbourhood are interred near this spot'. It was paid for by Alexander Cowan, whose heavily altered house of *c.* 1830 stands up-hill with a bay-windowed summer house. At the entry to the mills, Gothic, and also of *c.* 1830, the CHAPEL, with a bellcote and some traceried windows, and the SCHOOL, with cylindrical chimneys and inside a Gothic

* The original glossy brown varnish was stripped off the pews, and everything else in reach, in 1977.

fireplace of *c.* 1860, in the style of *Pilkington*, with a raised inscription 'Little Children Love One Another'.

Penicuik lies on the w bank of the river North Esk, 180 m. above sea level, in the foothills of the Pentlands whose bare outline appears between the houses and looming over the c20 suburban sprawl to the NW. John Clerk acquired the lands and barony of Penicuik in 1646, and about 1770 Sir James Clerk, the second baronet, laid out a new town on lines already suggested by his father Sir John. The plan remains, but c19 prosperity led to almost complete renewal as far as houses were concerned. A paper mill established at the riverside in 1709 and bought by Charles Cowan in 1779 grew mightily for a time but was closed in 1975. The old weaving industry came to an end much earlier. Coal mining has survived, and new industries have been established on the Eastfield Estate.

HIGH STREET. Only a few landmarks from Sir James Clerk's day – the portico of the church at the E end, and beside it the wings of the original manse, a good group but dwarfed by the Cowan Institute (*see* above). The ROYAL HOTEL on the corner of John Street was rebuilt in the early c19 and clumsily altered afterwards. The rest is nondescript Victorian or later. What survives to the w is the lie of the ground, which means that the N side stands up on a terrace with the OLD WELL, octagonal with a vase finial, by *J. A. Bell*, 1864, built at the expense and by the desire of the late Alexander Cowan. The RAILWAY TAVERN is a unique survival from the late c18. The s side, which maintains something like a Georgian regularity and has a good shopfront (long bow between pilasters) and chemist's sign at Nos. 5–7, slopes down to the corner of Bridge Street.

BRIDGE STREET starts with a detour into THE SQUARE, entirely rebuilt but with a nice early c19 pilastered shopfront at No. 24. Then on the w side the fancy mid c19 lodge of CAIRNBANK, a bargeboarded villa. The E side is unadventurous, with the exception of PARK END by *F. T. Pilkington*, *c.* 1862, three houses on the sloping street, a gap in the frontage bridged by a pointed arch. The end house has an arched corner porch resting on a big cylindrical shaft and sprouting an octagonal baywindow which is really a sort of dormer turret. Like the other dormers it has pink granite shafts, echoed in the earthenware flue pipes that are seen between the corner piers of the chimney stalks. Ruskinian carving abounds, and Ruskinian diversity; leafy capitals, little balls in the coved mouldings of arch stones, some of which are of pink stone. Where not otherwise enriched,

the whole thing is of rock-faced masonry. The separate tenement at the back, uncomfortably close, is of ashlar with rock-
faced bands. On both sides of the street are local authority
houses of the 1960s in an earnest combination of rubble and
harling, standing well on the slope. On the w side the South
Church (*see* above), Pilkington once more; he would make anything else look genteel.

WEST STREET. On the corner the baronial BURGH CHAMBERS
of 1916 and the Gothic SOUTH CHURCH HALLS of *c.* 1845.
On the N side No. 1 has a perfect shopfront of about the same
date, its five windows with the original glazing.

BOG ROAD has two notable villas. First, NAVAAR HOUSE
HOTEL (formerly RED GABLES), built for one of the Cowan
family *c.* 1910. Nonchalantly composed, but each section is
half-timbered on the upper storey, white-harled on the lower.
The gables are tilehung with red tiles like the roof, the one towards the road inset with classical medallions. To the S a little
tower with pyramidal roof and weathercock. The second villa,
CRAIGIE HOUSE HOTEL, was built in 1885 as a house for
Professor Ewart, the zoologist, by *Sir George Washington
Browne*. Snecked red rubble with smooth dressings, rather like
a rectory, with a Gothic front door and Gothic windows in the
huge buttress-ingle against the end gable. But then a big bay-
window on timber corbels carved as snakes and crocodiles, half-
timbered and pargetted on the gabled upper storey, with
curious bargeboards. There is also the former Free Church
MANSE at No. 18 (*see* above).

JOHN STREET. Nos. 41–47 on the E side are a good two-storey
terrace of *c.* 1845, of snecked rubble, with intricate lozenge glazing intact. Beyond them a series of substantial villas of the same
period. The R.C. church (*see* above) stands back behind a stolid
classical SCHOOL of *c.* 1850. John Street goes on towards Edinburgh through the middle of an interesting area of C20 housing.
Bowhill Gibson designed houses for the Town Council in 1927–
39; his chief contribution was the Carlops Avenue–Pentland
Terrace scheme to the w of the junction with Carlops Road.
R. J. Naismith of *Sir Frank Mears & Partners* finished the N
end of Pentland Terrace (1945) and then started work to the
E (1947–9) with long harled rows of quasi-Georgian design. The
housing he designed along John Street itself (1952–9) includes
the CORONATION CLOCK TOWER of 1953. The Ladywood
scheme on the w side is also his (1956); behind it is a large
estate built by the *Scottish Special Housing Association c.* 1950.

Other housing developments were provided by large contrac-
tors employing consultant architects, e.g. the Cuiken Avenue
scheme by *Louden* (*Peter Daniel*, architect) and two schemes
by *Harrison* (*James Gray*, architect), all in the early 1960s.

MARTYR'S CROSS, 1 km. NW. A small two-storey house of C17
origin with a candle-snuffered stair-turret, extended in 1748
and later known as a schoolhouse. Gothic being the educational
style, this use may date from *c.* 1800 when two of the gables
were given rudimentary pediments and Gothic windows. The
rubble walls were stripped of their harling *c.* 1960 and a tactful
addition put on in 1977.

SILVERBURN FARM, 3 km. W. Traditionally the sawmill of the
Penicuik estate, powered by the burn. CARNETHY, the cottage
at the nearby junction with Hopelands Road, has some nice vernacular stone carving with the monogram JDT and the date
1855; to the rear a profile portrait in relief of the young Queen
Victoria.

AUCHINDINNY HOUSE. *See* p. 83.
BEESLACK HOUSE. *See* p. 99.
BELLWOOD HOUSE. *See* p. 101
MAURICEWOOD HOUSE. *See* p. 320.
PENICUIK HOUSE, 1.5 km. SW. Penicuik* represents the ideal 81 & 82
of a Scots Palladian house in a romantic, yet classically inspired,
landscape. The grounds were laid out by *Sir John Clerk* whose
grandfather had bought the estate in 1646 along with the house
of Newbiggin. Sir John thought of remodelling the old house,
but came to the conclusion that it looked 'better in its antique
figure than if it was all new built'; his main architectural
achievement was Mavisbank House (*see* Loanhead) on another
Midlothian estate. It was his son *Sir James Clerk* the third
baronet, succeeding in 1755, who pulled down Newbiggin and
replaced it with a house to his own design, starting in 1761.
The end blocks were added by *David Bryce* in 1857. In 1899
the house was gutted by fire and its notable interiors were all
but lost. Sir James's stable block, whose plain portico and
Gibbsian spire are effectively related to it, has made a very good
house for the Clerks of the C20.

As a young man James Clerk, like his father, had been a law
student in Leyden and had gone on to Rome as an amateur
of architecture. He developed a practical ability much greater
than that of his father, and Penicuik shows him to have been
a disciplined designer of some originality. He consulted 'Mr

* Alistair Rowan: *Country Life*, 15 and 22 August 1968.

Adams' – probably *John Adam* who subsequently provided the timber for the house. But it was *John Baxter Sen.* who realized Sir James's perfectly competent drafts, first in finished drawings and then in the house itself, using yellow-grey sandstone from the Marfield quarry nearby. An inscription over the service entrance at the back of the house reads:

Ao. 1761 MASTER JOHN BAXTER SENR MASTER BUILDER
MASTER JAMES BLAIKIE MASTER CARPENTER

Three widely spaced windows each side of a hexastyle Ionic portico; a long attic interrupted only by thin strips that continue the vertical lines of the order; a basement enlivened by sideways stairs with intermediate landings; the FRONT is, in short, a stretched version of Palladio's Villa Capra. No refinements of texture, no token balustrades, and the minimum relief of the skyline with vases (now gone) over the portico by *George Anderson*, 1764. In the previous year he had been paid for the diagonally voluted Ionic capitals, the pedimental coat of arms and the Venetian windows at back and sides. The portico has a bold projection of two free columns. Beneath it, in the niches flanking the door, are two statues of druids carved by *Willie Jeans* in 1776, suitably primitive in execution. *Bryce*'s taller end blocks, whose crowning balustrades detract from the austerity of the house in its present form, must have looked less bulky when the whole thing was roofed. They faithfully reproduce the detail of the original, and at the BACK they are much less obtrusive, for here Clerk gave special importance to the projecting centre of the attic, which contained the library, with three arcaded windows and the merest hint of a pediment – a thin cornice very slightly tilted up towards the centre. As to the main storey, he gave it a Venetian window at each end and later employed *John Baxter Jun.* to remodel the windows of the dining room with moulded arches pushing up into pediments supported by consoles, a Roman mannerism which gave a new and rather nervous interest to the centre. The work was finished in 1778. From the central opening a bridge leaps on to the raised ground, the path then meeting a pedimented niche with a fountain before passing over another bridge. Very little survives within the house except the evidence of an old-fashioned symmetrical plan with twin cantilevered stairs of excellent construction in ovoidal wells on each side of the entry. Of *Alexander Runciman*'s scenes from Ossian painted in the cove of the dining room ceiling there is nothing. A square room whose brick vault has lost its plaster adds to the impression of a leafy Roman ruin.

The present house has been formed within the STABLE 83 COURT (including the former coach house, brewhouse and bakery), which is again by *Sir James Clerk* and *John Baxter Sen.* The front, seen obliquely from the ruined house, is of eleven arcaded bays, the end ones slightly advanced, the three centre ones brought forward by another arch-width to carry a simple pediment on which is mounted a steeple adapted from James Gibbs complete with a clock by *James Pringle*. It was all done by 1766, including the reproduction of 'Arthur's O'on' that surmounts the pedimented arch on the far side of the courtyard. What on earth is this? Arthur's Oven was the popular name for a building at Stenhouse, Stirlingshire, destroyed in 1743; visible from the Antonine Wall, it was probably a Roman shrine or victory monument. Here it is reproduced as a doocot. The conversion of the stable court as the new house (following the failure of the insurance claim for the full repair of the old one) was carried out by *Lessels & Taylor* and completed in 1902 to the wishes of Aymée Lady Clerk. The result is an example of antiquarian conservation in the best Clerk tradition. In the LIBRARY a moulded fireplace, presumably from the house of Newbiggin, dated 1662 and inscribed HEB. III 4 (for every house is builded by someone, but he that built all things is God). The wall niches in the DRAWING ROOM are the stable mangers left *in situ*, but the broken pedimented doorcases are from the old house, and so is the chimneypiece whose moulded frame is flanked by stiff caryatid figures supporting the shelf. A contemporary chimneypiece in a bedroom has an egg-and-dart frame, the shelf held up by blocks with guttae. Both are of white marble, presumably that shipped from Leghorn in 1766 and carved in part at least by *John Tasker*. Beams are exposed under the low ceilings, including lattice-webbed girders salvaged from *Bryce*'s extension of the old house.

John Clerk succeeded as second baronet in 1722, but began to plant the grounds from 1700 and continued until his death in 1755. The E avenue was formed in 1728, and by 1730 he had planted more than 300,000 trees. In that year he built the WALLED GARDEN to the W, and within it the little two-storey pavilion of ESKFIELD in brick with stone dressings and a pedimental gable with vases. In 1738 came the S avenue and the CENTURION'S BRIDGE over the Esk, humpbacked, with two side arches forming shelters like sentry-boxes. It leads to

ALLAN RAMSAY'S MONUMENT in Cauldshoulders Park. Sir
John wanted a feature here, but it was his son who built it in
1759 – an obelisk pierced with round holes over a round-headed
archway. The CHINESE GATE of fretted and painted timber
at the end of Cauldshoulders Avenue was erected by *James
Blaikie* in 1758. HURLEYCOVE and the Hurley Ponds were
made in 1741–3. Hurleycove is an artificial tunnel some 40 m.
long, entered by a rusticated arch and passing a little round
chamber on its way through the hill. On the wall above the stone
bench the inscription TENEBROSA OCCULTAQUE CAVE (Be-
ware of what is dark and hidden). Machicolated Roman
WATCH TOWER on Knight's Law, directly in front of the
house, of 1748–51. LODGE and GATES on the A701 by *Peddie
& Kinnear*, 1872–3.

PHANTASSIE *see* EAST LINTON

0070   PHILPSTOUN HOUSE   WL
                  5 km. WSW of South Queensferry

A harled, symmetrical house with crowstepped gables advanced
at each end, built for John Dundas, whose initials are carved
in the centre of the strapwork doorhead over the cornice of the
roll-moulded (former) front door. Chamfered stone window
dressings, the date 1676 over the middle one on the upper floor.
The original basement, which seems to have vaulted ceilings,
has been filled in. Simple wall-head moulding. SUNDIALS at
three of the angles. A staircase jamb, giving access right up to
the attic, projects from the centre of the back, where the
RCAHMS say there was a farm courtyard. Some internal finishings of the late C18, but most are of the early C20, when a
politely crowstepped extension was added to the N end. (DOO-
COT of lectern type with two chambers, and a stone inscribed
ID ED 1725.)

4060   PILMUIR HOUSE   EL
                      2 km. WSW of Bolton

A small but boldly individual house of 1624, orange-harled, with
two storeys and a dormered attic. In the middle of its single
range a square staircase tower, crowstepped like all the other
gables but rising a whole storey higher. On its top floor a cove-
ceilinged room served by a stair whose round turret bulges

out on the W side of the main tower, and bulges so far that it needs the support of a squinch in the angle. It also sets a roofing problem which is solved in pragmatic fashion. All this high-level excitement is balanced by a low-level extension to the E, its roof continuous with the slope of the main one. Over the moulded doorway on the front of the stair tower a dated stone panel which also bears the initials of William Cairns and his wife. In the early C18 a new front door was formed on main-storey level in the centre of the S front, the windows were given their thick astragals, and new pine finishings were installed in all the rooms. (The room at the W end on the main floor however still has its original ceiling of ribbed plaster, with moulded enrichments.)

The S front overlooks and adjoins the WALLED GARDEN. DOOCOT to the S, contemporary with the house. Of almost square lectern type, with 906 nesting boxes entered by holes half-way up the pitch of the roof. BEE-BOLES in the garden wall.

PINKIE HOUSE see MUSSELBURGH

PITTENDREICH HOUSE
2 km. NE of Lasswade

ML *3060*

By *David Bryce*, 1857, for Sir George Deas. Medium-size Jacobean baronial, but turretless, and dominated by crowstepped gables, two of them symmetrically composed on the entrance (E) front with a pair of corbelled chimneys and a central balustrade, two more on characteristically chamfered bays to the S and N. An ingeniously sunk office wing to the SW. The entrance is simplified externally but still has a little balustraded terrace and an angled stair leading down past the DOOCOT, C18, with a double-pitch roof and crowstep gables, to the lodge which is contemporary with the house. Indoors, a drawing room and library *en suite* along the S front, a thistle-corniced dining room to the NE. Their chimneypieces and overmantels were nicely up-dated in a C17–20 manner by *Lorimer & Matthew*, 1928. The owner was then *Douglas Strachan*, who did the three stained-glass panels in the upper sashes of the library. The staircase is not on the grand scale, but shows Bryce's flair for achieving lively detail through his craftsmen.

POGBIE *see* HUMBIE

PORT SETON *see* COCKENZIE

PRESTON

Preston means 'priests' town', for the monks of Newbattle and Holyrood had lands here. Today it is not so much a town or a village as an interesting incident alongside the road to North Berwick. Important buildings of the C17 and earlier have survived, but the only way to see them as a group is from a London-bound train passing to the S; to the SE is the STATION of *c.* 1845, with low-pitch gables. Nearly all the ordinary buildings of the old burgh have gone, and the others now find themselves on the fringe of a large area of C20 housing which joins Preston to Prestonpans (*see* p. 398). There has long been a division of importance between the two places, Preston having the mercat cross and Prestonpans the parish church. The battle at which Prince Charles Edward defeated Sir John Cope's Hanoverian army took place to the E of Preston.

ST GABRIEL (R.C.). 1965 by *Alison & Hutchison & Partners.* Basically circular, with white roughcast walls of eccentric profile. The chancel walls describe wider concentric arcs to the E; the porch does the same thing at the other end, faced by an opposite curve to form the glass-sided baptistery. – The STATIONS OF THE CROSS in terracotta and enamel by *Frederick Carson* are in tune with the simple drama of the interior, and so is the thick coloured glass of the lady chapel; some of the other furnishings are not.

99 MERCAT CROSS. The most handsome in Scotland, probably built just after 1617 when Preston was granted the privilege of holding a weekly market and an annual fair; more's the pity that it is now an isolated roadside monument. Round pilastered drum, 4·2 m. in diameter, with six shell-headed niches with seats; in the other two intervals doors, one into a chamber within the drum, the other to a winding stair up to the platform. Parapet corbelled out on an ingenious entablature, with Doric guttae under each of the eight spirally moulded waterspouts. The central shaft is an oval-section column; the unicorn on top holds a cartouche carved with a lion rampant. The well matched yellow sandstone is lightly weathered but the carving is still crisp, its quality equalling that of the best work of the time, e.g. at Winton House.

MARY MURRAY INSTITUTE (formerly Schaw's Hospital, i.e. School), to the E. Plain symmetrical Jacobean, roughcast with crisp stone dressings, by *William Burn*, 1830. The windows on the ground floor have hoodmoulds, those on the first floor pointed gables. Centre bay with a curvilinear gable. Doorway with a four-centred arch. Chimneystacks break forward from the end gables. The gabled profile to the rear (that is to the road) is more picturesquely irregular, though still symmetrical. Very plain interior, vestigially Grecian.

BANKTON HOUSE, to the S, the other side of the railway. The shell of an early C18 house with a basement and two storeys. Curvilinear wall-head gables to front and rear, and a pedimented front door reached by a bridging stair. The end gables are also shaped, and the house is so deep in plan that there is room within the roof for two attic storeys, the upper lit by single windows between the paired chimneystacks. This was the house of Col. James Gardiner, one of Cope's officers at the battle of Prestonpans (*see* above), who fell within sight of it. – MONUMENT, to the N. An obelisk with four lions at the base in memory of Col. Gardiner, by *A. Handyside Ritchie*, 1853.

HAMILTON HOUSE, adjoining the main street to the E. Property of the National Trust for Scotland. A two-storey house of double-L plan, rendered and white-painted with stone dressings, built by John Hamilton whose initials, with the date 1626, appear in the heraldic carving over the front door. The two jambs with crowstepped gables project forwards to form a courtyard (the low wall to the road is part of a successful restoration *c.* 1930). In one angle is the quasi-octagonal stair-turret and entrance, in the other the well, and a little round turret boldly corbelled out overhead. The two main first-floor dormers have moulded margins. Pedimented window to the stair-turret, with a thistle finial in relief. Below the pediment a hand points to the inscription PRAISED BE THE LORD MY STRENTH AND MY REDEIMER. The interior is unusual for its date, with the main rooms *en suite* on the ground floor. In the hall a wide fireplace, slim pilasters supporting an entablature with a monogrammed tablet in the middle. Two window embrasures beside it are united by the device of a large corbel holding up their twin arches. Moulded fireplaces in the dining room and (in the N jamb) the study. The former has wall cupboards with checked margins. The woodwork of the windows was decorated *c.* 1960 in imitation of the Northfield tempera work.

NORTHFIELD HOUSE, adjoining the main street to the w. Early 54

C17 and virtually intact, but based on a slightly earlier house
– a simple rectangle with a turnpike stair-turret and the main
door at the N W corner. In the kitchen in the vaulted basement
a segmental arched fireplace and an oven in the E gable. Then
a new owner, Joseph Marjoribanks, transformed the house both
inside and out. He added rooms to the W end, projecting so
as to form an L shape with the old turret in the angle. Flat-
ceilinged basement. New kitchen at the N end. On the S wall
head a crowstep-gabled DOOCOT shoots up at a dizzy angle,
and the skyline is further enlivened by dormers and by corbelled angle turrets with pointed roofs at the four main angles.
The whole roof is enfolded by swept slating. The turrets at the
E end (to whichever date they belong) are particularly effective,
one pushing out a little further from the roof than the other,
and the big kitchen chimney sticking up between them. The
harled walls are no less sculptural than the roofs.

The N barmkin wall runs along the roadside, a C19 baronial
bartizan making a gazebo at one end. The jambs of a moulded
archway which still form the entrance may be of the earlier date.
The house itself is entered by the new front door which Marjoribanks placed on the S front. It is inscribed under the pediment 'EXCEP THE LORD BUILD IN WANE BUILDS MAN', with
his initials and those of his wife, and the date 1611. Inside, he
or a somewhat later owner installed a scale-and-platt staircase
to the first floor where the early C17 tempera decoration of the
rooms (latterly subdivided) survives in uncommonly good condition – untouched since its discovery behind later plasterwork
in 1956. What are now the W room and the passage have a board
and joist ceiling painted with birds and fruit. The ceiling of
the NW room is decorated with fruit; the timber wall, divided
into compartments by the exposed frame, with bold sweeps of
leaves and flowers. Among them appear, in the uncovered part,
55 a hound, a cock, the leg of a deer and the brush of a fox. The
colours are red oxide and pale blue, fresh and quite matt in
texture, overlaid by rapid black line work of the utmost delicacy
and assurance. On the second floor, reached by an early C19
stair within the old angle turret, the whole of Marjoribanks'
W range is filled by a long drawing room. Over the early C19
chimneypiece a stone mantel of the early C17 from Woolmet
House, Midlothian, damaged by subsidence and finally demolished in 1954. Here also some fully intelligible tempera
work has been revealed: arcading in grisaille, keystones with
red lions' heads, a leafy ochre frieze. The architect of the admir-

ably conservative realization of Northfield since 1954 has been its owner, *W. Schomberg Scott*.

DOOCOT to the SE, now in a public space. Beehive type, but probably C17.

STEADING, mentioned here because it is just across the road. Mostly early C19, its pedimented dormers possibly a quotation from Hamilton House. Most of the square brick chimney has been taken down.

PRESTON HOUSE, to the E, forms no part of the public scene in Preston, but shows that the Hamiltons, who built it as their chief house after the fire in the Tower, were still in the forefront of architectural progress. It is only a fragment – the N wall of a late C17 house with a recessed three-bay centre in a long front, and twin pavilions, one still with its ogival roof. The most interesting features are the linking serpentine passages, concave where they curve out from the main front, convex where they abut the pavilions. Was this elegant solution ever produced elsewhere? Of this tantalizing frontage only the basement and main storey survive. GATES, to the E. A concave arrangement of rusticated piers, contemporary with the house.

PRESTON LODGE, at the E end of the main street. A Jacobean Gothic villa of *c.* 1850 with a shaped gable, bulkily extended *c.* 1890 in the same grey stone with a great show of cast-iron cresting on the roof-line.

PRESTON TOWER, to the NE. The shell of the C15 tower-house of the Hamiltons of Preston, enlarged upwards in the C17. The old tower is of L-plan with six storeys, corbelled at the wall head. Two big corbels project defensively over the entrance doors to basement and main storey, on the E side, not in the angle of the L. The slit windows on the S side show the position of the main stair. In 1626 the parapet with its corner bartizans was rebuilt, and within it was constructed a sort of two-storey house on the same L-plan, with Renaissance windows and a shaped wall head with swept-up merlons. Pedimented windows, triangular below, above segmental and bearing the initials SIDKH for Sir John and Dame Katherine Hamilton. (Inside, the RCAHMS note the fragment of an elaborate C15 fireplace and a possible C16 plaster cornice in the tunnel-vaulted hall. They also say – in 1924 – that the building has been conserved in recent years; an early use of the term in connection with buildings.)

DOOCOT, to the N. C17 lectern type, with three ball finials.

GATEWAY, to the E. Twin piers supporting a divided pediment, each part crudely scrolled.

91 A long baronial house, its entrance front (facing N to the sea) virtually all by *W. H. Playfair*. The W half of the S front is earlier. Even from this view it is not easy to see how it began. Prestongrange used to be called Newbattle Grange because it belonged to the abbey. The earliest datable part is the late C16 centre, extended to the E probably by Alexander Morison, a Lord of Session from 1626, linking the two parts with the corbelled stair-turret which has a step-off, also corbelled, at the top. The house was recast internally about 1750; the thick astragalled sashes given to the E extension are still there. The first stage of Playfair's work, begun in 1830, consists of a new block to the S and some development to the E end. These were early days for the real baronial revival; Burn's round-turreted Tyninghame of the previous year (*see* p. 456) may be compared with Playfair's bold cuboids and chamfers, the latter undeniably more positive in composition even though Burn was to become the master of a more antiquarian baronial style. Playfair's new block is of three storeys plus dormers. On to its corner is grafted an octagonal entrance tower with a pointed roof, an ogival-roofed stair-turret at one side. For the other side he designed a long main-storey balcony on brackets, very like Burn's at Tyninghame (both have unhappily decayed and been removed). As an outrigger to the W, a square turret with a chamfered base. Playfair's additions of 1850 to the E are more decisively baronial: a square tower recalling those of the C16, with tall gables very skilfully joined to it. On the S side it stands unobscured. A short link connects it to the older work (whose roof-line it shares), incorporating a Renaissance-style doorway with strapwork head which opens on to a square balustraded balcony and stair, the balustrade continuing to the E past the ground floor of the old work, which has now become a half-sunk basement.

The front door leads straight upstairs to the main storey in a single noble flight, with Tudor newels. Ahead is the drawing room, of mid C18 character except for the lovely neo-classical chimneypiece of *c.* 1810, in white statuary marble, with twin caryatid terms, a mask-and-foliage frieze and a central panel of putti playing a wedding game. Or rather, it was so till 1962, when everything except the arched pier-niche and its swagged enrichment was obscured by alterations. In the course of the work a board was raised on the floor above and found to be painted on the underside. A large board-and-joist ceiling was then discovered, dated 1581 and painted in red oxide on a grey ground with surprising grotesque motifs and figures. It could not stay at Prestongrange in suitable conditions, so the greater part of it was reinstated at Merchiston Tower (now part of Napier College) in Edinburgh. Adjoining it to the w is Playfair's dining room with a bay on each side of the house, its cranked but symmetrical plan according with its geometrical ceiling. The black marble chimneypiece likewise echoes the big bolection moulds of the doorcases. Similar care is taken with the quiet Renaissance design of Playfair's other chimneypieces throughout the house. But in the drawing room of his new s block, conventionally Grecian in its cornice, he re-used a splendid mid c18 example: the mantel of wood, with masks over inverted consoles, the inner architrave of beaded marble.

PRESTON HALL
6 km. ESE of Dalkeith

ML 3060

A large and highly finished house by *Robert Mitchell*, 1791. Mitchell was born in Aberdeen but practised from London; 'a man of limited invention but considerable refinement', says Mark Girouard,* and indeed this house is a showcase (a rather old-fashioned one at that) for many ideas that go back to Robert Adam. So is Moor Place, Herts., which seems to be next in importance among his surviving works. Yet there is also an awareness of contemporary developments and a considerable deftness in the ensemble. And the repetition of favourite details is a virtue when, as here, it gives homogeneity to the whole.

Alexander Callander returned to Scotland in 1786 having made a fortune in India. The estate (which he bought in 1789) included Crichton Castle (*see* p. 144) and the huge old house of Preston Hall, built in 1700 and overhauled and enlarged by *William Adam* in 1738. Callander died in 1792 before the completion of its replacement. A description of the new house must begin with the garden (s) elevation because in Mitchell's design it provided not only the show-front but the entrance. Centre

* *Country Life*, 31 August 1961.

block of seven bays with four plain pilasters, their capitals leafy and voluted, rising from the rusticated basement to support a bullseyed pediment; a balustrade above the cornice, a frieze of upright brackets below it. The (former) front door is reached by a stone-balustered perron staircase. A very long elevation stretches out symmetrically on each side. Mitchell's main block is not as long as the old one, but he seems to have retained Adam's far-flung pavilions because the present Callanders report that alterations to the windows have been revealed by internal repairs. Along this vast length Mitchell maintained the interest by giving a separate focus to each section: to the pavilions by means of balustraded centrepieces with domed and weathercocked templets (derived from Robert Adam's at Edinburgh's Register House); to the three-bay links by tabernacle centrepieces on which recline the over-lifesize figures of warriors, ancient and classical respectively. The N front became the entrance front in 1832. With its quadrant links it is well enough suited to its new role, though the blind arcade of the three middle bays was obscured by a porch of darker yellow sandstone than the rest.

The interior must be taken in its present-day order. The square ENTRANCE HALL that now introduces us to the house was originally its innermost sanctum, i.e. the library. It curiously combines a Soanic flat dome on pendentives with the intricate finishings which are more characteristic of Mitchell: the white marble chimneypiece, first of a good series, is decked with musical instruments and a centre panel of a female figure with a globe. The STAIRCASE is rather informally reached in the new arrangement. Its central position, with service stair to the W and pendentived corridor to the E, makes the deep plan virtually into a double-pile. It is the decorative as well as the spatial climax of the house, and there is some conflict between the two. Oval dome on pendentives, with top lantern, a panelled segmental vault at each end; beneath them on all four sides an opening with composite columns *in antis*, and four lifesize figures in *Coade* stone (each one different) bearing lamps. To this level the stair ascends in two main flights, the cantilevered steps shaped underneath, with iron balusters of great delicacy formed of lyres joined by thin swags. The most telling detail is the holding back of the balusters from the fascia of the landing at each end; the weakest is the intermediate pilaster sprouting from brackets part-way up the stairs. But any claim to neoclassical austerity was finally waived by the pretty pastoral wall decoration on first-floor level in the *grotesque* manner of *David Roberts*, c. 1830.

In the DRAWING ROOM at the SE corner a ceiling with a central umbrella surrounded by interwoven garlands and swags in the early Robert Adam manner (cf. Auchencruive, Ayrshire). At the ends, long painted panels depicting figures of Summer and Winter, with grisaille corner roundels of Justice and Prudence, Temperance and Fortitude. The decoration is dated *in situ* 1801, but the wall treatment of pale green powdered with stencilled motifs in gold must be of *c.* 1830. The tripartite window on the E side is an isolated classical feature flanked by composite columns and pilasters recalling (not for the first time in this house) the work of Mitchell's contemporary James Playfair (*see* Melville Castle). The chimneypiece of *c.* 1900, with babies sitting archly on Corinthian columns, was imported recently from Park Street, London. In the middle of the S front the MORNING ROOM (formerly the entrance hall), finished with elaborate austerity, the plane of the wall interrupted by blind arches with radiating husks over the doors, the frieze repeating the upright brackets of the exterior; Doric guttae underneath, plain paterae between them. In the late C19 the flat surface of the wall was given a comfortable, wholly interior character by a deep blue damask wallpaper of superb quality. The chimneypiece with caryatid terms was brought here from the drawing room. In the LIBRARY (former breakfast room) a frieze and ceiling in the Adam manner, and a chimneypiece with Orpheus and musical ladies in relief. Finally the DINING ROOM at the NW corner. The chimneypiece is a variant of the one in the morning room, with a long panel of putti and goats at a vintage, the ceiling a swagged oval, the sideboard recess framed and arched with an abundance of late C18 haberdashery. Altogether an elaborate farewell to the Adam manner.

The PARK was laid out to embower the house, and *Mitchell* exploited it with a TEMPLE on the knoll which closes the N vista; octagonal, swept inwards to eight thin columns and a dome. WALLED GARDEN to the W, probably by *Mitchell* too. Red brick, with two-storey octagonal pavilions, stone-dressed and pedimented, over the conservatory on the N wall. The garden itself still has its proper cruciform layout. On the outside of the S wall buttresses with lions and roses and an eccentrically shaped doorway dated 1888, which is a surprise in view of the chunky character of the carving. The STABLES to the NE have coupled columns and a pediment. Taller ends with thermal windows. LODGES to the S, twin blocks, with pedimented windows in blind arches. The pedestrian gates are in tabernacles supporting *Coade* stone lions; ironwork of spider's-web pattern below, spiked railings above. To the N a pair of GATEPIERS of *c.* 1700, with alternate courses of blocks and fluting, bearing vases. Elaborate wrought-iron arch between them.

9070   PRESTON HOUSE   WL
                        1 km. S of Linlithgow

A baronial house of considerable presence, very much in the manner of *David Bryce*, built *c.* 1840 in stugged ashlar. Unusual crowsteps, continuously moulded on their outer edge, the crowning stones with ogee Gothic finials. The asymmetrical entrance front has two such gables and a Renaissance doorpiece. At each end is a corbelled turret, a square one in Pinkie style, and a round one adjoining the smaller-scale offices. Then a screen with miniature arcades on each side of a big archway with a bellcote on top. The other two fronts are quite symmetrical, with the same square turrets at the ends. The long one, facing the splendid view to the N, has a pair of Bryce's favourite bay-windows, canted below and then corbelled out to the square under crowstepped gables. On the W front the ground floor has a large central bow which proves to be the conservatory, its mullioned glazing virtually continuous with that of the drawing room and dining room on either hand. All the large ground-floor windows have big horizontal panes between the mullions. The smaller ones have the conventional twelve lights. Jacobean interior with slim ribbed ceilings, the staircase leading quite modestly off the S side of the long central hall. Marble chimneypieces, quite plain except for two of the Louis XV kind in the drawing room and in the study which has the key position in the middle of the N front.

PRESTONKIRK *see* EAST LINTON

PRESTON MILL *see* EAST LINTON

3070   PRESTONPANS   EL

PARISH CHURCH, Kirk Street. One of the first post-Reformation kirks in Scotland,* built in 1596 by *John Davidson*. The round-

* The much more sophisticated Burntisland church in Fife dates from 1592

headed and roll-moulded s door belongs to that time, and so does the square w tower, knobbly and cream-washed. Its 28 broach roof and octagonal belfry may have been added as late as 1774 when the church was almost entirely recast and much enlarged. Running E and W, it has round-topped windows and a s jamb whose upper storey contained the Hamilton Loft; the outside stair is still there, and the lower level (perhaps the session house) is entered by its original doorway with heavily keystoned Gibbs surround. In 1911 the N jamb was added by *W. E. Wallace*, together with extensions to E and W for porches and a new gallery staircase – all quite congruously both outside and inside, where the main feature is the Wrenish casing of the ORGAN by *Ingram* of Edinburgh. The white marble FONT is of the same date but most of the other fittings are of 1891. – PAINTING in the N jamb (which has no gallery), possibly of the C18, showing a ship of the Royal Navy among fishing craft in a stormy sea. Frame with gilded shells and anchors. It belonged to the Fishermen's Society of Prestonpans. – In the sexton's lodge by the gate are MORTIFICATION PANELS of the late C17 and early C18, their lettering renewed in 1853. – MONUMENTS. On the gable of the former Hamilton Loft, a mid C18 wall-tabernacle to William Grant of Prestongrange. – In the churchyard, a collection of C17 and C18 stones in the local style, less numerous and more disturbed than those at Tranent. – In the E wall a small Ionic columned tabernacle with a pair of portrait heads in oval frames, one inscription defaced, the other recording John Hepburn † 1675. – To the s of this a larger one, with a coat of arms in its scrolly broken pediment, a skull and martial trophies below. It commemorates 'John Stuart of Phisgul ... barbarously murdered by four High-landers near the end of the Battle fought in the field of Preston, on the 21st Sept. 1745'.

GRANGE CHURCH (formerly Free Church), Ayres Wynd. 1878 by *R. Thornton Shiells*. A simple lanceted barn in grey sand-stone, but the front to the street has a porch with stair wings, plate tracery and a complicated bellcote at the head of the gable. Happy interior, its steep, wide four-bay roof on Gothic braces which rest delicately on slim iron shafts. – STAINED GLASS. Of the two pairs of lancets flanking the pulpit, *Ballantine & Gardiner* did one in 1896 and presumably did the other too; they have text panels surrounded respectively by twining vines and pomegranates, lilies and roses.

DESCRIPTION

Prestonpans is the seaward part of the burgh of Preston. There were twelve salt-pans here at the end of the C18, but the industry has recently died out along with others, like pottery and brick-making, that used the local coal. The town's historian C. E. Green described Prestonpans as 'one continuous village of old houses, set down with grotesque rather than picturesque irregularity'. That was in 1907, and the first part of his description is no longer true. But what gives the High Street its present scrappy look is the fragmentary state of the N (i.e. the sunlit) side which backs on to the firth. The landward side, though almost completely redeveloped, is in much better shape.

In HIGH STREET proper, the first building of any note is the FORTH TAVERN of 1908 on the s side, a nice pub with red masonry and a red-tiled roof with half-timbered oriels. The TOWN HALL, by *Peter Whitecross* of Prestonpans, 1896, has a red-dressed Renaissance gable to the street. On the opposite corner of New Street a tall baronial candle-snuffer of 1881. Then an outside stair at No. 141, possibly of the C17, and the painted baronial front of the RAILWAY TAVERN with its bowed and battlemented turret – probably an older house updated into a Victorian toy fort. Across Ayres Wynd some exemplary housing by *Adam Arnott* for East Lothian County Council, 1952, of squared red rubble with deftly slated roofs. It makes a good piece of townscape, to which some more local authority housing by *M. Watt* of Prestonpans, c. 1962, makes an adequate contribution – but more economically, in pebble-dash. It is worth going up AYRES WYND to see the PUBLIC LIBRARY of 1904, by *Whitecross* again, Scotch Queen Anne with an Art Nouveau twist, its red sandstone contrasting with the grey of the symmetrical Gothic SCHOOL by *J. & R. Farquharson*, 1881, whose flèche answers the pinnacle of the Grange Church opposite. Back in the High Street the next incident is a big but justified gap, leading up to the parish church, a trim garden with the MONUMENT to Thomas Alexander of Crimea fame, Director General of the Army Medical Department, a fine figure in full dress uniform by *William Brodie*, 1862.

On the N side there is precious little. Opposite the Ayres Wynd junction the WAR MEMORIAL with a statue of a Tommy in bonnet and greatcoat by *Birnie Rhind*, 1921. To the W of it a range of five pantiled sheds standing back from the street, reached through a masonry arch on the sea side. A cottage built out over the water behind No. 114 is the only other seaward building of note. To the E a large gap-site has been made into a dubious amenity with a portentously dreary shelter of rubble, built in 1959 to mark the bicentenary of Burns. A SCULPTURE in metal by *Frank Chorley*, c. 1963, which keeps it company has no obvious relevance to the place, but a little stone bartizan preserved at the back makes a good point of vantage for viewing the rocky shore. No. 98, BOAT-STONE HOUSE, with a heraldic panel dated 1630, owes its name to the inset relief of the fisherman's farewell which is similar to that at Dunbar harbour (*see* p. 189). The maltings and warehouses on both sides are ruinous.

HARLAW HILL, the next turning to the S, leads up to HARLAW HILL HOUSE, whose late C17 ogee-roofed tower was probably added to the slightly earlier L-plan house behind. To the E an C18 wing with scrolled skewputts. The road squeezes between its chamfered corner and that of an C18 house with rusticated quoins – altogether a townscape gem despite dereliction and alteration, and soon followed by the remains of another, the mid C18 No. 1 KIRK STREET, with moulded upper windows which look up the length of EAST LOAN. WINFIELDS on the W side was formerly the manse, baronially enlarged c. 1840. In its forecourt a pedimented garden doorway of the late C17 with a fleur-de-lys finial.

BEAM ENGINE at Prestongrange Colliery, near the coast road to 114 the W. Cornish type, i.e. the sort of engine that was used to pump water from the deep Cornish tin mines. Half the beam protrudes from the gable of a three-storey rusticated stone engine house. On the door the inscription MH (*Harvey & Co.* of Hayle, Cornwall) 1874. The capacity of the pump was increased in 1895 to 900 gallons (4000 l.) a minute, and it went on working till the closure of the colliery in 1952, a century after its opening. The adjacent brickworks, founded about the same time, have also closed.

DOOCOT at Dolphingstone, 2 km. SW, of C17 beehive type. It belonged to a large house of which a few fragments are noted by the RCAHMS.

DRUMMORE HOUSE. *See* p. 178.

PRESTONGRANGE. *See* p. 394.

RATHO

ML* *1070*

PARISH CHURCH(ST MARY). A medieval box embedded in
* Now Edinburgh.

later aisles. The s aisle of *c.* 1830 is bleakly Gothic, with three jagged gables and a gallery inside. On the N side two aisles of the C17. The E one (dated 1683) opens into the church through a wide segmental arch with trickily chamfered jambs. The residue is a basically Norman church. Much of the masonry is cubical ashlar. Immediately w of the s aisle is half a C12 door with scalloped capitals and a hoodmould with sawtooth decoration. One blocked C13 lancet in the w wall and three buttresses, the central one carrying a belfry. In the E wall a C15 window. No tracery, just three lights and the spandrels pierced. The interior was scraped in 1932 and an C18 gallery removed. – MONUMENTS. In the s porch a C13 tomb slab with a cross and sword, optimistically identified as belonging to one of the Knights Hospitaller who owned Ratho in the Middle Ages. – In the churchyard several headstones worth noticing, including Thomas Wilkie † 1679, William Anderson † 1756, and William Mitchell † 1809 'by a stroke from a thrashing machine', a panelled coffin formed of a single stone.

ST MARY (Episcopal), in the grounds of Dalmahoy House (*see* p. 166) and formerly its private chapel. By *John Henderson*, 1850. Buttressed E.E. with s porch and w belfry. Simple but well appointed interior. The chancel arch is painted with a text. Ribbed deep blue ceiling, powdered with stars. Stone altar on three shafts with foliage capitals, painted and gilded. Contemporary are the brown and cream floor tiles, the undistinguished memorial windows, and the brasswork, including three corona chandeliers – the one in the chancel double-tiered. – ORGAN by *Hamilton* of Edinburgh. – The RECTORY opposite the gates of Dalmahoy, likewise by *John Henderson*, is at the time of writing a restaurant.

ST MARY'S CHAPEL (R.C.), High Street. Gothic, by *James Fairley*, 1880.

RATHO HALL, 1 km. NW. Built *c.* 1800. Five windows long, with two storeys and a basement. Mainly of whin, but the front is ashlar, rather timid in its detail, including a Roman Doric doorpiece of thin proportions on a stepped-up platt. But the elaborate fanlight heralds a more lively interior with refined plasterwork. Gothic-glazed hall screen copiously trimmed with composition vines and ball-flowers in relief. The dining room, whose curved end has a Corinthian columned sideboard recess, is likewise decorated; six doorcases and a matching pine chimneypiece with delicate rope-moulded cornices exploit a repertoire of stock composition ornament. The graceful stair to the back has the same iron balusters as on the front steps, and a circular fan-centred ceiling.

RATHO PARK, 1 km. ENE. A severely picturesque Tudor house by *William Burn* for John Bonar of Ratho, 1824. Spindly corner turrets, stepped battlements, and mullioned windows identically disposed on two floors; an intimation of Jacobean in the shaped gables which all surmount projecting bays. It is planned as a compact rectangle with the main suite of rooms overlooking a balustraded terrace along the symmetrical s front, a lower-lying office court to the N, and, handy to both of them, an entrance tower in the East Barsham manner on the E side. The interior is austere Grecian – not an order to be seen as yet. Symmetrical entrance hall, long symmetrical saloon opening into the well staircase whose balustrade is of interlaced hoops. Along the s side a dignified sequence of drawing room, library and dining room. All have coffered ceilings except the last, which is a little less phlegmatic, with octagonal and square compartments. Upstairs the bathroom contains a marble bath in a pilastered timber aedicule. It is as old as the house, and the shower in the ceiling does not seem to be much newer. – STEADING and STABLES of 1836, also by *Burn*.

Ratho's distinctive building material is black whin, with sandstone dressings. Four houses on the N side of its single street, restored by the County Council in 1973, make a good focus at the T-junction where the road leads off to Dalmahoy. They include Nos. 58–60, of *c.* 1800, whose upper storey has a corbelled centrepiece and a pediment with strange vestigial bartizans at each end, and the former MASONIC LODGE to the W, late C18 with scrolled skewputts. At the E end the street is stopped by the gable of the Tudor SCHOOLHOUSE of *c.* 1840. BAIRD ROAD turns sharply N towards the Union Canal (opened in 1822) whose building brought work to Ratho's quarries and guests to the NEW INN which adjoins the humpbacked canal bridge. Baird Road has a good series of single-storey early C19 cottages on its E side and a prettily gabled SCHOOL of 1895 to the W. Its turn into the High Street is marked by the dormered single-storey cottage at the entry to THE LODGE, of *c.* 1840, with minimal Tudor Gothic detail.

ADDIESTOUN HOUSE. *See* p. 75.
DALMAHOY HOUSE. *See* p. 166.
NORTON HOUSE. *See* p. 369.

REDCOLL EL
3 km. NNW of Gladsmuir

An extremely severe house of *c.* 1824. Two storeys and basement, with tall piers of minimal projection at the corners. Unfluted Doric doorpiece reached by a bridging stair. Set-back one-storey wings with tripartite windows under segmental arches. Inside, a central well stair with curly snake and stem balusters and an oval dome light. Drawing-room chimneypiece of white statuary marble with detached Roman Doric columns and a graceful relief of Ganymede and the eagle in the middle.

LODGE. Of the same period, the front and end treated as blind arcades.

REDHOUSE CASTLE EL
3 km. SSW of Aberlady

A ruin, picturesquely untended. Redhouse was built by John Laing, Keeper of the Royal Signet, in two stages near in time but different in style: late C16 and early C17. Courtyard entered on the S through a roll-moulded archway. On the E side a single-storey (formerly two-storey) range, including a stone-roofed double lectern DOOCOT at the SE corner. To the N the earlier tower of four storeys and attic entered on ground-floor level by a roll-moulded door with the inscription NISI DOMINUS FRUSTRA; over it a heraldic tablet with supporting scrolls and a broken pediment. The turnpike stair is just inside.

Very soon afterwards this block was advanced some 3 m. to the N and given a big square tower at the NW corner. The new work is traditional in outline but consciously regular, with roll-moulded windows and straight string courses. The tower has its own entrance and turnpike stair, but three corbelled stair-turrets serve the upper floors, the one in the internal angle more simply moulded. To the N a pair of windows very close together. On the W side of the tower the windows are all double, with intermediate mullions, ending with a triangular-headed double dormer.

RICCARTON ML

Two lines of early C19 single-storey estate cottages are far enough apart for the A71 to rush between them, having just shaken off the encumbering suburbs of west Edinburgh, Sighthill and Wester Hailes.

HERMISTON HOUSE, to the W. A modest two-storey mansion whose baronial character can be attributed to *William Burn*, who lived here *c.* 1830. The S (entrance) front has an end jamb with canted sides corbelled out to the square, and an entrance turret in the internal angle. Then a pair of crowstep gables, and between them a GARGOYLE said to have come from Corstorphine parish church, Edinburgh, which Burn restored in 1828. In another gable a pedimented window that could belong to an earlier house, with the date 1633. Nothing of special interest inside; all was comfortably restored and modernized in 1955 by *Esmé Gordon*. LODGE of *c.* 1830.

HERMISTON FARM, adjoining. An C18 steading of grey rubble with timber lintels over the doors and cartshed openings. FARMHOUSE of the late C18.

HERIOT-WATT UNIVERSITY, 1 km. S. Something must be said of the site. It was formerly occupied by Riccarton House, whose nucleus was the C16 tower built by Sir Thomas Craig, an authority on feudal law; the Craigs of Riccarton have an important place in the history of Lothian estate improvement. *William Burn* designed a Jacobethan extension for James Gibson-Craig in 1823, but the house deteriorated as a result of wartime use in 1939–45, and it was demolished in 1956; the site was roughly that of the present University Library (*see* below). The County Council of Midlothian bought the estate, still well planted, and gave it to the university in 1967. The house stood to the SW of the lake. To the E of it was a quadrangular stable building, demolished in 1974. Few of the supporting buildings remain. The C18 WALLED GARDEN on the S side of the avenue, lined with red brick, has been surfaced for football. The symmetrical GARDENER'S COTTAGE (now the Chaplaincy Centre), with its deep eaves, is probably by *Burn*, and so is the N LODGE, with bargeboarded gables, on the A71.

Heriot-Watt University started in Edinburgh in 1821 as the School of Arts, for the spare-time teaching of science relevant to the trades. In 1851 it became known as the Watt Institution and School of Art (after James Watt), and in 1885 as the Heriot-Watt College, its extension in Chambers Street, Edinburgh, having been paid for by George Heriot's Trust. It received its charter in 1966. In 1968 *Alan Reiach, Eric Hall & Partners* drew up a development plan for an out-of-town campus, and all the buildings except the library are their work. The landscape designer is *A. E. Weddle*.

Seen from a distance on the rising ground to the S of the A71, this certainly has the look of a technological university: massive blank verticals for physical work, windowed horizontals for thought. What else does the Riccarton campus offer? Mainly an excellent discipline of layout and materials, made interesting by the site, which has a general slope towards the N, and by the established trees, which are absent only from the intimidating view we have already seen. Cost constraints are often mentioned as a reason for the monastic rigour of the buildings, but whatever the truth of this, the money has been well spent. The range of elements is small – chiefly long brick horizontals and brick stair-towers with chamfered corners. Brown rustic brick, laid with a precision that is rare in Scotland, is varied with exposed aggregate panels where a change is absolutely required, and there only. Window frames are brown and black, and the workshops are clad in drab green channelled aluminium sheet. The layout of the completed buildings is an L, continuously linked on first-floor level. They will be described starting at the SW corner.

LIBRARY (first phase so far completed) by *Sir Basil Spence, Glover & Ferguson*. A three-storey brick cuboid, the horizontal windows of the S front protected against high sunlight by massive concrete louvres. The E front with its canted walls is the only departure from the austere campus formula, and indeed the only hint of architectural swank to be seen as yet. The interior, with metal strip ceilings, is of simple virtuosity on every level; no impression of wall or even lintel obstructs the view of the trees outside. The library lies to the W of the main N–S axis and will eventually be linked to the administration building that will begin the sequence.

At the moment the axis starts with the BRIDGE, whose top and bottom form a projection of the HUGH NISBET BUILDING into which it runs. On this level the building has a lounge and dining room, a continuous space separated by a peninsular bar. The lounge has an open gallery on its inner side, the dining room is spanned by deep beams. Both enjoy the trees to the S and have a white cellular concrete ceiling overall, a vivid green carpet underfoot, and a brilliant yellow accent on the inverted triangle of the ascending staircase. The stair also goes down to the lower level, where the glass wall is notched back from the structural piers to form bays with benches. The main axis continues with CORE ONE, which begins as a covered shopping street, the display windows tied together with an up-and-down plastic moulding, brown and yellow and white. Then it serves the lecture theatres by way of seated assembly bays. The theatres themselves are white, with positively coloured seating.

The first of the technical blocks to be entered, the JAMES NASMYTH BUILDING, also offers the best spatial experience: the workshop with its variable display of machines, overlooked by the Exhibition Area. From now on all is very much in earnest; obscured glass stops the potential view from the narrow bridges joining one department to another.

Within the dominant L-plan, a residential oasis. Here the money constraint tells, for the RESIDENCES are spartan indeed; the rooms are good enough, but their hollow plastic doorcases amplify every coming and going like a sound-box. Could this have been avoided? An up-and-down serpentine path threads between the houses, which are of surprisingly intimate scale, cruciform, with a stair in the middle. The long E view from the nearby LAKE, bounded on the E side by a weir with a wide timber gangway, is marred by the scattered development of the RESEARCH PARK whose mediocrity is not the fault of the university's principal architects.

It is a good *ensemble* but it still lacks its main building, the hall, which is planned on the S side of the Avenue. How will the architects devise a suitable climax for this expert low-key performance? This part of the site is still empty except for the SPORTS CENTRE, whose blank N wall is one day to have other buildings in front of it. More residences are to be built to the SW.

ROCKVILLE see NORTH BERWICK

ROSEBERY HOUSE
2 km. SW of Temple

ML 3050

A nondescript house of modest size with an arched door and a big mullioned window, all the edges with square projecting quoins. Two gabled wings. In 1812–16 *William Atkinson* designed a Gothic house for the fourth Earl of Rosebery, but of this there is no sign; the ancillary buildings which are the main subject of this entry are all, in varying degrees, earlier.

LODGE. Late C17, square in plan, with rusticated quoins and pyramidal roof. Large window to the road, crudely carved at the head and protected with an iron grille of bellied profile. At the side a doorway with lugged moulding and cornice. This belonged to Clerkington House, built for the Hepburns who then owned the estate and demolished by them in 1805. It is now an outrigger of the entry to Rosebery, which is marked by GATEPIERS, pyramidal spikes on bowed plinths, simplified versions of the C17 piers at Moray House, Edinburgh, but probably of the first decade of the C19.

107   STEADING, straight across the road. Probably also of that period but acknowledging the style of *c.* 1700 with tall, thin, rusticated gatepiers with ball finials, flanked by long walls ending in battlemented pavilion fronts. Between them a fantastic clock tower: a pend with a depressed arch between two round ones, then a triangular-headed arcade, and finally above the clock stage a lofty pyramidal spire. The pend leads into a court with three depressed-arch cartshed openings on each side of the rear elevation.

2060   ROSEWELL   ML

PARISH CHURCH, at the S end of Main Street. Gothic in red and yellow brick, dated 1871. *Hardy & Wight* did some alterations in 1897.

38 ST MATTHEW (R.C.), at the N end of Main Street. A highly original church of yellow stock brick (replacing an earlier chapel) by *Archibald Macpherson*, finished in 1926. The site is large, cut off from the roadway by a wall with an arched and red-tiled gateway, and divided symmetrically by the nine-inch brick of the 'cloister' designed by *Reginald Fairlie*, 1935. The church stands in the middle with the PRIEST'S HOUSE attached to the N transept (compass points are given as if the church were correctly orientated). The main roof, red-tiled like the rest, stretches uninterrupted from the saddleback E belfry to the W gable, which is the first and chief surprise. It has a narrow canted bay in the middle, so the steep slope of the roof produces a very odd profile like the bow of a ship, emphasized by a wall-head course of tiles and cement, with slanted eaves over the side walls of the bay. These are continuous with the reveals of the doors on each side, which have wilfully unfinished ogee heads of pink stone, left in block form. The lower half of the bay, defined by windows and corbelling, proves to be the baptistery; the upper half belongs to the W gallery, with narthex underneath.

Wide nave with an open, dark stained roof. Brick arcades of five bays on brick-and-a-half-square piers, set diagonally and

corbelled out with the aid of single stone blocks. No fancy glass
– indeed no rest for the eye at all, except for the Stations of
the Cross inset over the piers. There is no crossing; the arcade
presses on past the transepts, which have axial arches from
which springs a median arch. 'One has to see such things done
before he can believe in their success', says *The Builder*. The
transepts have brick altars to the E, and the progress of the nave
is ended by the brick chancel arch, awkwardly wide but revealing the wide termination: three arches, of which the two outer are
niches for statues (possibly from the previous chapel). The
central arch penetrates the base of the bell-tower. This revela-
tory space is interrupted by a crudely Gothic skeleton arcade
and lit by concealed windows on each side. Altar rail and pulpit
can hardly be called furnishings, for they are formed of uniform
moulded brick units.

ROSEWELL INSTITUTE, across the street from the parish
church. By *James McLachlan* for the Lothian Coal Company,
1919. A concave portico of paired Roman Doric columns links
two partitions across the end of the main hall.

ROSEWELL TAVERN, Carnethie Street. Built *c.* 1920. The lofty
interior is the main thing, with arched pitch-pine roof and clearstorey windows.

CASTLE VIEW, to the W. A tall gabled villa of patterned Whitehill
brick, red and yellow, dated 1869. It was built for Mr Hood
who bought the colliery from the Ramsays.

ROSEWELL MAINS, to the S. An early C19 steading made over
for industrial use, cluttered with makeshift constructions and
at the time of writing derelict.

For the rest, Rosewell is a late C19 village of single-storey red brick
terraces which one might call a small town if it had more of
the commercial trappings usually associated with that term.
Architecturally, this deprivation is perhaps fortunate – at least
for the time being.

ST JOSEPH'S HOSPITAL (WHITEHILL). *See* p. 421.

HAWTHORNDEN CASTLE. *See* p. 248.

MIDFIELD HOUSE. *See* 326.

ROSLIN   ML *2060*

ST MATTHEW'S CHAPEL (Episcopal). The church of a college
established by William Sinclair, third Earl of Orkney – in 1450,
according to an inscription on the N clearstory cornice. Building
may actually have started earlier, as a note of *c.* 1447 in the *Scoti-*

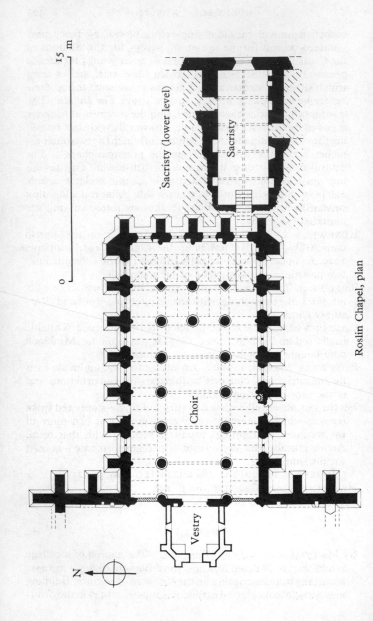

Roslin Chapel, plan

chronicon mentions Earl William 'in fabricando sumptuosam structuram apud Roslyn'. For the subsequent progress of the work there is no documentation at all. The chapel was intended to be cruciform, but in the end only the choir was built, together with some parts of the E transept walls. The foundations of the rest of the transept and the nave were uncovered at various times in the C19. The present length is 21 m. With the transept and nave it would come to around 55 m. The only other private collegiate church planned on this scale was Trinity College Church in Edinburgh, a royal foundation. However, Roslin is famous not for its size but for the decorative stone carving that covers almost every part of the building. In any context this would be remarkable, but it is so much more so in late medieval Scotland when even the most ambitious buildings can be plain to the point of severity. Yet the individual decorative forms used at Roslin are drawn, almost without exception, from the stock of Late Gothic foliage types, and the detailed character of the ornament is much less individual than its application to the building. Carving arranged in bands or blocks defines the main lines of the design; more strictly architectural forms like mouldings and shafts remain small in scale and unenterprising in detail. But there is no question of ornament concealing structure, for, as we shall see, the structure is extremely simple. Basically, the technique is one of encrustation, which has nothing in common with the general Late Gothic principle of multiplying small-scale architectural members, what Panofsky called 'overmembrification'. But if the methods of Roslin can be analysed, the visual effects they produce are all but impossible to describe. The sculpture has a denseness and repetitiousness that resembles cake-icing or topiary more than carving in stone. In the description, therefore, almost no attempt will be made to characterize foliage types, and figural sculpture will be discussed only in terms of its subject matter.

It is often suggested that Roslin owes its exotic character to the influence of Portugal or Spain, and the idea seems to be supported by a comment in Father Hay's notes on the Sinclairs to the effect that the third Earl imported craftsmen from abroad. But Father Hay was so much given to embellishing what he undoubtedly found in documents now lost that the authority of his statement is slight. There is in fact nothing at Roslin that need be attributed to direct foreign influences, and, moreover, the comparisons with Spain or Portugal will not work because the relevant buildings there are too late, i.e. late c15 and after. All the same, it remains true that for comparably fantastic and sculpture-encrusted Gothic one must go to Belém or Batalha or S. Juan de los Reyes in Toledo.

21   EXTERIOR. The chapel consists of an aisled choir of five bays with a straight ambulatory opening into four E chapels. This is not a c15 type of E end so much as a reproduction of one used widely by the Cistercians in the late c12 and, possibly under Cistercian influence, at Glasgow Cathedral c. 1230. For Roslin the immediate source was probably the destroyed late c12 church at the Cistercian abbey of Newbattle, just 8 km. away. This is by no means the only instance of a c15 Scots designer turning to the Early Gothic past when circumstances demanded a specially imposing solution. The five bays of the choir proper are marked out from the ambulatory and chapels by a tall clearstory. The design of the lower storey is more or less uniform throughout. All windows here are two-light except over the N and S doors. The W bays of the aisles are blank. The tracery is mostly simple and flowing, but several windows have the odd motif of a saltire cross. Mullions with twin shafts and two sets of shafts to the jambs with image niches squeezed between. Window heads and labels are lined with thick foliage, sometimes in trails, sometimes in square lumps. Even the surface of the tracery is ornamented, mostly with foliage but in a few cases with dogtooth. On the outer faces of the buttresses niches alternately of a normal and a richer than normal pattern. Between the buttresses of the E wall run stone benches, apparently original. What were they for? Were they an ecclesiastical equivalent of the window seats in medieval secular buildings? The view from here over the river North Esk is superb, although a high wall prevents one from enjoying it while seated. Only the E chapels and ambulatory preserve their crested parapets. The pinnacles here are cylindrical, those of the aisles square. Some have niches (that can never have held statues), but mostly their ornamentation is flat, geometric, and almost devoid of period character. N and S doors protected by shallow segmental porches slung between the buttresses with big, jolly gargoyles projecting above the arches. The S door is the richer, with three orders of shafts, an ogee hoodmould and pinnacles. The N door is square-headed.

The clearstory windows are taller and more sparsely decorated than the aisle windows. There is no tracery and the jambs are without niches. Hoodmoulds continued as string courses between the windows. The E window has tracery of

1861, but the probability is that there was none here originally. On the s side the cornice has square blocks with the Sinclair engrailed cross, i.e. a cross with the edges scalloped in reverse. The N cornice has engrailed crosses on shields alternating with single letters and the date of 1450 mentioned earlier. The flatness of the clearstory is offset by flying buttresses – purely decorative, for the tunnel-vault exerts for its whole length an even outward thrust which could only be counteracted by some form of continuous abutment or absorbed, as here, by thick clearstorey walls; so it follows that the flyers, particularly such thin flyers, are useless. The big pinnacles from which they spring stand no more than a couple of feet behind the pinnacles of the aisle buttresses, yet squeezed in between them is a further double rank of diminutive flyers, all just as if there were an outer aisle beneath! Did the Roslin mason design his buttresses with tongue in cheek? Or had he seen the two ranks of flyers at Melrose and decided to reproduce them here regardless of their original context?

The aisle roofs have at some stage obscured part of the clearstory windows (see the raggle on the transept walls and the renewed course on the clearstory itself). While it is obvious that this cannot have been the original arrangement, the ornament of the outer buttresses is carefully stopped so as to clear a sloping roof. Presumably the aisles were at first covered by a pitched roof with a central ridge and a gutter below the clearstory.

The remains of the TRANSEPTS must be described with the exterior. They include only some parts of the E walls. Externally each is divided by buttresses into two bays, but inside they were treated as a single bay. To allow for high retables (cf. e.g. Haddington) there were going to be no E windows. The corbels for the retables are still in place, along with parts of the altars and aumbries with outsize pinnacles. The centre, corresponding to the choir and aisles, is partly obscured by the tall Roslinesque vestry and organ chamber of 1880 by *Andrew Kerr*; the stodgy statues proclaim its date. On either side are the blocked entrances to the aisles, with lintels constructed as flat arches and shallow relieving arches. Shafts with bell bases and foliage capitals. Large and small fleurons on the lintels. By the vestry on the s side a figure of St Christopher and on the N side St Sebastian. The vestry hides a very tall arch and a solid screen pierced by a straight-headed door like those to the aisles. The screen is integral with the structure of the W wall (cf.

Lincluden). Outside the aisle entrances triple vault shafts rise to
choir clearstory level, and above them the wall curves inwards
– details which have been taken to imply that the nave was meant
to be covered by a single barrel-vault 10.7 m. wide. It would
spring from the same level as the choir vault but rise considerably higher, and the transept vaults would cut into it at a lower
level. However, a less outlandish reconstruction is possible if
one takes account of the evident rebuilding of the W gable, perhaps when the bellcote was added. Then one can argue that
the corbels directly over the parapet of the vestry carried vaulting like the shafts to l. and r. From this it follows that there
were going to be nave arcades, but no N and S crossing arches.

20   The INTERIOR is surprisingly tall in its proportions. The
bay design does not exploit this fact particularly, but no doubt
the vertical lines were stronger when there were statues in the
two tiers of niches between the upper windows. Two storeys:
tall arcades and a clearstory about two-thirds as tall. The piers
are bundles of sixteen shafts separated by small projections,
though one does not read them as clustered piers in the late
C12 or early C13 sense, but rather as columns decorated with
a kind of convex fluting. The bell bases and capitals with bushy
foliage discourage the isolation of the shafts as distinct elements. The arch mouldings are a series of shallow hollows and
demi-rolls between bands of foliage that start from pieces of
grotesque sculpture, mostly animals. The hoodmoulds, with
foliage and sporadic fleuron, do not reach down to the arch
springings. Image niche in the spandrel in the E wall. The piers
dividing the ambulatory and the E chapels are distinguished
from the rest by their spectacular decoration. That on the N
has eight shafts, alternately keeled and covered with leaf carving. The S pier is known as the 'Prentice Pillar' from the end-
lessly repeated and quite recent story of the apprentice who
carved it and was killed by the jealous master mason. Reeded
core with four strips of foliage that start from each of the cardinal points and turn through 180 degrees. Twisted columns are
ultimately an Antique motif, but there are plenty of C15
continental examples designed on the Roslin principle
(Brunswick Cathedral aisles, 1469; St-Séverin, Paris, c. 1490).
The realization of the idea at Roslin is uniquely luxuriant. On
the base winged serpents with entwined necks bite their own
tails.

The decoration of clearstory, aisle and ambulatory windows
repeats exactly their external treatment. The string course i

the aisles steps up between each window and comes to a sudden end in the w bays. In the w wall is the intended E crossing arch. Two plain chamfered orders framed by a continuation of the string course below the clearstory windows. The lower two-thirds now opens into an organ gallery and the rest is glazed. C19 parapet at the foot of the arch. So much for the internal surfaces of the walls. We must now turn to the vaults which, better than anything else, reveal the Scottishness of Roslin and its independence from the Gothic style as understood in most European countries. As noted before, the vault over the main span is of the pointed tunnel variety common in smaller Scots Late Gothic churches. It is the only instance of a tunnel-vault set on a clearstory, and, needless to say, such a combination runs counter to the basic premises of Gothic architecture. But again the structural primitivism is overlaid by an amazing effusion of ornament. The bays are marked by transverse arches covered with a sort of pendant cresting made up of fleurs-de-lys alternating with indeterminate vegetal sprouts. Each compartment is closely patterned with a single motif – e.g. stars, squares, flowers – carved in shallow relief and resembling nothing so much as batches of pastry cut-outs on trays. The vaults of the aisles and the ambulatory are pointed tunnels set at r. angles to the main axis and carried on massive lintels decorated with foliage and occasionally figure sculpture. The lintels are flat arches, but their supporting role is an illusion, and in the N aisle the top coping has been left off so that one can see the shallow segmental arches that really take the weight. Transverse tunnels were in the late C15 an extraordinary anachronism. The idea goes back at least to the C9 (Aachen, Palatine Chapel) and was often used by the Cistercians in the first half of the C12. At Roslin it need not be seen as a recrudescence of the Romanesque; it is more probably due to the designer's familiarity with the forms of the contemporary Scots vernacular and an exceptional willingness to use them in a church context. The lintel construction would come from fireplaces, while pointed tunnel-vaults were a commonplace in military and domestic work. Except in the w bays the vaults are carved with the Sinclair engrailed cross – a notably self-confident piece of heraldic display, even for the late Middle Ages.

The eastern chapels have the only rib-vaults in the building.* They are quadripartite with two lots of ridge ribs, but this simple description conveys nothing of their overwhelming

---

* Although the transepts were intended to have them.

visual impact. They are indeed the decorative crescendo of the whole chapel, and a decidedly cacophonous one. The ribs have thick hanging cusps between strips of foliage. The transverse ribs have two orders, which makes their thickness nearly equal to the distance between them and the centres of the bays. At the intersections pendant bosses of a disagreeable sagging profile. Even more disturbing are the fat pendants at the springings that point diagonally downwards. They rest on strange cone-shaped brackets above the proper capitals of the wall-shafts. The final vaulting oddity covers the probable SACRISTY, a rectangular room some 11 m. long reached down a flight of steps in the SE corner. Here the engrailed cross is carved on a semi-circular tunnel-vault to form a longitudinal ridge rib and four transverse ribs. In the S wall an aumbry, a piscina, and a fire-place, and in both side walls cupboards and doors leading to demolished rooms. The altar, which incorporates a medieval mensa, is flanked by corbels, one with the Sinclair cross, the other with the arms of Earl William and his wife Elizabeth Douglas.

SCULPTURE. The many small-scale figural carvings at Roslin are nowhere of specially high quality, and their placing takes no account of their subject matter. Only religious subjects are listed here. EAST CHAPELS AND AMBULATORY. Below the niches in the E wall, busts of angels (nearly all replaced in a restoration by *David Bryce* of 1860–1*). – In the head of a N ambulatory window, Apostles. – Above the capitals of the piers, angels playing musical instruments including a bagpipe with a single drone. – On the capital of the central pier an un-identified scene with figures and a tree. – On the northernmost chapel diagonal vault rib, the Dance of Death. – On a boss of the second chapel from the N, Virgin and Child with the Three Living and Three Dead. – On the aumbry in the southernmost chapel, Vernicle. – SOUTH AISLE. S wall, busts of angels (most renewed in 1861). – In the head of the easternmost window, twelve figures of which six hold books. – In the head of the

---

* Bryce's carver was *Laurence Baxter*. *The Builder* reported that all badly decayed stones were replaced and almost the whole of the carving was retooled and sharpened. The *Building News* gave a more emotive account: parts of the stone cleaned with acids, others rechiselled – flayed – destroying the original proportions of the mouldings, and altering entirely the character of the orna-ment, a third of the cusps on the nave vault restored in cement. The interior was thoroughly cleaned by the former Ministry of Works in 1957 without recourse to any of these methods.

second window from the E, nine angels, probably standing for the Nine Orders of Angels. – Below the lintels flanking the S door, Christ before Pilate (E) and the Carrying of the Cross with St Veronica (W). – Below the N end of the westernmost lintel, Resurrection. – On the second arcade arch from the W, Apostles. – On the easternmost lintel W face, inscription based on I Esdras, i, 10–12: *forte est vinum fortior est rex fortiores sunt mulieres super omnia vincit veritas*. – On the second lintel from the E, the Seven Acts of Mercy (E face) and the Seven Deadly Sins (W face). – NORTH AISLE. Below the second lintel from the E, Agnus Dei. – Below the fourth lintel from the E, Crucifixion (N end) and (?) Man of Sorrows (S end). – On the second lintel from the E (E face), Tree of Jesse (much contracted; but note David harping on the l.). – SACRISTY. Miscellaneous fragments including the upper parts of two statues of ecclesiastics. *See* p. 525 22

MONUMENTS. Between the easternmost piers of the N arcade an incised slab with a knight in mid C15 armour. The surviving heraldry has no known connection with the Sinclairs. – On the N aisle W wall George Earl of Caithness † 1582. Round arch on pilasters. Ogee hood. – C13 coffin lid with the name William de Sinclair inscribed much later. – DRAWINGS. Incised on the N and S walls of the sacristy several preparatory drawings including cusped arches and a pinnacle. – STAINED GLASS. An extensive scheme by *Clayton & Bell*, from 1885, with saints in the clearstorey, biblical scenes below. Some windows are in good repair, e.g. the high W window (Christ in Majesty), but others are sadly faded. – In the baptistery a memorial window (SS. Andrew and George) by *William Wilson*, 1951, and one by *A. Carrick Whalen* (St Francis), 1970. – In the sacristy the Transfiguration by *Patrick Pollen*, 1954. – MONUMENT, in the churchyard to the E. Gothic, with admirably sensitive carving and figures, all in red sandstone, by *W. Birnie Rhind*, 1899. – The N ENTRANCE to the churchyard is made up of oddments, at least some of them late medieval and potentially from the castle. Square-headed door framed by angle roll and fine fleuron. Balanced on this a gablet(?) covered with a sort of dogtooth, a blank shield with helm and mantling, and a C19 cross.

PARISH CHURCH (former Free Church), Penicuik Road. A snecked rubble Gothic church by *Thornton Shiells & Thomson*, dated 1880, with staircase wings and a protuberant bellcote. The interior, though of the same date, is earlier in spirit: slim iron shafts with leafy bell capitals supporting a clearstorey. One gallery.

PARISH CHURCH (former), Manse Road. Dated 1826. An oblong kirk of ashlar with rusticated quoins, the centre advanced and pedimented between two tall round-headed windows. Later porch. The building became the church hall in 1935.

Roslin is an extended crossroads village, the SE limb leading to the castle and chapel past COLLEGEHILL HOUSE (the former Rosslyn Inn) which bears the retrospective date 1660 over the door. Its chief internal interest is in the staircase, whose cut-out wooden balusters are probably of the early C18. The gabled and bay-windowed ROYAL HOTEL at the crossing is by the engineer *Archibald Sutter*, dated 1868.

ROSSLYNLEE HOSPITAL, 2.5 km. SSW. The original E-plan asylum by *W. L. Moffat*, 1871, faces NE. It is 'plain Italian' (*Building News*), with two storeys of squared snecked rubble and deep eaves. Large plain additions by *R. Rowand Anderson*, 1898, in variegated red ashlar include two monumental blocks which make an impressive symmetrical frontage to the SW. Staff accommodation in new and converted cottages was provided by *A. Murray Hardie* in 1920.

ROSLIN CASTLE. The site gave Roslin its name, which means 'the rock on the falls'; the rock is a spur which pushes southward into a loop of the river North Esk. On this eminence the C15 castle of the Sinclairs makes a picturesque ruin from whose fine square ashlar the hand of the restorer has so far been withheld. The C16–17 E range is an equally pleasant surprise for another reason: domestic in scale, with finishings of above average quality, it is still habitable.

BRIDGE. In the C15 the high natural causeway giving access to the rock from the N was breached, the gap presumably being crossed by a drawbridge between ashlar piers of which only the one to the S remains unaltered. On top of it the remains of a C16 gateway. A permanent bridge was built later (still in the C15 say the RCAHMS), consisting of two deep lateral walls with semicircular arches which carried a wooden structure between them. Only the arch to the E survives; the other was replaced by a new and much higher segmental arch in the late C16. The N pier on this side is made in diminishing stages and turns at an obtuse angle to line up with what was evidently another abutment. A squinch arch had to be built to take this very narrow bridge round the corner. Down from this dizzy height a road runs under the bridge, crossing the loop of the river with a stone bridge to the E, a wooden one to the N. Vestiges of both can still be seen.

N RANGE. Just enough is left, mainly of the C15, to show that it gave entry through a pend into the courtyard. C16 windows and bartizan turret.

W RANGE. What is left of this C15 work is tantalizing indeed: a long W wall of great height, founded on six deeply splayed archways (one door, the rest windows). It is uncommonly fine, but poses questions about floor levels and structure which are not fully answered by the regular (but very small) holes for joists between the arches, or by any other signs. Right at the head of the wall is a round, moulded corbel, and a drawing in Father Hay's History of the St Clairs suggests that there was a row of these supporting a wall-walk. On the outside (W) of the wall a majestic row of buttresses, splayed to a rounded edge. Hay shows them as rising to support a series of open bartizans on the outer side of the wall-walk; to their structural purpose there are no clues. At its S end this range ended in a tower of which only the SW quarter is left, with machicolations at the head of the boldly curved wall. Much of the rest of the stonework must be inside the natural-looking hillock at its foot; for this destruction the Earl of Hertford (1544) was at least partly responsible.

E RANGE. Built of rubble with massive freestone quoins to replace the E curtain wall of the courtyard. It is a much more impressive piece of work than at first appears, for it is not built on the plateau but against its E face, so that three full storeys descend into the glen below courtyard level. Square tower attached to the SE corner. The foundation is naked rock, cut as a battered base. Windows with rounded margins except on the courtyard front. Wide gun loops below the windows at the S end, mere holes to the E. Two little squinch windows in the angles where the tower meets the main building, nicely trimmed at top and bottom, light a garderobe and the narrow turnpike stair that descends from the hall. Inside, the plans of the three lowest floors are virtually identical. A corridor along the W side gives access to a range of rooms which are longitudinally tunnel-vaulted. Steps lead up to the shot holes in the window embrasures. At the N end of each corridor is a full-width room, similarly vaulted, the kitchen on the lower level, the bakehouse above it, both with fireplaces and drained sinks. Vertical communication is provided in various ways: small square holes in the vaults of the end rooms for verbal contact, and large ones at the foot of the stairs, apparently for a hoist.

The stair itself runs up through all five storeys, in straight scales from front to back, with an intermediate wall half-way along the building.

A new paragraph to describe the part that shows above ground, a work of much more refinement, with intricate stone dressings on the harled two-storey frontage overlooking the courtyard. The doorway, with a frame for a heraldic panel, is in the middle, and the whole thing was roughly symmetrical if we assume that the s part, now ruined, had a big dormer window to balance the one which still survives; the gateway to the chapel (*see* above) may well be formed of that very dormer. The N part, still complete, has the eccentrically placed windows of the staircase and, at the end, a turnpike-stair-turret corbelled out just above the ground. The enrichment is of high quality, all of grey freestone. Moulded base course, all the original apertures framed by a deeply cut roll moulding whose internal curve is relieved by delicate quatrefoils. The doorway has, in addition, a thin serpentine foliage pattern and under the cornice the raised inscription 'SWS [for Sir William Sinclair] 1622'. The remaining dormer head is heraldic, with finials. There is also a dormer with concentric semicircles on the E side of the building.

Indoors, the HALL on the ground floor at the s end has been cut in two. The surviving part is open to the weather but still has a couple of outstanding features: a wide fireplace in what was the centre of the W wall, carved in a similar manner to the external work and bearing the initials and shield of Sir William Sinclair and the date 1597; and a sink with a nicely arched drain-hole in the reveal of the window opposite. The rest of the room was cut off in the early C18 and panelled with pine; subsequently, as a kitchen, it was given a coal range bearing the Carron Ironworks mark. In the DRAWING ROOM at the N end some late C17 panelling (afterwards modified with such C18 features as arched openings). Its original ceiling, within a regular cornice, is divided into nine square compartments by plaster ribs whose chamfers are moulded with curly foliage, fruits and animals. Each square is decorated with diagonal leaves except for the middle one which has a shield with mermaid and (?) unicorn, the initials SWS and the date 1622. The fireplace, like others in the building, is probably of the early C18. Moulded frame, rounded at the corners. Late C17 panelling in the rooms upstairs.

RUCHLAW HOUSE
0.5 km. W of Stenton

EL *6070*

Early C17, though the date on two resited dormer heads with the initials and heraldry of Archibald Sydserff is 1663. Harled, of three storeys, on an L-plan, with crowstepped gables and a moulded eaves course. The turret in the angle was replaced *c*. 1700 with one of rectangular plan to house a more spacious stair. Its dividing wall is topped with a wooden balustrade. In the drawing room on the first floor the post-Union coat of arms of James VI and Anne of Denmark, painted in tempera.

DOOCOT, to the SW. C17, lectern type.

ST GERMAINS
2 km. NE of Tranent

EL *4070*

A seven-bay N front in the late C18 manner just like a house in Edinburgh's Queen Street, with an engaged four-column door-piece against a rusticated ground floor, but with a central pediment. This shallow range was an addition to an earlier C18 house which can still be seen behind it. A further addition was made *c*. 1820. Little of the interior finishings survived the sub-division *c*. 1950, but there are an Adamesque frieze and cornice at the head of the staircase, and on the second floor a columned screen leads to a pretty round room complete with chimney-piece.

Alongside the house to the W a steeply pedimented STABLE BLOCK of two storeys.

DOOCOT to the S, cylindrical and battlemented.

ST JOSEPH'S HOSPITAL
1 km. SE of Rosewell

ML *2060*

Originally WHITEHILL, a large Tudor-Jacobean revival house of prodigious authority by *William Burn* and *David Bryce* for Wardlaw Ramsay, 1844. The builder was *David Wallace* and the estate provided the hard white stone, now weathered to pale grey, which accentuates the bold massing and lively detail. Whitehill is of two mullion-windowed storeys plus an attic that is not always in evidence and a shallow basement that is allowed a little more daylight to the S and W. The N (actually NNW) front is the most splendid. Over a Renaissance porte-cochère 92 the centrepiece is crowned with a cartouche surrounded by strapwork in a scrolled gable and guarded by two heraldic beasts. It is flanked by recessed bays and then by two towers, similar in their crowstep gables and square corner turrets, dissimilar in that the one to the E is enlarged by the addition of a dominant tower with bowed oriel. The other fronts are virtually symmetrical but no less dynamic. That to the E, with the main range of rooms, has a long and busy skyline with dormers between the crowstep gables. The central focus is on the ground floor, where a single-storey bow of trefoil plan projects further than the tall canted bays on each side of it; the wall at ground level is otherwise effectively blank. The S front, again symmetrical, returns to the theme of tower and gable eccentrically juxtaposed. Between the two towers the centre bow rises to the full height of the balustraded parapet, acknowledging their duality with its central knife-edge. It is triangular with a round bow on each face, like a diagonal cut across one of the Montacute gazebos. Three-dimensionally the whole composition is united not only by these consistent themes but by the ranks of twisted chimneys that group and regroup on the skyline behind the gables and the ogee roofs of tower and turret. The stable and office block, or rather court, projects from the W side of the entrance front. The four-centred entrance arch is now unhappily built up. Neither the external fire escape to the E nor the extensive hospital extensions to the S and W reflect any credit on their designers.

As to the interior, suspended ceilings now obscure the sumptuous originals reportedly damaged by mining subsidence. The Jacobean staircase hall and its big fireplace survive, hideously painted, in the centre of the house, and so do two chimneypieces in the suite of state rooms along the E front: drawing room, library, dining room. The main bedrooms are on the S front, the family rooms off the entrance hall to the NW.

LODGE on the road just N of Rosewell. Matching the house, with a spacious drive-in.

SALTCOATS CASTLE   EL
1 km. S of Gullane

Late C16. The armorial stone of the builder, Patrick Levingtoun of Saltcoats, now mounted over the front door of a nearby cottage, probably came from over the door of the castle, and the date must be 1592 (the second digit crudely recut as a 3). It is a fragmentary ruin, but its arched W end is a landmark, five storeys high, with two square corner turrets corbelled out from the round. Very fancy gun loops in the N one. The segmental arch connecting them is apparently later, but it makes the building look older, and the big centre window adds to the illusion that this is a monumental entrance, Dirleton-style. In the wall overhead a formidable row of plain gargoyles that may have drained a parapet wall. Only the s wall survives of a lower and narrower block, later extended still further to the E, running back from this screen-like tower, with a corbelled stair-turret on the s side in the internal angle where they meet. Traces of barrel-vaulting in the basement. Large first-floor windows. The door seems to have been at the W end of the N wall. A walled courtyard extends to the N, with a vaulted kitchen remaining from a N range of buildings, and to the W, where there is a rebuilt well head. Further to the N a ruined DOOCOT of lectern type which could be contemporary with the castle.

SALTOUN HALL   EI. 4060
2 km. NW of East Saltoun

Castellated Gothic on a large scale, by *William Burn* from 1817 on a basis of older work. The house faces N. The earliest part is the range on the W, at an obtuse angle to match a bend of the Saltoun Water. In 1769 Lord Fletcher was adding a two-storey wing along what is now the s front; at its E end was a Venetian-windowed library over an arcaded greenhouse. All that is left of it is an inscribed tablet now in the gallery (*see* below) which announces that 'This Library was built A.D. 1779 to contain that excellent collection of books made by his Uncle of Illustrious Memory whose name he bore.' This wing and the old block formed an L, and Fletcher put a 'great stair' in the angle. In 1803 *Robert Burn* added corner turrets at the angles and castellated the whole thing, but William Burn's vast enlargements obliterated his father's work as well as that of the C18. His new front to the N has a bleak magnificence: hood-moulded windows between square towers, a Perp arcaded porch stretched across on the ground floor, the great Perp lantern of the saloon looming up behind, with stepped and chimneyed battlements. To the E is the transformed library wing, a solitary round turret marking the change to two storeys from the three of the main block. This is the only show front, but the s side was given a canted bay and a garden door in a new square turret.

The interior provides a spectacular Gothic revival sequence, rib-vaulted throughout. The porch leads into the hall, with a billiard room to the l. Then comes the SALOON which ousted the C18 staircase, 25 m. high and oblong in plan, contracted into a square by vaulted side bays with crenellated landings. Dummy windows in the walls to N and S. Straight ahead to the S a black marble Gothic chimneypiece with corner turrets and a centre bartizan. Within the square, pendentive vaults with heraldic shields soar up to support a circular balcony. Above it a ribbed ceiling with a central pendant. All this is within the oblong shell seen from outside. The double staircase to the E, with its own rectangular lantern, communicates on ground-floor level with the LIBRARY, which Burn demoted to this position. It is of three rib-vaulted compartments, the middle one square and bay-windowed, each with a central pendant. The Gothic chimneypiece is of veined black marble, and so is that of the STUDY, whose panelling is of the C20. Burn built a corridor in the form of a Gothic gallery on to the N side of this range, but the most surprising incident is his recasting of the rooms to the W in the calmest Grecian manner; the dining room in the old part, the little oval ANTEROOM and then the DRAWING ROOM with its serene compartmented ceiling, the last two *en suite* with the Gothic library. On the first floor over the library a notable BEDROOM with a central vault on arched bays, three of them quite shallow, the fourth opening into the canted bay-window. Saltoun Hall was subdivided into flats in 1967.

STABLES. Late C18. The centre block is arched and pedimented on both sides, with a domed octagonal clock tower. Arched windows in the end pavilions, niches in the links. The building is now a single house. Behind it, a square CISTERN with blank arches and a shallow dome.

GATEWAY on the same axis. Of the later C19, unused.

GAS WORKS. 1870, with fancy bargeboards and square chimney, by *J. Edmundson & Co.*

DOOCOT. Of two stages, square in plan and elaborately castellated; perhaps by *Robert Burn.*

NORTH LODGE. In the same style; twin lodges linked by a bridge in 1935.

SOUTH LODGE. Picturesque Scottish Baronial by *W. Beattie Brown,* 1913.

SAMUELSTON see HADDINGTON

SEACLIFF   EL 6080
5 km. E of North Berwick

The melancholy ruin of an early house in *David Bryce*'s mature baronial style, designed for George Sligo on the basis of a long house that already existed. The date is 1841. It was enlarged after 1850, burned out and abandoned in the C20. Purposeful asymmetry is the keynote, with a square tower dominating the sea front to the N, two gables to the S, one of them Bryce's favourite type corbelled out from a canted bay, the other more importantly treated with a mullioned bay over the entrance and twin cylindrical bartizans. The bartizans at the far ends of the house however are square (*see* Pinkie House, Musselburgh, p. 336). A long conservatory extended to the W.

SETON   EL 4070

ST MARY AND HOLY CROSS. Almost hidden by trees and the high wall round the policies of Seton House. From the E the church appears a cruciform Late Gothic building with an apsidal choir, boldly projecting transepts and a low crossing tower carrying a truncated stone spire. So it comes as a disappointment to find that the nave has vanished except for the lowest courses of its N and S walls. The simple initial picture is further complicated by the foundations of a rectangular building protruding westwards from under the S transept. Fortunately, however, the successive phases can be followed quite closely thanks to the history of the Seton family written by George Maitland *c.* 1560. The unaisled parish church first mentioned in the C13 is represented by the ruined side walls of the nave which continued at least as far as the E walls of the transepts. The foundations under the S transept belong to a chapel built in or after 1434 by Catharine St Clair, wife of the first Lord Seton. The choir and sacristy were largely the work of the third Lord († 1478), the fourth Lord vaulted the W part of the choir and founded a college in 1492, and the choir was roofed with stone slabs and furnished by the fifth Lord († 1513). His widow Lady Janet Seton added the N transept by 1541 and the S one in 1545, so making 'ane perfyt and proportionat croce church'. The nave disappeared later, probably after 1580 when the parish was joined with Tranent. The spire was evidently never finished, for Maitland says that Lady Janet 'biggit up the steeple as ye see it now to ane grit hight swa that it wants little of compleiting'.

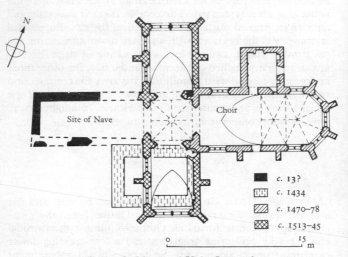

Seton, St Mary and Holy Cross, plan

N

Site of Nave

Choir

■ *c.* 13?
▦ *c.* 1434
▨ *c.* 1470–78
▧ *c.* 1513–45

0   15
                      m

The choir is of three bays plus a three-sided apse. The broad, spreading proportions are offset to some extent by the buttresses, carefully detailed but lacking pinnacles. Windows with deep twice-chamfered splays and simple flowing tracery, mostly of two lights, but of three in the w bays and the centre window of the apse. In the central bay on the s a round-headed priest's doorway, now blocked. Above it much blank wall and a small armorial panel. The sacristy projecting from the middle of the N wall is still slab-roofed, as are the transepts, of two bays each and showing their later date only in small details, e.g. paterae in the cornice instead of foliage trails. The E walls are blank, as so often in late medieval Scottish churches. The windows of the N, s and w walls are similar to those in the choir, though larger. The thick ugly centre mullions of the N and s windows recur in the W windows at Haddington and King's College Chapel, Aberdeen, both also of the early C16. Tower of one low storey lit by single lancets. Stair-turret at the E corner of the S face. The spire is octagonal in plan and the transition to the square is made by widening the cardinal faces until they reach the corners and tapering the diagonal faces into steeply sloping inverted triangular surfaces. The result is quite different from English broach-spires, though many of the kind exist in France, most of them of timber. A Scottish parallel, also timber, is at St John, Perth. Of the nave one can say only that it had a wooden roof and no vault.

The interior is completely tunnel-vaulted except for the crossing, which has a plain rib-vault. The E half of the choir vault, its surface ribs springing from corbels, was built by the third Lord Seton who 'pendit [the choir] as far as it is with rum-braces'. The plain part was built later by his son. There was no question of ribs being intended farther W because the western-most transverse rib makes no provision for a continuation of the ridge rib. The choir is well lit, as the windows penetrate into the springing of the vault. The E arch of the crossing belongs to the third Lord's work, and is more finely detailed than Lady Janet's three arches. Originally it was simply the chancel arch between the choir and the old nave, a small piece of whose N wall can still be seen from the transept, just E of the N crossing arch. Here also is visible the original NW buttress of the choir incorporated into the S end of the E wall of the transept. The corresponding traces on the S side are hidden by the stair-turret. Lady Janet's crossing, like those at Dunglass and South Queensferry, reads as a separate spatial compartment. The limiting factors here were the narrowness of the existing arch into the choir and even more the narrowness of the old nave. The sacristy has a pointed barrel-vault and is divided by a wooden floor, apparently the medieval arrangement. Fireplace in the N wall.

SEDILIA. A single recess set rather high in the wall. Three-centred arch on shafts. – PISCINA. Like an image niche, with a gabled and pinnacled canopy and a foliage corbel under the bowl. – PISCINA (S transept). Ogee-headed with broken cusping and pinnacles, the bowl carried on the bust of a demon with bat's wings. – FONT. Fragment of an octagonal bowl with shields on each face. – MONUMENTS. In the choir, a segmental recess with foliage trail and deep mouldings flanked by big buttresses. Highly finished effigies of a man in plate armour and a lady. One would assume this to be the monument of the builder of the choir, the third Lord Seton † 1478, but he is known to have been buried at the Blackfriars in Edinburgh. However, the armour seems too early for the fourth Lord († 1508). – On the N transept N and S transept S walls, empty round-headed recesses coeval with the building. – N transept E wall: James Ogilvie of Birnes † 1617. Big inscription with a skinny pediment over and paired pilasters and foliage drops either side. – S transept E wall: James Earl of Perth † 1611. Very good indeed, though damaged in 1715. Large wall-tablet framed by detached marble columns standing on a bulgy base that originally carried two kneeling figures (a fragment of one is in the choir). Deep cornice with coffering, pilasters with arabesque and rich swags of fruit. Above the cornice an armorial panel in a round-headed frame. Many traces of colour. The main inscription is lost, but on the base is the epitaph composed by William Drummond of Hawthornden:

> In steed of epitaphes and airye praise,
> This monument a ladye chaste did raise,
> To her lord's living fame and after death,
> Her bodye doth unto this place bequeath,
> To rest with his till God's shrill trumpet sound,
> Thogh tyme her lyf no tyme her love can bound.

Both this monument and that to James Ogilvie of Birnes were in the choir until 1878, when the Earl of Wemyss unblocked and restored the windows.

ARCHITECTURAL FRAGMENTS from Seton Palace. A small collection of pediments and other enriched features, vigorously carved in the Scots Renaissance manner of Winton House, have been set up near the chapel. The splendid palace of the Setons appears to have been built on an L-plan with a tall square tower and plenty of pediments on the roofline. William Mackenzie bought it in ruinous condition and cleared the site for the building of Seton House. However the C17 garden walls survive with their round corner towers, and so do the remains of Seton Mill to the N.

SETON HOUSE. Seton was built (on the site of the old palace, see above) for the Edinburgh lawyer Alexander Mackenzie who had acquired the land from the York Buildings Company (see Cockenzie House, p. 137). The architect was *Robert Adam*, 1789, and it is the most perfectly executed of the castle type

which he developed in Scotland over the last fifteen years of
his life. Wedderburn (1770) and Caldwell (1773) can hardly be
included, though both are battlemented and Caldwell even has
little bartizans stuck on to the corners of what is basically an
ordinary Georgian house. Culzean (1777) is really the first, for
it has a multiplicity of corner towers and a scenic forecourt,
and it later acquired a third characteristic feature of the Adam
castle style, the central round tower dominating the back elevation. Airthrey (1790) is not Adam's last castle but it represents
the final development in which this tower, which had evolved
from the Georgian bow, takes over and engulfs the whole plan
of the house in a big half-circle. Seton comes between, and
marks the high point in Adam's synthesis of neo-classical geometry and picturesque diversity. Like all his castles it is basically symmetrical not only in elevation but in plan, with the staircase in the middle and rooms of varied shapes filling out the
projections and swellings of the outer wall.

   The castle, for it obviously is that, was built by *Adam &*
Thomas Russell, masons, who started work in April 1790 and
seem to have finished by the end of the year. The stone is varicoloured, with grey predominating at the bottom but eventually
running out, even for the fully dressed margins, warm yellow
and brown towards the top, the main wall areas being laid in
more or less consistent courses and roughly tooled in various
ways. A delightful effect; but all this evidence, and some
fragments of very thin harling on the rear elevation, suggests
that it was all originally covered up, except for the margins and
other definitive surfaces like the parapets. From the s, Seton
appears as a cluster of blunt-topped towers rising from behind
a low screen of much greater width. The latter consists of the
stables and offices, placed right in front of the castle to play
their part in the scenic ensemble: two U-plan ranges turning
their backs on each other, with a quadrant-cornered forecourt
in between. Both have square corner towers and severe fenestration with small thermal windows sparingly disposed. The
FORECOURT, entered through an archway between two of the
convex quadrants, is enclosed by their concave faces and those
of their two fellows on the far side; all are arcaded. The full
three-storey height of the castle is now seen. It is not large (its
solid could be fitted into the courtyard's void) but makes its
effect by a powerful assembly of tall towers: square ones flanking the entrance, round ones rising over the quadrant screens 86
at each end, and the implication of more square ones round

the corners. The detail – string courses, windows and unbattle-
mented parapets – is predominantly horizontal except at the
centre, where steps run up to the front door with its wide segmental fanlight, filigree-glazed, the slightly bowed glass original. In the two storeys above it modified Venetian windows
whose outer lights are elliptical-headed. Finally a vestigial
Scots wall-walk and a crowstep gable.

To the back the solid geometry of the main block, supplemented by a basement on the falling ground, is fully evident.
Canted ends with the projecting corners that previously gave
the impression of towers. In their middle bays simple Venetian
windows of conventional design. The climax is the half-round
tower that bursts from the centre of the main N front, its windows once again of enlivened Venetian type, with oval-headed
sidelights. The whole is flanked by the rear walls of the service
ranges, each with the grave, unseeing eyes of three blank
thermal windows.

Quite a small house fills this outward form; basically two
rooms on the main axis and one to each side. First the oblong
ENTRANCE HALL on whose frieze Mackenzie stag-heads are
substituted for Doric ox-skulls. The white marble chimneypiece with double consoled ends and delicate reliefs of corn and
vine may well have been moved here from the dining room.
This room is also the stair-well, with straight flights on three
sides, a delicate trellis balustrade and oval-section handrail.
The first-floor landing has been enlarged to take in the space,
and the daylighting, of the front room – an effective device,
but lacking the articulation which Adam would have given it,
probably with a columned screen. Such a screen does exist on
the top level, where an extra landing leads to what was presumably the library with its splendid sea view; only the entablature
has been queerly embellished in the C20 with plaster reliefs of
quite unsuitable character on the soffit. Other ornament of this
kind, more or less unrelated to any possible C18 work, crops
up in other rooms but is mostly too obvious to mention. Beyond
the entrance hall, the DRAWING ROOM whose bow end fills
the N tower. Delicate griffons on the marble chimneypiece,
winged sphinxes on the frieze. A moulded pelmet unfortunately
obscures the lively window shapes. The DINING ROOM to the
W of the hall fits into the canted side of the house. It has two
bowed ends and a garlanded frieze (the wall set forward and
the reproduction chimneypiece are of the C20). Here as elsewhere the corner towers are used for lobbies and cupboards.

The remainder of the rooms, where not altered, are of charming lightweight Adam character.

SILVERBURN see PENICUIK

SKATERAW see INNERWICK

SNAWDON see GARVALD

SOUTHFIELD
EL 4070
3.5 km. NW of Gladsmuir

Small but handsome, says the New Statistical Account. Built c. 1804, it has a bullseyed pediment over the three centre bays, and a Roman Doric doorpiece with a fluted lintel.

SOUTH QUEENSFERRY
WL 1070

ST MARY (Episcopal), at the w end. Originally the church of a Carmelite friary sometimes said to have been founded as early as 1330. The present building cannot be dated before 1441, when James Dundas of Dundas granted a piece of land 'lying in the town of the ferry . . . for the church of St Mary the Virgin and for the construction of certain buildings to be erected there in the form of a monastery'. Seen from the street the church has very little of the monastic about it – indeed, with its choir, transept, tower, and traces of a nave, it looks the archetypal smaller collegiate church. Walking round to the N side one finds no transept, only a plain wall that shows traces of the lean-to roof of a cloister; so there can be no question of a N transept having existed and been destroyed. This peculiar lopsided plan was something of a speciality of British friaries, for it existed at the St Andrews Dominicans, at many places in Ireland and at one or two in England and Wales. It sometimes indicates that the transept was added later where it would not interfere with the cloister, but there is nothing at Queensferry to suggest that the church is not all of a piece. It is of low, broad proportions, and the lack of buttressing imparts a certain boxiness. Walls of coursed brown rubble, with ashlar reserved for the tower. The choir has a stone-slabbed roof and windows which are either lancets or two-light with minimal tracery; the E wall has both sorts plus an image niche, several blank shields and the corbels for a belfry. Only the S transept S window is more enterprising, square-headed, the lights with cusped ogee tops (cf. Dunglass chancel). The tower, quite plain, was no doubt higher originally. On the W wall traces of the nave pulled down as late as c. 1820.* It was shorter than the choir and had windows like the S transept S window and a wooden roof of low pitch.

Inside, the crossing, transept and choir are firmly separated spatial compartments. Round E and S crossing arches with moulded imposts and slight chamfers. Blocked W arch of two orders with capitals. The jambs of the E arch have the marks of a low coped wall, presumably a choir screen. Under the tower a semicircular tunnel-vault runs N–S. In the choir a pointed tunnel-vault with corbels at springing level that may have carried the floor of an upper chamber lit by the two E lancets. In the E wall an AUMBRY, in the S wall a PISCINA and basket-arched SEDILIA with outsize cusping (cf. the recesses inside the W tower at Linlithgow).

After the Reformation St Mary became the parish church. It was abandoned in 1635 when the new one was finished (see below). In 1890 Seymour & Kinross restored the building and presumably added the W porch. – FONT, in the transept. Of stone, a big square basin on a cusped octagonal pedestal and steps, in memory of Charlotte Mary Dundas † 1905. – Many other memorials to the family of Dundas (see Dundas Castle). – In the chancel on the E wall a royal COAT OF ARMS of C18 character, on the N wall a SLAB from the tomb of George Dundas † c. 1600 and his wife Dame Katherine Oliphant, resited here in 1893. – In the transept a WALL TABLET carved as a draped curtain, to George Dundas of Deescroft, Baillie to the Laird of Dundas, † 1710. – STAINED GLASS. On the S side of the nave two lights (SS. James and John) by James Ballantine & Son. – In the transept three lights (Adoration and Death of the Virgin) of 1891. – At the E end three lights (the Ascension) by Mayer & Co. of Munich, 1904. – FURNISHINGS. Gordon Russell chairs, altar rail and simple pulpit installed by Ian G. Lindsay, 1963.

PARISH (former Free) CHURCH, The Loan. 1893–4. Gothic, with rectilinear tracery and a stone spirelet to one side. Plain, scissor-roofed interior. – Under the W gallery two PANELS painted with the heraldry of Queen Margaret, brought from the Old Parish Church. – HALL attached to the S side. Harled; a good simple job by T. Harley Haddow, 1972.

* It is shown in a painting of c. 1840 in the S transept.

OLD PARISH CHURCH (former), The Vennel. A plain rectangular kirk of 1633 with doorways to N and S, round-headed with fluted margins; the former bears the date. W gable corbelled to support the stocky original bellcote. Later W door. The building was 'renovated' by *P. MacGregor Chalmers* in 1898. Some fixtures survived the conversion to office use *c.* 1962. – STAINED GLASS. At the E end Christ and Jacob, 1898. – On the S side two lights (the Nativity, Christ in the carpenter's shop), after 1899, and two more (Moses and St Paul) of 1949. – C18 GATEPIERS at the entry to the adjoining churchyard, rusticated, with ball finials. – MONUMENTS. John Hutton † 1684, with a lurid *memento mori*. – Two six-legged C18 table-tombs with anchors and navigational instruments. – The children of Henry Steel, Shipmaster in Queensferry, 1755, with the relief of a ship.

TOLBOOTH TOWER. Queensferry's senior building, and a nice termination at the W end of the High Street. Harled with stone dressings, C17, remodelled *c.* 1720, the Jubilee Clock incorporated in the pyramidal slate roof *c.* 1887. Adjoining it to the E the ROSEBERY MEMORIAL HALL, Scots Renaissance by *Sydney Mitchell & Wilson*, opened in 1894. In the wall at the base of the tolbooth a cast-iron PLAQUE dated 1817 incorporating a public fountain, with a testimonial to Lord Rosebery for providing this amenity and a bleaching-green for the burgh.

SCOTSTOUN HOUSE, Kirkliston Road. 1965 by *Ove Arup & Partners* as their own office. Regular concrete piers with big sheets of glass between them and continuous clearstory windows along the top; then a flat roof carried outwards on projecting I-beams. The shell of an early C19 stable clock is preserved as a screen and an ornament. More screening is provided by luxurious tree-planting.

DUDDINGSTON HOUSE. *See* p. 180.

DUNDAS CASTLE. *See* p. 190.

South Queensferry lies along the S side of the Firth of Forth, looking across to Fife between the vast construction of the rail bridge and the nonchalant suspended curves of the road bridge (for both of these *see* below). The first section is the EDINBURGH ROAD. The HAWES INN, with twin crowstepped gables of the C17, was extended to the W in the early C19, then to the E in 1893 by *Sydney Mitchell & Wilson*. The HAWES PIER was used by the ferry. Designed by *Rennie & Stevenson*, 1809–18, it has a little octagonal lighthouse with rusticated base.

The town really begins at the road's w end, where it is narrowed
to the s by a splayed row of houses, to the N by the baronial
SEALSCRAIG HOTEL, its back beetling over the rocks. After
a brief widening it is again cramped by a splay corner.

103 The HIGH STREET now begins. It is sited on a very narrow shelf
between the water and the sharp rise to the s, and is consistently
notable in townscape if not in individual buildings. The N side
starts with Nos. 59–61, a symmetrical three-storey block of
c. 1820 in droved ashlar. Then the less urban harled No. 58
pushes out and covers the start of a long modern gap; not a
serious leak, for there are plenty of buildings on the s side to
enjoy the view. On the lower pavement level a long row of early
C19 pilastered shopfronts, only slightly the worse for wear.
Their roof is the upper pavement. On this level No. 9 with its
bargeboarded gable is a gay introduction to a continuous Georgian row dominated by the three-storey ST HELENS of c. 1790,
its doorpiece cornice matched by that of LABURNUM HOUSE.
The terrace ends when BLACK CASTLE comes forward to the
old narrow street line. End gables with big crowsteps. Three
scrolly pedimented dormers to the N, one dated 1626. Beyond
it is the way up to the parish church (see above). The FORTH
BRIDGE HOTEL at No. 36 is evidence of an earlier widening;
although its character is mainly of c. 1900 the corbelling at
second-floor level accords with one or other of the two dated
stones, 1674 and 1683. EAST TERRACE and MID TERRACE
with its good iron railing with spears and pineapples carry on
the earlier idiom. WEST TERRACE leads along to the Rosebery
Memorial Hall and Tolbooth Tower (see above), after which
the municipal housing of HILL COURT, 1964 by *Wheeler &
Sproson*, is set up on stilts above yet another raised terrace to
allow the pavement underneath; round the corner it is enlivened by the light-catching windows of a concertina front, and
by a polygonal glazed staircase. Meantime the N side has recom-
menced with the baronial CLYDESDALE BANK, c. 1880, and
continues with a good low-rise sequence, especially No. 29 of
c. 1770 with a Gibbs-surround central doorpiece and scrolled
skewputts (the shops are rather later) and a presently neglected
house of c. 1700 with a lugged and moulded doorpiece. This
whole sequence curves gently to the r. and ends with PLEW-
LANDS HOUSE, 1641 (property of the National Trust for Scotland), restored externally and adapted internally for housing
purposes by *Basil Spence* in 1956. The staircase jamb is set
slightly apart from the internal angle of the L-plan. The

house successfully stood in the way of a proposed new service road to the red brick distillery that appears from a distance to dominate the town. The other important building in HOPE-TOUN STREET is No. 2, *c.* 1820, with a shopfronted bow. On its near side the OLD HARBOUR, founded in the C16 but built in its present form by *Rennie & Stevenson* in 1809–18. The High Street vista is effectively ended by the solid, low-set mass of the priory church (*see* above). Up-hill in THE LOAN, No. 8 is rectory-Gothic of *c.* 1870.

HOUSING. The HOPETOUN ROAD area was developed by the Town Council from 1920 with semi-detached houses by *William Scott* of Linlithgow. SCOTSTOUN PARK to the SE was developed for the *Scottish Special Housing Association* by *Robert Matthew, Johnson-Marshall & Partners*, 1968. The predominant type is the staggered row of two-storey houses; white dash walls with a weatherboarded centre section to each house. Link walls and boarded carports are well used to tie the blocks together. SHOPPING CENTRE and QUEEN'S RETREAT BAR by *Marshall Morrison & Associates*, 1970. The external aspect is like a small fortress, with few windows and rounded corners, but this is not altogether inappropriate. The well laid red brickwork has kept its appearance remarkably well.

ECHLINE FARM, to the SW. Late C18–early C19. In poor condition at the time of writing and worth mentioning only because it is known to have been repaired by *James Paterson*, wright, in 1778 and *Davud Udny*, builder, in 1791. The barn with the large pantiled piend roof is probably the one that was built in 1789. Long row of late C18 cottages with a pantiled roof sticking up into three peaks to meet the higher ridges of the extensions to the rear.

THE FORTH RAIL BRIDGE, to the E. Elegant in its structural logic and totally purposeful in its form, this prodigious steel bridge was built to carry the North British and associated railways across the firth between South and North Queensferry. The total distance between the cliffs on each side is just over 2.5 km. and the twin tracks are 47 m. above the high-tide level of the busy water leading to Grangemouth and the naval docks at Rosyth. The designers were *John Fowler* (his best known works in Britain are the Metropolitan and District Railways in London) and *Benjamin Baker*, his partner and former assistant. Baker had an artisan training, and his subsequent work as a designer was characterized by an unusual combination of vision and honesty. 'Where no precedent exists, the successful engineer is he who makes the fewest mistakes.' He also had a

proper sense of loyalty to his predecessors, repairing their work
rather than replacing or modifying it (e.g. the bridges of Telford). What architect is his equal? The contract was let to
Tancred, Arrol & Co. in December 1882 and work began in
the following year. On 24 January 1890 the Marchioness of
Tweeddale drove the first train across the bridge, and on 4
March the Prince of Wales declared the bridge open. In the
company was Gustave Eiffel, whose tower for the Paris Universal Exhibition is exactly contemporary with the bridge and
structurally related to it.

At South Queensferry, whose slight promontory is answered
by that of North Queensferry on the Fife coast, the Firth of
Forth changes recognizably to the River Forth. A double tunnel
was planned in 1805, a light chain bridge in 1818, 'so light indeed that on a dull day it would hardly have been visible, and
after a heavy gale probably no longer to be seen on a clear day
either'.* Nothing came of it, and even the aggressive spread
of the railways was for a time halted s of the Forth. Thomas
Bouch's 1865 scheme for a suspension rail bridge from Blackness to Charleston (4 km.) was abandoned in favour of a system
of boat-trains in which the passengers were frequently seasick.
Bouch again was the designer of a bridge with widely separated
tracks for which the contract was signed in 1873, but by 1879
only the preparatory work had been done, including the start
of a monstrous central tower on the island of Inchgarvie. The
collapse of his Tay Bridge in that same year led to an exhaustive
inquiry by the railway companies into the best method of securing a Forth crossing. In 1882 a fresh Act of Parliament auth-
orized Baker & Fowler's cantilever bridge.

The system of a central lattice truss between cantilevers had
been foreshadowed theoretically by Barton, of St Pancras (London) fame, in 1855, and this idea of a 'discontinuous span' had
long been discussed. It was successfully used for the bridge at
Poznan, Poland, in 1876, but for a single span of only 46 m.
The Forth Bridge has two main spans, each of 523 m., on each
side of the central tower based on Inchgarvie island. The three
towers with their balanced cantilevers are like huge stress-dia-
grams, painted dull red‡; lattice girders for tension members,

* The long article by W. Westhofen in *Engineering*, 28 February 1890,
supplies this pleasantry along with a great quantity of information and drawings.

‡ Dull red is indeed the present colour, but Westhofen says that the top
coat was originally 'a bright Indian or Persian red, which, however, darkens
considerably in a short time'.

tubes for compression members and those that combine both roles. Stability is the reason for the inward batter of the whole structure, and also for the broader stance of the central tower, whose cantilevers lack the anchorage of stone piers. The outer cantilevers, since they have no intermediate trusses to carry, are equivalently loaded with a dead weight of metal within these piers, which are of rock-faced masonry. Each has an arch through which a train in either direction, having traversed the approach viaduct on its rock-faced supports, penetrates the steel forest of the cantilevers. The simple trusses that carry the track seem quite incidental to them. The clearest function of this bridge is to withstand sea and storm. To its other job, the provision of the direct route to the N and E of Scotland across this formidable natural barrier, it is somewhat aloof. The bridge is seen at its simplest, in pure, distant elevation, from Hopetoun House to the W; at its most complex and powerful from the old ferry pier by the Hawes Inn, or best of all from the water.

THE FORTH ROAD BRIDGE, to the W. *Mott, Hay & Anderson* 4 began their report on the feasibility and siting of the road bridge in 1926. The Joint Board set up in 1947 confirmed their appointment as consulting engineers together with *Freeman, Fox & Partners*, *Giles Gilbert Scott & Partners* being the consultant architects. The site was one of those originally recommended, using the Mackintosh Rock on the N side to support one of the two towers of a suspension bridge. Treasury authority was given in 1958, and the Queen opened the bridge in 1964. It is not a pioneer work of its kind like the rail bridge, and indeed its design owed much to previous experience – not least to the lesson of the Tacoma Bridge, U.S.A., which collapsed as a result of rhythmic movement induced by wind pressure. This is one reason for the absence of continuous surfaces to the sides, which in turn contributes to the main quality of the bridge if it is seen as a work of architecture. The carriageway, unlike that of the rail bridge, is predominant, rising and falling in an easy curve 1830 m. in length between the box girders of the approach viaducts. The main span accounts for just over 1000 m. of this. The only other elements are the two steel towers, 150 m. high, simply latticed between their slightly tapering legs, which carry saddles for the cables whose calligraphic curve complements that of the carriageway and then disappears underneath it to anchorages in the rock. The only suspicion of 'applied architecture' is in the design of the arched concrete piers, whose job is not only to carry the last girders of the approach but to take the eccentric strain of the cables before they run to ground. The dual carriageway is supported by lattice trusses, elegantly pointed at the extreme ends. The experience of crossing it, attaining the greatest height at the furthest distance from land, is made less exciting (but doubtless safer) by the steel grid crash-barriers blocking the sideways and downwards view; the slightly later Severn Bridge improved on this. Cross-girders outside the trusses support a track for cyclists and pedestrians. Undoubtedly the best way to see the bridge, and the views from it, is to walk. The ADMINISTRATION BUILDING at the S end, with curved-up eaves that are not inappropriate to the levitation effect of the bridge itself, is by *Giles Gilbert Scott & Partners*. *Wheeler & Sproson* added the garages for service vehicles in 1969, tactfully concealing them to avoid clutter.

3060   SOUTHSIDE HOUSE   ML
                         5 km. SE of Dalkeith

(A C17 L-plan house romanticized *c.* 1840 when the corner turrets, corbelled out on first-floor level, were extended upwards. A re-used lintel is inscribed PE AC (Patrick Ellis of Plewlands and his wife) 1640–4.

SOUTRA *see* FALA AND SOUTRA

SPITTAL *see* ABERLADY

6070   SPOTT   EL

PARISH CHURCH. A little T-plan kirk which may have taken its present form in 1790 or (more likely) in 1809 when *John Mason* was in charge of repairs. Bellcote at the SW end. C17 burial aisle left over from an earlier church. The porch was added in 1848, and the old jougs hung up outside the door. Quite plain inside, with box pews. – PULPIT, in the centre of the long wall. Mid C18; Corinthian columns supporting a sounding-board with carved entablature. – STAINED GLASS in the SW window before 1967 ('He healed those that had need of healing'). – MONUMENT. In the churchyard a headstone to the infant children of Patrick Nisbet, mason, † 1742, the attributes of his craft in the pediment, which is supported by puny half-columns.
Apart from the church, the oldest building is the L-plan MANSE, built in 1805 by *William Lamb*, wright, of Linton, and *James*

Hannan of Tyninghame. It was enlarged in 1812 by *John Mason* of Spott. It is colour-washed, but the rest of this loose-knit estate village is of deep pink sandstone. *Robert Bell* was said to have designed the farm at the s w end 'and other buildings' in 1833. *John Mason Jun.* built the SCHOOL in the previous year: an exceptionally pretty building with small square glazing throughout, jutting out from the schoolhouse, which has a pedimented door under a big gable. But the cottages are like those at Tyninghame, with tilted stone hoods over the doors. The 'square' of cottages at the farm end, newly built in 1835, is at the time of writing derelict.

SPOTT HOUSE, to the E. A choice site indeed, on a sw spur of Doon Hill and naturally moated by a fork in the Spott Burn; but this has been culverted on the w side, possibly before 1830, when *William Burn* recast the building, making it a miniature Tyninghame in sandstone of a somewhat paler pink. The w (entrance) front is all Burn's except for the block to the N which he crowned with two crowstepped gables and prolonged with an entrance bay and a Jacobean doorpiece. The new dormered block to the s is set forward from it, and at the join he placed a tall round stair-turret with swept-in candle-snuffer roof. Square Tudor chimneys, set diagonally. Spott has been diversely occupied since the C13, and the other fronts hint at a complex history. But the only characteristic early details are the nicely moulded chamfers of the C17 windows in the N block, which has a later bell-cast roof. The s block, founded on massive under-building, some of whose lower chambers are built up, has round turrets of the C17 or earlier. Burn completely transformed the interior, though there is still a turnpike stair whose C17 bottle nosing is returned down the edges. His main stair is Jacobean, his rooms Grecian with plain chimneypieces, all on a modest scale.

STABLE COURT. Dated 1856, with a little Italian belfry on the crowstep gable of the centre range, the remnants of Georgian rusticated quoins on one wing. It overlooks the house, with prettily walled and terraced gardens between.

DOOCOT. C18 lectern type with crowstep gables and two large chambers.

LODGE, by the village. Gothic, with bracketed eaves, *c.* 1830.

EASTER BROOMHOUSE, 1.5 km. NE. A much altered red sandstone steading of 1825 with cartsheds at the entry, worthy of mention because it is known to have been designed by *W. & J. Lamb*; mason *Thomas Hamilton*, wright *Thomas Henderson*, the cost £560. Contemporary farmhouse. Four 'cot houses' at one foot of the road by *William Lamb*, 1828, with inclined hoods over the doors. The gables are later. To the S a STANDING STONE, 2.7 m. high, with three cup-marks on the W face.

PARISH CHURCH. By *William Burn*, 1829. The New Statistical Account relates that Mrs Ferguson asked the heritors to subscribe £900. She paid far more, and got Burn to build a modern Gothic church to her taste with a magnificent tower; no galleries inside, but a PULPIT in the centre with the family seat opposite. So it is a T-plan kirk, very lean and spiky, with a crocketed E tower. The neo-Jacobean family loft survives, and so does Burn's segmental ceiling with transverse ribs. But in 1892 *James Jerdan* resited the pulpit and communion table at the W end, turning the pews to face them. – STAINED GLASS. In the W window five lights (the Virgin and Child with SS. Paul, Andrew, Columba and Peter, with Old Testament figures beneath) by *C. E. Kempe*, 1888. – On the N side, W end, two lights (Righteousness and Faith) by *Ballantine & Gardiner*, 1892. – On the S side, W end, two lights (Faith and Hope, Charity), 1898, and adjacent to them another two (an angel and a Christian warrior), 1910, both by *Ballantine & Gardiner*, who also supplied tinted glass for Jerdan's reconstruction. – MONUMENTS, in the churchyard. A fair selection from the C17 and C18 including a table-top to John Dodds † 1677 with C18 and C19 inscriptions added.

OLD PARISH CHURCH. A C16 fragment. It was a plain rectangle with a S door whose jambs and segmental arch are moulded with a double roll. Attached to the W end a tower of two stages with a saddleback roof with crowstepped gables. – FONT at the E end. Plain and cylindrical. – FINIAL nearby, gableted on all four sides, with thin foliage carving. A cross has been inserted (perhaps correctly) in the hole in the middle.

Stenton means stane-toun, probably in reference to the surrounding terrain. But the village also has its own characteristic building stone, of a deep pink colour that goes well with the orange pantiles of the less pretentious houses. Almost the only thing not built of it is the ROOD WELL at the E end, a little cylindrical well-head with a conical roof in lapping courses like slates, topped with a rope-moulded ring and leafy finial. Then comes the parish church and, across the road, the former MANSE, reconstructed after a fire in 1820. Its arcaded upper storey suggests at least the influence of *Sir Robert Smirke* (*see* Whittingehame House). ST MARY'S (*c.* 1800) pushes out into view towards the East Green with the outside-stair cottage known as the Church Officer's House. Further on, past a doorway dated 1750, the two-storey, slate-roofed JOINER'S HOUSE of 1692. Next comes the MID GREEN, bounded by a small steading with octagonal horse-mill, and after it a narrow length of street, with another steading behind, ending with the late C18 SCHOOL HOUSE. Finally the street opens out into the triangular WEST GREEN with the BOARD SCHOOL built in 1878.

Stenton is distinguished for its well defined spaces and its simple hierarchy of buildings, pride of place being given to the churches.

BIEL HOUSE. *See* p. 101.

RUCHLAW HOUSE. *See* p. 421.

STEVENSON HOUSE

EL *5070*

2 km. ENE of Haddington

A plain quadrangular house of three storeys built round a courtyard, apparently in the early C17. A moulded doorway of that period leads into one of the three (originally four) turnpike stair towers in the internal angles, and there are glass checks in the upper parts of some of the window reveals on the E side. It is thus an interesting and uncommon adaptation of the 'palace' plan for the house of a lesser landowner. Externally its present aspect is of late Georgian regularity, and any other evidence of earlier work has disappeared under the harling which covers all except the pair of ashlar bows built *c.* 1820 on the S front. About that time corridors were formed round the inner sides of the courtyard.

Apart from a moulded stone fireplace (defaced) in a corner bedroom, the earlier internal work is the late C17 STAIRCASE to the S of the entrance hall, climbing up three sides of the well, with panelled newels, a moulded rail, and big stone balusters that are continued in timber along the landing. Deep coved ceiling, a thin acanthus leaf poking up into each corner. The ground-floor rooms are not (or no longer) stone-vaulted, and the main rooms are on the first floor. Along the S front, first the drawing room, which has late C17 panelling and diagonally voluted Ionic pilasters flanking a late C18 chimneypiece. Two round-headed frames with key-blocks camouflage the nonalignment of the w windows. The bracketed cornice has been reproduced in the bow window. Then the (former) dining room and a bedroom, both with pretty Edwardian chimneypieces. In 1934 the corridor along two sides was lined with woodwork from the Red Star liner S.S. Columbia. There is more in the library on the second floor, and its late c17 character is perfectly suitable. The house was repaired and restored in 1946–50 and the early c19 laundry wing and coach house to the n were repaired and converted as separate houses by *Mary Tindall* in 1952 and 1956, with great ingenuity and without overdoing the mannerisms of that period. She subsequently converted a number of cottages on the estate, including the TRUST COTTAGE of 1856 in the walled garden.

5070   STONEYPATH TOWER   EL
                    1 km. E of Garvald

The crumbling ruin of the c15 tower of the Lyells of Stoneypath, the ground falling into a deep ravine to the w. L-plan, of orangey-red rubble with irregular freestone dressings, the long sides to the s, where the door was in the section later rebuilt, and E, where there is a projecting stone at the n end, carved as a bearded head. The hall filled the whole of the s range and the stair was in the angle, wholly merged in the great thickness of the wall. At its head was once a domical stone roof which surprised MacGibbon and Ross.

4040   STOW   ML*

Stow in Old English means place – usually a holy or consecrated place. When the Scots conquered Lothian in 1018 the ancient church of St Mary of Wedale passed into the diocese of St Andrews and so into Midlothian. It was famous throughout the Middle Ages for its privilege of sanctuary and for the fragments of an image of the Virgin supposedly brought from Jerusalem by King Arthur. Wedale (valley of sorrow) is the old name for the valley of the Gala Water. The A7 follows its meanderings quite closely on the E side without a crossing, but bridges were necessary to connect this road to the older one on the w bank. Buildings in this area, such as they are, are concentrated in or near the valley and the main walling material is dark grey whin.

* Now Borders Region.

The Stow Hills, once clothed by part of the Ettrick Forest, are now bald and bleak, supporting a few sheep farms only.

ST MARY OF WEDALE PARISH CHURCH. 1873 by *Wardrop & Brown*. E.E. and Dec in pink and yellow sandstone, and a welcome sight on its hillock amongst the hills. The three-stage pinnacled tower, plus spire, is attached to what seems to be the w end but is actually the N, the illusion of a cruciform plan being helped by the five-sided apse at the other end and a transept in between. But round the other side there is no corresponding transept – only a rose-windowed gable and the vestry. Once inside, the puzzle is explained. Pulpit and communion table are not sited in the apse, which ends merely in a family pew, but under the rose window. So it is a T-plan kirk after all, uniformly roofed in open timber. Yet the balance of ideas is nicely maintained, the 'nave' being emphasized by a shallow gallery and by an arcaded aisle of two bays which provides two more private pews. – COMMUNION TABLE and CHAIRS of oak, 1912 by *John Taylor* of Edinburgh. – ORGAN by *Ingram & Co.*, 1905. – STAINED GLASS. Wheel and flanking windows (Ruth and the parable of the Sower) of *c.* 1875. – In the transept many New Testament scenes, flanked by the Stoning of Stephen and Paul in Athens, 1912 by *James Ballantine*; deep colours effectively contrasted with pale green and brown scumbled ground. – In the apse two lights (SS. Margaret and Luke) of 1967 by *William Wilson*.

OLD PARISH CHURCH. Disused since the opening of the new church in 1876 and now a ruin. Some of the red ashlar of the late C15 church can be seen on the N nave wall, and it projects buttress-wise at the SW corner where there is a section of the old base course. In the C17 the church was largely rebuilt in a mixture of rubble and freestone, with a round-topped and hoodmoulded S door, a S aisle with a fireplace (and formerly a gallery above) and an outside stair giving access by a doorway dated 1660 to galleries on the N, E and W sides. In the W wall two mullioned windows, and above them a double light with loop tracery; its margins set forward from the rubble wall confirm its C17 date. C18 bellcote at the gable head; 1771 is the date on one of the windows.

To the SE are fragments of the BISHOP'S PALACE.

Stow itself, though hardly more than a village, boasts a formidably baronial TOWN HALL of 1885 in which style is a long way ahead of function. The early C19 MANSIONLEA HOTEL bordering the road has a strong family resemblance to other houses of that period in the neighbourhood (*see* Burnhouse and Torquhan).

BRIDGES. STOW (Gala Water). 1654–5. Three main arches of rubble, diminishing from E to W; disused and broken. – LUGGATE (Luggate Water), 1.5 km. SW. Late C18, with three segmental arches and rounded cutwaters; mentioned in the New Statistical Account. – FERNIEHURST (Gala Water), 3 km. SSW. 1823. – BOWLAND (Gala Water), 5 km. SSW. Dated 1815, with four arches.

TORSONCE HOUSE. *See* p. 451.

FARMS. CROOKSTON NORTH MAINS, 9 km. NNW. Possibly late C18. Entirely of grey whinstone with swept angles. A square court for sheep, with a slated piend roof all round. – CROOKSTON SOUTH MAINS, 8 km. NNW. Dated 1814 in the pediment over a flat rusticated arch. Whin walls with sandstone dressings. – TORSONCE MAINS, 1 km. SW. Late C19. An impressive three-storey block (animal shed downhill, stable uphill and lofts on top) of red and yellow brick, overlooking the A7.

SUNNYSIDE *see* EAST LINTON

SYDSERF HOUSE   EL
              3.5 km. SSW of North Berwick

A pantiled, L-plan house of the early C18. The outside stair is probably later, for by the early C19 it had already become workers' dwellings.

TANTALLON CASTLE   EL
              3 km. E of North Berwick

40 A singular site indeed: a headland pointing NE into the Forth, with waves breaking at the foot of the cliffs on three sides. Across the landward neck, the huge curtain wall of reddish sandstone with a tower at each end and another in the middle. At its foot a ditch, and then a larger one which cuts off a generous slice of the headland to form a bailey. Then a ravelin pointing SW, the only way an attacker could come. The outermost ditch beyond it may have been made by a besieging force.

The castle was probably built by William, first Earl of Douglas, *c.* 1370. It is a castle of enclosure with the big SW curtain for defence, a NW range for the main accommodation. Another

wall on the SE side seems to have been intended, but not built.
The approach runs between the large ditch and a burn, and
is first confronted by the gun-looped spur of the C16 OUTER
GATE. In the bailey a DOOCOT of C17 lectern type. The SW
front, with its curtain wall 15.2 m. high, seems even larger
because it has lost so much of its shape, the mid tower having
been crudely reinforced in the C16, the end ones torn open by
General Monk's cannon in 1651, and the whole thing savagely
weathered. The present aspect of the MID TOWER dates from
soon after 1529 when the castle was surrendered to James V.
The Master of Works' Accounts for 1537–9 record building in
progress under *John Skrimgeour*, with *George Sempill* as master
mason. They advanced the base of the tower some 3.5 m., with
rounded corners against artillery, using greenish stone banded
with red, burying the old barbican and covering the twin jambs
and turrets of the old front which had become insecure after
the king's bombardment.

In the entry the picture is clearer, with signs of the old drawbridge and portcullis. The original entry was spacious, albeit
punctuated by doors and yetts: a pointed arch on the outside,
with recessed mouldings, and a round one to the courtyard.
Both were altered by simply blocking them up, and providing
smaller openings to one side. In the courtyard a new stair-tower
was built to the l. Its green sandwich masonry was not bonded
into the older work and has parted company with it. The rooms
it serves are apparently original; they had been reached by a
stair within the wall. All of them, above the ground floor, had
timber floors that have now disappeared to show a series of
canopied fireplaces. Two corner bartizans remain on the courtyard side, and from the courtyard one enters the twin staircases
within the 3.7 m. thickness of the CURTAIN WALL. The slits
seen on the main front give them light, and their first straight
flights are remarkable for their ceilings: a series of transverse
arches slightly deeper than the steps. The soffits of the turnpike
stairs are treated with the same sort of laborious care, and the
wall-walk is eventually reached, behind the big crenellations.
The round DOUGLAS TOWER to the W has a pit prison in the
basement, and timber-floored rooms with vaulted garderobes
above. The EAST TOWER is D-shaped, with stone-benched
rooms; the one on the third floor had a barred window and
access to the walk on the head of the SE wall which was not
built. The NW range is of no great splendour. The hall over
the vaulted basement has corbels indicating a (probably

subsequent) lateral division, and the further part, evidently of
the C16, had a kitchen and bakehouse in the basement. Little
pointed windows in the top storey. To the NW the remains of
the SEA GATE, covering a cleft in the headland. The WELL to
the E of the mid tower, in the courtyard, 32.3 m. deep, was excavated by Sir Walter Hamilton Dalrymple at the end of the C19.
In 1924 the castle was given to the Office of Works.

OLD PARISH CHURCH. Temple takes its name from the
Knights Templar, who had their main Scottish house here from
the mid C12 until their suppression in 1312. However, the existing building cannot be the Templars' church: its arrangements
are purely those of a parish church, and moreover its stylistic
character indicates a date after the Templar period, mid
C14 at the earliest. It consists of one long room, roofless but
otherwise complete. The best index of date is in the window
tracery: intersecting in the N and E windows, a single circle in
the S window. In theory such patterns belong to the period
c. 1280–1310 (cf. Elgin Cathedral choir), but here the details
are simplified in typically Late Gothic ways, notably by the
omission of cusps and of the arched head to the centre light
of the S window. The lancets W of the traceried windows, the
plinth and the priest's door all hark back to C13 prototypes.
C17 or C18 bellcote on the E gable, but what the RCAHMS
regards as the original gable cross is now on one of the churchyard gatepiers. Gabled buttresses on the E and S walls, remains
of one later buttress of unexplained breadth at the E end of the
N wall. The westernmost third of the church has been plainly
rebuilt at some time after the Reformation, re-using axe-
dressed ashlar of an unmistakably Romanesque kind. Might it
have been taken from a demolished C12 W tower? In the W wall
a window with Y-tracery and a round-headed door. In the N
wall a door to a former W gallery. Inside, most windows have
finely moulded rear-arches. E window with attached shafts. Indications of another three-light window W of the priest's door.
A jamb of the N nave door is visible at the W extremity of the
medieval work. In the S wall damaged SEDILIA with two very
C13-looking trefoiled heads. – MONUMENTS. Below the NE
window a segmental tomb niche contemporary with the building (cf. the moulded capitals with those of the E window). It
belonged in all probability to whoever paid for the church. –

In the churchyard a round-topped headstone with an urn. On one side the attributes of death, and an inscription to John Craig, Farmer in Outerstoun, † 1742; on the other his full-length portrait in high relief – a fine figure in long coat, bonnet 26 and knotted scarf, flanked by his two sons on a smaller scale.

PARISH CHURCH. 1832 by *Thomas Brown* of Uphall, T-plan Gothick without much desire to drop the k, though there are crisp stone mullions in the windows, neatly placed buttresses with gableted tops and a skinny but perilous bellcote corbelled from the W gable. The church is being converted into a house (1977). – MANSE across the road. Built for the old church, repaired in 1790 and 1805, and now pleasantly chaotic with bargeboarded C19 additions. The RCAHMS reports the discovery of a C13 basement course, possibly associated with the claustral buildings, during alterations in 1928.

Temple consists of a string of houses climbing up each side of a quiet main road. The two earliest are probably Nos. 21 (1760) and 25 (1761). Both are dated over the doors, and the lintel of No. 25 is a flat arch. The old and new parish churches are downhill towards the South Esk. At the riverside is one gable of an old mill. Just above it, MILL HOUSE, dated 1710 in the pediment over its lugged front door. Deep skews suggest that it may have been thatched. The skew to the W has a sundial skewputt and a moulded outer edge which returns across the base of the chimney stalk. The chimney at the other end rises from a projecting ingle on which two vertical stones mark the end of a chute for ashes. Inside, a stone stair rises straight from front to back. Bolection-moulded fireplace on the first floor to the W with a cornice and a pulvinated frieze. The one downstairs was probably the same.

GATEWAY, to the E of the village. An arched entrance of the late C17 with chevron rustication on the base and on alternate courses. It led to Temple House.

ROSEBERY FARM, 2 km. SW. *See* Rosebery House.

THORNTONLOCH *see* INNERWICK

THURSTON MAINS *see* INNERWICK

TORPHICHEN   WL 9070

PRECEPTORY CHURCH. Torphichen was the only Scottish house of the Knights of St John of Jerusalem otherwise known

as Hospitallers. The first mention occurs in a document normally dated to 1168, but what sort of buildings existed then we
do not know. Towards the very end of the c12 a church was
built which consisted of a choir, transepts and nave (all aisleless)
plus a central tower. In the c15 the transepts and crossing were
greatly heightened, and remodelled. The choir and nave, which
remained wooden-roofed and low, have disappeared almost
completely, although the nave survived as the parish church
until it was replaced in 1756 by the present building. The transepts were used after the Reformation as the court house of the
Regality of Torphichen, a fact which must explain their preservation.

The exterior should be examined in an anti-clockwise
sequence, starting with the evidence for the choir. This consists
of no more than some traces of the eaves cornice, and on the
N side a piece of the string course that ran beneath the windows.
The length of the choir is not known. The blocked crossing
arch is c15, but the central tower is still of c. 1200, with the
obvious exception of the saddleback roof. The E and W faces
have each a minuscule pair of lancets under a vesica, that on
the W displaced by a c16 or c17 mullioned window. In the N
transept E wall a large window of three lights and two encircled
quatrefoils. Beneath the sill a reset length of c12 string course.
The N wall shows traces of the E conventual range. Of the range
itself only two pier bases remain; otherwise the monastic buildings are a matter of markings in the grass. Nothing about their
planning calls for special comment. The cloister was entered
from the N transept by a door with a three-sided head (cf. e.g.
St Salvator's Chapel, St Andrews; Huntly Castle). To the r.
of this another door leads to the upper chamber of the tower.*
The nave is reduced to the lowest courses of the N wall, just
enough to show that the N door projected from the wall and
had finely moulded and still non-waterholding bases to the
outer order and a filleted roll without bases to the inner order.
The string course of the S transept W wall, which is still basically
late c12, is cut by the roof-line of a low aisle which opened into
the transept through a plain segmental arch.* Two original eaves
corbels in the angle with the former nave. Large S window of
four lights with three cusped circles, the smallest at the top.
The angle buttresses look absurdly low unless one agrees with
the RCAHMS that the raising of the transepts was done some
time after the initial stage of remodelling. In the E wall and close

* The S nave was four bays long with octagonal piers.

to the crossing one small lancet with more string course below and a blind quatrefoil either side.

The interior is an impressive spatial sequence of three strongly marked and nearly equal bays. The N transept is slightly shorter than the other and probably still of the late C12 length. Quadripartite vault with ridge ribs, one carrying an inscription referring to Sir Andrew Meldrum, Preceptor of Torphichen in the 1430s. The crossing belongs to the same phase. Crossing piers with fat shafts, some with fillet. Elided capitals and bases. The low W crossing arch is still late C12. The blocking wall has recently been moved back to reveal three orders facing W as against the one towards the crossing. Presumably the E face was kept flat to allow choir stalls to fit against it. Alternatively, the richer treatment of the W face may mean that the arch was a chancel arch in the parish church sense, in which case the choir and transepts would be later (though only slightly later) additions. The detail is characteristically Transitional and well-finished. Keeled and coursed innermost shafts, the others plain and detached. Capitals with plain broad leaves and waterleaf. The label continues as a string course. The S transept was evidently rebuilt some time after the rest as the rib profiles are different. The SW rib springs from a re-used C12 corbel. It remains to ask the question: why were the transepts rebuilt and not the liturgically more important choir? Is it possible that the transepts were conceived as monumental versions of the private transeptal chapels in parish churches like Borthwick or Corstorphine? The central placing of the tomb niche in the S transept and the inscription to Sir Andrew Meldrum in the N transept would tend to confirm this interpretation. From the rooms over the transepts can be seen parts of lancets that formerly lit the tower. Here also are collected some C15 double bell capitals and bases from the cloister arcades.

PAINTING. In the S transept below the E lancet pieces of a foliate diaper pattern. – Over the W crossing arch red lines simulating ashlar. – On the W wall of the S transept, incised in the plaster and hence difficult to locate, a working DRAWING showing the setting out of voussoirs. – MONUMENT to Sir George Dundas † 1532 in the blocking wall of the W crossing arch. Two narrow panels out of an original four arranged as a rectangular frame. One has Renaissance arabesques and trophies, the other a skeleton in a shroud and scrolls recording the erection of the monument by Sir George's nephew and successor as Preceptor, Sir Walter Lindsay. 23

PARISH CHURCH, adjoining the preceptory. A T-plan kirk of
1756 with round-headed windows, scrolled skewputts and a
birdcage bellcote. The pews and galleries in all three jambs were
installed in 1803. The pulpit with its sounding-board and
twisted stair balusters may be earlier. All the woodwork has
been painted pale grey.* – MONUMENT, in the churchyard.
Walter Gowans † 1859, by *James Gowans* his son. A garland
looped informally over the round top of the stone.

Torphichen is a road-junction village, sadly fragmented, but the
SQUARE still has some character. In the middle of the irregular
space is the octagonal JUBILEE FOUNTAIN of 1897, with an
ogee cap. On the N side a pair of stone dormered cottages
flanked by single-storey wings, that to the l. with an artisan
doorpiece with simple columns. One house to the W is dated
1802. To the E are the stone walls of GLEBE HOUSE, with trees
on the slope behind; this is the beginning of the Bathgate Hills.
On the S ROCK COTTAGES, a harl and timber terrace by *Reiach
& Hall*, 1963, mount the slope with something of the assurance
shown by the Georgian cottages of HIGH BRAE. On the N side
are three housing developments: from the inter-war period
the pebbledashed GREENSIDE round a very large green; and
the white-harled NORTH GATE and BOW YETT by *Reiach
& Hall*, the latter running from the square to the preceptory.

WALLHOUSE, to the W. A crenellated Gothic front of c. 1840,
strangely austere because it has pointed hoodmoulds over the
square-topped windows of the upper floor. Spindly octagonal
turrets at the ends. In 1855 *J. Maitland Wardrop* added a porch,
and over it a bay-window with blind tracery in the upper part.
He also extended the frontage and built a stair-tower off-centre
at the back, causing trouble with the surrounding chimneys,
which had to be heightened. All this and the office buildings
to the rear are in slightly yellower sandstone than the original
building. The interior is entirely of 1855. Large stained-glass
window depicting the medieval Master of Torphichen on the
stair. Chimneypieces of oak and coarsely classical except the
one in the drawing room to the S, of Louis XV type in white
marble. To the NE an octagonal, castellated Tudor TOWER of
c. 1840; a ruin.

CRAIGEND FARM, 1 km. N. An unusually large farmhouse of
c. 1800. Three storeys. Anta doorpiece in a segmental arch and
tripartite windows above. Round dome-topped gatepiers to
the court behind.

* The interior is in process of alteration (1977).

CAIRNPAPPLE HILL. *See* p. 128.
CATHLAW HOUSE. *See* p. 136.

TORQUHAN HOUSE
3 km. NNW of Stow

ML* *4040*

Built in 1823 in coursed whin, with sandstone dressings of great refinement. Roman Doric doorpiece in a pedimented centre. Single-storey pavilions with Venetian windows. *Kinnear & Peddie* carried out alterations in 1885, but this date is too early for the pretty interior, which is apparently Edwardian.

TORSONCE HOUSE
1 km. SSW of Stow

ML* *4040*

By *David Bryce Jnr.*, *c.* 1868. Tall and hard, with braced gables and iron balconies, it became more friendly when mullioned windows and an inconsequential turret were added to the E front. Bryce interiors in the library and on the first floor. The rest was transformed *c.* 1900, including the charming sequence of drawing room, hall, sitting room and dining room, the last with Jacobean pilasters and an ingle. Moulded plasterwork in the manner of Lorimer; but neither the date nor the architect of these changes is known.

TORSONCE MAINS *see* STOW

TOWNHEAD *see* GIFFORD

TRABROUN *see* GLADSMUIR

TRANENT
EL *4070*

OLD PARISH CHURCH, Church Street. Built by *John Simpson*, mason, in 1800 over fragments of the pre-Reformation church which belonged to the abbey of Holyrood. It had transepts and a central tower. At the base of the W and S walls some late C15 masonry. In the S wall part of a roll-moulded doorway. On the N side two buttresses and the ruined mortuary aisle of the Cadells of Cockenzie are of pre-Reformation date. The new

* Now Borders Region.

church has round-headed windows. Attached to the E end a
tower in two stages, the lower with lunette windows for the
landing of the gallery stair, the upper with little pointed windows, battlements and pyramidal corner finials. The inside was
completely recast in 1953 by *Leslie Grahame Thomson*, who removed the galleries. Smooth shiny walls sweep up without a
break into a flattened vault. To the W a chancel of similar but
smaller section. The organ to the N is totally concealed. This
spartan simplicity is effectively relieved by good wrought-iron
lights and oak pews and furnishings. – STAINED GLASS. Venetian W window by *Margaret Chilton*, 1953, working with *Marjorie Kemp* in the centre light (Christ and the four Evangelists),
and *John Blyth* in the outer ones (coal mining and agriculture).
– Centre S window by *William Wilson*, 1966 (Blessed art thou
amongst women). – The churchyard has a countryfied
approach, though its outlook to the N is filled by the power
station and its dependencies. In it, an unusually good collection
of MONUMENTS. To the S of the church the large slab of Alexander Crawfurd, priest of Tranent and Clerk to the Chapel
Royal † *c.* 1489, with an incised pattern of a cross on a stepped
base. – Then from the general period of *c.* 1700 a wealth of pedimented tabernacle monuments, bizarrely eroded, and scrolly
headstones carved in high relief with skulls and crossbones and
much gusto. – Best of all, two rather later table stones with
Rococo tops, on six legs with arches which have distinctive
pendant centres; the Seton monument has acanthus balusters
of square section at the corners and a portrait bust in high relief
on the S side. – DOOCOT, to the N of the churchyard. Of the
double lectern variety in three stages, with a stone over the door
inscribed 'DAVID SITOUN 1587'.

ST MARTIN OF TOURS (R.C.), at the E end. A harled octagonal
church with a brick porch. A cross forms a flèche to its shallow-
pitch copper roof on laminated wood arches. By *G. R. M. Kennedy*, 1967.

ST JOSEPH'S SCHOOL, 1 km. N. Ionic and austere, by *William
Burn*, 1821; built as George Stiel's Hospital, it is virtually a
country house. The simply moulded cornice of the portico continues that of the house. Four unfluted Greek Ionic columns,
those at the ends with diagonal corner volutes. Behind them
are antae which break solidly forward from the three flanking
bays on each side, and they rest on walls which project forwards
to contain the solemn stair. All in grey ashlar, polished portico
against droved walling. Basement windows with segmental

heads. The internal arrangements have been obscured by later alteration, though the twin staircases remain. The building was acquired by the R.C. Church in 1884, and in 1896 a large E wing was extended backwards from the main block. W wing, containing the chapel, of 1914. The single-storey bungalows were built in 1909, Ogilvie House in 1966. Later additions and alterations by *Bamber, Gray & Partners*.

Until the C17 Tranent was the head of a large parish embracing Prestonpans, Pencaitland and Gladsmuir. It has been associated with coal mining since the early C13, when the Lord of Tranent granted mines and a quarry to the monks of Newbattle. The lower seams began to be worked in the early C18, and from 1722 there was a wooden tramway to the port of Cockenzie, replaced by an iron railway in 1815. Tranent itself is still a mining town, and a small one, though swelled by C20 rehousing. BRIDGE STREET and HIGH STREET are part of the A1 and their buildings have been continuously redeveloped, but they still form an almost unbroken line in which a small, two-storey scale has been maintained. At the point where the street name changes and Church Street comes in from the N, the WAR MEMORIAL by *T. Aikman Swan*, 1923, stands in for a mercat cross. The sinuous main street is punctuated by pubs which appear, as you round each bend, at the end of the next stretch. The only ones worth noting are the late C19 CROWN INN with its fat candle-snuffer turret in High Street, and the BRIG INN at the E end, built in the early C19 by the bridge spanning the old coal railway. *John MacLachlan* added its gabled upper storey in 1897. Between the two is the BACK MARKER which forms part of the CIVIC SQUARE redevelopment by East Lothian County Council, designed by *Douglas Sanderson*, 1969. The square adjoins the High Street and provides a real centre for Tranent, with shops and flats as well as the upstairs pub. In its centre is the PUBLIC LIBRARY, nicely detailed with a single octagonal space covered by laminated arch beams and roofed in copper. CHURCH STREET leads first to TRANENT TOWER, apparently of the late C16, a three-storey ruin with a square staircase turret and unusually small windows. Then the former WISHART CHURCH of *c.* 1830 with a flat classical front, its width exaggerated by the long, curiously humped parapet. Further down, No. 205, an early C19 cottage with a pretty porch whose finial is an insurance mark. An armorial cartouche is mounted over a gateway to one side, a pointed arch incorporated in the wall to the other. THE LODGE, No. 246, flanking the approach to the parish church, has a simple pedimented porch.

ST GERMAINS. *See* p. 421.

ST GERMAINS. *See* p. 421.

5070   TRAPRAIN LAW   EL
                    6 km. E of Haddington

2 This isolated ridge was one of the capitals of the tribe known as the Votadini. The situation and the size of the site make it an interesting monument to visit, though the remains of the rampart at the bottom of the hill and those of the later wall higher on the hillside are not in themselves remarkable. A hoard of Roman silver (now in the National Museum of Antiquities in Edinburgh) was found in 1919.

The LOTH STONE, 300 m. SSW, which stands to a height of 2.4 m., was originally situated 47.5 m. to the S of its present position. It is said to have marked the grave of the fictitious king Loth, after whom the Lothians are supposed to be named; no burials were discovered during excavations in 1860 and 1948.

TYNEFIELD *see* EAST LINTON

TYNEHOLM *see* PENCAITLAND

6070   TYNINGHAME   EL

OLD PARISH CHURCH (ST BALDRED), in the grounds of Tyninghame House (*see* p. 456). St Baldred is supposed to have lived at Tyninghame as an anchorite and died in 756 or 757. The monastery which existed here in the C9 owned lands stretching from Lammermoor to Inveresk, in other words modern East Lothian. Tyninghame was sacked by the Danish King of Northumbria in 941, and nothing more is heard of the monastery thereafter. What exists today is the ruin of a mid C12 parish church which continued in use till the village was cleared in 1761. It makes an extraordinary sight marooned among the flower beds of Tyninghame House, and hardly less odd is the way that all plain masonry has been removed, leaving a skeleton of arches and shafts like some outsize demonstration model. Fortunately enough is left to show that Tyninghame was once the equal of the infinitely more celebrated Dalmeny. The plan is in fact virtually identical with Dalmeny's: an oblong nave, narrower W tower, square chancel and semicircular apse.

Nothing of the nave or the tower stands to any height. The chancel and apse arches are carried on groups of three shafts. The vanished ribs of the apse vault sprang from coupled shafts with annulets two-thirds of the way up. On either side of the chancel arch is an altar recess (cf. e.g. Castle Rising, Norfolk). In detail Tyninghame and Dalmeny are not particularly close, yet they cannot be widely separated in time. Of the two, Tyninghame is perhaps the more resourceful in its choice of decorative motifs, although figural carving is absent. Chancel arch with two orders of chevron separated by a band of billet and framed by a hoodmould decorated with paired semicircles. The soffit of the inner order is treated as a series of lozenges. The capitals and their abaci are covered with a pattern of overlapping scales exactly as in the nave wall arcading at Dunfermline. Other Dunfermline motifs are the volute capitals and the palmette-decorated abaci of the apse arch. The apse vault shafts have scalloped capitals – though not of the ordinary variety – and abaci with fancy chip carving. Who can have paid for these splendours? We know the Bishops of St Andrews owned both the church and the lordship, but is this in itself sufficient explanation? There is no reason to think the church was anything more than parochial. – MONUMENT. In the S chancel wall a C15 tomb recess. Pointed arch, worn female effigy.

Tyninghame is the very model of an estate village. On the E side of the main road the harled FACTOR'S HOUSE, *c.* 1800, and the lodge and arched gateway of the big house which are presumably by *William Burn, c.* 1830. Opposite is the crowstepped SAWMILL, with undershot water-wheel still *in situ,* built in 1828 by *Thomas Hannan,* mason, and the engineer *George Sked.* It has diamond-paned windows. The road is joined by an uphill branch to East Linton, the main street of the village, all of pink sandstone except the two harled rows by *Ian Arnott,* 1939. The random rubble block on the corner, formerly the inn, is the oldest building. Most of the C19 work is by *Thomas Hannan* again, and it has a delightfully varied relationship with the road line, its quality enhanced by good planting (including two espaliered trees against triangular gables) and confirmed by good maintenance. In 1836 *Hannan* built the (former) SCHOOL and adjoining schoolmaster's house, enlarging them in 1852. In 1841 he was paid for some cottages which are probably WIDOWS' ROW, five of them round a half square. The centre house is inscribed 'rebuilt 1840' under the nice artisan-classical pediment. His grandest building is the BAKER'S

HOUSE of 1842 (now the Village Hall), a long block with a similar pediment over its front door and ventilated gables for storage in the attic, reached by a loading door round the back. In 1854 *James Hannan* built some cottages which would seem to be the row at the w end with pointed stone dormers; the wright, as at the Baker's House and school extension, was *Thomas Henderson*. The POST OFFICE, with a corbelled chimney stalk to the road, and the semi-courtyard of the SMITH'S HOUSE to the N of it, with canted porches in the angles, share the family resemblance.

TYNINGHAME BRIDGE, on the main road to the s. Originally built in 1778, *Andrew Meikle** 'giving advice and attendance', and excellently rebuilt for a wider roadway by *Blyth & Blyth*, engineers, in 1931.

LAWHEAD, 1 km. WNW. Tudor farmhouse and adjacent cottages of 1838-40 by *Thomas Hannan*, mason, and *Thomas Henderson*, wright. *Francis Buchan* did some work at the steading in 1796, but the main feature of the present building is an arched entrance incorporating flight holes for pigeons, dated 1858.

TYNINGHAME HOUSE

90 A precocious baronial essay in rosy pink sandstone by *William Burn*, 1829. The Earls of Haddington have had Tyninghame since 1628, and in the early C19 the house was 'a plain old Scottish mansion of large size' (Small's *Castles and Mansions*), whose C17 character is conveyed by a sketch in the library and whose extent is clearly shown in the drawings for Burn's transformation. Looking at the plan, the surprise is that he kept so much and added so little. The old house was built round three sides of a courtyard open to what is approximately the s, the oldest part the thick-walled N and W ranges (i.e. the gallery, the ante-room and part of the drawing room). It subsequently rambled out to the SE and expanded to the N. Apart from the bay-windows, Burn's only significant additions to the plan were the porch, the lengthened w range (enlarging the drawing room) and a new corridor alongside the SE projection, where he also put on some new turrets; those of the w range were there already.

The elevations are a different story. The walls were almost entirely refaced, and although the pattern of the large new

---

* Was he the millwright and inventor of the same name? He seems to have had engineering knowledge.

mullioned windows is quite regular, the other details are clearly designed for romantic outline and dynamic mass – a combination which was to be the hallmark of the Baronial revival with a capital B, as opposed to the more static and obviously less pretentious C17 baronial on which it was (in this case quite literally) based. At Tyninghame the courtyard, where some old masonry is still visible, still has some of the accidental quality of the original. The two dummy pepperpots added to the E side of the SE extension represent the simplest sort of baronial allusion, familiar for the past fifty years. Their swept-in candle-snuffer roofs are another feature of the earlier revival. The W side of the house goes a stage further; here baronial elements are used to achieve a dynamic balance between the two unequal but similarly organized walls on each side of the circular turret. Much of the detail is of course Tudor or Jacobean in flavour: the chimneys, the bay-windows and even the crowsteps which are bracketed in outline (*see* Winton House, p. 472). The eccentrically placed tower balconies are vital to the balance of the whole, and so is – or rather was – the continuous balcony at main-storey level, which gave lightness and overall continuity. Unfortunately it became eroded and had to be removed *c.* 1960, but a small section of it remains at the SE corner. The entrance (N) front moves right into the Baronial idiom. The house already had three blocks pushing forward. Burn organized them with a powerful build-up towards the r. and a different gable treatment on each, and added the single-storey porch as a further projection between the second and third. The heraldic doorpiece is a replacement by *W. Schomberg Scott*, 1961. To the l. the composition subsides further, the office buildings being dominated by a little square clock tower corbelled out from the gable end of a row of cottages which Burn recast, with nine dormers on the S front. An older square tower of unknown purpose stands to the N of the yard.

The main rooms, eclectic but perfectly assured, are the most beautiful of their time in Scotland. The layout is spaciously informal, the detail frankly composite, e.g. in the cornices – some consisting of a near-Gothic line of sinuous stalk and foliage, others of delicate openwork shells over heavy egg-and-dart. Doorcases with plain bolection mouldings throughout. The principal floor is reached by a straight flight from the porch, then a shorter one which is properly part of the main STAIR-CASE: a Jacobean well-stair, powerfully cross-beamed, with compartmented plaster soffits. The ceiling at its head has the

classical type of cornice, with Rococo enrichment in the
corners. In the GALLERY the original paper, deep lacquer red
lightly powdered with informal flock sprays of leaves and
flowers. French Rococo chimneypiece of red speckled marble.
The woodwork is dark stained and part gilded, as are the overdoors by *Jackson* of London, successfully added *c.* 1960. To the
N the DINING ROOM, heavily cross-beamed in plaster. Each
section has a foliage cornice of extreme delicacy. The c18 white
marble chimneypiece, a monumental importation from a
demolished house* in Suffolk, has big Corinthian pilasters
flanking the overmantel and curly-headed fireplace, a heavy
cornice breaking forward at their heads. Then the main suite
of three rooms along the w side. The ANTEROOM opens off
the end of the gallery. Grecian ochre marble chimneypiece,
quite plain except for the moulded antae supporting the lintel.
The paper, again original, pale green damask overprinted in
gold with another light leaf pattern, this time more formal, is
continued into the adjoining DRAWING ROOM, whose great
length is relieved by the slightly different treatment of its two
halves. The nearer (in fact the older part) has cross beams
centred about the first chimneypiece; the further has a clear
ceiling, and spreads out into a square bay at the end and a large
canted bay opposite the second chimneypiece, a pair to the first,
of white marble and quite small-scale, with exquisite Grecian
relief on a very plain ground. To the N of the anteroom the
LIBRARY, its ceiling, the most original single part of the house,
geometrically divided by a transverse oval containing a longitudinal one. Their soffits and those of the supporting arcs and
circles are progressively recessed and lined with fine Grecian
mouldings, and the centre of each compartment is marked with
a rosette. Bookcases with jambs and lintels with simple inset
panels. Chimneypiece of French type like that of the gallery,
but deep red. From the gallery's upper end opens a corridor
with WALL PAINTINGS in *trompe l'œil* architectural frames by
William McLaren, 1967, showing East Lothian scenes and the
attributes and interests of the Earl and Countess of Haddington. At the end LADY HADDINGTON'S DRAWING ROOM,
with mid c18 finishings from Elie House, Fife. The marble
chimneypiece has an owl and a monkey in relief over the end
lugs, and garlands of fruit and flowers between. Complex wood
overmantel with Corinthian columns supporting a carved
broken pediment, mirror plates between. Doorcase *en suite*.

* Probably Rushbrooke Hall.

Pyramidal bookcases by *John Fowler*. Concerning the other rooms all that is here relevant is that they are finished in straightforward fashion, Burn having efficiently removed all trace of earlier work.

The PARK is a pioneer work of landscape, not architecture, so it cannot be described here. Its chief creator is commemorated by an OBELISK sited to the W of the house on a promontory of the ha-ha. Its inscription reads

TO THE MEMORY OF THOMAS VITH EARL OF HADDINGTON
BORN 1680 DIED 1735
WHO AT A PERIOD OF THE GREATEST NATIONAL DEPRESSION
HAD FORESIGHT AND ENERGY
TO SET THE EXAMPLE OF PLANTING ON AN EXTENSIVE SCALE
AND TO BE AN ACTIVE AND SUCCESSFUL PROMOTER OF
AGRICULTURAL IMPROVEMENT
AND TO HIS WIFE
HELEN SISTER OF THE FIRST EARL OF HOPETOUN
1677–1768
OF WHOSE VALUED SUGGESTIONS AND ASSISTANCE
HER HUSBAND HAS LEFT AN AMPLE RECORD
1856

Downhill from the obelisk is the WALLED GARDEN, entered by way of the APPLE WALK which extends its tree-vault along the whole lower end. Doorway with an C18 Gibbs surround on the outside, but on the inside a flat-arched Renaissance doorpiece dated 1666. The central walk, a wide lawn lined with yew and punctuated by classical statues of the C20, ascends to the conservatory. The garden walls are crowned with stove-urns of the late C18. On the W side of the house the centrepiece of *Burn*'s Italian garden layout is a reproduction of the C17 Newbattle Abbey sundials; or so one would say if the crowning obelisk did not seem to be well weathered and genuine. Further to the W an openwork timber ARBOUR of *c.* 1960, Sino-Gothic, with an ogee top, and to the N a battlemented Gothic SUMMER HOUSE of the same period. In the courtyard a Venetian WELL HEAD, dated 1586, with the winged lion of St Mark.

STABLES. A courtyard mostly by *Burn*, 1833, with crowsteps and coroneted entry. But the S range is older, and incorporates fragments of chip-carved masonry from the old parish church.

UNION CANAL *see* KIRKLISTON, LINLITHGOW *and* RATHO

UPHALL

St Nicholas Parish Church, Ecclesmachan Road. The w tower, nave and chancel are still mostly C12 in their masonry but the Norman details are of 1878.* The one exception is the s door of the nave, which has one order of shafts, scalloped capitals and a roll moulding on the soffit of the arch. Blank tympanum, perhaps not original. The proportions of the whole are tall and narrow. In the lengthened chancel two E lancets, presumably C13 but widened, and a C15 s window; no tracery, just three lights and pierced spandrels. The tunnel-vaulted aisle of the Shairps of Houstoun, added *c.* 1620, has round-headed windows and bold half-round mouldings and corbel course. Then the Buchan loft to the N, of which only the outside stair is left, with the date 1644. This and other N additions were removed in 1878 when the N aisle was added, making the plan into a T. Inside, it looks into the nave through a triple arcade with scalloped capitals. The present scraped and rubbly look is due to *A. Lorne Campbell*, who in 1937 removed the post-Reformation galleries, revealed the pointed arch of the water stoup at the s door and the masonry of the plain round arch into the tower, and designed the new woodwork. – In the tower, the burial place of the Erskines, Earls of Buchan, a WALL TABLET to Thomas, Lord Erskine, Lord Chancellor of England, and the Hon. Henry Erskine, Lord Advocate of Scotland, † 1823 and 1817 at Almondell. – In the Shairp Aisle more tablets and a little marble URN containing the heart of Walter Shairp † 1787 in St Petersburg where he was H.M. Consul General. – War memorial TABLET in the nave by *J. Jeffrey Waddell*, 1922. – STAINED GLASS. At the E end two lights (Nativity and Ascension) by *William Wilson*, 1962. – On the s side a war memorial window (Resurrection, with the attributes of the Passion) designed by *P. MacGregor Chalmers*, 1922. – MONUMENTS in the churchyard. To the SE a good early C18 group. Table-top with Adam and Eve and a tree loaded with apples. – Headstone (broken in the time between our two visits) with a man and wife in relief; others with trade symbols. – To the SW a table-top to Margaret Aitken † 1730. – Opposite the s door a head-

* *Wardrop & Reid* made plans for a new church in 1865. It was not built, but they did the restoration.

stone dated 1721, carved with a graceful foliated wreath and a pair of skulls. – Beside it, a headstone of frightening simplicity: on one side a weaver's shuttle, on the other a mask within a loom and the inscription AH. IG 1710 with MEMENTO MORI in much more elegant characters. – To the NE a monument to Lieut.-Col. John Drysdale † 1865, with sword and hat in bronze, by *John Steell*, 1866.

Uphall used to be called Strathbrock (valley of badgers, as in Broxburn, the straggling C19 industrial village that adjoins it). The main street has a good sloping site, but its character is tenuous indeed, depending not on the church, which is 0.5 km. up the Ecclesmachan road, but almost entirely on the bland authority of the OATRIDGE HOTEL, *c.* 1810, with advanced and pedimented centre and a wide pilastered doorpiece. The main C20 contribution is the SCHOOL PLACE housing development by *Wheeler & Sproson*, 1963. The four-storey part adjoining the street is quite large in scale, with staircases glazed from top to bottom. It stands well on its site – a new and different architectural presence – but its white harling and paintwork need maintenance to look their best.

FREE CHURCH, on the S side of the street. Red sandstone, with a Perp traceried front, by *J. Graham Fairley*, 1896.

HOUSTOUN HOUSE, 0.5 km. SW. A tall, plain house of L plan, built for the advocate Sir Thomas Shairp from 1600; congruous C18 additions and a sympathetically contrasting C20 extension. The original main block is on the S side. Its ground floor is vaulted, and the old kitchen fireplace and bake-oven are in the E gable. It has four storeys, the bedroom jamb to the NE squeezing five storeys into the same height. In the internal angle was the turnpike stair-turret with the main entrance door in its base. In 1737 another jamb was built to the NW, with the new segmentally arched kitchen fireplace in its N gable. Between the two jambs a scale-and-platt staircase was built, reached by an entrance door inserted in the S front; this is now a window once more, for the front door was moved yet again *c.* 1830 – this time to the E side, with a single-storey porch. A service stair was also added at the NE. So the house is now virtually a solid square in plan. Screen walls form a courtyard to the N, connecting it with the Woman House, which seems to be of the original date. This contained the domestic offices: brewhouse, bakehouse and dairy in the vaulted ground floor, the servants' quarters above, reached by an outside stair.

Within the house, the dining room to the SE on the first floor

has a heavy cornice probably of the early C18, as are the Corinthian pilasters flanking the later chimneypiece. The former
library to the W of it was panelled in 1725, and the basket-arched
chimneypiece of dove grey marble was inserted in 1741. The
room to the NW has mid C18 panelling but the chimneypiece
is of *c.* 1820. On second-floor level all the rooms have plaster
cornices and wood panelling of the early C18, with a generous
provision of closets in the wall. The 1737 stair has turned
balusters and ball finials, and a small stair with a flat, cut-out
balustrade leads down to the top bedroom in the NE jamb; this
became necessary with the loss of the original turnpike stair
with its ability to step off at any required height.

After the untimely death of the architect and historian Ian
G. Lindsay, who had owned Houstoun from 1943, *Wheeler &
Sproson* were responsible for the conversion to its present use
as a hotel in 1970. They removed the C19 porch, and all that
now cuts across the C17 E elevation of the house is a cantilevered
lead fascia joining it to a slate-hung bedroom block which in
no way interferes with the integrity of the original (further
extensions contemplated at the time of writing may have a less
happy effect). COACH HOUSE and STABLES dated 1736. DOO-
COT on the E approach, of C17 lectern type. SUNDIAL on a
square baluster dated 1757. The yews in the garden were
planted in 1722.

UTTERSHILL CASTLE *see* PENICUIK

3060   VOGRIE HOUSE   ML
                        2 km. SW of Pathhead

93 Designed for the Dewar family of whisky fame by *Andrew Heiton
    Jun.* of Perth, 1875, and since the demolition of Castleroy, near
    Dundee, his finest surviving work. Baronial in its main elements
    of tower and bay, it nevertheless rejects all orthodox historical
    trimmings and pursues one clear objective – the expression of
    simple mass and structure by means of the stone surface. Thus
    window margins, relieving arches and quoins are all absorbed
    into lightly stugged masonry of mathematical flatness. Once
    you get used to this, much contemporary work in the later Vic-
    torian baronial style – turreted and string-coursed to the limit
    – seems over-dressed in comparison. String courses in a sense
    there are, but they are used to mark the decisive recession and
    advance of the wall plane; the strange device of reverse corbel-

ling, on the two octagon-based towers that are constrained inwards to a round form, has the same effect. So do the deep, cusped bargeboards of the gables, but they do it by force of contrast, oddly mocking the close-knit masonry underneath. Most remarkable of all, the upstairs windows have fixed upper sashes whose many divisions are without glass (the movable sash behind is glazed with a single sheet) so that no reflective plane compromises the dominating wall.

This great mass, with bedroom and service wing forming a lower outrigger to the NE, has a perfectly simple plan, each slice running right through the house. First the vestibule, with a lobby beyond. Then the long HALL with an Imperial staircase at the far end, the ceiling carried by two pairs of segmental arches. These focus attention on the doors into the two rooms at the SW end, which form the last slice: the bayed DRAWING ROOM with its deep cornice of formidably erect plaster leaves, and the DINING ROOM whose roof is supported on corbels representing, in four heads, the ages of man. The detail is of an idiom common to many revolutionary architects of the C19; the pylon chimneypiece of the hall, the chip-carved stair newels like those of 'Greek' Thomson, the equivocally Gothic doorpieces that disown the wall.

Beyond the house are the STABLES, in the prettiest Gothic of *c.* 1825. The New Statistical Account says that they are 'built in a style of taste and splendour indicating what the proprietor would have done to the house had his scheme been completed'. Whatever the house was like, it is indeed a relief that Heiton's tough masterpiece did not replace anything so irresponsibly happy as the stables. They consist of a U-plan block with stepped gables. A tower capped with a spiky octagon rises from the back, nicely obstructed by a Gothic arched screen wall canted forwards between the gables. All this suggests an attribution to *R. & R. Dickson*.

LODGE. Dated 1896, in an ordinary picturesque style which betrays nothing of the surprises to come.

VOGRIE GRANGE. A late C18 farm consisting of two simply pedimented ranges with a lectern DOOCOT as a plain centrepiece between them.

WEST BARNS EL 6070

The A1 makes a promising entrance over the Biel Water, which is fronted by two Georgian houses: the harled LOTHIAN

COTTAGE to the N, WEST BARNS COTTAGE in grey ashlar with an Ionic doorpiece, c. 1810, to the S. But the only coherent part of the village is a string of C18–19 houses along the N side of the road, including the INN. On the S side the READING ROOM of 1901: otherwise at the time of writing a scene of dereliction, the ruined brewery awaiting redevelopment which could well include the restoration of the few remaining vernacular houses. The decent housing further S was designed by the County Architect *F. W. Hardie* in 1931.

BIELSIDE HOUSE, to the N. A large Italianate villa by *R. Rowand Anderson*, 1866, with an Ionic loggia between pavilions, a tower behind. Further to the rear the round stump of a WINDMILL, of harled rubble, with a stone stair spiralling up the outside.

WEST BEARFORD *see* HADDINGTON

0060   WEST CALDER   ML

OLD PARISH CHURCH. Built in 1643, three years before West Calder became a separate parish from that of Midcalder, it became ruinous after its abandonment in 1880. Long and plain, the round-headed windows now filled in. Two small windows on the N side are obscured by a later turnpike stair that must have served a gallery or more likely a pulpit. Square bellcote with ball finial on the W gable. The walls buttressed in the mid C18.

PUBLIC LIBRARY, near the church. Queen Anne Art Nouveau in red and yellow sandstone with shaped gables, by *William Baillie* of Glasgow, 1903.

The CHURCHES of West Calder are unremarkable; gables and flanking spires are the rule. Not so the two CO-OPERATIVE STORES in the HIGH STREET: on the S side in grey stone by *J. Graham Fairley*, 1884, with a clock on the corner; on the N side a taller block in red and yellow with crowstep gables and iron-crested centrepiece, by *William Baillie*, 1913. A good pub is the COMMERCIAL INN to the E. Timber frontage with suppressed bay-windows and excellent iron grilles. In the middle a broken pediment with the date 1905. At the centre a group of shops and flats designed by *E. Thompson* for Midlothian County Council, 1964, with harled walls, sawtooth gables and rubble trim. In HARBURN ROAD to the SE, No. 65 is a 'cottage' by *Edward Gatney* of Wallsend-on-Tyne, 1914. Plasterwork by *W. Ferguson & Son*, Newcastle.

West Calder spreads to the E along the A71, first to POLBETH, which consists entirely of C20 housing. The most interesting are the timber houses by *Carr & Howard*, 1939. LIMEFIELD HOUSE to the S is early C19. Five bays, the three middle ones advanced and pedimented. Columned and fanlit doorpiece. Then BELLSQUARRY, which has a red and yellow SCHOOL of 1909 with four Queen Anne gables. The ELM TREE INN is early C19. The neighbouring house, of *c.* 1880, has lots of quirky cast-ironwork.

HARWOOD, 0.5 km. to the S. A three-bay farmhouse of two storeys and attic, with a moulded and corniced door. The New Statistical Account gives its date as 1768.

HERMAND HOUSE, 1 km. to the E. A five-bay house of 1797 built for George Fergusson, son of Sir James Fergusson of Kilkerran, Ayrshire; he became a judge in 1799 with the title of Lord Hermand. Three storeys and basement, pedimented tripartite doorpiece. Contemporary STABLE BLOCK, with an archway in the tall pedimented centre. Farm buildings sloping downhill from it. In the wall of the WALLED GARDEN an apsidal arbour with pointed windows.

WESTER CAUSEWAYEND *see* MIDCALDER

WESTFIELD HOUSE   ML 0060
2.5 km. ENE of West Calder

A small five-bay house of *c.* 1760, harled, with stone dressings. Paired chimneystacks and round-headed windows at the end gables. The doorpiece and the attached wings with pedimental gables were added *c.* 1800. In the W wing the drawing room with a contemporary upright leaf cornice and a timber chimneypiece enriched with thistles. FARM BUILDINGS immediately to the E inscribed with the dates 1838 and 1839, two parallel blocks, the S one with copious ledges and flight holes for birds. A square pavilion further to the E, similarly provided, has a niche containing a stone pineapple which may have come from one of the rusticated piers of the E gate.

WEST FORTUNE see ATHELSTANEFORD

WHITBURGH HOUSE   EL
3 km. WNW of Humbie

A medium-sized but very elaborate neo-classical house of three storeys, built *c.* 1810. Advanced centre with an apsidal porch of four Roman Doric columns *in antis* with a bowed stairway. Niched ends with blank ovals above. The columned wings forming an open loggia with a canted end to the W, a drawing room to the E, may date from *c.* 1914 when *Hippolyte J. Blanc* carried out alterations. (The interiors appear to be of equal elaboration.)

DOOCOT in front of the house. Two harled storeys and a conical slated roof, probably C18.

GATES. Channelled piers, probably contemporary with the house, with older urns.

WHITBURN   WL

PARISH (SOUTH) CHURCH, Manse Road, on a hillock to the S of the town. A cross-plan kirk with bellcote and a weathered sundial on the S gable. Two reset keystones on the N jamb and adjoining porch announce that it was built in 1729, the roof finished in May 1730. A third stone of similar shape is inscribed 'rebuilt 1959', i.e. the roof was replaced and the interior recast after the fire of 1955. C19 Gothic skews all by *Dick Peddie & McKay*. Attached to the E side the C18 pedimented burial enclosure of the Baillies of Polkemmet. – MONUMENTS, in the churchyard. To the W, two late table-tops, one to the Rev. John Brown † 1833, the other of *c.* 1827 to a family of Wilsons, with cast-iron balusters supporting a single iron sheet engraved in copperplate writing. – A few early C18 headstones.

BRUCEFIELD CHURCH, East Main Street. 1964 by *Rowand Anderson, Kininmonth & Paul*. Effective if not always functionally expressive. A white-harled convex shell fronting the main street contains the chancel; a convex one to the side street makes a niche for a concrete cross and also supports the porch. Well detailed interior with a raked floor and a ceiling of dark varnished boards which here and there push their way out to make bellied fascias on the outside.

LONGRIDGE CHURCH, 2 km. S. 1840 by *Robert Black* of Glasgow. A spiky Gothic gable with a central bellcote faces the road.

PUBLIC BATHS, Main Street. Of concrete blocks, with mono-pitch channelled steel gables to the street. By *Tom Duncan* of *Rowand Anderson, Kininmonth & Paul*, 1973.

WHITBURN ACADEMY, Shanks Road, to the NE. 1967 by *Wheeler & Sproson*. Four-storey classroom block of storey-height precast units assembled chequerboard fashion. Extended later by a different firm.

YOUTH AND COMMUNITY CENTRE, near the parish church. In red brick, by *William Nimmo & Partners*, 1975.

Whitburn was already established before the coal and iron boom of the early C19, and even its C20 buildings are of some quality, but the overall effect is very bitty. EAST MAIN STREET begins with a chimney gable of swept profile, the round skewputts prettily inscribed 18,13. The TOWN HOUSE next door is late Georgian, the chimney gable ingeniously extended into an ogee-topped belfry. Further on, an excellent development of houses, flats and shops in dark red brick with four four-storey towers fronting the street. This is MILLBANK, by *Alec Somer-ville* of *Gordon, Duncan & Somerville*, 1969.

WHITE CASTLE
3.2 km. SE of Garvald

EL 6060

An accessible and impressive multivallate fort.

WHITEHILL *see* ST JOSEPH'S HOSPITAL

WHITEKIRK

EL 5080

PARISH CHURCH. In the C12 Whitekirk was simply a parish church belonging to Holyrood Abbey, but by *c.* 1300 miracles of healing were being performed at a nearby well and pilgrims came in large numbers (supposedly more than 15,000 in 1413). James I placed Whitekirk under his protection and built pil-grims' hostels. In 1435 Aeneas Silvius Piccolomini, the future Pope Pius II, walked here barefoot through snow to give thanks for his deliverance from shipwreck in the Forth. James IV was a frequent visitor, as he was to other pilgrimage centres, but in 1537 James V granted the pilgrims' hostels to Oliver Sinclair, who demolished them. The church became parochial once more and survived almost without alteration until 1914, when it was set on fire by suffragettes. The walls sustained little damage, but some good C17 furnishings were lost. A careful

restoration was carried out by *Robert Lorimer*. Yet for all
its eventful history, Whitekirk is an unassuming church, aisleless and cruciform with a squat central tower. Two-bay choir
with prominent buttresses and plain, deep window embrasures.
The only medieval tracery is in the s window. The E wall is
blank except for a small oculus high up (renewed correctly after
1914) and a small armorial panel with foliage on the frame.
Crozier behind a shield whose arms have been identified as
those of Abbot Crawford of Holyrood (1460–83). This is not
reconcilable in any obvious way with a record that Adam Hepburn of Hailes Castle built the choir in 1439. The N transept
has no old features and the s transept is of 1830, much rebuilt
by Lorimer. Central tower with small two-light openings, a
stair-turret at the NW corner and a low slated spire recessed
behind a corbelled parapet. The N wall of the nave opens into
a shallow rectangular projection (hardly an aisle) added in 1832
and rewindowed by Lorimer. The s porch has a large, roughly
detailed arch, a canopied niche over diagonal buttresses and,
inside, a tunnel-vault with surface ribs. Agreeably spacious and
uncluttered interior. Plain pointed tunnel-vault over the
choir. The crossing is entirely Lorimer's but reproduces the
old design. Short, wide piers and round arches (both
chamfered), moulded imposts and rib-vault with ridge ribs.
Also by Lorimer the ceiled wagon roof over the nave and transepts. The texture of the wood makes it appear older than it is.
– COMMUNION TABLE, PULPIT, LECTERN and FONT all by
Lorimer. – STAINED GLASS. In the W window four lights (the
Resurrection with saints and angels) by *C. E. Kempe* after 1889;
a survival from the fire. – In the N aisle four windows (St
Andrew and three others) by *Kenneth Parsons*, 1916. His are
also the moody seraphim in hot colours in the three mouchettes
of the round s transept window.

MANSE. Built in 1796 but given its present aspect, dark whinstone with grey stone dressings and a ground-floor arcade, by
Robert Brown, 1837.

TITHE BARN, to the N of the church. A long three-storey
block with crowstepped ends. The W end is the tower built
c. 1540 by Oliver Sinclair with stone from the pilgrims' houses,
extended in the following century.

NEWBYTH HOUSE. *See* p. 350.

WHITTINGEHAME

EL 6070

James Balfour acquired Whittingehame in 1817, built the new house and rebuilt the church, and then established a new model village to the N W of the former. It consists of a school house and a string of cottages, all in red sandstone *c*. 1840, with a mixture of crowstepped and deep-eaved gables. REDCLIFF, a busy Jacobean house with a bargeboarded lodge, was built about the same time. Balfour himself is commemorated by a roadside OBELISK of 1858, 2.5 km. to the W.

PARISH CHURCH, to the W. 1820,* supplanting an older church of 1722. Spiky battlemented Gothic, T-plan, in red sandstone, with a W tower. To the NE is the burial enclosure of the Buchan Sydserfs of Ruchlaw (*see* p. 421) with an Ionic pilastered front; C18, but probably restored. Some good headstones of the late C17 show that there was a still earlier church.

WHITTINGEHAME TOWER, to the SW of the church. Built by one of the Douglas family who became Earls of Morton. Here Bothwell and Lethington are said to have proposed to the fourth Earl, later Regent Morton, the assassination of Darnley; this would have been in 1567 and the tower is distinctly earlier, late C15 or early C16. It is rectangular in plan, with a staircase jamb to the N. Three storeys, with a boldly corbelled and crenellated parapet within which stands a cap-house over the main block. At the foot of the stair is the entrance, moulded with a roll and equivalent hollow. In a shield superimposed on the lintel the arms of Douglas of Whittingehame. (In the hall on the first floor a C17 ribbed and moulded plaster ceiling in which birds are conspicuous. Massive brackets for the main beams. The egg-and-dart door frames may be later.)

The WALLED GARDEN has a pavilion like a temple with an order of antae dated 1905, and gates with brick piers dated 1914.

PAPPLE, 2 km. SW of the village. A mid C19 farm steading with cattle courts and a dormered Jacobethan front. Entrance arch with corbelled doocot and pyramidal slated roof. The farmhouse is of the late C18.

WHITTINGEHAME HOUSE. A big rectilinear house of pale Cullalo stone by *Sir Robert Smirke* for James Balfour, 1817, with additions and alterations by *William Burn* ten years later. The New Statistical Account called it 'a splendid mansion of Grecian architecture'. The main block, entered on the NE front,

* 'Messrs *Barclay & Lamb*' provided plans and specifications for repairs in 1820.

is actually astylar except for the porches. What makes it interesting is that Smirke built it all up from slabs of one-bay thickness in such a way as to give depth to the centre part and length to the side parts, and to the whole thing an intriguing variety of scale and silhouette. Burn in 1827 used the same stone, but managed to make what was already a dry composition into a boring one – by the massive piers that flank the centre bay, obscuring the crispness of Smirke's slabs and planes, and by a deep plinth and balustrade overall. At the NW end Smirke had built a kitchen and office court on basement level, and a conservatory (only its arcaded rear wall now stands) and a pedimented Greek Doric loggia on the garden front. Burn gave this wing an extra storey on the entrance front, and attached a portico exactly the same as that of Smirke's loggia – but a rather pointless one, for it has no doorway and the rooms behind it are nothing special. It seems to have been much later that the porches of the main block were altered – probably in 1871, when the balustrades were added to the garden terrace. The semicircular porch on the garden front became a bow window with antae in place of columns; and behind and beneath the entrance portico a long canted bay was threaded with fiendish ingenuity. *Farquharson* of Haddington added the glazed corridor in the NW wing in 1896.

Though somewhat impaired by Burn's work on the outside, Smirke's cross-axial system still prevails within. The ENTRANCE HALL with its black Doric chimneypiece leads through an anta screen across the central corridor into the SALOON (so marked on Smirke's plan), whose coffered ceiling has guilloche ribs. The length of the lofty, anta-punctuated corridor on the long axis, with five saucer domes, is matched by that of the vast LIBRARY on the garden side, with its ceiling in five coffered sections. On the entrance side is the DINING ROOM, transformed in the late C19 (possibly by Eustace Balfour), with oak panelling and a lusciously ribbed and bracketed plaster ceiling. The room beyond it, in Burn's single-storey extension, is a second LIBRARY. Its ceiling is Grecian, as is the first, but less austere, with a diagonal ribbed centre surrounded by laurel moulding. The stairwell, which finishes the long axis in the other direction, is an awe-inspiring space with a triple blind arcade in the Baroque manner mounted high on the far wall; the arches were for the display of large pieces of oriental porcelain on the three heavily scrolled brackets. Burn was also responsible for the huge DRAWING ROOM at the S corner

with its coffered ceiling in six sections, and probably for forming yet a third LIBRARY in what had originally been 'Mr
Balfour's Room' to the left of the hall.

STABLES. Apparently to *Smirke*'s design. Two parallel
ranges, mainly of pink sandstone, with pedimented centres.
The range towards the house has a blind arcade on the ground
floor of its grey stone frontage. Intermediate block with pedimented ends.

LODGES. Of those which could be by *Smirke* the most interesting is the E lodge, L-shaped, with a pediment on each
gable, the walls articulated by antae. The porch in the angle has
a single unfluted Greek Doric column.

WILLIAMSCRAIGS
2 km. s w of Linlithgow

WL 9070

Baronial of *c.* 1880 with rockfaced stonework. The main feature
is a portentous build-up of vestigial turrets over the central
front door which has been functionally supplanted by a new
porch to one side.

WINCHBURGH
WL 0070

Winchburgh tells its own story. To the s of the road a severe gridiron of miners' rows whose names recall their landlords, the
Hopes of Hopetoun. They were built in brick in the 1890s, with
sills, lintels, and gable brackets of red stone. Those to the s survey a landscape of pit spoil, with the ruin of Niddry Castle. See p. 525
They are the foremost examples of their kind in Lothian, but
will their value as a housing resource be sufficient to save them?
To the E two single-storey SCHOOLS, one extended and the
other designed from the start by *James Jerdan & Son*, 1903 and
1907. In the middle a pompous POLICE STATION by *William
Scott* of Linlithgow, 1904, and quite separate to the w a little
Gothic MISSION CHURCH and manse of 1891.

GLENDEVON FARM, 1 km. w. 1820 by *James Anderson* for the
Earl of Hopetoun. The plan of the farm buildings consists of
a central passage with stables on each side, flanked by cattle
courts. The axial passage runs N to s, and there are cartsheds
along the s side.

4060   WINTON HOUSE   EL
                      1 km. NW of Pencaitland

Until it was forfeited in 1715, Winton was the junior house of
the Setons who lived in Seton Place (*see* p. 428). They were
given the Earldom of Winton in 1600 and about that time the
first Earl repaired the house, which had been burnt by Hertford. The second Earl employed the King's Master Mason
William Wallace to enlarge and embellish it in 1620–7.
Although the exterior is partly obscured by *John Paterson*'s
additions of *c.* 1805, Winton is still one of the finest houses of
the Anglo-Scots Renaissance.

  The carcase of the old house is still there: a rubble-built block
on the steep N bank of the river Tyne, with a jamb at the E
end of the N side, and a stair-turret in the angle. Wallace added
another jamb at the W end, a square tower whose lower part
contains a more spacious turnpike stair to the first floor. For
architectural display he concentrated on the skyline, with rows
of twisty chimneys (those at the gables set rather oddly behind
the crowstep profile), window heads and finials. The only show
front is that to the N, which must have overlooked an entrance
58   courtyard. The existing stair-turret in the angle was refaced in
ashlar and carried up to emerge above the wall head as a full
octagon with an ogee-capped roof, the slates on the inward splay
being cut in a fancy pattern. Presumably the front door had
always been in its base and still remained there, but the stairs
inside have been altered. The new tower, also of ashlar and
rounded at the corners, has two full stages above the wall head
and then a frieze overlaid with bracketed and gargoyled panels.
Above the cornice a large arcade, like a tower-head balustrade
but actually much too big. A round turret corbelled out in the
angle carries a little stair from the first floor to the roof, and
ends with an ogee cap. The windows have tabernacle frames
with strapwork or pedimented heads, and the whole of this front
is horizontally organized by means of string courses which
sometimes acts as sills, sometimes as cornices. The focus of the
whole composition in the wall between the two jambs, where
the windows are at last in balance. Centred in the lower section,
now built over, was a panel (now built into the E terrace), carved
with the royal arms and the inscription JACOBUS PRIMUS
BRITANNIAE MAGNAE ET FRANCIAE ET HIBERNIAE REX.
A trio of chimneys on the wall head above. The one in the centre
has straight instead of twisted flutes, with tiers of acanthus

leaves. The s front towards the river owes its extra storey to
the fall of the ground. It is harled, with stone string courses.
Broken pediments above the windows at the wall head.

Paterson's additions might have been much worse, given that
he was obliged to deepen a house only one room thick, rather
than lengthen it. To the n he built over the courtyard; a single-
storey battlemented screen of cardboard aspect with octagonal
corner turrets, and a two-storey canted centrepiece with a
Gothic doorway running back to the older house. Neither these
nor the canted bays to E and W are too much of a challenge
to Wallace's richer stonework.

The entrance leads into the OCTAGON HALL, prettily niched
and vaulted with pencil-thin shafts and plaster ribs ascending
to the round lantern which has a classical frieze of seahorses.
A vaulted anteroom is followed by the DINING ROOM at the
NE corner, refitted after a fire in 1881. Now for *Wallace*'s interiors. The STUDY in the E jamb has a rose in the middle of its
ribbed ceiling, and a frieze of birds, roses, pears and pomegranates. The LIBRARY (or KING CHARLES'S ROOM) is hardly
bigger but crammed with decoration. The eccentric arrangement certainly suggests a bedroom. A vast fireplace shoved
against one corner is topped by a string course with voluted
ends like a stretched Ionic capital and then a big jolly pediment
filled with strapwork, which overlaps an arcaded plaster frieze
of potted plants. The pattern of the ceiling ribs is far from rest-
ful. Its main lines are carried down into gadrooned or scrolled
pendants, its compartments filled with the attributes of the
United Kingdom with the arms of Scotland in the central
square. The DRAWING ROOM has a similar ceiling but without
pendants, its much larger area devoted to the heraldry of the
family. A vegetable frieze runs all around, interrupted only by
the arms on the chimneybreast. Here a second frieze surmounts
a wide stone fireplace with Roman Doric columns. In the fireplace frieze are seahorses which were to be quoted by Paterson
(*see* above). The main lintel is weakly defined by a lower architrave, on its keystone the monogram of the third Earl, George
Seton, and his wife Anne Hay. The corbel that pushes into the
room at the base of the upper turnpike on the N side is a
reminder of the organic Scots tradition that was now being
ousted. In the BEDROOMS on the first floor the ribbed ceilings
are less grand, but lighter and more imaginative. At the SE
corner of the basement is the pre-Wallace KITCHEN, with a
fireplace arch some 4 m. wide. The names of some of the C17

craftsmen are known from accounts, though unattached to particular jobs (or possibly to Winton at all, for there was also a
town house in Edinburgh): *John White*, plasterer (Alexander
White worked at The Binns), *David Stone*, wright, and *William
Pedden*, mason. The glazier *James Maistertoune* also appears.
The older windows have glass checks in the upper parts of the
reveals, and there is a late C18 report on the dereliction of the
stained glass in what is called the long gallery, but no old glazing
survives.

SOUTH GATES (*see* Pencaitland). C17, possibly from elsewhere.

NORTH LODGE. Twin castellated towers of the early C19,
the gap between them bridged by *Gilbert Ogilvy* who designed
the LAUNDRY in 1928.

4060

WOODCOTE PARK   ML
2.5 km. WSW of Fala

By *James Morris* of *Morris & Steedman*, 1970. A long simple form
made up of three cubes in a row, fully glazed on both storeys
and articulated by eight white piers, the W cube glazed to the
sky. Nearby is a red sandstone corner turret, a relic of the house
by *David Bryce* for Lord Woodcote, 1854, demolished in 1971.
– LODGE. Of *c.* 1820, with Gothic windows.

WOODEND *see* ABERCORN

WOODHOUSELEE   ML
3 km. N of Penicuik

Woodhouselee was an C18 house on the site of the old Fulford
Castle, and *George Meikle Kemp*, architect of the Scott Monument in Edinburgh, designed a wing in 1843. Everything was
demolished in 1965 except the early C19 STABLES which are
planned as a courtyard with curious Gothic windows in the
gables, ogee-headed lancets grouped in threes.

YESTER *see* GIFFORD

GLOSSARY

Particular types of an architectural element are often defined under the name of the element itself, e.g. for 'dog-leg stair' see STAIR. Literal meanings, where specially relevant, are indicated by the abbreviation *lit.*

ABACUS (*lit.* tablet): flat slab forming the top of a capital, *see* Orders (fig. 16).

ABUTMENT: the meeting of an arch or vault with its solid lateral support, or the support itself.

ACANTHUS: formalized leaf ornament with thick veins and frilled edge, e.g. on a Corinthian capital.

ACHIEVEMENT OF ARMS: in heraldry, a complete display of armorial bearings.

ACROTERION (*lit.* peak): pointed ornament projecting above the apex or ends of a pediment.

ADDORSED: description of two figures placed symmetrically back to back.

AEDICULE (*lit.* little building): term used in classical architecture to describe the unit formed by a pair of orders, an entablature, and usually a pediment, placed against a wall to frame an opening.

AFFRONTED: description of two figures placed symmetrically face to face.

AGGER (*lit.* rampart): Latin term for the built-up foundations of Roman roads.

AGGREGATE: small stones added to a binding material, e.g. in harling or concrete.

AISLE (*lit.* wing): (1) passage alongside the nave, choir or transept of a church, or the main body of some other building, separated from it by columns or piers; (2) (Scots) projecting wing of a church for special use, e.g. by a guild or by a landed family whose burial place it may contain.

AMBULATORY (*lit.* walkway): aisle at the E end of a chancel, usually surrounding an apse and therefore semicircular or polygonal in plan.

ANNULET (*lit.* ring): shaft-ring (q.v.).

ANSE DE PANIER (*lit.* basket handle): basket arch (*see* Arch).

ANTA: classical order of oblong section employed at the ends of a colonnade which is then called *In Antis. See* Orders (fig. 16).

ANTEFIXAE: ornaments projecting at regular intervals above a classical cornice. *See* Orders (fig. 16).

ANTHEMION (*lit.* honeysuckle): classical ornament like a honeysuckle flower (*see* fig. 1).

Fig. 1. Anthemion and Palmette Frieze

APSE: semicircular (i.e. apsidal) extension of an apartment. A term first used of the magistrate's end of a Roman basilica, and thence especially of the vaulted semicircular or polygonal end of a chancel or a chapel.

ARABESQUE: light and fanciful surface decoration. *See* Grotesque.

ARCADE: series of arches supported by piers or columns. *Blind Arcade:* the same applied to the surface of a wall. *Wall Arcade:* in medieval churches, a blind arcade forming a dado below windows.

ARCH: for the various forms *see* fig. 2. The term *Basket Arch* refers to a basket handle and is sometimes applied to a three-centred or depressed arch as well as the type with a flat middle. *Transverse Arch:* across the main axis of an interior space. A term used especially for the arches between the compartments of tunnel-

or groin-vaulting. *Diaphragm Arch:* transverse arch with solid spandrels spanning an otherwise wooden-roofed interior. *Chancel Arch:* across the w end of a chancel. *Relieving Arch:* incorporated in a wall, to carry some of its weight, some way above an opening. *Strainer Arch:* inserted across an opening to resist any inward pressure of the side members. *Triumphal Arch:* Imperial Roman monument whose elevation supplied a motif for many later classical compositions.

ARCHITRAVE: (I) formalized lintel, the lowest member of the classical entablature (*see* Orders, fig. 16); (2) moulded frame of a door or window. Also *Lugged* (Scots) or *Shouldered Architrave*, whose top is prolonged into lugs (*lit.* ears).

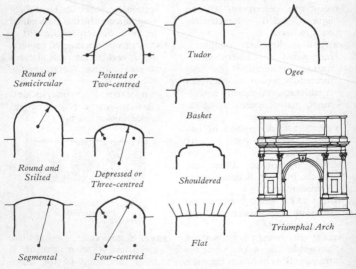

Round or Semicircular

Pointed or Two-centred

Tudor

Ogee

Round and Stilted

Depressed or Three-centred

Basket

Shouldered

Segmental

Four-centred

Flat

Triumphal Arch

Fig. 2.   Arch

ARCHIVOLT: continuous moulding of an arch.

ARRIS (*lit.* stop): sharp edge at the meeting of two surfaces.

ASHLAR: masonry of large blocks wrought to even faces and square edges. *Droved Ashlar* (Scots) is finished with sharp horizontal tool-marks.

ASTRAGAL (*lit.* knuckle): moulding of round section, and hence (Scots) wooden glazing-bar between window panes.

ASTYLAR: term used to describe an elevation that has no columns or similar vertical features.

ATLANTES: male counterparts of caryatids, often in a more demonstrative attitude of support. In sculpture, a single figure of the god Atlas may be seen supporting a globe.

ATTACHED: description of a shaft or column that is partly merged into a wall or pier.

ATTIC: (1) small top storey, especially behind a sloping roof; (2) in classical architecture, a storey above the main cornice, as in a triumphal arch.

AUMBRY: recess or cupboard to hold sacred vessels for Mass.

BAILEY: open space or court of a stone-built castle; *see also* Motte-and-Bailey.

BALDACCHINO: tent-like roof supported by columns, e.g. over some monuments of the C17–18.

BALLFLOWER: globular flower of three petals enclosing a small ball. A decoration used in the first quarter of the C14.

BALUSTER (*lit.* pomegranate): hence a pillar or pedestal of bellied form. *Balusters:* vertical supports of this or any other form, for a handrail or coping, the whole being called a *Balustrade*. *Blind Balustrade:* the same with a wall behind.

BARBICAN: outwork defending the entrance to a castle.

BARGEBOARDS: boards, often carved or fretted, hanging clear of the wall under sloping eaves.

BARMKIN (Scots): enclosing wall.

BARONY: *see* Burgh.

BARROW: burial mound.

BARTIZAN (*lit.* battlement): corbelled turret, square or round, at the top angle of a building.

BASE: moulded foot of a column or other order. For its use in classical architecture *see* Orders (fig. 16). *Elided Bases:* bases of a compound pier whose lower parts are run together, ignoring the arrangement of the shafts above. Capitals may be treated in the same way.

BASEMENT: lowest, subordinate storey of a building, and hence the lowest part of an elevation, below the piano nobile.

BASILICA (*lit.* royal building): a Roman public hall; hence an aisled church with a clearstory.

BASTION: projection at the angle of a fortification.

BATTER: inward inclination of a wall.

BATTLEMENT: fortified parapet with upstanding pieces called merlons along the top. Also called Crenellation.

BAYS: divisions of an elevation or interior space as defined by any regular vertical features.

BAY-WINDOW: window in a recess, with a consequent projection on the outside, named according to the form of the latter. A *Canted Bay-window* has a straight front and bevelled sides.

A *Bow Window* is curved. An *Oriel Window* does not start from the ground.

BEAKER: type of pottery vessel used in the late third and early second millennia B.C.

BEAKHEAD: Norman ornamental motif consisting of a row of bird or beast heads with beaks biting usually into a roll moulding.

BELFRY (*lit.* tower): (1) bell-turret set on a roof or gable (*see also* Bellcote); (2) room or stage in a tower where bells are hung; (3) bell-tower in a general sense.

BELL-CAST: *see* Roof.

BELLCOTE: belfry as (1) above, with the character of a small house for the bell(s), e.g. *Bird-cage Bellcote:* framed structure, usually of stone.

BERM: level area separating ditch from bank on a hill fort or barrow.

BILLET (*lit.* log or block) FRIEZE: Norman ornament consisting of small blocks placed at regular intervals (*see* fig. 3).

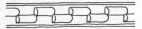

Fig. 3. Billet Frieze

BIVALLATE: of a hill fort: defended by two concentric banks and ditches.

BLIND: *see* Arcade, Balustrade, Portico.

BLOCKED: term applied to columns etc. that are interrupted by regular projecting blocks, e.g. to the sides of a Gibbs surround (*see* fig. 10).

BLOCKING COURSE: plain course of stones, or equivalent, on top of a cornice and crowning the wall.

BOLECTION MOULDING: mould-ing covering the joint between two different planes and over-lapping the higher as well as the lower one, especially on panel-ling and fireplace surrounds of the late C17 and early C18.

BOND: in brickwork, the pattern of long sides (stretchers) and short ends (headers) produced on the face of a wall by laying bricks in a particular way (*see* fig. 4).

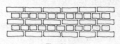

English

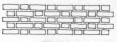

Flemish

Fig. 4. Bond

BOSS: knob or projection usually placed to cover the intersection of ribs in a vault.

BOW WINDOW: *see* Bay-window.

BOX PEW: pew enclosed by a high wooden back and ends, the latter having doors.

BRACE: *see* Roof (fig. 22).

BRACKET: small supporting piece of stone, etc., to carry a project-ing horizontal member.

BRESSUMER (*lit.* breast-beam): big horizontal beam, usually set forward from the lower part of a building, supporting the timber superstructure.

BRETASCHE (*lit.* battlement): de-fensive wooden gallery on a wall.

BROCH (Scots): circular tower-like structure, open in the middle, the double wall of drystone masonry linked by slabs forming internal galleries at varying levels; found in w and n Scotland and probably dating from the earliest centuries of the Christian era.

BRONZE AGE: in Britain, the period from *c*. 2000 to 600 B.C.

BUCRANIUM: ox skull.

BULLSEYE WINDOW: small circular window, e.g. in the tympanum of a pediment.

BURGH: formally constituted town with trading privileges. *Royal Burghs*, which still hold this courtesy title, monopolized imports and exports till the C17 and paid duty to the Crown. *Burghs of Barony* were founded by secular or ecclesiastical barons to whom they paid duty on their local trade.

BUT-AND-BEN (Scots, *lit.* outer and inner rooms): two-room cottage.

BUTTRESS: vertical member projecting from a wall to stabilize it or to resist the lateral thrust of an arch, roof or vault. For different types used at the corners of a building, especially a tower, *see* fig. 5. A *Flying Buttress* transmits the thrust to a heavy abutment by means of an arch or half-arch.

Angle

Diagonal

Set-back

Clasping

Fig. 5. Buttresses at a corner

CABLE MOULDING or ROPE MOULDING: originally a Norman moulding, imitating the twisted strands of a rope.

CALEFACTORY: room in a monastery where a fire burned for the comfort of the monks.

CAMBER: slight rise or upward curve in place of a horizontal line or plane.

CAMPANILE: free-standing bell-tower.

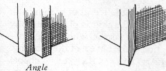

Block or Cushion   *Scalloped*   *Waterleaf*

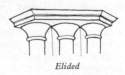

Elided

Crocket   *Bell*   *Stiff-leaf*

Fig. 6. Capitals

CANDLE-SNUFFER ROOF: conical roof of a turret.

CANES: see Quarries.

CANOPY: projection or hood over an altar, pulpit, niche, statue, etc.

CANTED: tilted, generally on a vertical axis to produce an obtuse angle on plan, e.g. of a canted bay-window.

CAP-HOUSE (Scots): (1) small chamber at the head of a turnpike stair, opening onto the parapet walk; (2) chamber rising from within the parapet walk.

CAPITAL: head or top part of a column or other order; for classical types see Orders (fig. 16); for medieval types see fig. 6. *Elided Capitals:* capitals of a compound pier whose upper parts are run together, ignoring the arrangement of the shafts below.

CARTOUCHE: tablet with ornate frame, usually of elliptical shape and bearing a coat of arms or inscription.

CARYATIDS (*lit.* daughters of the village of Caryae): female figures supporting an entablature, counterparts of Atlantes.

CASEMENT: (1) window hinged at the side; (2) in Gothic architecture, a concave moulding framing a window.

CASTELLATED: battlemented.

CAVETTO: concave moulding of quarter-round section.

CELURE or CEILURE: panelled and adorned part of a wagon roof above the rood or the altar.

CENOTAPH (*lit.* empty tomb): funerary monument which is not a burying place.

CENSER: vessel for the burning of incense, frequently of architectural form.

CENTERING: wooden support for the building of an arch or vault, removed after completion.

CHAMBERED TOMB: burial mound of the Neolithic Age having a stone-built chamber and entrance passage covered by an earthen barrow or stone cairn.

CHAMFER (*lit.* corner-break): surface formed by cutting off a square edge, usually at an angle of forty-five degrees.

CHANCEL (*lit.* enclosure): that part of the E end of a church in which the altar is placed, usually applied to the whole continuation of the nave E of the crossing.

CHANTRY CHAPEL: chapel attached to, or inside, a church, endowed for the celebration of masses for the soul of the founder or some other individual.

CHECK (Scots): rebate.

CHERRY-CAULKING or CHERRY-COCKING (Scots): masonry technique using a line of pin stones in the vertical joints between blocks.

CHEVET (*lit.* head): French term for the E end of a church (chancel and ambulatory with radiating chapels).

CHEVRON: zigzag Norman ornament.

CHOIR: (1) the part of a church where services are sung; in monastic churches this can occupy the crossing and/or the easternmost bays of the nave, but in cathedral churches it is usually in the E arm: (2) the E arm of a cruciform church (a usage of long standing though liturgically anomalous).

CIBORIUM: canopied shrine for the reserved sacrament.

CINQUEFOIL: see Foil.

CIST: stone-lined or slab-built grave. First appears in Late Neolithic times. It continued to be used in the Early Christian period.

CLAPPER BRIDGE: bridge made of large slabs of stone, some built up to make rough piers and other longer ones laid on top to make the roadway.

CLASSIC: term for the moment of highest achievement of a style.

CLASSICAL: term for Greek and Roman architecture and any subsequent styles inspired by it.

CLEARSTORY: upper storey of the nave walls of a church, pierced by windows.

CLOSE (Scots): courtyard or passage giving access to a number of buildings.

COADE STONE: artificial (cast) stone made in the late C18 and the early C19 by Coade and Sealy in London.

COB: walling material made of mixed clay and straw.

COFFERING: sunken panels, square or polygonal, decorating a ceiling, vault or arch.

COLLAR: see Roof (fig. 22).

COLLEGIATE CHURCH: a church endowed for the support of a college of priests, especially for the singing of masses for the soul of the founder. Some collegiate churches were founded in connection with universities, e.g. three at St Andrews and one at King's College, Aberdeen.

COLONNADE: range of columns.

COLONNETTE: small column.

COLUMN: in classical architecture, an upright structural member of round section with a shaft, a capital and usually a base. See Orders (fig. 16).

COLUMNA ROSTRATA: column decorated with carved prows of ships to celebrate a naval victory.

COMMENDATOR: one who holds the revenues of an abbey *in commendam* (medieval Latin for 'in trust' or 'in custody') for a period in which no regular abbot is appointed. During the Middle Ages most Commendators were bishops, but in Scotland during and after the Reformation they were laymen who performed no religious duties.

COMPOSITE: see Orders.

CONDUCTOR (Scots): down-pipe for rainwater; see also Rhone.

CONSERVATION: a modern term employed in two, sometimes conflicting, senses: (1) work to prolong the life of the historic fabric of a building or other work of art, without alteration; (2) work to make a building or a place more viable. Good conservation is a combination of the two.

CONSOLE: ornamental bracket of compound curved outline (*see* fig. 7). Its height is usually greater than its projection, as in (*a*).

COOMB CEILING or COMB CEILING (Scots): ceiling whose

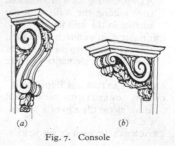

(*a*)   (*b*)

Fig. 7. Console

slope corresponds to that of the roof.

COPING (*lit.* capping): course of stones, or equivalent, on top of a wall.

CORBEL: block of stone projecting from a wall, supporting some feature on its horizontal top surface. *Corbel Course:* continuous projecting course of stones fulfilling the same function. *Corbel Table:* series of corbels to carry a parapet or a wall-plate; for the latter *see* Roof (fig. 22).

CORBIE-STEPS (Scots, *lit.* crow-steps): *see* Gable (fig. 9).

CORINTHIAN: *see* Orders (fig. 16).

CORNICE: (1) moulded ledge, decorative and/or practical, projecting along the top of a building or feature, especially as the highest member of the classical entablature (*see* Orders, fig. 16); (2) decorative moulding in the angle between wall and ceiling.

CORPS-DE-LOGIS: French term for the main building(s) as distinct from the wings or pavilions.

COUNTERSCARP BANK: small bank on the down-hill or outer side of a hill-fort ditch.

COURSE: continuous layer of stones etc. in a wall.

COVE: concave soffit like a hollow moulding but on a larger scale. A *Cove Ceiling* has a pronounced cove joining the walls to a flat surface in the middle.

CREDENCE: in a church or chapel, a side table, often a niche, for the sacramental elements before consecration.

CRENELLATION: *see* Battlement.

CREST, CRESTING: ornamental finish along the top of a screen, etc.

CROCKETS (*lit.* hooks), CROCKET-ING: in Gothic architecture, leafy knobs on the edges of any sloping feature. *Crocket Capital: see* Capital (fig. 6).

CROSSING: in a church, central space opening into the nave, chancel and transepts. *Crossing Tower:* central tower supported by the piers at its corners.

CROWSTEPS (Scots): squared stones set like steps to form a skew; *see* Gable (fig. 9).

CRUCK (*lit.* crooked): piece of naturally curved timber combining the structural roles of an upright post and a sloping rafter, e.g. in the building of a cottage, where each pair of crucks is joined at the ridge.

CRYPT: underground room usually below the E end of a church.

CUPOLA (*lit.* dome): (1) small polygonal or circular domed turret crowning a roof; (2) (Scots) small dome or skylight as an internal feature, especially over a stairwell.

CURTAIN WALL: (1) connecting wall between the towers of a castle; (2) in modern building, thin wall attached to the main structure, usually outside it.

CURVILINEAR: *see* Tracery.

CUSP: projecting point formed by the foils within the divisions of Gothic tracery, also used to decorate the soffits of the Gothic arches of tomb recesses, sedilias, etc.

CYCLOPEAN MASONRY: built with large irregular polygonal stones, but smooth and finely jointed.

DADO: lower part of a wall or its decorative treatment; *see also* Pedestal (fig. 17).

DAGGER: *see* Tracery.

DAIS, or DEIS (Scots): raised platform at one end of a room.

DEC (DECORATED): historical division of English Gothic architecture covering the period from *c.* 1290 to *c.* 1350.

DEMI-COLUMNS: engaged columns, only half of whose circumference projects from the wall.

DIAPER (*lit.* figured cloth): repetitive surface decoration.

DISTYLE: having two columns; cf. Portico.

DOGTOOTH: typical E.E. decoration applied to a moulding. It consists of a series of squares, their centres raised like pyramids and their edges indented (*see* fig. 8).

Fig. 8. Dogtooth

DONJON: *see* Keep.

DOOCOT (Scots): dovecot. Freestanding doocots are usually of *Lectern* type, rectangular in plan with single-pitch roof, or *Beehive* type, circular in plan and growing small towards the top.

DORIC: *see* Orders (fig. 16).

DORMER WINDOW: window standing up vertically from the slope of a roof and lighting a room within it. *Dormer Head:* gable above this window, often formed as a pediment.

DORTER: dormitory; sleeping quarters of a monastery.

DOUBLE PILE: *see* Pile.

DRESSINGS: features made of smoothly worked stones, e.g. quoins or string courses, projecting from the wall which may be of different material, colour or texture.

DRIPSTONE: moulded stone projecting from a wall to protect the lower parts from water; *see also* Hoodmould.

DROVED ASHLAR: *see* Ashlar.

DRUM: (1) circular or polygonal vertical wall of a dome or cupola; (2) one of the stones forming the shaft of a column.

DRYSTONE: stone construction without mortar.

DUN (Scots): a small stone-walled fort.

E.E. (EARLY ENGLISH): historical division of English Gothic architecture covering the period 1200–1250.

EASTER SEPULCHRE: recess with tomb-chest, usually in the wall of a chancel, the tomb-chest to receive an effigy of Christ for Easter celebrations.

EAVES: overhanging edge of a roof; hence *Eaves Cornice* in this position.

ECHINUS (*lit.* sea-urchin): lower part of a Greek Doric capital; *see* Orders (fig. 16).

EDGE-ROLL: moulding of semicircular or more than semicircular section at the edge of an opening.

ELEVATION: (1) any side of a building; (2) in a drawing, the same or any part of it, accurately represented in two dimensions.

ELIDED: term used to describe (1) a compound architectural feature, e.g. an entablature, in which some parts have been omitted; (2) a number of similar parts which have been combined to form a single larger one (*see* Capital, fig. 6).

EMBATTLED: furnished with battlements.

EMBRASURE (*lit.* splay): small splayed opening in the wall or battlement of a fortified building.

ENCAUSTIC TILES: glazed and decorated earthenware tiles used for paving.

EN DÉLIT (*lit.* in error): term used in Gothic architecture to describe attached stone shafts whose grain runs vertically instead of horizontally, against normal building practice.

ENGAGED: description of a column that is partly merged into a wall or pier.

ENTABLATURE: in classical architecture, collective name for the three horizontal members (architrave, frieze and cornice) above a column; *see* Orders (fig. 16).

ENTASIS: very slight convex deviation from a straight line; used on classical columns and sometimes on spires to prevent an optical illusion of concavity.

ENTRESOL: mezzanine storey within or above the ground storey.

EPITAPH (*lit.* on a tomb): inscription in that position.

ESCUTCHEON: shield for armorial bearings.

EXEDRA: apsidal end of an apartment; *see* Apse.

FERETORY: (1) place behind the high altar where the chief shrine of a church is kept; (2) wooden or metal container for relics.

FESTOON: ornament, usually in high or low relief, in the form of a garland of flowers and/or fruit, hung up at both ends; *see also* Swag.

FEU (Scots): land granted, e.g. by sale, by the *Feudal Superior* to the *Vassal* or *Feuar*, on conditions that include the annual payment of a fixed sum of *Feu-duty*. The paramount superior of all land is the Crown. Any subsequent proprietor of the land becomes the feuar and is subject to the same obligations. Although many superiors have disposed of their feudal rights, others, both private and corporate, still make good use of the power of feudal control which has produced many well-disciplined developments in Scotland.

FIBREGLASS (or glass-reinforced plastic): synthetic resin reinforced with glass fibre, formed in moulds, often simulating the outward appearance of traditional materials.

FILLET: narrow flat band running down a shaft or along a roll moulding.

FINIAL: topmost feature, e.g. above a gable, spire or cupola.

FLAMBOYANT: properly the latest phase of French Gothic architecture, where the window tracery takes on undulating lines, based on the use of flowing curves.

FLATTED: divided into apartments. But flat (Scots) is also used with a special colloquial meaning. 'He stays on the first flat' means that he lives on the first floor.

FLÈCHE (*lit.* arrow): slender spire on the centre of a roof.

FLEUR-DE-LYS: in heraldry, a formalized lily as in the royal arms of France.

FLEURON: decorative carved flower or leaf.

FLOWING: *see* Tracery (Curvilinear).

FLUTING: series of concave grooves, their common edges sharp (arris) or blunt (fillet).

FOIL (*lit.* leaf): lobe formed by the cusping of a circular or other shape in tracery. *Trefoil* (three), *Quatrefoil* (four), *Cinquefoil* (five) and *Multifoil* express the number of lobes in a shape; *see* Tracery (fig. 25).

FOLIATED: decorated, especially carved, with leaves.

FORE- (Scots, *lit.* in front): *Forebuilding:* structure protecting an entrance. *Forestair:* external stair, usually unenclosed.

FOSSE: ditch.

FRATER: refectory or dining hall of a monastery.

FREESTONE: stone that is cut, or can be cut, in all directions, usually fine-grained sandstone or limestone.

FRESCO: painting executed on wet plaster.

FRIEZE: horizontal band of ornament, especially the middle member of the classical entablature; *see* Orders (fig. 16). *Pulvinated Frieze* (*lit.* cushioned): frieze of bold convex profile.

FRONTAL: covering for the front of an altar.

GABLE: (1) peaked wall or other vertical surface, often triangular, at the end of a double-pitch roof; (2) (Scots) the same, very often with a chimney at the apex, but also in a wider sense: end wall, of whatever shape. *See* fig. 9. *Gablet:* small gable. *See also* Roof, Skew.

GADROONING: ribbed ornament, e.g. on the lid or base of an urn, flowing into a lobed edge.

GAIT (Scots) or GATE: street, usually with a prefix indicating its use, direction or destination.

GALILEE: chapel or vestibule usually at the W end of a church enclosing the porch; *see also* Narthex.

GALLERY: balcony or passage, but with certain special meanings, e.g. (1) upper storey above the aisle of a church, looking through arches to the nave; also called tribune and often erroneously triforium. (2) balcony or mezzanine, often with seats, overlooking the main interior space of a building. (3) external walkway projecting from a wall.

GARDEROBE (*lit.* wardrobe): medieval privy.

GARGOYLE: water spout projecting from the parapet of a wall or tower, often carved into human or animal shape.

Skewputt

Skew Gable   *Crowstep Gable*

Dutch Gable   *Curvilinear or Shaped Gable at wall-head*

Fig. 9.   Gables

GAZEBO (jocular Latin, 'I shall gaze'): lookout tower or raised summer house overlooking a garden.

GEOMETRIC: historical division of English Gothic architecture covering the period *c.* 1250–90. *See also* Tracery. For another meaning, *see* Staircase.

GIBBS SURROUND: C18 treatment of door or window surround, seen particularly in the work of James Gibbs (1682–1754) (*see* fig. 10).

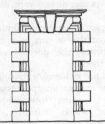

Fig. 10. Gibbs Surround

GNOMON: vane or indicator casting a shadow on to a sundial.

GROIN: sharp edge at the meeting of two cells of a cross-vault; *see* Vault (fig. 26a).

GROTESQUE (*lit.* grotto-esque): classical wall decoration of spindly, whimsical character adopted from Roman examples, particularly by Raphael, and further developed in the C18.

GUILLOCHE: running classical ornament formed by a series of circles with linked and interlaced borders (see fig. 11).

GUN LOOP: opening for a firearm.

GUTTAE: *see* Orders (fig. 16).

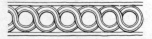

Fig. 11. Guilloche

HAGIOSCOPE: *see* Squint.

HALF-TIMBERING: timber framing with the spaces filled in by plaster, stones or brickwork.

HALL CHURCH: (1) church whose nave and aisles are of equal height or approximately so. (2) (Scots C20): church convertible into a hall.

HAMMERBEAM: *see* Roof.

HARLING (Scots, *lit.* hurling): wet dash, i.e. a form of roughcasting in which the mixture of aggregate and binding material (e.g. lime) is dashed onto a rubble wall as protection against weather.

HEADER: *see* Bond.

HENGE: ritual earthwork with a surrounding bank and ditch, the bank being on the outer side.

HERITORS (Scots): proprietors of a heritable subject, especially church heritors who till 1925 were responsible for each parish church and its manse.

HERM (*lit.* the god Hermes): male head or bust on a pedestal.

HERRINGBONE WORK: masonry or brickwork in zigzag courses.

HEXASTYLE: term used to describe a portico with six columns.

HILL FORT: Iron Age earthwork enclosed by a ditch and bank system; in the later part of the period the defences multiplied in size and complexity. They vary in area and are usually built with careful regard to natural elevations or promontories.

HOODMOULD or label: projecting moulding above an arch or lintel to throw off water.

HORSE-WALK: circular or polygonal farm building in which a central shaft is turned by a horse to drive agricultural machinery.

HUNGRY JOINTS: *see* Pointing.

HUSK GARLAND: festoon of nut-shells diminishing towards the ends (*see* fig. 12).

Fig. 12. Husk Garland

HYPOCAUST (*lit.* under-burning): Roman underfloor heating system. The floor is supported on pillars and the space thus formed is connected to a flue.

Fig. 13. Keel Moulding

Fig. 14. Key Pattern

ICONOGRAPHY: description of the subject matter of works of the visual arts.

IMPOST (*lit.* imposition): horizontal moulding at the spring of an arch.

IN ANTIS: *see* Anta.

INDENT: (1) shape chiselled out of a stone to match and receive a brass; (2) in restoration, a section of new stone inserted as a patch into older work.

INGLENOOK (*lit.* fire-corner): recess for a hearth with provision for seating.

INTERCOLUMNIATION: interval between columns.

IONIC: *see* Orders (fig. 16).

JAMB (*lit.* leg): (1) one of the straight sides of an opening; (2) (Scots) wing or extension adjoining one side of a rectangular plan, making it into an L or T plan.

KEEL MOULDING: *see* fig. 13.

KEEP: principal tower of a castle. Also called Donjon.

KEY PATTERN: *see* fig. 14.

KEYSTONE: middle and topmost stone in an arch or vault.

KINGPOST: *see* Roof (fig. 22).

LABEL: *see* Hoodmould. *Label Stop:* ornamental boss at the end of a hoodmould.

LADY CHAPEL: chapel dedicated to the Virgin Mary (Our Lady).

LAIGH, or LAICH (Scots): low.

LAIRD (Scots): landowner.

LANCET WINDOW: slender pointed-arched window.

LANTERN: a small circular or polygonal turret with windows all round crowning a roof (*see* Cupola) or a dome.

LAVATORIUM: in a monastery, a washing place adjacent to the refectory.

LEAN-TO: term commonly applied not only to a single-pitch roof but to the building it covers.

LESENE (*lit.* a mean thing): pilaster without base or capital. Also called pilaster strip.

LIERNE: *see* Vault (fig. 26b).

LIGHT: compartment of a window.

LINENFOLD: Tudor panelling ornamented with a conventional representation of a piece of linen laid in vertical folds. The piece is repeated in each panel.

LINTEL: horizontal beam or stone bridging an opening.

LOFT: two special senses: (1) *Organ Loft* in which the organ, or sometimes only the console (keyboard), is placed; (2) (Scots) reserved gallery in a church, e.g. a *Laird's Loft*, or a *Trades Loft* for members of one of the incorporated trades of a burgh.

LOGGIA: sheltered space behind a colonnade.

LONG-AND-SHORT WORK: quoins consisting of stones placed with the long sides alternately upright and horizontal, especially in Saxon building.

LOUIS: convenient term used in the antique trade to describe a curvaceous chimneypiece of Louis XV character.

LOUVRE: (1) opening, often with lantern over, in the roof of a room to let the smoke from a central hearth escape; (2) one of a series of overlapping boards to allow ventilation but keep the rain out.

LOZENGE: diamond shape.

LUCARNE(*lit.* dormer): small window in a roof or spire.

LUCKENBOOTH (Scots): lock-up booth or shop.

LUGGED: *see* Architrave.

LUNETTE (*lit.* half or crescent moon): (1) semicircular window; (2) semicircular or crescent-shaped surface.

LYCHGATE (*lit.* corpse-gate): wooden gate structure with a roof and open sides placed at the entrance to a churchyard to provide space for the reception of a coffin.

LYNCHET: long terraced strip of soil accumulating on the downward side of prehistoric and medieval fields due to soil creep from continuous ploughing along the contours.

MACHICOLATIONS (*lit.* mashing devices): on a castle, downward openings through which missiles can be dropped, under a parapet or battlement supported by deep corbels.

MAINS (Scots): home farm on an estate.

MAJOLICA: ornamented glazed earthenware.

MANSARD: *see* Roof (fig. 21).

MANSE: house of a minister of religion, especially in Scotland.

MARGINS (Scots): dressed stones at the edges of an opening. 'Back-set margins' (RCAHMS) is a misleading term because they are actually set forward from a rubble-built wall to act as a stop for the harling. Also called Rybats.

MARRIAGE LINTEL (Scots): on a house, a door or window lintel carved with the initials of the owner and his wife and the date of the work – only coincidentally of their marriage.

MAUSOLEUM: monumental tomb, so named after that of Mausolus, king of Caria, at Halicarnassus.

MEGALITHIC(*lit.* of large stones): archaeological term referring to the use of such stones, singly or together.

MERCAT (Scots): market. The *Mercat Cross* was erected in a Scottish burgh, generally in a wide street, as the focus of market activity and local ceremonial. Most examples are of post-Reformation date and have heraldic or other finials (not crosses), but the name persisted.

MERLON: *see* Battlement.

MESOLITHIC: term applied to the Middle Stone Age, dating in Britain from *c.*5000 to *c.*3500 B.C., and to the hunting and gathering activities of the earliest communities. *See also* Neolithic.

METOPES: spaces between the triglyphs in a Doric frieze; *see* Orders (fig. 16).

MEZZANINE: (1) low storey between two higher ones; (2) low upper storey within the height of a high one, not extending over its whole area.

MISERERE: *see* Misericord.

MISERICORD (*lit.* mercy): shelf placed on the underside of a hinged choir stall seat which, when turned up, provided the occupant with support during long periods of standing. Also called Miserere.

MODILLIONS: small consoles at regular intervals along the underside of some types of classical cornice.

MORT-SAFE (Scots): device to assure the security of a corpse or corpses: (1) iron frame over a grave; (2) building or room where bodies were kept during decomposition.

MOTTE: steep mound forming the main feature of C11 and C12 castles.

MOTTE-AND-BAILEY: post-Roman and Norman defence system consisting of an earthen mound (motte) topped with a wooden tower within a bailey, with enclosure ditch and palisade, and with the rare addition of an internal bank.

MOUCHETTE: motif in curvilinear tracery, a curved version of the dagger form, specially popular in the early C14; *see* Tracery (fig. 25).

MOULDING: ornament of continuous section; *see* the various types.

MULLION: vertical member between the lights in a window opening.

MULTI-STOREY: modern term denoting five or more storeys.

MULTIVALLATE: of a hill fort: defended by three or more concentric banks and ditches.

MUNTIN: post forming part of a screen.

NAILHEAD MOULDING: E.E. ornamental motif, consisting of small pyramids regularly repeated (*see* fig. 15).

Fig. 15. Nailhead Moulding

NARTHEX: enclosed vestibule or covered porch at the main entrance to a church; *see also* Galilee.

NECESSARIUM: medieval euphemism for latrines in a monastery.

NEOLITHIC: term applied to the New Stone Age, dating in Britain from the appearance of the first settled farming communities from the continent *c.*3500 B.C. until the beginning of the Bronze Age. *See also* Mesolithic.

NEWEL: central post in a circular or winding staircase; also the principal post when a flight of stairs meets a landing.

NICHE (*lit.* shell): vertical recess in a wall, sometimes for a statue.

NIGHT STAIR: stair by which monks entered the transepts of their church from their dormitory to celebrate night services.

NOOK-SHAFT: shaft set in an angle formed by other members.

NORMAN: *see* Romanesque.

NOSING: projection of the tread of a step. A *Bottle Nosing* is half-round in section.

OBELISK: lofty pillar of square section tapering at the top and ending pyramidally.

OGEE: double curve, bending first one way and then the other. *Ogee* or *Ogival Arch*: *see* Arch.

ORATORY: small private chapel in a house.

ORDER: (1) upright structural member formally related to others, e.g. in classical architecture a column, pilaster, or anta; (2) one of a series of recessed arches and jambs forming a splayed opening. *Giant* or *Colossal Order*: classical order whose height is that of two or more storeys of a building.

ORDERS: in classical architecture, the differently formalized versions of the basic post-and-lintel structure, each having its own rules of design and proportion. For examples of the main types *see* fig. 16. Others include the primitive Tuscan, which has a

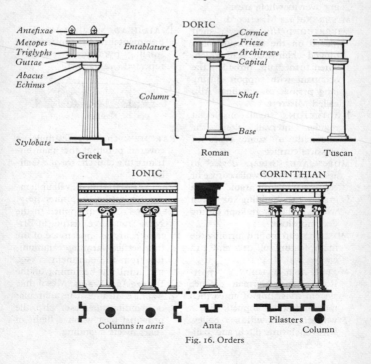

Fig. 16. Orders

plain frieze and simple torus-moulded base, and the Composite, whose capital combines Ionic volutes with Corinthian foliage. *Superimposed Orders:* term for the use of Orders on successive levels, usually in the upward sequence of Doric, Ionic, Corinthian.

Fig. 17. Pedestal

ORIEL: *see* Bay-window.

OVERHANG: projection of the upper storey(s) of a building.

OVERSAILING COURSES: series of stone or brick courses, each one projecting beyond the one below it; *see also* Corbel course.

Pₐₗᵢₘₚₛₑₛₜ PALIMPSEST (*lit.* erased work): re-use of a surface, e.g. a brass for another engraving or a wall for another painting.

PALLADIAN: architecture following the ideas and principles of Andrea Palladio, 1508–80.

PALMETTE: classical ornament like a symmetrical palm shoot; for illustration *see* Anthemion, fig. 1.

PANTILE: roof tile of curved S-shaped section.

PARAPET: wall for protection at any sudden drop, e.g. on a bridge or at the wall-head of a castle; in the latter case it protects the *Parapet Walk* or wall walk.

PARCLOSE: *see* Screen.

PARGETING (*lit.* plastering): usually of moulded plaster panels in half-timbering.

PATERA (*lit.* plate): round or oval ornament in shallow relief, especially in classical architecture.

PEDESTAL: in classical architecture, a stand sometimes used to support the base of an order (*see* fig. 17).

PEDIMENT: in classical architecture, a formalized gable derived from that of a temple, also used over doors, windows, etc. For the generally accepted meanings of *Broken Pediment* and *Open Pediment see* fig. 18.

Pediment

Broken   *Open*

Fig. 18. Pediments

PEEL (*lit.* palisade): stone tower, e.g. near the Scottish–English border.

PEND (Scots): open-ended passage through a building on ground level.

PENDANT: hanging-down feature of a vault or ceiling, usually ending in a boss.

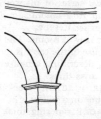

Fig. 19. Pendentive

PENDENTIVE: spandrel between adjacent arches supporting a drum or dome, formed as part of a hemisphere (*see* fig. 19).

PEPPERPOT TURRET: bartizan with conical or pyramidal roof.

PERISTYLE: in classical architecture, a range of columns all round a building, e.g. a temple, or an interior space, e.g. a courtyard.

PERP (PERPENDICULAR): historical division of English Gothic architecture covering the period from *c.* 1335–50 to *c.* 1530.

PERRON: see Stair.

PIANO NOBILE: principal floor, usually with a ground floor or basement underneath and a lesser storey overhead.

PIAZZA: open space surrounded by buildings; in the C17 and C18 sometimes employed to mean a long colonnade or loggia.

PIEND: *see* Roof.

PIER: strong, solid support, frequently square in section. *Compound Pier:* of composite section, e.g. formed of a bundle of shafts.

PIETRA DURA: ornamental or scenic inlay by means of thin slabs of stone.

PILASTER: classical order of oblong section, its elevation similar to that of a column. *Pilastrade:* series of pilasters, equivalent to a colonnade. *Pilaster Strip: see* Lesene.

PILE: a row of rooms. The important use of the term is in *Double Pile*, describing a house that is two rows thick.

PILLAR PISCINA: free-standing piscina on a pillar.

PINNACLE: tapering finial, e.g. on a buttress or the corner of a tower, sometimes decorated with crockets.

PINS (Scots): small stones pushed into the joints between large ones, a technique called cherry-caulking.

PISCINA: basin for washing the communion or mass vessels, provided with a drain; generally set in or against the wall to the s of an altar.

PIT PRISON: sunk chamber with access above through a hatch.

PLAISANCE: summer house, pleasure house near a mansion.

PLATT (Scots): platform, doorstep or landing. *Scale-and-Platt Stair: see* Stair.

PLEASANCE (Scots): close or walled garden.

PLINTH: projecting base beneath a wall or column, generally chamfered or moulded at the top.

POINTING: exposed mortar joints of masonry or brickwork. The finished form is of various types, e.g. *Flush Pointing, Recessed Pointing. Bag-rubbed Pointing* is flush at the edges and gently recessed in the middle of the joint. *Hungry Joints* are either without any pointing at all, or deeply recessed to show the outline of each stone. *Ribbon Pointing* is a nasty practice in the modern vernacular, the joints being formed with a trowel so that they stand out.

POPPYHEAD: carved ornament of leaves and flowers as a finial for the end of a bench or stall.

PORCH: covered projecting entrance to a building.

PORTCULLIS: gate constructed to rise and fall in vertical grooves at the entry to a castle.

PORTE COCHÈRE: porch large enough to admit wheeled vehicles.

PORTICO: in classical architecture, a porch with detached columns or other orders. *Blind Portico:* the front features of a portico attached to a wall so that it is no longer a proper porch.

POSTERN: small gateway at the back of a building.

POTENCE (Scots): rotating ladder for access to the nesting boxes of a round doocot.

PREDELLA: in an altarpiece the horizontal strip below the main representation, often used for a number of subsidiary representations in a row.

PRESBYTERY: the part of the church lying E of the choir. It is the part where the altar is placed.

PRESS (Scots): cupboard.

PRINCIPAL: *see* Roof (fig. 22).

PRIORY: monastic house whose head is a prior or prioress, not an abbot or abbess.

PROSTYLE: with a row of columns in front.

PULPITUM: stone screen in a major church provided to shut off the choir from the nave and also as a backing for the return choir stalls.

PULVINATED: *see* Frieze.

PURLIN: *see* Roof (fig. 22).

PUTHOLE or PUTLOCK HOLE: putlocks are the short horizontal timbers on which during construction the boards of scaffolding rest. Putholes or putlock holes are the holes in the wall for putlocks, and often are not filled in after construction is complete.

PUTTO: small naked boy (plural: putti).

QUADRANGLE: inner courtyard in a large building.

QUARRIES (*lit.* squares): (1) square (or sometimes diamond-shaped) panes of glass supported by lead strips which are called *Canes;* (2) square floor-slabs or tiles.

QUATREFOIL: *see* Foil.

QUEENPOSTS: *see* Roof (fig. 22).

QUIRK: sharp groove to one side of a convex moulding, e.g. beside a roll moulding, which is then said to be quirked.

QUOINS: dressed stones at the angles of a building. When rusticated they may be alternately long and short.

RADIATING CHAPELS: chapels projecting radially from an ambulatory or an apse; *see* Chevet.

RAFTER: *see* Roof (fig. 22).

RAGGLE: groove cut in masonry, especially to receive the edge of glass or roof-covering.

RAKE: slope or pitch.

RAMPART: stone wall or wall of earth surrounding a castle, fortress, or fortified city. *Rampart Walk:* path along the inner face of a rampart.

RANDOM: *see* Rubble.

REBATE: rectangular section cut out of a masonry edge.

REBUS: a heraldic pun, e.g. a fiery cock as a badge for Cockburn.

REEDING: series of convex mouldings; the reverse of fluting.

REFECTORY: dining hall (or frater) of a monastery or similar establishment.

REREDORTER (*lit.* behind the dormitory): medieval euphemism for latrines in a monastery.

REREDOS: painted and/or sculptured screen behind and above an altar.

RESPOND: half-pier bonded into a wall and carrying one end of an arch.

RETABLE: altarpiece; a picture or piece of carving standing behind and attached to an altar.

RETROCHOIR: in a major church, an aisle between the high altar and an E chapel, like a square ambulatory.

REVEAL: the inward plane of a jamb, between the edge of an external wall and the frame of a door or window that is set in it.

RHONE (Scots): gutter along the eaves for rainwater; see also Conductor.

RIB-VAULT: see Vault.

Fig. 20. Rinceau

RINCEAU (lit. little branch) or antique foliage: classical ornament, usually on a frieze, of leafy scrolls branching alternately to left and right (see fig. 20).

RISER: vertical face of a step.

ROCK-FACED: term used to describe masonry which is cleft to produce a natural, rugged appearance.

ROCOCO (lit. rocky): latest phase of the Baroque style, current in most Continental countries between c. 1720 and c. 1760, and showing itself in Britain mainly in playful, scrolled decoration, especially plasterwork.

ROLL MOULDING: moulding of semicircular or more than semicircular section.

ROMANESQUE: that style in architecture which was current in the C11 and C12 and preceded the Gothic style (in England often called Norman). (Some scholars extend the use of the term Romanesque back to the C10 or C9.)

ROOD: cross or crucifix, usually over the entry into the chancel. The Rood Screen beneath it may have a Rood Loft along the top, reached by a Rood Stair.

ROOF: for external forms see fig. 21; for construction and components see fig. 22. Wagon Roof: lined with timber on the inside, giving the appearance of a curved or polygonal vault.

ROPE MOULDING: see Cable Moulding.

Single-Pitch Double-Pitch Bell-cast M Mansard

Piend (Scots) or Hipped Gambrel or Gabled Hip Jerkin Head or Hipped Gable Cat-Slide Helm

Fig. 21. Roof Forms

ROSE WINDOW: circular window with patterned tracery about the centre.

ROTUNDA: building circular in plan.

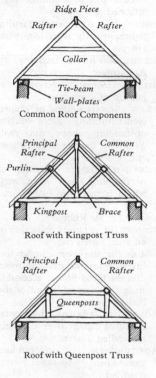

Common Roof Components

Roof with Kingpost Truss

Roof with Queenpost Truss

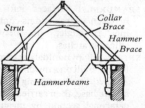

Hammerbeam Roof

Fig. 22. Roof Construction

ROUND (Scots): useful term employed by the RCAHMS for a bartizan, usually roofless.

RUBBLE: masonry whose stones are wholly or partly in a rough state. *Coursed Rubble:* of coursed stones with rough faces. *Random Rubble:* of uncoursed stones in a random pattern. *Snecked Rubble* has courses frequently broken by smaller stones (snecks).

RUSTICATION: treatment of joints and/or faces of masonry to give an effect of strength. In the most usual kind the joints are recessed by V-section chamfering or square-section channelling. *Banded Rustication* has only the horizontal joints emphasized in this way. The faces may be flat but there are many other forms, e.g. *Diamond-faced*, like a shallow pyramid, *Vermiculated*, with a stylized texture like worms or worm-holes, or *Glacial*, like icicles or stalactites. *Rusticated Columns* may have their joints and drums treated in any of these ways.

RYBATS (Scots): *see* Margins.

SACRAMENT HOUSE: safe cupboard for the reserved sacrament.

SACRISTY: room in a church for sacred vessels and vestments.

SALTIRE or ST ANDREW'S CROSS: with diagonal limbs. As the flag of Scotland it is coloured white on a blue ground.

SANCTUARY: (1) area around the main altar of a church (*see* Presbytery); (2) sacred site consisting of wood or stone uprights enclosed by a circular bank and ditch. Beginning in the Neolithic, they were elaborated in the succeeding Bronze Age. The best known examples are Stonehenge and Avebury.

SARCOPHAGUS (*lit.* flesh-consuming): coffin of stone or other durable material.

SARKING (Scots): boards laid on the rafters (*see* Roof, fig. 22) to support the covering, e.g. metal or slates.

SCAGLIOLA: composition imitating marble.

SCALE-AND-PLATT (*lit.* stair and landing): *see* Stair (fig. 24).

SCARCEMENT: extra thickness of the lower part of a wall, e.g. to carry a floor.

SCARP: artificial cutting away of the ground to form a steep slope.

SCREEN: in a church, usually at the entry to the chancel; *see* Rood Screen and Pulpitum. *Parclose Screen:* separating a chapel from the rest of the church.

SCREENS or SCREENS PASSAGE: screened-off entrance passage between the hall and the kitchen in a medieval house, adjoining the kitchen, buttery, etc.; *see also* Transe.

SCUNTION (Scots): equivalent of a reveal on the indoor side of a door or window opening.

SECTION: view of a building, moulding, etc. revealed by cutting across it.

SEDILIA: seats for the priests (usually three) on the S side of the chancel of a church; a plural word that has become a singular, collective one.

SESSION HOUSE (Scots): room or separate building for meetings of the elders who form a kirk session.

SET-OFF: *see* Weathering.

SGRAFFITO: scratched pattern, often in plaster.

SHAFT: upright member of round section, especially the main part of a classical column. *Shaft-ring:* motif of the C12 and C13 consisting of a ring like a belt round a circular pier or a circular shaft attached to a pier.

SHEILA-NA-GIG: female fertility figure, usually with legs wide open.

SHOULDERED: *see* Arch (fig. 2), Architrave.

SILL: horizontal projection at the bottom of a window.

SKEW (Scots): sloping or shaped stones finishing a gable which is upstanding above the roof. *Skewputt:* bracket at the bottom end of a skew.

SLATE-HANGING: covering of overlapping slates on a wall, which is then said to be *slate-hung*.

SNECKED: *see* Rubble.

SOFFIT (*lit.* ceiling): underside of an arch, lintel, etc.

SOLAR (*lit.* sun-room): upper living room or withdrawing room of a medieval house, accessible from the high table end of the hall.

SOUNDING-BOARD: horizontal board or canopy over a pulpit; also called Tester.

SOUTERRAIN: underground stone-lined passage and chamber.

SPANDRELS: surfaces left over between an arch and its containing rectangle, or between adjacent arches.

SPIRE: tall pyramidal or conical feature built on a tower or turret. *Broach Spire:* starting from a square base, then carried into an octagonal section by means of triangular faces. *Needle Spire:* thin spire rising from the centre of a tower roof, well inside the parapet. *Helm Spire: see* Roof (fig. 21).

SPIRELET: *see* Flèche.

SPLAY: chamfer, usually of a reveal or scuntion.

SPRING: level at which an arch or vault rises from its supports. *Springers:* the first stones of an arch or vaulting-rib above the spring.

SQUINCH: arch thrown across an angle between two walls to support a superstructure, e.g. a dome (*see* fig. 23).

Fig. 23. Squinch

SQUINT: hole cut in a wall or through a pier to allow a view of the main altar of a church from places whence it could not otherwise be seen. Also called Hagioscope.

STAIR: see fig. 24. The term *Perron* (*lit.* of stone) applies to the external stair leading to a doorway, usually of double-curved plan as shown. *Spiral, Turnpike* (Scots) or *Newel Stair:* ascending round a central supporting newel, usually in a circular shaft. *Flying Stair:* cantilevered from the wall of a stairwell, without newels. *Geometric Stair:* flying stair whose inner edge describes a curve. *Well Stair:* term applied to any stair contained in an open well, but generally to one that climbs up three sides of a well, with corner landings.

STALL: seat for clergy, choir, etc., distinctively treated in its own right or as one of a row.

STANCHION: upright structural member, of iron or steel or reinforced concrete.

STEADING (Scots): farm building or buildings. A term most often used to describe the principal group of agricultural buildings on a farm.

STEEPLE: a tower together with a spire or other tall feature on top of it.

STOUP: vessel for the reception of holy water, usually placed near a door.

STRAINER: *see* Arch.

▲

Dog-leg or Scale-and-Platt

▲

Imperial

▲

T-plan

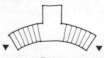

▼　　　　　▼

Perron

Fig. 24. Stair

STRAPWORK: C16 and C17 decoration used also in the C19 Jacobean revival, resembling interlaced bands of cut leather.

STRING COURSE: intermediate stone course or moulding projecting from the surface of a wall.

STUCCO (*lit.* plaster): (1) smooth external rendering of a wall etc.; (2) archaic term for plasterwork.

STUDS: intermediate vertical members of a timber-framed wall or partition.

STUGGED (Scots): of masonry that is hacked or picked as a key for rendering; used as a type of surface finish in the C19.

STYLOBATE: solid structure on which a colonnade stands.

SWAG (*lit.* bundle): like a festoon, but also a cloth bundle in relief, hung up at both ends.

TABERNACLE (*lit.* tent): (1) canopied structure, especially on a small scale, to contain the reserved sacrament or a relic; (2) architectural frame, e.g. of a monument on a wall or free-standing, with flanking orders. Also called an Aedicule.

TAS-DE-CHARGE: stone(s) forming the springers of more than one vaulting-rib.

TERMINAL FIGURE or TERM: upper part of a human figure growing out of a pier, pilaster, etc. which tapers towards the bottom.

TERRACOTTA: moulded and fired clay ornament or cladding, usually unglazed.

TESSELLATED PAVEMENT: mosaic flooring, particularly Roman, consisting of small *Tesserae* or cubes of glass, stone, or brick.

TESTER (*lit.* head): bracketed canopy, especially over a pulpit, where it is also called a sounding-board.

TETRASTYLE: term used to describe a portico with four columns.

THERMAL WINDOW (*lit.* of a Roman bath): semicircular, with two mullions.

THREE-DECKER PULPIT: pulpit with clerk's stall below and reading desk below the clerk's stall.

TIE-BEAM: see Roof (fig. 22).

TIERCERON: see Vault (fig. 26b).

TILE-HANGING: see Slate-hanging.

TIMBER FRAMING: method of construction where walls are built of timber framework with the spaces filled in by plaster or brickwork. Sometimes the timber is covered over with plaster or boarding laid horizontally.

TOLBOOTH (Scots): tax office containing a burgh council chamber and a prison.

TOMB-CHEST: chest-shaped stone coffin, the most usual medieval form of funerary monument.

TOUCH: soft black marble quarried near Tournai.

TOURELLE: turret corbelled out from the wall.

TOWER HOUSE (Scots): compact fortified house with the main hall raised above the ground and at least one more storey above it. A medieval Scots type continuing well into the C17 in its modified forms, the L plan and so-called Z plan, the former having a jamb at one corner, the latter at each diagonally opposite corner.

TRACERY: pattern of arches and

geometrical figures supporting the glass in the upper part of a window, or applied decoratively to wall surfaces or vaults. *Plate Tracery* is the most primitive form of tracery, being formed of openings cut through stone slabs or plates. In *Bar Tracery* the openings are separated not by flat areas of stonework but by relatively slender divisions or bars which are constructed of voussoirs like arches. Later developments of bar tracery are classified according to the character of the decorative patterns used. For generalized illustrations of the main types *see* fig. 25.

TRANSE (Scots): passage, especially screens passage.

TRANSEPTS (*lit.* cross-enclosures): transverse portions of a cross-shaped church.

TRANSOM: horizontal member between the lights in a window opening.

TREFOIL: *see* Foil.

TRIBUNE: *see* Gallery (1).

TRICIPUT, SIGNUM TRICIPUT: sign of the Trinity expressed by three faces belonging to one head.

TRIFORIUM (*lit.* three openings): middle storey of a church treated as an arcaded wall passage or blind arcade, its height corresponding to that of the aisle roof.

TRIGLYPHS (*lit.* three-grooved tablets): stylized beam-ends in the Doric frieze, with metopes between; *see* Orders (fig. 16).

TRIUMPHAL ARCH: *see* Arch.

TROPHY: sculptured group of arms or armour as a memorial of victory.

TRUMEAU: stone mullion supporting the tympanum of a wide doorway.

Plate   *Geometric*   *Y*

Reticulated   *Flowing or Curvilinear*   *Loop*

Perpendicular

Dagger

Quatrefoil   *Mouchette*

Fig. 25. Tracery

Tunnel or Barrel *Pointed Tunnel* *Pointed Tunnels with Surface Ribs*

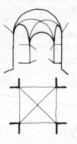

Groin *Quadripartite* *Sexpartite* *Fan*

Fig. 26. (a) Vaults

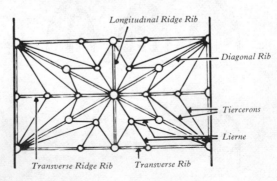

Longitudinal Ridge Rib

Diagonal Rib

Tiercerons

Lierne

Transverse Ridge Rib *Transverse Rib*

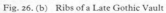

Fig. 26. (b) Ribs of a Late Gothic Vault

TUMULUS (*lit.* mound): barrow.

TURNPIKE: *see* Stair.

TURRET: small tower, often attached to a building.

TUSCAN: *see* Orders (fig. 16).

TYMPANUM (*lit.* drum): as of a drum-skin, the surface framed by an arch or pediment.

UNDERCROFT: vaulted room, sometimes underground, below the main upper room.

UNIVALLATE: of a hill fort: defended by a single bank and ditch.

VASSAL: *see* Feu.

VAULT: ceiling of stone formed like arches (sometimes imitated in timber or plaster); *see* fig. 26. *Tunnel-* or *Barrel-Vault*: the simplest kind of vault, in effect a continuous semicircular arch. *Pointed Tunnel-Vaults* are frequent in Scottish late medieval architecture but otherwise rare. A Scottish peculiarity is the *Pointed Tunnel-Vault with Surface Ribs* which are purely decorative in intention. *Groin-Vaults* (usually called *Cross-Vaults* in classical architecture) have four curving triangular surfaces produced by the intersection of two tunnel-vaults at right angles. The curved lines at the intersections are called groins. In *Quadripartite Rib-Vaults* the four sections are divided by their arches or ribs springing from the corners of the bay. *Sexpartite Rib-Vaults* are most often used over paired bays. The main types of rib are shown in fig. 26b: *transverse ribs*, *wall ribs*, *diagonal ribs*, and *ridge*

ribs. *Tiercerons* are extra, decorative ribs springing from the corners of a bay. *Liernes* are decorative ribs in the crown of a vault which are not linked to any of the springing points. In a *stellar vault* the liernes are arranged in a star formation as in fig. 26b. *Fan-vaults* are peculiar to English Perpendicular architecture and differ from rib-vaults in consisting not of ribs and infilling but of halved concave cones with decorative blind tracery carved on their surfaces.

VAULTING-SHAFT: shaft leading up to the springer of a vault.

VENETIAN WINDOW: *see* fig. 27.

VERANDA(H): shelter or gallery against a building, its roof supported by thin vertical members.

VERMICULATION: *see* Rustication.

VESICA (*lit.* bladder): usually of a window, with curved sides and pointed at top and bottom like a rugger-ball.

VESTIBULE: anteroom or entrance hall.

VILLA: originally (1) Roman country-house-cum-farmhouse, developed into (2) the similar

Fig. 27. Venetian Window

C16 Venetian type with office wings, made grander by Palladio's varied application of a central portico. This became an important type in C18 Britain, often with the special meaning of (3) a country house which is not a principal residence. Gwilt (1842) defined the villa as 'a country house for the residence of opulent persons'. But devaluation had already begun, and the term implied, as now, (4) a more or less pretentious suburban house.

VITRIFIED: hardened or fused into a glass-like state.

VITRUVIAN SCROLL: running ornament of curly waves on a classical frieze. (*See* fig. 28.)

Fig. 28. Vitruvian Scroll

VOLUTES: spiral scrolls on the front and back of a Greek Ionic capital, also on the sides of a Roman one. *Angle Volute:* pair of volutes turned outwards to meet at the corner of a capital.

VOUSSOIRS: wedge-shaped stones forming an arch.

WAINSCOT: timber lining on an internal wall.

WALLED GARDEN: C17 type whose formal layout is still seen in the combined vegetable and flower gardens of C18 and C19 Scotland. They are usually sited at a considerable distance from a house.

WALL-PLATE: *see* Roof (fig. 22).

WATERHOLDING BASE: type of Early Gothic base in which the upper and lower mouldings are separated by a hollow so deep as to be capable of retaining water.

WEATHERBOARDING: overlapping horizontal boards, covering a timber-framed wall.

WEATHERING: inclined, projecting surface to keep water away from wall and joints below.

WEEPERS: small figures placed in niches along the sides of some medieval tombs; also called mourners.

WHEEL WINDOW: circular window with tracery of radiating shafts like the spokes of a wheel; *see also* Rose Window.

WYND (Scots): subsidiary street or lane, often running into a main street or gait.

YETT (Scots, *lit.* gate): hinged openwork gate at a main doorway, made of wrought-iron bars alternately penetrating and penetrated.

INDEX OF PLATES

INDEX OF ARTISTS

INDEX OF PLACES

ADDENDA

JANUARY 1978

p. 162 [Dalkeith.] LUGTON, just to the N of Bridgend. The village has the good stone walls characteristic of the ducal policies of Dalkeith, and the houses are a mixture of the C18–20. The latest is an ingenious group of three, built in concrete blocks by *Henry Wylie*, 1976. WALLED GARDEN at the Dalkeith end of the village. Properly the walled garden of Dalkeith House, this huge area is half occupied by two schools, LUGTON and WESTFIELD, built by the local authority *c.* 1972. The other half is grassed, so from the schools one looks across the green to the red brick garden wall, with a silhouette of trees and church spires beyond.

p. 166 [Dalkeith.] Another farm. SHERIFFHALL, 1.5 km. NW of the town, has a mid C18 farmhouse and barn, connected by a garden wall. The DOOCOT consists of the now isolated staircase tower of Sheriffhall House, complete with C16 doorway, windows and gun-loops. It has a little lantern on top through which the pigeons entered.

p. 417 [Roslin Chapel.] One of the stones of this lintel has been put up the wrong way round so that Giving Drink to the Thirsty appears among the Seven Deadly Sins (*see* plate 22) and Gluttony among the Seven Acts of Mercy!

p. 471 [Winchburgh.] NIDDRY CASTLE, 1 km. SE by the Niddry Burn. The ruin of a four-storey L-plan tower built *c.* 1500 by George, fourth Lord Seton, who was killed at Flodden. The entry is in the angle, and from it the turnpike stair ascends within the thickness of the wall. Towards the end of the C16 the wall head and corbelling were rebuilt and a further storey added above the parapet, with deeply splayed dormers which had boat-shaped profiles. These have disappeared, and the only distinctive feature of the later work to have survived is the round corner turret in the angle, high above the ground. Niddry was acquired in the mid C17 by the Hopes of Hopetoun and is now surrounded by the spoil from their coalmines. To the E a rectangular GARDEN WALL, probably of the C18.

223